PHILIP'S

ST AS

Co wall

C000164418

First published in 2003 by

Philip's, a division of
Octopus Publishing Group Ltd
2-4 Heron Quays, London E14 4JP

Second edition 2006
First impression 2006
CORBA

ISBN-10 0-540-08849-8 (pocket)
ISBN-13 978-0-540-08849-2 (pocket)

Printed by Toppan, China

Contents

II **Key to map pages**

IV **Route planning**

VIII **Administrative and Postcode boundaries**

1 **Key to map symbols**

2 **Street maps** at 1⅓ inches to 1 mile

104 **Street maps** at 2⅔ inches to 1 mile

148 **Street map of Plymouth city centre** at 5⅓ inches to 1 mile

150 **Index** of towns and villages

154 **Index** of streets, hospitals, industrial estates, railway stations, schools, shopping centres, universities and places of interest

Digital Data

The exceptionally high-quality mapping found in this atlas is available as digital data in TIFF format, which is easily convertible to other bitmapped (raster) image formats.

The index is also available in digital form as a standard database table. It contains all the details found in the printed index together with the National Grid reference for the map square in which each entry is named.

For further information and to discuss your requirements, please contact Philip's on 020 7644 6932 or james.mann@philips-maps.co.uk

Key to map pages

149 Map pages at 5⅓ inches to 1 mile

128 Map pages at 2⅔ inches to 1 mile

100 Map pages at 1⅓ inches to 1 mile

Scale

0 5 10 15 20 25 km

0 5 10 15 miles

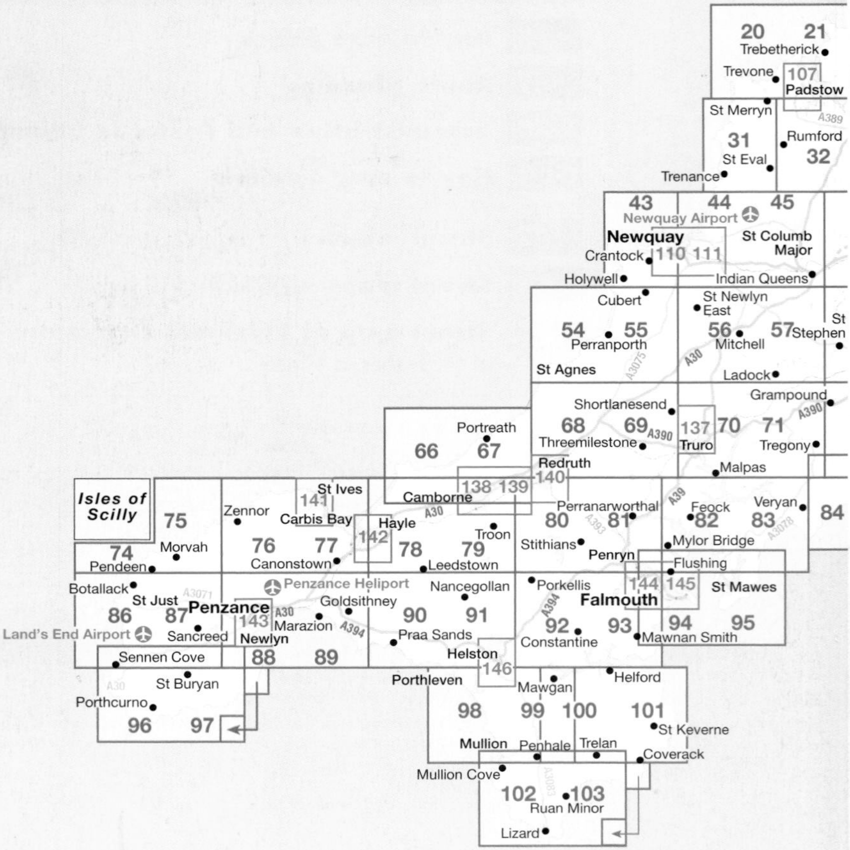

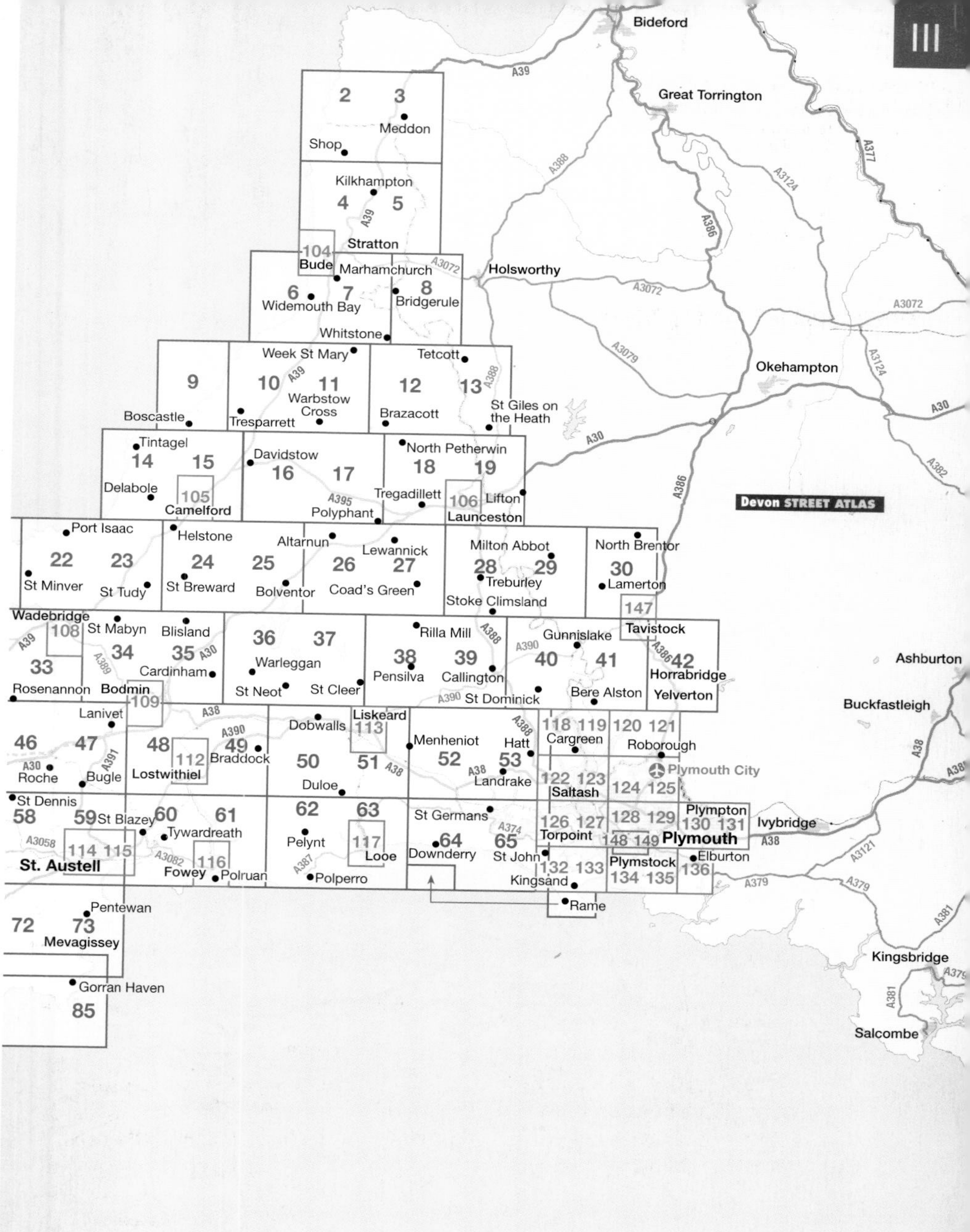
Devon STREET ATLAS
Bideford
Great Torrington
Holsworthy
Okehampton
Ashburton
Buckfastleigh
Ivybridge
Kingsbridge
Salcombe
A39
A377
A388
A3124
A386
A3072
A3079
A30
A382
A38
A3121
A379
A381
2
3
Meddon
Shop
Kilkhampton
4
5
Stratton
104
Bude
Marhamchurch
6
7
8
Widemouth Bay
Bridgerule
Whitstone
9
Boscastle
Week St Mary
10
11
Warbstow Cross
Tresparrett
Tetcott
12
13
Brazacott
St Giles on the Heath
Tintagel
14
15
Delabole
105
Camelford
Davidstow
16
17
A395
Polyphant
North Petherwin
18
19
Tregadillett
106
Lifton
Launceston
Port Isaac
22
23
St Minver
St Tudy
Helstone
24
25
St Breward
Altarnun
Bolventor
26
27
Lewannick
Coad's Green
Milton Abbot
28
29
Treburley
Stoke Climsland
North Brentor
30
Lamerton
147
Tavistock
Wadebridge
108
St Mabyn
Blisland
33
34
35
Rosenannon
Bodmin
Cardinham
109
36
37
Warleggan
St Neot
St Cleer
Rilla Mill
38
39
Pensilva
Callington
A390
St Dominick
Gunnislake
40
41
Bere Alston
42
Horrabridge
Yelverton
Lanivet
46
47
Roche
Bugle
A391
48
112
Lostwithiel
49
Braddock
Dobwalls
50
Duloe
Liskeard
113
51
Menheniot
52
Landrake
Hatt
53
118
119
Cargreen
120
121
Roborough
Plymouth City
122
123
Saltash
124
125
St Dennis
58
59
St Blazey
60
61
Tywardreath
A3058
114
115
St. Austell
A3082
116
Fowey
Polruan
62
63
Pelynt
117
Looe
A387
Polperro
St Germans
A374
64
65
Downderry
St John
126
127
Torpoint
128
129
148
149
Plymouth
Plympton
130
131
132
133
Kingsand
Plymstock
134
135
136
Elburton
Rame
Pentewan
72
73
Mevagissey
Gorran Haven
85

Route planning

Scale

0 — 5 — 10 km

0 — 1 — 2 — 3 — 4 — 5 — 6 miles

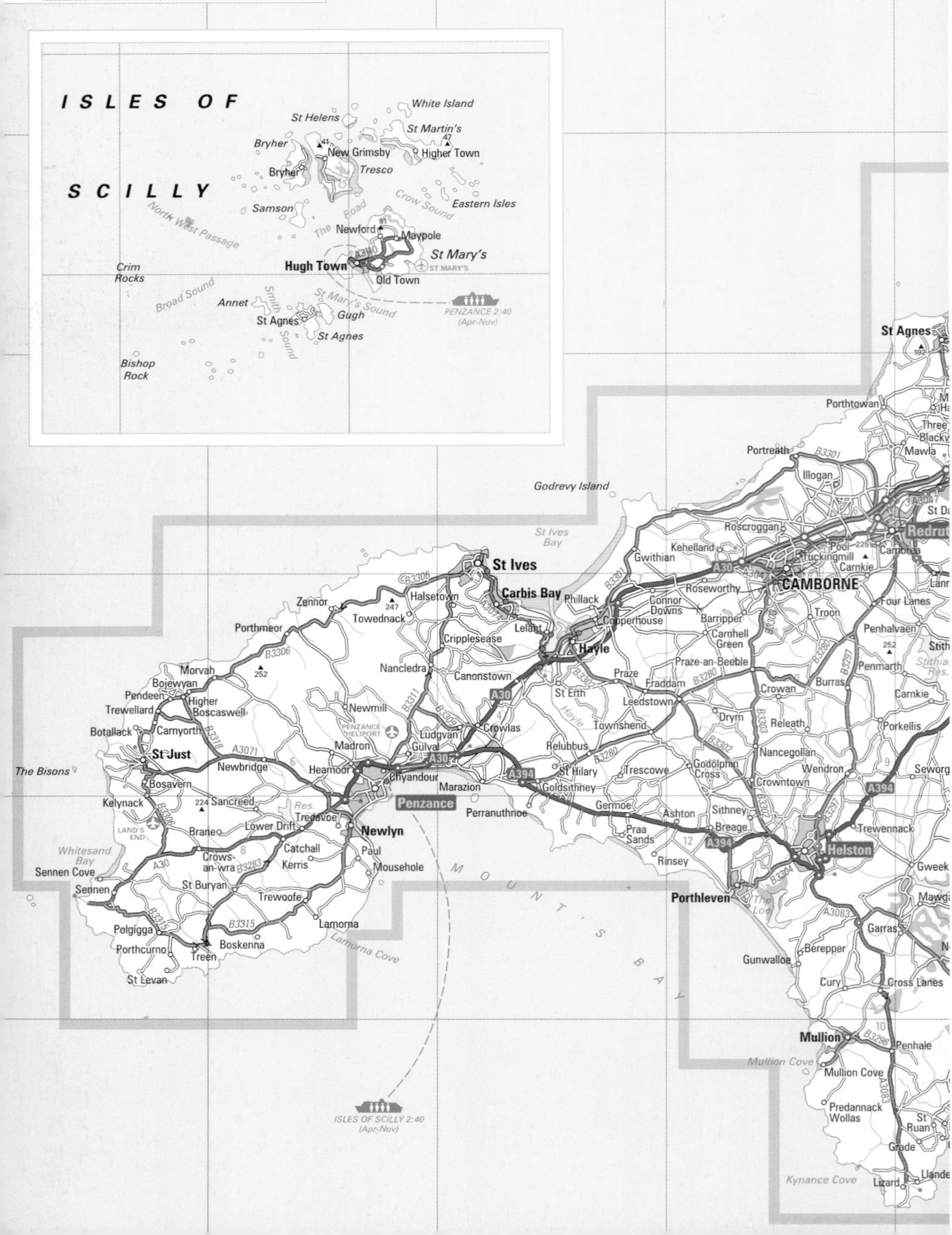

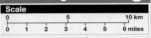

Porthcothan
Little Petherick
Whitecross
Trevanson
Wadebridge
St Mabyn
St Issey
St Breock
Egloshayle
Penrose
St Ervan
Rumford
Tredinnick
St Jidgey
Burlawn
Helland
Washaway
Bodmin Forest
St Eval
Trenance
Cardinham
Bodmin
Ruthernbridge
Nanstallon
St Mawgan
Trevarrian
Rosenannon
St Lawrence
WATERGATE BAY
Talskiddy
Withiel
Tregurrian
St Wenn
NEWQUAY
St Columb Major
Tregonetha
Lanivet
Newquay Bay
Fistral Bay
Porth
St Columb Minor
Trebyan
Pentire
Belowda
Victoria
Sweethouse
Trebudannon
Lockengate
Redmoor
Newquay
Colan
Quintrell Downs
Mountjoy
Ruthvoes
West Pentire
Crantock
Tregoss
Bilberry
Lane
Trevarren
Roche
Lostwithiel
Kestle Mill
St Columb Road
Indian Queens
Trezaise
Bugle
Holywell
Carines
Fraddon
Penhale
Lanlivery
St Dennis
Cubert
Ligger or Perran Bay
Penhale Sands
Mount
Rejerrah
St Newlyn East
Gummow's Shop
St Enoder
Retew
Whitemoor
Luxulyan
Milltown
Stenalees
Treviscoe
Nanpean
Penwithick
Penpillick
Rose
Summercourt
Carthew
Perranporth
Mitchell
Brighton
Trethosa
Foxhole
Trethurgy
St Blazey
Golant
Goonhavern
Carclaze
Bolingey
Carland Cross
High Street
Boscoppa
Tywardreath
Perranzabuloe
Trelassick
St Stephen
St Austell
Par
Trevellas
Zelah
Trewoon
Holmbush
Polkerris
Menabilly
Fowey
Mithian
St Allen
New Mills
Coombe
St Mewan
Callestick
St Erme
Trispen
Ladock
Grampound Road
Charlestown
Goonbell
Marazanvose
Sticker
Polgooth
Porthpean
Polruan
ST. AUSTELL BAY
Hewas Water
Allet
Probus
Grampound
Trenarren
Shortlanesend
Burrows
Tresillian
Creed
Pentewan
Kenwyn
Truro
Mevagissey Bay
Tresawle
St Ewe
Polmassick
Kestle
Scorrier
Chacewater
Threemilestone
Merther
Tregony
Mevagissey
Portmellon
Baldhu
Kea
St Clement
Trevarrick
Twelve Heads
Ruan Lanihorne
Gorran Churchtown
St Michael Caerhays
Malpas
Bissoe
St Michael Penkevil
Gorran Haven
Carharrack
Playing Place
Old Kea
Lamorran
Carnon Downs
Gwennap
Porthholland
Boswinger
Treworga
Trelissick
Philleigh
Penare
Perranarworthal
Penpol
Veryan
Portloe
Veryan Bay
Devoran
Feock
Ponsanooth
Treworlas
Carne
Gerrans Bay
Trewithian
Burnthouse
Mylor Bridge
St Just in Roseland
Carrick Roads
Gerrans
Portscatho
Penryn
Flushing
Rame
Longdowns
Mabe Burnthouse
Falmouth
St Mawes
Bohortha
Budock Water
Treverva
Penjerrick
Falmouth Bay
Constantine
Mawnan Smith
Porth Navas
Helford Passage
Mawnan
Helford River
Helford
St Anthony
Manaccan
St Martins
Porthallow
Tregidden
Porthoustock
St Keverne
Traboe
Trelan
Coverack
Gwenter
Kuggar
Ruan Minor
Cadgwith
A30
A39
A389
A3059
A392
A3075
A3058
A3076
A390
A391
A38
A3078
A394
A393
A3082
B3276
B3274
B3275
B3279
B3285
B3284
B3277
B3298
B3289
B3292
B3287
B3273
B3268
B3269
B3293
B3294

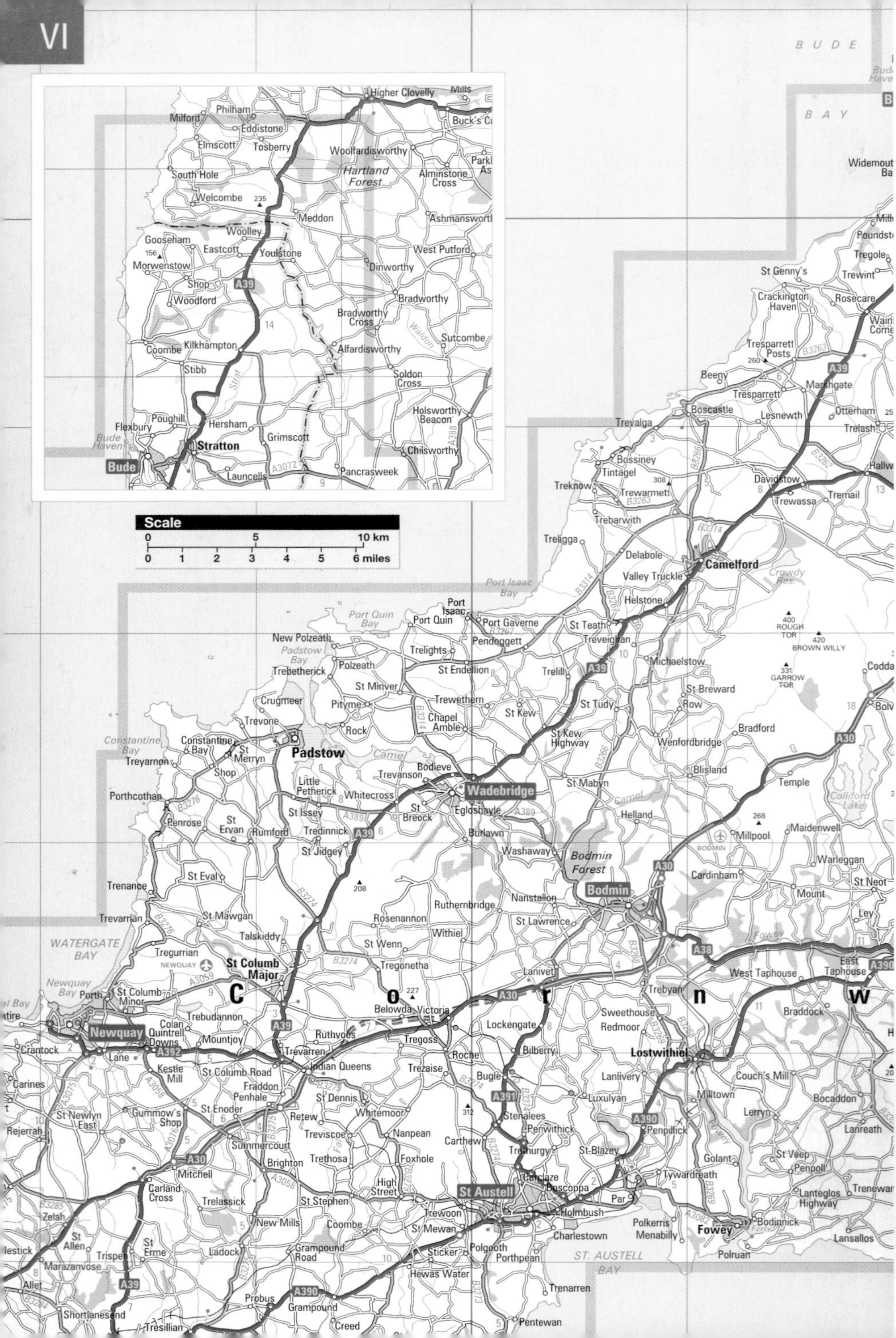

Scale
0
5
10 km
0
1
2
3
4
5
6 miles
BUDE
BAY
Higher Clovelly
Mills
Philham
Milford
Eddistone
Buck's Cross
Elmscott
Tosberry
Woolfardisworthy
Hartland Forest
South Hole
Alminstone Cross
Welcombe
235
Meddon
Ashmansworthy
Woolley
Gooseham
156
Eastcott
Youlstone
West Putford
Morwenstow
Dinworthy
Shop
A39
Woodford
Bradworthy
Bradworthy Cross
14
Waldon
Sutcombe
Coombe
Kilkhampton
Alfardisworthy
Stibb
Strat
Soldon Cross
Poughill
Holsworthy Beacon
Flexbury
Hersham
Bude Haven
Stratton
Grimscott
A388
Chilsworthy
Bude
A3072
Launcells
Pancrasweek
9
Widemouth Bay
Millook
Poundstock
Tregole
St Gennys
Trewint
Crackington Haven
Rosecare
Wainhouse Corner
Tresparrett Posts
260
B3263
Beeny
A39
Marshgate
Tresparrett
Boscastle
Otterham
Trevalga
Lesnewth
Trelash
Bossiney
B3266
B3262
Tintagel
308
Davidstow
Treknow
Trewarmett
Tremail
B3263
Trewassa
Trebarwith
B3314
Treligga
Delabole
Camelford
Valley Truckle
Crowdy Res.
Port Isaac Bay
B3314
B3267
Helstone
Port Quin Bay
Port Isaac
Port Quin
Port Gaverne
St Teath
400 ROUGH TOR
420 BROWN WILLY
New Polzeath
Pendoggett
Treveighan
Padstow Bay
Trelights
Michaelstow
331 GARROW TOR
Trebetherick
Polzeath
St Endellion
Trelill
A39
St Minver
St Breward
Crugmeer
Pityme
Trewethern
St Tudy
B3314
Row
Trevone
Rock
Chapel Amble
St Kew
St Kew Highway
Bradford
Constantine Bay
Constantine Bay
St Merryn
Padstow
Camel
Wenfordbridge
A30
Treyarnon
Shop
Bodieve
B3266
Trevanson
Blisland
Little Petherick
Wadebridge
St Mabyn
Temple
Porthcothan
B3276
Whitecross
Colliford Lake
St Issey
St Breock
Egloshayle
A389
Camel
Helland
St Ervan
Penrose
Rumford
Tredinnick
A39
Burlawn
268
Millpool
Maidenwell
St Jidgey
Washaway
BODMIN
Bodmin Forest
Warleggan
A30
St Eval
208
Trenance
B3274
Nanstallon
Bodmin
Cardinham
St Neot
Mount
Ruthernbridge
Trevarrian
St Mawgan
Rosenannon
St Lawrence
B3276
Withiel
Fowey
Talskiddy
WATERGATE BAY
St Wenn
B3268
A38
Tregurrian
NEWQUAY
St Columb Major
B3274
Tregonetha
Lanivet
East Taphouse
A390
A3059
West Taphouse
Newquay Bay
Porth
St Columb Minor
C
o
227
r
Trebyan
n
w
Belowda
Victoria
A30
Braddock
Newquay
Colan
Trebudannon
Sweethouse
Quintrell Downs
Ruthvoes
Lockengate
Redmoor
Crantock
Mountjoy
A39
Tregoss
Lostwithiel
Lane
A392
Trevarren
Roche
Bilberry
Kestle Mill
St Columb Road
Indian Queens
Trezaise
Lanlivery
Couch's Mill
Carines
A3075
Fraddon
Penhale
Bugle
A391
Luxulyan
Milltown
Bocaddon
A3058
St Dennis
Whitemoor
312
St Newlyn East
Gummow's Shop
St Enoder
Retew
Stenalees
A390
Lerryn
Rejerrah
A3076
B3275
Treviscoe
Nanpean
Penwithick
Penpillick
Lanreath
Summercourt
Carthew
Trethurgy
St Blazey
Golant
St Veep
A30
Trethosa
Foxhole
Penpoll
Mitchell
Brighton
A3058
High Street
B3279
Carclaze
Tywardreath
Carland Cross
St Austell
Boscoppa
Lanteglos Highway
Trenewan
B3285
Trelassick
St Stephen
B3269
Zelah
Par
Holmbush
New Mills
Coombe
Trewoon
Polkerris
Bodinnick
St Allen
St Erme
St Mewan
Menabilly
A3082
Fowey
Lansallos
Charlestown
Trispen
Ladock
Grampound Road
Sticker
Polgooth
Polruan
Marazanvose
Porthpean
ST. AUSTELL BAY
A39
B3275
Hewas Water
B3273
Allet
A390
Trenarren
Probus
Grampound
Shortlanesend
Tresillian
Creed
Pentewan

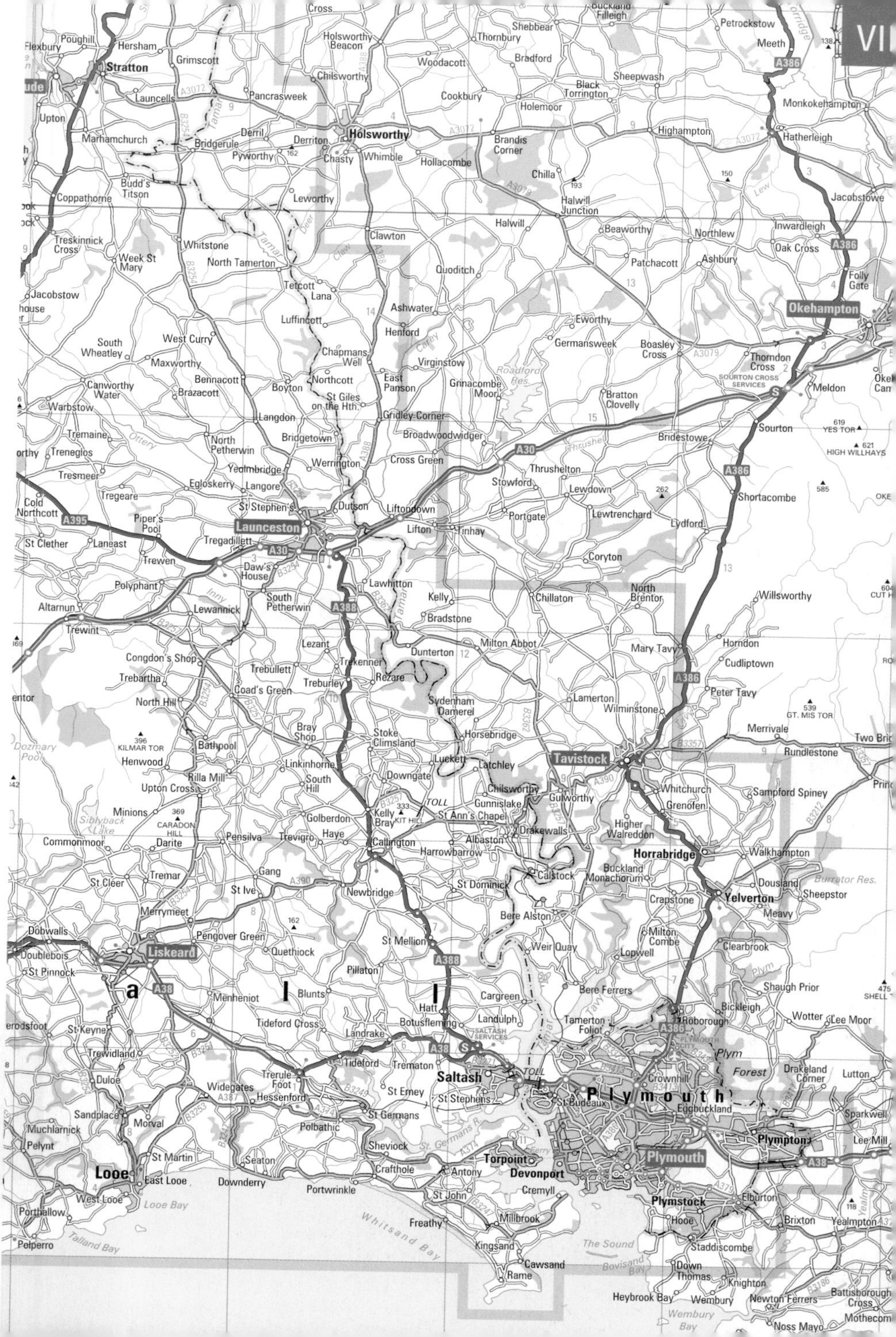
Cross
Buckland Filleigh
Shebbear
Petrockstow
Poughill
Flexbury
Hersham
Holsworthy Beacon
Thornbury
Meeth
A386
Stratton
Grimscott
Woodacott
Bradford
Chilsworthy
Sheepwash
A3072
Launcells
Pancrasweek
Cookbury
Black Torrington
Holemoor
Monkokehampton
Upton
Holsworthy
Derril
Highampton
Hatherleigh
Marhamchurch
Bridgerule
Derriton
Brandis Corner
Pyworthy
162
Chasty
Whimble
Hollacombe
Chilla
193
150
Budd's Titson
A3079
Coppathorne
Leworthy
Halwill Junction
Jacobstowe
Halwill
Beaworthy
Inwardleigh
Treskinnick Cross
Clawton
Northlew
Oak Cross
Whitstone
Week St Mary
North Tamerton
Patchacott
Ashbury
Quoditch
Folly Gate
Tetcott
Lana
Jacobstow
13
Okehampton
Ashwater
Luffincott
Henford
Eworthy
Germansweek
Boasley Cross
South Wheatley
West Curry
Chapmans Well
Thorndon Cross
Maxworthy
Virginstow
Sourton Cross Services
Canworthy Water
Bennacott
Northcott
East Panson
Grinacombe Moor
Roadford Res.
Meldon
Brazacott
Boyton
St Giles on the Hth.
Bratton Clovelly
Warbstow
Langdon
Gridley Corner
Sourton
619 Yes Tor
Tremaine
North Petherwin
Bridgetown
Broadwoodwidger
Bridestowe
621 High Willhays
Treneglos
Werrington
Cross Green
A30
Thrushelton
Tresmeer
Yeolmbridge
Stowford
Egloskerry
Langore
Lewdown
262
A386
585
Tregeare
St Stephen's
Dutson
Liftondown
Shortacombe
Cold Northcott
A395
Piper's Pool
Launceston
Lifton
Tinhay
Portgate
Lewtrenchard
Lydford
St Clether
Laneast
Tregadillett
Trewen
Daw's House
B3254
Lawhitton
Coryton
Polyphant
South Petherwin
Kelly
Chillaton
North Brentor
Willsworthy
Altarnun
Lewannick
A388
Bradstone
Trewint
Lezant
Milton Abbot
Mary Tavy
Horndon
Congdon's Shop
Trekenner
Dunterton
Cudliptown
Trebullett
Rezare
Trebartha
Treburley
Coad's Green
Sydenham Damerel
Lamerton
Peter Tavy
North Hill
Wilminstone
539 Gt. Mis Tor
Bray Shop
Stoke Climsland
Horsebridge
Merrivale
Two Bridges
396 Kilmar Tor
Dozmary Pool
Bathpool
Henwood
Linkinhorne
Luckett
Latchley
Tavistock
Rundlestone
Rilla Mill
South Hill
Downgate
Chilsworthy
Gulworthy
Whitchurch
Upton Cross
Gunnislake
Grenofen
Sampford Spiney
Minions
369 Caradon Hill
Siblyback Lake
Golberdon
Kelly Bray
333 Kit Hill
Toll
St Ann's Chapel
Higher Walreddon
Commonmoor
Darite
Pensilva
Trevigro
Haye
Drakewalls
Albaston
Callington
Harrowbarrow
Horrabridge
Walkhampton
Tremar
Gang
Calstock
Buckland Monachorum
St Cleer
St Ive
A390
Newbridge
St Dominick
Yelverton
Dousland
Burrator Res.
Sheepstor
Merrymeet
Crapstone
Meavy
Dobwalls
Pengover Green
162
Bere Alston
St Mellion
Milton Combe
Clearbrook
Doublebois
Liskeard
Quethiock
Weir Quay
Lopwell
St Pinnock
Pillaton
A388
Shaugh Prior
475 Shell Top
A38
Menheniot
Blunts
Cargreen
Bere Ferrers
Hatt
Landulph
Bickleigh
Wotter
Lee Moor
St Keyne
Tideford Cross
Botusfleming
Tamerton Foliot
Roborough
Landrake
Saltash Services
Trewidland
Tideford
Trematon
Saltash
Toll
Plymouth
Crownhill
Plym Forest
Drakeland Corner
Lutton
Trerule Foot
Duloe
Widegates
Hessenford
St Erney
St Stephens
St Budeaux
Egg Buckland
Sandplace
Morval
St Germans
Polbathic
Sparkwell
Muchlarnick
Pelynt
Sheviock
Plympton
Lee Mill
St Martin
Seaton
Torpoint
Devonport
Plymouth
Looe
East Looe
Downderry
Crafthole
Antony
A38
Portwrinkle
Cremyll
West Looe
Looe Bay
St John
Plymstock
Elburton
Porthallow
Millbrook
Hooe
Brixton
Yealmpton
Freathy
Whitsand Bay
Talland Bay
Polperro
Kingsand
The Sound
Staddiscombe
Cawsand
Bovisand Bay
Down Thomas
Rame
Knighton
Heybrook Bay
Wembury
Newton Ferrers
Battisborough Cross
Wembury Bay
Noss Mayo
Mothecombe

Major administrative and Postcode boundaries

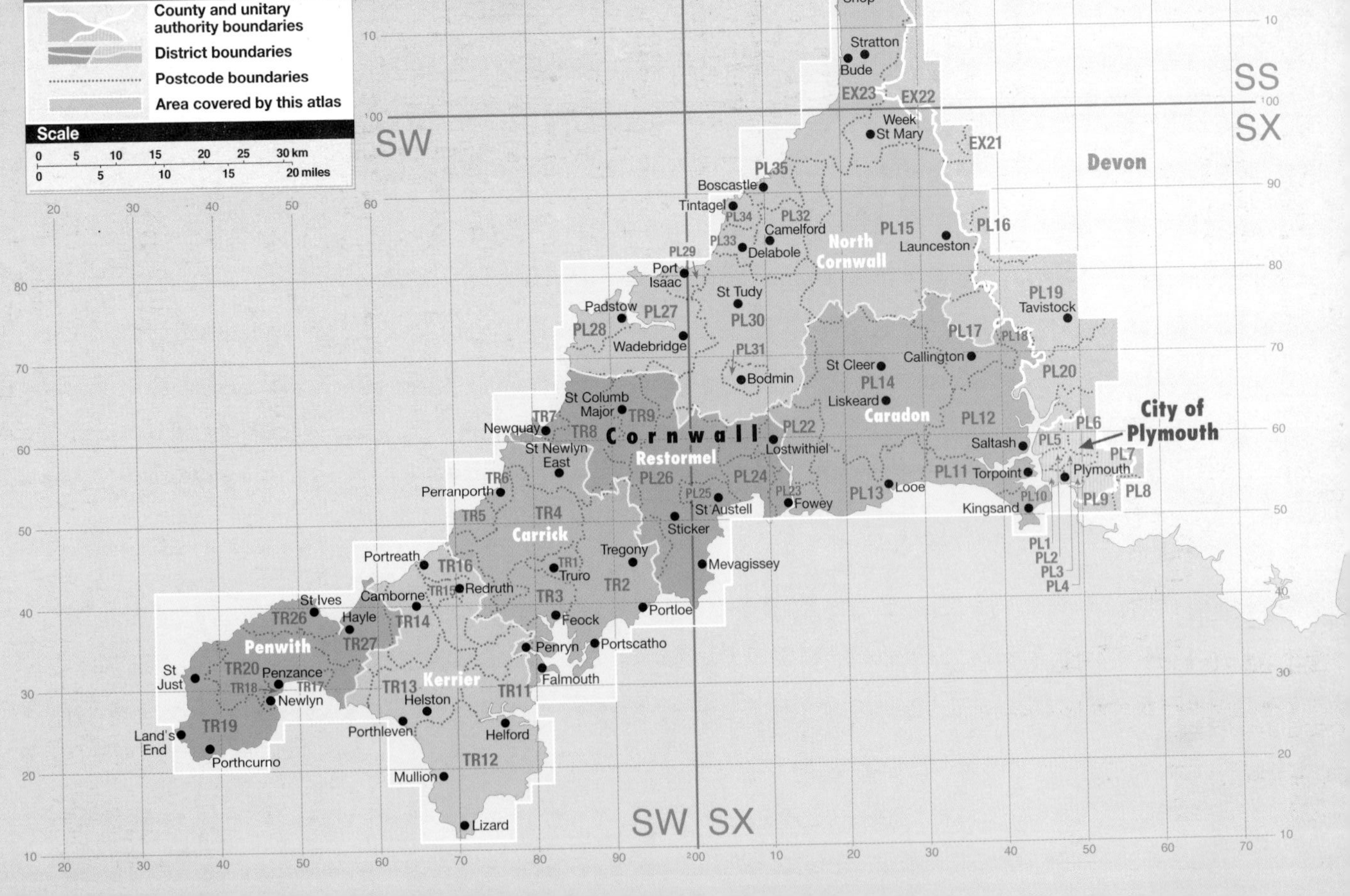
County and unitary authority boundaries
District boundaries
Postcode boundaries
Area covered by this atlas
Scale
0 5 10 15 20 25 30 km
0 5 10 15 20 miles
SS
SW
SX
Devon
Cornwall
North Cornwall
Caradon
Restormel
Carrick
Kerrier
Penwith
City of Plymouth
Shop
Stratton
Bude
Week St Mary
Boscastle
Tintagel
Camelford
Delabole
Launceston
Port Isaac
St Tudy
Padstow
Wadebridge
Bodmin
Tavistock
Callington
St Cleer
Liskeard
St Columb Major
Newquay
St Newlyn East
Lostwithiel
Saltash
Torpoint
Plymouth
Kingsand
Looe
Fowey
St Austell
Sticker
Perranporth
Mevagissey
Tregony
Truro
Portreath
Redruth
Camborne
St Ives
Hayle
Feock
Portloe
Penryn
Portscatho
Falmouth
St Just
Penzance
Newlyn
Helston
Porthleven
Helford
Land's End
Porthcurno
Mullion
Lizard
EX39
EX23
EX22
EX21
PL35
PL34
PL33
PL32
PL29
PL15
PL16
PL27
PL28
PL30
PL31
PL19
PL17
PL18
PL20
PL14
PL12
PL22
PL6
PL5
PL7
PL8
PL9
PL10
PL11
PL13
PL23
PL24
PL25
PL26
PL1
PL2
PL3
PL4
TR7
TR8
TR9
TR6
TR5
TR4
TR16
TR15
TR1
TR2
TR3
TR26
TR27
TR14
TR20
TR18
TR17
TR13
TR11
TR19
TR12

Key to map symbols

- **Motorway** with junction number (22a)
- **Primary route** – dual/single carriageway
- **A road** – dual/single carriageway
- **B road** – dual/single carriageway
- **Minor road** – dual/single carriageway
- **Other minor road** – dual/single carriageway
- **Road under construction**
- **Tunnel, covered road**
- **Rural track, private road or narrow road in urban area**
- **Gate or obstruction to traffic** (restrictions may not apply at all times or to all vehicles)
- **Path, bridleway, byway open to all traffic, road used as a public path**
- **Pedestrianised area**
- DY7 **Postcode boundaries**
- **County and unitary authority boundaries**
- **Railway, tunnel, railway under construction**
- **Tramway, tramway under construction**
- **Miniature railway**
- Walsall **Railway station**
- **Private railway station**
- South Shields **Metro station**
- **Tram stop, tram stop under construction**
- **Bus, coach station**
- **Ambulance station**
- **Coastguard station**
- **Fire station**
- **Police station**
- **Accident and Emergency entrance to hospital**
- H **Hospital**
- **Place of worship**
- i **Information Centre** (open all year)
- **Shopping Centre**
- P P&R **Parking, Park and Ride**
- PO **Post Office**
- **Camping site, caravan site**
- **Golf course, picnic site**
- Prim Sch **Important buildings, schools, colleges, universities and hospitals**
- **Built up area**
- **Woods**
- River Medway **Water name**
- **River, weir, stream**
- **Canal, lock, tunnel**
- **Water**
- **Tidal water**
- *Church* **Non-Roman antiquity**
- ROMAN FORT **Roman antiquity**
- 87 / 237 **Adjoining page indicators and overlap bands**
  The colour of the arrow and the band indicates the scale of the adjoining or overlapping page (see scales below)

Acad	**Academy**	Inst	**Institute**	Recn Gd	**Recreation Ground**
Allot Gdns	**Allotments**	Ct	**Law Court**	Resr	**Reservoir**
Cemy	**Cemetery**	L Ctr	**Leisure Centre**	Ret Pk	**Retail Park**
C Ctr	**Civic Centre**	LC	**Level Crossing**	Sch	**School**
CH	**Club House**	Liby	**Library**	Sh Ctr	**Shopping Centre**
Coll	**College**	Mkt	**Market**	TH	**Town Hall/House**
Crem	**Crematorium**	Meml	**Memorial**	Trad Est	**Trading Estate**
Ent	**Enterprise**	Mon	**Monument**	Univ	**University**
Ex H	**Exhibition Hall**	Mus	**Museum**	W Twr	**Water Tower**
Ind Est	**Industrial Estate**	Obsy	**Observatory**	Wks	**Works**
IRB Sta	**Inshore Rescue Boat Station**	Pal	**Royal Palace**	YH	**Youth Hostel**
		PH	**Public House**		

Enlarged mapping only

- **Railway or bus station building**
- **Place of interest**
- **Parkland**

■ The small numbers around the edges of the maps identify the 1 kilometre National Grid lines

■ The dark grey border on the inside edge of some pages indicates that the mapping does not continue onto the adjacent page

The scale of the maps on the pages numbered in blue is 4.2 cm to 1 km • 2⅔ inches to 1 mile • 1: 23810

0 – ¼ – ½ – ¾ – 1 mile
0 – 250 m – 500 m – 750 m – 1 kilometre

The scale of the maps on pages numbered in green is 2.1 cm to 1 km • 1⅓ inches to 1 mile • 1: 47620

0 – ¼ – ½ – ¾ – 1 mile
0 – 250m – 500m – 750m – 1 kilometre

The scale of the maps on pages numbered in red is 8.4 cm to 1 km • 5⅓ inches to 1 mile • 1: 11900

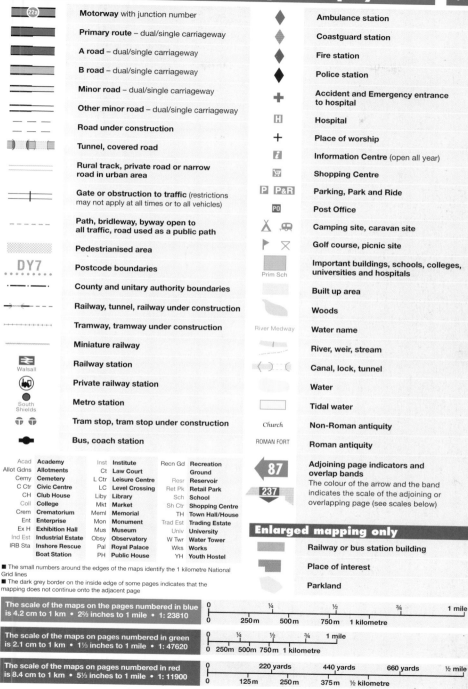

0 – 220 yards – 440 yards – 660 yards – ½ mile
0 – 125 m – 250 m – 375 m – ½ kilometre

Scale: 1⅓ inches to 1 mile
0 ¼ ½ mile
0 250m 500m 750m 1 km

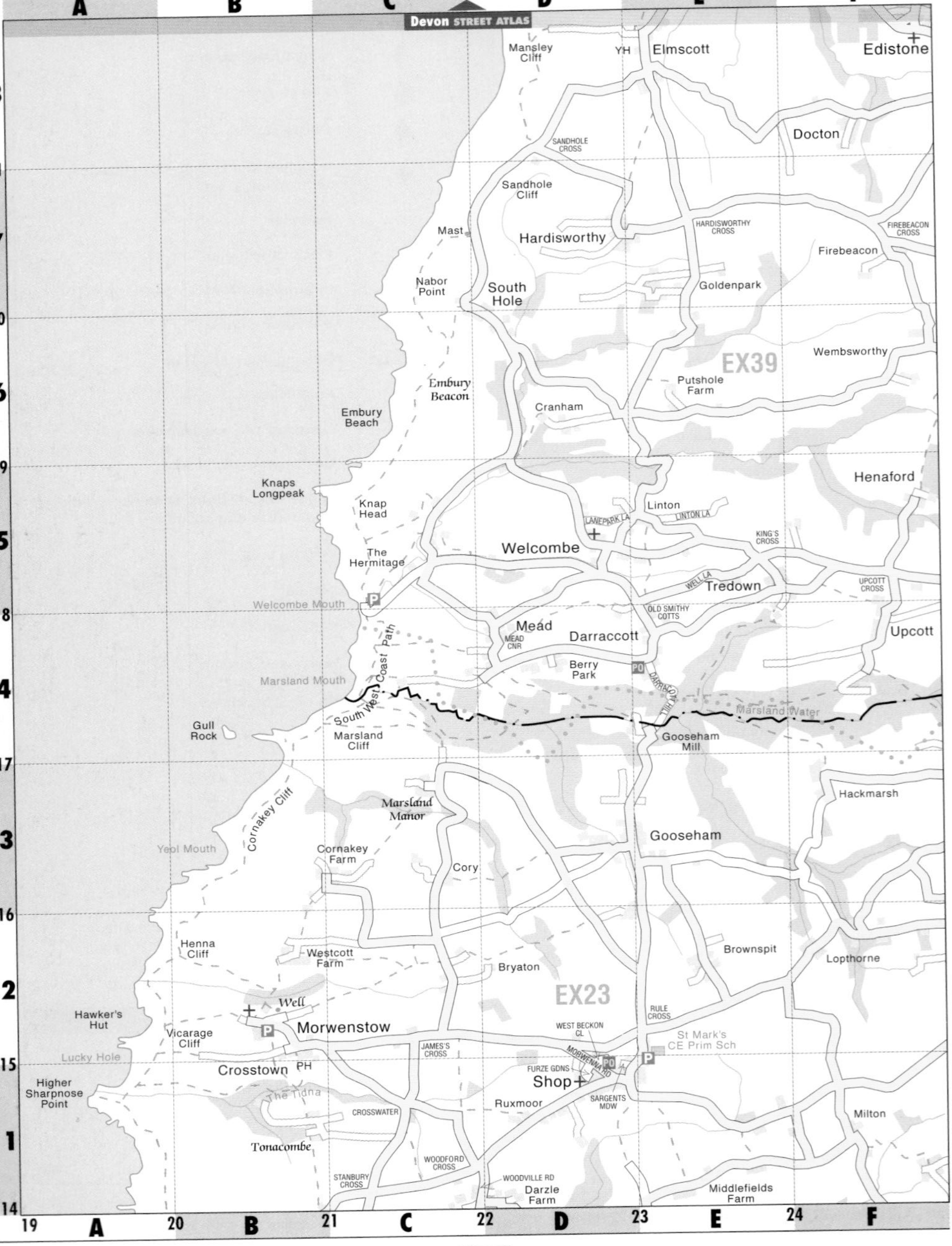

A B C D E F
Devon STREET ATLAS
8
21
7
20
6
19
5
18
4
17
3
16
2
15
1
14
19 A 20 B 21 C 22 D 23 E 24 F
Mansley Cliff
YH
Elmscott
Edistone
Docton
SANDHOLE CROSS
Sandhole Cliff
Mast
Hardisworthy
HARDISWORTHY CROSS
FIREBEACON CROSS
Firebeacon
Nabor Point
South Hole
Goldenpark
Wembsworthy
EX39
Putshole Farm
Embury Beacon
Embury Beach
Cranham
Henaford
Knaps Longpeak
Knap Head
Linton
LANEPARK LA
LINTON LA
KING'S CROSS
The Hermitage
Welcombe
WELL LA
Tredown
UPCOTT CROSS
Welcombe Mouth
OLD SMITHY COTTS
Mead
Darracott
Upcott
MEAD CNR
Berry Park
PO
DARRACOTT HILL
Marsland Mouth
South West Coast Path
Marsland Water
Gull Rock
Marsland Cliff
Gooseham Mill
Hackmarsh
Marsland Manor
Cornakey Cliff
Gooseham
Yeol Mouth
Cornakey Farm
Cory
Henna Cliff
Westcott Farm
Brownspit
Bryaton
Lopthorne
EX23
Well
Hawker's Hut
RULE CROSS
Vicarage Cliff
Morwenstow
WEST BECKON CL
St Mark's CE Prim Sch
Lucky Hole
JAMES'S CROSS
MORWENNA RD
PO
Crosstown
PH
FURZE GDNS
Shop
Higher Sharpnose Point
The Tidna
Ruxmoor
SARGENTS MDW
Milton
CROSSWATER
Tonacombe
WOODFORD CROSS
STANBURY CROSS
WOODVILLE RD
Darzle Farm
Middlefields Farm

4

Scale: 1⅓ inches to 1 mile
0 ¼ ½ mile
0 250m 500m 750m 1 km

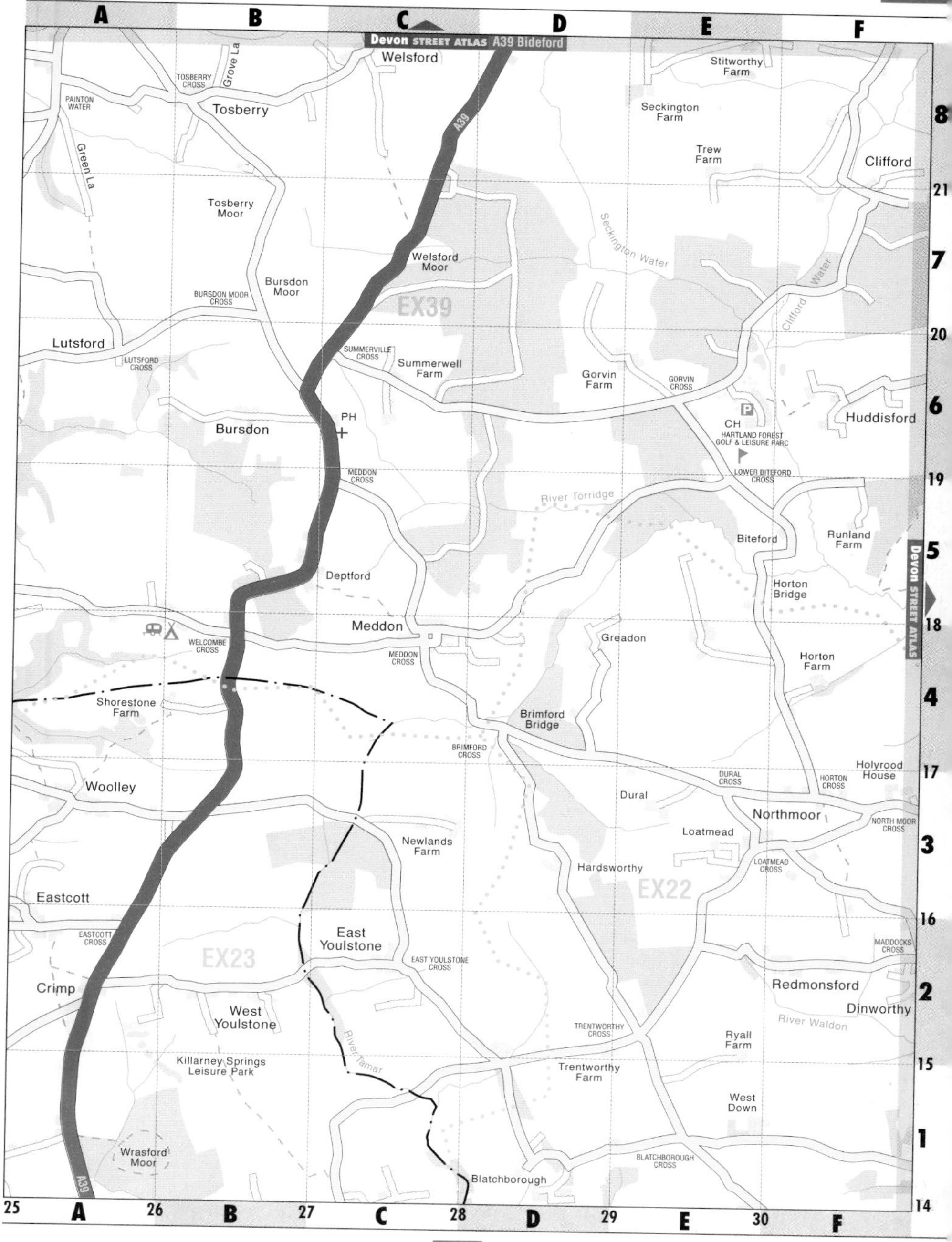

5

2

Scale: 1⅓ inches to 1 mile
0 ¼ ½ mile
0 250m 500m 750m 1 km

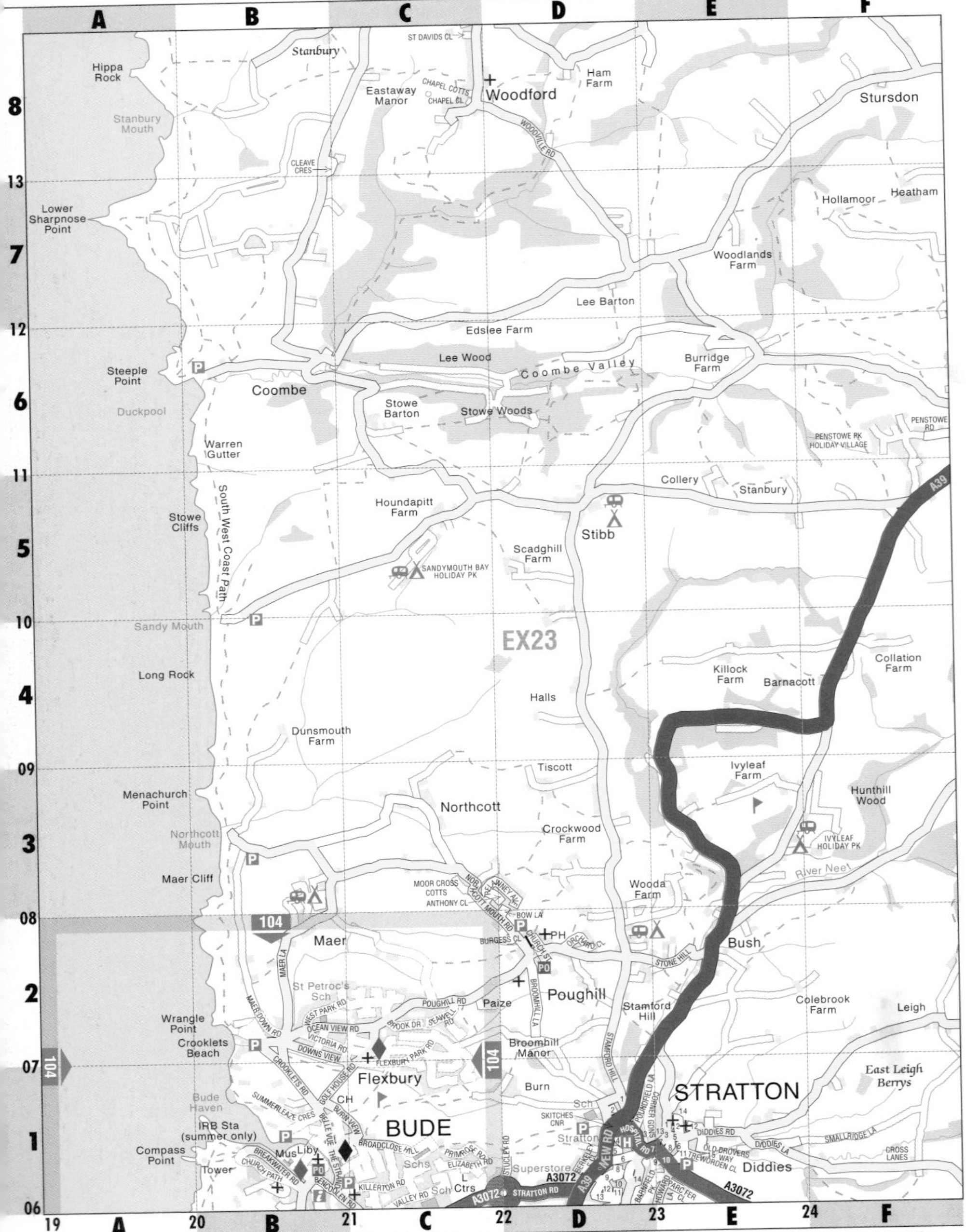

A
B
C
D
E
F
8
7
6
5
4
3
2
1
13
12
11
10
09
08
07
06
19
20
21
22
23
24
Hippa Rock
Stanbury
Stanbury Mouth
ST DAVIDS CL
Eastaway Manor
CHAPEL COTTS
CHAPEL CL
Woodford
Ham Farm
Stursdon
WOODVILLE RD
CLEAVE CRES
Lower Sharpnose Point
Hollamoor
Heatham
Woodlands Farm
Lee Barton
Edslee Farm
Lee Wood
Coombe Valley
Burridge Farm
Steeple Point
Coombe
Duckpool
Stowe Barton
Stowe Woods
PENSTOWE RD
PENSTOWE PK HOLIDAY VILLAGE
Warren Gutter
Collery
Stanbury
A39
South West Coast Path
Stowe Cliffs
Houndapitt Farm
Stibb
Scadghill Farm
SANDYMOUTH BAY HOLIDAY PK
Sandy Mouth
EX23
Long Rock
Killock Farm
Barnacott
Collation Farm
Halls
Dunsmouth Farm
Tiscott
Ivyleaf Farm
Menachurch Point
Northcott
Hunthill Wood
Crockwood Farm
Northcott Mouth
IVYLEAF HOLIDAY PK
River Neet
Maer Cliff
MOOR CROSS COTTS
ANTHONY CL
Wooda Farm
BOW LA
104
Maer
BURGESS CL
CHURCH ST
PH
ORCHARD CL
PO
STONE HILL
Bush
MAER LA
St Petroc's Sch
BROOMHILL LA
Poughill
Paize
POUGHILL RD
WEST PARK RD
MAER DOWN RD
OCEAN VIEW RD
BROOK DR
SEAWELL RD
Stamford Hill
Colebrook Farm
Leigh
Wrangle Point
Crooklets Beach
VICTORIA RD
DOWNS VIEW
FLEXBURY PARK RD
Broomhill Manor
STAMFORD HILL
Flexbury
CROOKLETS RD
GOLF HOUSE RD
Burn
POUNDFIELD LA
CORNER GDNS
East Leigh Berrys
STRATTON
Bude Haven
SUMMERLEAZE CRES
CH
BURN VIEW
BELLE VUE
Sch
SKITCHES CNR
HOSPITAL RD
DIDDIES RD
IRB Sta (summer only)
BUDE
BROADCLOSE HILL
Stratton
NEW RD
DIDDIES LA
SMALLRIDGE LA
Compass Point
Mus
Liby
BREAKWATER RD
THE STRAND
PRIMROSE
ELIZABETH RD
STUCLEY RD
Superstore
BERKELEY
OLD DROVERS WAY
TREWORDEN CL
Diddies
CROSS LANES
Tower
CHURCH PATH
Schs
A3072
BARNFIELD PK
HOWARD LA
PARC FER CL
BENCOOLEN RD
KILLERTON RD
VALLEY RD
Sch
L Ctrs
STRATTON RD

6

For full street detail of the highlighted area see page 104.

7

D1
1 POUNDFIELD HILL
2 POUNDFIELD CL
3 BAY TREE COTTS
4 WARD CL
5 BENTLEY DR
6 UNION HILL
7 BRIDGE ST
8 WOODLEY CL
9 ST MICHAEL'S RD
10 GLADWELL GDNS
11 ST PETERS RD
12 ST ANDREW'S RD
13 ST OLAF'S RD
14 BOWDEN

E1
1 MAIDEN ST
2 COT HILL
3 MARKET ST
4 CHURCH SQ
5 CHURCH ST
6 GIBRALTER SQ
7 FORE ST
8 OLD POST OFFICE HILL
9 THE LEAT
10 HOWELL'S RD
11 SPICERS LA
12 SANCTUARY LA
13 BIDEFORD MEWS
14 TOWNSEND
15 HUNTFIELD GDNS

Scale: 1⅓ inches to 1 mile
0 ¼ ½ mile
0 250m 500m 750m 1 km

3

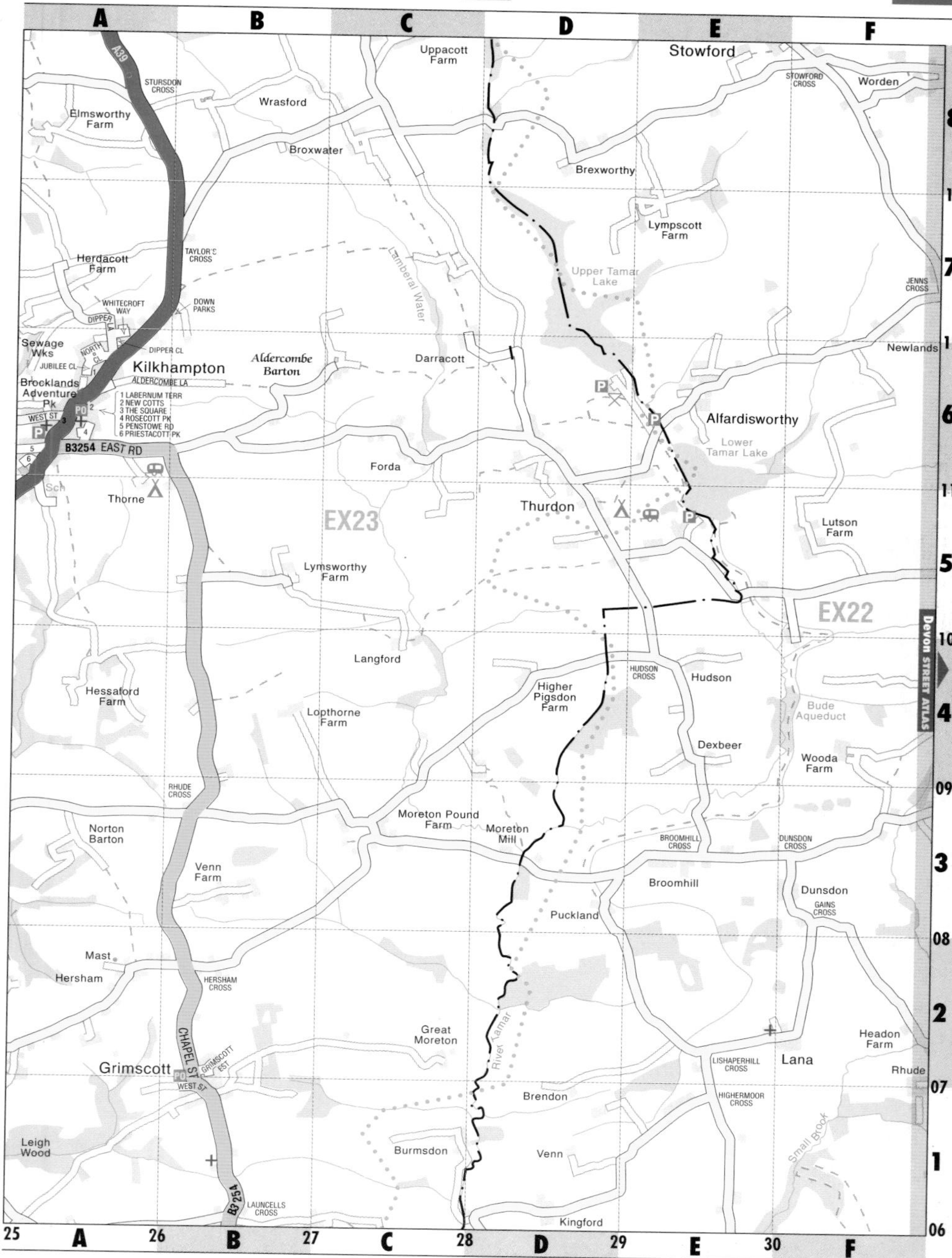
A
B
C
D
E
F
Uppacott Farm
Stowford
STURSDON CROSS
STOWFORD CROSS
Worden
Elmsworthy Farm
Wrasford
A39
Broxwater
Brexworthy
Lympscott Farm
Herdacott Farm
TAYLOR'S CROSS
Lamberal Water
Upper Tamar Lake
JENNS CROSS
WHITECROFT WAY
DOWN PARKS
DIPPER LA
Sewage Wks
NORTH CL
DIPPER CL
Newlands
JUBILEE CL
Kilkhampton
Aldercombe Barton
Darracott
Brocklands Adventure Pk
ALDERCOMBE LA
1 LABERNUM TERR
2 NEW COTTS
3 THE SQUARE
4 ROSECOTT PK
5 PENSTOWE RD
6 PRIESTACOTT PK
WEST ST
PO
Alfardisworthy
Lower Tamar Lake
B3254 EAST RD
Forda
Sch
Thorne
Thurdon
EX23
Lutson Farm
Lymsworthy Farm
EX22
Langford
HUDSON CROSS
Hudson
Devon STREET ATLAS
Hessaford Farm
Higher Pigsdon Farm
Bude Aqueduct
Lopthorne Farm
Dexbeer
Wooda Farm
RHUDE CROSS
Moreton Pound Farm
Moreton Mill
Norton Barton
BROOMHILL CROSS
DUNSDON CROSS
Venn Farm
Broomhill
Dunsdon
GAINS CROSS
Puckland
Mast
Hersham
HERSHAM CROSS
Great Moreton
Headon Farm
River Tamar
CHAPEL ST
GRIMSCOTT EST
LISHAPERHILL CROSS
Lana
Grimscott
Rhude
Brendon
HIGHERMOOR CROSS
Leigh Wood
Small Brook
Burmsdon
Venn
B3254
LAUNCELLS CROSS
Kingford
8
13
7
12
6
11
5
10
4
09
3
08
2
07
1
06
25
26
27
28
29
30

7
8

4

For full street detail of the highlighted area see page 104.

Scale: 1⅓ inches to 1 mile
0 ¼ ½ mile
0 250m 500m 750m 1 km

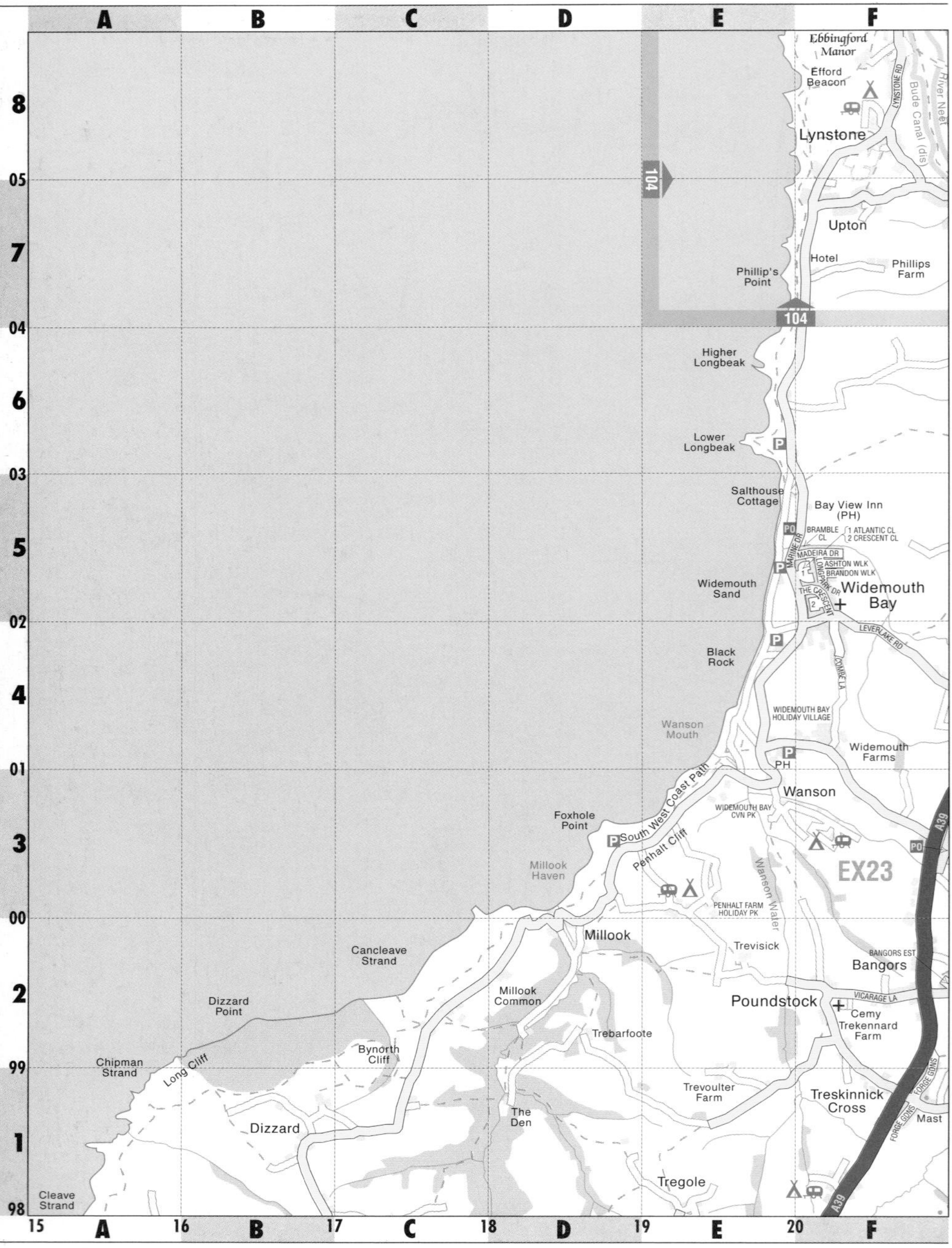

A
B
C
D
E
F
8
05
7
04
6
03
5
02
4
01
3
00
2
99
1
98
15
16
17
18
19
20
Ebbingford Manor
Efford Beacon
LYNSTONE RD
River Neet
Bude Canal (dis)
Lynstone
104
Upton
Hotel
Phillips Farm
Phillip's Point
104
Higher Longbeak
Lower Longbeak
Salthouse Cottage
Bay View Inn (PH)
BRAMBLE CL
1 ATLANTIC CL
2 CRESCENT CL
MARINE DR
MADEIRA DR
ASHTON WLK
BRANDON WLK
LONGPARK DR
THE CRESCENT
Widemouth Sand
Widemouth Bay
LEVERLAKE RD
Black Rock
CYMBRE LA
WIDEMOUTH BAY HOLIDAY VILLAGE
Wanson Mouth
Widemouth Farms
PH
Wanson
South West Coast Path
WIDEMOUTH BAY CVN PK
Foxhole Point
A39
Penhalt Cliff
EX23
Millook Haven
Wanson Water
PENHALT FARM HOLIDAY PK
Millook
Trevisick
Cancleave Strand
BANGORS EST
Bangors
Millook Common
Poundstock
VICARAGE LA
Dizzard Point
Cemy
Trekennard Farm
Trebarfoote
Bynorth Cliff
Chipman Strand
Long Cliff
Trevoulter Farm
Treskinnick Cross
FORGE GDNS
The Den
Mast
Dizzard
Tregole
Cleave Strand
A39

10
11

Scale: 1⅓ inches to 1 mile
0 ¼ ½ mile
0 250m 500m 750m 1 km

For full street detail of the highlighted area see page 104.

4 8 5

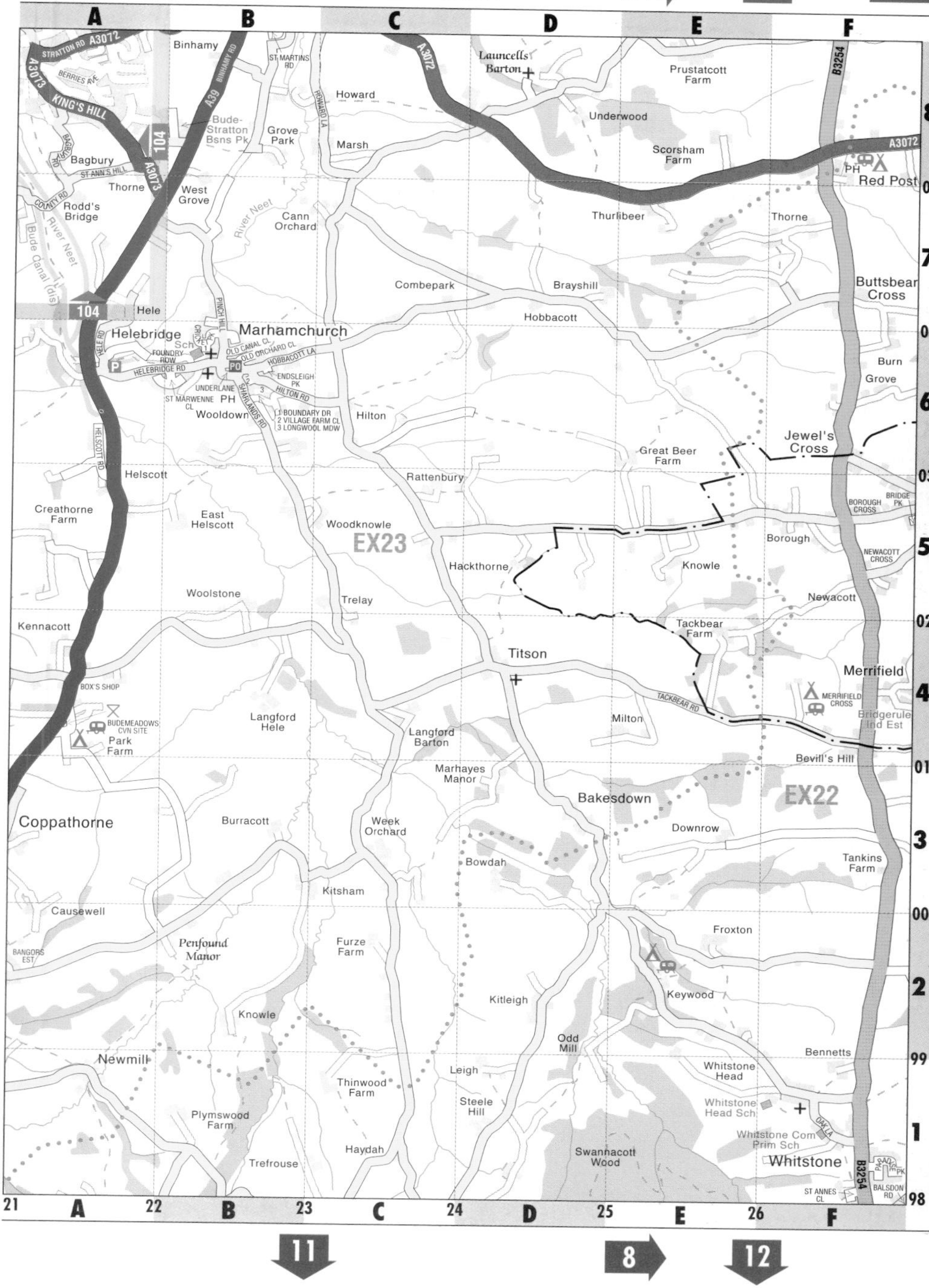

11 8 12

7
5

Scale: 1⅓ inches to 1 mile

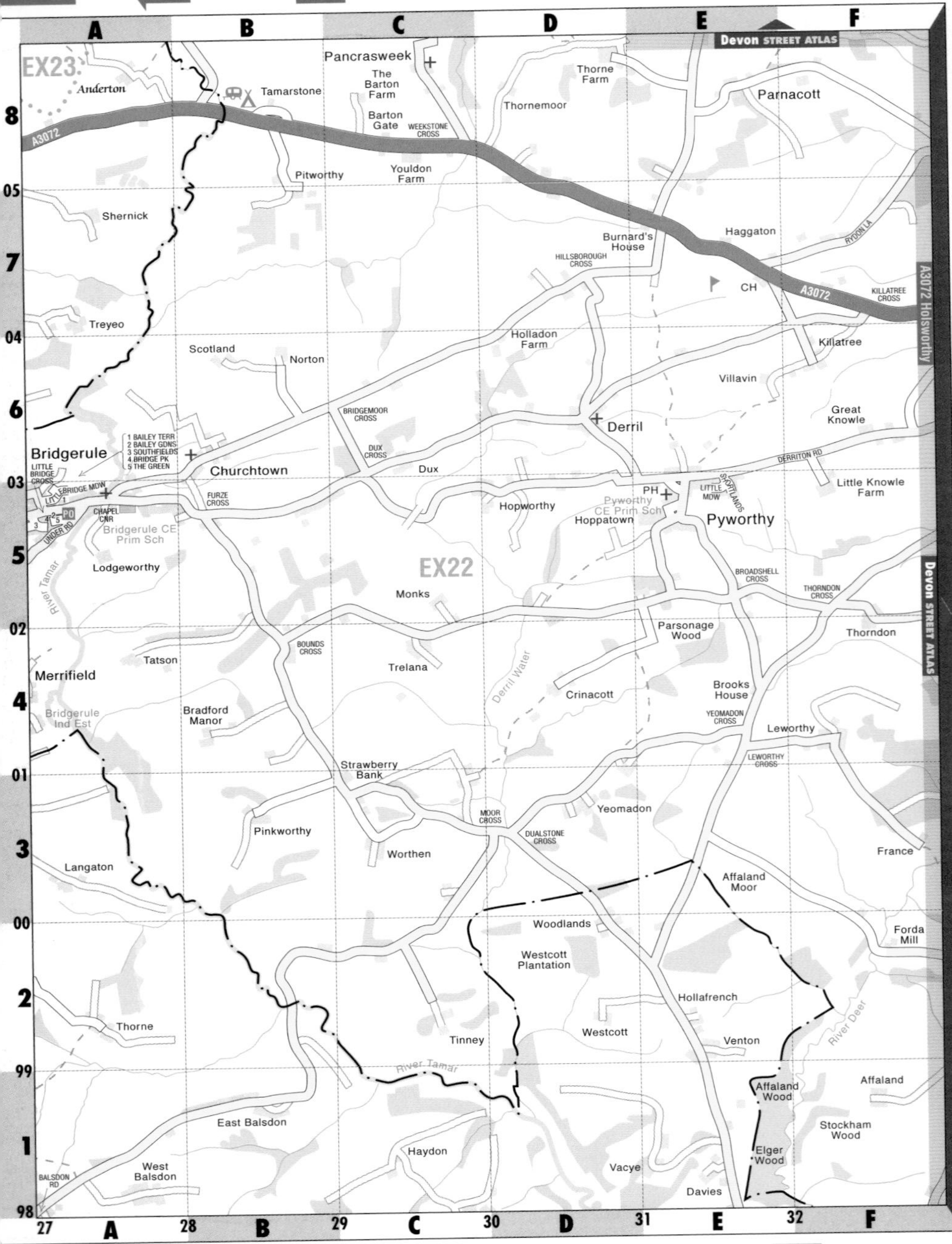

7
12
13

Scale: 1⅓ inches to 1 mile
0 ¼ ½ mile
0 250m 500m 750m 1 km
10
A B C D E F
8
97
7
96
6
95
5
94
4
93
3
92
2
91
1
90
07 08 09 10 11 12
14
15
10
Cambeak
Voter Run
EX23
High Cliff
Rusey Beach
Rusey Cliff
Buckator
Gull Rock
Beeny Sisters
Fire Beacon Point
Seals Hole
South West Coast Path
Beeny
Beeny Cliff
Trebyla Farm
B3263
Pentargon
Hillsborough
Tremorle
Trewannett
C2
1 HOLLOWELL HO
2 BRIDGE WLK
3 THE OLD MILL
VALENCY ROW
Penally Point
Penally Hill
PENALLY TERR
Meachard
YH
Mus
Penally House
Harbour
PENALLY HILL
PENALLY CT
C1
1 PENTARGON RD
2 EGLOS VIEW
3 TREFLEUR CL
4 LANGFORDS MDW
5 FORRABURY HILL
6 CLOVER LANE CL
7 WHITE SMOCK MDW
8 DOCTORS HILL
9 GUNPOOL LA
10 DUNN ST
Visitor Ctr
MARINE TERR
NEW RD
OLD RD
Tresuck
PL35
Newmills
River Valency
Willapark
Forrabury
Mast
Trafalgar Farm
Short Island
Grower Rock
Boscastle
B3263
PO
Sch
FORE ST
Firebeacon Hill
Ladies Window
CAMBEAK
GREEN LA
POTTERS LA
UNDERRD
BUTTS LA
Home Farm
Trebiffin
Long Island
Welltown Manor
TINTAGEL RD
BARNPARK RD
PARADISE RD
B3266
MOUNT PLEASANT
Trewold
Trevalga
WILLAPARK VIEW
GIBBS LA
HIGH ST
Paradise House
B3263
B3266

9
6

Scale: 1⅓ inches to 1 mile
0 ¼ ½ mile
0 250m 500m 750m 1 km

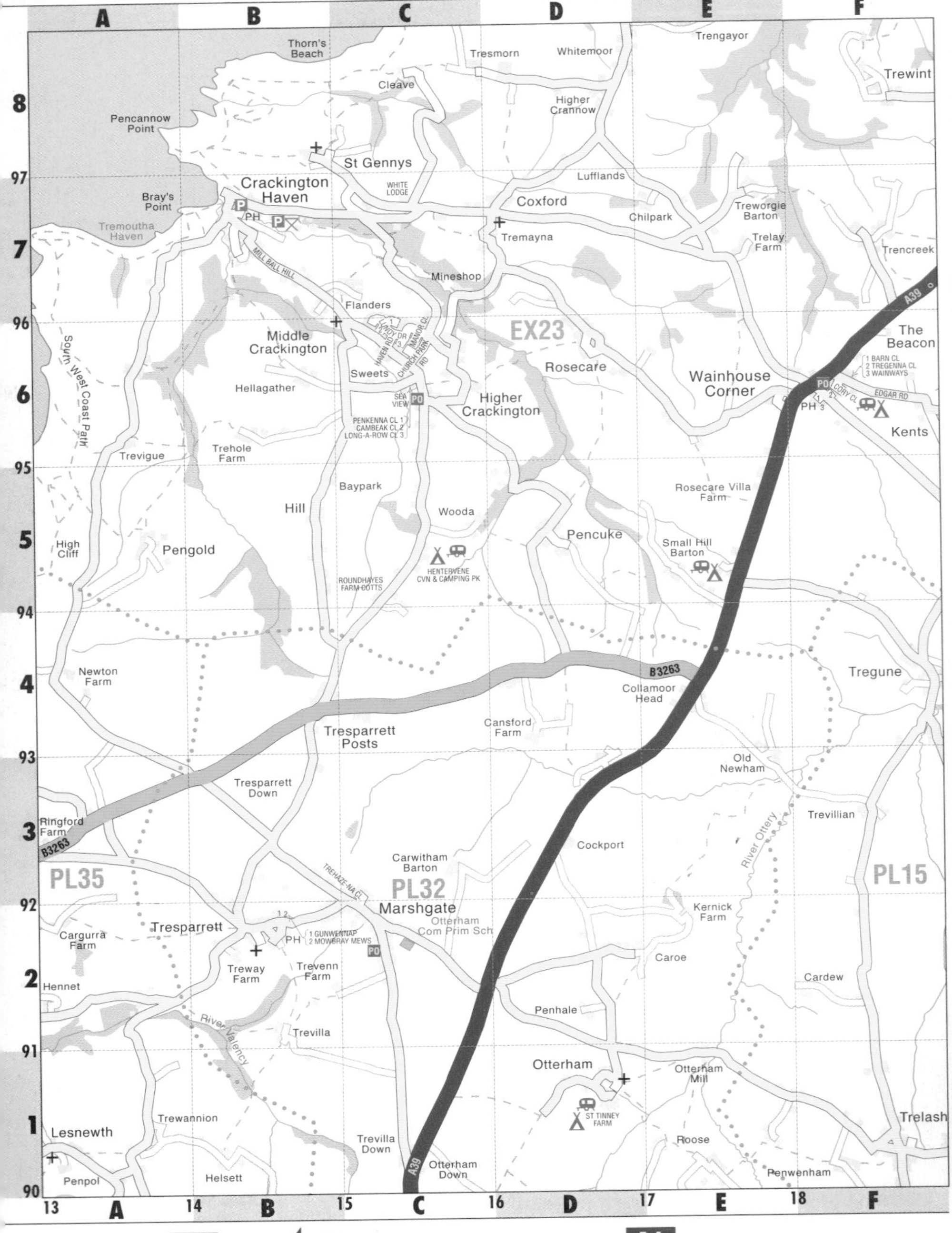

15
9
16

Scale: 1⅓ inches to 1 mile
0 ¼ ½ mile
0 250m 500m 750m 1 km

6
7
12

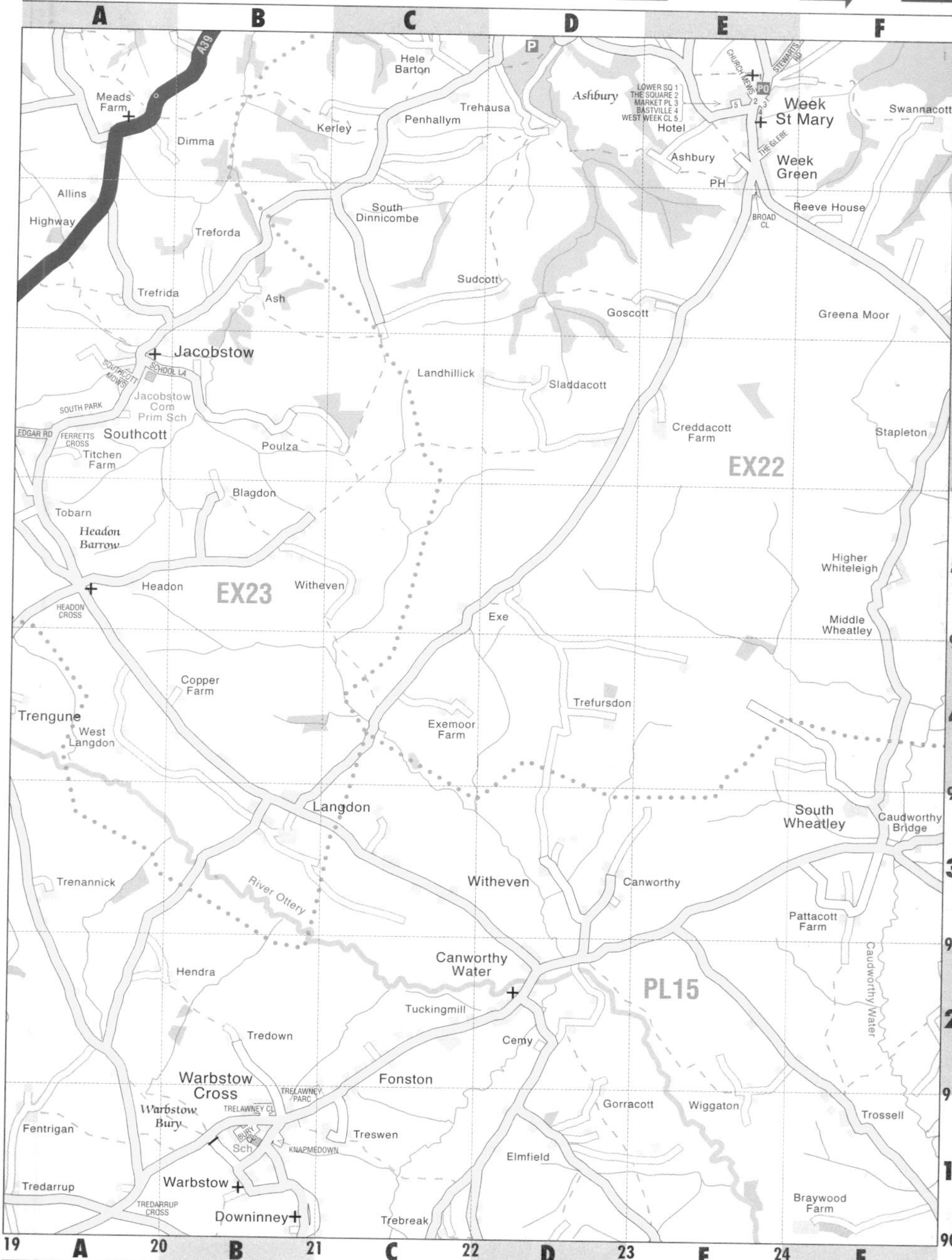

16
17
12

7
11
8

Scale: 1⅓ inches to 1 mile
0 ¼ ½ mile
0 250m 500m 750m 1 km

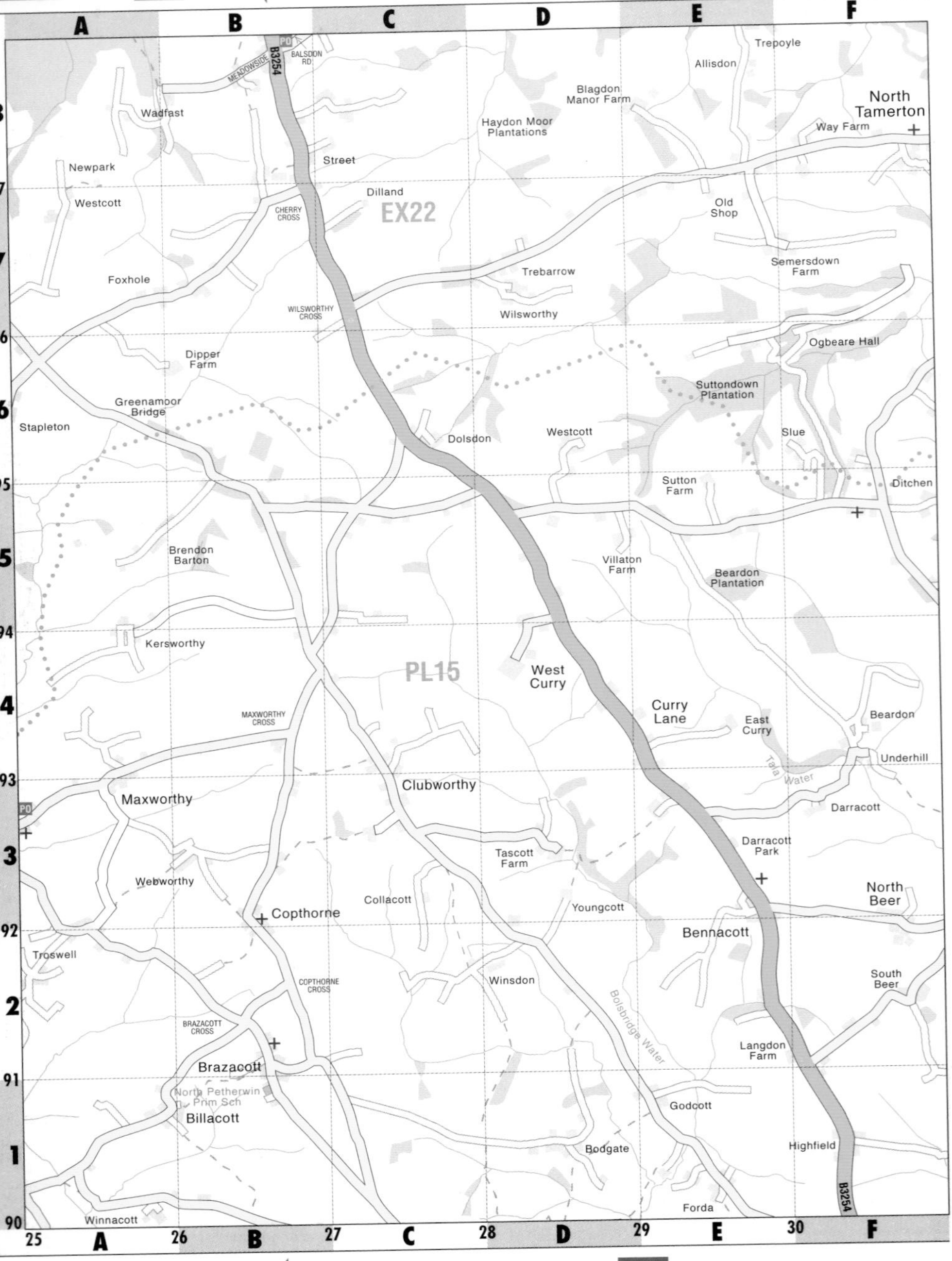

17
11
18

Scale: 1⅓ inches to 1 mile
0 ¼ ½ mile
0 250m 500m 750m 1 km

8

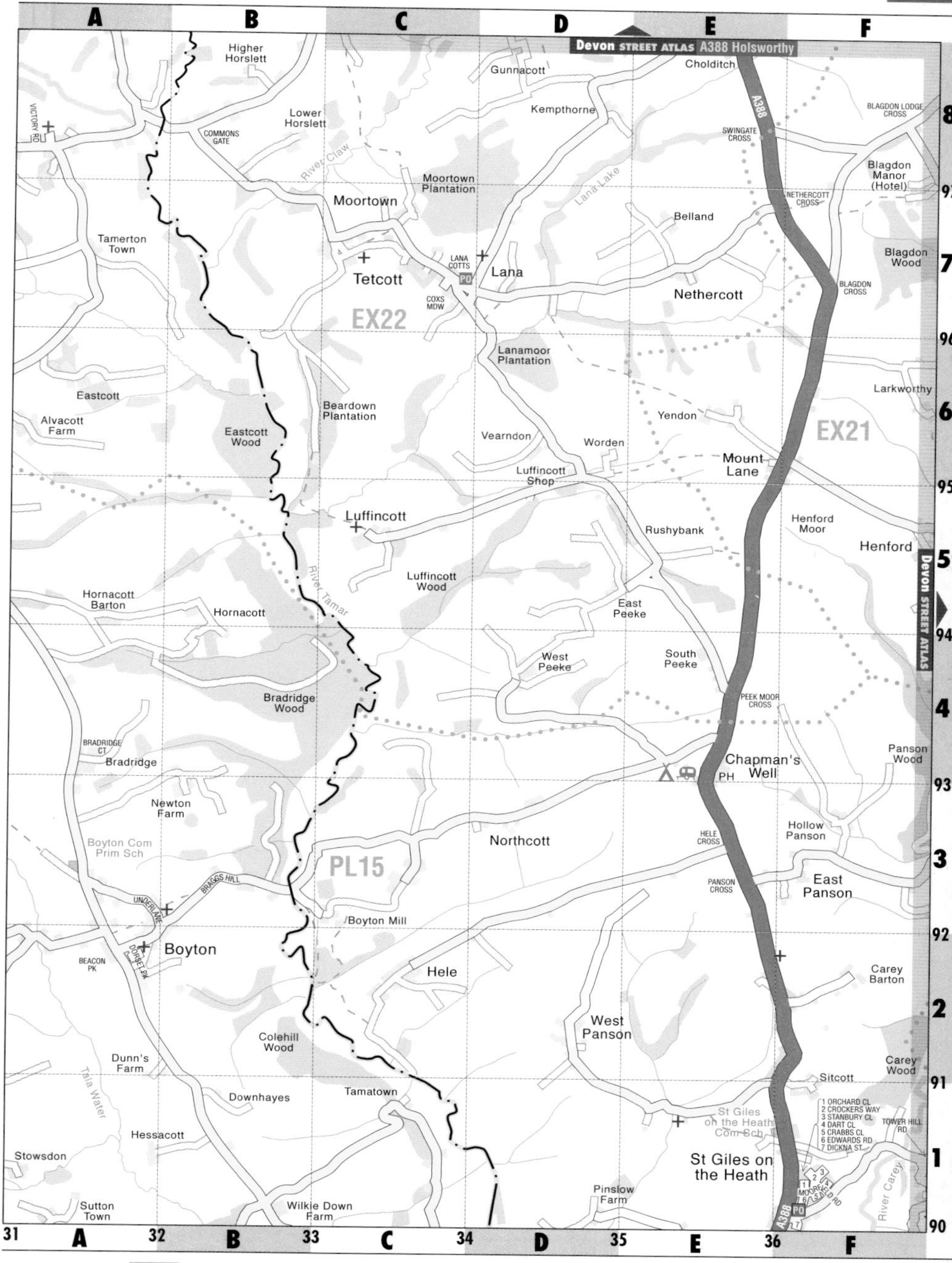

18

19

9

Scale: 1⅓ inches to 1 mile

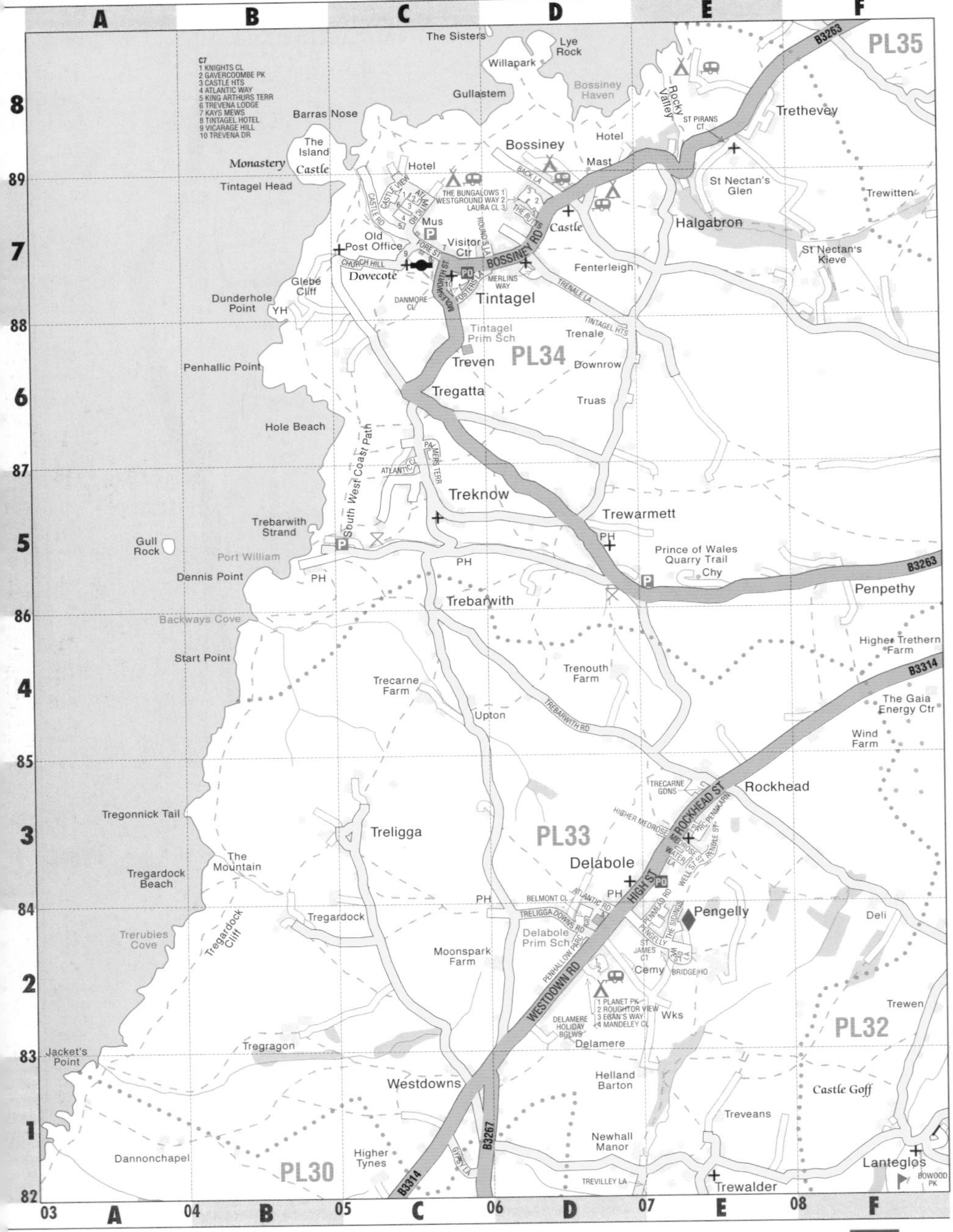

A
B
C
D
E
F
8
89
7
88
6
87
5
86
4
85
3
84
2
83
1
82
03
04
05
06
07
08
C7
1 KNIGHTS CL
2 GAVERCOOMBE PK
3 CASTLE HTS
4 ATLANTIC WAY
5 KING ARTHURS TERR
6 TREVENA LODGE
7 KAYS MEWS
8 TINTAGEL HOTEL
9 VICARAGE HILL
10 TREVENA DR
The Sisters
Lye Rock
Willapark
Gullastem
Bossiney Haven
Rocky Valley
B3263
PL35
Trethevey
ST PIRANS CT
Barras Nose
The Island
Monastery
Castle
Tintagel Head
Hotel
Bossiney
Mast
BACK LA
THE BUNGALOWS 1
WESTGROUND WAY 2
LAURA CL 3
THE BUTTS
Castle
St Nectan's Glen
Trewitten
Halgabron
St Nectan's Kieve
CASTLE VIEW
CASTLE RD
ATLANTIC RD
Mus
Old Post Office
Visitor Ctr
FORE ST
CHURCH HILL
Dovecote
BOSSINEY RD
MOLESWORTH ST
FOSTERS LA
ROUND'S LA
PO
MERLINS WAY
Fenterleigh
TRENALE LA
Glebe Cliff
Dunderhole Point
YH
DANMORE CL
Tintagel
TINTAGEL HTS
Trenale
Tintagel Prim Sch
PL34
Treven
Downrow
Penhallic Point
Tregatta
Truas
Hole Beach
South West Coast Path
PALMERS TERR
ATLANTIC CL
Treknow
Trewarmett
Trebarwith Strand
Gull Rock
Port William
PH
Prince of Wales Quarry Trail
Chy
Dennis Point
Penpethy
Trebarwith
Backways Cove
Start Point
Higher Trethern Farm
Trenouth Farm
Trecarne Farm
B3314
Upton
TREBARWITH RD
The Gaia Energy Ctr
Wind Farm
TRECARNE GDNS
Rockhead
ROCKHEAD ST
HIGHER MEDROSE
PARC PENHALLOW
Tregonnick Tail
Treligga
PL33
MEDROSE ST
WATER LA
RENDLE ST
The Mountain
Delabole
Tregardock Beach
HIGH ST
BELMONT CL
ATLANTIC RD
PENMEAD RD
THE SIDINGS
Pengelly
Deli
Tregardock
TRELIGGA DOWNS RD
Delabole Prim Sch
PENGELLY
ST JAMES CT
WELL ST
Trerubies Cove
Tregardock Cliff
Moonspark Farm
PENHALLOW PARC
Cemy
BRIDGE HO
WESTDOWN RD
1 PLANET PK
2 ROUGHTOR VIEW
3 EGAN'S WAY
4 MANDELEY CL
Wks
Trewen
DELAMERE HOLIDAY BGLWS
Delamere
PL32
Jacket's Point
Tregragon
Westdowns
Helland Barton
Castle Goff
Treveans
B3267
Newhall Manor
Dannonchapel
Higher Tynes
GYPSY LA
PL30
TREVILLEY LA
Lanteglos
Trewalder
BOWOOD PK

23

24

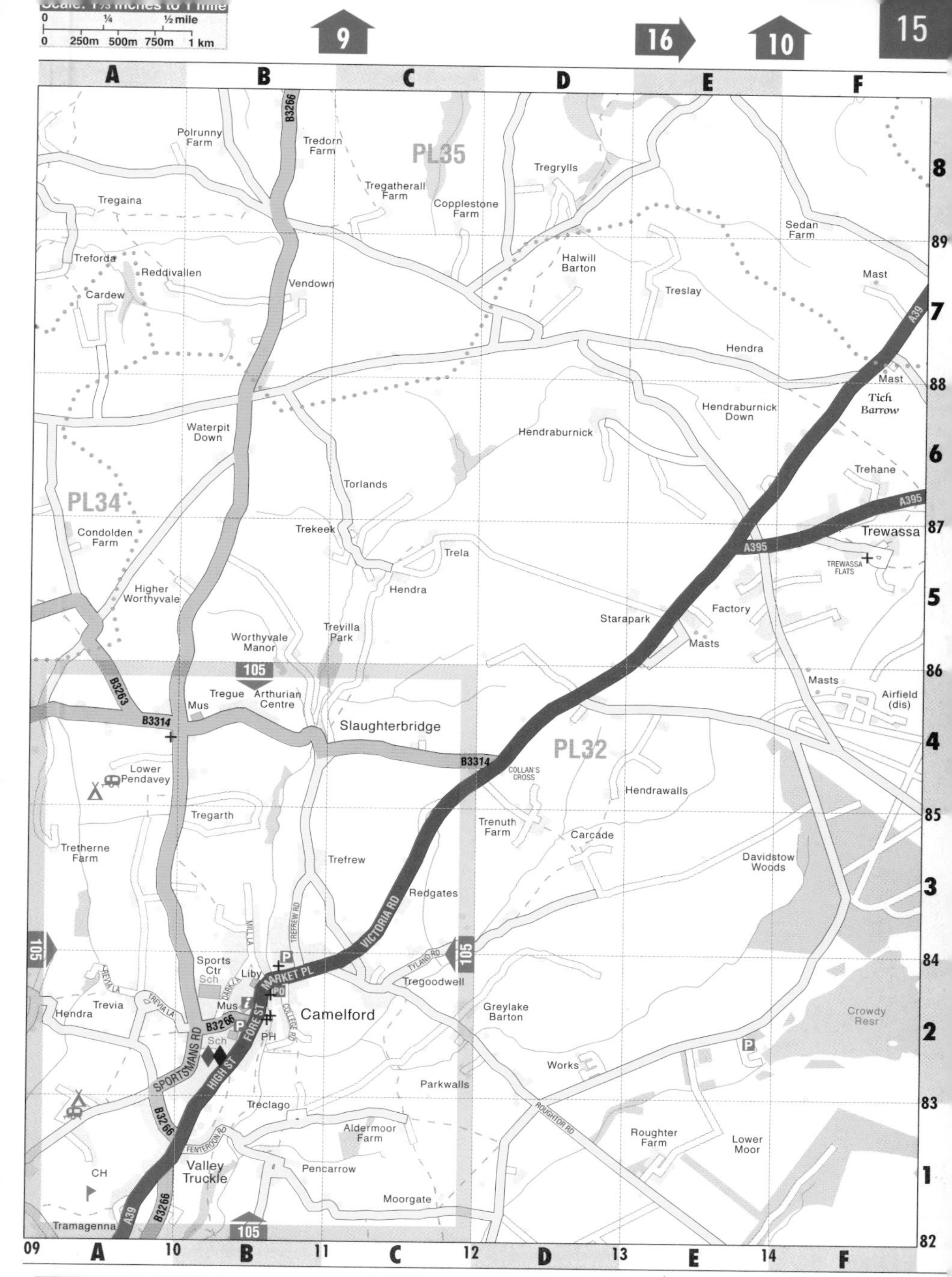

For full street detail of the highlighted area see page 105.

15 10 11

Scale: 1⅓ inches to 1 mile
0 ¼ ½ mile
0 250m 500m 750m 1 km

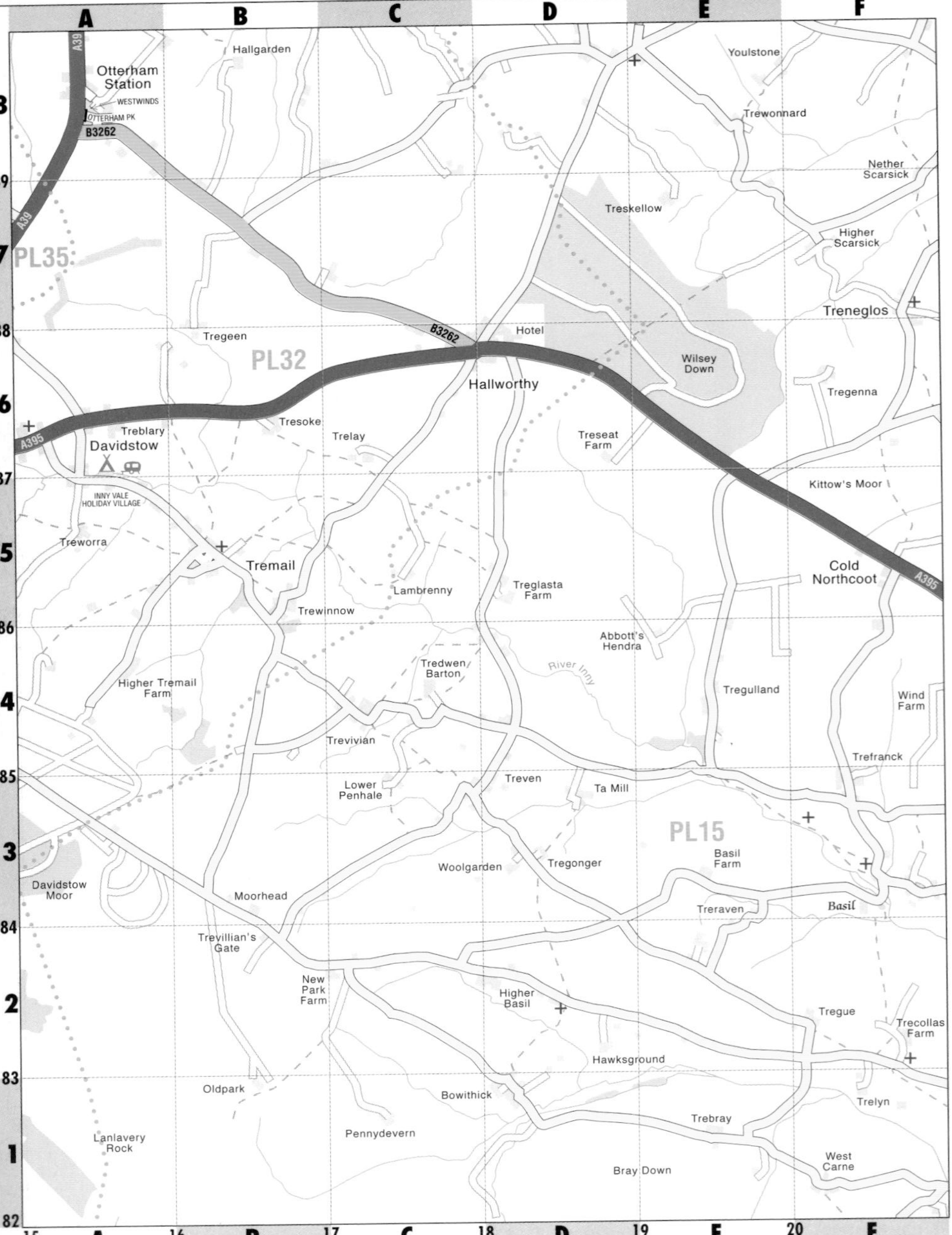

15 25 26

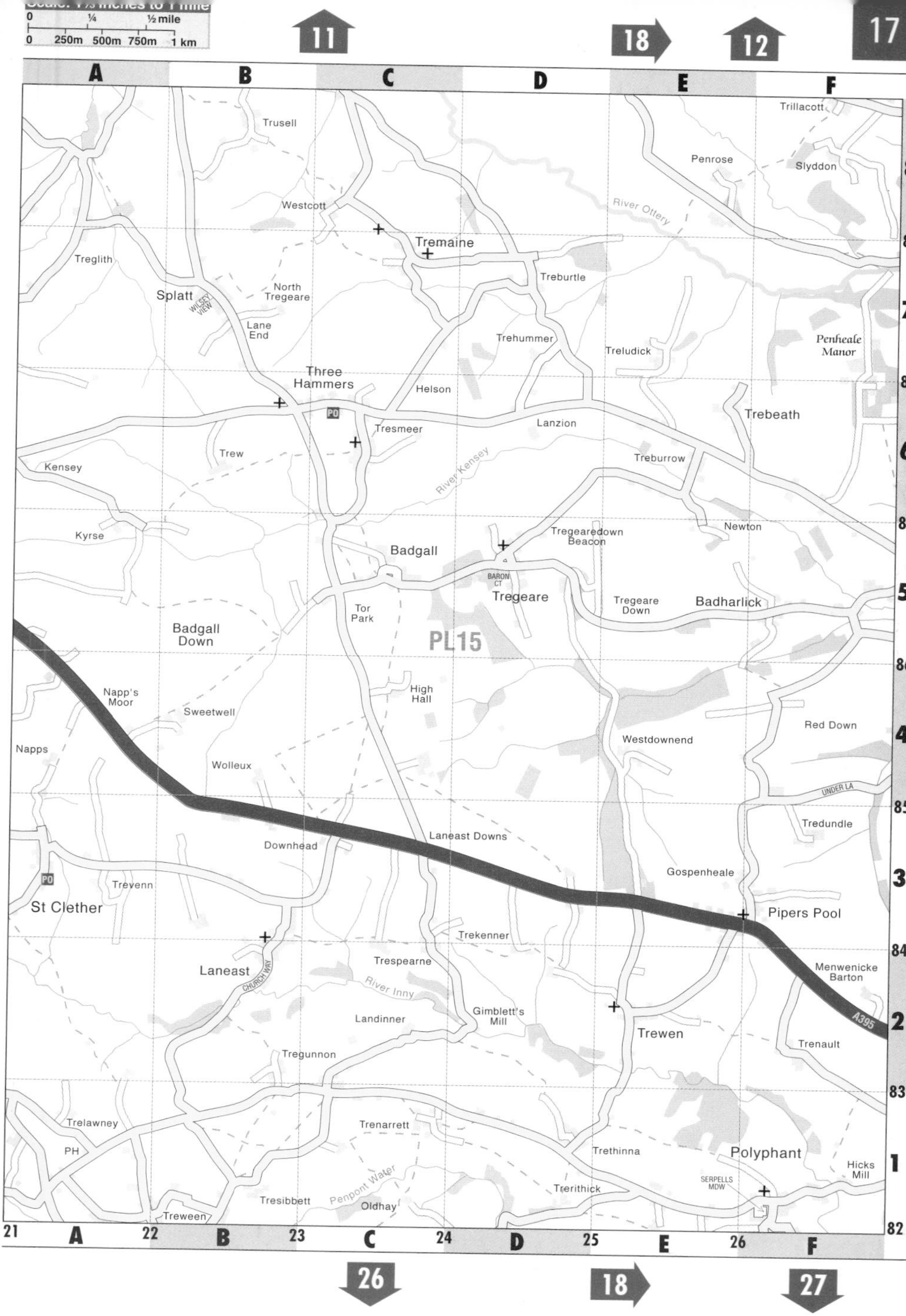
Scale: 1⅓ inches to 1 mile
0 ¼ ½ mile
0 250m 500m 750m 1 km
11
18
12
A B C D E F
8 89 7 88 6 87 5 86 4 85 3 84 2 83 1 82
21 22 23 24 25 26
Trusell
Trillacott
Penrose
Slyddon
Westcott
River Ottery
Tremaine
Treglith
Treburtle
Splatt
WILSEY VIEW
North Tregeare
Lane End
Trehummer
Treludick
Penheale Manor
Three Hammers
Helson
Trebeath
PO
Lanzion
Tresmeer
Trew
Kensey
Treburrow
River Kensey
Newton
Kyrse
Badgall
Tregearedown Beacon
BARON CT
Tregeare
Tregeare Down
Badharlick
Tor Park
Badgall Down
PL15
Napp's Moor
High Hall
Sweetwell
Red Down
Napps
Westdownend
Wolleux
UNDER LA
Tredundle
Laneast Downs
Downhead
Gospenheale
PO
Trevenn
St Clether
Pipers Pool
Trekenner
Menwenicke Barton
Trespearne
Laneast
CHURCH WAY
River Inny
Gimblett's Mill
Landinner
A395
Trewen
Trenault
Tregunnon
Trelawney
Trenarrett
PH
Trethinna
Polyphant
Hicks Mill
Penpont Water
Treweek
Tresibbett
Oldhay
SERPELLS MDW
Treween
26
18
27

17 12 13

Scale: 1⅓ inches to 1 mile
0 ¼ ½ mile
0 250m 500m 750m 1 km

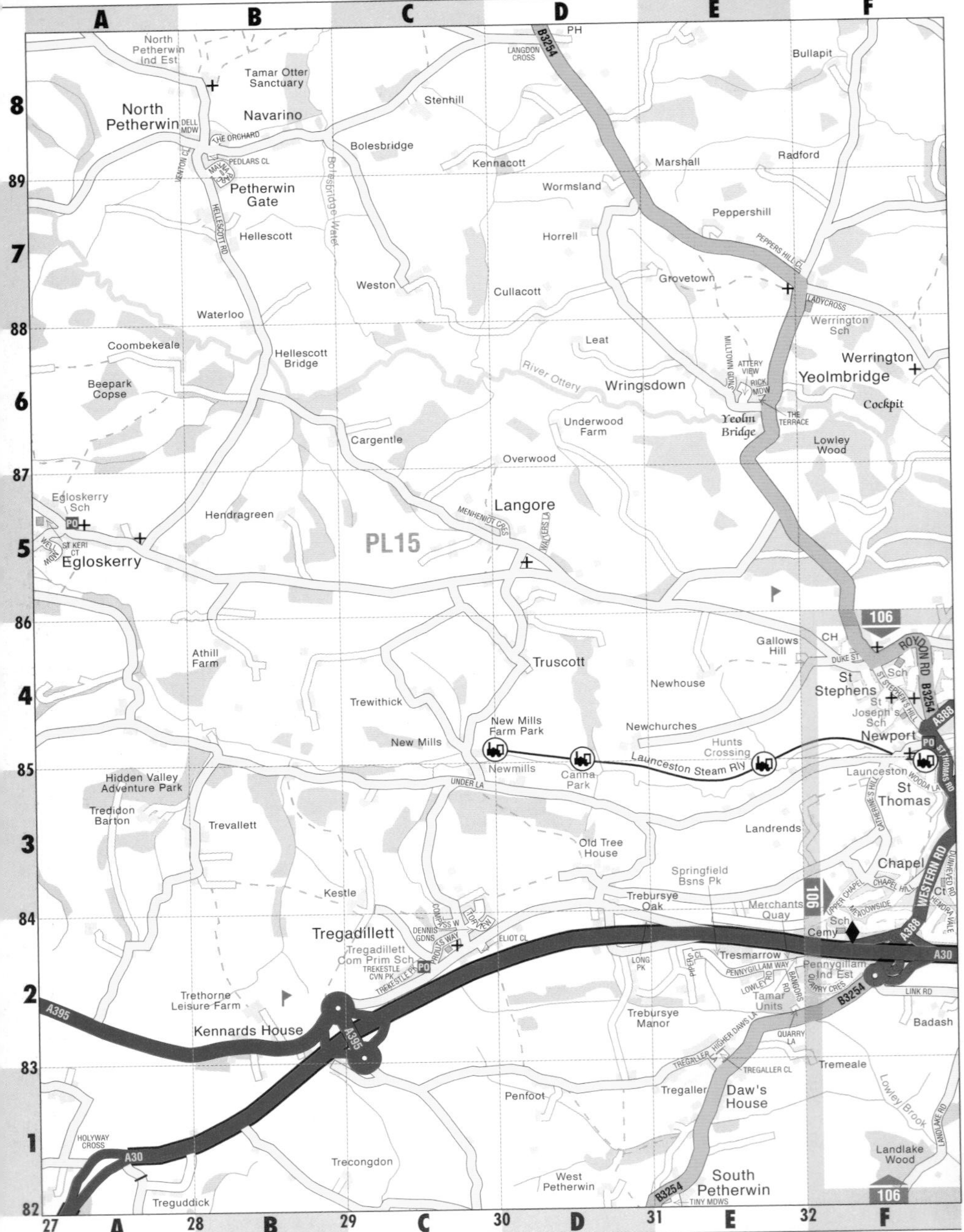

17 27

For full street detail of the highlighted area see page 106.

28

Scale: 1⅓ inches to 1 mile
0 ¼ ½ mile
0 250m 500m 750m 1 km

13

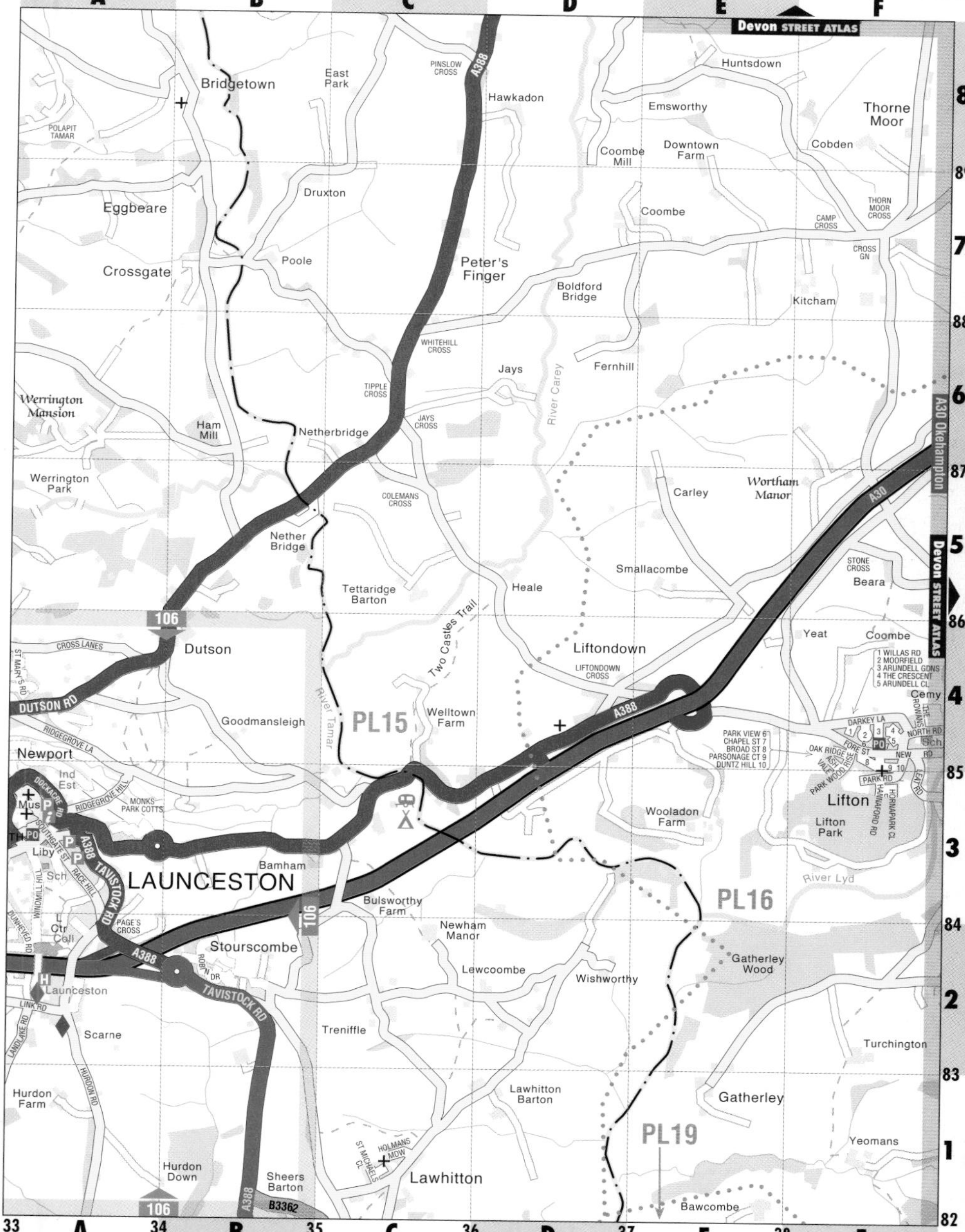

For full street detail of the highlighted area see page 106.

28

29

Scale: 1⅓ inches to 1 mile
0 ¼ ½ mile
0 250m 500m 750m 1 km

31

32

For full street detail of the highlighted area see page 107.

32

22

33

21

Scale: 1⅓ inches to 1 mile
0 ¼ ½ mile
0 250m 500m 750m 1 km

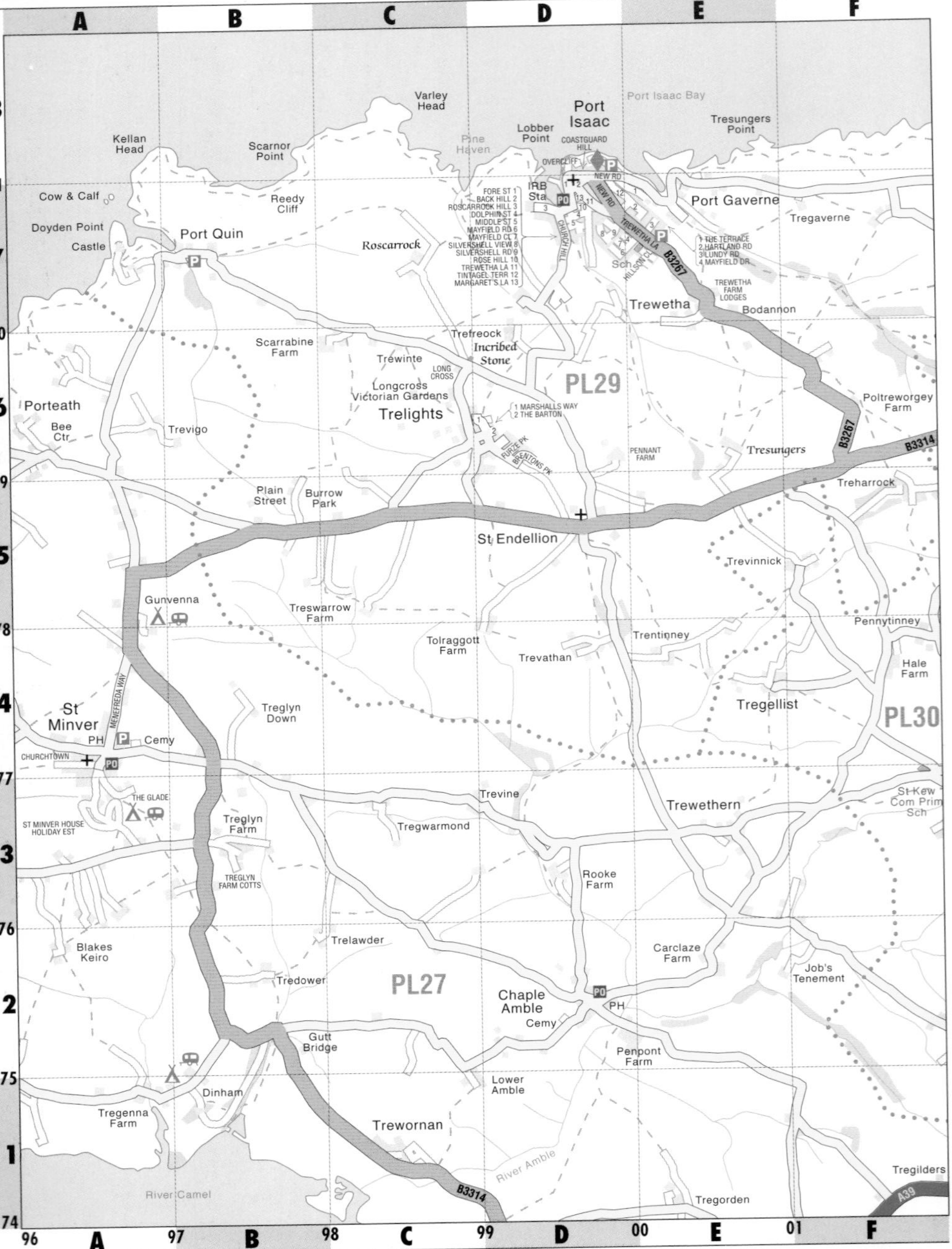
A
B
C
D
E
F
8
81
7
80
6
79
5
78
4
77
3
76
2
75
1
74
96
97
98
99
00
01
Port Isaac Bay
Varley Head
Port Isaac
Kellan Head
Scarnor Point
Pine Haven
Lobber Point
COASTGUARD HILL
Tresungers Point
OVERCLIFF
NEW RD
Cow & Calf
Reedy Cliff
IRB Sta
PO
Port Gaverne
Tregaverne
Doyden Point
Castle
Port Quin
Roscarrock
FORE ST 1
BACK HILL 2
ROSCARROCK HILL 3
DOLPHIN ST 4
MIDDLE ST 5
MAYFIELD RD 6
MAYFIELD CL 7
SILVERSHELL VIEW 8
SILVERSHELL RD 9
ROSE HILL 10
TREWETHA LA 11
TINTAGEL TERR 12
MARGARET'S LA 13
CHURCH HILL
TREWETHA LA
HILLSON CL
B3267
Sch
1 THE TERRACE
2 HARTLAND RD
3 LUNDY RD
4 MAYFIELD DR
TREWETHA FARM LODGES
Trewetha
Bodannon
Scarrabine Farm
Trefreock
Incribed Stone
Trewinte
LONG CROSS
PL29
Longcross Victorian Gardens
Trelights
1 MARSHALLS WAY
2 THE BARTON
Poltreworgey Farm
Porteath
Bee Ctr
Trevigo
FURZE PK
BRENTONS PK
PENNANT FARM
Tresungers
B3314
Treharrock
Plain Street
Burrow Park
St Endellion
Trevinnick
Gunvenna
Treswarrow Farm
Pennytinney
Tolraggott Farm
Trentinney
Trevathan
Hale Farm
St Minver
MENEFREDA WAY
Treglyn Down
Tregellist
PL30
PH
Cemy
CHURCHTOWN
Trevine
Trewethern
St Kew Com Prim Sch
THE GLADE
ST MINVER HOUSE HOLIDAY EST
Treglyn Farm
Tregwarmond
TREGLYN FARM COTTS
Rooke Farm
Blakes Keiro
Trelawder
Carclaze Farm
Job's Tenement
Tredower
PL27
Chaple Amble
Gutt Bridge
Penpont Farm
Lower Amble
Dinham
Tregenna Farm
Trewornan
River Amble
Tregilders
River Camel
Tregorden
A39

21
33
34

Scale: 1⅓ inches to 1 mile
0 ¼ ½ mile
0 250m 500m 750m 1 km

14
24

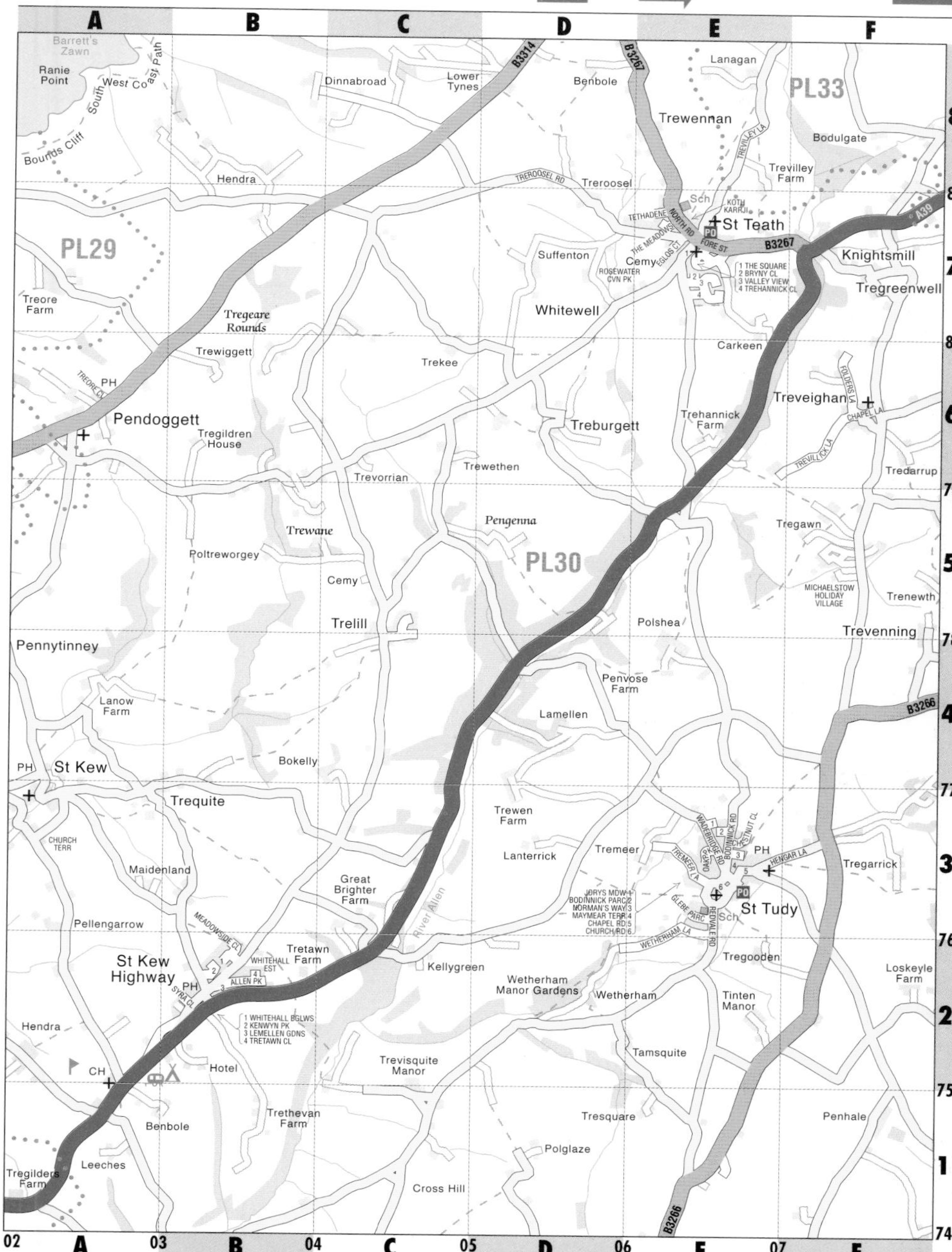

34
24
35

14
23
15

Scale: 1⅓ inches to 1 mile
0 ¼ ½ mile
0 250m 500m 750m 1 km

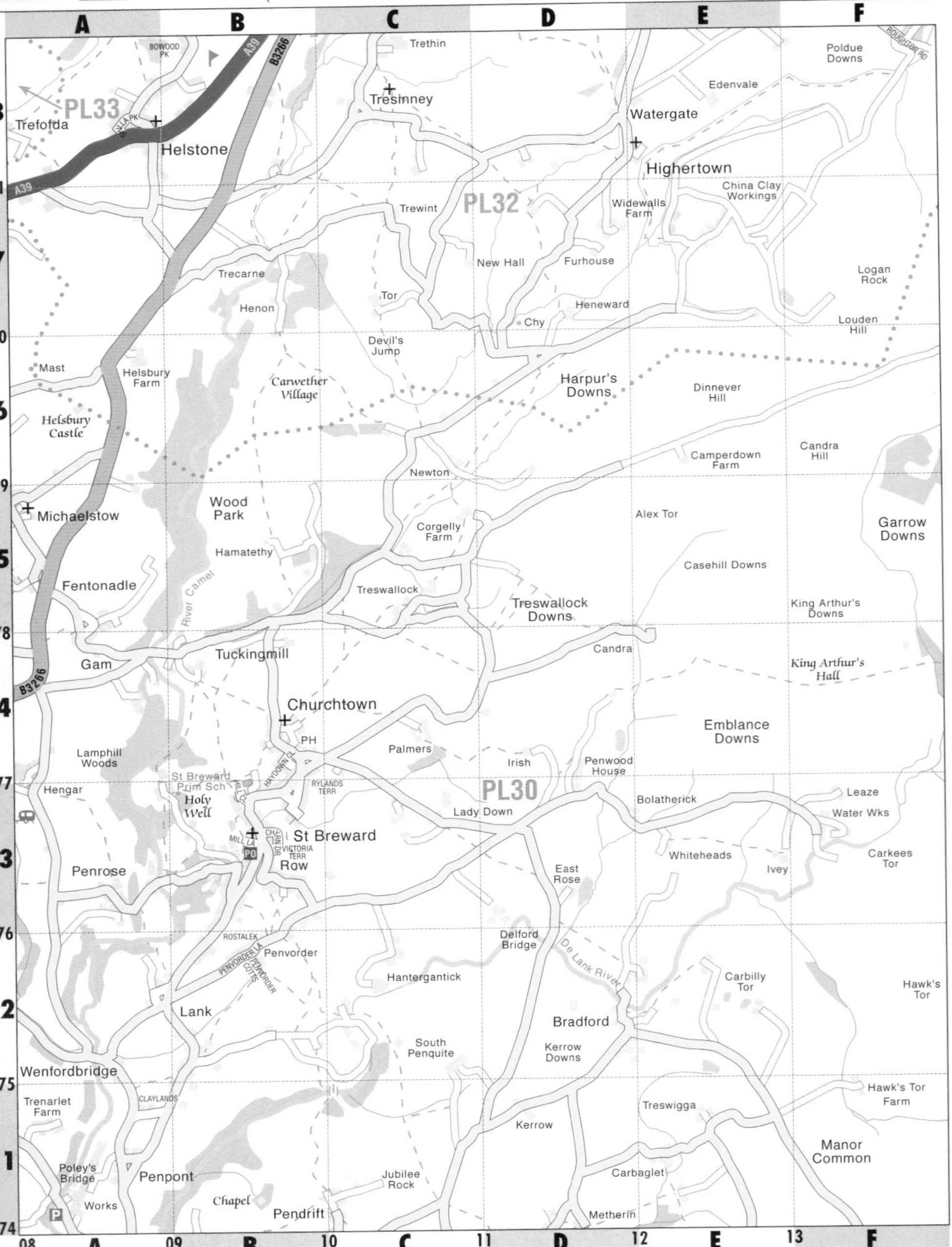

23
35
36

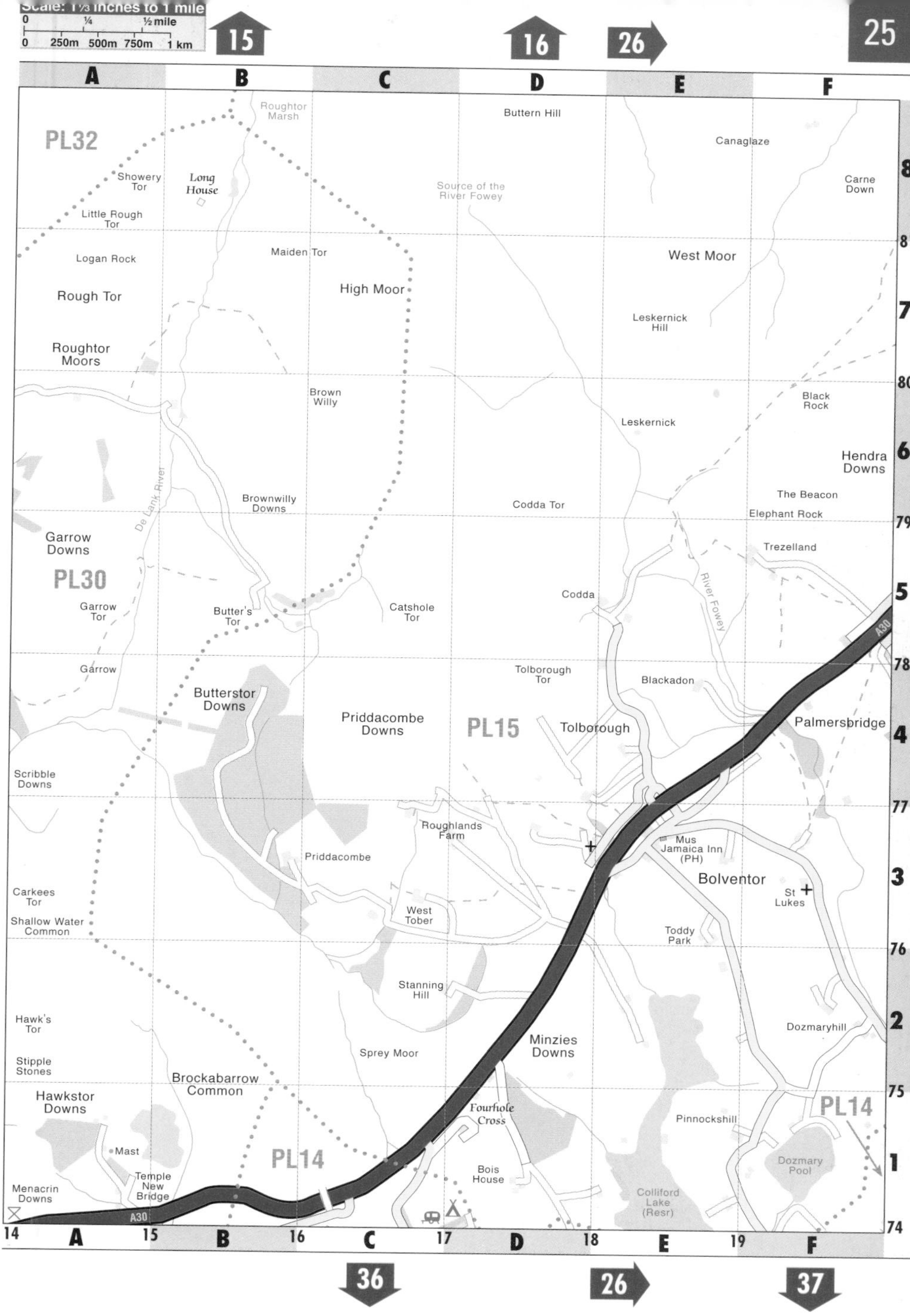
Scale: 1⅓ inches to 1 mile
0 ¼ ½ mile
0 250m 500m 750m 1 km
15
16
26
A
B
C
D
E
F
PL32
Roughtor Marsh
Buttern Hill
Canaglaze
Showery Tor
Long House
Source of the River Fowey
Carne Down
8
Little Rough Tor
81
Logan Rock
Maiden Tor
West Moor
Rough Tor
High Moor
7
Leskernick Hill
Roughtor Moors
80
Brown Willy
Black Rock
Leskernick
6
Hendra Downs
De Lank River
The Beacon
Brownwilly Downs
Codda Tor
Elephant Rock
79
Garrow Downs
Trezelland
PL30
River Fowey
Codda
5
Garrow Tor
Butter's Tor
Catshole Tor
A30
78
Garrow
Tolborough Tor
Blackadon
Butterstor Downs
Priddacombe Downs
PL15
Tolborough
Palmersbridge
4
Scribble Downs
77
Roughlands Farm
Mus
Jamaica Inn (PH)
Priddacombe
3
Bolventor
Carkees Tor
St Lukes
West Tober
Shallow Water Common
Toddy Park
76
Stanning Hill
Hawk's Tor
2
Dozmaryhill
Sprey Moor
Minzies Downs
Stipple Stones
Brockabarrow Common
75
Hawkstor Downs
Fourhole Cross
PL14
Pinnockshill
Mast
1
PL14
Dozmary Pool
Bois House
Temple New Bridge
Menacrin Downs
Colliford Lake (Resr)
A30
74
14
A
15
B
16
C
17
D
18
E
19
F
36
26
37

16
25
17
Scale: 1⅓ inches to 1 mile
0 ¼ ½ mile
0 250m 500m 750m 1 km

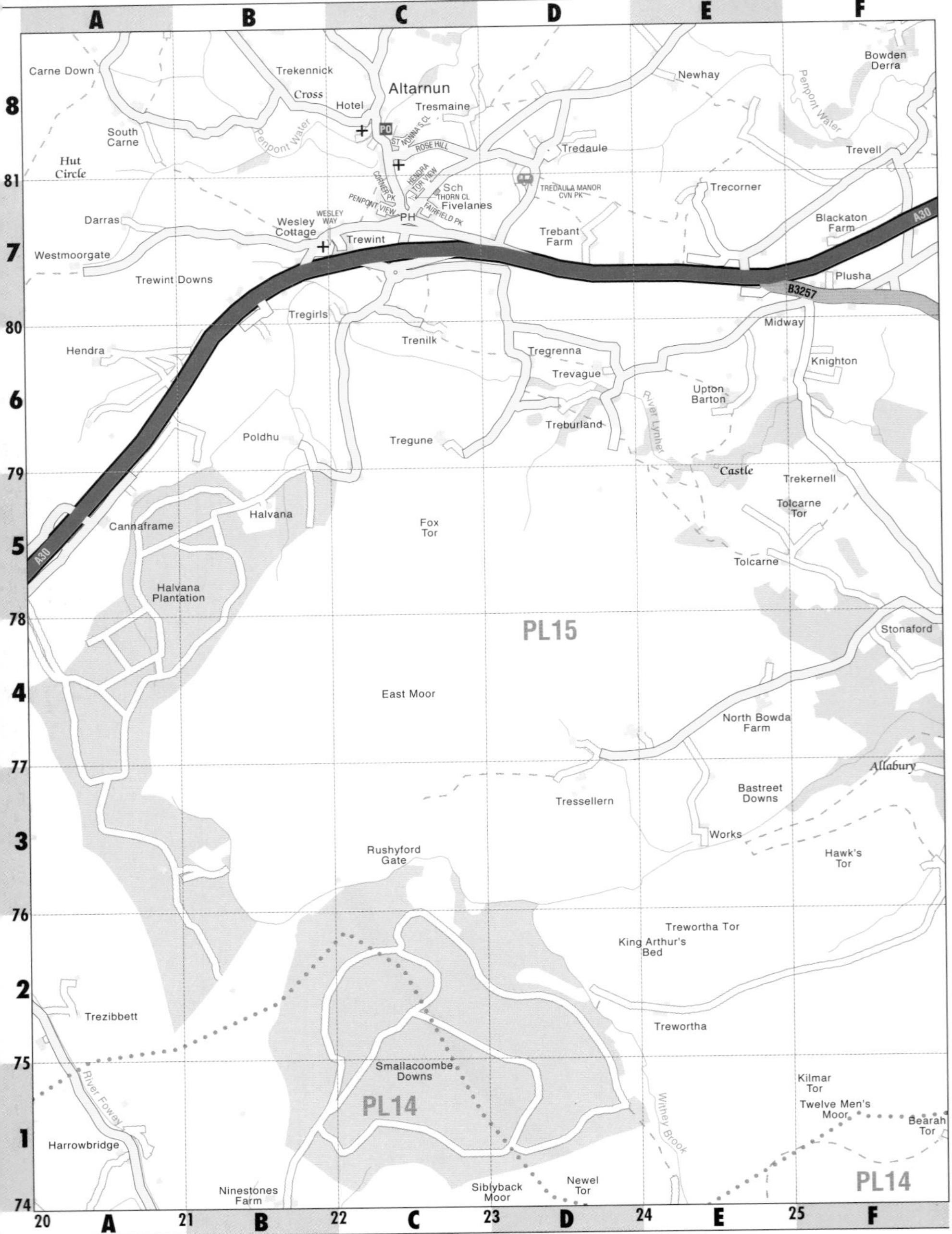

25
37
38

Scale: 1⅓ inches to 1 mile
0 ¼ ½ mile
0 250m 500m 750m 1 km

17 18 28

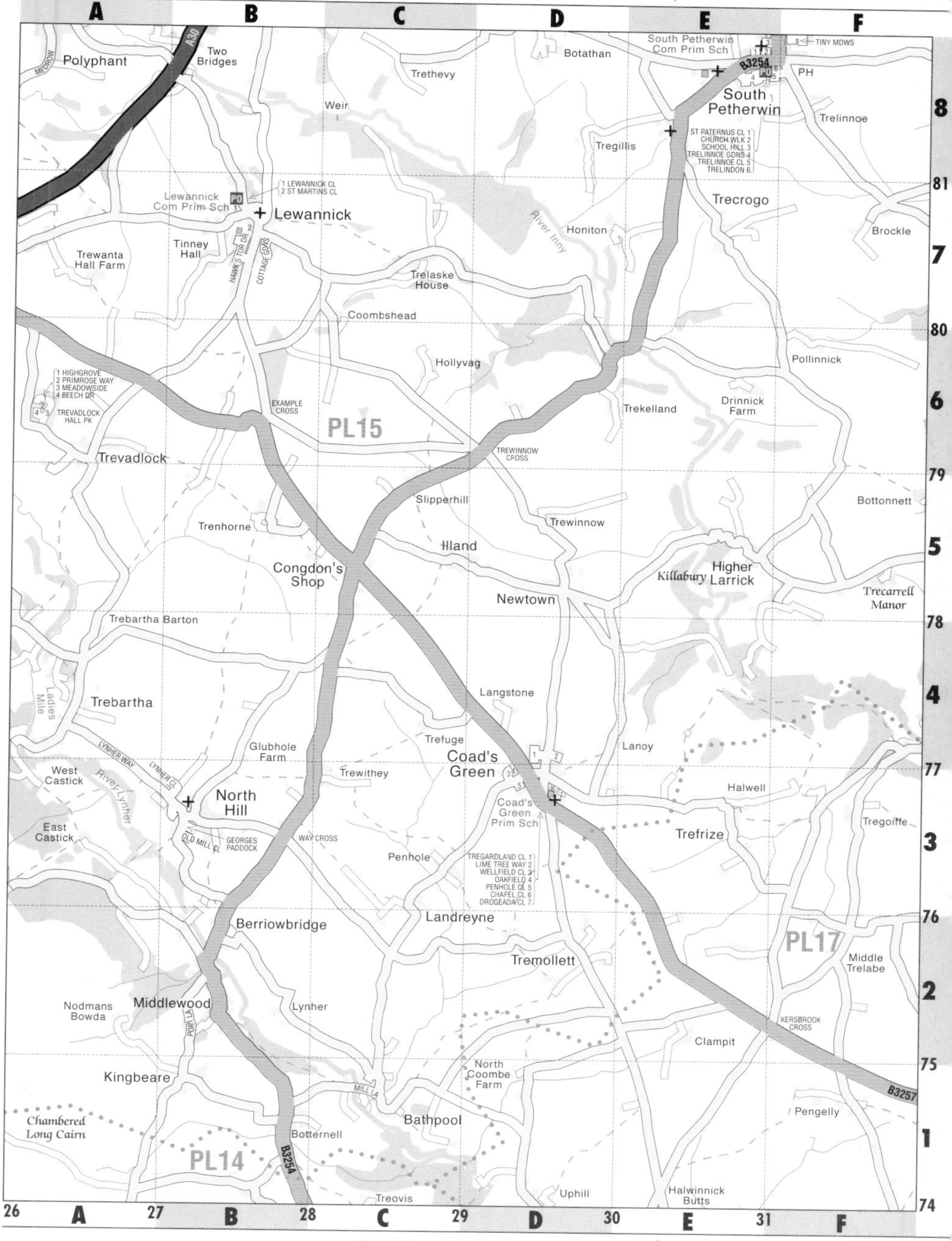

38 28 39

18
27
19

Scale: 1⅓ inches to 1 mile
0 ¼ ½ mile
0 250m 500m 750m 1 km

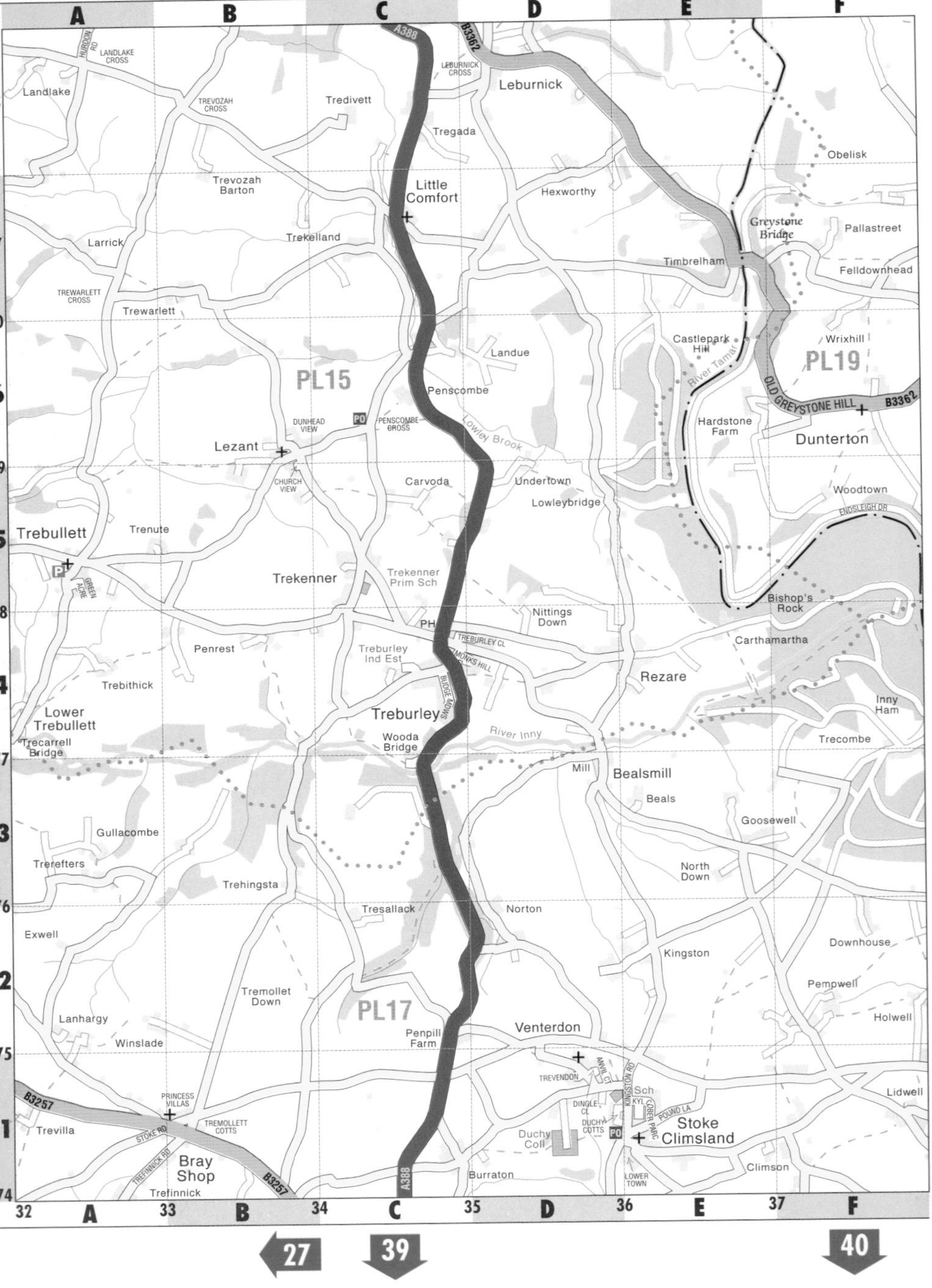

27
39
40

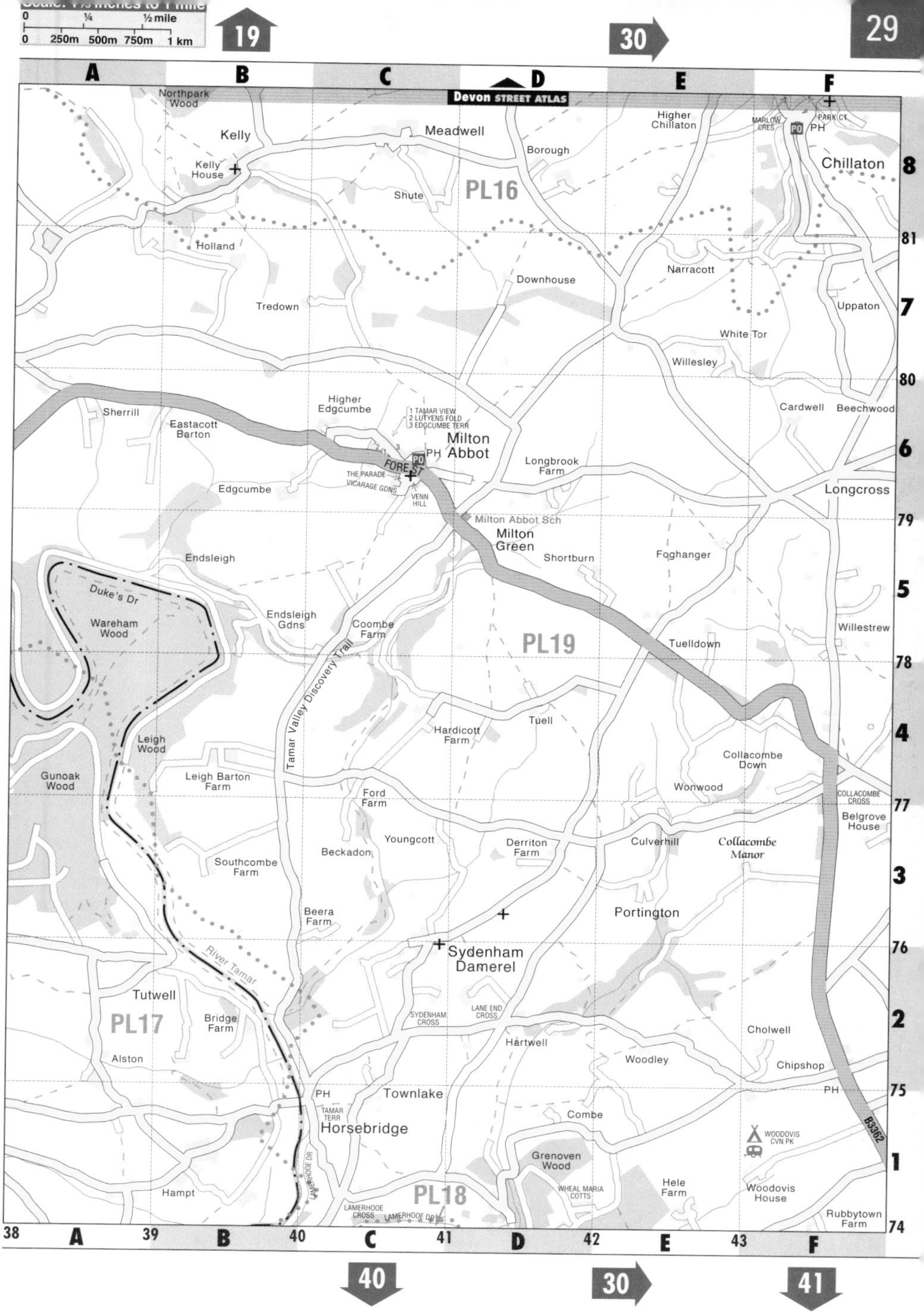

Scale: 1⅓ inches to 1 mile
0 ¼ ½ mile
0 250m 500m 750m 1 km
19
30
Devon STREET ATLAS
A B C D E F
Northpark Wood
Kelly
Kelly House
Meadwell
Borough
Higher Chillaton
MARLOW CRES
PARK CT
PO
PH
Chillaton
PL16
Shute
Holland
Narracott
Downhouse
Tredown
Uppaton
White Tor
Willesley
Higher Edgcumbe
1 TAMAR VIEW
2 LUTYENS FOLD
3 EDGCUMBE TERR
Cardwell
Beechwood
Sherrill
Eastacott Barton
Milton Abbot
FORE ST
THE PARADE
VICARAGE GDNS
VENN HILL
Longbrook Farm
Longcross
Edgcumbe
Milton Abbot Sch
Milton Green
Shortburn
Foghanger
Endsleigh
Duke's Dr
Wareham Wood
Endsleigh Gdns
Coombe Farm
PL19
Tuelldown
Willestrew
Tamar Valley Discovery Trail
Hardicott Farm
Tuell
Collacombe Down
Leigh Wood
Gunoak Wood
Leigh Barton Farm
Ford Farm
Wonwood
COLLACOMBE CROSS
Belgrove House
Youngcott
Derriton Farm
Culverhill
Collacombe Manor
Southcombe Farm
Beckadon
Portington
Beera Farm
Sydenham Damerel
River Tamar
Tutwell
PL17
Bridge Farm
SYDENHAM CROSS
LANE END CROSS
Cholwell
Alston
Hartwell
Woodley
Chipshop
PH
Townlake
PH
TAMAR TERR
Horsebridge
Combe
WOODOVIS CVN PK
B3362
Grenoven Wood
LAMERHOOE DR
Hampt
PL18
WHEAL MARIA COTTS
Hele Farm
Woodovis House
LAMERHOOE CROSS
LAMERHOOE DR
Rubbytown Farm
8 81 7 80 6 79 5 78 4 77 3 76 2 75 1 74
38 39 40 41 42 43
40
30
41

Scale: 1⅓ inches to 1 mile
0 ¼ ½ mile
0 250m 500m 750m 1 km

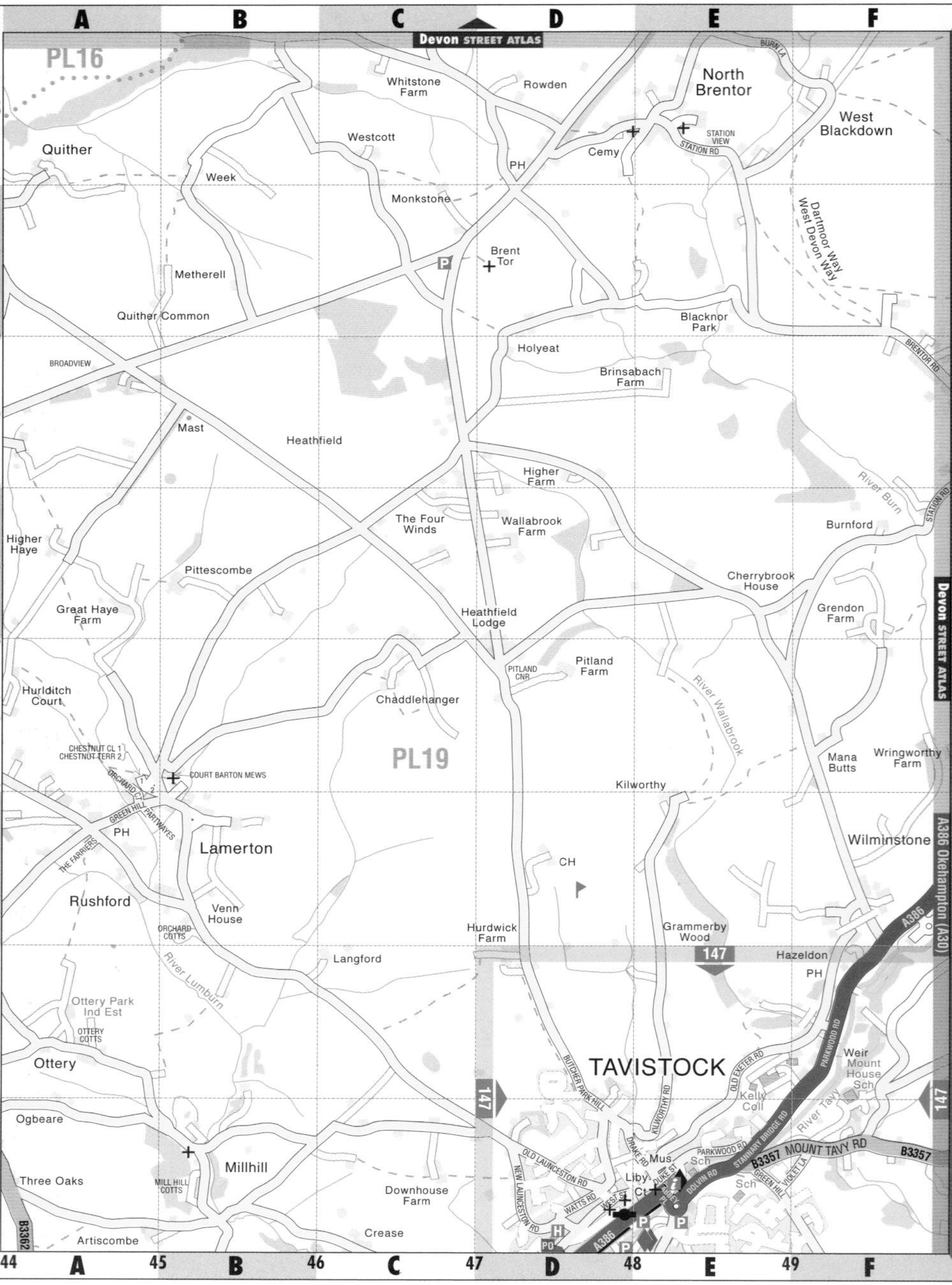
A
B
C
D
E
F
Devon STREET ATLAS
PL16
Whitstone Farm
Rowden
North Brentor
West Blackdown
Quither
Westcott
Cemy
STATION VIEW
STATION RD
BURN LA
PH
Week
Monkstone
Dartmoor Way
West Devon Way
Brent Tor
Metherell
Quither Common
Blacknor Park
Holyeat
BROADVIEW
BRENTOR RD
Brinsabach Farm
Mast
Heathfield
Higher Farm
River Burn
STATION RD
Higher Haye
The Four Winds
Wallabrook Farm
Burnford
Pittescombe
Cherrybrook House
Great Haye Farm
Heathfield Lodge
Grendon Farm
PITLAND CNR
Pitland Farm
Hurlditch Court
Chaddlehanger
River Wallabrook
CHESTNUT CL 1
CHESTNUT TERR 2
COURT BARTON MEWS
PL19
Mana Butts
Wringworthy Farm
ORCHARD CT
GREEN HILL
PARTWAYES
Kilworthy
PH
Lamerton
THE FARRIERS
Wilminstone
A386 Okehampton (A30)
CH
Rushford
Venn House
ORCHARD COTTS
Hurdwick Farm
Grammerby Wood
A386
River Lumburn
Langford
147
Hazeldon
PH
Ottery Park Ind Est
OTTERY COTTS
Ottery
BUTCHER PARK HILL
TAVISTOCK
OLD EXETER RD
PARKWOOD RD
Weir
Mount House Sch
Kelly Coll
KILWORTHY RD
River Tavy
147
Ogbeare
DRAKE RD
STANNARY BRIDGE RD
PARKWOOD RD
B3357 MOUNT TAVY RD
B3357
OLD LAUNCESTON RD
Mus
Sch
Millhill
Liby
Ct
DOLVIN RD
GREEN HILL
VIOLET LA
Three Oaks
MILL HILL COTTS
NEW LAUNCESTON RD
WATTS RD
Downhouse Farm
Sch
B3362
Crease
Artiscombe
H
PO
A386
P
8
81
7
80
6
79
5
78
4
77
3
76
2
75
1
74
44
45
46
47
48
49

For full street detail of the highlighted area see page 147.

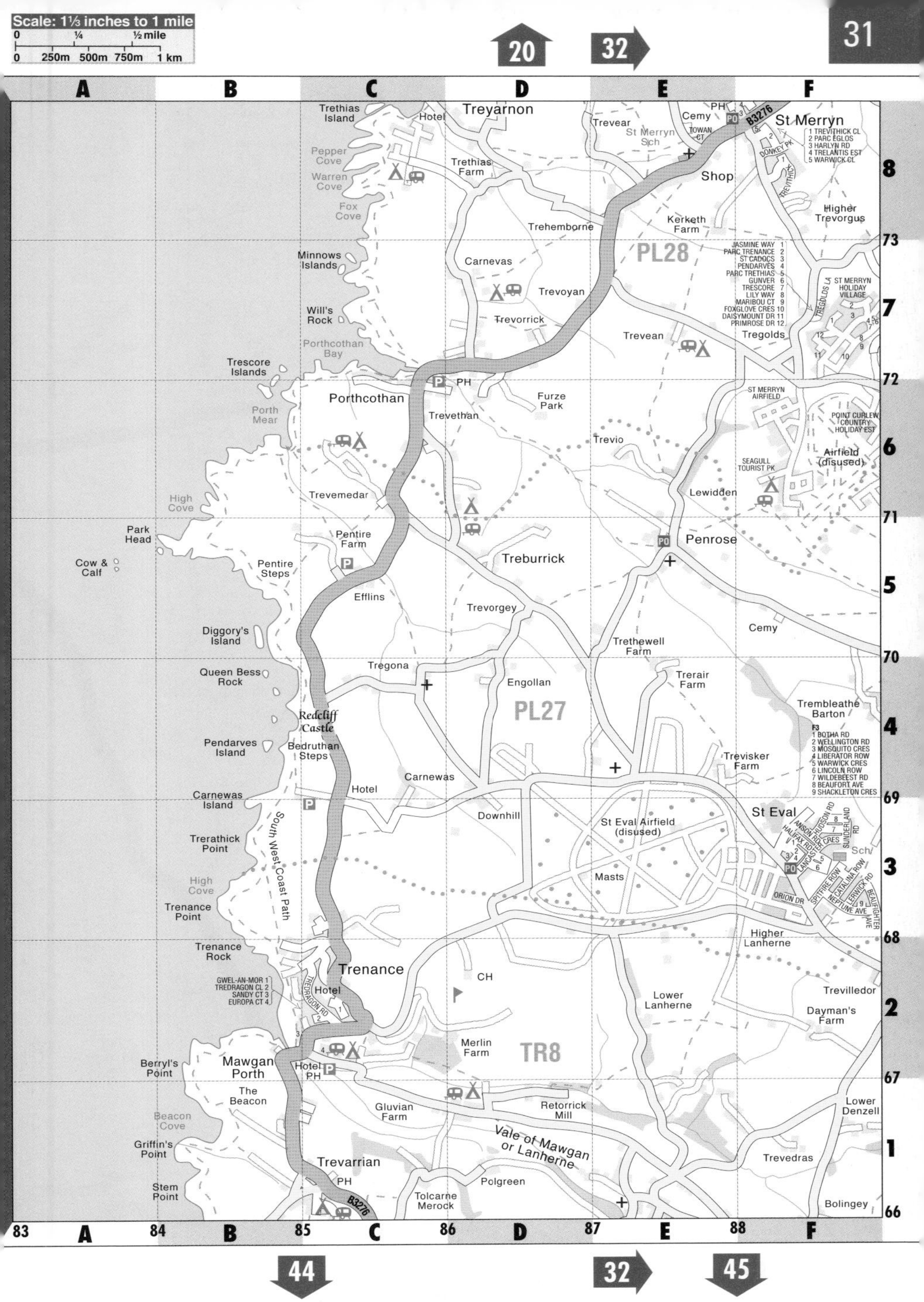
Scale: 1⅓ inches to 1 mile
0 ¼ ½ mile
0 250m 500m 750m 1 km
20
32
Treyarnon
Trethias Island
Hotel
Pepper Cove
Warren Cove
Fox Cove
Trethias Farm
Trevear
St Merryn Sch
Cemy
TOWAN CT
PH
PO
B3276
St Merryn
1 TREVITHICK CL
2 PARC EGLOS
3 HARLYN RD
4 TRELANTIS EST
5 WARWICK CL
DONKEY PK
TREVITHICK
Shop
Higher Trevorgus
Trehemborne
Kerketh Farm
PL28
JASMINE WAY 1
PARC TRENANCE 2
ST CADOCS 3
PENDARVES 4
PARC TRETHIAS 5
GUNVER 6
TRESCORE 7
LILY WAY 8
MARIBOU CT 9
FOXGLOVE CRES 10
DAISYMOUNT DR 11
PRIMROSE DR 12
ST MERRYN HOLIDAY VILLAGE
TREGOLDS LA
Minnows Islands
Carnevas
Trevoyan
Will's Rock
Trevorrick
Trevean
Tregolds
Porthcothan Bay
Trescore Islands
PH
Porthcothan
Furze Park
ST MERRYN AIRFIELD
POINT CURLEW COUNTRY HOLIDAY EST
Porth Mear
Trevethan
Trevio
Airfield (disused)
SEAGULL TOURIST PK
Lewidden
High Cove
Trevemedar
Park Head
Pentire Farm
Penrose
Cow & Calf
Pentire Steps
Treburrick
Efflins
Trevorgey
Cemy
Diggory's Island
Trethewell Farm
Queen Bess Rock
Tregona
Engollan
Trerair Farm
Trembleathe Barton
Redcliff Castle
PL27
F3
1 BOTHA RD
2 WELLINGTON RD
3 MOSQUITO CRES
4 LIBERATOR ROW
5 WARWICK CRES
6 LINCOLN ROW
7 WILDEBEEST RD
8 BEAUFORT AVE
9 SHACKLETON CRES
Pendarves Island
Bedruthan Steps
Trevisker Farm
Carnewas
Hotel
Carnewas Island
Downhill
St Eval
St Eval Airfield (disused)
ANSON RD
HUDSON RD
HALIFAX RD
SUNDERLAND RD
LANCASTER CRES
Trerathick Point
South West Coast Path
Sch
Masts
High Cove
SPITFIRE ROW
CATALINA ROW
LERWICK RD
BEAUFIGHTER AVE
NEPTUNE AVE
ORION DR
Trenance Point
Higher Lanherne
Trenance Rock
Trenance
GWEL-AN-MOR 1
TREDRAGON CL 2
SANDY CT 3
EUROPA CT 4
TREDRAGON RD
Hotel
CH
Trevilledor
Lower Lanherne
Dayman's Farm
Merlin Farm
TR8
Berryl's Point
Mawgan Porth
Hotel
PH
The Beacon
Gluvian Farm
Retorrick Mill
Lower Denzell
Beacon Cove
Vale of Mawgan or Lanherne
Griffin's Point
Trevarrian
Trevedras
PH
Polgreen
Stem Point
Tolcarne Merock
B3276
Bolingey
A B C D E F
8 73 7 72 6 71 5 70 4 69 3 68 2 67 1 66
83 84 85 86 87 88
44
32
45

20
31
For full street detail of the highlighted area see page 107.
21

Scale: 1⅓ inches to 1 mile
0 ¼ ½ mile
0 250m 500m 750m 1 km

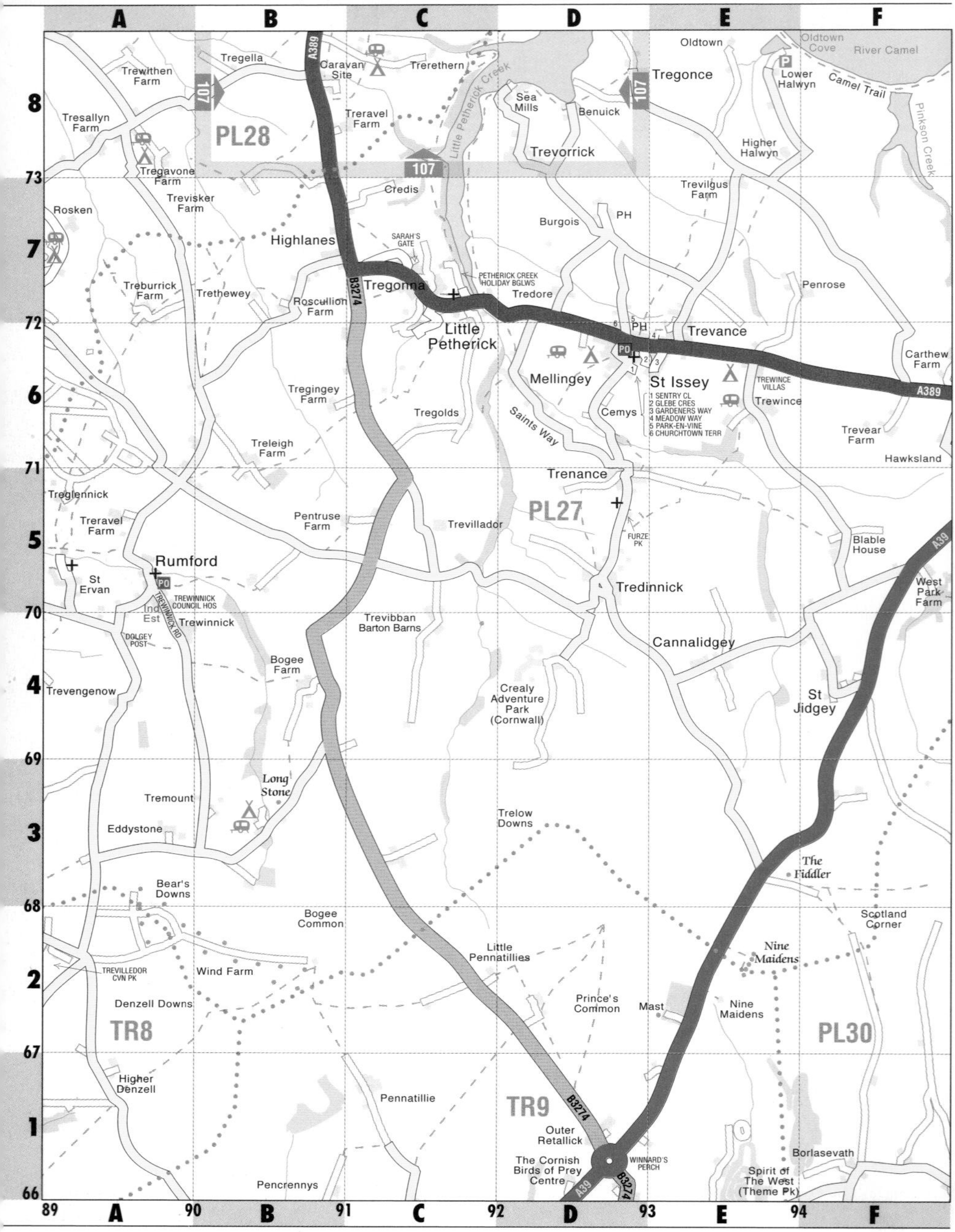

31
45
46

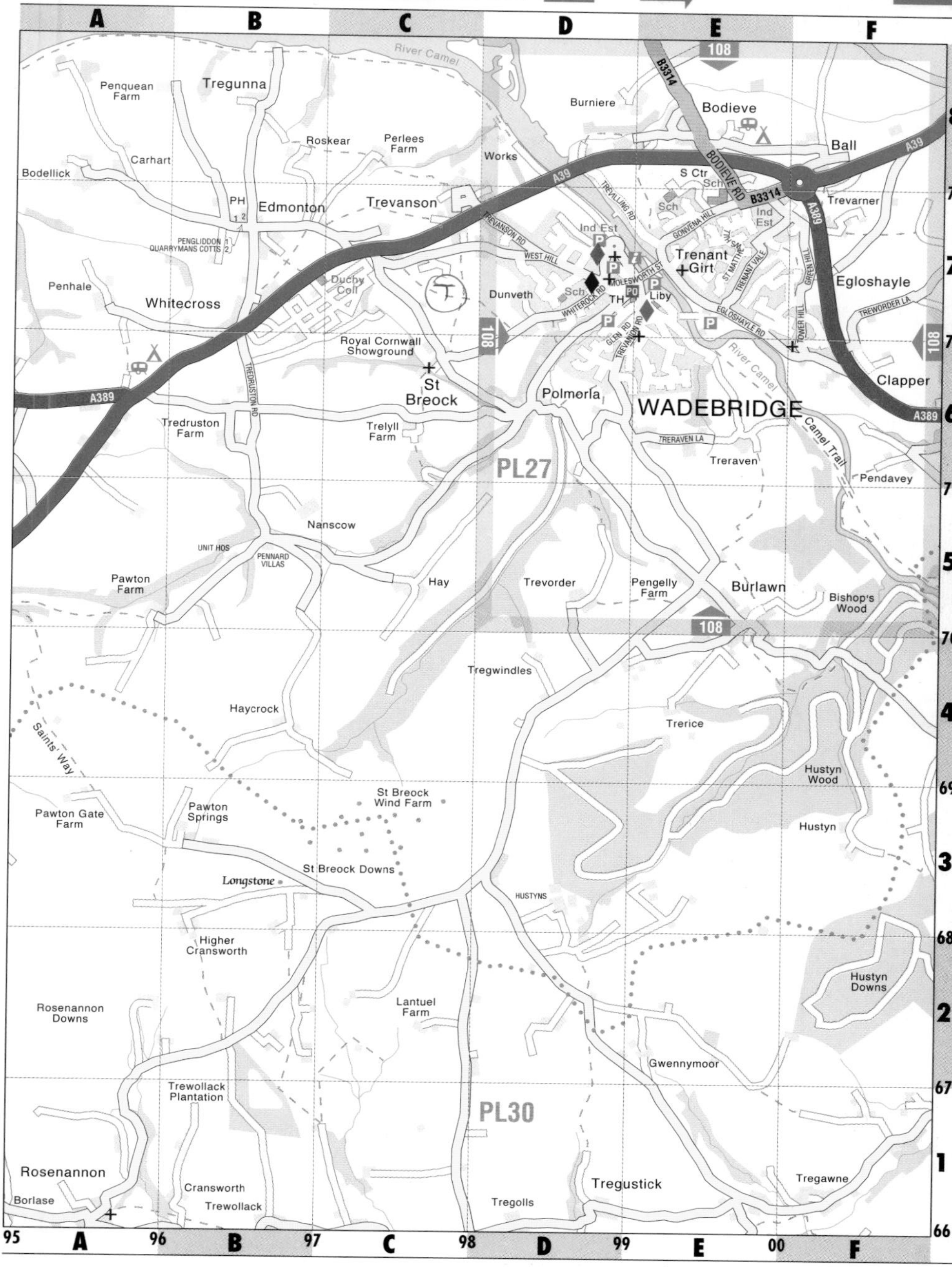
A B C D E F
River Camel
108
B3314
Penquean Farm
Tregunna
Burniere
Bodieve
Roskear
Perlees Farm
Ball
Carhart
Works
A39
Bodellick
S Ctr
Sch
BODIEVE RD
B3314
PH
Edmonton
Trevanson
TREVILLING RD
Sch
Ind Est
Trevarner
PENGLIDDON
QUARRYMANS COTTS
TREVANSON RD
Ind Est
GONVENA HILL
WEST HILL
Trenant
Girt
Penhale
Duchy Coll
MOLESWORTH ST
ST MATTHEW
TRENANT VALE
GREEN HILL
Egloshayle
Whitecross
Dunveth
Sch
WHITEROCK RD
TH
Liby
EGLOSHAYLE RD
TREWORDER LA
Royal Cornwall Showground
GLEN RD
TREVANION RD
TOWER HILL
River Camel
Clapper
St Breock
A389
TREDRUSTON RD
Polmorla
WADEBRIDGE
A389
Tredruston Farm
Trelyll Farm
TREVAVEN LA
Camel Trail
Treraven
PL27
Pendavey
Nanscow
UNIT HOS
PENNARD VILLAS
Pawton Farm
Hay
Trevorder
Pengelly Farm
Burlawn
Bishop's Wood
Tregwindles
Haycrock
Trerice
Saints' Way
Hustyn Wood
St Breock Wind Farm
Pawton Gate Farm
Pawton Springs
Hustyn
St Breock Downs
Longstone
HUSTYNS
Higher Cranswoth
Hustyn Downs
Rosenannon Downs
Lantuel Farm
Gwennymoor
Trewollack Plantation
PL30
Rosenannon
Tregawne
Cranswoth
Tregustick
Borlase
Trewollack
Tregolls
8 73 7 72 6 71 5 70 4 69 3 68 2 67 1 66
95 96 97 98 99 00

22
33
23

Scale: 1⅓ inches to 1 mile
0 ¼ ½ mile
0 250m 500m 750m 1 km

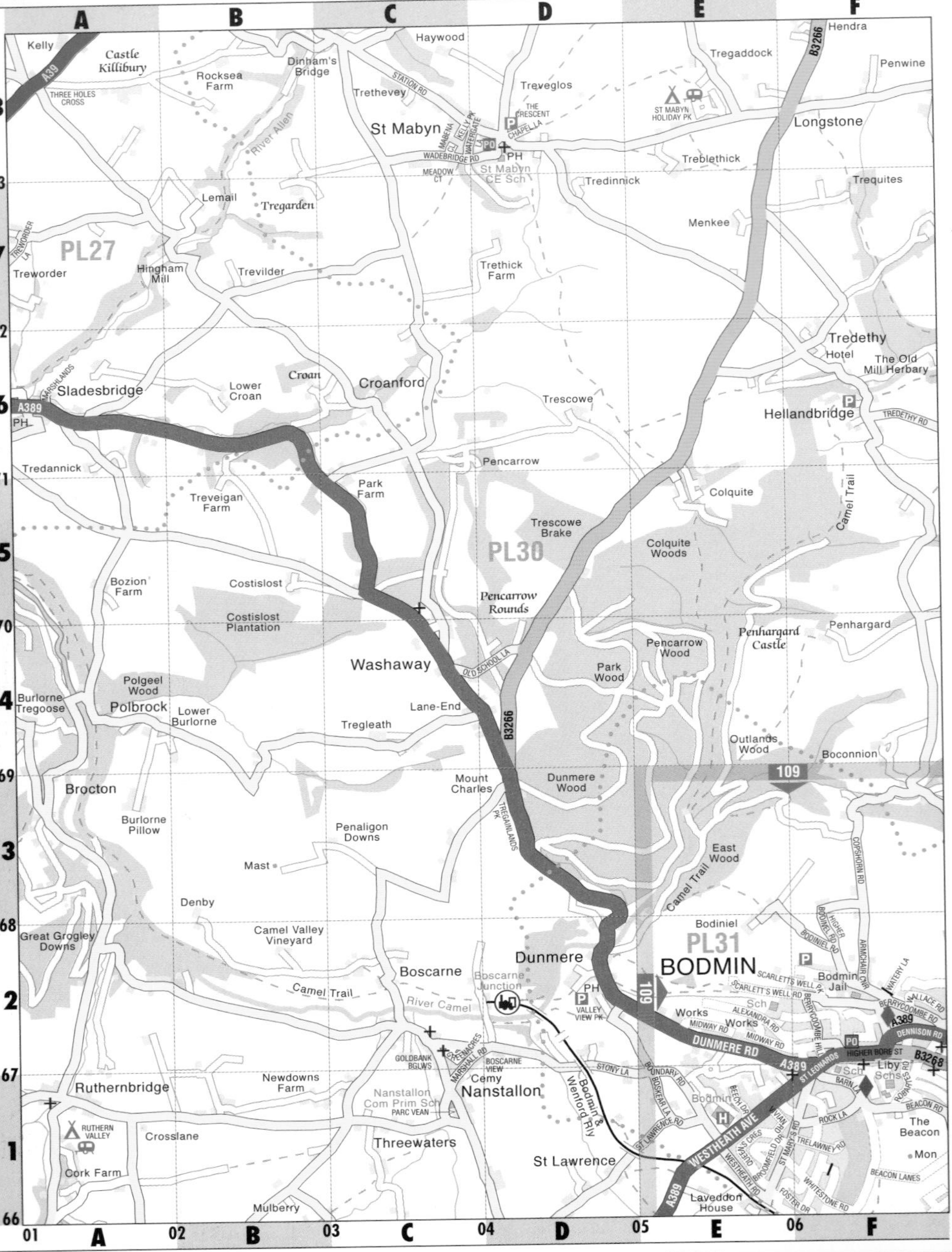
A
B
C
D
E
F
Kelly
A39
Castle Killibury
THREE HOLES CROSS
Rocksea Farm
Dinham's Bridge
Haywood
STATION RD
Trethevey
St Mabyn
Treveglos
THE CRESCENT
CHAPEL LA
Tregaddock
ST MABYN HOLIDAY PK
B3266
Hendra
Penwine
Longstone
River Allen
MABENA CL
KELLY PK
WATERGATE LA
PO
PH
WADEBRIDGE RD
MEADOW CT
St Mabyn CE Sch
Treblethick
Tredinnick
Trequites
Lemail
Tregarden
Menkee
TREWORDER LA
PL27
Treworder
Hingham Mill
Trevilder
Trethick Farm
Tredethy
Hotel
The Old Mill Herbary
MARSHLANDS
Sladesbridge
A389
PH
Lower Croan
Croan
Croanford
Trescowe
Hellandbridge
TREDETHY RD
Tredannick
Pencarrow
Park Farm
Treveigan Farm
Colquite
Camel Trail
Trescowe Brake
Colquite Woods
PL30
Bozion Farm
Costislost
Pencarrow Rounds
Costislost Plantation
Penhargard Castle
Penhargard
Pencarrow Wood
Washaway
OLD SCHOOL LA
Park Wood
Polgeel Wood
Burlorne Tregoose
Polbrock
Lower Burlorne
Lane-End
Tregleath
Outlands Wood
Boconnion
109
Brocton
Mount Charles
Dunmere Wood
TREGAINLANDS PK
Burlorne Pillow
Penaligon Downs
East Wood
COPSHORN RD
Mast
Denby
Bodiniel
BODINIEL RD
HIGHER BODINIEL RD
ARMCHAIR CNR
Great Grogley Downs
Camel Valley Vineyard
PL31
Dunmere
BODMIN
Boscarne
Boscarne Junction
SCARLETTS WELL PK
SCARLETT'S WELL RD
Bodmin Jail
WATERY LA
Camel Trail
River Camel
VALLEY VIEW PK
Works
ALEXANDRA RD
BERRYCOOMBE HILL
BERRYCOOMBE RD
WALLACE RD
MIDWAY RD
DUNMERE RD
HIGHER BORE ST
DENNISON RD
B3268
GOLDBANK BGLWS
GREENACRES
MARSHALL RD
BOSCARNE VIEW
STONY LA
BOUNDARY RD
A389
ST LEONARDS
Liby
Schs
BARN LA
ROBARTES RD
BEACON RD
Newdowns Farm
Ruthernbridge
Cemy
Nanstallon
Nanstallon Com Prim Sch
PARC VEAN
Bodmin & Wenford Rly
BOSKEAR LA
Bodmin
BEACH DR
H
WESTHEATH AVE
ROCK LA
The Beacon
RUTHERN VALLEY
Crosslane
Threewaters
St Lawrence
ST LAWRENCE RD
TRELAWNEY RD
Mon
Cork Farm
BEACON LANES
A389
Laveddon House
FOSTER DR
WHITESTONE RD
Mulberry
8
73
7
72
6
71
5
70
4
69
3
68
2
67
1
66
01
02
03
04
05
06

33
47
48
For full street detail of the highlighted area see page 109.

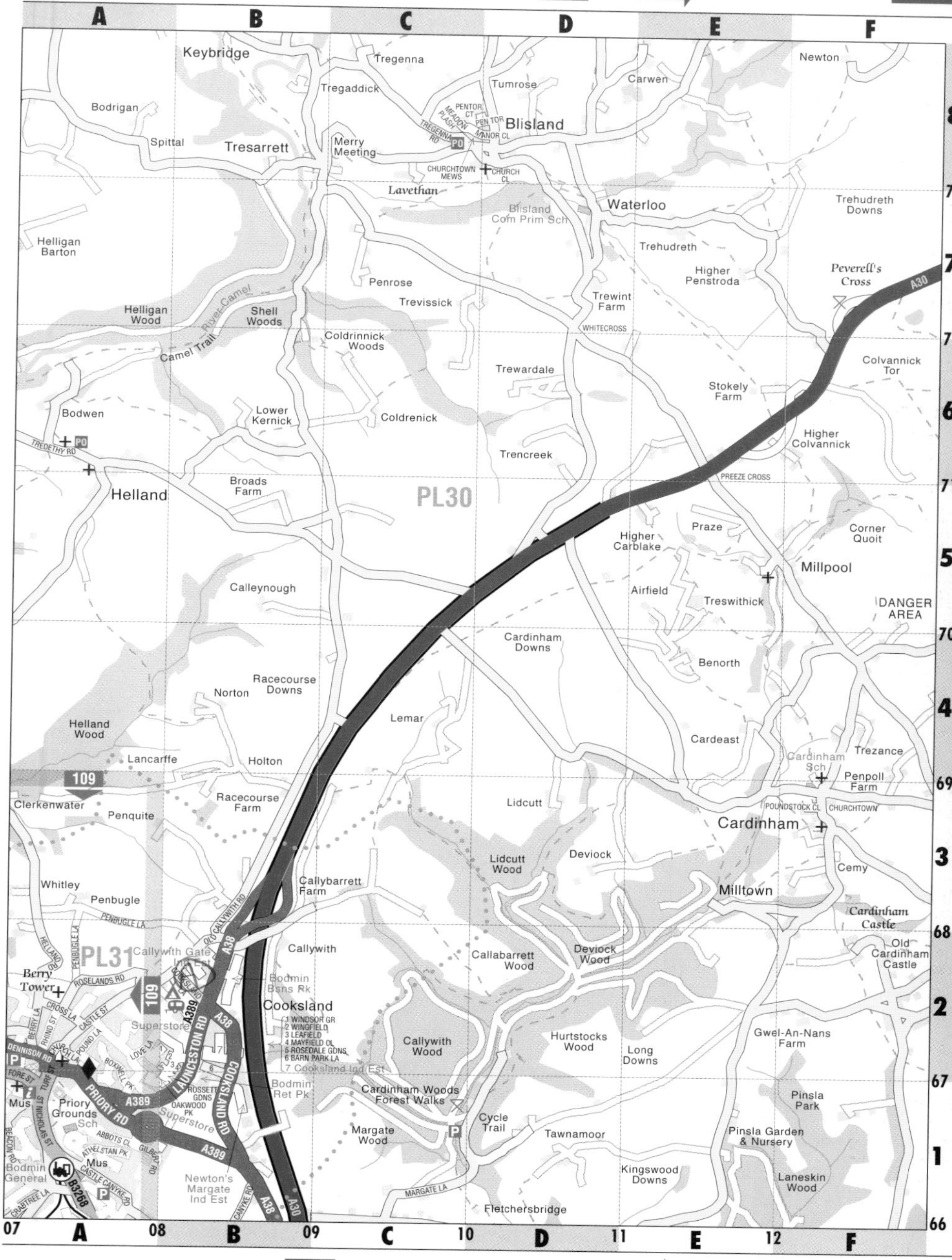
A
B
C
D
E
F
Keybridge
Tregenna
Tregaddick
Tumrose
Carwen
Newton
Bodrigan
Spittal
Tresarrett
Merry Meeting
PENTOR CT
MEADON PLASH
PEN TOR
TREGENNA RD
Blisland
MANOR CL
PO
CHURCHTOWN MEWS
CHURCH CL
Lavethan
Blisland Com Prim Sch
Waterloo
Trehudreth Downs
Helligan Barton
Trehudreth
Higher Penstroda
Peverell's Cross
A30
Penrose
Trevissick
Trewint Farm
Helligan Wood
River Camel
Shell Woods
Camel Trail
Coldrinnick Woods
WHITECROSS
Trewardale
Stokely Farm
Colvannick Tor
Bodwen
Lower Kernick
Coldrenick
Higher Colvannick
TREDETHY RD
Trencreek
PREEZE CROSS
Helland
Broads Farm
PL30
Higher Carblake
Praze
Corner Quoit
Millpool
Calleynough
Airfield
Treswithick
DANGER AREA
Cardinham Downs
Benorth
Racecourse Downs
Norton
Lemar
Helland Wood
Cardeast
Lancarffe
Holton
Cardinham Sch
Trezance
109
Penpoll Farm
Clerkenwater
Penquite
Racecourse Farm
Lidcutt
POUNDSTOCK CL
CHURCHTOWN
Cardinham
Lidcutt Wood
Deviock
Cemy
Whitley
Callybarrett Farm
Milltown
Penbugle
Cardinham Castle
PENBUGLE LA
OLD CALLYWITH RD
Old Cardinham Castle
HELLAND RD
PENBUGLE LA
PL31
Callywith Gate Ind Est
A38
Callywith
Callabarrett Wood
Deviock Wood
Berry Tower
ROSELANDS RD
109
Bodmin Bsns Pk
A389
Cooksland
CROSS LA
CASTLE ST
BERRY LA
RHIND ST
Superstore
1 WINDSOR GR
2 WINGFIELD
3 LEAFIELD
4 MAYFIELD CL
5 ROSEDALE GDNS
6 BARN PARK LA
7 Cooksland Ind Est
Callywith Wood
Hurtstocks Wood
Long Downs
Gwel-An-Nans Farm
DENNISON RD
POUND LA
LOVE LA
BOXWELL PK
LAUNCESTON RD
COOKSLAND RD
FORE ST
TURF ST
Mus
Priory Grounds
PRIORY RD
A389
ROSSETT GDNS
OAKWOOD PK
Bodmin Ret Pk
Cardinham Woods Forest Walks
Pinsla Park
Sch
Superstore
ST NICHOLAS ST
BEACON RD
ABBOTS CL
ATHELSTAN PK
GILBERT RD
A389
Margate Wood
Cycle Trail
Tawnamoor
Pinsla Garden & Nursery
Bodmin General
Mus
B3268
CASTLE CANYKE RD
Newton's Margate Ind Est
Kingswood Downs
Laneskin Wood
CRABTREE LA
CANYKE RD
A38
A30
MARGATE LA
Fletchersbridge
07
A
08
B
09
C
10
D
11
E
12
F
66
67
68
69
70
71
72
73
1
2
3
4
5
6
7
8

Scale: 1⅓ inches to 1 mile
0 ¼ ½ mile
0 250m 500m 750m 1 km

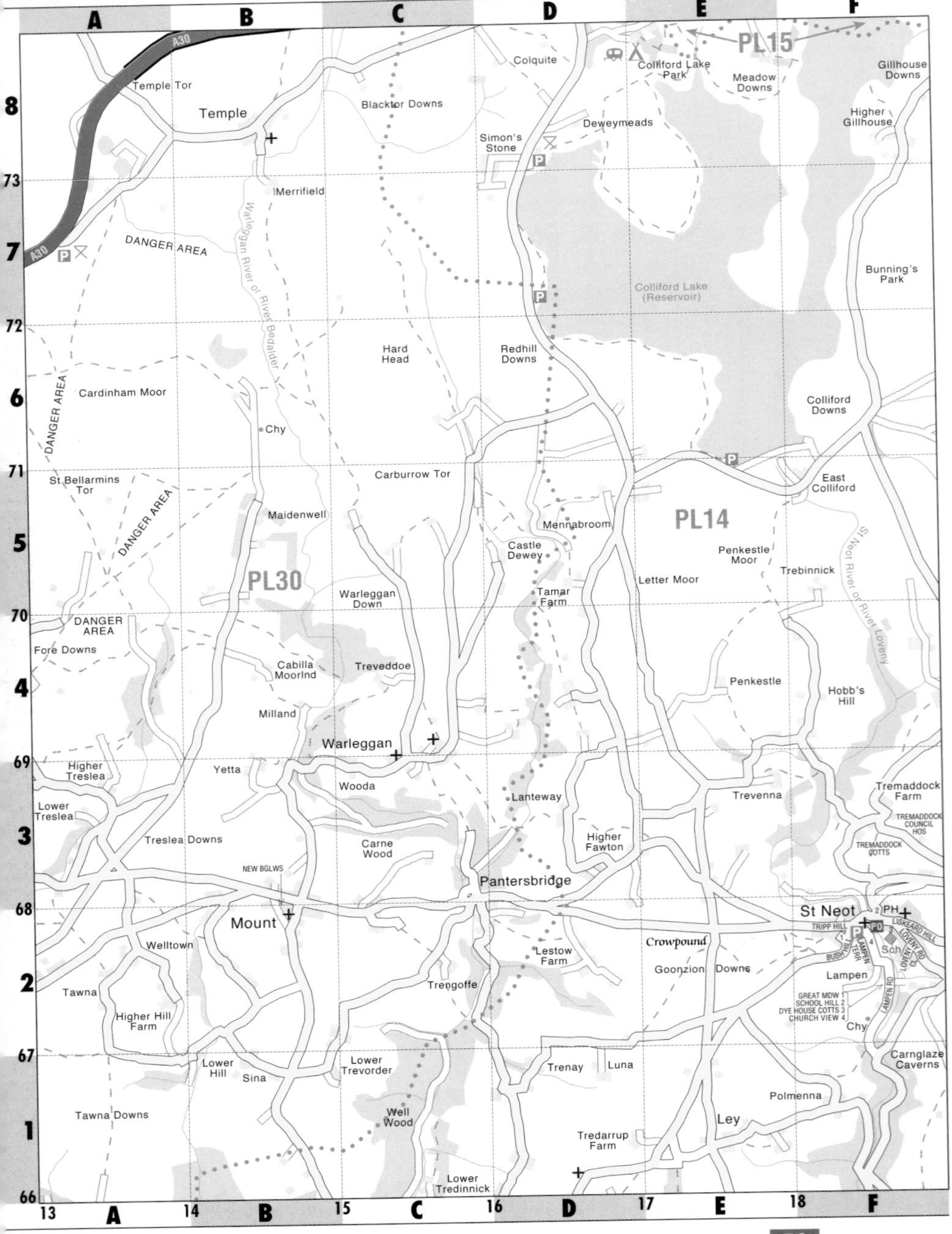

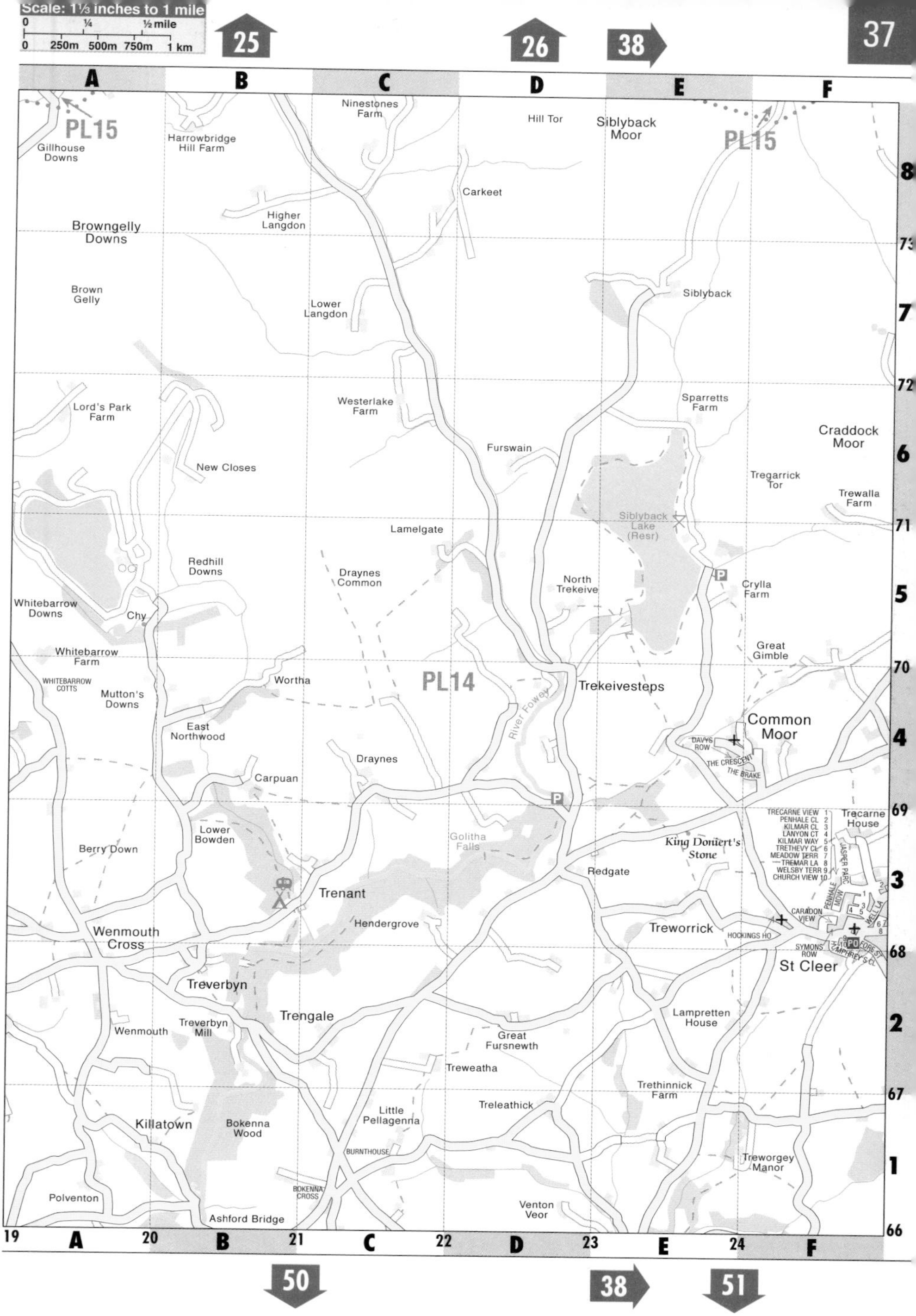
Scale: 1⅓ inches to 1 mile
0 ¼ ½ mile
0 250m 500m 750m 1 km
25
26
38
A
B
C
D
E
F
PL15
Gillhouse Downs
Harrowbridge Hill Farm
Ninestones Farm
Hill Tor
Siblyback Moor
PL15
Carkeet
Higher Langdon
Browngelly Downs
Brown Gelly
Lower Langdon
Siblyback
Lord's Park Farm
Westerlake Farm
Sparretts Farm
Craddock Moor
New Closes
Furswain
Tregarrick Tor
Trewalla Farm
Siblyback Lake (Resr)
Lamelgate
Redhill Downs
Draynes Common
North Trekeive
Crylla Farm
Whitebarrow Downs
Chy
Great Gimble
Whitebarrow Farm
WHITEBARROW COTTS
Wortha
PL14
Trekeivesteps
Mutton's Downs
River Fowey
East Northwood
Common Moor
DAVYS ROW
THE CRESCENT
THE BRAKE
Draynes
Carpuan
TRECARNE VIEW 1
PENHALE CL 2
KILMAR CL 3
LANYON CT 4
KILMAR WAY 5
TRETHEVY CL 6
MEADOW TERR 7
TREMAR LA 8
WELSBY TERR 9
CHURCH VIEW 10
Trecarne House
Lower Bowden
Golitha Falls
King Doniert's Stone
JASPER PARC
Berry Down
Redgate
Trenant
PENHALE MDW
WELL LA
CARADON VIEW
Hendergrove
Treworrick
HOCKINGS HO
Wenmouth Cross
SYMONS ROW
HUMPHREY'S CL
FORE ST
St Cleer
Treverbyn
Trengale
Lampretten House
Wenmouth
Treverbyn Mill
Great Fursnewth
Treweatha
Trethinnick Farm
Treleathick
Little Pellagenna
Killatown
Bokenna Wood
BURNTHOUSE
Treworgey Manor
BOKENNA CROSS
Polventon
Venton Veor
Ashford Bridge
8
73
7
72
6
71
5
70
4
69
3
68
2
67
1
66
19
20
21
22
23
24
50
38
51

26 37 27

Scale: 1⅓ inches to 1 mile

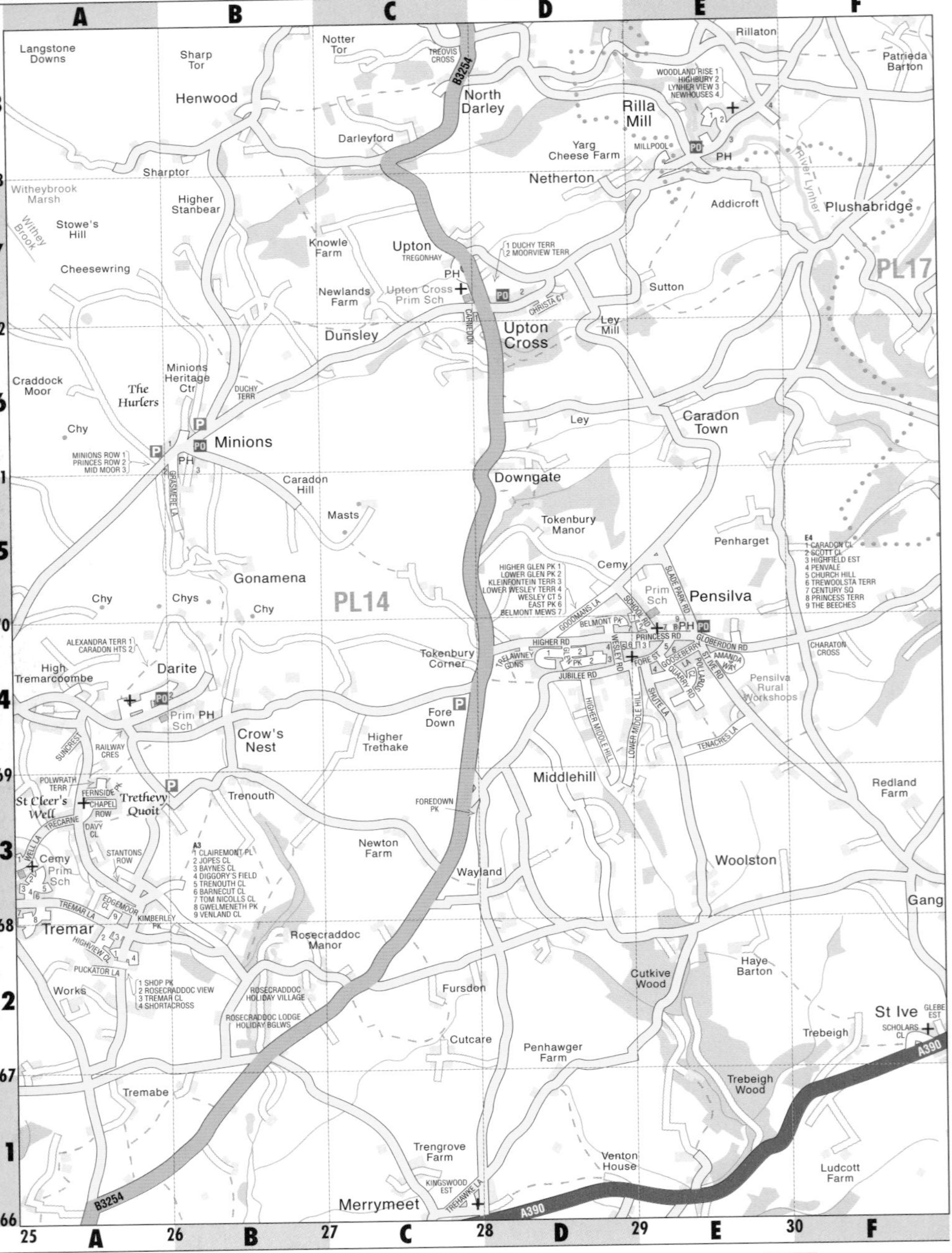

37 51 52

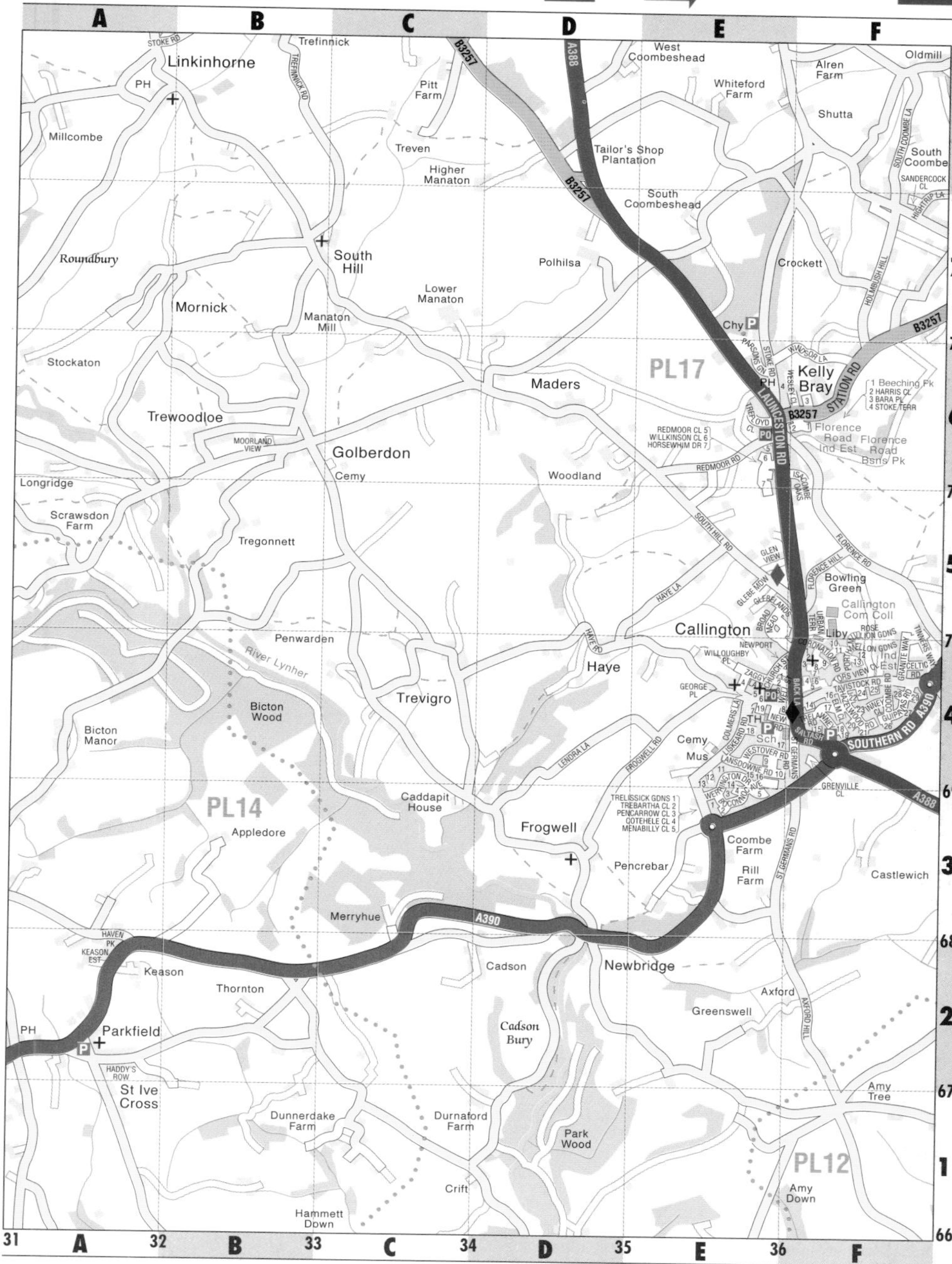

E4
1 MOWHAY LA
2 COMPTON RD
3 LONGMAN'S LA
4 VALENTINE ROW
5 TILLIE ST
6 FORE ST
7 WEST END SQ
8 BISCOMBES LA
9 CARADON CL
10 CHEQUETTS CL
11 GODOLPHIN PK
12 BAKEHOUSE LA
13 TRELOWARREN CT
14 PENTILLIE GDNS
15 TRERICE CT
16 WHITEFORD CL
17 TRETHURGY GDNS
18 CHANTRY PK
19 MARKET SQ

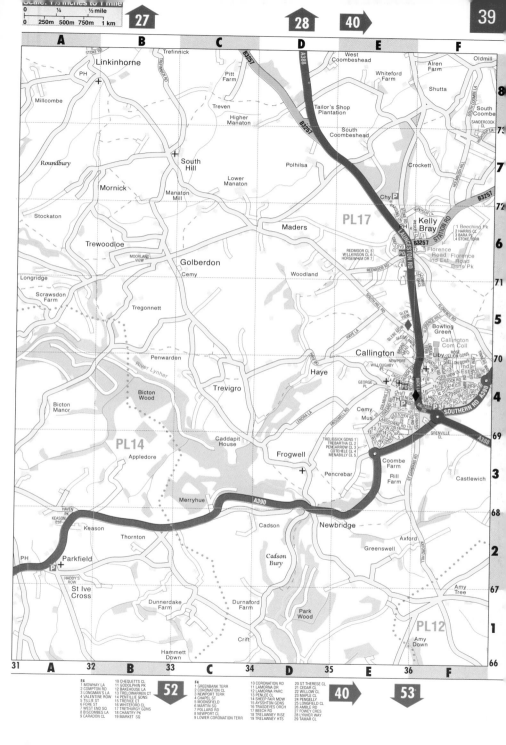

F4
1 GREENBANK TERR
2 CORONATION CL
3 NEWPORT TERR
4 CHAPEL ST
5 MOONSFIELD
6 MARTIN SQ
7 POLLARD RD
8 NEWPORT CL
9 LOWER CORONATION TERR
10 CORONATION RD
11 LAMORNA DR
12 LAMORNA PARC
13 PENLEE CL
14 SHEEP FAIR MDW
15 AYSSHTON GDNS
16 TRASDEVES ORCH
17 BEECH RD
18 TRELAWNEY RISE
19 TRELAWNEY HTS
20 ST THERESE CL
21 CEDAR CL
22 WILLOW CL
23 MAPLE CL
24 PENGELLY
25 LONGFIELD CL
26 AMBLE RD
27 FOWEY CRES
28 LYNHER WAY
29 TAMAR CL

28 39 29

Scale: 1⅓ inches to 1 mile

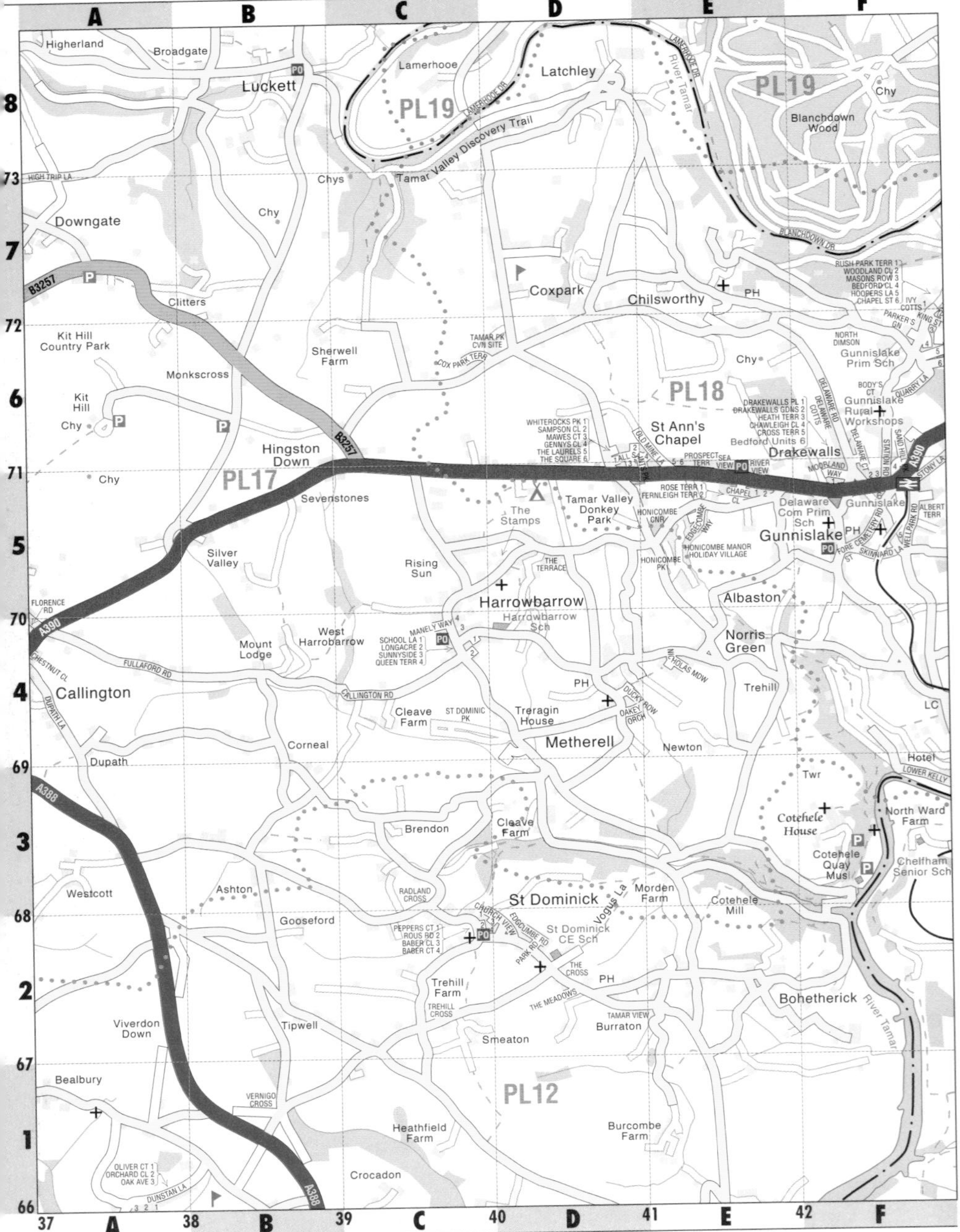

39 53 118

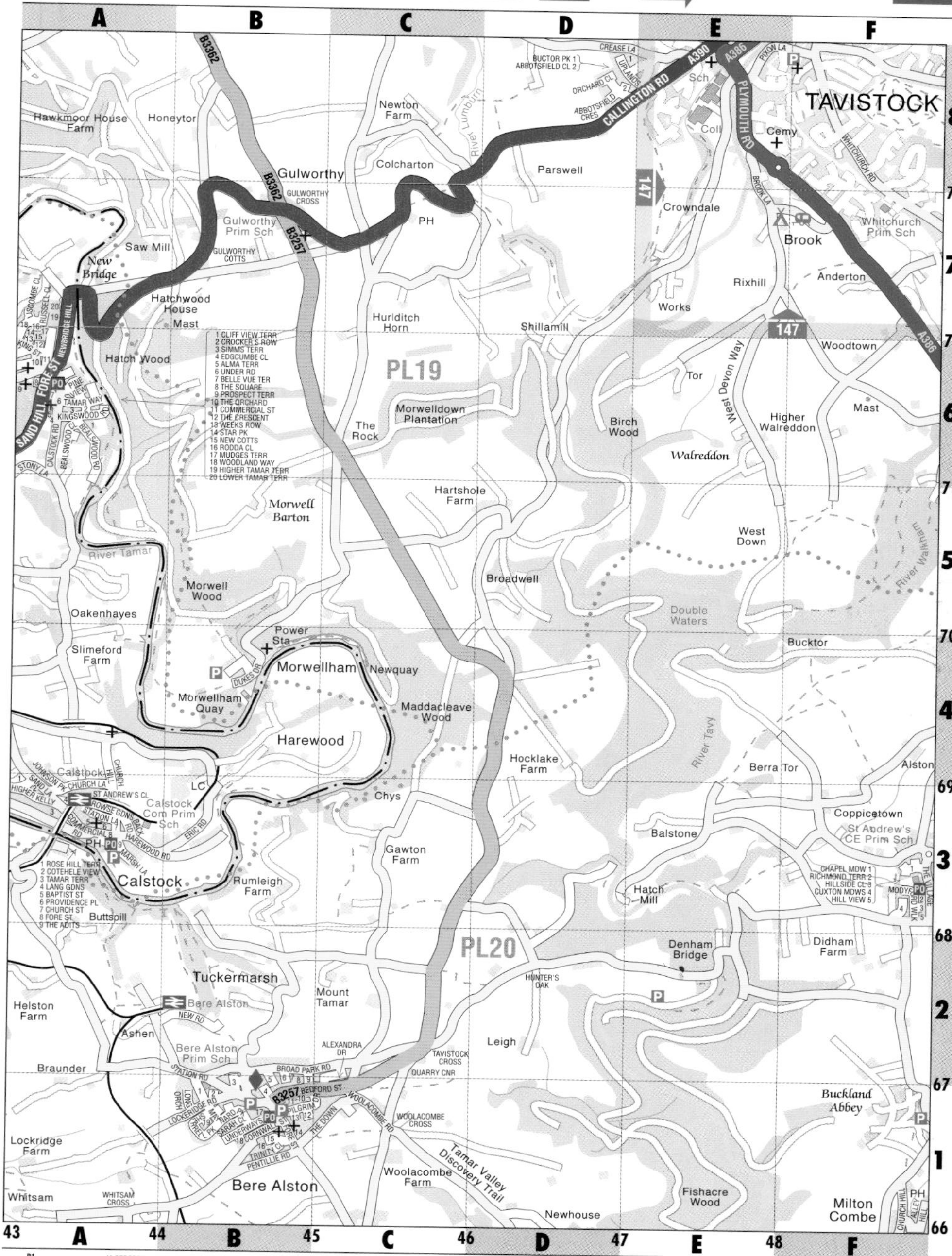

B1
1 POUNDS PARK RD
2 JOHNSON CL
3 DRAKE'S PK
4 CHAPEL ST
5 WEST VIEW RD
6 BEDFORD PL
7 BEDFORD VILLAS
8 PARK LA
9 WHITEHALL DR
10 BEDFORD PK
11 PILGRIM CT
12 ST ANDREWS CL
13 LANGMAN CT
14 EDGCUMBE TERR
15 MARYTHORNE RD
16 THE SQUARE
17 THE CLOSE
18 TAMAR CL
19 MAYFLOWER CL

For full street detail of the highlighted area see page 147.

Scale: 1⅓ inches to 1 mile
0 ¼ ½ mile
0 250m 500m 750m 1 km

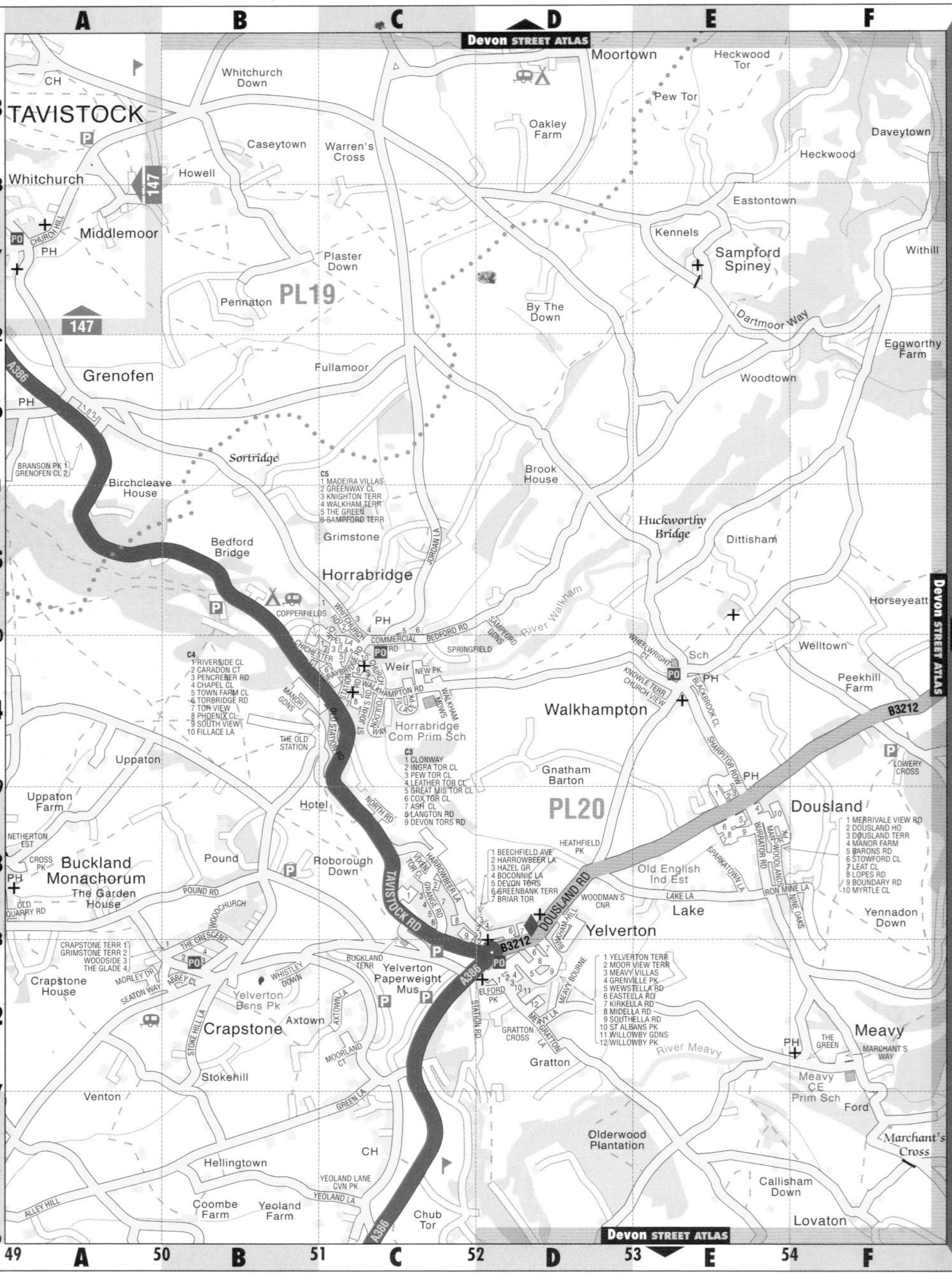

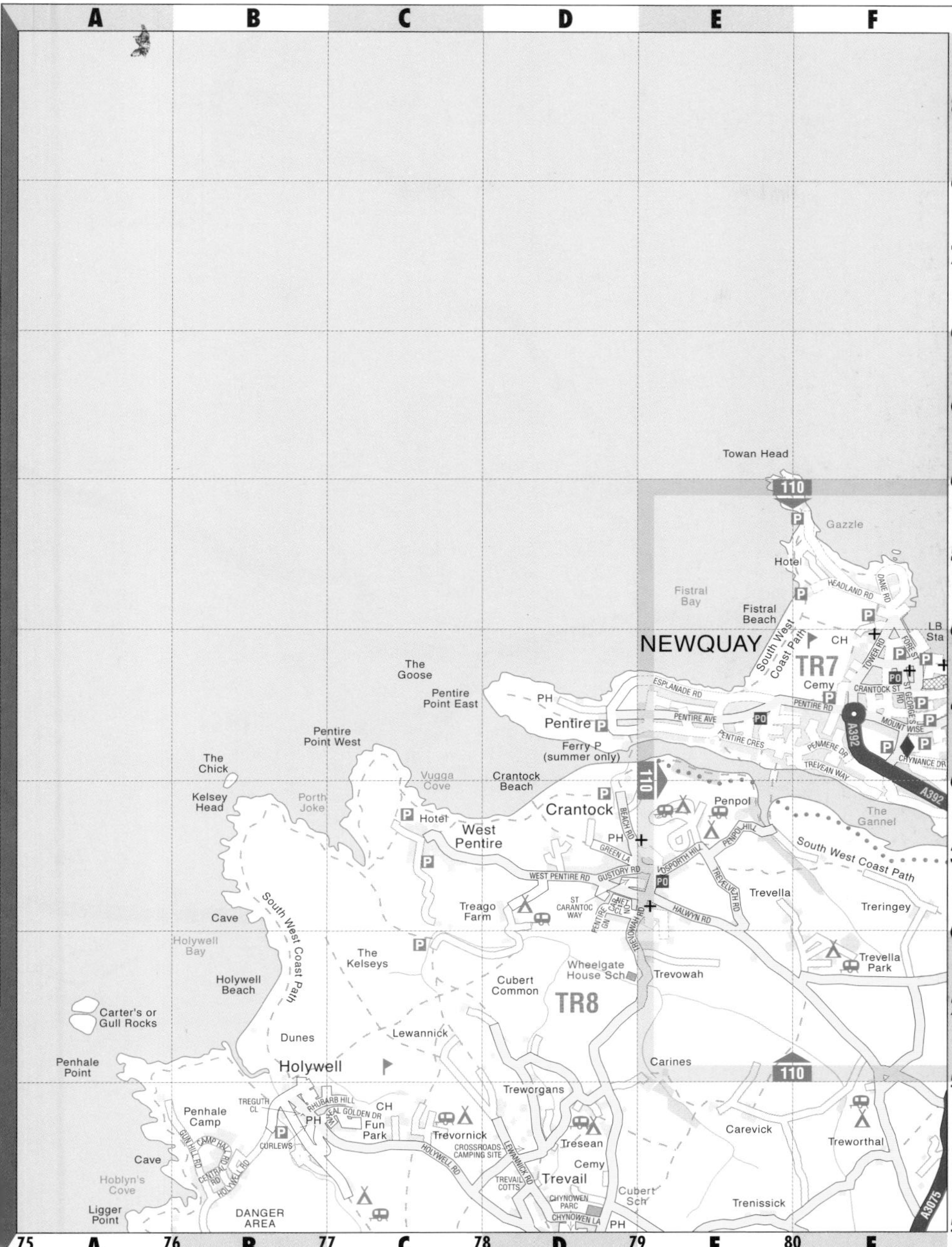
A B C D E F
8
65
7
64
6
63
5
62
4
61
3
60
2
59
1
58
75 76 77 78 79 80
Towan Head
110
Gazzle
Hotel
HEADLAND RD
DANE RD
Fistral Bay
Fistral Beach
NEWQUAY
South West Coast Path
CH
LB Sta
TOWER RD
FORE ST
TR7
Cemy
CRANTOCK ST
ST GEORGE'S RD
ESPLANADE RD
PENTIRE RD
PENTIRE AVE
PENTIRE CRES
MOUNT WISE
PENMERE DR
TREVEAN WAY
CHYNANCE DR
A392
The Gannel
The Goose
Pentire Point East
PH
Pentire
Ferry P (summer only)
Pentire Point West
The Chick
Kelsey Head
Porth Joke
Vugga Cove
Crantock Beach
Crantock
Penpol
Hotel
West Pentire
BEACH RD
GREEN LA
PENPOL HILL
VOSPORTH HILL
South West Coast Path
WEST PENTIRE RD
GUSTORY RD
TREVELVETH RD
Trevella
Treringey
Treago Farm
ST CARANTOC WAY
PENTIRE GN
HALWYN RD
TREVOWAH RD
Cave
Holywell Bay
South West Coast Path
The Kelseys
Wheelgate House Sch
Trevowah
Trevella Park
Holywell Beach
Cubert Common
TR8
Carter's or Gull Rocks
Dunes
Lewannick
Penhale Point
Holywell
Carines
Treworgans
Penhale Camp
TREGUTH CL
RHUBARB HILL
GOLDEN DR
CH
PH
Fun Park
Trevornick
CROSSROADS CAMPING SITE
LEWANNICK RD
Tresean
Carevick
Treworthal
CURLEWS
CAMP HAL RD
GUN HILL RD
CENTRAL RD
HOLYWELL RD
Cave
Cemy
Trevail
TREVAIL COTTS
Hoblyn's Cove
CHYNOWEN PARC
CHYNOWEN LA
Cubert Sch
Trenissick
A3075
Ligger Point
DANGER AREA
PH

For full street detail of the highlighted area see page 110.

43

31

Scale: 1⅓ inches to 1 mile
0 ¼ ½ mile
0 250m 500m 750m 1 km

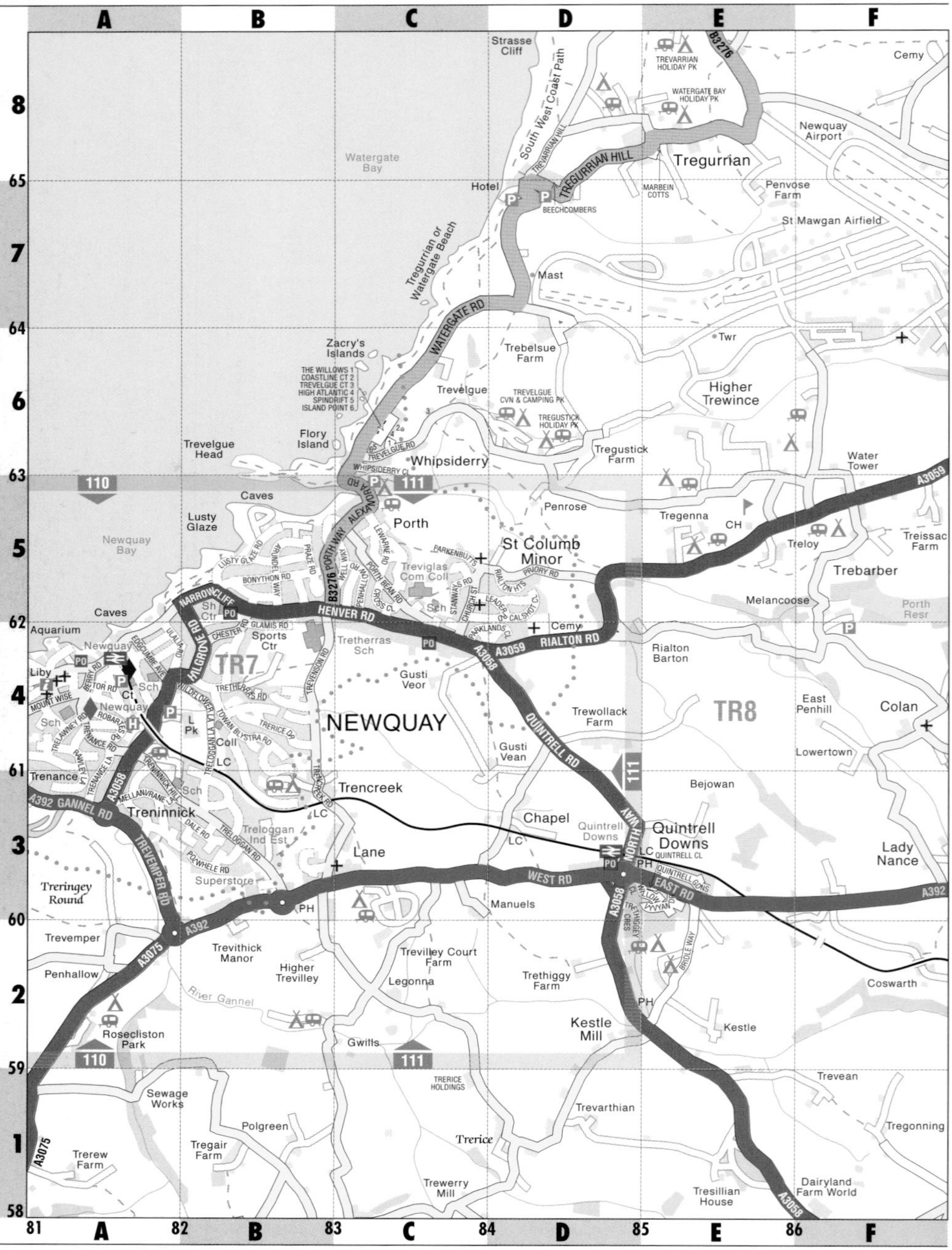
A
B
C
D
E
F
8
65
7
64
6
63
5
62
4
61
3
60
2
59
1
58
81
82
83
84
85
86
Strasse Cliff
South West Coast Path
TREVARRIAN HILL
B3276
TREVARRIAN HOLIDAY PK
WATERGATE BAY HOLIDAY PK
Cemy
Newquay Airport
Watergate Bay
Tregurrian
TREGURRIAN HILL
Hotel
MARBEIN COTTS
BEECHCOMBERS
Penvose Farm
St Mawgan Airfield
Tregurrian or Watergate Beach
Mast
WATERGATE RD
Zacry's Islands
THE WILLOWS 1
COASTLINE CT 2
TREVELGUE CT 3
HIGH ATLANTIC 4
SPINDRIFT 5
ISLAND POINT 6
Trebelsue Farm
Twr
Higher Trewince
Trevelgue
TREVELGUE CVN & CAMPING PK
TREGUSTICK HOLIDAY PK
Trevelgue Head
Flory Island
TREVELGUE RD
Whipsiderry
WHIPSIDERRY CL
Tregustick Farm
Water Tower
A3059
110
111
Caves
Lusty Glaze
Porth
ALEXANDRA RD
Penrose
Tregenna
CH
Treloy
Treissac Farm
Newquay Bay
LUSTY GLAZE RD
ARUNDEL WAY
PRAZE RD
PORTH WAY
WELL WAY
LEWARNE RD
PARKENBUTTS
St Columb Minor
BONYTHON RD
B3276
Treviglas Com Coll
PORTH BEAN RD
PENHALLOW RD
CROSS CL
RIALTON HTS
PRIORY RD
Trebarber
NARROWCLIFF
Sh Ctr
PO
HENVER RD
Sch
STANWAYS RD
CHURCH ST
LEADER RD
CALSHOT CL
PARKLANDS CL
Melancoose
Caves
Aquarium
GLAMIS RD
CHESTER RD
Sports Ctr
Tretherras Sch
Cemy
A3059
RIALTON RD
Porth Resr
Rialton Barton
Newquay
ULALIA RD
EDGCUMBE AVE
HILGROVE RD
TR7
Liby
PO
BERRY RD
TOR RD
Ct
Sch
MOUNT WISE
Newquay
ROBARTES RD
TRETHERRAS RD
WILDFLOWER LA
TREVENSON RD
Gusti Veor
A3058
QUINTRELL RD
Trewollack Farm
TR8
East Penhill
Colan
Sch
TRELAWNEY RD
TREVANCE RD
RAWLEY LA
L Pk
Coll
TOWAN BLYSTRA RD
TRERICE DR
TRELOGGAN LA
NEWQUAY
Gusti Vean
Lowertown
LC
Trenance
TRENANCE LA
A3058
TRENINNICK HILL
MELLANVRANE LA
Sch
TRENCREEK RD
Trencreek
111
Bejowan
A392 GANNEL RD
Treninnick
DALE RD
TRELOGGAN RD
Treloggan Ind Est
LC
Chapel
Quintrell Downs
Quintrell Downs
NORTH WAY
LC
QUINTRELL CL
Lady Nance
TREVEMPER RD
POLWHELE RD
Lane
PO
PH
QUINTRELL GDNS
Treringey Round
Superstore
WEST RD
EAST RD
A392
PH
Manuels
TRETHIGGEY CRES
60
A392
Trevemper
A3075
Trevithick Manor
Treviley Court Farm
BRIDLE WAY
Penhallow
Higher Trevilley
Legonna
Trethiggy Farm
Coswarth
River Gannel
PH
Kestle Mill
Kestle
Rosecliston Park
Gwills
110
111
Trevean
TRERICE HOLDINGS
Sewage Works
Trevarthian
Polgreen
Tregonning
A3075
Tregair Farm
Trerice
Trerew Farm
Trewerry Mill
Tresillian House
Dairyland Farm World
A3058

For full street detail of the highlighted area see pages 110 and 111.

43

56

Scale: 1⅓ inches to 1 mile
0 ¼ ½ mile
0 250m 500m 750m 1 km

31
32
46

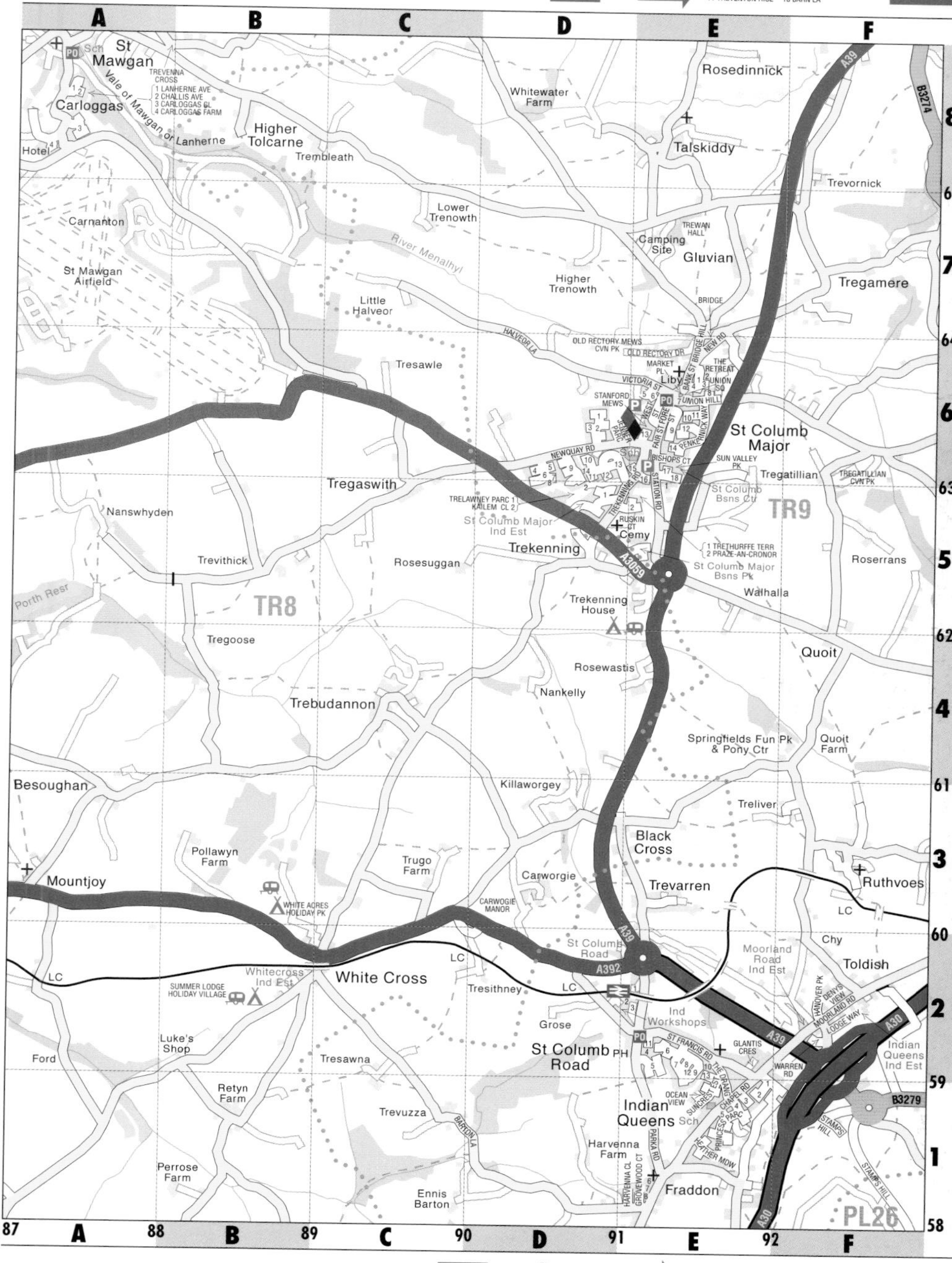

57
46

32 45 33

Scale: 1⅓ inches to 1 mile
0 ¼ ½ mile
0 250m 500m 750m 1 km

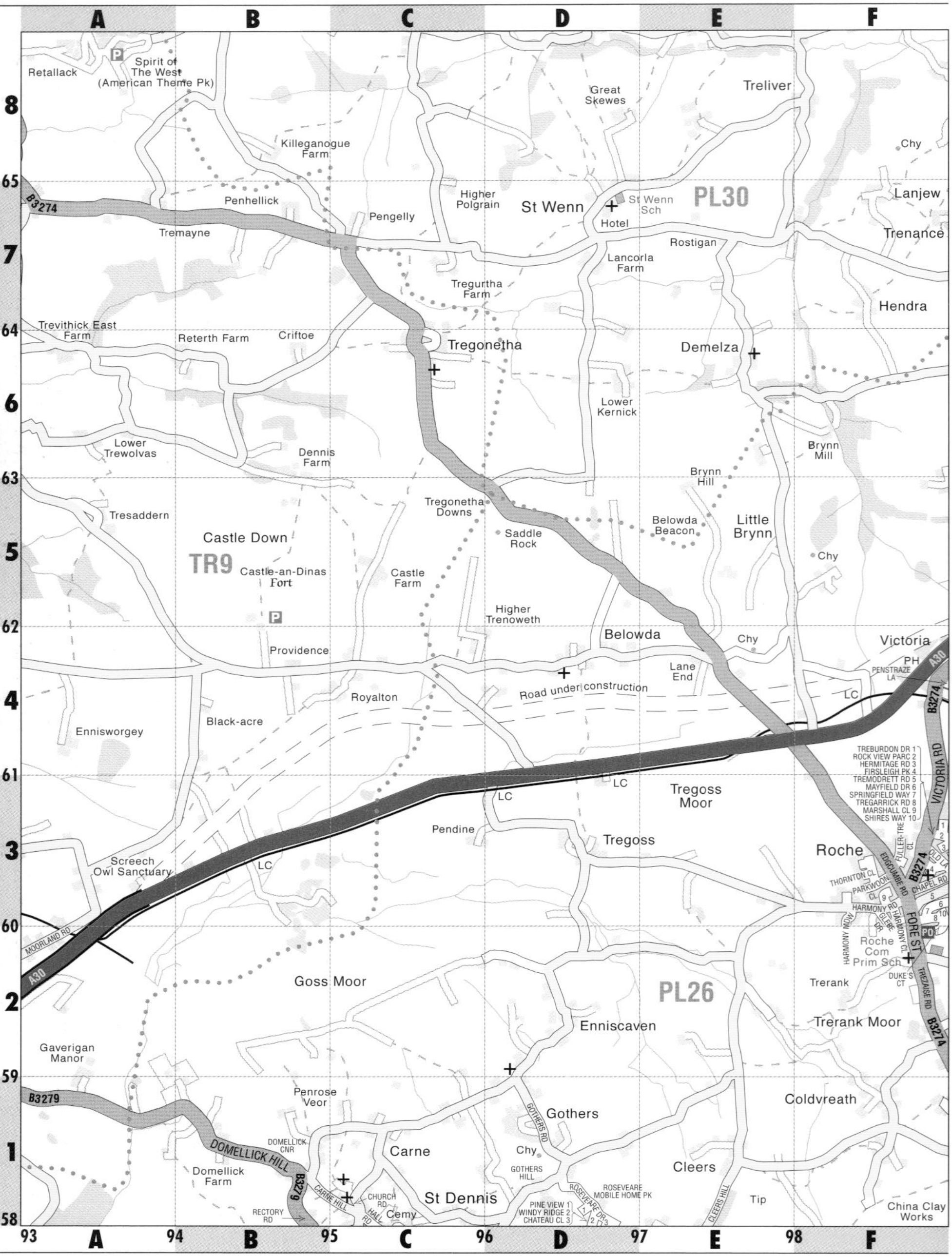

45 58

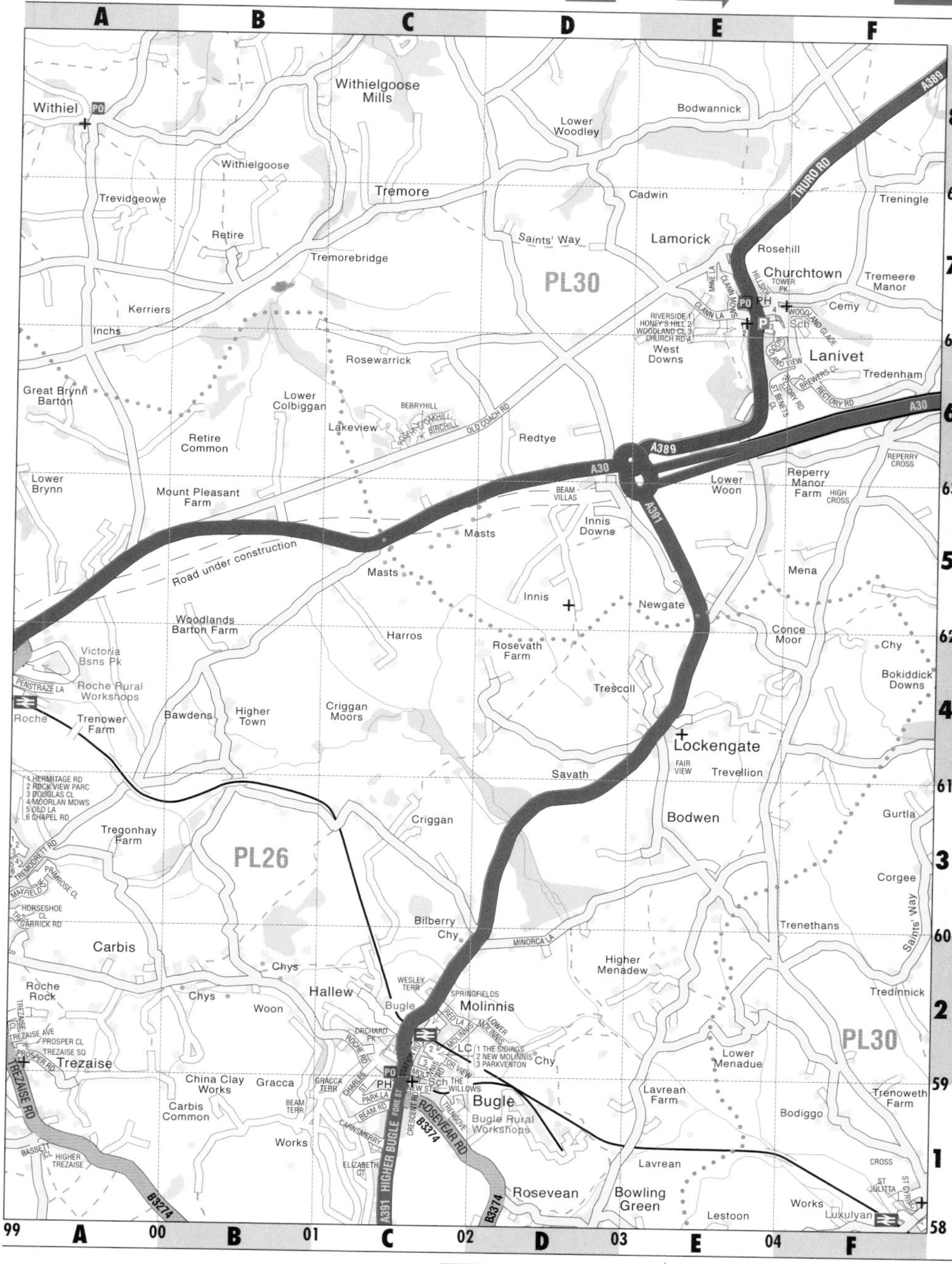
A
B
C
D
E
F
Withiel
PO
Withielgoose Mills
Lower Woodley
Bodwannick
A389
8
Withielgoose
Tremore
Trevidgeowe
Cadwin
TRURO RD
65
Treningle
Retire
Saints' Way
Lamorick
Rosehill
Tremorebridge
7
PL30
Churchtown
Tremeere Manor
TOWER PK
MINE LA
CLANN MDWS
HILLSIDE
Kerriers
CLANN LA
PO
PH
WOODLAND GLADE
Cemy
RIVERSIDE 1
HONEY'S HILL 2
WOODLAND CL 3
CHURCH RD 4
P
Sch
Inchs
64
West Downs
Lanivet
Rosewarrick
Tredenham
LAND VIEW
BREWERS CL
RECTORY RD
ST BENETS CL
Great Brynn Barton
Lower Colbiggan
BERRYHILL
OAKHILL
BIRCHILL
OLD COACH RD
A30
6
Lakeview
Retire Common
Redtye
A389
REPERRY CROSS
A30
Lower Brynn
Lower Woon
Reperry Manor Farm
HIGH CROSS
63
Mount Pleasant Farm
BEAM VILLAS
A391
Innis Downs
Masts
Road under construction
5
Masts
Mena
Innis
Newgate
Woodlands Barton Farm
Harros
Conce Moor
62
Rosevath Farm
Chy
Victoria Bsns Pk
PENISTRAZE LA
Roche Rural Workshops
Bokiddick Downs
Trescoll
Roche
Trenower Farm
Bawdens
Higher Town
Criggan Moors
4
Lockengate
FAIR VIEW
Trevellion
Savath
1 HERMITAGE RD
2 ROCK VIEW PARC
3 DOUGLAS CL
4 MOORLAN MDWS
5 OLD LA
6 CHAPEL RD
61
Criggan
Gurtla
Tregonhay Farm
Bodwen
TREMODRETT RD
PL26
3
PRIMROSE CL
MAYFIELD
Corgee
HORSESHOE CL
TREGARRICK RD
Trenethans
Bilberry
Chy
MINORCA LA
60
Saints' Way
Carbis
Higher Menadew
Chys
WESLEY TERR
Roche Rock
Tredinnick
Hallew
SPRINGFIELDS
Chys
Woon
Bugle
Molinnis
2
TREZAISE CL
TREZAISE AVE
PROSPER CL
TREZAISE SQ
ORCHARD PK
LC
1 THE SIDINGS
2 NEW MOLINNIS
3 PARKVENTON
PL30
Trezaise
PROSPER RD
Chy
Lower Menadue
China Clay Works
Gracca
GRACCA TERR
PO
PH
Sch
THE WILLOWS
59
Carbis Common
BEAM TERR
BEAM RD
PARK LA
NEW ST
Bugle
Lavrean Farm
Trenoweth Farm
TREZAISE RD
Bodiggo
Bugle Rural Workshops
CARNSMERRY
B3374
ROSEVEAR RD
HIGHER BUGLE
FORE ST
STATION RD
CRESCENT RD
TRENGOVE
BASSETT CL
HIGHER TREZAISE
Works
1
ELIZABETH CT
Lavrean
CROSS
B3274
A391
Rosevean
B3374
Bowling Green
ST JULITTA
ST CYRICS
Works
Luxulyan
Lestoon
58

34
47
35

D8
1 ISLAND LANES
2 PAARDEBURG RD
3 LUCKNOW RD S
4 Walker Lines Ind Est
5 Carminow Rd Ind Est

Scale: 1⅓ inches to 1 mile
0 ¼ ½ mile
0 250m 500m 750m 1 km

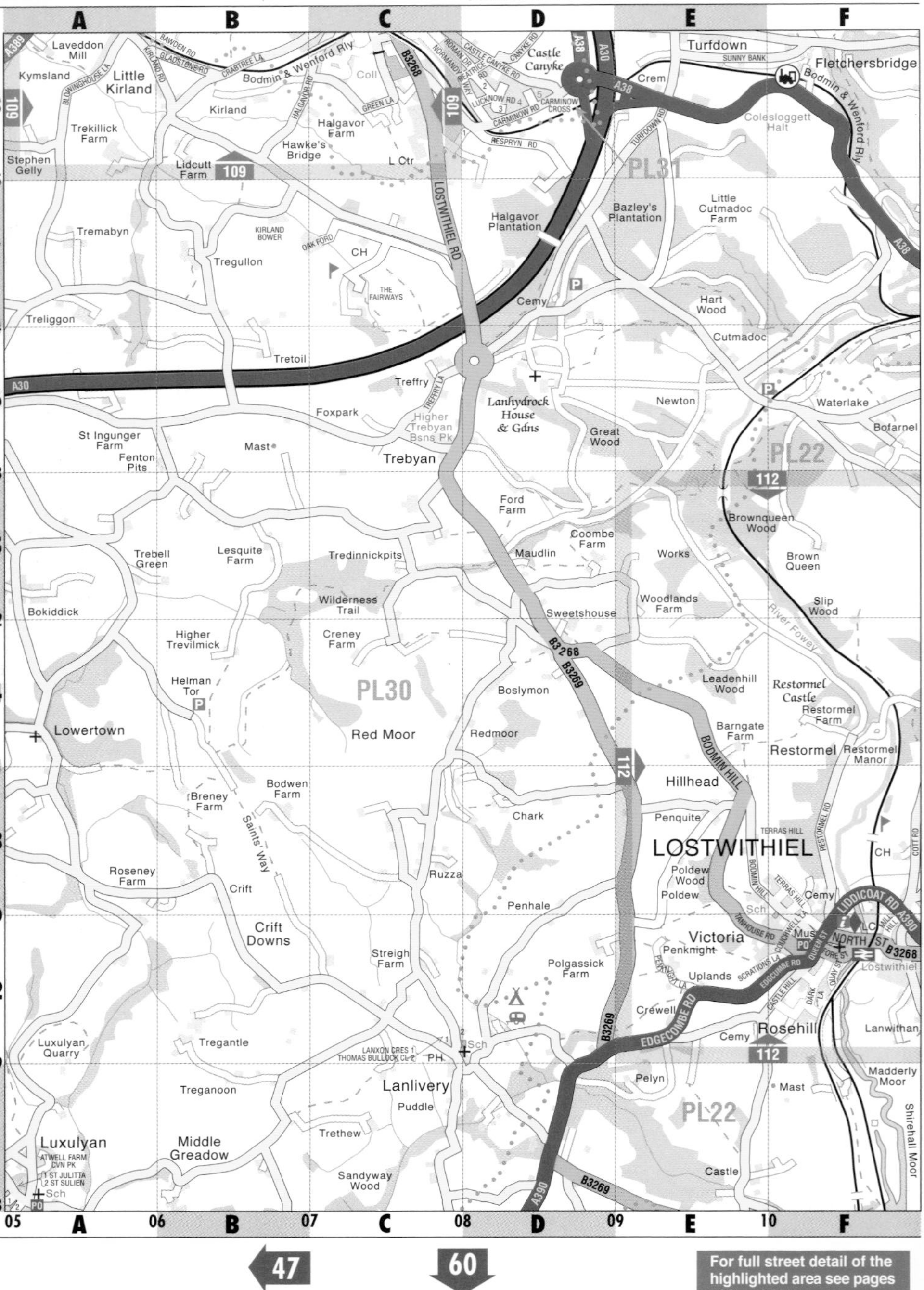

47
60

For full street detail of the highlighted area see pages 109 and 112.

Scale: 1⅓ inches to 1 mile
0 ¼ ½ mile
0 250m 500m 750m 1 km

35 36 50

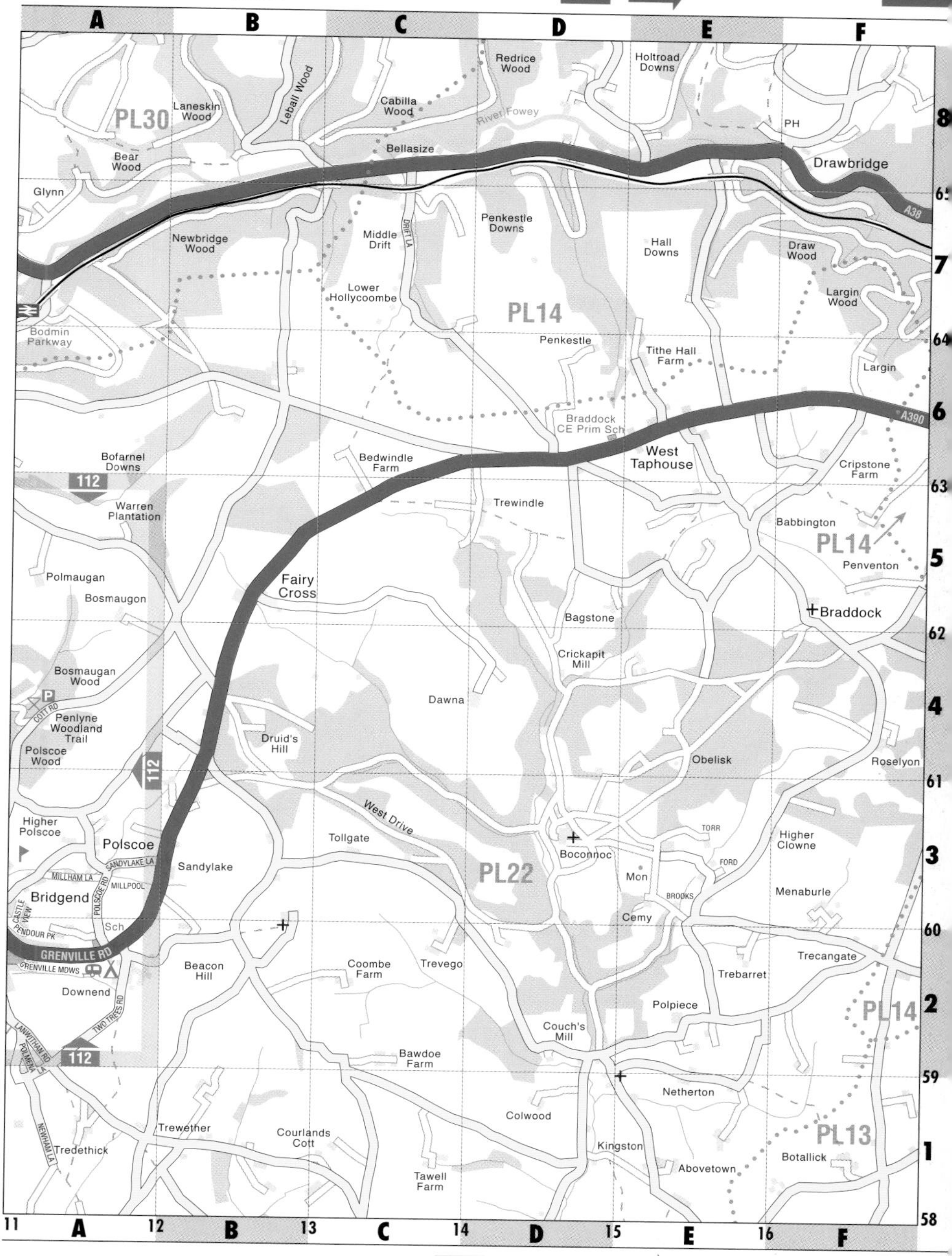

61 50

36 49 37

Scale: 1⅓ inches to 1 mile
0 ¼ ½ mile
0 250m 500m 750m 1 km

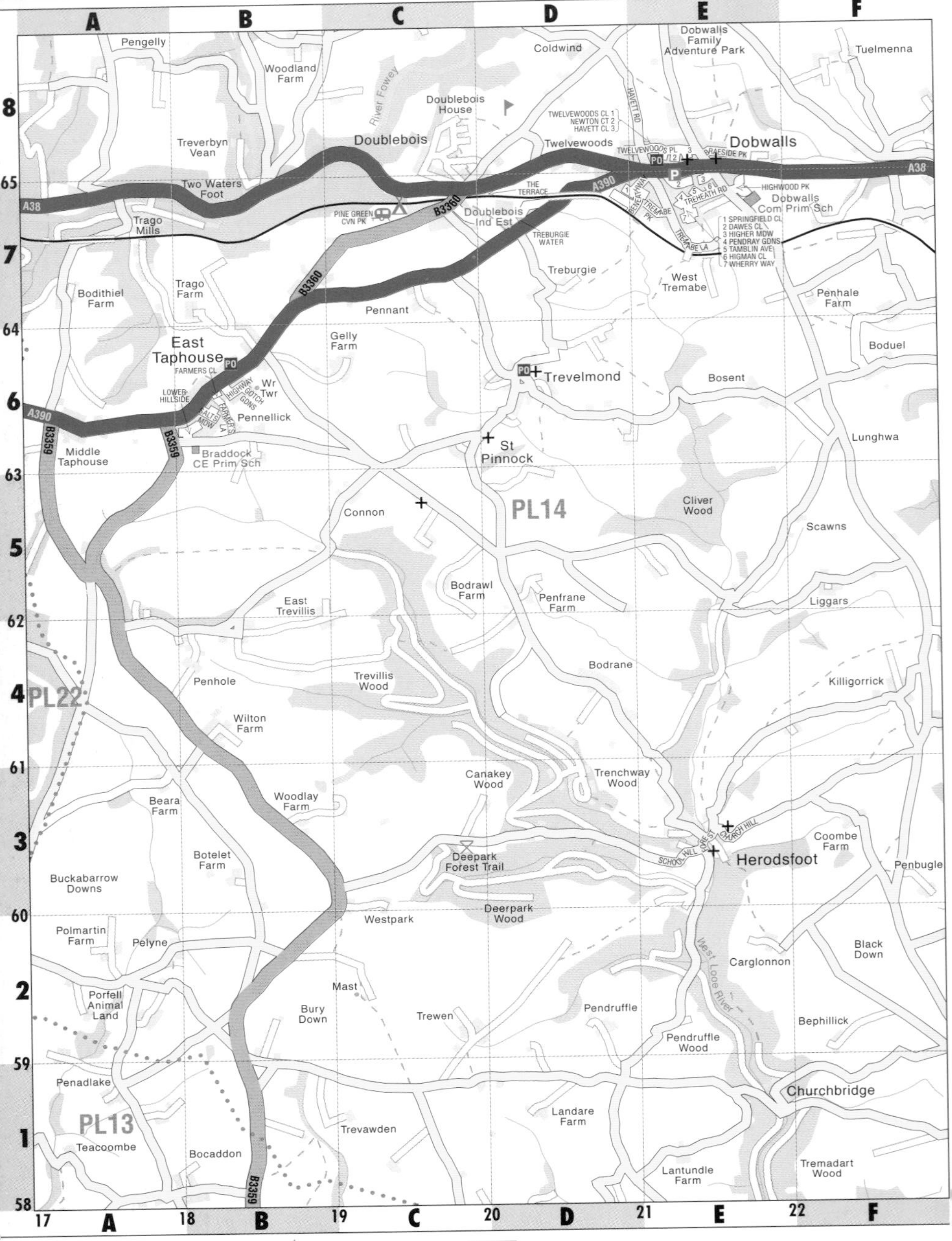

49 62

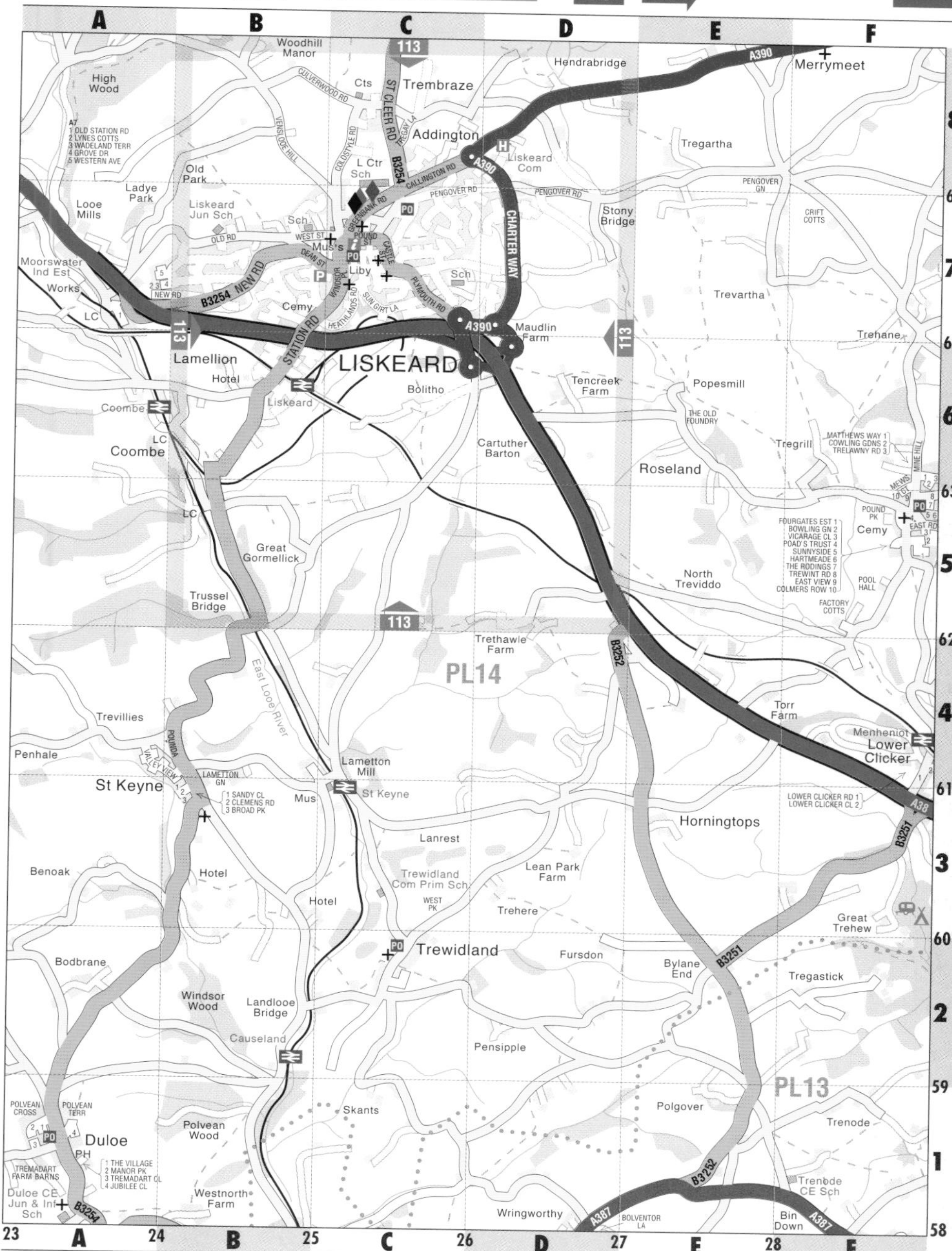
A B C D E F
8 7 6 5 4 3 2 1
65 64 63 62 61 60 59 58
23 24 25 26 27 28
113
Woodhill Manor
High Wood
Cts
Trembraze
Hendrabridge
Merrymeet
A390
CULVERWOOD RD
ST CLEER RD
VENSLOE HILL
COLDSTYLE RD
TREGAY LA
Addington
A7
1 OLD STATION RD
2 LYNES COTTS
3 WADELAND TERR
4 GROVE DR
5 WESTERN AVE
Tregartha
Old Park
Ladye Park
Looe Mills
L Ctr
Sch
B3254
CALLINGTON RD
Liskeard Com
PENGOVER RD
PENGOVER GN
CRIFT COTTS
Liskeard Jun Sch
GREENBANK RD
PO
Stony Bridge
CHARTER WAY
OLD RD
Sch
WEST ST
Mus's
POUND ST
DEAN ST
CASTLE ST
Moorswater Ind Est
Works
NEW RD
B3254 NEW RD
WINDSOR PL
Liby
Sch
Trevartha
P
Cemy
HEATHLANDS RD
SUN GIRT LA
PLYMOUTH RD
LC
STATION RD
A390
Maudlin Farm
Trehane
Lamellion
LISKEARD
Hotel
Liskeard
Bolitho
Tencreek Farm
Popesmill
Coombe
THE OLD FOUNDRY
LC
Coombe
Cartuther Barton
Tregrill
MATTHEWS WAY 1
COWLING GDNS 2
TRELAWNY RD 3
MINE HILL
Roseland
MEWS
LC
POUND PK
EAST RD
FOURGATES EST 1
BOWLING GN 2
VICARAGE CL 3
POAD'S TRUST 4
SUNNYSIDE 5
HARTMEADE 6
THE RODINGS 7
TREWINT RD 8
EAST VIEW 9
COLMERS ROW 10
Cemy
Great Gormellick
North Treviddo
POOL HALL
Trussel Bridge
FACTORY COTTS
Trethawle Farm
B3252
PL14
East Looe River
Trevillies
Torr Farm
POUNDA
Menheniot
Lower Clicker
Penhale
VALLEY VIEW
LAMETTON GN
Lametton Mill
St Keyne
1 SANDY CL
2 CLEMENS RD
3 BROAD PK
Mus
St Keyne
LOWER CLICKER RD 1
LOWER CLICKER CL 2
A38
Horningtops
B3251
Lanrest
Benoak
Hotel
Trewidland Com Prim Sch
Lean Park Farm
Hotel
WEST PK
Trehere
Great Trehew
Trewidland
Fursdon
Bodbrane
Bylane End
Tregastick
Windsor Wood
Landlooe Bridge
Causeland
Pensipple
PL13
Skants
Polgover
POLVEAN CROSS
POLVEAN TERR
Polvean Wood
Trenode
Duloe
PH
1 THE VILLAGE
2 MANOR PK
3 TREMADART CL
4 JUBILEE CL
TREMADART FARM BARNS
Duloe CE Jun & Inf Sch
Westnorth Farm
Wringworthy
A387
BOLVENTOR LA
Trenode CE Sch
Bin Down

38
51
39

Scale: 1⅓ inches to 1 mile
0 ¼ ½ mile
0 250m 500m 750m 1 km

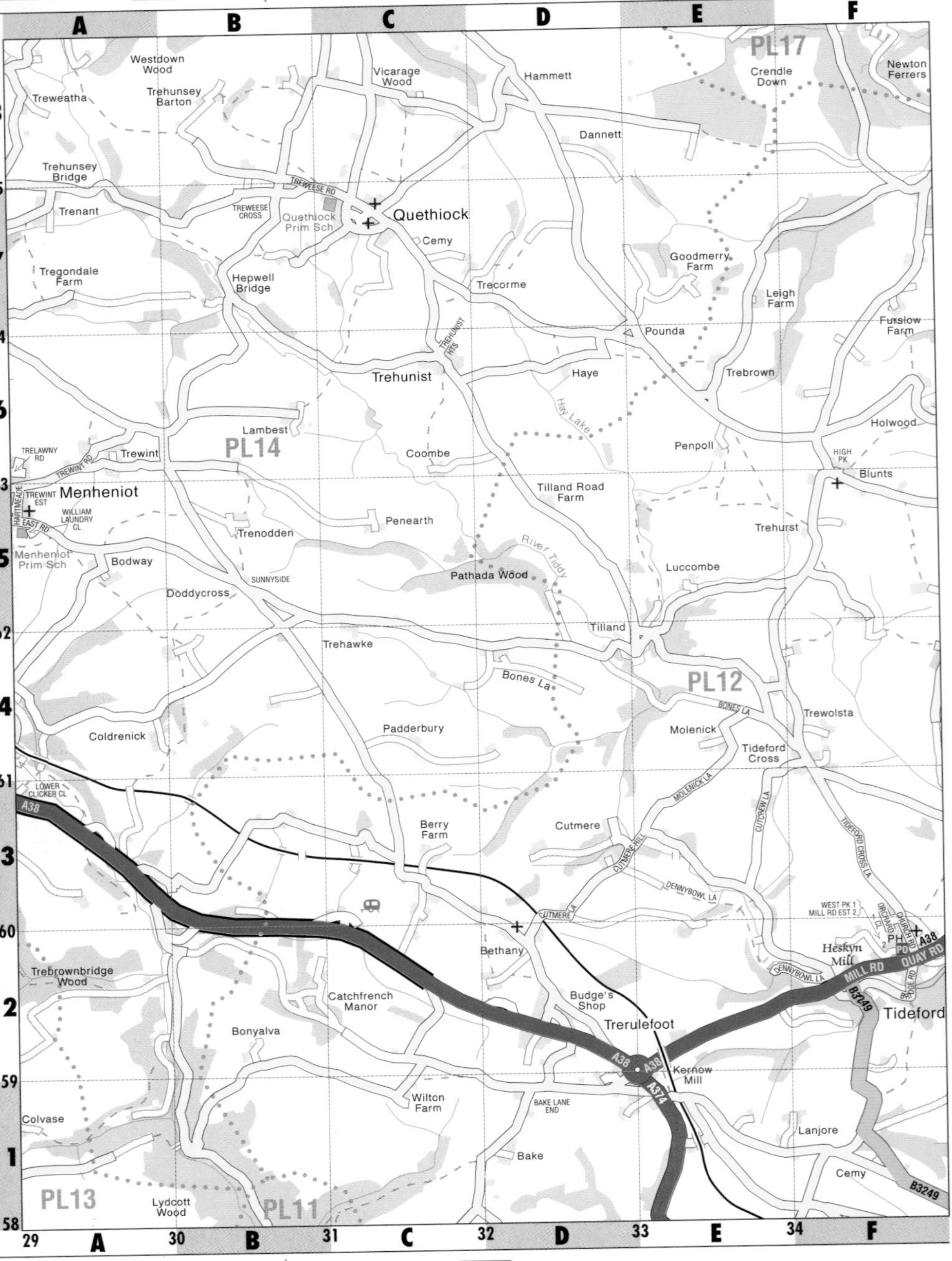

Scale: 1⅓ inches to 1 mile
0 ¼ ½ mile
0 250m 500m 750m 1 km

39 40 118

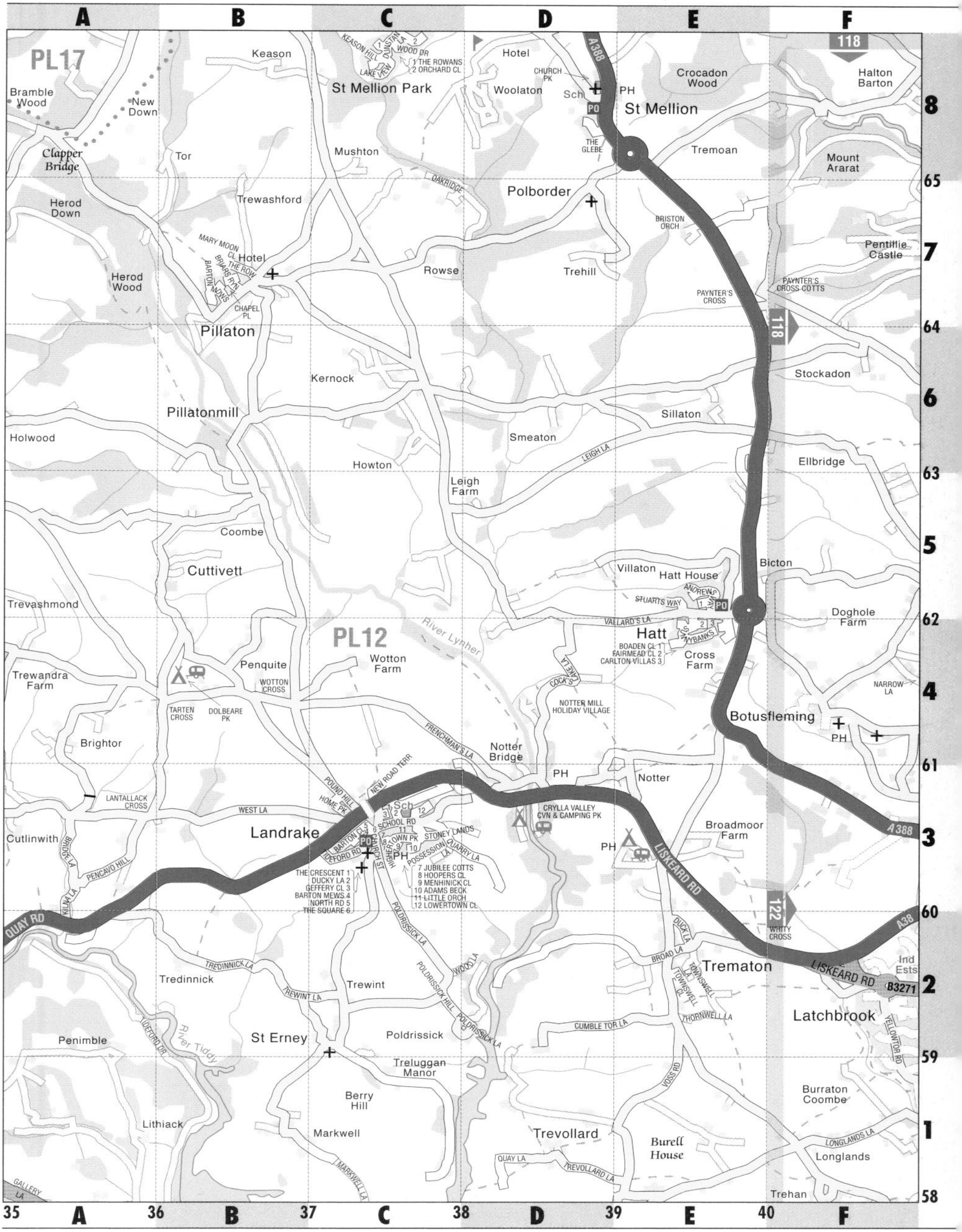

65 122

Scale: 1⅓ inches to 1 mile
0 ¼ ½ mile
0 250m 500m 750m 1 km

A
B
C
D
E
F
8
57
7
56
6
55
5
54
4
53
3
52
2
51
1
50
69
70
71
72
73
74
Shag Rock
Shafts (dis)
Cligga Head
Cligga Workshops 1
ST GEORGE'S TERR 2
B3285
ST GEORGE'S HILL
Shafts (dis)
Hotel
TR6
Bawden Rocks
Hanover Cove
South West Coast Path
Anchor
Airfield
Green Island
Trevellas Porth
Cross Coombe
Chy
Newdowns Head
Trevaunance Cove
Trevellas
Crams
New Downs
Chy
Heritage Trail
Blue Hills
Trevellas Coombe
Blowinghouse
St Agnes Head
Shafts (dis)
PH
PERRAN VIEW HOLIDAY PK
Carn Gowla
TREVAUNANCE CL
Wheal Kitty Workshops
TR5
Higher Bal
Wheal Kitty
Mithian Sch
Chy
Peterville
GOONLAZE TERR
Barkla Shop
TOWN HILL
B3285
St Agnes Sch
PH
Tubby's Head
Chy
St Agnes Beacon
Liby
Mithian
BEACON RD
BEACON FARM
St Agnes
Mus
B3277
Chy
Cemy
Goonown
WHITWORTH CL
GOONVREA RD
PENWINNICK RD
GOONOWN RD
WATER LA
BRITISH RD
VICARAGE RD
ROSEMUNDY
QUAY RD
ROCKY LA
WHEAL FRIENDLY LA
WHEAL KITTY LA
WHEAL KITTY
BEACON DR
A
B
C
D
E
F

C1
1 BRECON CL
2 BEACONSFIELD PL
3 WHITE'S CL
4 ANGWIN AVE
5 CHURCHTOWN
6 CHEGWYN GDNS
7 KEMP'S CL
8 BOLSTER CL
9 PENWINNICK CL

68

D1
1 PENGARTH
2 CASTLE MDWS
3 CASTLE MEADOWS CT
4 PENWINNICK PARC
5 MIDDLEGATES
6 GRENVILLE DR
7 LAMBOURNE AVE
8 ATLANTIC MEWS
9 HIGHFIELD CT
10 THE OLD SCHOOL
11 STIPPY STAPPY

Scale: 1⅓ inches to 1 mile
0 ¼ ½ mile
0 250m 500m 750m 1 km

43
56

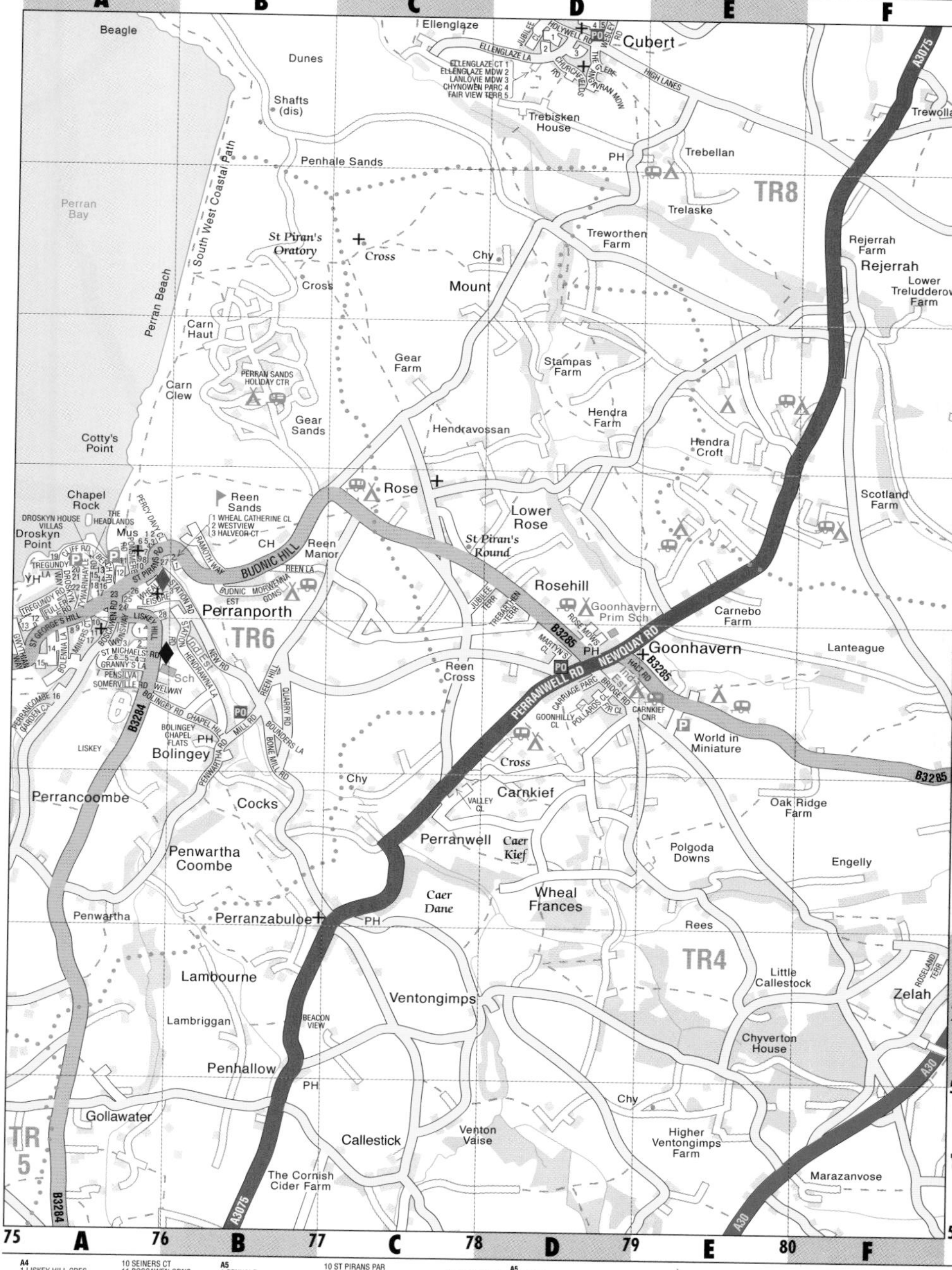

A B C D E F
8 7 6 5 4 3 2 1
57 56 55 54 53 52 51 50
75 76 77 78 79 80
Beagle
Dunes
Shafts (dis)
Ellenglaze
Cubert
JUBILEE CL
HOLYWELL RD
WESLEY RD
ELLENGLAZE LA
CHURCHFIELDS RD
THE GLEBE
TRENGOVRAN MDW
HIGH LANES
ELLENGLAZE CT 1
ELLENGLAZE MDW 2
LANLOVIE MDW 3
CHYNOWEN PARC 4
FAIR VIEW TERR 5
Trebisken House
A3075
Trewolla
PH
Trebellan
Penhale Sands
TR8
Perran Bay
Trelaske
South West Coastal Path
Treworthen Farm
St Piran's Oratory
Cross
Chy
Rejerrah Farm
Rejerrah
Lower Treludderow Farm
Perran Beach
Mount
Carn Haut
Gear Farm
Stampas Farm
Carn Clew
PERRAN SANDS HOLIDAY CTR
Gear Sands
Hendra Farm
Hendravossan
Hendra Croft
Cotty's Point
Chapel Rock
Reen Sands
Rose
Lower Rose
Scotland Farm
DROSKYN HOUSE VILLAS
THE HEADLANDS
Droskyn Point
Mus
1 WHEAL CATHERINE CL
2 WESTVIEW
3 HALVEOR CT
CH
Reen Manor
St Piran's Round
RAMOTH WAY
BUDNIC HILL
REEN LA
YH
TREGUNDY LA
ST PIRANS RD
BUDNIC EST
MORWENNA GDNS
Rosehill
Carnebo Farm
Perranporth
Goonhavern Prim Sch
TR6
B3285
ROSE MDWS
MARTYN'S CL
PH
NEWQUAY RD
Goonhavern
Lanteague
ST GEORGE'S HILL
LISKEY HILL
ST MICHAELS RD
GRANNY'S LA
PENSILVA
SOMERVILLE RD
Sch
WELWAY
HENDRAWNA LA
NEW RD
REEN HILL
QUARRY RD
Reen Cross
PERRANWELL RD
CARRIAGE PARC
BRIDGE RD
HALT RD
Ind Est
PERRANCOMBE GARDEN CT
B3284
BOLINGEY RD
CHAPEL HILL
MILL RD
BOUNDERS LA
BONE MILL RD
GOONHILLY CL
POLLARDS CL
FR CL
CARNKIEF CNR
World in Miniature
BOLINGEY CHAPEL FLATS
LISKEY
Bolingey
PENWARTHA RD
Cross
B3285
Chy
Carnkief
Perrancoombe
VALLEY CL
Oak Ridge Farm
Cocks
Perranwell
Caer Kief
Polgoda Downs
Penwartha Coombe
Engelly
Caer Dane
Wheal Frances
Penwartha
Perranzabuloe
PH
Rees
TR4
ROSELAND TERR
Lambourne
Little Callestock
Zelah
Ventongimps
BEACON VIEW
Lambriggan
Chyverton House
Penhallow
A30
PH
Chy
Gollawater
TR5
Callestick
Venton Vaise
Higher Ventongimps Farm
The Cornish Cider Farm
Marazanvose
B3284
A3075
A30

A4
1 LISKEY HILL CRES
2 SUNNYSIDE
3 HENTAL
4 LAMORNE CL
5 TREVALGA CL
6 TREVIAN CL
7 NAMPARA CT
8 UPPER HILLCREST
9 LOWER HILLCREST
10 SEINERS CT
11 BOSCAWEN GDNS
12 TREDINNICK WAY
13 ST GEORGES HILL CL
14 HIGHER BOLENNA
15 COOMBE VIEW
16 WHITE WALLS CT
17 BOSCAWEN CT

A5
1 PENHALE
2 PENVENEN
3 WHEAL RAMOTH
4 ROSEMULLION
5 VENTONVAISE
6 SAND-BAY HOLIDAY FLATS
7 EUREKA VALE
8 TREGONNING CT
9 PONSMERE CT
10 ST PIRANS PAR
11 GOLDEN SANDS
12 BEACH LA
13 HERONS CT
14 THE GOUNCE
15 ST PIRANS HO
16 POPLARS CT
17 HANOVER CL
18 LOWER TYWARNHAYLE
19 DROSKYN CASTLE

69

A5
20 TREGUNDY CT
21 TREGUNDY CL
22 DROSKYN CL
23 TYWARNHAYLE SQ
24 MITCHELLS CNR
25 WHEAL LEISURE CL
26 MARINE CT
27 JOSEPH'S CT
28 RIDGEWAY

56

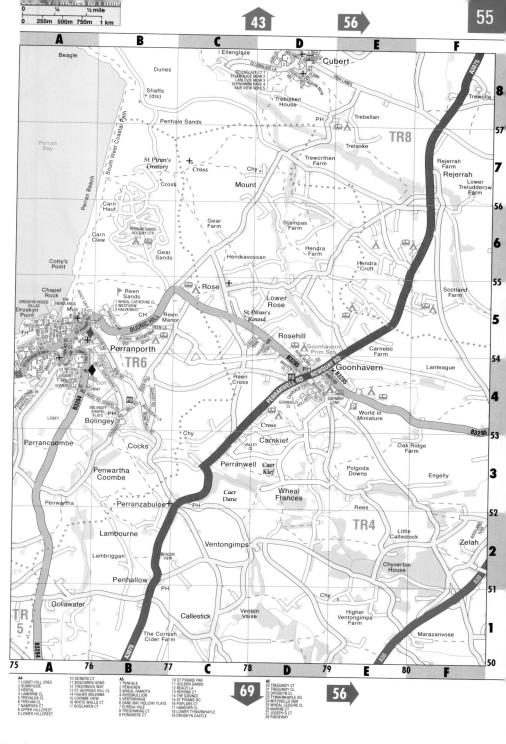

55
44

Scale: 1⅓ inches to 1 mile

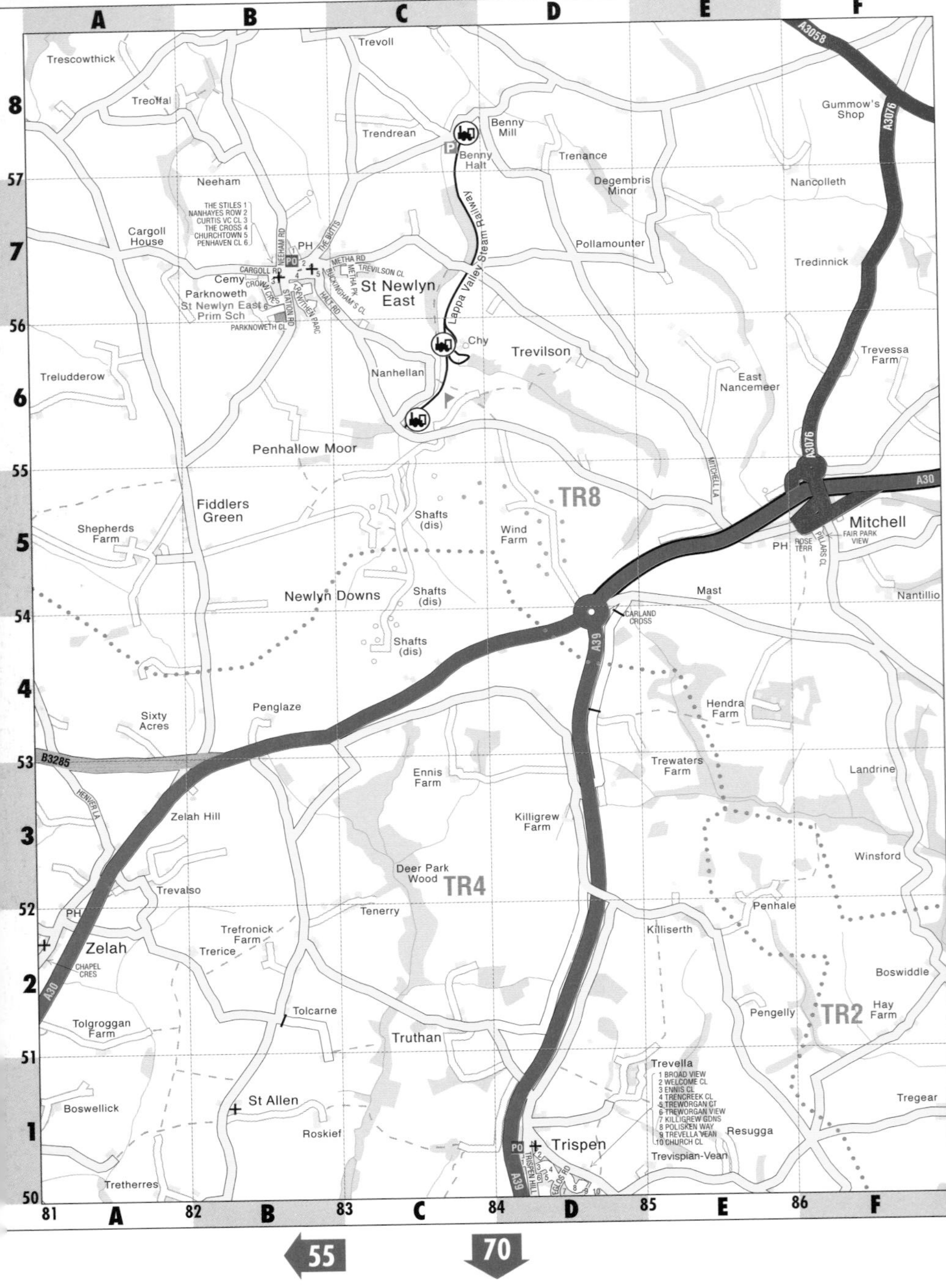

55
70

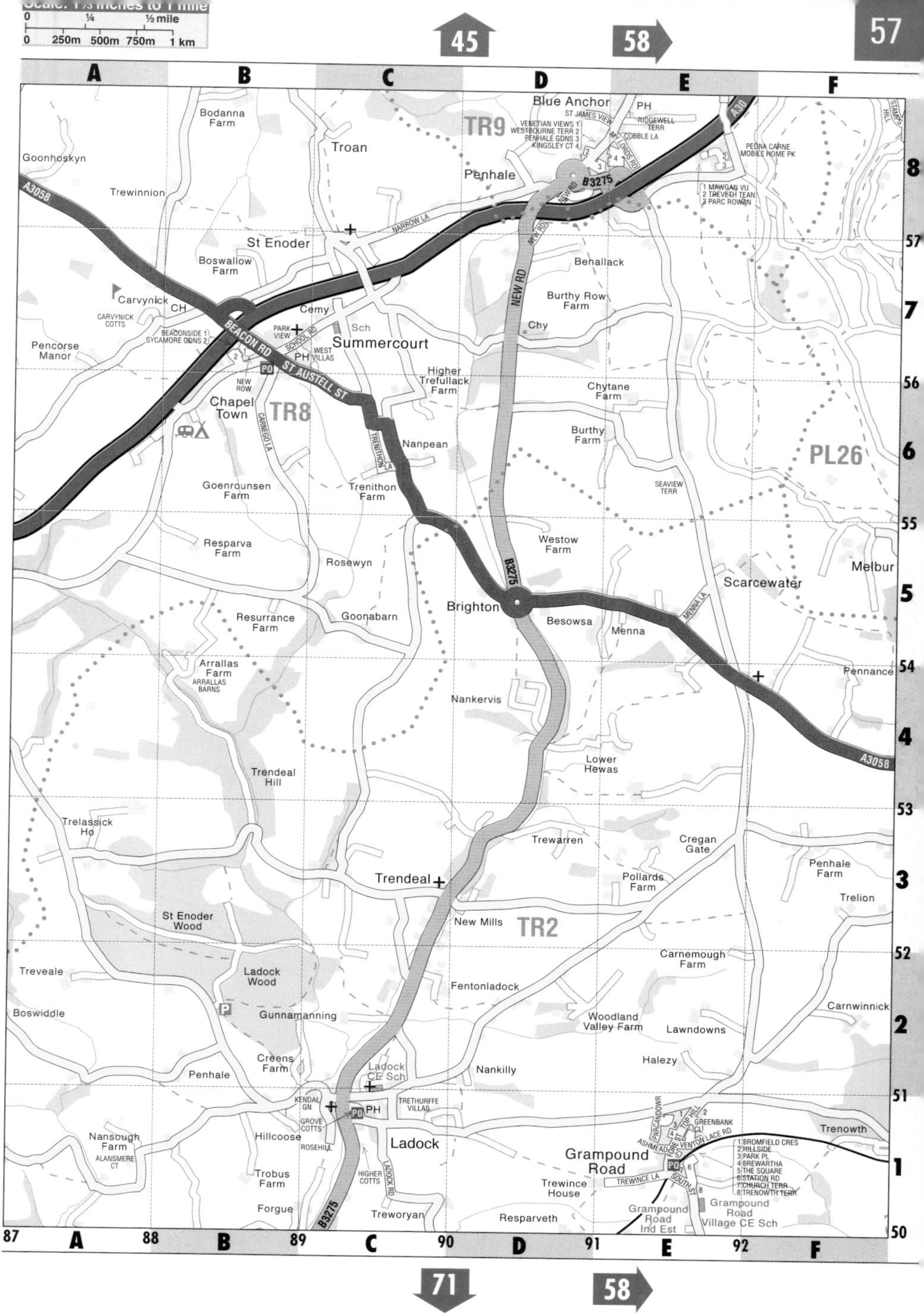
Scale: 1⅓ inches to 1 mile
0 ¼ ½ mile
0 250m 500m 750m 1 km
45
58
A B C D E F
Blue Anchor
TR9
Troan
Penhale
Goonhoskyn
Bodanna Farm
Trewinnion
A3058
St Enoder
Boswallow Farm
Carvynick
CH
Cemy
Summercourt
Sch
Pencorse Manor
Chapel Town
TR8
Nanpean
Trenithon Farm
Goenrounsen Farm
Resparva Farm
Rosewyn
Goonabarn
Brighton
Resurrance Farm
Arrallas Farm
ARRALLAS BARNS
Nankervis
Trendeal Hill
Trelassick Ho
Trendeal
New Mills
TR2
St Enoder Wood
Treveale
Ladock Wood
Boswiddle
Gunnamanning
Fentonladock
Creens Farm
Penhale
Ladock CE Sch
Nankilly
Ladock
Hillcoose
Nansough Farm
Trobus Farm
Forgue
Treworyan
Resparveth
Grampound Road
Trewince House
Grampound Road Ind Est
Grampound Road Village CE Sch
Benallack
Burthy Row Farm
Chy
Higher Trefullack Farm
Chytane Farm
Burthy Farm
Westow Farm
Besowsa
Menna
Scarcewater
Melbur
PL26
Pennance
Lower Hewas
Trewarren
Cregan Gate
Pollards Farm
Penhale Farm
Trelion
Carnemough Farm
Woodland Valley Farm
Lawndowns
Halezy
Carnwinnick
Trenowth
PEDNA CARNE MOBILE HOME PK
1 MAWGAN VU
2 TREVETH TEAN
3 PARC ROWAN
VENETIAN VIEWS 1
WESTBOURNE TERR 2
PENHALE GDNS 3
KINGSLEY CT 4
ST JAMES VIEW
RIDGEWELL TERR
COBBLE LA
MY LORDS RD
NEW RD
B3275
A30
NARROW LA
BEACON RD
ST AUSTELL ST
SCHOOL RD
PARK VIEW
WEST VILLAS
BEACONSIDE 1
SYCAMORE GDNS 2
CARVYNICK COTTS
NEW ROW
CARNEGO LA
TRENITHON LA
SEAVIEW TERR
MENNA LA
KENDAL GN
GROVE COTTS
ROSEHILL
TRETHURFFE VILLAS
HIGHER COTTS
LADOCK RD
ALANSMERE CT
PARCANDOWR
FORE ST
TOP HILL
GREENBANK CL
VENTON LACE RD
ASHMEAD
SOUTH ST
TREWINCE LA
1 BROMFIELD CRES
2 HILLSIDE
3 PARK PL
4 BREWARTHA
5 THE SQUARE
6 STATION RD
7 CHURCH TERR
8 TRENOWTH TERR
PO
PH
P
8 57 7 56 6 55 5 54 4 53 3 52 2 51 1 50
87 88 89 90 91 92
71
58

57
46

Scale: 1⅓ inches to 1 mile

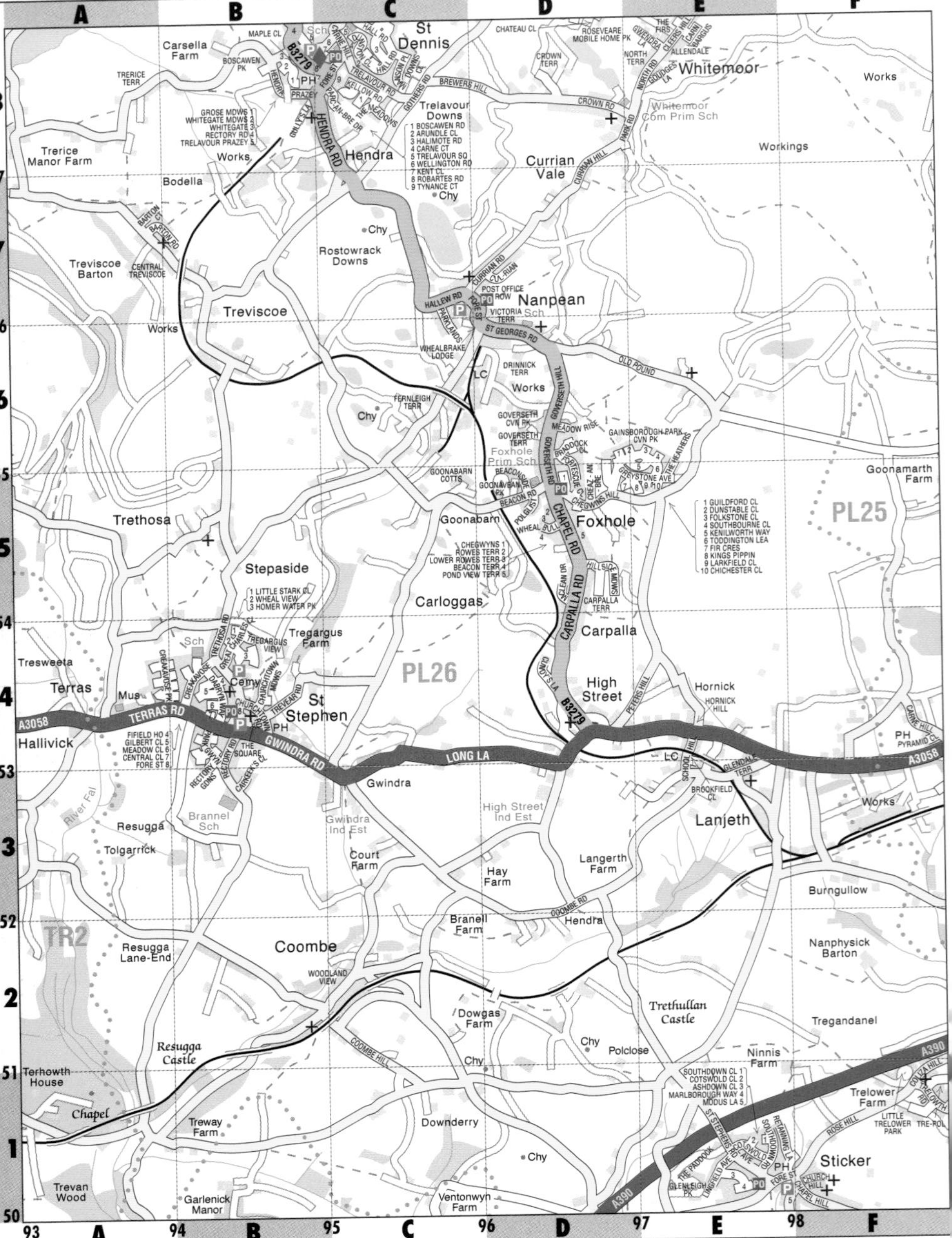

57
72

Scale: 1⅓ inches to 1 mile
0 ¼ ½ mile
0 250m 500m 750m 1 km

47

D7
1 MEADOW RISE
2 MONTGOMERY RD
3 CANNAMANNING RD
4 TEDDER RD
5 MOUNTBATTEN RD
6 PENWITHICK PK

60

D7
7 HELENA CT
8 PENTREVAH RD
9 ASHLEY CL
10 CHURCHILL WAY
11 GROSE HILL CRES
12 TREGARTH

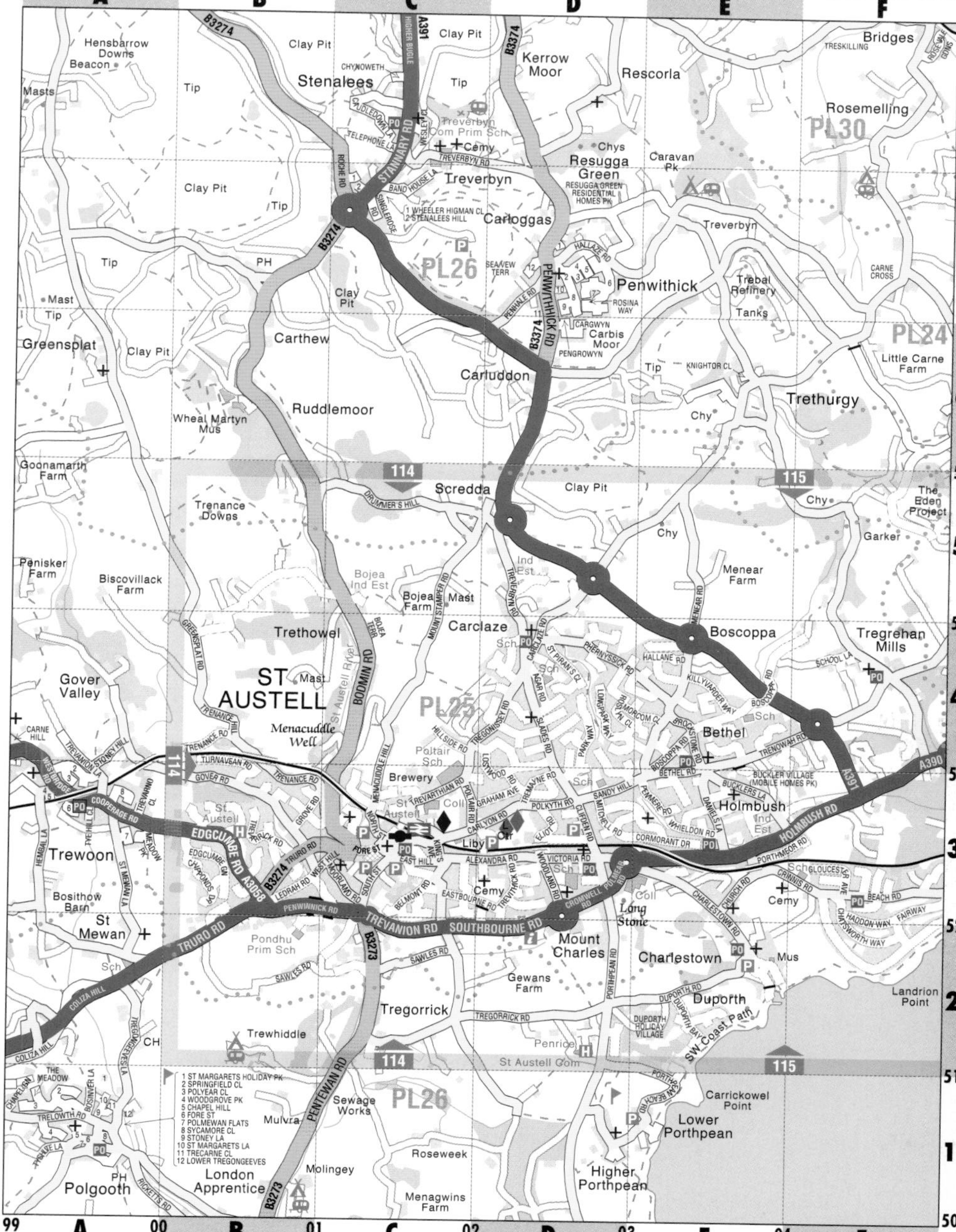

A3
1 TREMEWAN
2 TREVANION RD
3 ST ANNE'S RD
4 HEMBAL RD
5 HEMBAL CL
6 THE GREEN
7 SOCOTRA DR
8 COOPERAGE GDNS

73

60

For full street detail of the highlighted area see pages 114 and 115.

59
48

Scale: 1⅓ inches to 1 mile
0 ¼ ½ mile
0 250m 500m 750m 1 km

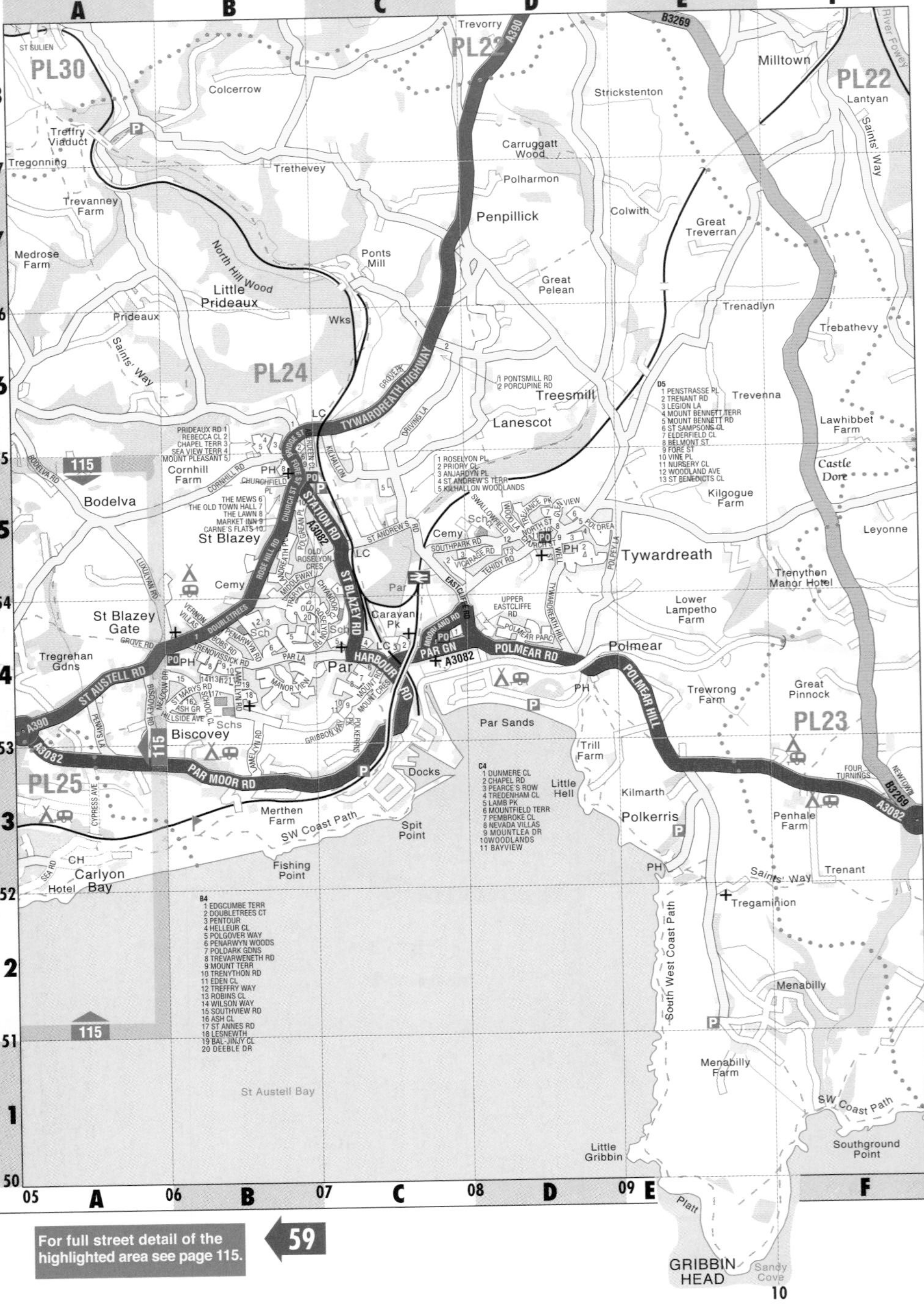
A
B
C
D
E
F
8
57
7
56
6
55
5
54
4
53
3
52
2
51
1
50
05
06
07
08
09
10
PL30
PL22
PL22
PL24
PL25
PL23
ST SULIEN
Colcerrow
Trevorry
A390
B3269
Milltown
River Fowey
Lantyan
Strickstenton
Saints' Way
Treffry Viaduct
Tregonning
Trethevey
Carruggatt Wood
Polharmon
Trevanney Farm
Penpillick
Colwith
Great Treverran
Medrose Farm
Ponts Mill
North Hill Wood
Little Prideaux
Great Pelean
Prideaux
Wks
Trenadlyn
Trebathevy
Saints' Way
GROVER
TYWARDREATH HIGHWAY
1 PONTSMILL RD
2 PORCUPINE RD
Treesmill
D5
1 PENSTRASSE PL
2 TRENANT RD
3 LEGION LA
4 MOUNT BENNETT TERR
5 MOUNT BENNETT RD
6 ST SAMPSONS CL
7 ELDERFIELD CL
8 BELMONT ST
9 FORE ST
10 VINE PL
11 NURSERY CL
12 WOODLAND AVE
13 ST BENEDICTS CL
Trevenna
Lawhibbet Farm
LC
Lanescot
PRIDEAUX RD 1
REBECCA CL 2
CHAPEL TERR 3
SEA VIEW TERR 4
MOUNT PLEASANT 5
BRIDGE ST
ABERDEEN CL
DRIVING LA
KILHALLON
BODELVA RD
115
Cornhill Farm
CORNHILL RD
PH
CHURCHFIELD PL
FORE ST
CHURCH ST
STATION RD
1 ROSELYON PL
2 PRIORY CL
3 ANJARDYN PL
4 ST ANDREW'S TERR
5 KILHALLON WOODLANDS
Castle Dore
Kilgogue Farm
Bodelva
THE MEWS 6
THE OLD TOWN HALL 7
THE LAWN 8
MARKET INN 9
CARNE'S FLATS 10
A3082
ST ANDREW'S RD
SWALLOWFIELD
WOODLA
TRUANCE PK
GLEN VIEW
POL DREA
Sch
Leyonne
St Blazey
ROSE HILL RD
ANDREATH PL
POLGREAN PL
OLD ROSELYON CRES
LC
Cemy
SOUTHPARK RD
VICARAGE RD
TEHIDY RD
NORTH ST
CHURCH ST
WELL
PH
POLPEY LA
Tywardreath
LUXULYAN RD
Cemy
MIDDLEWAY
TRENYTHON
CHYANDOUR CL
ST BLAZEY RD
Par
EASTCLIFFE RD
Trenython Manor Hotel
Lower Lampetho Farm
VERNON VILLAS
DOUBLETREES
St Blazey Gate
Caravan Pk
MOORLAND RD
UPPER EASTCLIFFE RD
POLMEAR PARC
TYWARDREATH HILL
GROVE RD
Sch
PENARWYN RD
BOBS RD
TRENOVISSICK RD
PAR LA
HARBOUR RD
LC
PAR GN
PO
POLMEAR RD
Polmear
A3082
Tregrehan Gdns
ST AUSTELL RD
ST MARYS RD
MEADOW DR
ASH GR
SCHOOL CL
LAMELYN RD
HILLSIDE AVE
MANOR VIEW
MOUNT RD
MOUNT CRES
POLMEAR HILL
Trewrong Farm
Great Pinnock
BISCOVEY RD
A390
PENNYS LA
Schs
Biscovey
GRIBBON WAY
POLKERRIS
PK
Par Sands
PH
A3082
PAR MOOR RD
LAMELYN RD
Trill Farm
Docks
C4
1 DUNMERE CL
2 CHAPEL RD
3 PEARCE'S ROW
4 TREDENHAM CL
5 LAMB PK
6 MOUNTFIELD TERR
7 PEMBROKE CL
8 NEVADA VILLAS
9 MOUNTLEA DR
10WOODLANDS
11 BAYVIEW
Little Hell
Kilmarth
FOUR TURNINGS
NEWTOWN
B3269
A3082
CYPRESS AVE
Merthen Farm
Polkerris
Penhale Farm
SW Coast Path
Spit Point
SEA RD
CH
Carlyon Bay
Hotel
Fishing Point
PH
Saints' Way
Trenant
Tregaminion
B4
1 EDGCUMBE TERR
2 DOUBLETREES CT
3 PENTOUR
4 HELLEUR CL
5 POLGOVER WAY
6 PENARWYN WOODS
7 POLDARK GDNS
8 TREVARWENETH RD
9 MOUNT TERR
10 TRENYTHON RD
11 EDEN CL
12 TREFFRY WAY
13 ROBINS CL
14 WILSON WAY
15 SOUTHVIEW RD
16 ASH CL
17 ST ANNES RD
18 LESNEWTH
19 BAL-JINJY CL
20 DEEBLE DR
South West Coast Path
Menabilly
115
Menabilly Farm
St Austell Bay
SW Coast Path
Southground Point
Little Gribbin
Platt
GRIBBIN HEAD
Sandy Cove

For full street detail of the highlighted area see page 115.

59

49
62

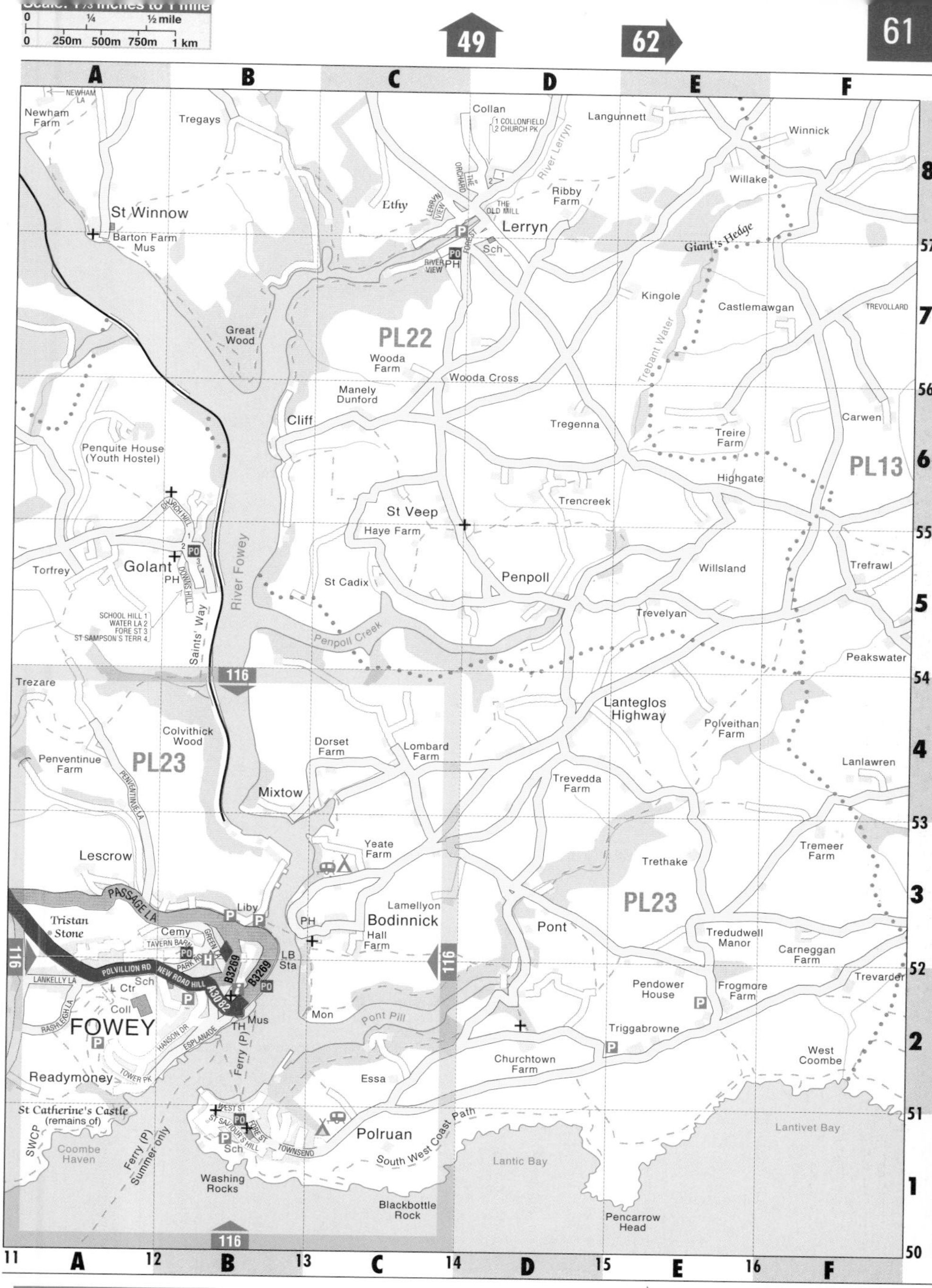

For full street detail of the highlighted area see page116.

62

61
50
Scale: 1⅓ inches to 1 mile
0 ¼ ½ mile
0 250m 500m 750m 1 km

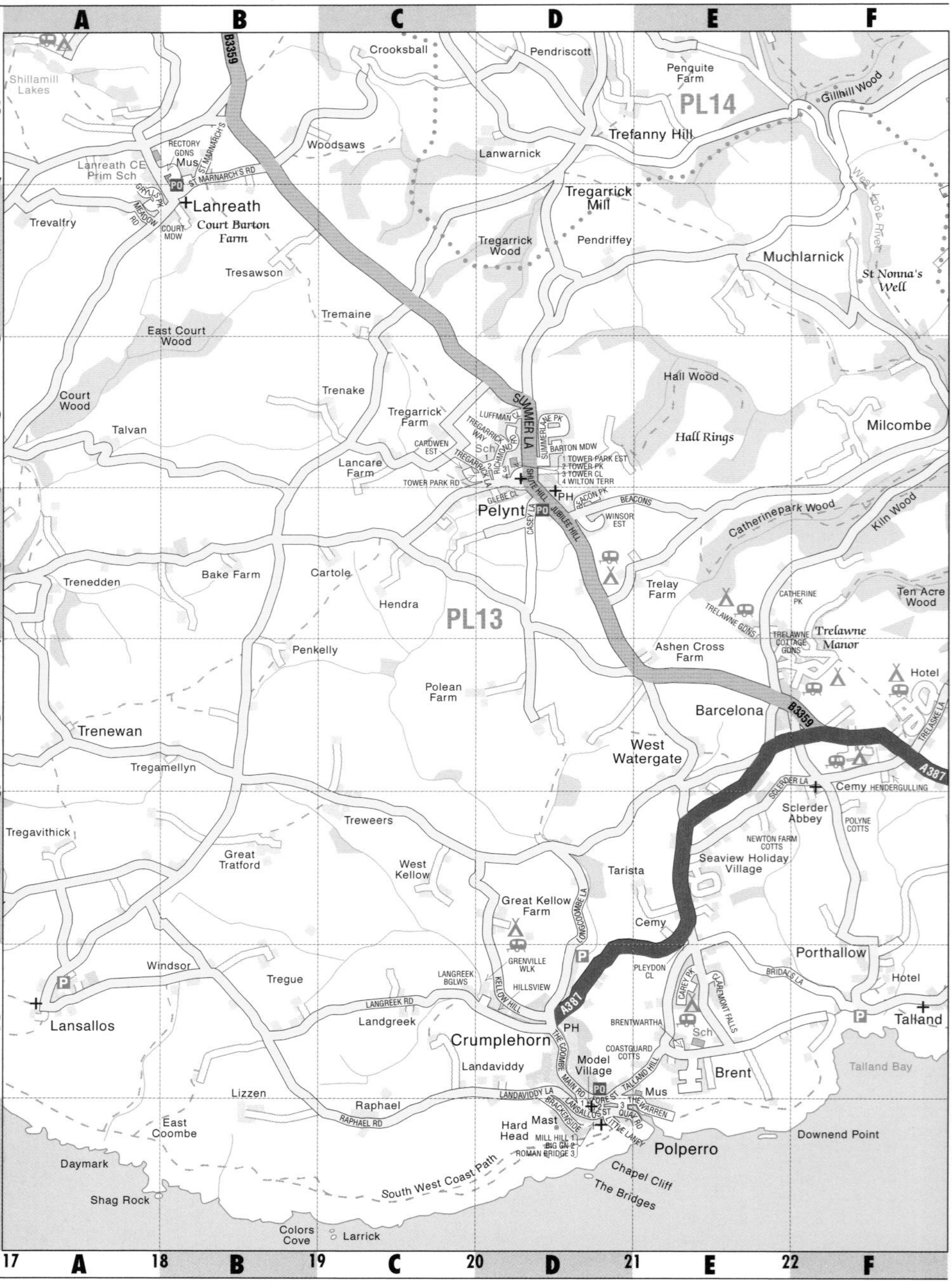
A B C D E F
8 57 7 56 6 55 5 54 4 53 3 52 2 51 1 50
17 18 19 20 21 22
B3359
A387
PL14
PL13
Shillamill Lakes
Crooksball
Pendriscott
Penquite Farm
Gillhill Wood
Trefanny Hill
Woodsaws
Lanwarnick
Rectory Gdns
Mus
St Marnarch's Rd
Lanreath CE Prim Sch
PO
Lanreath
Court Barton Farm
Meadow Rd
Court Mdw
Trevalfry
Tregarrick Mill
West Looe River
Tregarrick Wood
Pendriffey
Muchlarnick
St Nonna's Well
Tresawson
Tremaine
East Court Wood
Hall Wood
Court Wood
Trenake
Tregarrick Farm
Summer La
Luffman Cl
Summerlane Pk
Barton Mdw
Milcombe
Talvan
Hall Rings
Cardwen Est
Tregarrick Way
Richmond Rd
Sch
1 Tower Park Est
2 Tower Pk
3 Tower Cl
4 Wilton Terr
Lancare Farm
Tower Park Rd
Glebe Cl
Shute Hill
PH
Beacon Pk
Beacons
Pelynt
Casey La
Jubilee Hill
Winsor Est
Catherinepark Wood
Kiln Wood
Trenedden
Bake Farm
Cartole
Hendra
Trelay Farm
Catherine Pk
Ten Acre Wood
Trelawne Gdns
Trelawne Cottage Gdns
Trelawne Manor
Penkelly
Ashen Cross Farm
Hotel
Polean Farm
Barcelona
Trelaske La
Trenewan
West Watergate
Tregamellyn
Sclerder La
Cemy
Hendergulling
Sclerder Abbey
Polyne Cotts
Tregavithick
Treweers
Newton Farm Cotts
Seaview Holiday Village
Great Tratford
West Kellow
Tarista
Great Kellow Farm
Longcoombe La
Cemy
Grenville Wlk
Pleydon Cl
Porthallow
Windsor
Langreek Bglws
Kellow Hill
Hillsview
Tregue
Carey Pk
Claremont Falls
Bridals La
Hotel
Langreek Rd
Lansallos
Landgreek
Brentwartha
Talland
Crumplehorn
The Coombe
Coastguard Cotts
Model Village
Talland Bay
Landaviddy
Main Rd
Talland Hill
Brent
Lizzen
Landaviddy La
Fore St
Mus
Raphael
Lansallos St
Quay Rd
The Warren
Raphael Rd
Brackenside
East Coombe
Hard Head
Mast
Mill Hill
Big Gn
Roman Bridge
Little Laney
Downend Point
Polperro
Daymark
South West Coast Path
Chapel Cliff
The Bridges
Shag Rock
Colors Cove
Larrick

61

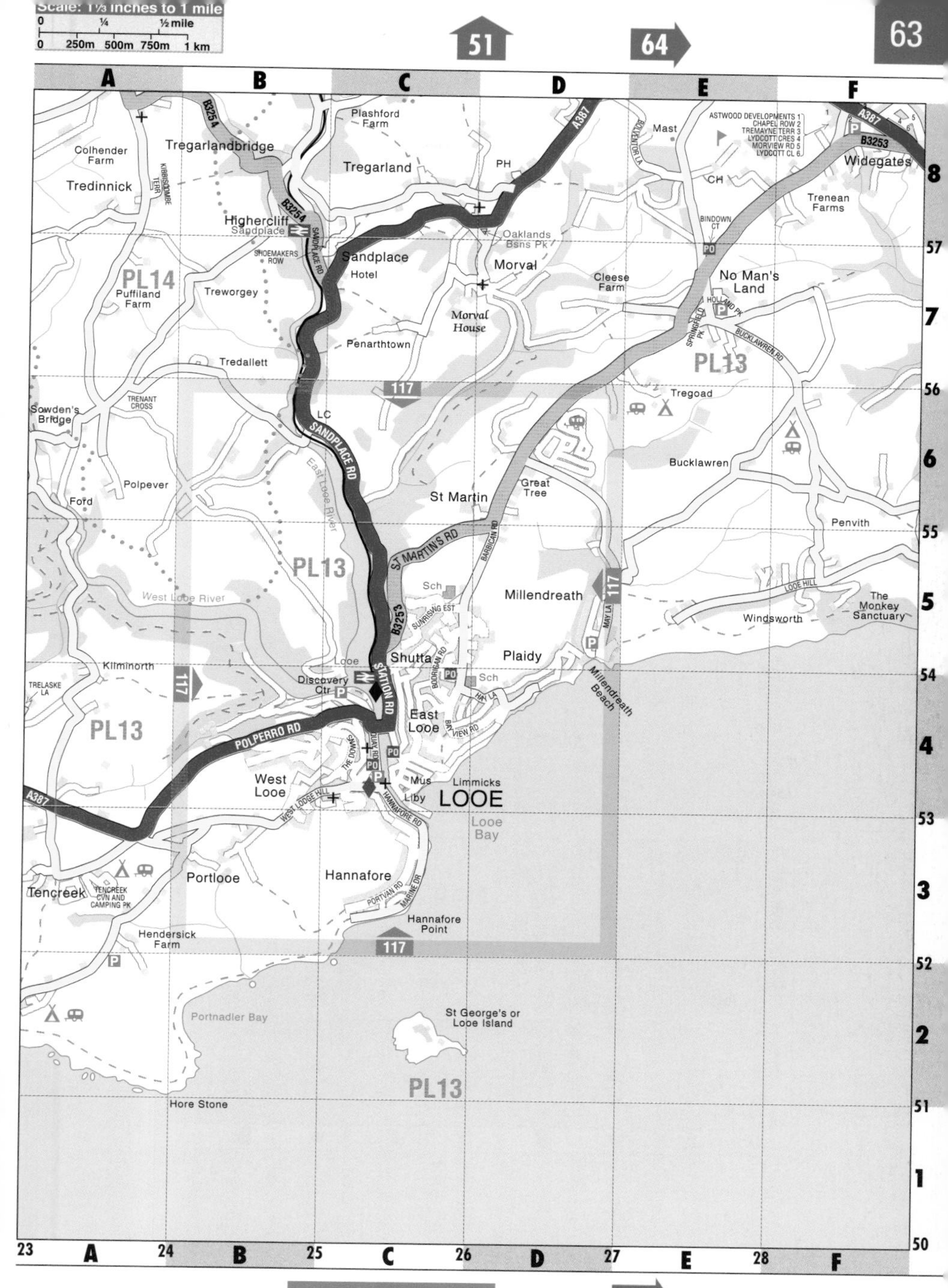

For full street detail of the highlighted area see page 117.

64

63
52

Scale: 1⅓ inches to 1 mile
0 ¼ ½ mile
0 250m 500m 750m 1 km

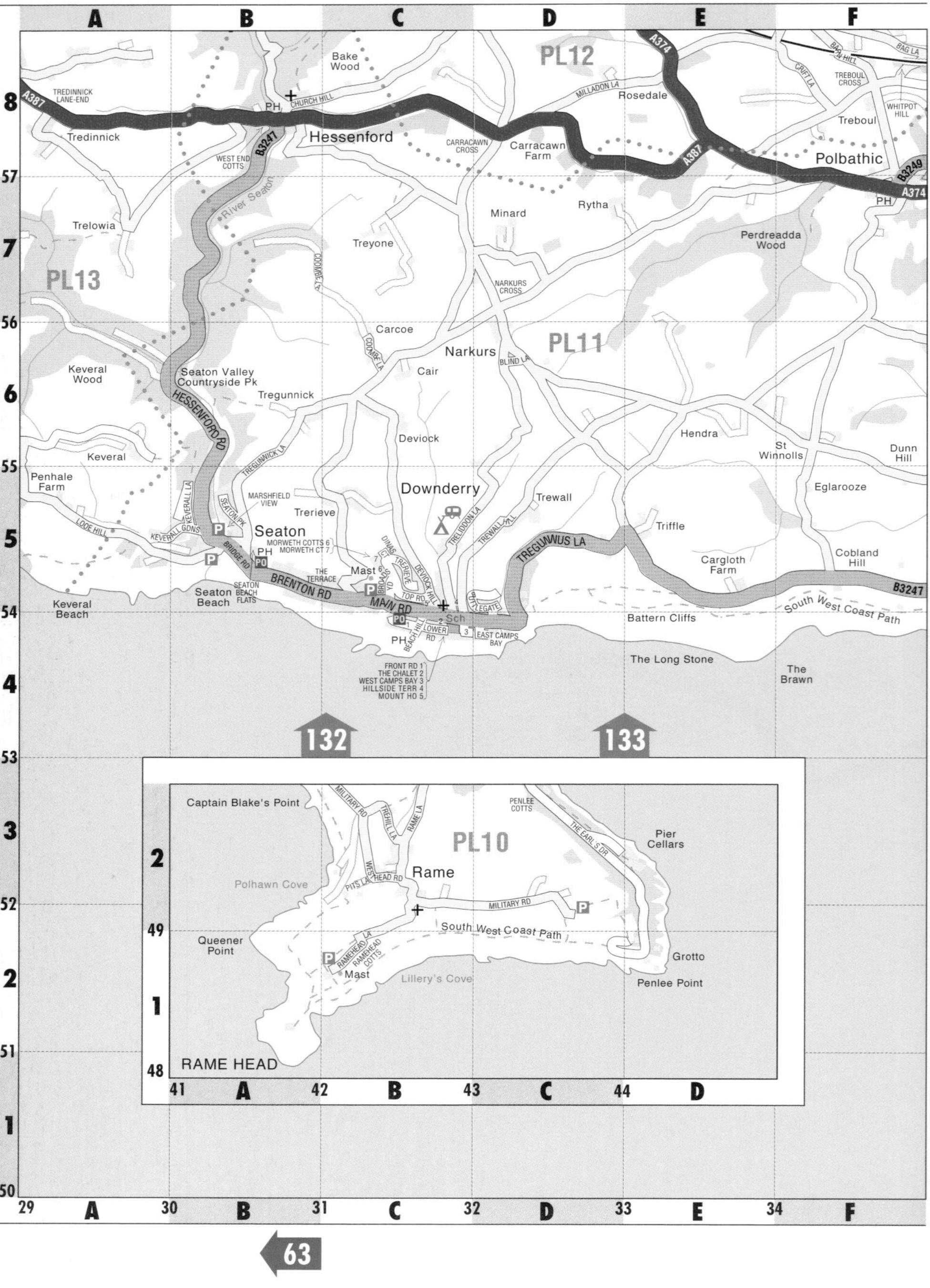

63

53
126

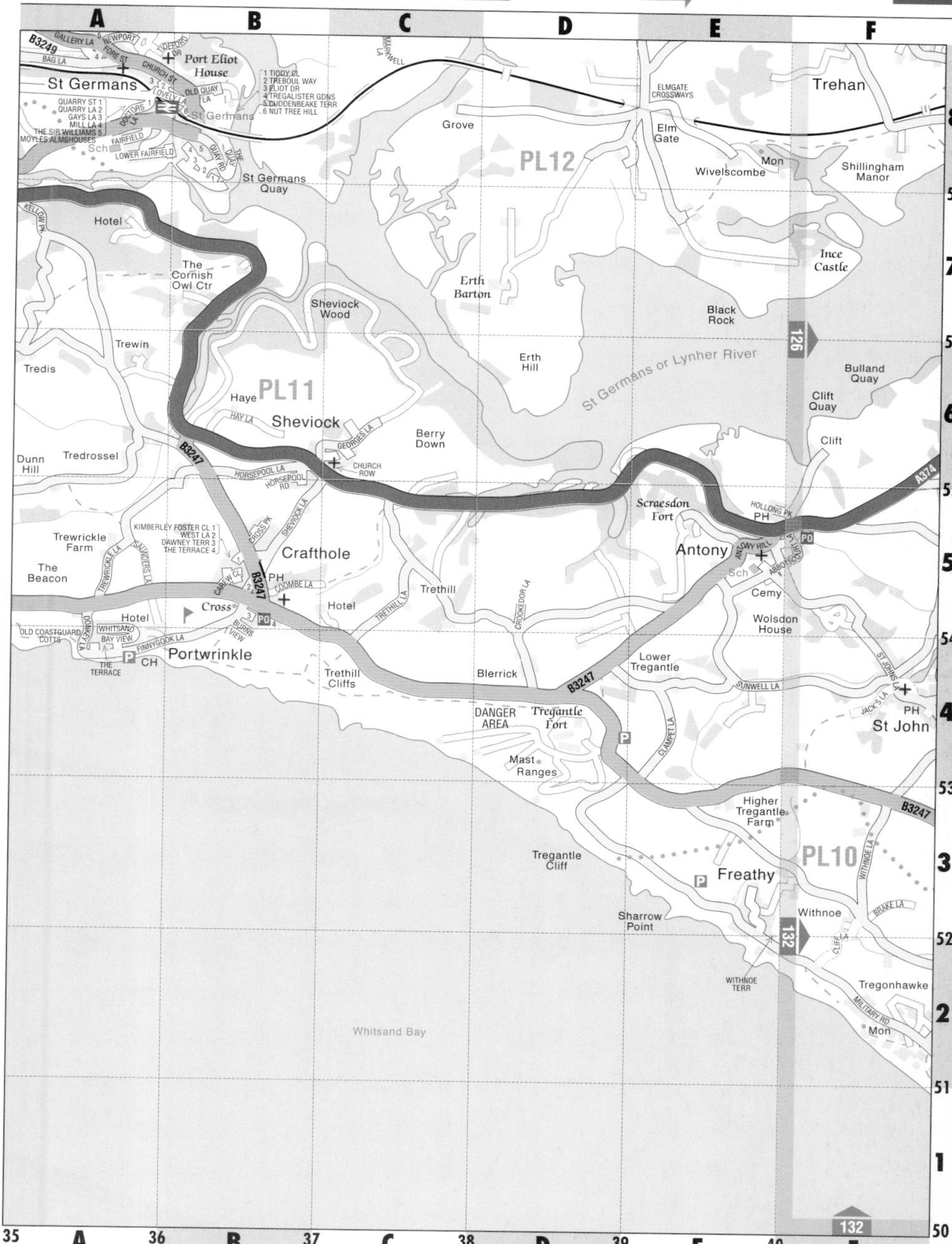

132

For full street detail of the highlighted area see pages 126 and 132.

Scale: 1⅓ inches to 1 mile

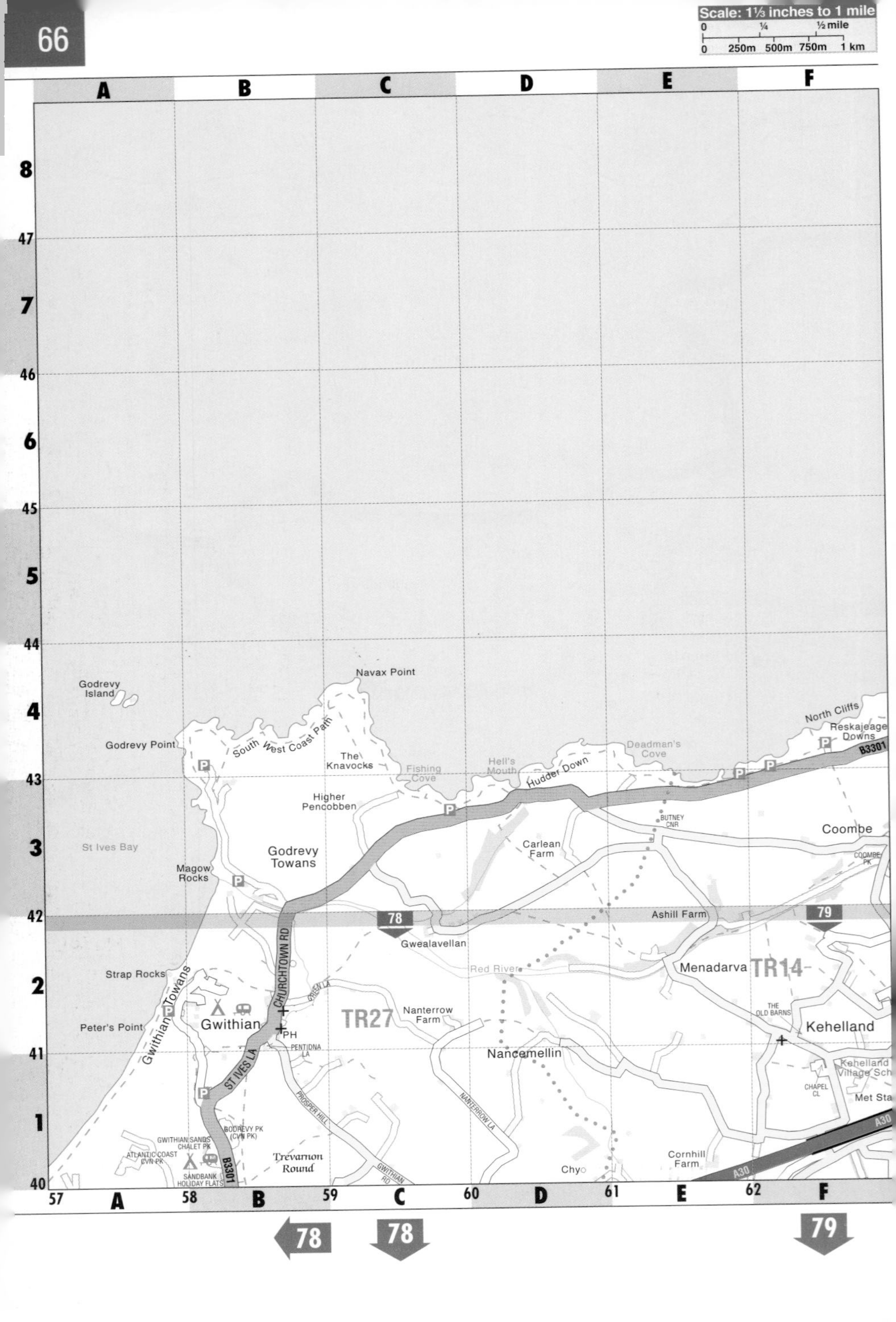

A
B
C
D
E
F
8
47
7
46
6
45
5
44
4
43
3
42
2
41
1
40
57
58
59
60
61
62
Godrevy Island
Navax Point
Godrevy Point
South West Coast Path
The Knavocks
Fishing Cove
Hell's Mouth
Hudder Down
Deadman's Cove
North Cliffs
Reskajeage Downs
B3301
Higher Pencobben
BUTNEY CNR
Coombe
St Ives Bay
Godrevy Towans
Carlean Farm
Magow Rocks
COOMBE PK
78
Ashill Farm
79
CHURCHTOWN RD
Gwealavellan
Strap Rocks
Red River
Menadarva
TR14
GREEN LA
Gwithian Towans
TR27
Nanterrow Farm
THE OLD BARNS
Kehelland
Peter's Point
Gwithian
PH
PENTIDNA LA
Nancemellin
Kehelland Village Sch
ST IVES LA
PROSPER HILL
NANTERROW LA
CHAPEL CL
Met Sta
GODREVY PK (CVN PK)
GWITHIAN SANDS CHALET PK
ATLANTIC COAST CVN PK
SANDBANK HOLIDAY FLATS
Trevarnon Round
GWITHIAN RD
Chy
Cornhill Farm
A30

78
78
79

Scale: 1⅓ inches to 1 mile
0 ¼ ½ mile
0 250m 500m 750m 1 km

E4
1 CORONATION RD
2 VENTONRAZE TERR
3 ROBARTES TERR
4 HARMONY TERR
5 ALEXANDRA CL
6 TREFORTHLAN CL
7 TREFORTHLAN
8 ILLOGAN PK
9 SUNNYSIDE PARC
10 KESTRAL WAY
11 BOSVEAN GDNS
12 POLDARK RD
13 PENCARROW RD
14 PENWARTHA VEAN
15 PENWARTHA RD
16 LAMANVA CL
17 LAMANVA RD
18 TREVELTHAN RD
19 VALLEY VIEW
20 VALLEY GDNS
21 FORTH DALL
22 LOWER MERRITTS HILL
23 BEACON VIEW PK

68

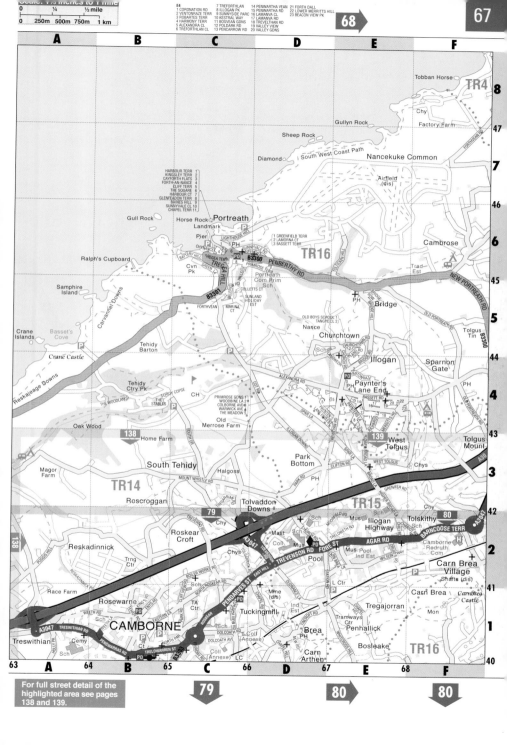

For full street detail of the highlighted area see pages 138 and 139.

79

80

80

67
54

Scale: 1⅓ inches to 1 mile
0 ¼ ½ mile
0 250m 500m 750m 1 km

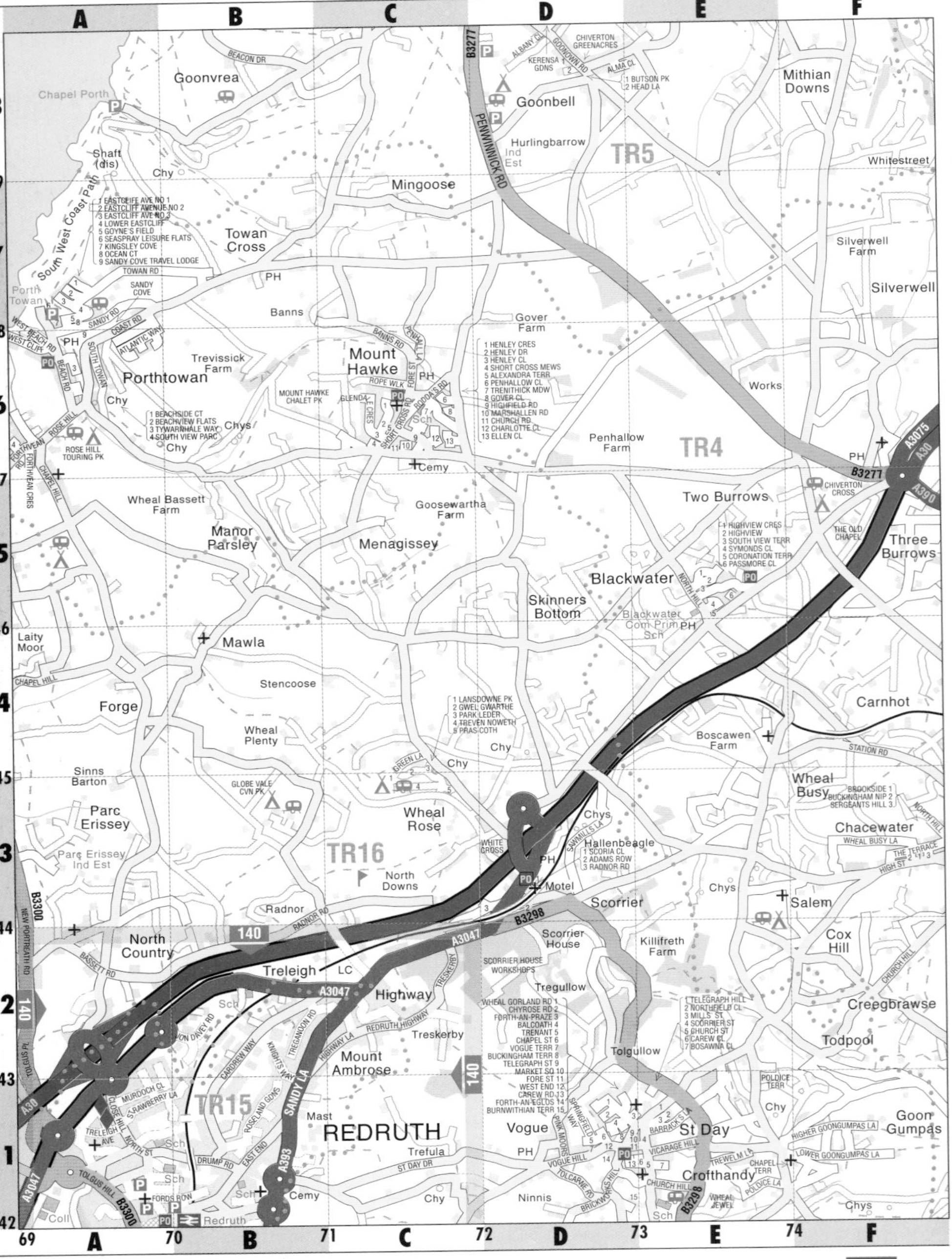

For full street detail of the highlighted area see page 140.
67
80
81

Scale: 1⅓ inches to 1 mile

55
70

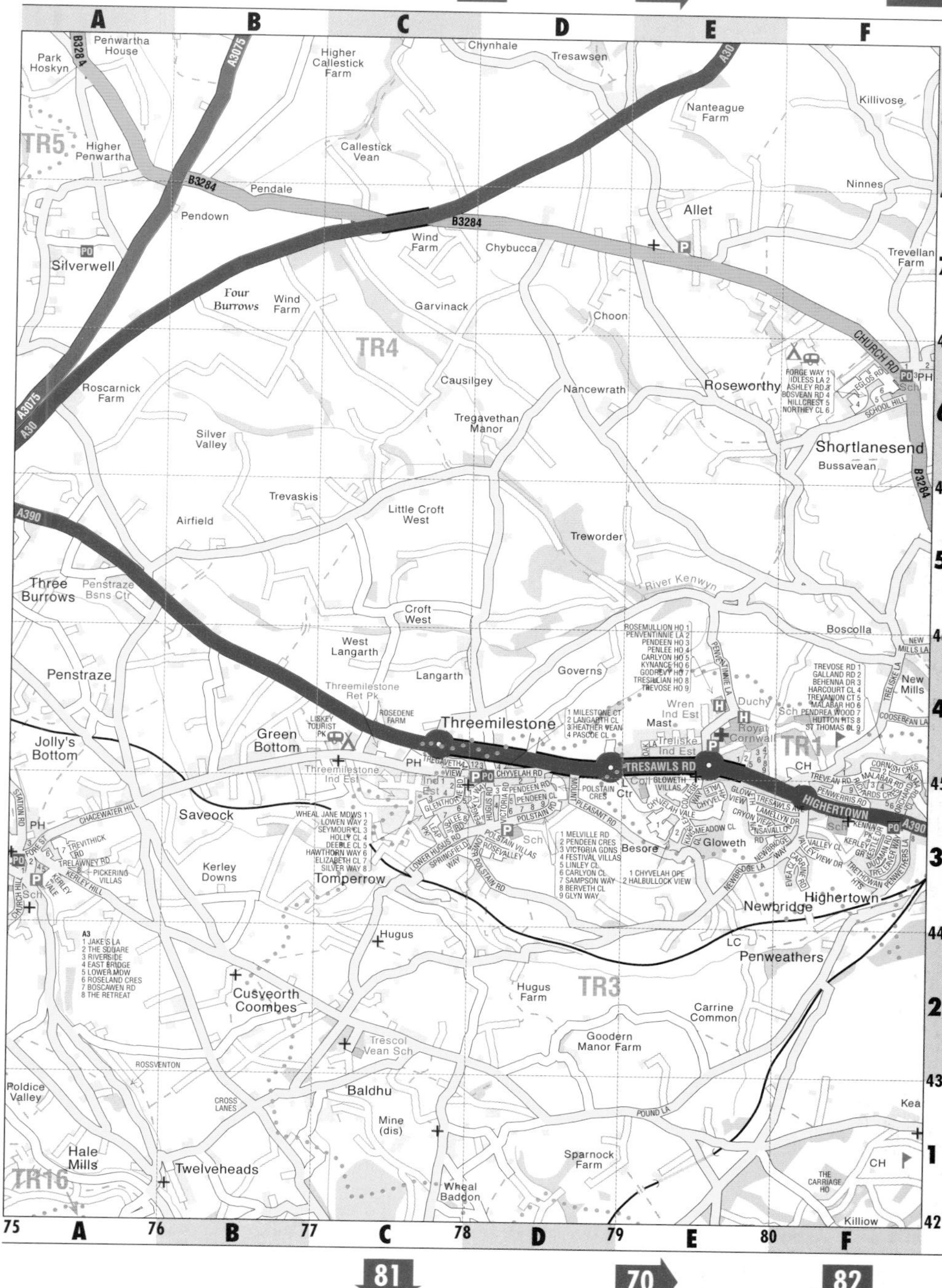

81
70
82

69
56

Scale: 1⅓ inches to 1 mile
0 ¼ ½ mile
0 250m 500m 750m 1 km

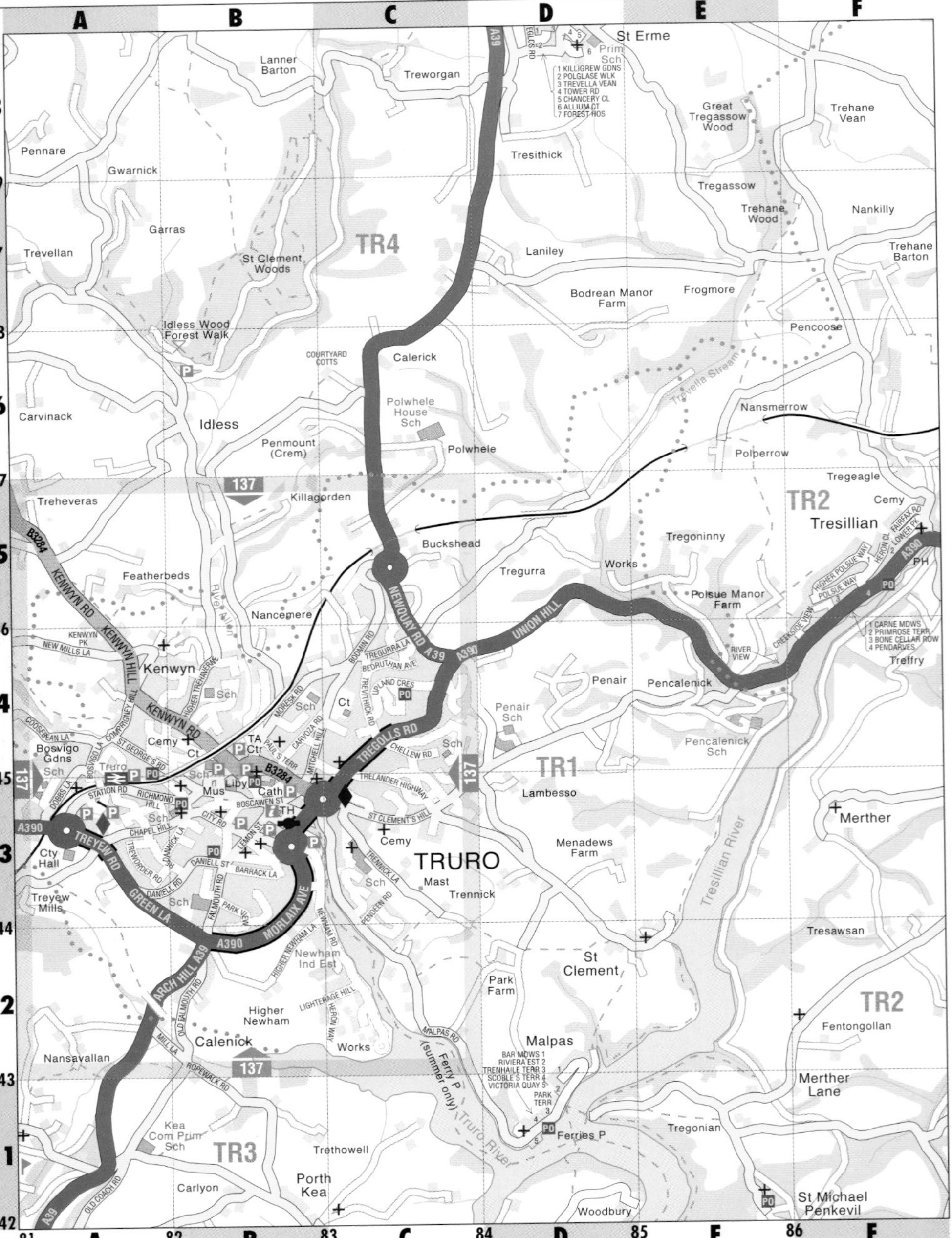

69
82
83
For full street detail of the highlighted area see page 137.

Scale: 1⅓ inches to 1 mile
0 ¼ ½ mile
0 250m 500m 750m 1 km

57
72

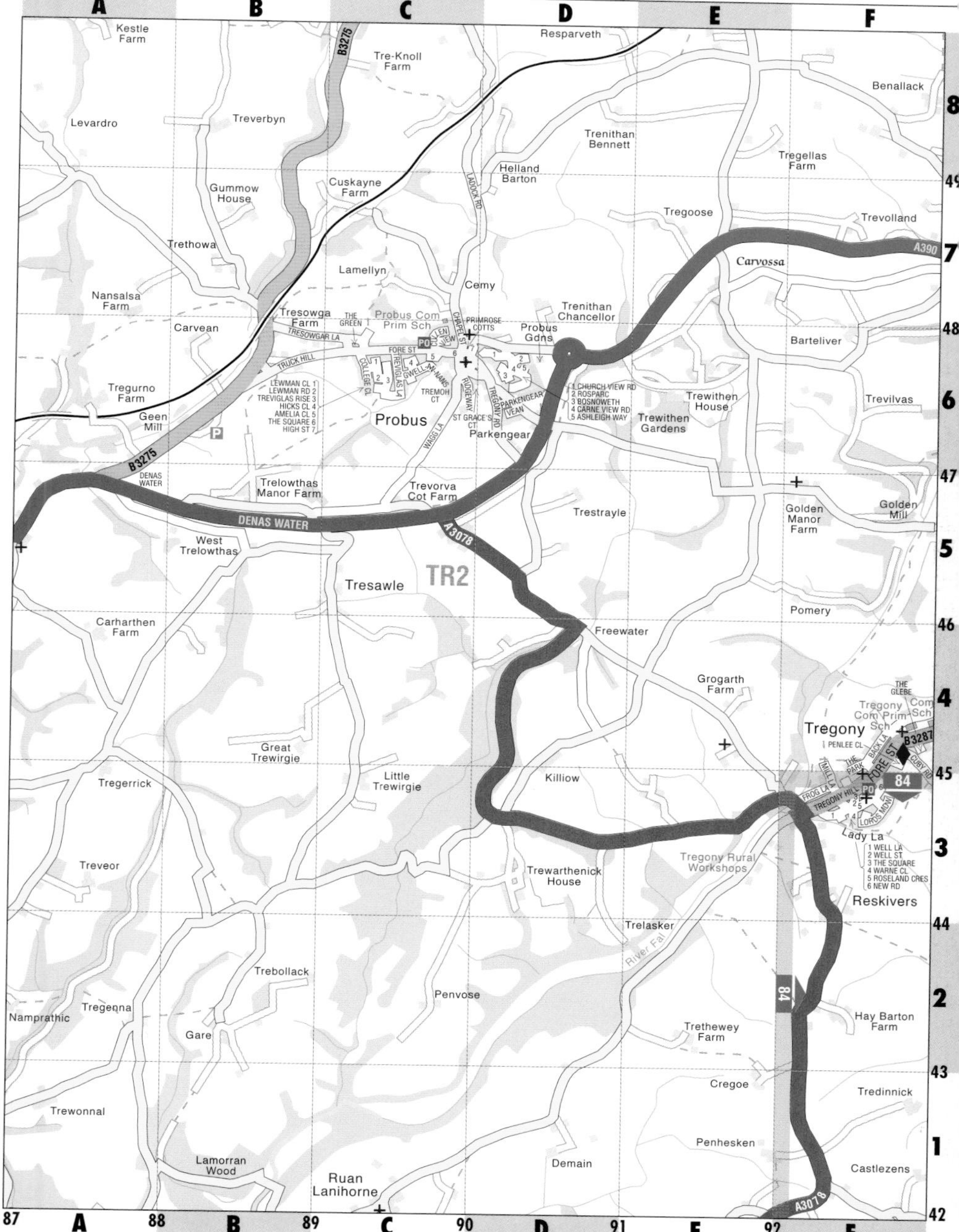

83
72
84

71
58

Scale: 1⅓ inches to 1 mile
0 ¼ ½ mile
0 250m 500m 750m 1 km

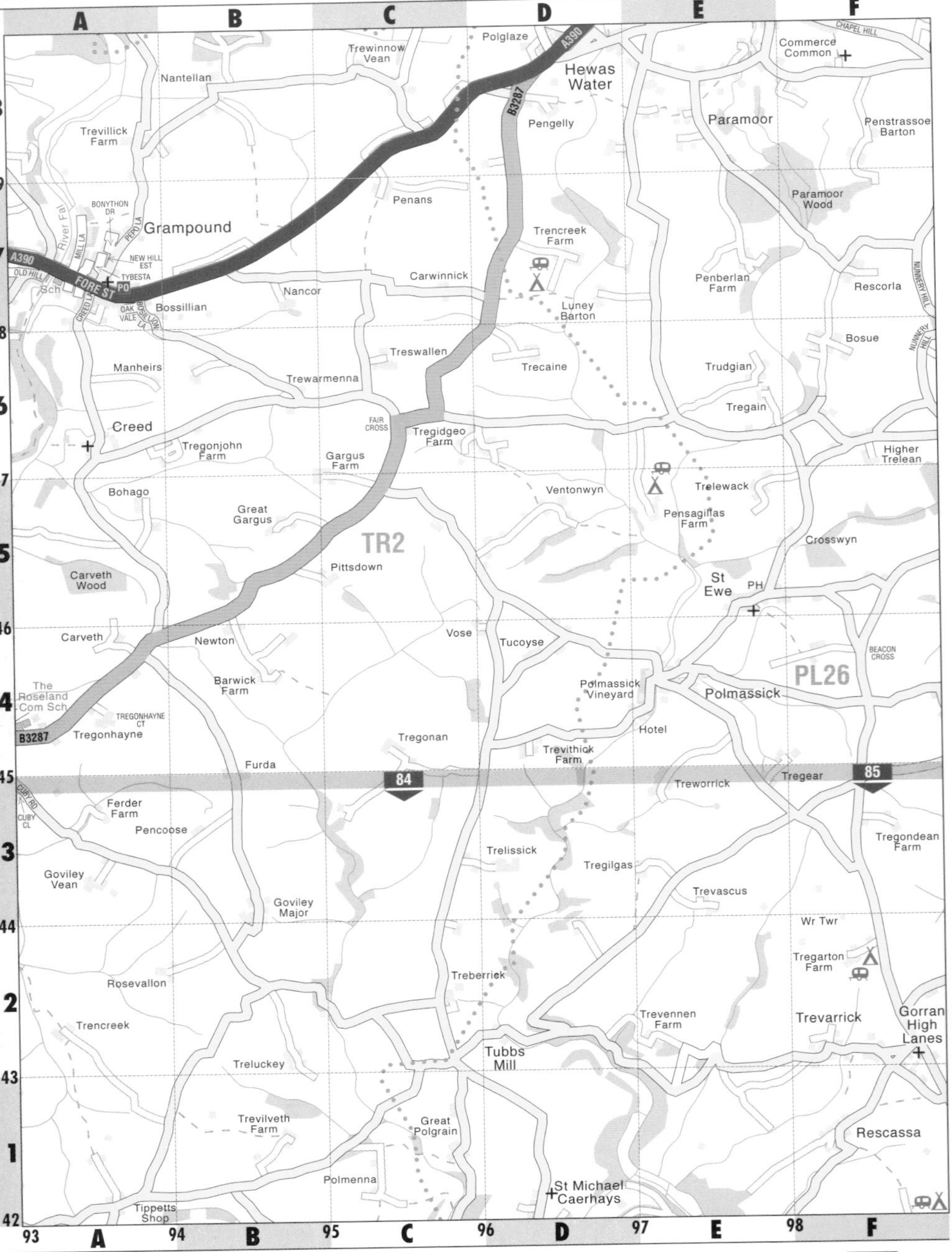

71
84
85

Scale: 1⅓ inches to 1 mile
0 ¼ ½ mile
0 250m 500m 750m 1 km

59

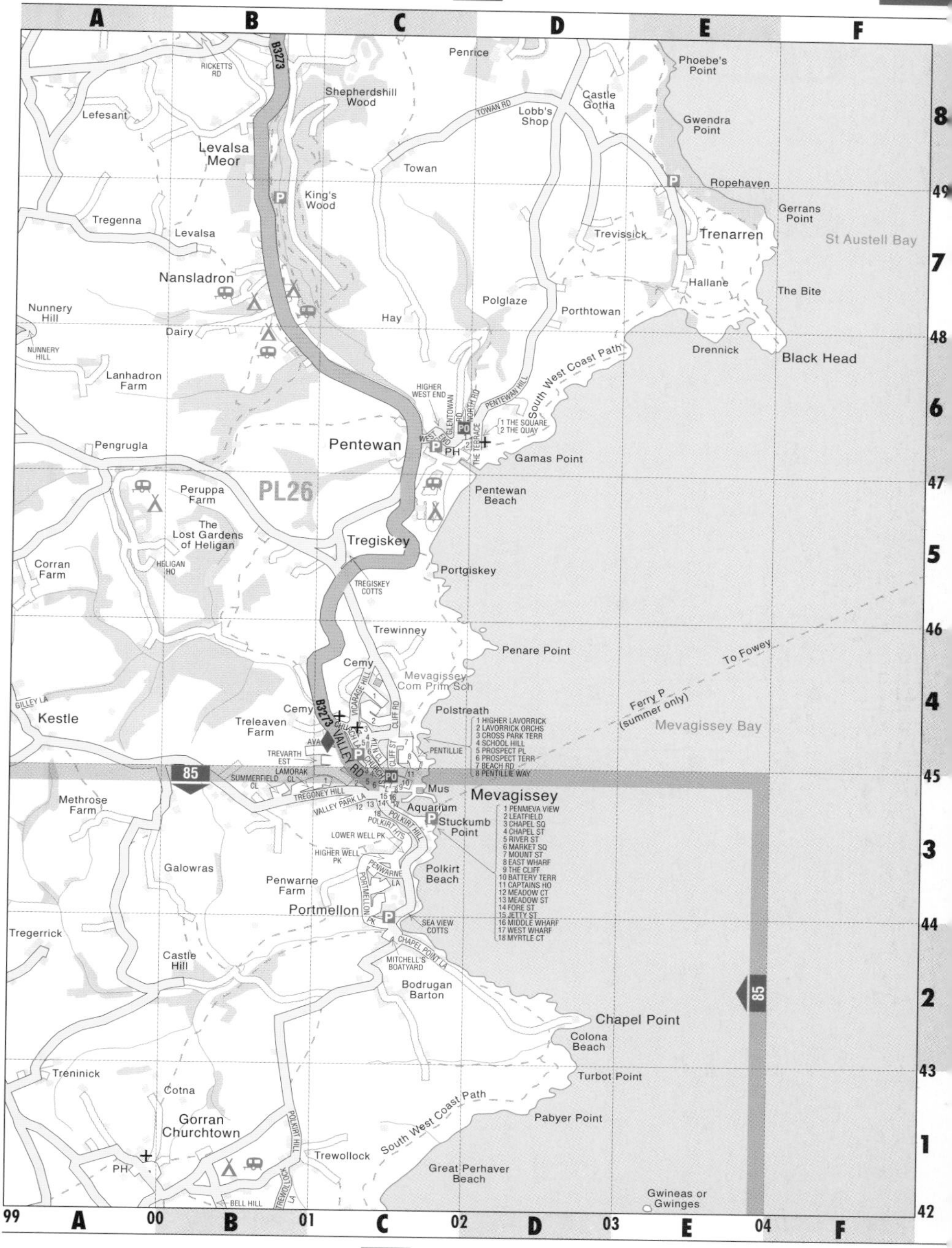

85

Scale: 5¼ miles to 1 inch

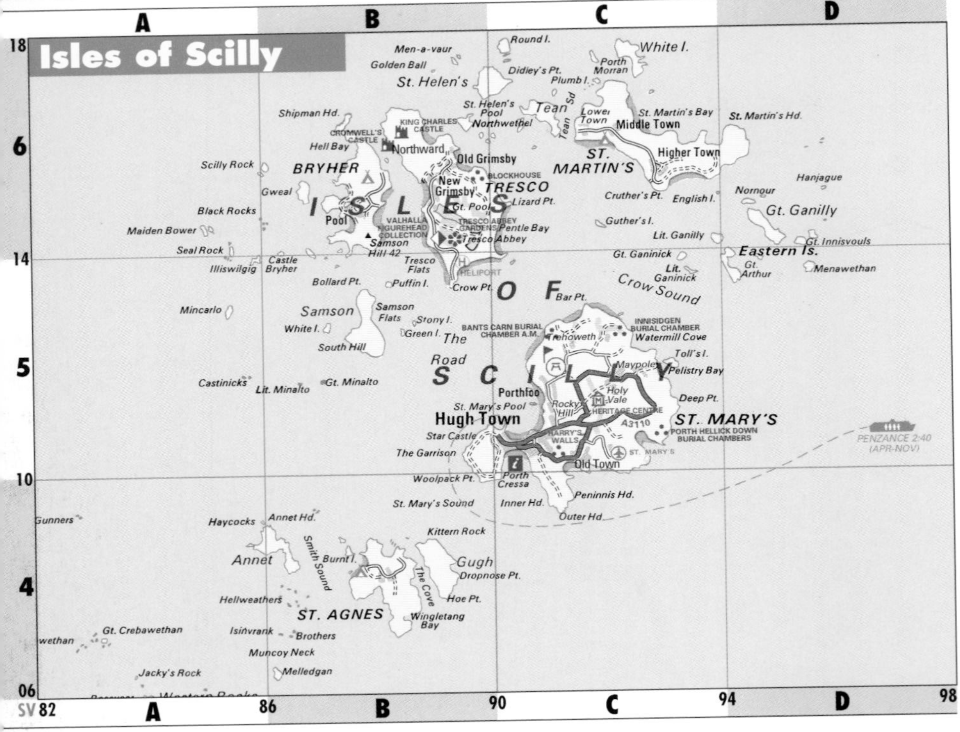

Scale: 1⅓ inches to 1 mile

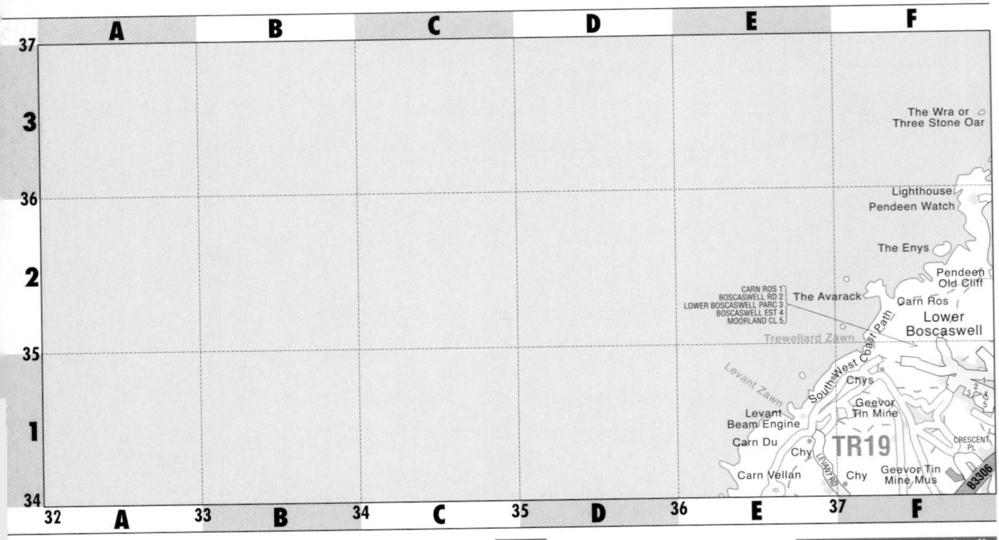

86

76

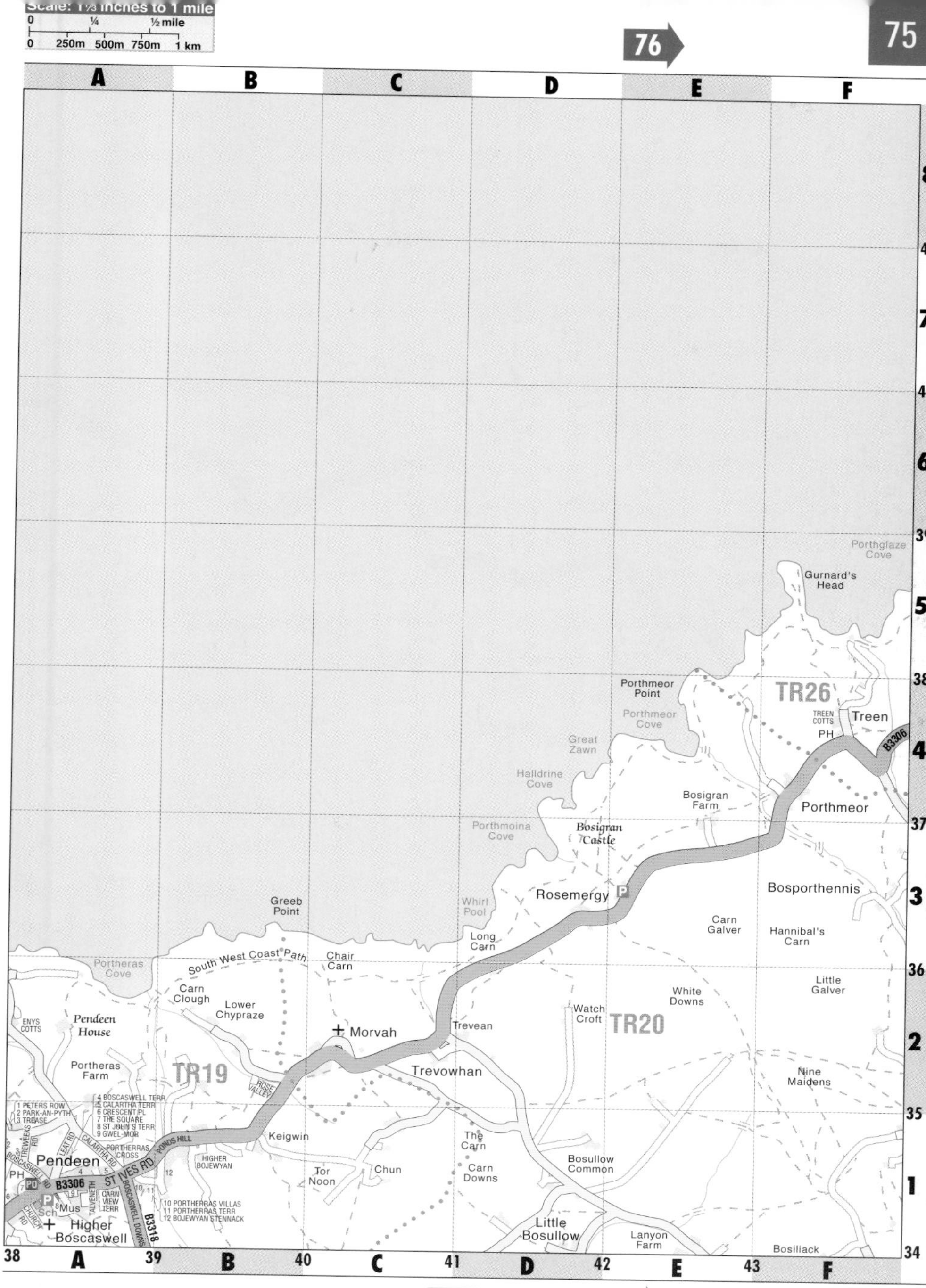
Scale: 1⅓ inches to 1 mile
0 ¼ ½ mile
0 250m 500m 750m 1 km
A B C D E F
8 41 7 40 6 39 5 38 4 37 3 36 2 35 1 34
38 39 40 41 42 43
Porthglaze Cove
Gurnard's Head
Porthmeor Point
Porthmeor Cove
TR26
TREEN COTTS
Treen
PH
B3306
Great Zawn
Halldrine Cove
Bosigran Farm
Porthmeor
Porthmoina Cove
Bosigran Castle
Rosemergy
P
Bosporthennis
Greeb Point
Whirl Pool
Carn Galver
Hannibal's Carn
Long Carn
Portheras Cove
South West Coast Path
Chair Carn
Little Galver
Carn Clough
Lower Chypraze
White Downs
Watch Croft
TR20
ENYS COTTS
Pendeen House
Morvah
Trevean
Portheras Farm
TR19
ROSE VALLEY
Trevowhan
Nine Maidens
1 PETERS ROW
2 PARK-AN-PYTH
3 TREASE
4 BOSCASWELL TERR
5 CALARTHA TERR
6 CRESCENT PL
7 THE SQUARE
8 ST JOHN'S TERR
9 GWEL-MOR
TREWEEKS RD
LEAT RD
CALARTHA RD
PORTHERRAS CROSS
PONDS HILL
Keigwin
The Carn
Pendeen
BOSCASWELL RD
ST IVES RD
HIGHER BOJEWYAN
PH
PO
B3306
TALVENETH
CARN VIEW TERR
BOSCASWELL DOWNS
B3318
Tor Noon
Chun
Carn Downs
Bosullow Common
10 PORTHERRAS VILLAS
11 PORTHERRAS TERR
12 BOJEWYAN STENNACK
P
Sch
Mus
CHURCH RD
Higher Boscaswell
Little Bosullow
Lanyon Farm
Bosiliack

87

76

75

Scale: 1⅓ inches to 1 mile
0 ¼ ½ mile
0 250m 500m 750m 1 km

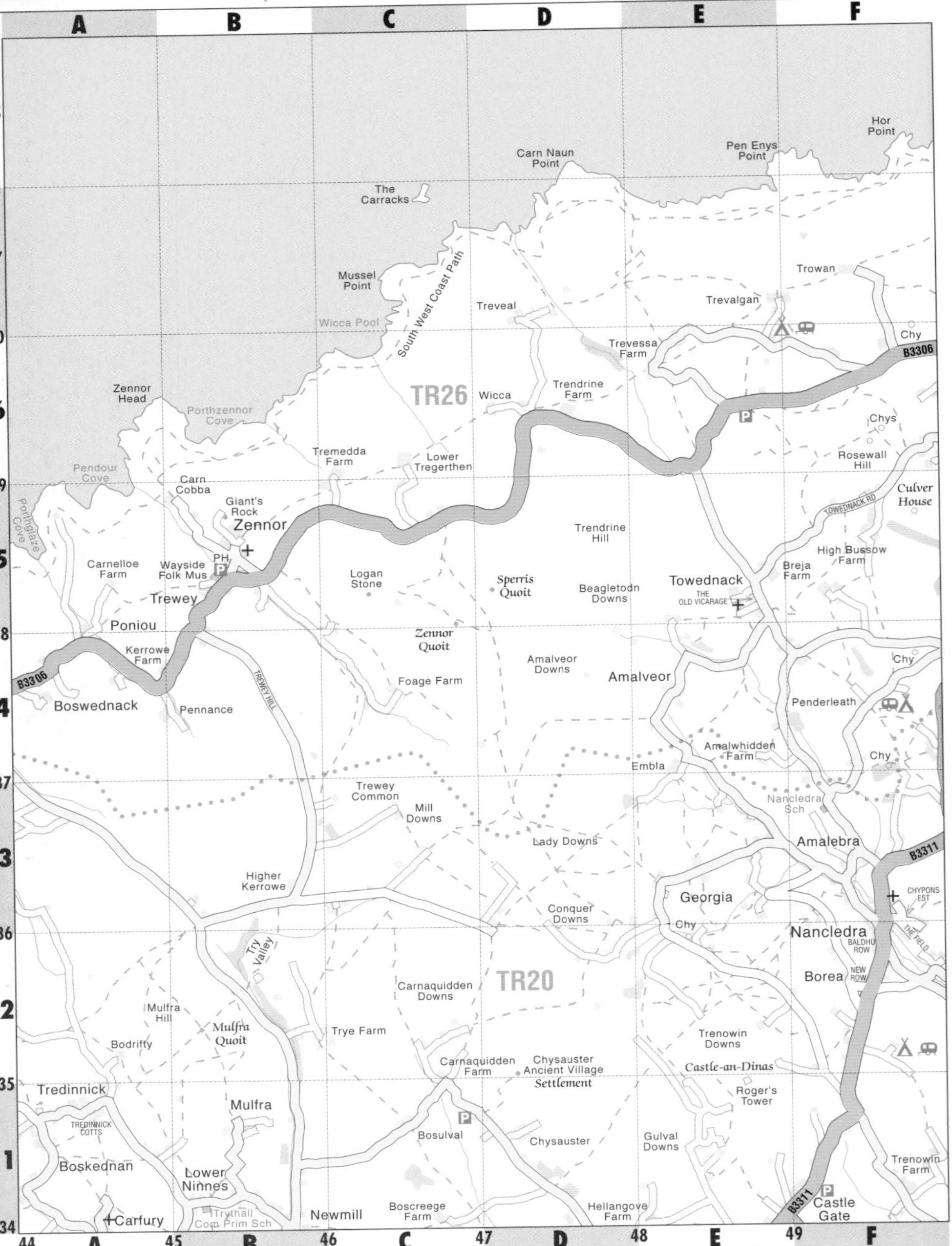

75

88

0 ¼ ½ mile
0 250m 500m 750m 1 km

78

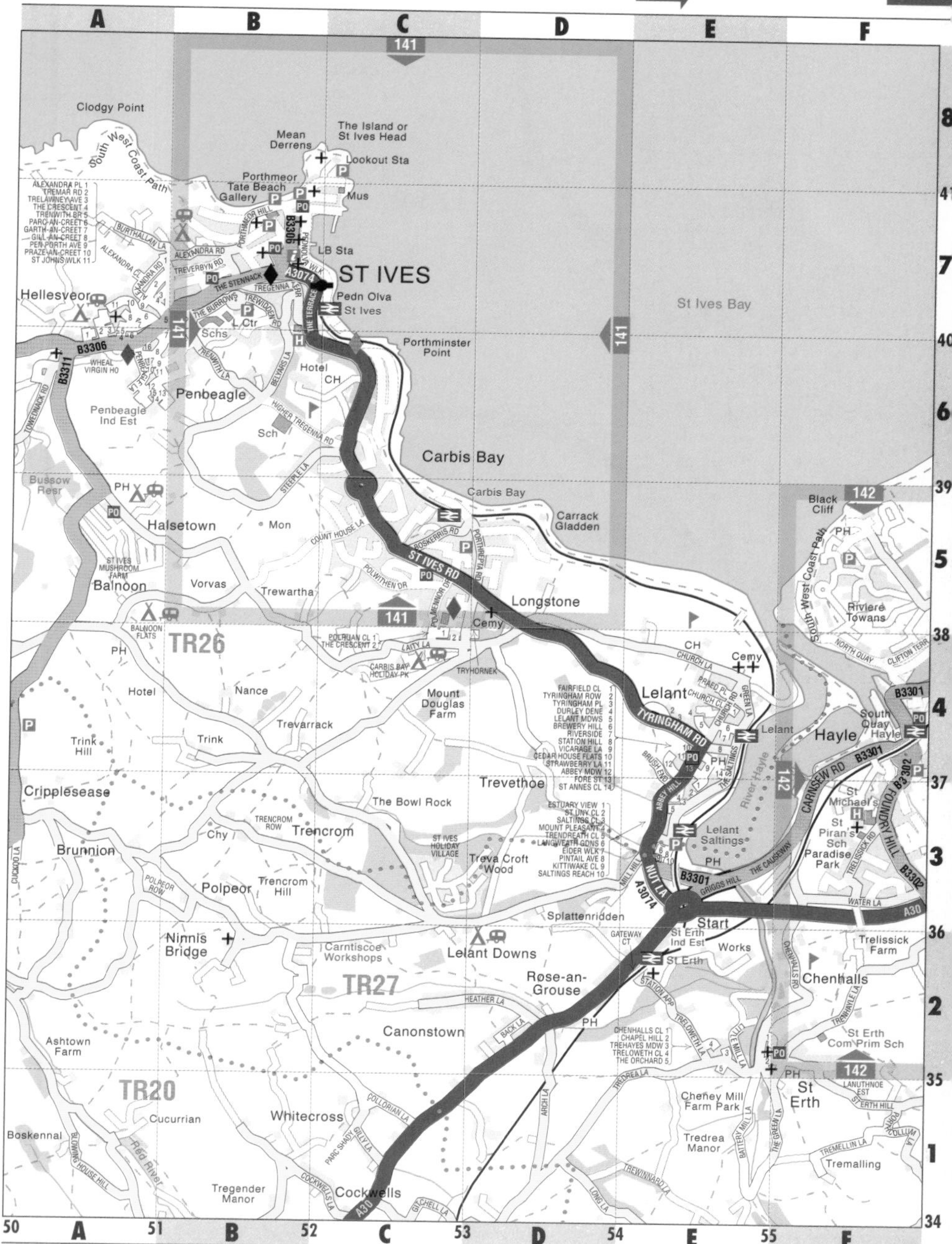

A6
1 CHY-AN-DOUR CL
2 HELLESVEAN
3 HELLESVEAN CL
4 PARC-AN-STAMPS
5 CROWS-AN-EGLOS
6 PARC-AN-FORTH
7 PENBEAGLE TERR
8 PENBEAGLE CRES
9 CORVA RD
10 PRIORS CL
11 CORVA CL
12 PORTHIA RD
13 CARNSTABBA RD
14 ALAN HARVEY CL
15 JUBILEE CT
16 TINNERS WAY
17 PENBEAGLE CL

89

78

For full street detail of the highlighted area see pages 141 and 142.

77
66

Scale: 1⅓ inches to 1 mile
0 ¼ ½ mile
0 250m 500m 750m 1 km

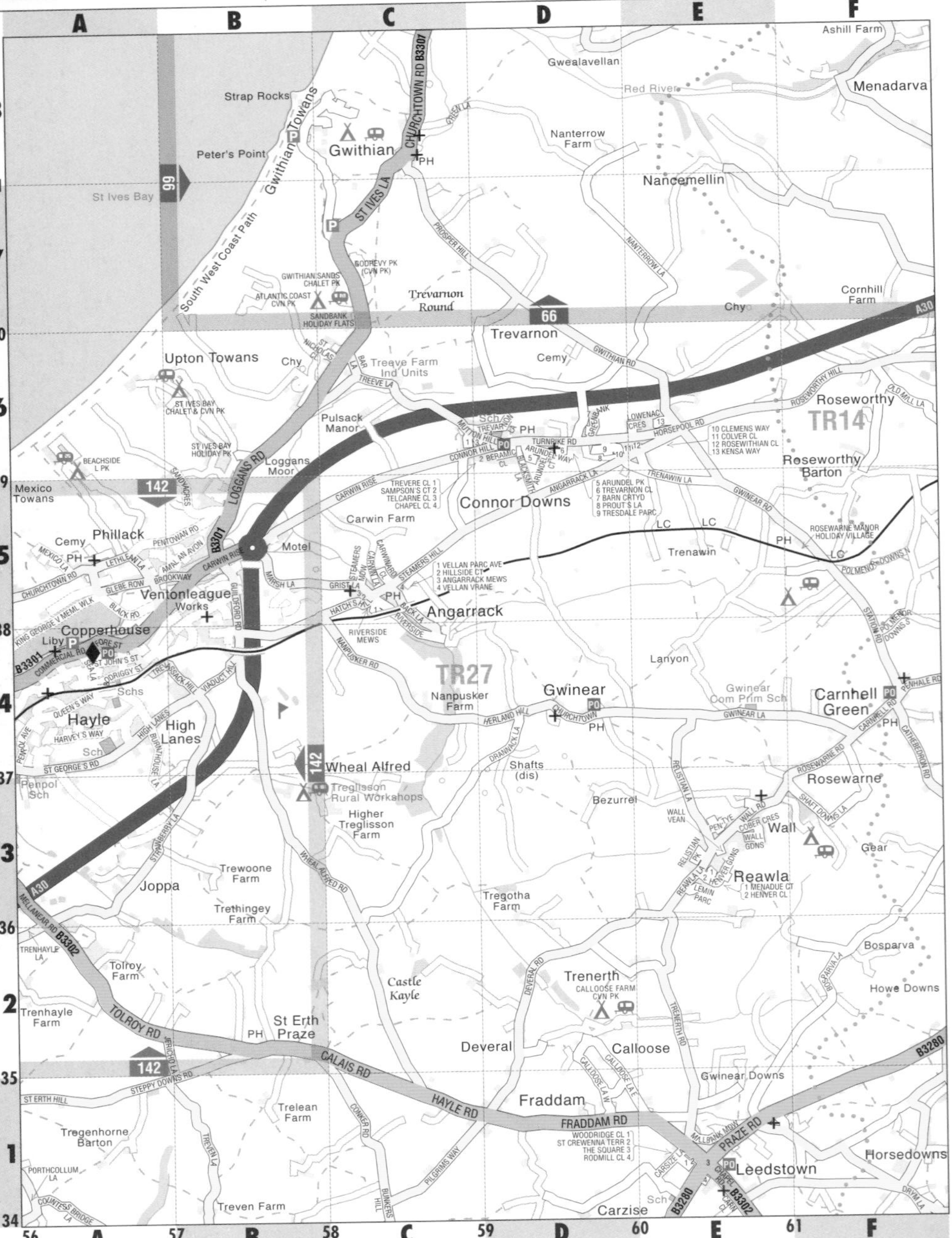
A B C D E F
8
41
7
40
6
39
5
38
4
37
3
36
2
35
1
34
56 57 58 59 60 61
Ashill Farm
Gwealavellan
Red River
Menadarva
Strap Rocks
Gwithian Towans
Gwithian
CHURCHTOWN RD B3307
GREEN LA
PH
Nanterrow Farm
Peter's Point
Nancemellin
St Ives Bay
ST IVES LA
PROSPER HILL
NANTERROW LA
South West Coast Path
GODREVY PK (CVN PK)
GWITHIAN SANDS CHALET PK
ATLANTIC COAST CVN PK
SANDBANK HOLIDAY FLATS
Trevarnon Round
Cornhill Farm
Chy
A30
Trevarnon
Cemy
GWITHIAN RD
Upton Towans
Chy
Treeve Farm Ind Units
TREEVE LA
ST IVES BAY CHALET & CVN PK
Pulsack Manor
Sch
PH
TURNPIKE RD
LOWENAC CRES
HORSEPOOL RD
ROSEWORTHY HILL
Roseworthy
TR14
OLD MILL LA
10 CLEMENS WAY
11 COLVER CL
12 ROSEWITHIAN CL
13 KENSA WAY
Roseworthy Barton
ST IVES BAY HOLIDAY PK
BEACHSIDE L PK
Loggans Moor
LOGGANS RD
CONNOR HILL
ARUNDEL WAY
TRENAWIN LA
GWINEAR RD
Mexico Towans
142
TREVERE CL 1
SAMPSON'S CT 2
TELCARNE CL 3
CHAPEL CL 4
Connor Downs
ANGARRACK LA
5 ARUNDEL PK
6 TREVARNON CL
7 BARN CRTYD
8 PROUT'S LA
9 TRESDALE PARC
Carwin Farm
CARWIN RISE
LC
ROSEWARNE MANOR HOLIDAY VILLAGE
Cemy
Phillack
PENTOWAN RD
B3301
Motel
Trenawin
PH
LC
POLMENOR DOWNS
MEXICO LA
PH
LETHLEAN LA
CHURCHTOWN RD
GLEBE ROW
BROOKWAY
MARSH LA
GRIST LA
STEAMERS HILL
1 VELLAN PARC AVE
2 HILLSIDE CT
3 ANGARRACK MEWS
4 VELLAN VRANE
Ventonleague
Works
BLACK RD
HATCH'S HILL
PH
Angarrack
RIVERSIDE
RIVERSIDE MEWS
STATION HILL
Copperhouse
Liby
P
PO
FORE ST
COMMERCIAL RD
B3301
ST JOHN'S ST
TR27
Lanyon
NANPUSKER RD
Schs
Nanpusker Farm
Gwinear
PO
Gwinear Com Prim Sch
Carnhell Green
PO
PENHALE RD
QUEEN'S WAY
Hayle
HARVEY'S WAY
High Lanes
HERLAND HILL
CHURCHTOWN
PH
GWINEAR LA
PH
Sch
DRANNACK LA
Shafts (dis)
ROSEWARNE RD
ST GEORGE'S RD
Wheal Alfred
Rosewarne
Penpol Sch
Treglisson Rural Workshops
Higher Treglisson Farm
RELISTIAN LA
Bezurrel
WALL VEAN
PEN-TYE
WALL RD
COBER CRES
WALL GDNS
Wall
Gear
STRAWBERRY LA
Trewoone Farm
WHEAL ALFRED RD
Reawla
1 MENADUE CT
2 HENVER CL
A30
Joppa
Tregotha Farm
Trethingey Farm
MELLANEAR RD
B3302
Bosparva
TRENHAYLE LA
Tolroy Farm
Castle Kayle
DEVERAL RD
Trenerth
CALLOOSE FARM CVN PK
TRENERTH RD
Howe Downs
Trenhayle Farm
TOLROY RD
St Erth Praze
PH
Deveral
Calloose
142
CALAIS RD
B3280
STEPPY DOWNS RD
Gwinear Downs
ST ERTH HILL
HAYLE RD
Fraddam
FRADDAM RD
Trelean Farm
CONNEAR RD
WOODRIDGE CL 1
ST CREWENNA TERR 2
THE SQUARE 3
RODMILL CL 4
PRAZE RD
MALLBANK MDW
Tregenhorne Barton
TREVEN LA
PILGRIMS WAY
CARZISE
PO
Leedstown
Horsedowns
PORTHCOLLUM LA
Sch
COUNTESS BRIDGE LA
Treven Farm
BUNKERS HILL
Carzise
B3280
B3302
DRYM LA

For full street detail of the highlighted area see page 142.

77
90

Scale: 1⅓ inches to 1 mile
0 ¼ ½ mile
0 250m 500m 750m 1 km

66 67 80

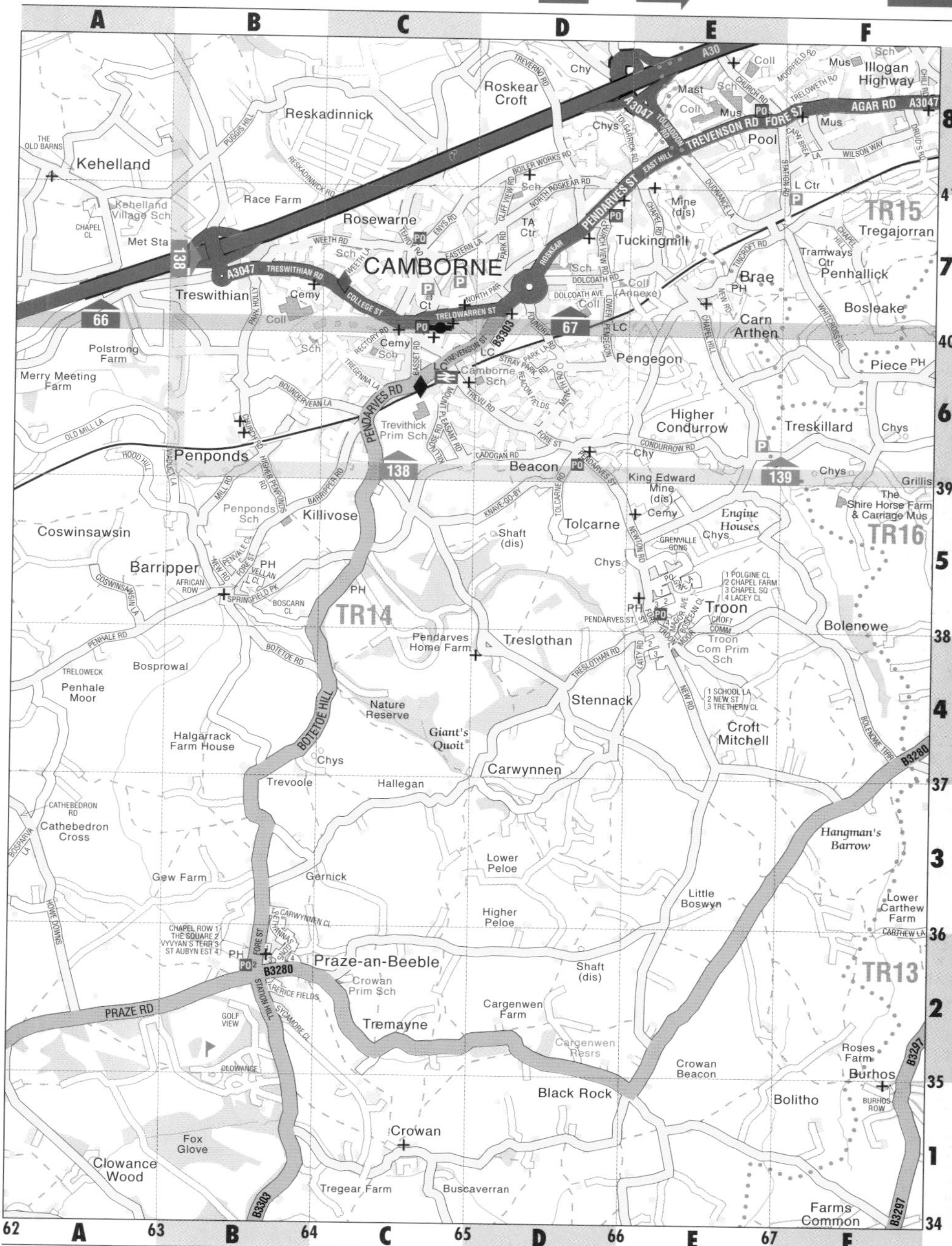

91 80

For full street detail of the highlighted area see pages 138 and 139.

67
79
68

Scale: 1⅓ inches to 1 mile
0 ¼ ½ mile
0 250m 500m 750m 1 km

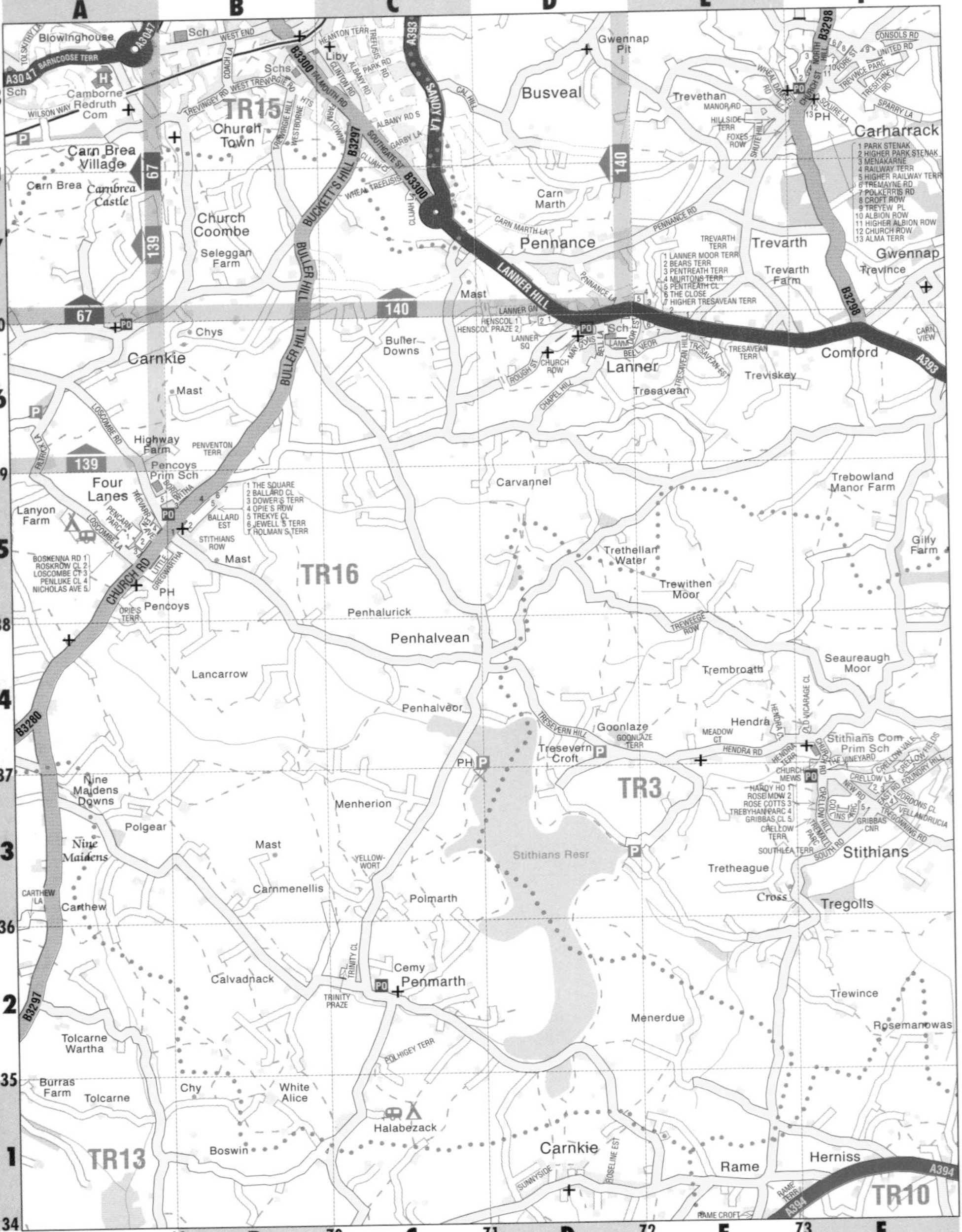

79
92

For full street detail of the highlighted area see pages 139 and 140.

F7
1 WEST CNR
2 COWLING RD
3 WOON LA
4 FORTH NOWETH
5 STRETYN
6 MANSE RD

F7
7 PARC-AN-GWARRY
8 FIR GR
9 PARKANCREEG
10 TRELAWNE CL
11 AGAR MDWS
12 HALWYN CL
13 CARNON CRES
14 ALEXANDER CT

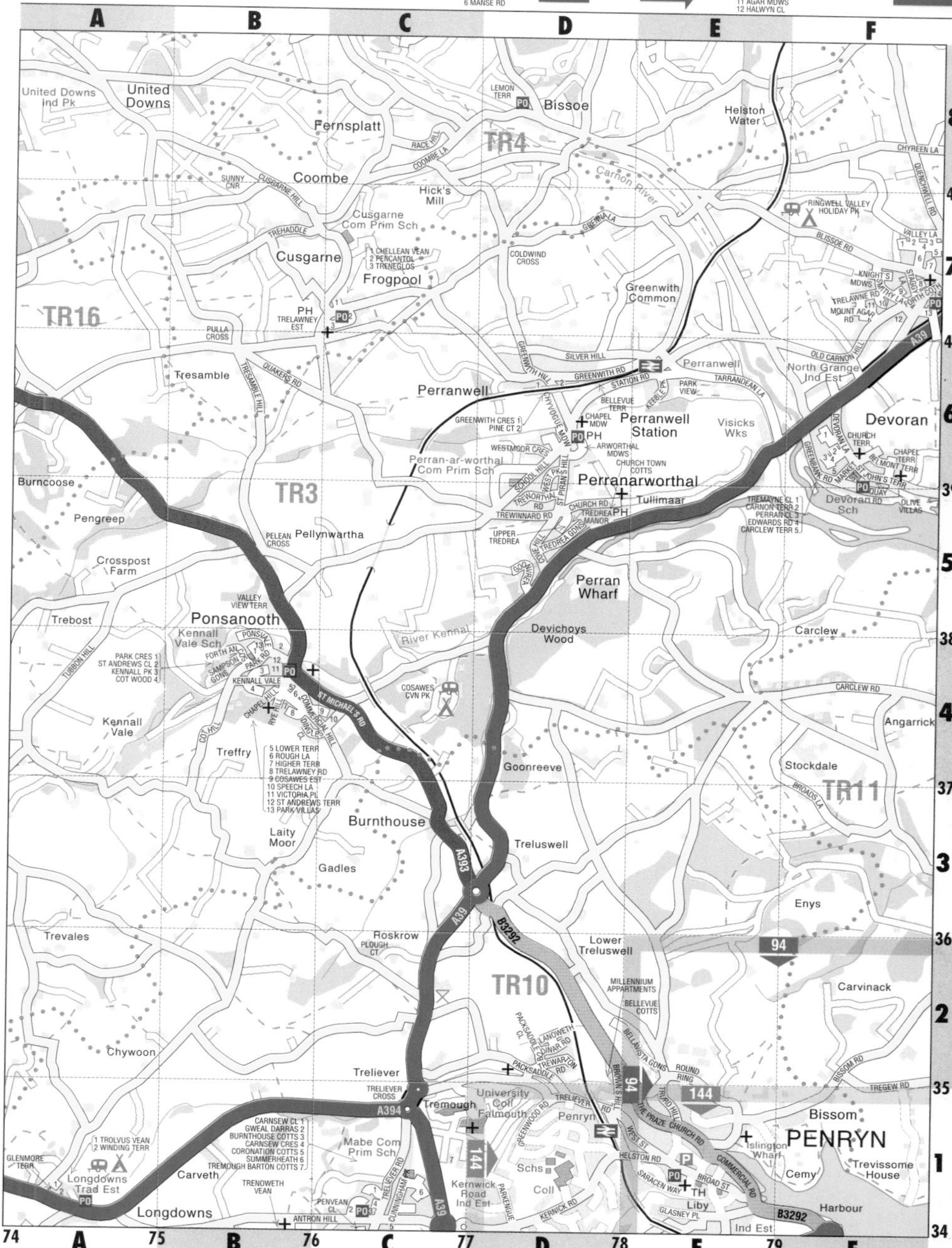

For full street detail of the highlighted area see page 144.

Scale: 1⅓ inches to 1 mile
0 ¼ ½ mile
0 250m 500m 750m 1 km

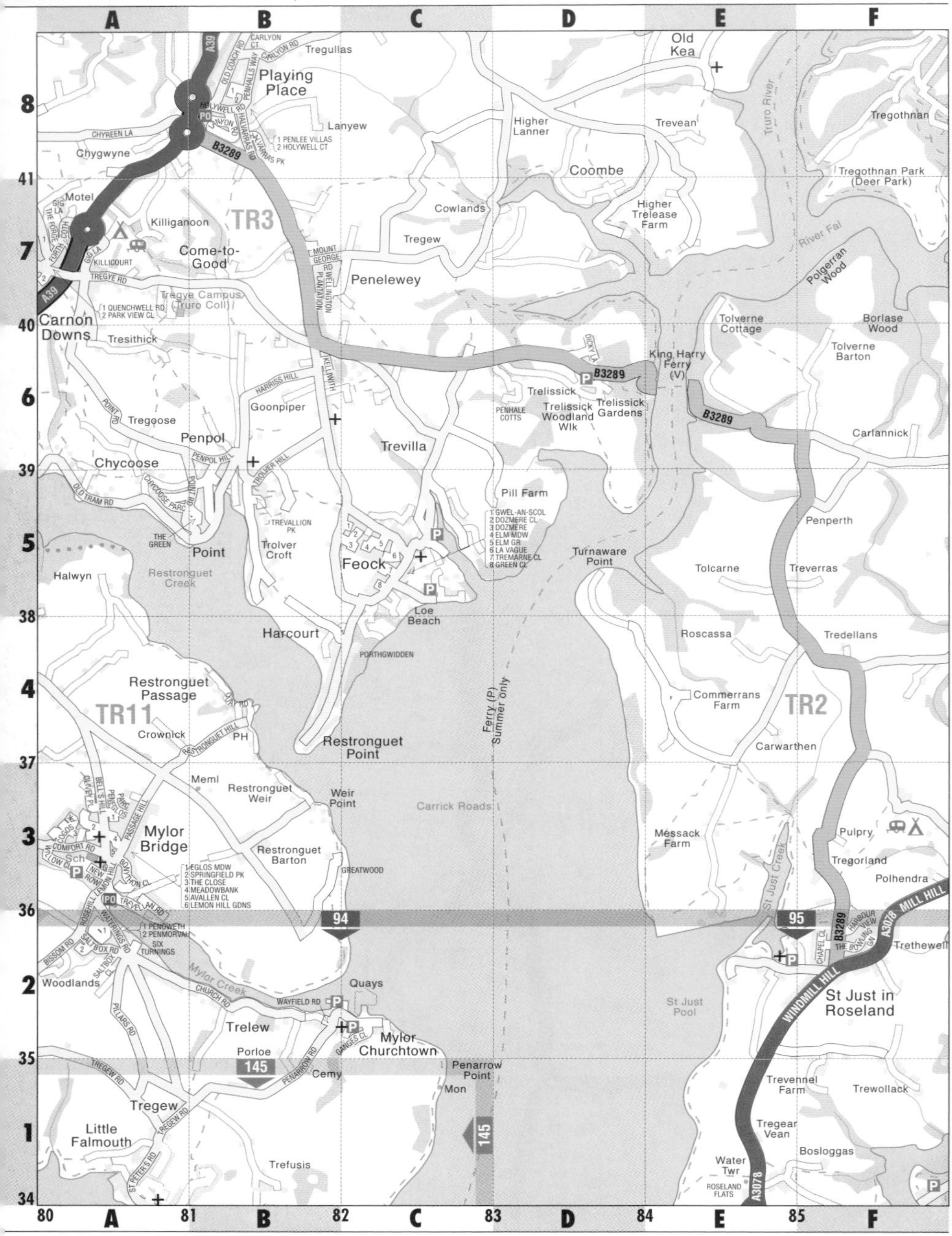

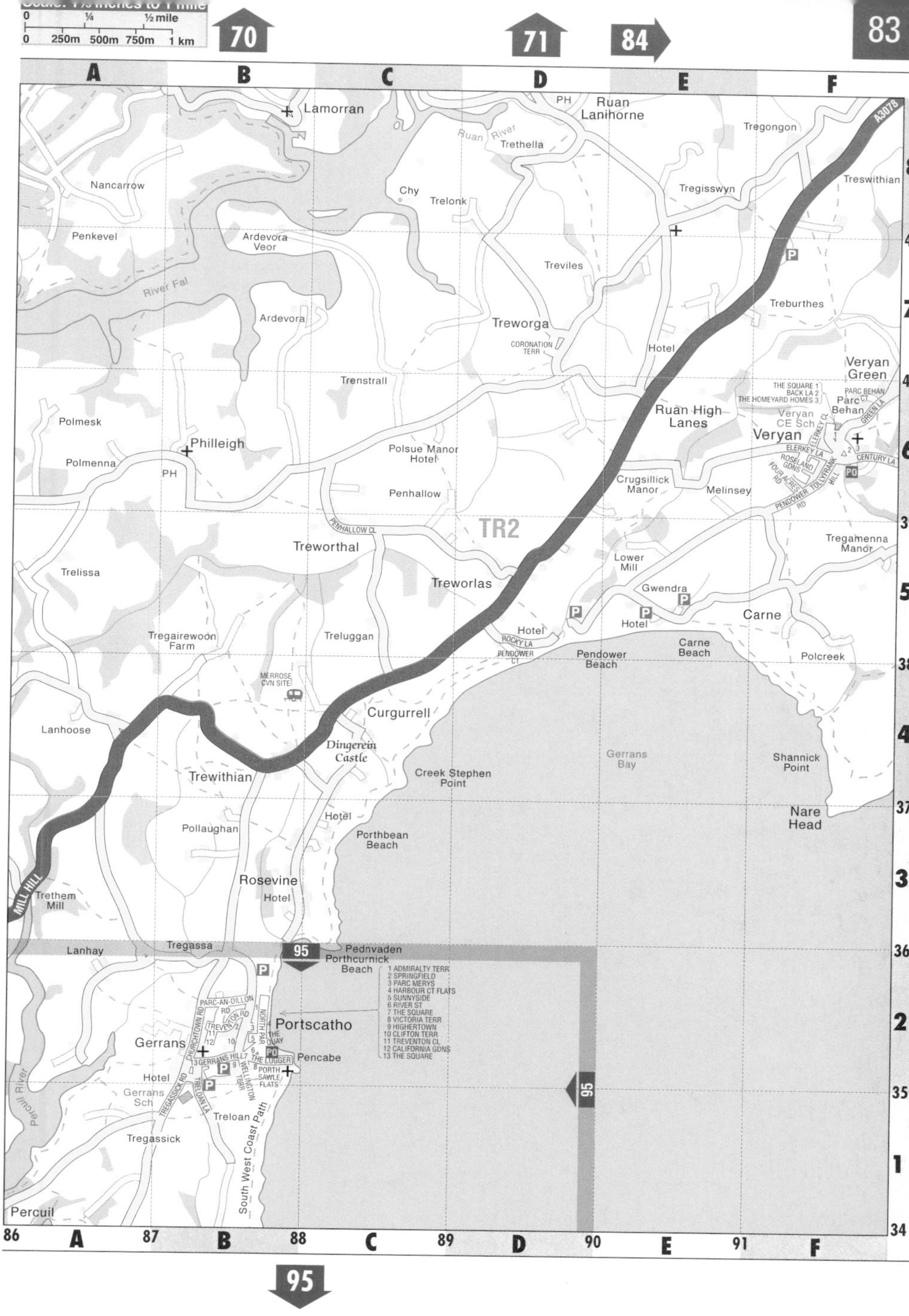
Scale: 1½ inches to 1 mile
0 ¼ ½ mile
0 250m 500m 750m 1 km
70
71
84
A B C D E F
Lamorran
PH
Ruan Lanihorne
Ruan River
Trethella
Tregongon
A3078
Nancarrow
Chy
Trelonk
Tregisswyn
Treswithian
Penkevel
Ardevora Veor
Treviles
River Fal
Ardevora
Treworga
Treburthes
CORONATION TERR
Hotel
Veryan Green
Trenstrall
THE SQUARE 1
BACK LA 2
THE HOMEYARD HOMES 3
PARC BEHAN CT
Parc Behan
Ruan High Lanes
Veryan CE Sch
Polmesk
Phillieigh
Veryan
Polsue Manor Hotel
ELERKEY LA
ELERKEY CL
GREEN LA
CENTURY LA
ROSELAND GDNS
FOUR ACRES RD
TOLLYFRANK HILL
Polmenna
PH
Crugsillick Manor
Melinsey
PENDOWER RD
PO
Penhallow
PENHALLOW CL
TR2
Treworthal
Tregamenna Manor
Trelissa
Lower Mill
Treworlas
Gwendra
Carne
Hotel
Hotel
Tregairewoon Farm
Treluggan
ROCKY LA
PENDOWER CT
Pendower Beach
Carne Beach
Polcreek
MERROSE CVN SITE
Curgurrell
Lanhoose
Dingerein Castle
Gerrans Bay
Shannick Point
Trewithian
Creek Stephen Point
Nare Head
Hotel
Pollaughan
Porthbean Beach
Rosevine
Hotel
MILL HILL
Trethem Mill
Lanhay
Tregassa
95
Pednvaden
Porthcurnick Beach
1 ADMIRALTY TERR
2 SPRINGFIELD
3 PARC MERYS
4 HARBOUR CT FLATS
5 SUNNYSIDE
6 RIVER ST
7 THE SQUARE
8 VICTORIA TERR
9 HIGHERTOWN
10 CLIFTON TERR
11 TREVENTON CL
12 CALIFORNIA GDNS
13 THE SQUARE
PARC-AN-DILLON RD
TREVENTON RD
CHURCHTOWN RD
NORTH PAR
Portscatho
THE QUAY
Gerrans
GERRANS HILL
THE LUGGER
Pencabe
WELLINGTON TERR
PORTH SAWLE FLATS
Hotel
Gerrans Sch
TREGASSICK RD
TRELOAN LA
Percuil River
Treloan
South West Coast Path
Tregassick
Percuil
8 41 7 40 6 39 5 38 4 37 3 36 2 35 1 34
86 A 87 B 88 C 89 D 90 E 91 F
95

71 71 72

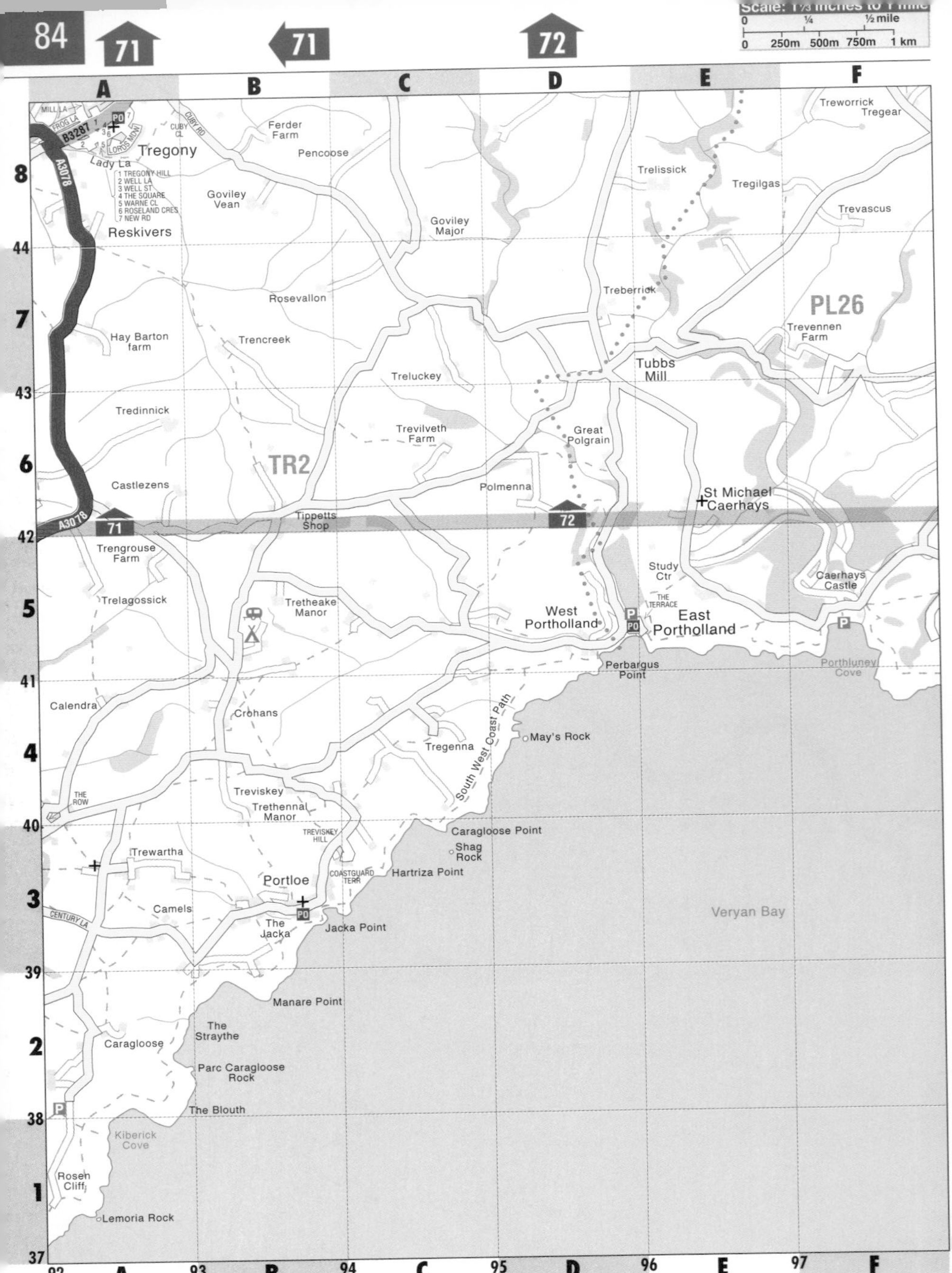
Scale: 1⅓ inches to 1 mile
0 ¼ ½ mile
0 250m 500m 750m 1 km
A B C D E F
8 7 6 5 4 3 2 1
44 43 42 41 40 39 38 37
92 93 94 95 96 97
Tregony
Lady La
1 TREGONY HILL
2 WELL LA
3 WELL ST
4 THE SQUARE
5 WARNE CL
6 ROSELAND CRES
7 NEW RD
MILL LA
FROG LA
B3287
LOROS MDW
CUBY CL
CUBY RD
A3078
Ferder Farm
Pencoose
Goviley Vean
Reskivers
Goviley Major
Treworrick
Tregear
Trelissick
Tregilgas
Trevascus
Treberrick
PL26
Rosevallon
Hay Barton farm
Trencreek
Trevennen Farm
Tubbs Mill
Treluckey
Tredinnick
Trevilveth Farm
Great Polgrain
TR2
Castlezens
Polmenna
St Michael Caerhays
Tippetts Shop
71
72
Trengrouse Farm
Study Ctr
Caerhays Castle
Trelagossick
Tretheake Manor
West Portholland
THE TERRACE
East Portholland
Perbargus Point
Porthluney Cove
Calendra
Crohans
South West Coast Path
May's Rock
Tregenna
THE ROW
Treviskey
Trethennal Manor
Caragloose Point
TREVISKEY HILL
Shag Rock
Trewartha
Portloe
COASTGUARD TERR
Hartriza Point
Camels
CENTURY LA
The Jacka
Jacka Point
Veryan Bay
Manare Point
The Straythe
Caragloose
Parc Caragloose Rock
The Blouth
Kiberick Cove
Rosen Cliff
Lemoria Rock

83

Scale: 1⅓ inches to 1 mile
0 ¼ ½ mile
0 250m 500m 750m 1 km

72 73

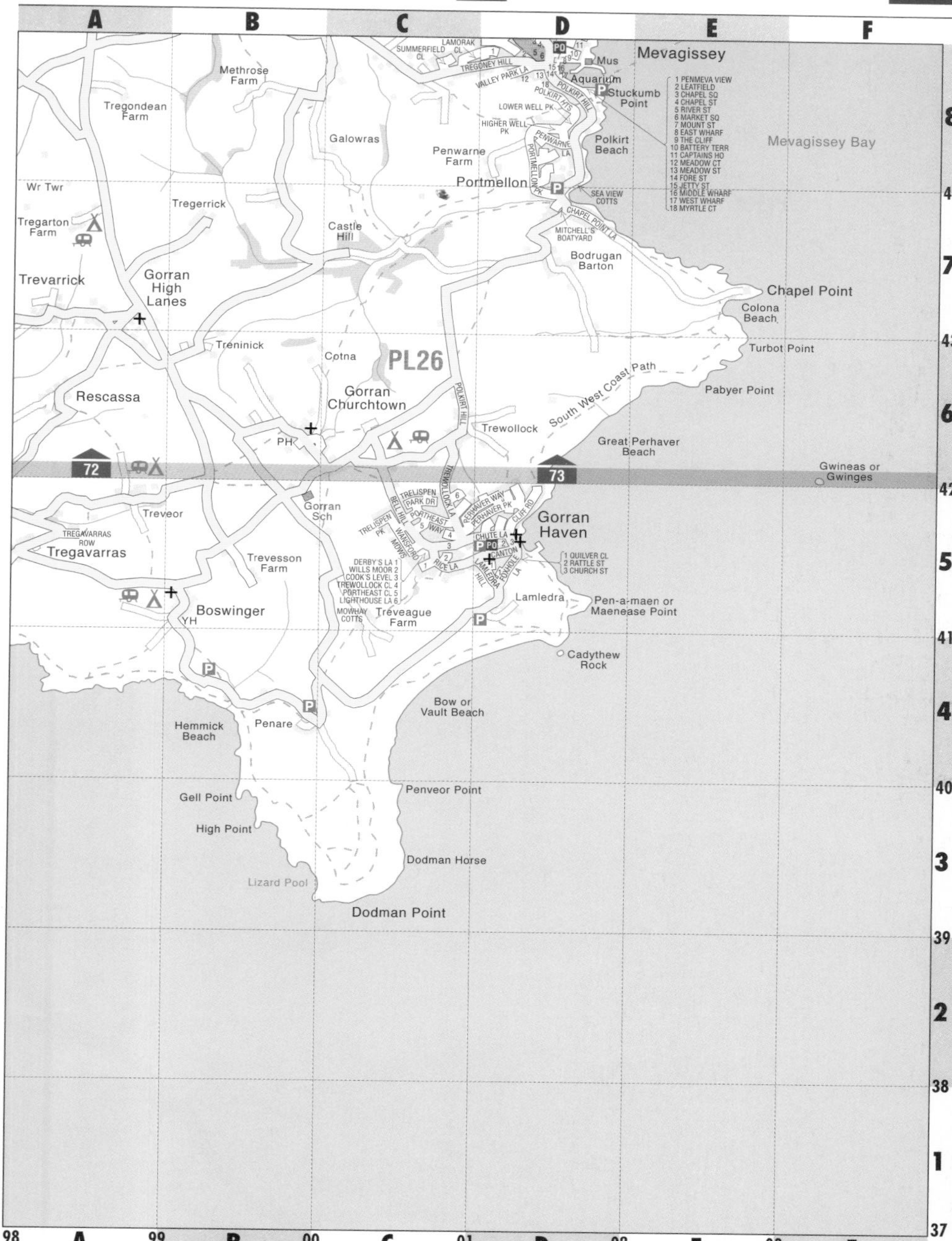
A
B
C
D
E
F
Mevagissey
Mus
Aquarium
Stuckumb Point
Mevagissey Bay
Polkirt Beach
SUMMERFIELD CL
LAMORAK CL
TREGONEY HILL
VALLEY PARK LA
POLKIRT HTS
POLKIRT HILL
LOWER WELL PK
HIGHER WELL PK
PENWARNE LA
PORTMELLON PK
SEA VIEW COTTS
1 PENMEVA VIEW
2 LEATFIELD
3 CHAPEL SQ
4 CHAPEL ST
5 RIVER ST
6 MARKET SQ
7 MOUNT ST
8 EAST WHARF
9 THE CLIFF
10 BATTERY TERR
11 CAPTAINS HO
12 MEADOW CT
13 MEADOW ST
14 FORE ST
15 JETTY ST
16 MIDDLE WHARF
17 WEST WHARF
18 MYRTLE CT
Methrose Farm
Tregondean Farm
Galowras
Penwarne Farm
Portmellon
Wr Twr
Tregerrick
Tregarton Farm
Castle Hill
CHAPEL POINT LA
MITCHELL'S BOATYARD
Bodrugan Barton
Chapel Point
Colona Beach
Trevarrick
Gorran High Lanes
Treninick
Cotna
PL26
Turbot Point
South West Coast Path
Pabyer Point
Rescassa
Gorran Churchtown
POLKIRT HILL
Trewollock
PH
Great Perhaver Beach
72
73
Gwineas or Gwinges
TREWOLLOCK LA
TRELISPEN PARK DR
PERHAVER WAY
PERHAVER PK
CLIFF RD
Gorran Haven
Treveor
Gorran Sch
BELL HILL
PORTHEAST WAY
TRELISPEN PK
WANSFORD MDWS
CHUTE LA
CANTON
TREGAVARRAS ROW
Tregavarras
Trevesson Farm
DERBY'S LA 1
WILLS MOOR 2
COOK'S LEVEL 3
TREWOLLOCK CL 4
PORTHEAST CL 5
LIGHTHOUSE LA 6
RICE LA
LAMLEDRA HILL
FOXHOLE LA
1 QUILVER CL
2 RATTLE ST
3 CHURCH ST
Lamledra
Pen-a-maen or Maenease Point
Boswinger
YH
MOWHAY COTTS
Treveague Farm
Cadythew Rock
Bow or Vault Beach
Hemmick Beach
Penare
Penveor Point
Gell Point
High Point
Dodman Horse
Lizard Pool
Dodman Point
8
44
7
43
6
42
5
41
4
40
3
39
2
38
1
37
98
99
00
01
02
03

74

Scale: 1⅓ inches to 1 mile

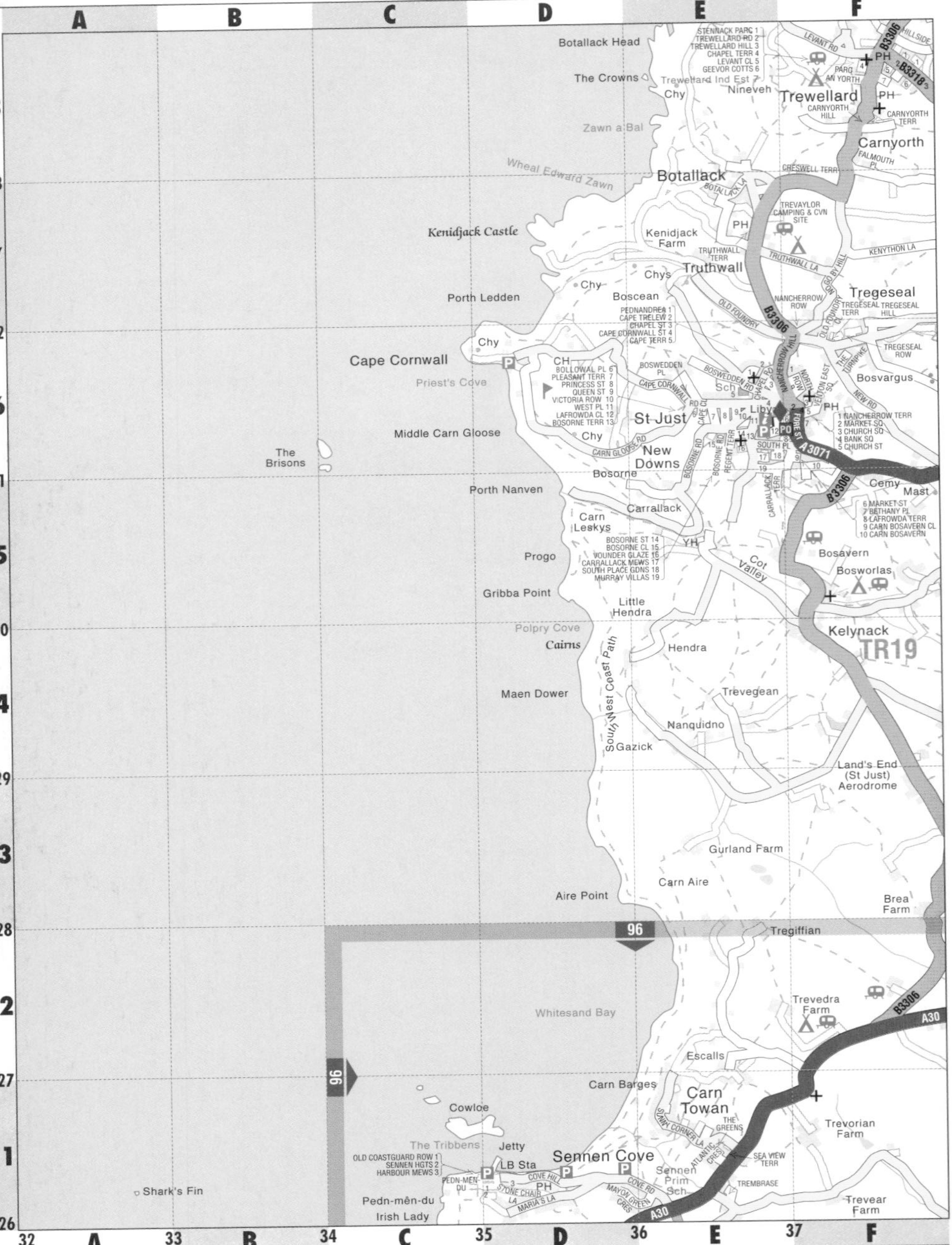

Botallack Head
The Crowns
Trewellard Ind Est
Chy
Nineveh
Trewellard
Zawn a Bal
Carnyorth
Wheal Edward Zawn
Botallack
Kenidjack Castle
Kenidjack Farm
Truthwall
Chys
Chy
Boscean
Tregeseal
Porth Ledden
Cape Cornwall
Priest's Cove
St Just
Bosvargus
Middle Carn Gloose
The Brisons
New Downs
Bosorne
Porth Nanven
Cemy
Mast
Carn Leskys
Carrallack
Progo
Bosavern
Bosworlas
Cot Valley
Gribba Point
Little Hendra
Polpry Cove
Cairns
Kelynack
TR19
Hendra
Maen Dower
Trevegean
South West Coast Path
Nanquidno
Gazick
Land's End (St Just) Aerodrome
Gurland Farm
Carn Aire
Aire Point
Brea Farm
Tregiffian
Whitesand Bay
Trevedra Farm
Escalls
Carn Barges
Carn Towan
Cowloe
Trevorian Farm
The Tribbens
Jetty
Sennen Cove
LB Sta
Shark's Fin
Sennen Prim Sch
Pedn-mên-du
Irish Lady
Trevear Farm
B3306
A3071
A30
B3318
96

96

0 ¼ ½ mile
0 250m 500m 750m 1 km

75 88

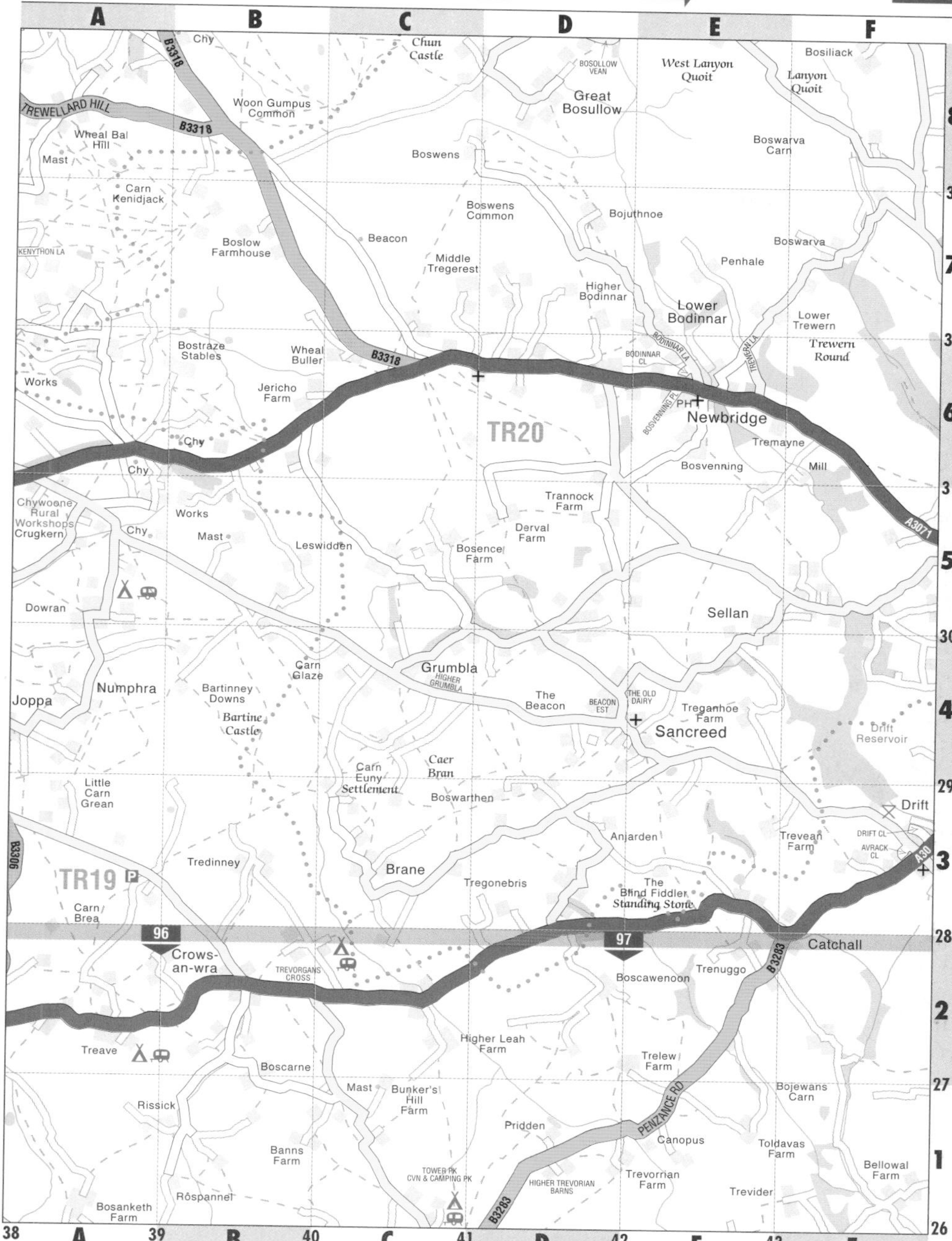

96 97 88

87
76

Scale: 1⅓ inches to 1 mile
0 ¼ ½ mile
0 250m 500m 750m 1 km

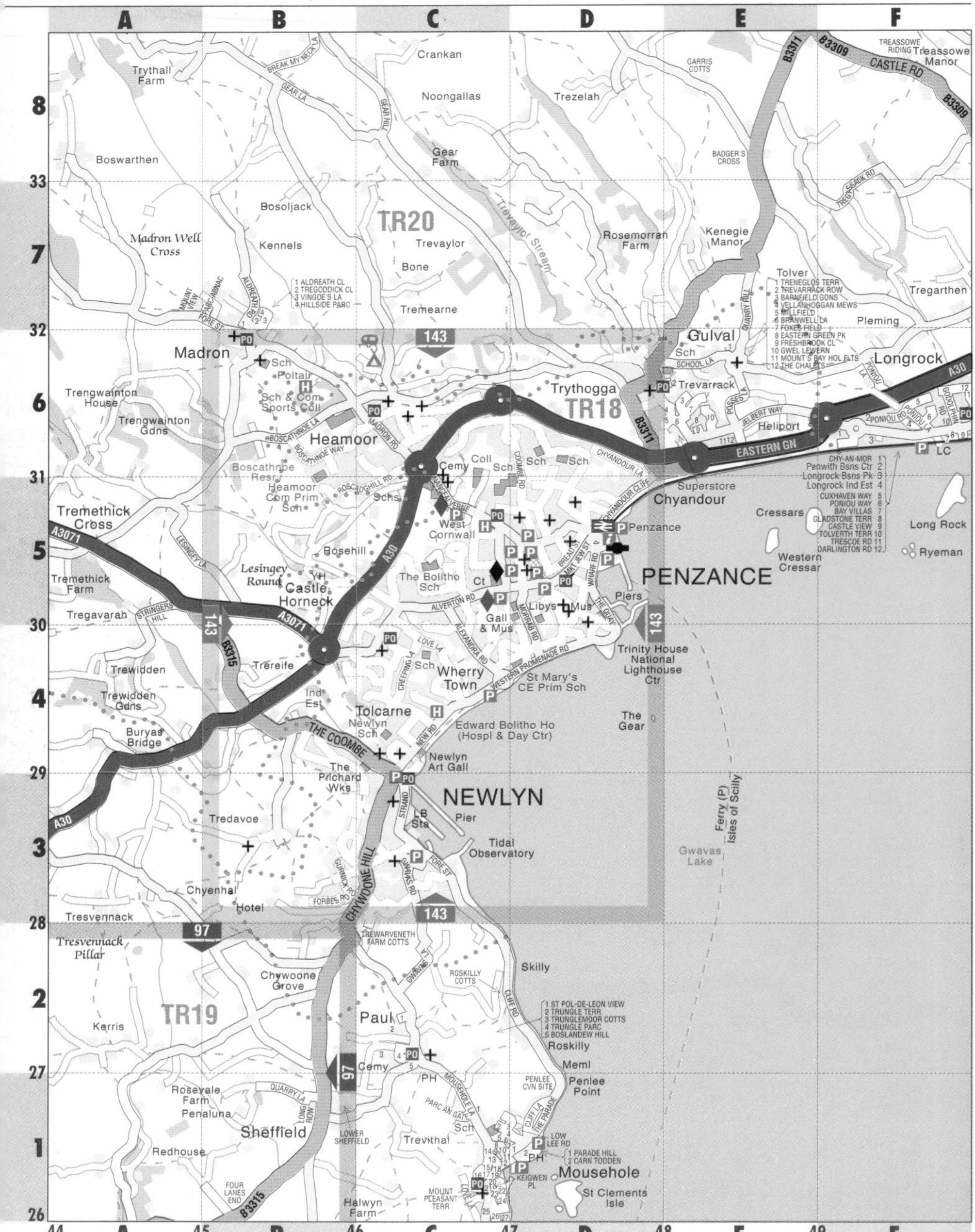

97
87

C1
1 LYNWOOD COTTS
2 PREVENNA RD
3 GWELENYS RD
4 PARKRYN RD
5 FOXES LA
6 MARCWHEAL
7 DUMBARTON TERR
8 SOUTHVIEW TERR
9 DUCK ST

For full street detail of the highlighted area see page 143

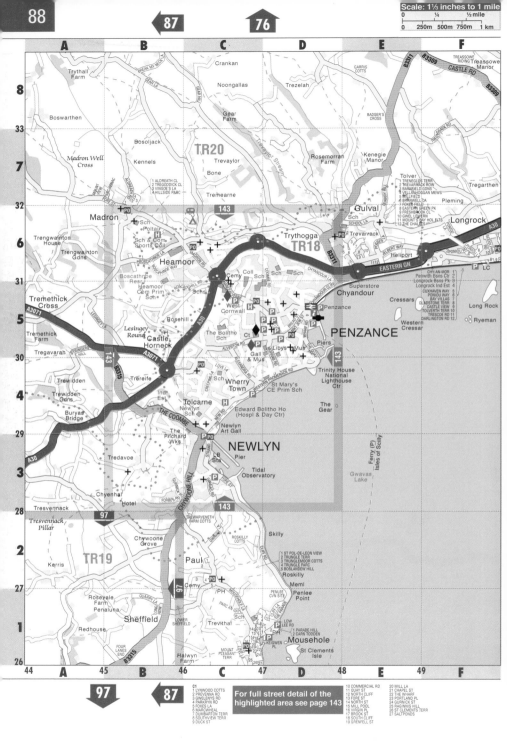

10 COMMERCIAL RD
11 QUAY ST
12 NORTH CLIFF
13 FORE ST
14 NORTH ST
15 MILL POOL
16 VIRGIN PL
17 BROOK ST
18 SOUTH CLIFF
19 GRENFELL ST
20 MILL LA
21 CHAPEL ST
22 THE WHARF
23 PORTLAND PL
24 GURNICK ST
25 RAGINNIS HILL
26 ST CLEMENTS TERR
27 SALTPONDS

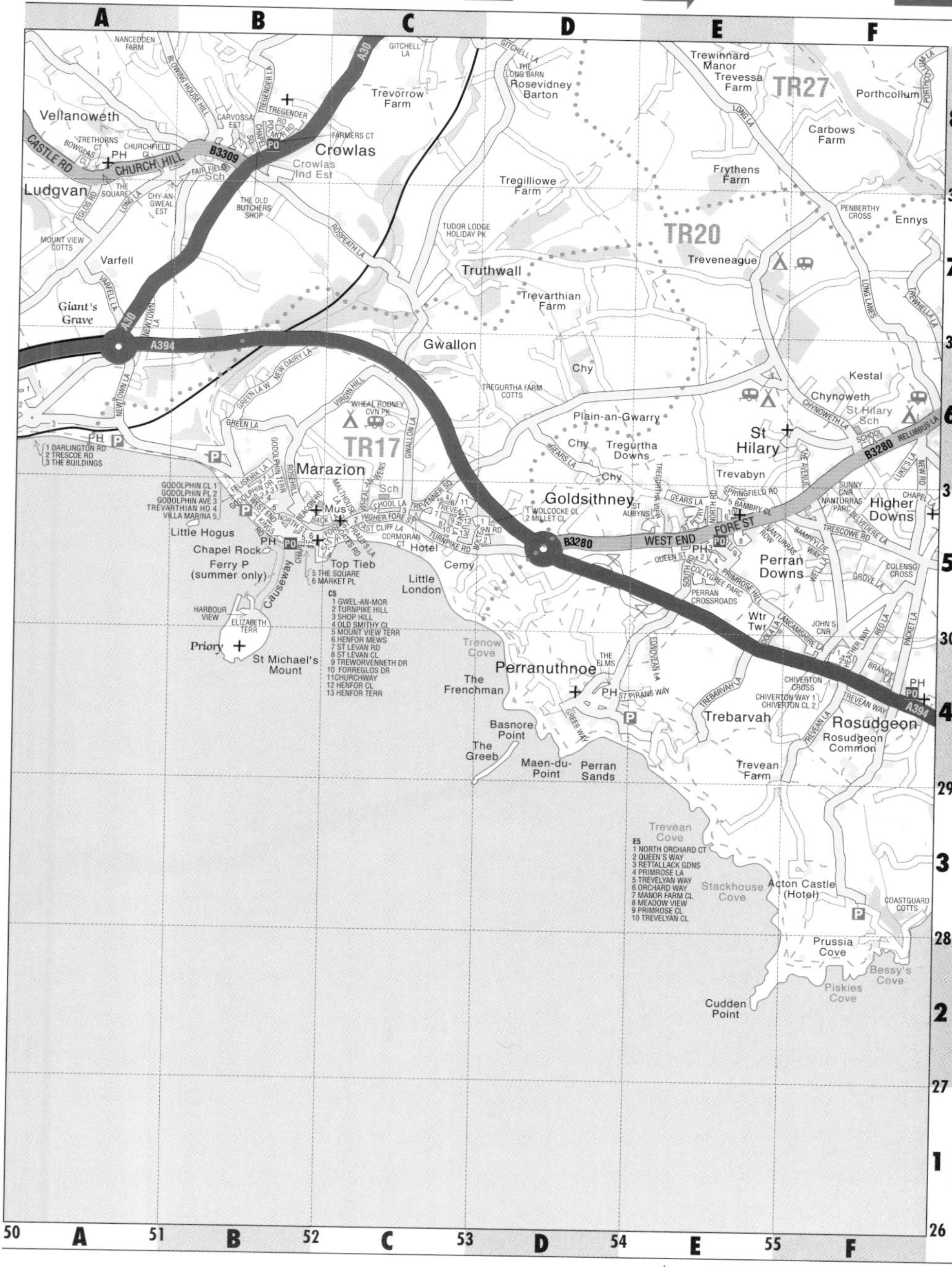
A
B
C
D
E
F
Nancedden Farm
Blowing House Hill
Tregender La
Tregender Rd
Tregender
Gitchell La
The Long Barn
Rosevidney Barton
Trewinnard Manor
Trevessa Farm
TR27
Porthcollum
Vellanoweth
Trethorns Ct
Carvossa Est
Churchfield Cl
Polmor Rd
Farmers Ct
Crowlas
Crowlas Ind Est
Trevorrow Farm
Carbows Farm
Castle Rd
Church Hill
B3309
Fair Field
Sch
PO
PH
Ludgvan
Eglos Rd
The Square
Long La
Chy-an-Gweal Est
The Old Butchers Shop
Tregilliowe Farm
Frythens Farm
Mount View Cotts
Varfell
Varfell La
Rospeath La
Tudor Lodge Holiday Pk
TR20
Penberthy Cross
Ennys
Treveneague
Truthwall
Trevarthian Farm
Long Lanes
Trewhella La
Giant's Grave
A30
Newtown La
A394
Gwallon
Chy
Kestal
New Dairy La
Green La W
Virgin Hill
Wheal Rodney Cvn Pk
Tregurtha Farm Cotts
Chynoweth
Chynoweth La
St Hilary Sch
School La
Relubbus La
Green La
Plain-an-Gwarry
St Hilary
1 Darlington Rd
2 Trescoe Rd
3 The Buildings
TR17
Gwallon La
Godolphin Terr
Rosehill
Marazion
Gears La
Chy
Tregurtha Downs
Trevabyn
B3280
Godolphin Cl 1
Godolphin Pl 2
Godolphin Ave 3
Trevarthian Ho 4
Villa Marina 5
Mus
Sch
Chy
Goldsithney
Springfield Rd
Sunny Cnr
Nanturras Parc
Higher Downs
Luke's La
New Rd
Chapel La
1 Wolcocke Cl
2 Millet Cl
St Aubyns
Tregurtha View
Gears La
North Rd
Bambry Cl
Little Hogus
Fore St
West End
Trescowe Rd
Belvedere La
Chapel Rock
Ferry P (summer only)
Causeway
Top Tieb
5 The Square
6 Market Pl
Hotel
Cormoran Ct
Turnpike Rd
Cemy
Queen St
Nanturras Row
Bampfylde Way
Perran Downs
Colenso Cross
Grove La
Little London
South Rd
Collygree Parc
Primrose Hill
Well La
Perran Crossroads
Harbour View
Elizabeth Terr
Priory
St Michael's Mount
C5
1 Gwel-an-Mor
2 Turnpike Hill
3 Shop Hill
4 Old Smithy Cl
5 Mount View Terr
6 Henfor Mews
7 St Levan Rd
8 St Levan Cl
9 Treworvenneth Dr
10 Forreglos Dr
11 Churchway
12 Henfor Cl
13 Henfor Terr
Trenow Cove
Perranuthnoe
The Elms
Wtr Twr
Lancamshire La
John's Cnr
Heather Way
Red La
Packet La
Brandy La
The Frenchman
St Pirans Way
Greeb Way
Trebarvah La
Chiverton Cross
Chiverton Way 1
Chiverton Cl 2
Trevean Way
Trevean La
A394
Trebarvah
Rosudgeon
Rosudgeon Common
Basnore Point
The Greeb
Maen-du-Point
Perran Sands
Trevean Farm
Trevean Cove
E5
1 North Orchard Ct
2 Queen's Way
3 Rettallack Gdns
4 Primrose La
5 Trevelyan Way
6 Orchard Way
7 Manor Farm Cl
8 Meadow View
9 Primrose Cl
10 Trevelyan Cl
Stackhouse Cove
Acton Castle (Hotel)
Coastguard Cotts
Prussia Cove
Bessy's Cove
Piskies Cove
Cudden Point
8
33
7
32
6
31
5
30
4
29
3
28
2
27
1
26
50
51
52
53
54
55

89
78

Scale: 1⅓ inches to 1 mile
0 ¼ ½ mile
0 250m 500m 750m 1 km

89

Scale: 1⅓ inches to 1 mile
0 ¼ ½ mile
0 250m 500m 750m 1 km

79 92

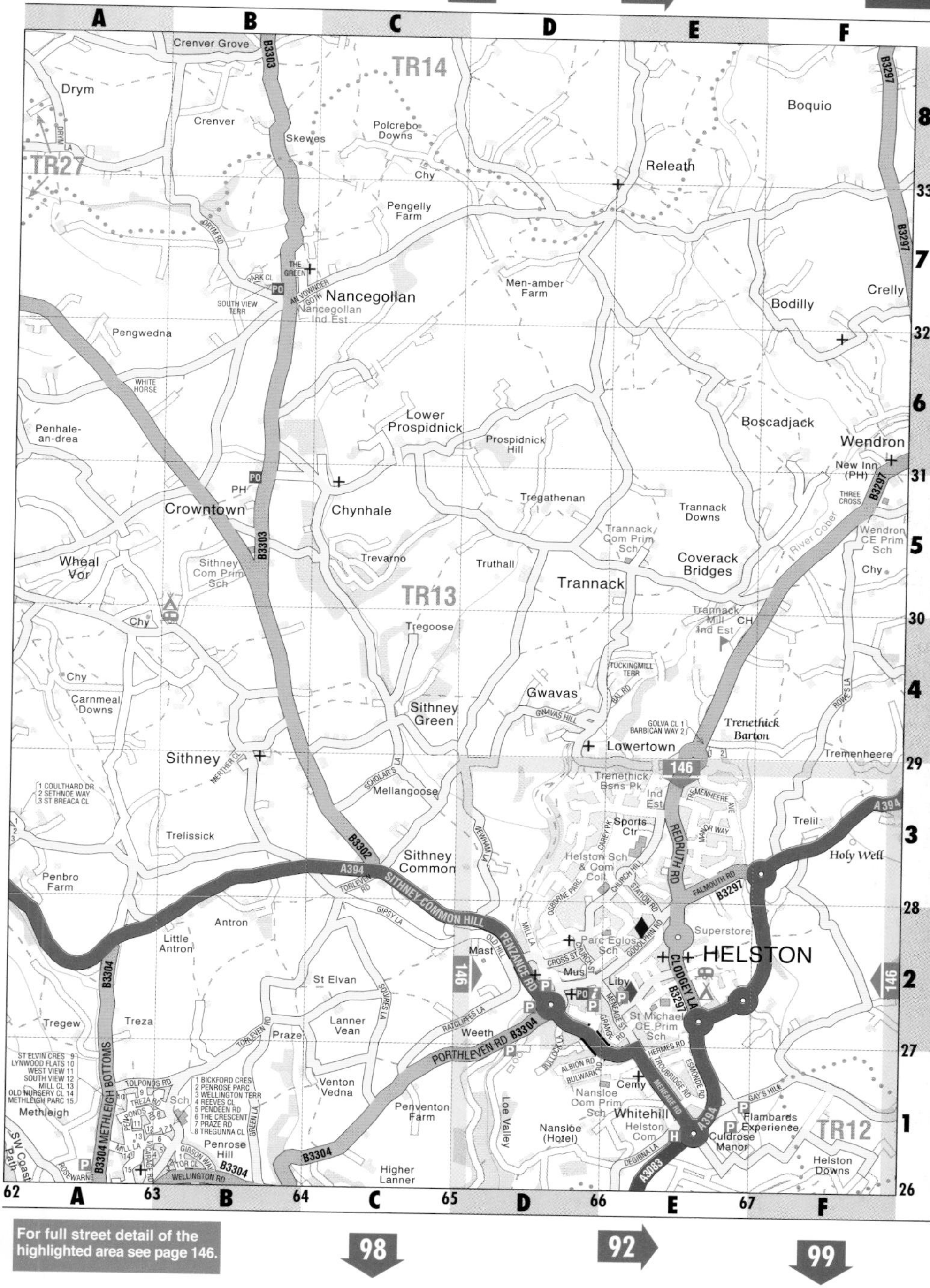

For full street detail of the highlighted area see page 146.

98 92 99

91
80

Scale: 1⅓ inches to 1 mile
0 ¼ ½ mile
0 250m 500m 750m 1 km

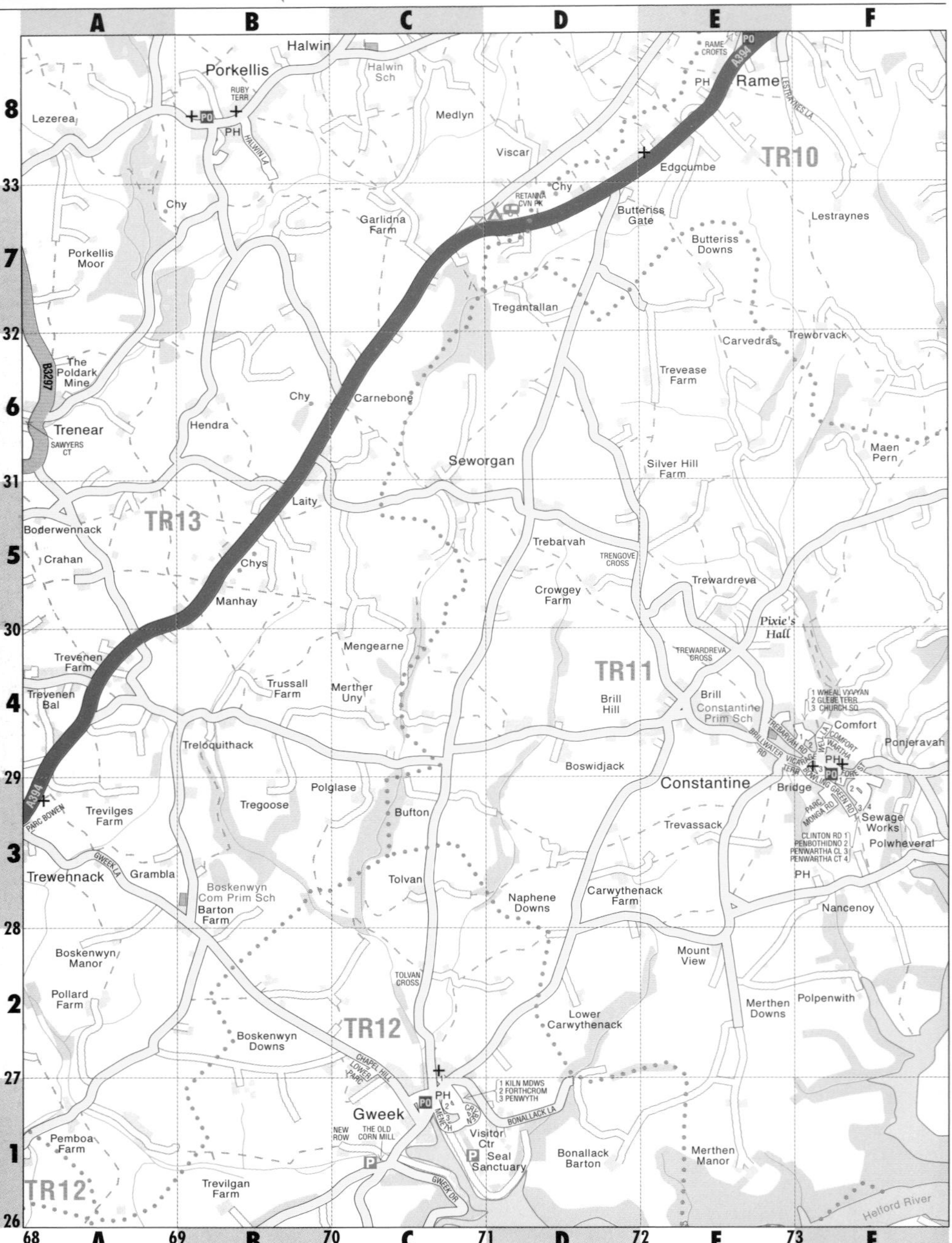

91
99
100

Scale: 1⅓ inches to 1 mile
0 ¼ ½ mile
0 250m 500m 750m 1 km

81
94

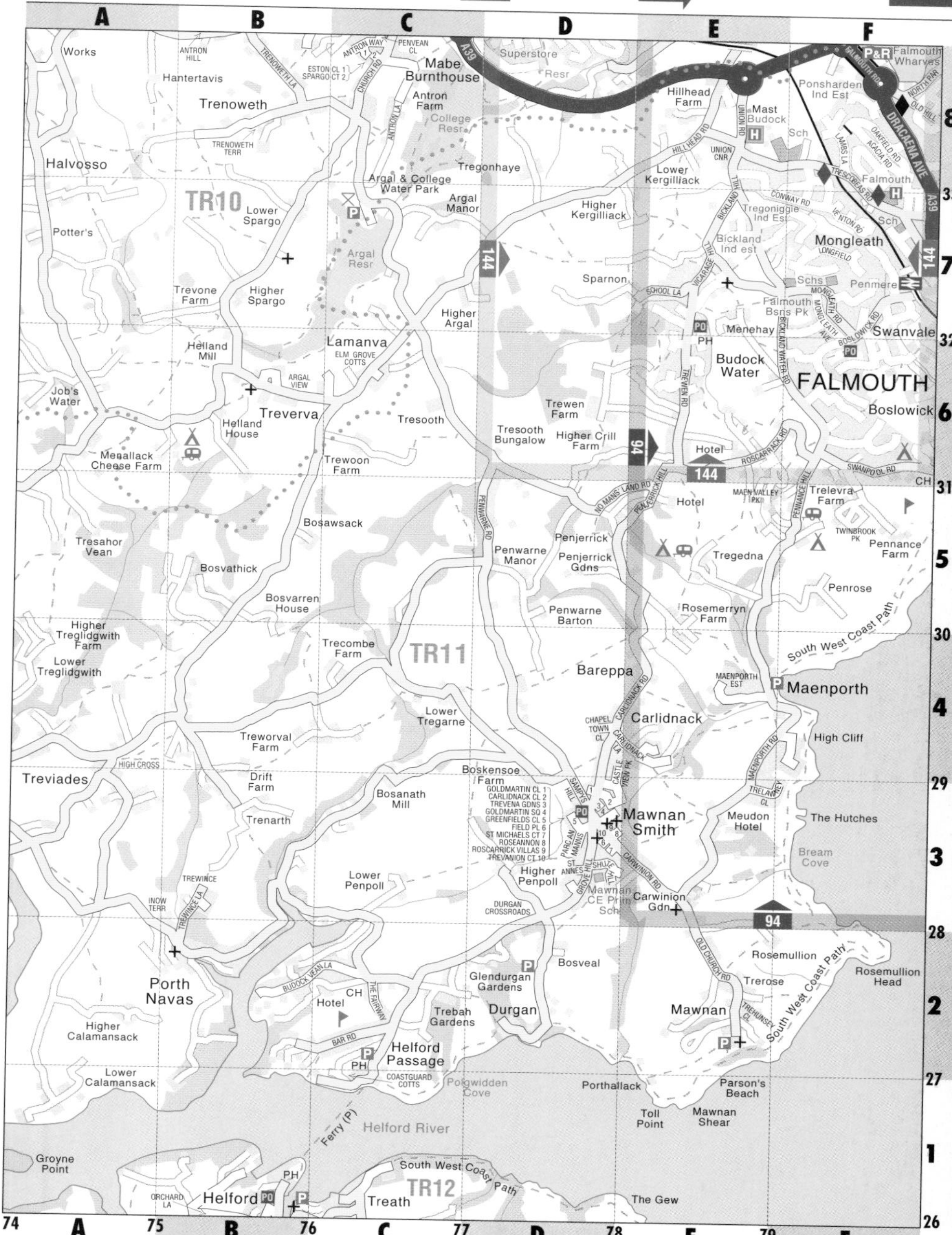

100
101

For full street detail of the highlighted area see page 144.

81
81
For full street detail of the highlighted area see pages 144 and 145.
82

Scale: 1⅓ inches to 1 mile
0 ¼ ½ mile
0 250m 500m 750m 1 km

93
93

Scale: 1⅓ inches to 1 mile
0 ¼ ½ mile
0 250m 500m 750m 1 km

82
83

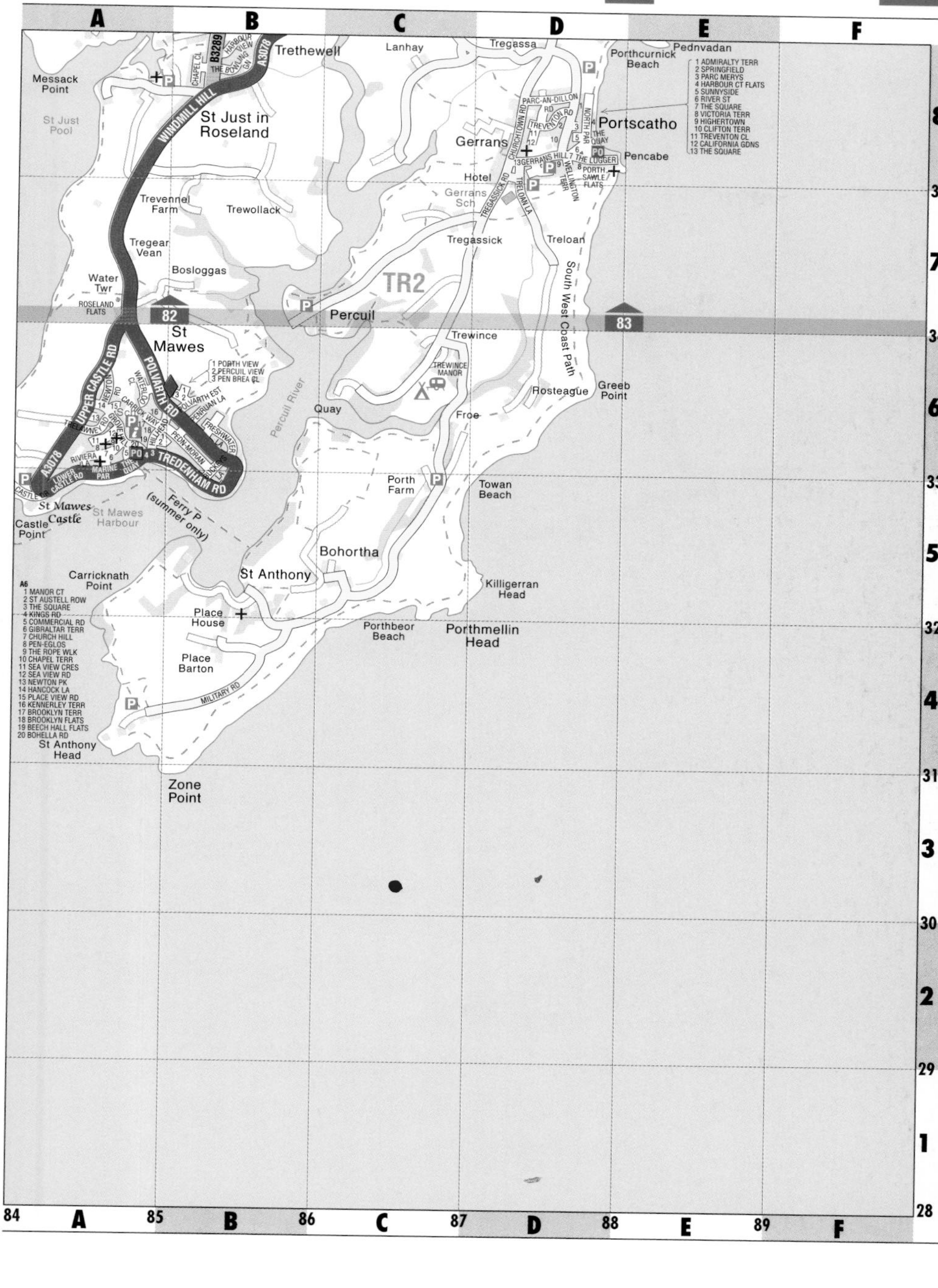
A
B
C
D
E
F
8
35
7
34
6
33
5
32
4
31
3
30
2
29
1
28
84
85
86
87
88
89
Messack Point
St Just Pool
Trethewell
Lanhay
Tregassa
Pednvadan
Porthcurnick Beach
1 ADMIRALTY TERR
2 SPRINGFIELD
3 PARC MERYS
4 HARBOUR CT FLATS
5 SUNNYSIDE
6 RIVER ST
7 THE SQUARE
8 VICTORIA TERR
9 HIGHERTOWN
10 CLIFTON TERR
11 TREVENTON CL
12 CALIFORNIA GDNS
13 THE SQUARE
CHAPEL CL
B3289
HARBOUR VIEW
THE BOWLING GN
A3078
WINDMILL HILL
St Just in Roseland
Gerrans
Portscatho
PARC-AN-DILLON RD
TREVENTON RD
CHURCHTOWN RD
NORTH PAR
THE QUAY
GERRANS HILL
THE LUGGER
WELLINGTON TERR
PORTH SAWLE FLATS
PO
Pencabe
Hotel
Gerrans Sch
TREGASSICK RD
TRELOAN LA
Trevennel Farm
Trewollack
Tregassick
Treloan
Tregear Vean
Bosloggas
Water Twr
ROSELAND FLATS
TR2
South West Coast Path
Percuil
82
83
St Mawes
Trewince
1 PORTH VIEW
2 PERCUIL VIEW
3 PEN BREA CL
UPPER CASTLE RD
POLVARTH RD
NEWTON RD
WATERLOO CL
CARRICK WAY
POLVARTH EST
PENRUAN LA
TRELAWNEY RD
GROVE HILL
HILLHEAD
PEN-MORAN
FRESHWATER LA
RIVIERA LA
MARINE PAR
THE QUAY
TREDENHAM RD
LOWER CASTLE RD
CASTLE DR
DOCK LA
TREWINCE MANOR
Percuil River
Quay
Rosteague
Greeb Point
Froe
Porth Farm
Towan Beach
St Mawes Castle
St Mawes Harbour
Castle Point
Ferry P (summer only)
Bohortha
St Anthony
Carricknath Point
Killigerran Head
A6
1 MANOR CT
2 ST AUSTELL ROW
3 THE SQUARE
4 KINGS RD
5 COMMERCIAL RD
6 GIBRALTAR TERR
7 CHURCH HILL
8 PEN-EGLOS
9 THE ROPE WLK
10 CHAPEL TERR
11 SEA VIEW CRES
12 SEA VIEW RD
13 NEWTON PK
14 HANCOCK LA
15 PLACE VIEW RD
16 KENNERLEY TERR
17 BROOKLYN TERR
18 BROOKLYN FLATS
19 BEECH HALL FLATS
20 BOHELLA RD
Place House
Porthbeor Beach
Porthmellin Head
Place Barton
MILITARY RD
St Anthony Head
Zone Point

Scale: 1⅓ inches to 1 mile

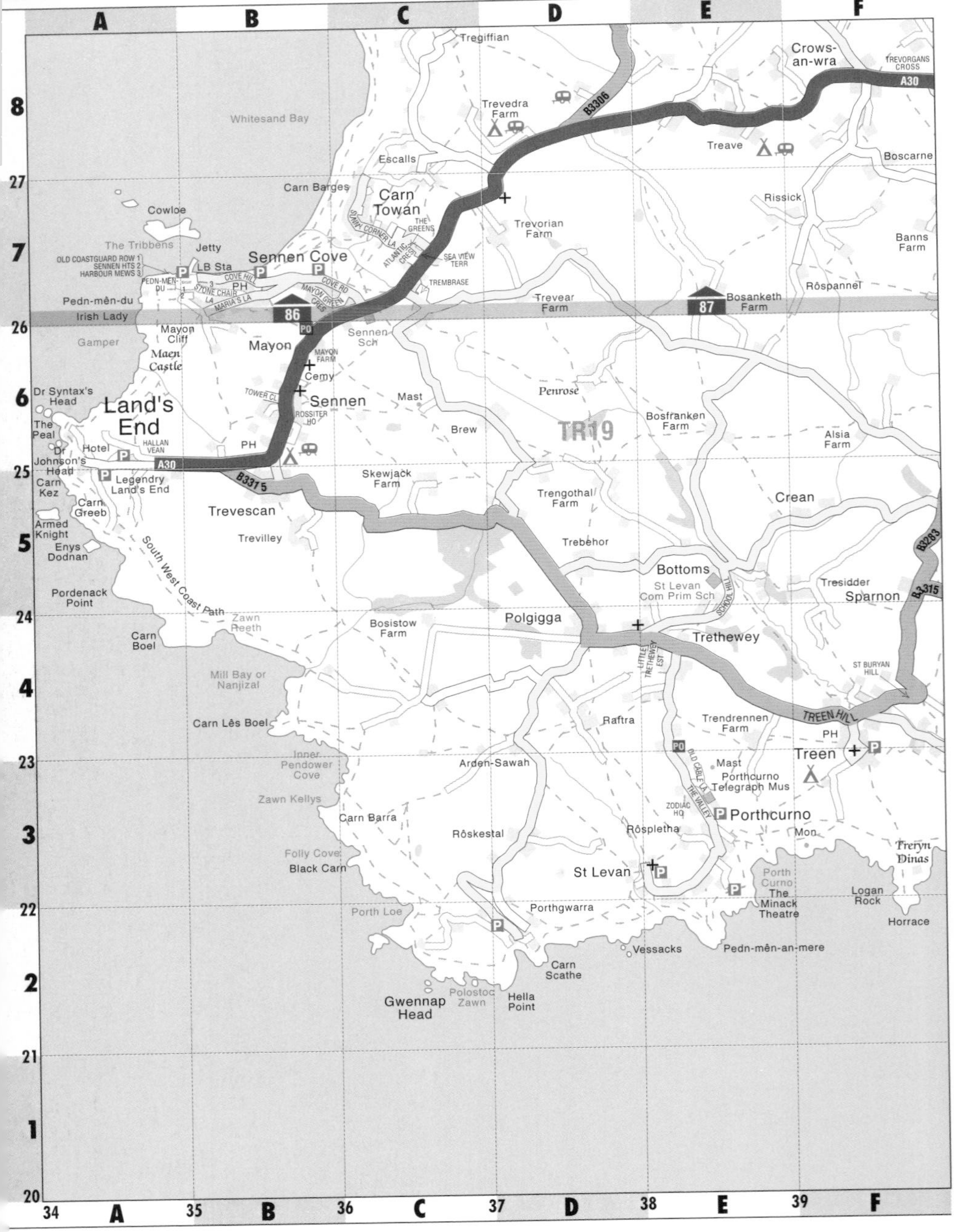

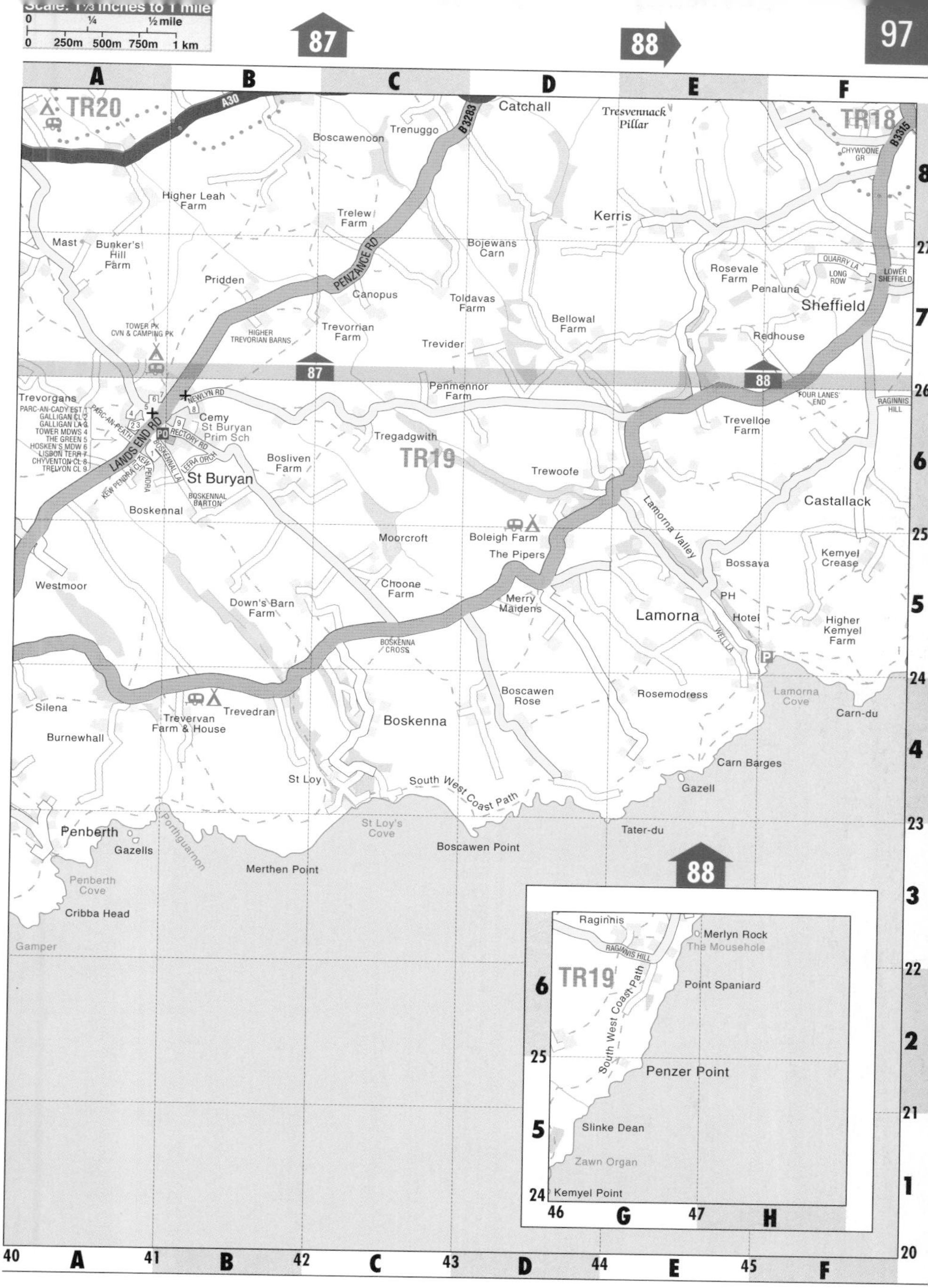
Scale: 1⅓ inches to 1 mile
0 ¼ ½ mile
0 250m 500m 750m 1 km
87
88
A B C D E F
TR20
A30
B3283
Catchall
Tresvennack Pillar
TR18
B3315
CHYWOONE GR
Boscawenoon
Trenuggo
Higher Leah Farm
Trelew Farm
Kerris
Mast
Bunker's Hill Farm
Bojewans Carn
QUARRY LA
LOWER SHEFFIELD
LONG ROW
Rosevale Farm
Penaluna
Pridden
PENZANCE RD
Canopus
Toldavas Farm
Sheffield
Bellowal Farm
TOWER PK CVN & CAMPING PK
HIGHER TREVORIAN BARNS
Trevorrian Farm
Trevider
Redhouse
Penmennor Farm
FOUR LANES' END
RAGINNIS HILL
Trevorgans
PARC-AN-CADY EST 1
GALLIGAN CL 2
GALLIGAN LA 3
TOWER MDWS 4
THE GREEN 5
HOSKEN'S MDW 6
LISBON TERR 7
CHYVENTON CL 8
TRELYON CL 9
NEWLYN RD
PARC-AN-PEATH
Cemy
St Buryan Prim Sch
RECTORY RD
LANDS END RD
BOSKENNAL LA
KEW PENDRA
KEW PENDRA CL
LEFRA ORCH
Tregadgwith
Trevelloe Farm
TR19
Bosliven Farm
Trewoofe
St Buryan
BOSKENNAL BARTON
Boskennal
Lamorna Valley
Castallack
Moorcroft
Boleigh Farm
The Pipers
Kemyel Crease
Bossava
Westmoor
Choone Farm
PH
Merry Maidens
Down's Barn Farm
Lamorna
Hotel
Higher Kemyel Farm
WELL LA
BOSKENNA CROSS
Silena
Boscawen Rose
Rosemodress
Lamorna Cove
Carn-du
Trevedran
Trevervan Farm & House
Boskenna
Burnewhall
Carn Barges
St Loy
South West Coast Path
Gazell
St Loy's Cove
Porthguarnon
Tater-du
Penberth
Gazells
Boscawen Point
Merthen Point
Penberth Cove
Cribba Head
Gamper
Raginnis
Merlyn Rock
The Mousehole
RAGINNIS HILL
TR19
Point Spaniard
South West Coast Path
Penzer Point
Slinke Dean
Zawn Organ
Kemyel Point
46 G 47 H
6 25 5 24
40 A 41 B 42 C 43 D 44 E 45 F
8 27 7 26 6 25 5 24 4 23 3 22 2 21 1 20

For full street detail of the highlighted area see page 146.

Scale: 1⅓ inches to 1 mile
0 ¼ ½ mile
0 250m 500m 750m 1 km

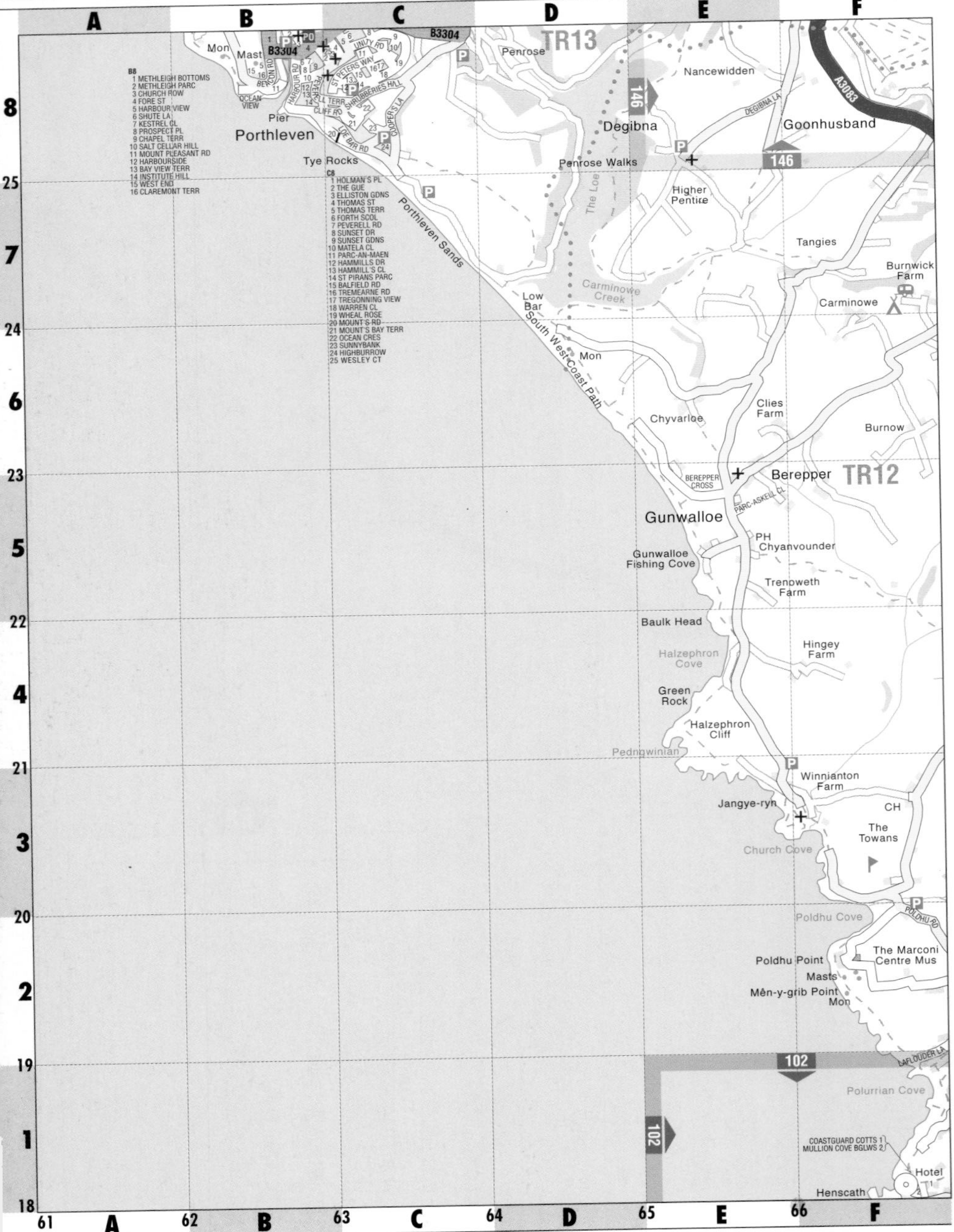
A
B
C
D
E
F
8
25
7
24
6
23
5
22
4
21
3
20
2
19
1
18
61
62
63
64
65
66
B3304
Mon
Mast
OCEAN VIEW
BEACON RD
HARBOUR RD
PEVERELL TERR
ST PETERS WAY
UNITY RD
SHRUBBERIES HILL
CLIFF RD
COOPER'S LA
LOE BAR RD
Pier
Porthleven
Tye Rocks
B8
1 METHLEIGH BOTTOMS
2 METHLEIGH PARC
3 CHURCH ROW
4 FORE ST
5 HARBOUR VIEW
6 SHUTE LA
7 KESTREL CL
8 PROSPECT PL
9 CHAPEL TERR
10 SALT CELLAR HILL
11 MOUNT PLEASANT RD
12 HARBOURSIDE
13 BAY VIEW TERR
14 INSTITUTE HILL
15 WEST END
16 CLAREMONT TERR
C8
1 HOLMAN'S PL
2 THE GUE
3 ELLISTON GDNS
4 THOMAS ST
5 THOMAS TERR
6 FORTH SCOL
7 PEVERELL RD
8 SUNSET DR
9 SUNSET GDNS
10 MATELA CL
11 PARC-AN-MAEN
12 HAMMILLS DR
13 HAMMILL'S CL
14 ST PIRANS PARC
15 BALFIELD RD
16 TREMEARNE RD
17 TREGONNING VIEW
18 WARREN CL
19 WHEAL ROSE
20 MOUNT'S RD
21 MOUNT'S BAY TERR
22 OCEAN CRES
23 SUNNYBANK
24 HIGHBURROW
25 WESLEY CT
Porthleven Sands
Penrose
TR13
Nancewidden
146
Degibna
DEGIBNA LA
Goonhusband
A3083
146
Penrose Walks
The Loe
Higher Pentire
Tangies
Burnwick Farm
Carminowe
Carminowe Creek
Low Bar
South West Coast Path
Mon
Clies Farm
Chyvarloe
Burnow
BEREPPER CROSS
Berepper
TR12
PARC-ASKELL CL
Gunwalloe
PH
Chyanvounder
Gunwalloe Fishing Cove
Trenoweth Farm
Baulk Head
Hingey Farm
Halzephron Cove
Green Rock
Halzephron Cliff
Pedngwinian
Winnianton Farm
Jangye-ryn
CH
The Towans
Church Cove
POLDHU RD
Poldhu Cove
The Marconi Centre Mus
Poldhu Point
Masts
Mên-y-grib Point
Mon
102
LAFLOUDER LA
Polurrian Cove
102
COASTGUARD COTTS 1
MULLION COVE BGLWS 2
Hotel
Henscath

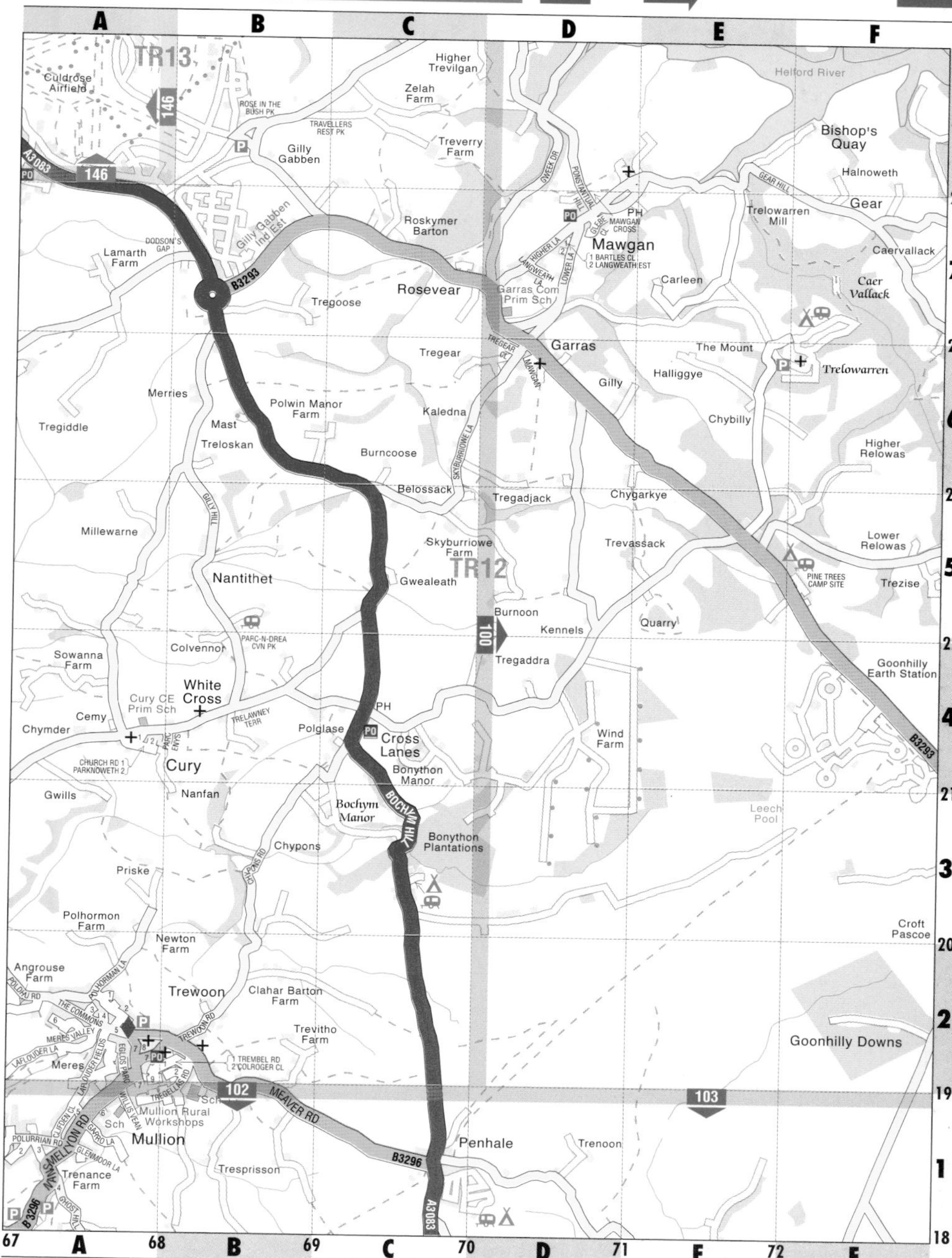
A
B
C
D
E
F
TR13
Culdrose Airfield
146
ROSE IN THE BUSH PK
TRAVELLERS REST PK
Gilly Gabben
Higher Trevilgan
Zelah Farm
Treverry Farm
Helford River
Bishop's Quay
Halnoweth
GEAR HILL
Gear
A3083
PO
Gilly Gabben Ind Est
DODSON'S GAP
Lamarth Farm
B3293
Roskymer Barton
Rosevear
Tregoose
GWEEK DR
PONSTANTIAL HILL
PO
PH
MAWGAN CROSS
GLEBE
HIGHER LA
LANGWEATH LA
LOWER LA
Mawgan
1 BARTLES CL
2 LANGWEATH EST
Carleen
Trelowarren Mill
Caervallack
Caer Vallack
Garras Com Prim Sch
TREGEAR CL
MAWGAN
Garras
The Mount
Trelowarren
Tregear
Gilly
Halliggye
Merries
Polwin Manor Farm
Kaledna
Chybilly
Tregiddle
Mast
Treloskan
Burncoose
SKYBURRIOWE LA
Higher Relowas
Belossack
Tregadjack
Chygarkye
GILLY HILL
Millewarne
Skyburriowe Farm
Trevassack
Lower Relowas
TR12
Nantithet
Gwealeath
PINE TREES CAMP SITE
Trezise
Burnoon
Quarry
PARC-N-DREA CVN PK
Kennels
Sowanna Farm
Colvennor
100
Tregaddra
Goonhilly Earth Station
White Cross
Cury CE Prim Sch
PH
TRELAWNEY TERR
Cemy
Chymder
PARC ENYS
Polglase
PO
Cross Lanes
Wind Farm
B3293
CHURCH RD 1
PARKNOWETH 2
Cury
Bonython Manor
Gwills
Nanfan
Bochym Manor
BOCHYM HILL
Leech Pool
Chypons
Bonython Plantations
CHYPONS RD
Priske
Polhormon Farm
Croft Pascoe
Newton Farm
Angrouse Farm
POLHORMAN LA
POLDHU RD
THE COMMONS
Trewoon
Clahar Barton Farm
TREWOON RD
MERES VALLEY
Trevitho Farm
Goonhilly Downs
LAFLOUDER LA
LAFLOUDER FIELDS
EGLOS PARC
Meres
1 TREMBEL RD
2 COLROGER CL
TREGELLAS RD
Sch
102
MEAVER RD
103
CLIFDEN CL
WILLIS VEAN
Mullion Rural Workshops
Sch
GARRO LA
POLURRIAN RD
Mullion
Penhale
Trenoon
B3296
GLENMOOR LA
Tresprisson
Trenance Farm
B3296
GHOST HILL
A3083
8
25
7
24
6
23
5
22
4
21
3
20
2
19
1
18
67
68
69
70
71
72

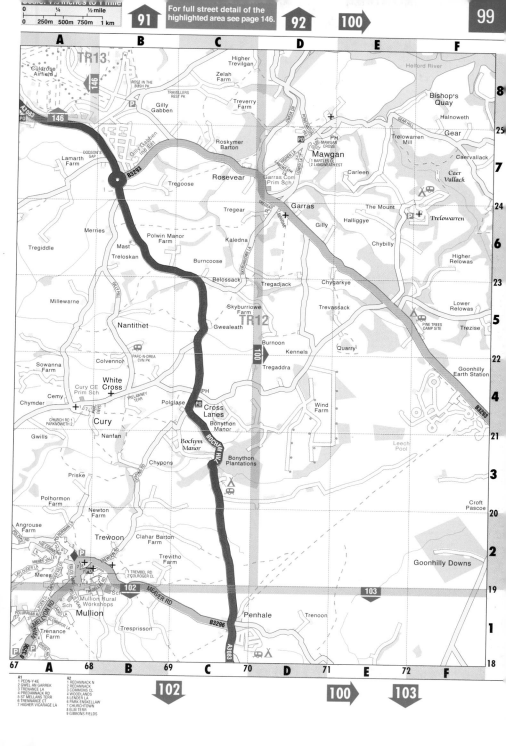

99 92 93

Scale: 1⅓ inches to 1 mile

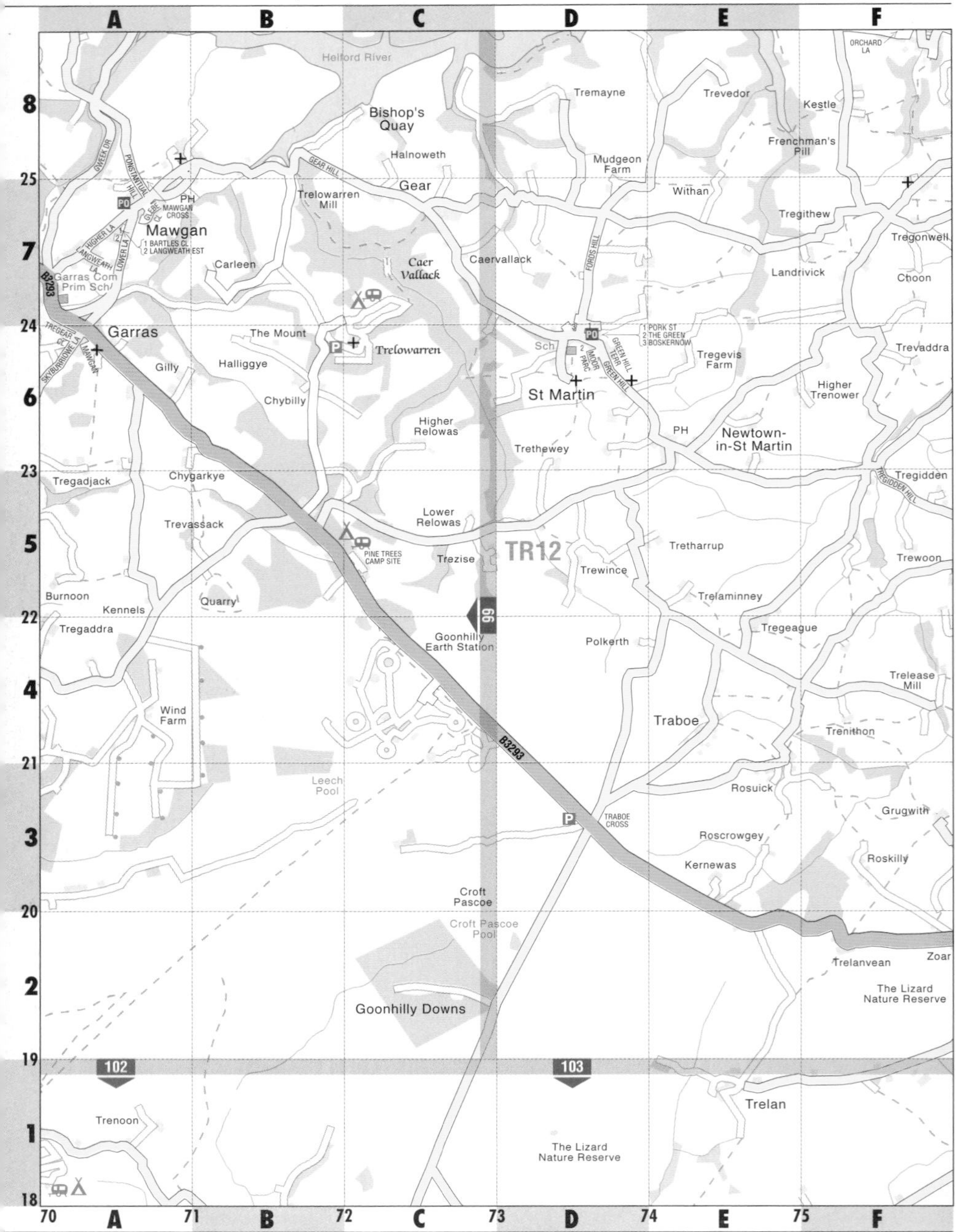

102 99 103

93

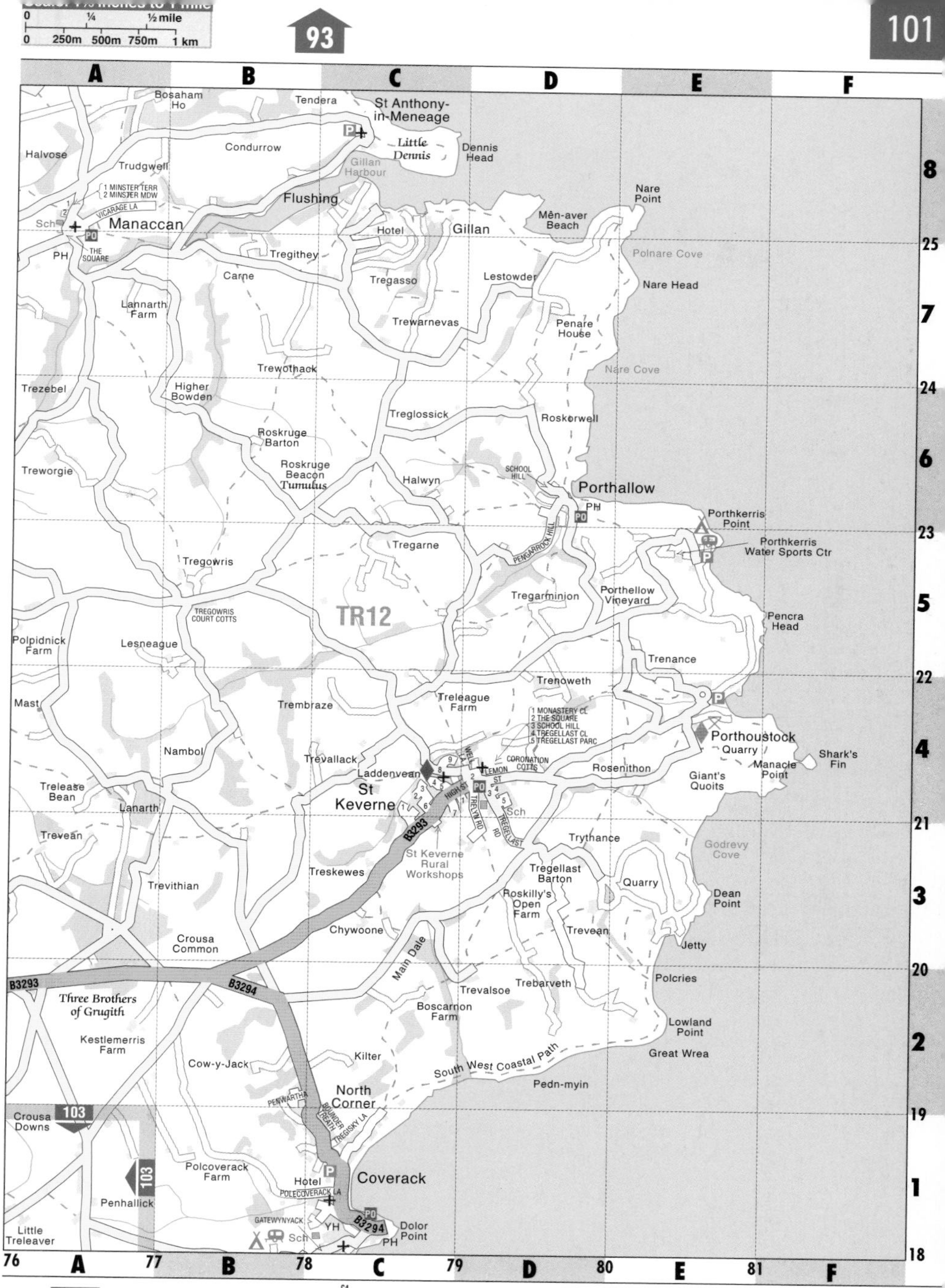
0 ¼ ½ mile
0 250m 500m 750m 1 km
A
B
C
D
E
F
Bosaham Ho
Tendera
St Anthony-in-Meneage
Little Dennis
Dennis Head
Halvose
Condurrow
Trudgwell
Gillan Harbour
1 MINSTER TERR
2 MINSTER MDW
Flushing
VICARAGE LA
Nare Point
Sch
Manaccan
Mên-aver Beach
Hotel
Gillan
PH
THE SQUARE
Tregithey
Polnare Cove
Carne
Lestowder
Nare Head
Tregasso
Lannarth Farm
Trewarnevas
Penare House
Trewothack
Nare Cove
Trezebel
Higher Bowden
Treglossick
Roskorwell
Roskruge Barton
Roskruge Beacon
Tumulus
Treworgie
Halwyn
SCHOOL HILL
Porthallow
PH
Porthkerris Point
Tregarne
Porthkerris Water Sports Ctr
Tregowris
PENGARROCK HILL
Porthellow Vineyard
Tregarminion
TREGOWRIS COURT COTTS
TR12
Pencra Head
Polpidnick Farm
Lesneague
Trenance
Trenoweth
Mast
Trembraze
Treleague Farm
1 MONASTERY CL
2 THE SQUARE
3 SCHOOL HILL
4 TREGELLAST CL
5 TREGELLAST PARC
Porthoustock
Quarry
Shark's Fin
Nambol
Trevallack
CORONATION COTTS
Rosenithon
Manacle Point
Laddenvean
LEMON ST
Giant's Quoits
Trelease Bean
St Keverne
HIGH ST
TREVYLN RD
TREGELLAST RD
Sch
Lanarth
Trevean
B3293
Trythance
St Keverne Rural Workshops
Godrevy Cove
Treskewes
Tregellast Barton
Trevithian
Quarry
Roskilly's Open Farm
Dean Point
Chywoone
Trevean
Crousa Common
Jetty
Main Dale
B3293
B3294
Polcries
Trevalsoe
Trebarveth
Three Brothers of Grugith
Boscarnon Farm
Lowland Point
Kestlemerris Farm
Great Wrea
Kilter
Cow-y-Jack
South West Coastal Path
Pedn-myin
North Corner
PENWARTHA
BOUNDER TREATH
TREGISKY LA
Crousa Downs
103
Polcoverack Farm
Coverack
Hotel
POLCOVERACK LA
Penhallick
GATEWYNYACK
YH
B3294
Dolor Point
Sch
PH
Little Treleaver
76
77
78
79
80
81
8
25
7
24
6
23
5
22
4
21
3
20
2
19
1
18

103

C4
1 TRESKEWES EST
2 TREVALLACK VIEW
3 TREVALLACK PARC
4 LANHEVERNE PARC
5 DOCTORS HILL
6 POLVENTON PARC
7 PENMENNER EST
8 COMMERCIAL RD
9 TREGONNING PARC

98
99

Scale: 1⅓ inches to 1 mile

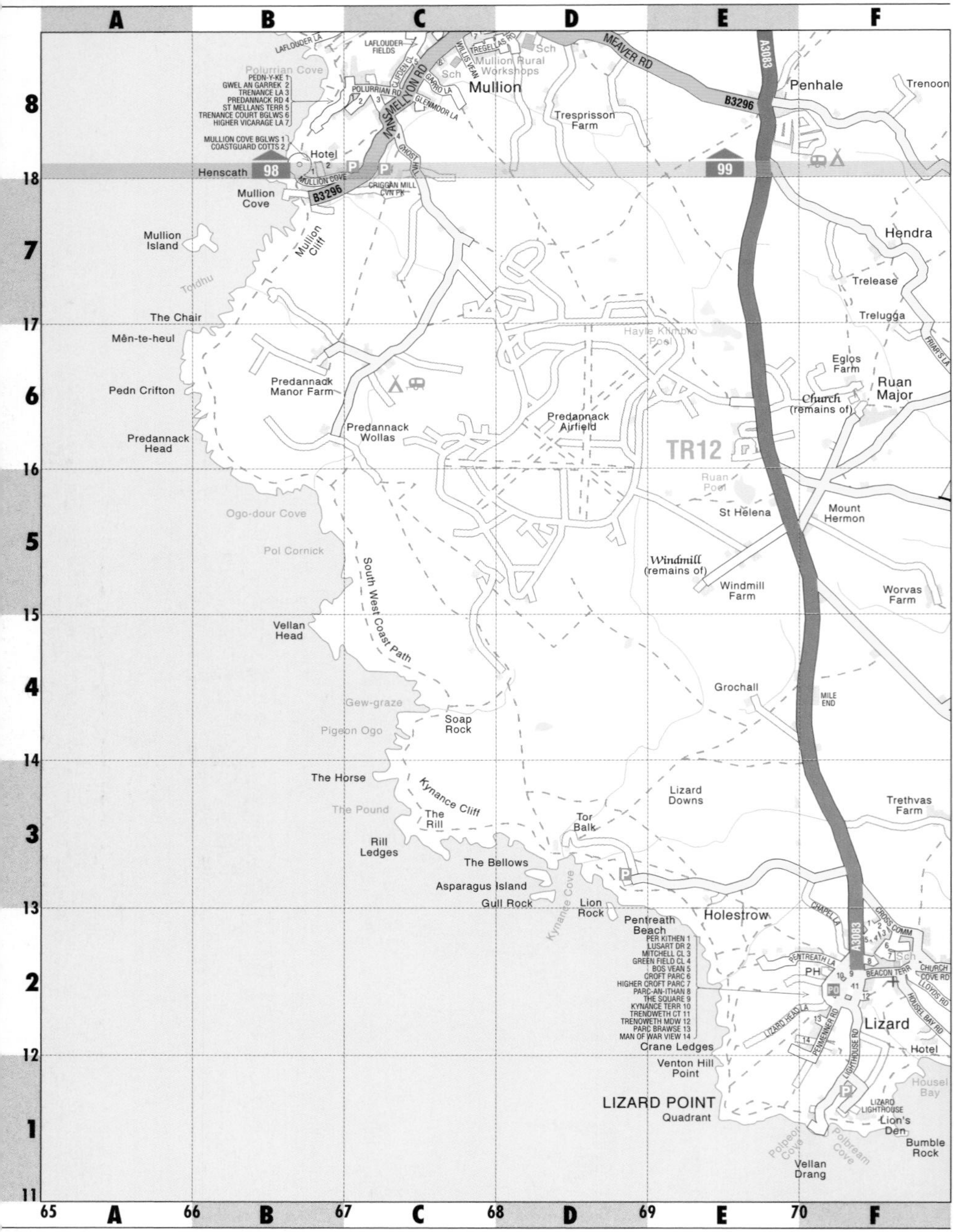
A
B
C
D
E
F
Mullion
Polurrian Cove
Mullion Rural Workshops
Sch
LAFLOUDER LA
LAFLOUDER FIELDS
POLURRIAN RD
CLIFDEN CL
NANSMELLYON RD
WILLIS VEAN
TREGELLAS RD
GARRO LA
GLENMOOR LA
GHOST HILL
MEAVER RD
B3296
A3083
PEDN-Y-KE 1
GWEL AN GARREK 2
TRENANCE LA 3
PREDANNACK RD 4
ST MELLANS TERR 5
TRENANCE COURT BGLWS 6
HIGHER VICARAGE LA 7
MULLION COVE BGLWS 1
COASTGUARD COTTS 2
Hotel
Henscath
98
99
MULLION COVE
CRIGGAN MILL CVN PK
Mullion Cove
Mullion Island
Mullion Cliff
Toldhu
Penhale
Trenoon
Tresprisson Farm
Hendra
Trelease
Trelugga
FRIAR'S LA
The Chair
Mên-te-heul
Pedn Crifton
Predannack Head
Predannack Manor Farm
Predannack Wollas
Predannack Airfield
Hayle Kimbro Pool
Eglos Farm
Ruan Major
Church (remains of)
TR12
Ruan Pool
St Helena
Mount Hermon
Ogo-dour Cove
Pol Cornick
South West Coast Path
Windmill (remains of)
Windmill Farm
Worvas Farm
Vellan Head
Grochall
MILE END
Gew-graze
Soap Rock
Pigeon Ogo
The Horse
Kynance Cliff
The Pound
The Rill
Rill Ledges
Tor Balk
Lizard Downs
Trethvas Farm
The Bellows
Asparagus Island
Gull Rock
Kynance Cove
Lion Rock
Pentreath Beach
Holestrow
PER KITHEN 1
LUSART DR 2
MITCHELL CL 3
GREEN FIELD CL 4
BOS VEAN 5
CROFT PARC 6
HIGHER CROFT PARC 7
PARC-AN-ITHAN 8
THE SQUARE 9
KYNANCE TERR 10
TRENOWETH CT 11
TRENOWETH MDW 12
PARC BRAWSE 13
MAN OF WAR VIEW 14
CHAPEL LA
CROSS COMM
PENTREATH LA
BEACON TERR
CHURCH COVE RD
LLOYDS RD
HOUSEL BAY RD
LIZARD HEAD LA
PENMENNER RD
LIGHTHOUSE RD
PH
PO
Lizard
Hotel
Crane Ledges
Venton Hill Point
LIZARD POINT
Quadrant
Housel Bay
LIZARD LIGHTHOUSE
Lion's Den
Bumble Rock
Polpeor Cove
Polbream Cove
Vellan Drang
8
18
7
17
6
16
5
15
4
14
3
13
2
12
1
11
65
66
67
68
69
70

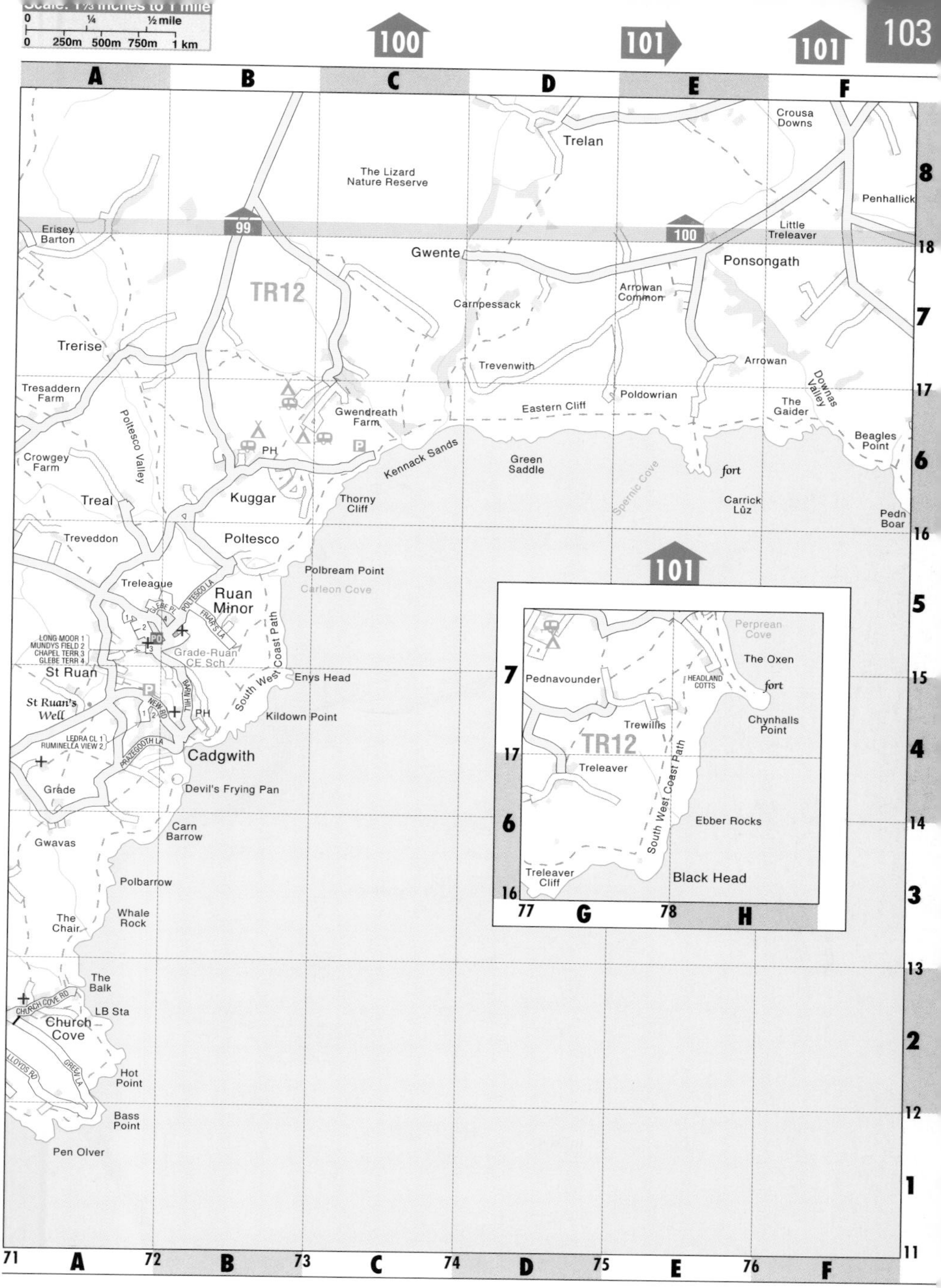
Scale: 1⅓ inches to 1 mile
0 ¼ ½ mile
0 250m 500m 750m 1 km
100
101
101
99
100
101
The Lizard Nature Reserve
Trelan
Crousa Downs
Penhallick
Erisey Barton
Gwente
Little Treleaver
Ponsongath
TR12
Carnpessack
Arrowan Common
Trerise
Trevenwith
Arrowan
Downas Valley
Tresaddern Farm
Poltesco Valley
Gwendreath Farm
Poldowrian
Eastern Cliff
The Gaider
Beagles Point
PH
Kennack Sands
Crowgey Farm
Green Saddle
Spernic Cove
fort
Treal
Kuggar
Thorny Cliff
Carrick Lûz
Pedn Boar
Treveddon
Poltesco
Polbream Point
Carleon Cove
Treleague
POLTESCO LA
GLEBE PL
Ruan Minor
FRIAR'S LA
LONG MOOR 1
MUNDYS FIELD 2
CHAPEL TERR 3
GLEBE TERR 4
PO
Grade-Ruan CE Sch
South West Coast Path
St Ruan
Enys Head
BARN HILL
St Ruan's Well
NEW RD
PH
Kildown Point
LEDRA CL 1
RUMINELLA VIEW 2
PRAZEGOOTH LA
Cadgwith
Grade
Devil's Frying Pan
Carn Barrow
Gwavas
Polbarrow
The Chair
Whale Rock
The Balk
CHURCH COVE RD
LB Sta
Church Cove
LLOYDS RD
GREEN LA
Hot Point
Bass Point
Pen Olver
Perprean Cove
The Oxen
Pednavounder
HEADLAND COTTS
fort
Trewillis
Chynhalls Point
TR12
Treleaver
South West Coast Path
Ebber Rocks
Treleaver Cliff
Black Head
77 G 78 H
A B C D E F
71 72 73 74 75 76
8 7 6 5 4 3 2 1
18 17 16 15 14 13 12 11

4 4

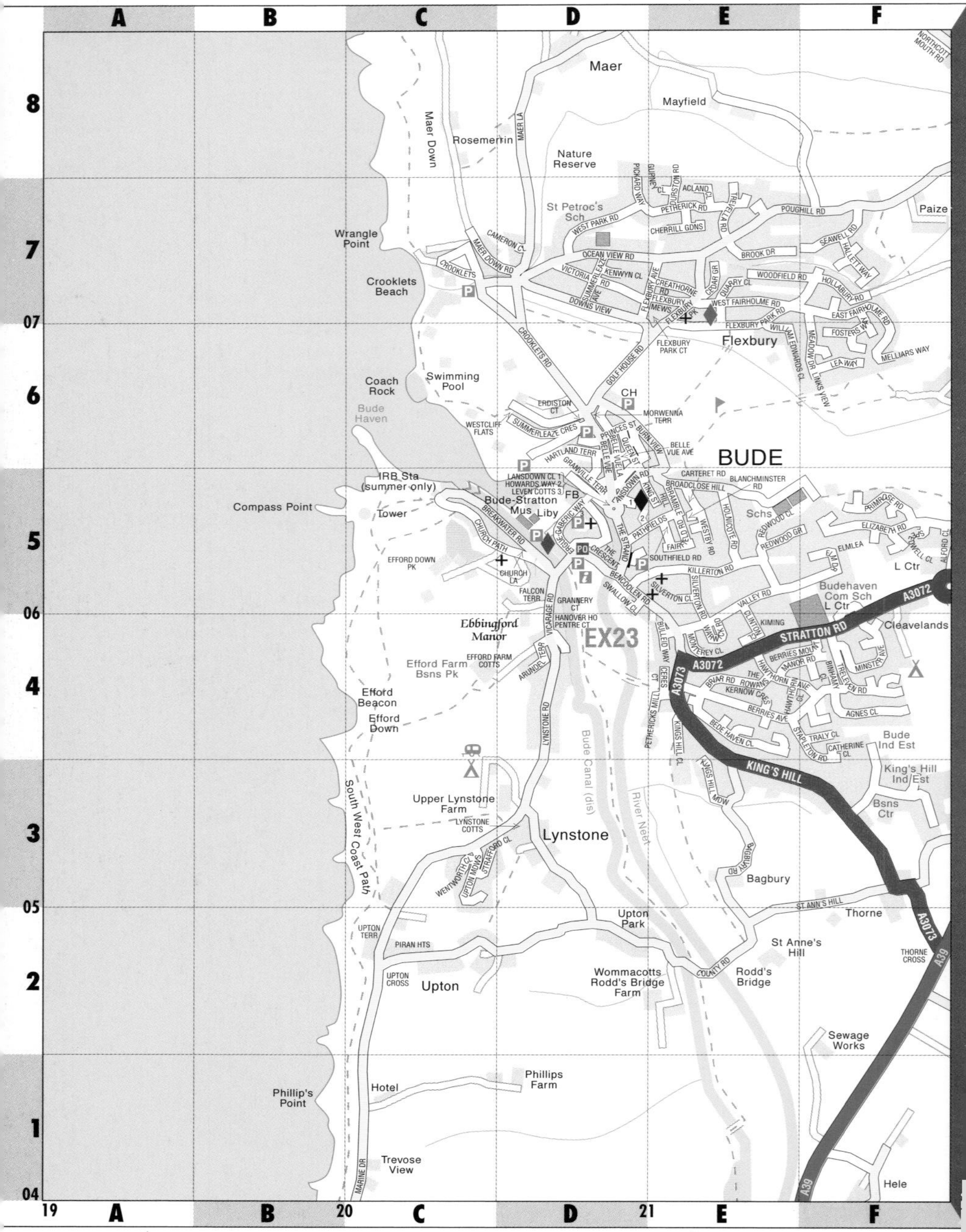

A B C D E F
8 7 07 6 5 06 4 3 05 2 1 04
19 20 21
Maer
Mayfield
Maer Down
Rosemerrin
MAER LA
Nature Reserve
St Petroc's Sch
PICKARD WAY
GURNEY CL
DURSTON RD
ACLAND CL
PETHERICK RD
TREVELLA RD
POUGHILL RD
Paize
WEST PARK RD
CHERRILL GDNS
SEAWELL RD
HALLETT WAY
CAMERON CL
MAER DOWN RD
OCEAN VIEW RD
BROOK DR
Wrangle Point
CROOKLETS
VICTORIA RD
SUMMERLEAZE AVE
KENWYN CL
FLEXBURY AVE
CREATHORNE RD
CEDAR GR
QUARRY CL
WOODFIELD RD
HOLLABURY RD
Crooklets Beach
DOWNS VIEW
FLEXBURY MEWS
FLEXBURY PK
WEST FAIRHOLME RD
EAST FAIRHOLME RD
FLEXBURY PARK RD
FOSTERS WAY
FLEXBURY PARK CT
Flexbury
WILLIAM EDWARDS CL
MEADOW DR
LINKS VIEW
LEA WAY
MELLIARS WAY
CROOKLETS RD
GOLF HOUSE RD
Coach Rock
Swimming Pool
CH
ERDISTON CT
MORWENNA TERR
Bude Haven
WESTCLIFF FLATS
SUMMERLEAZE CRES
PRINCES ST
BURN VIEW
BELLE VUE AVE
HARTLAND TERR
BELLE VUE
QUEEN ST
BUDE
GRANVILLE TERR
LANSDOWN CL 1
HOWARDS WAY 2
LEVEN COTTS 3
IRB Sta (summer only)
CARTERET RD
BLANCHMINSTER RD
LANSDOWN RD
KING ST
BROADCLOSE HILL
Compass Point
Tower
Bude-Stratton Mus
Liby
FB
BRAMBLE HILL
HOLNICOTE RD
WESTBY RD
Schs
REDWOOD CL
PRIMROSE RD
BREAKWATER RD
CHURCH PATH
GABERIC WAY
THE STRAND
PATHFIELDS
ELIZABETH RD
REDWOOD GR
ELMLEA
EFFORD DOWN PK
THE CRESCENT
SOUTHFIELD RD
ELM DR
L Ctr
CHURCH LA
BENCOOLEN RD
KILLERTON RD
Budehaven Com Sch
L Ctr
A3072
FALCON TERR
GRANNERY CT
SWALLOW CL
SILVERTON CL
SILVERTON RD
VALLEY RD
Ebbingford Manor
HANOVER HO
PENTRE CT
VICARAGE RD
EX23
KIMING
CLINTON RD
STRATTON RD
Cleavelands
Efford Farm Bsns Pk
EFFORD FARM COTTS
ARUNDEL TERR
BULLEID WAY
MONTEREY CL
BERRIES MOUNT
MANOR RD
BINHAMY CL
MINSTER AVE
CERES CT
A3073
BRIAR RD
ROWANS
THE HAWTHORN AVE
TRELEVEN RD
Efford Beacon
KERNOW CRES
Efford Down
LYNSTONE RD
Bude Canal (dis)
PETHERICKS MILL
KINGS HILL CL
BERRIES AVE
BEDE HAVEN CL
AGNES CL
STAPLETON RD
TRALY CL
CATHERINE CL
Bude Ind Est
KING'S HILL
King's Hill Ind Est
South West Coast Path
Upper Lynstone Farm
River Neet
KINGS HILL MDW
Bsns Ctr
LYNSTONE COTTS
STRAFFORD CL
Lynstone
WENTWORTH CL
UPTON MDWS
BAGBURY RD
Bagbury
ST ANN'S HILL
Thorne
A3073
UPTON TERR
Upton Park
PIRAN HTS
St Anne's Hill
THORNE CROSS
A39
COUNTY RD
UPTON CROSS
Upton
Wommacotts Rodd's Bridge Farm
Rodd's Bridge
Sewage Works
Phillips Farm
Hotel
Phillip's Point
Trevose View
MARINE DR
A39
Hele

6 6 7 7

14
15
15

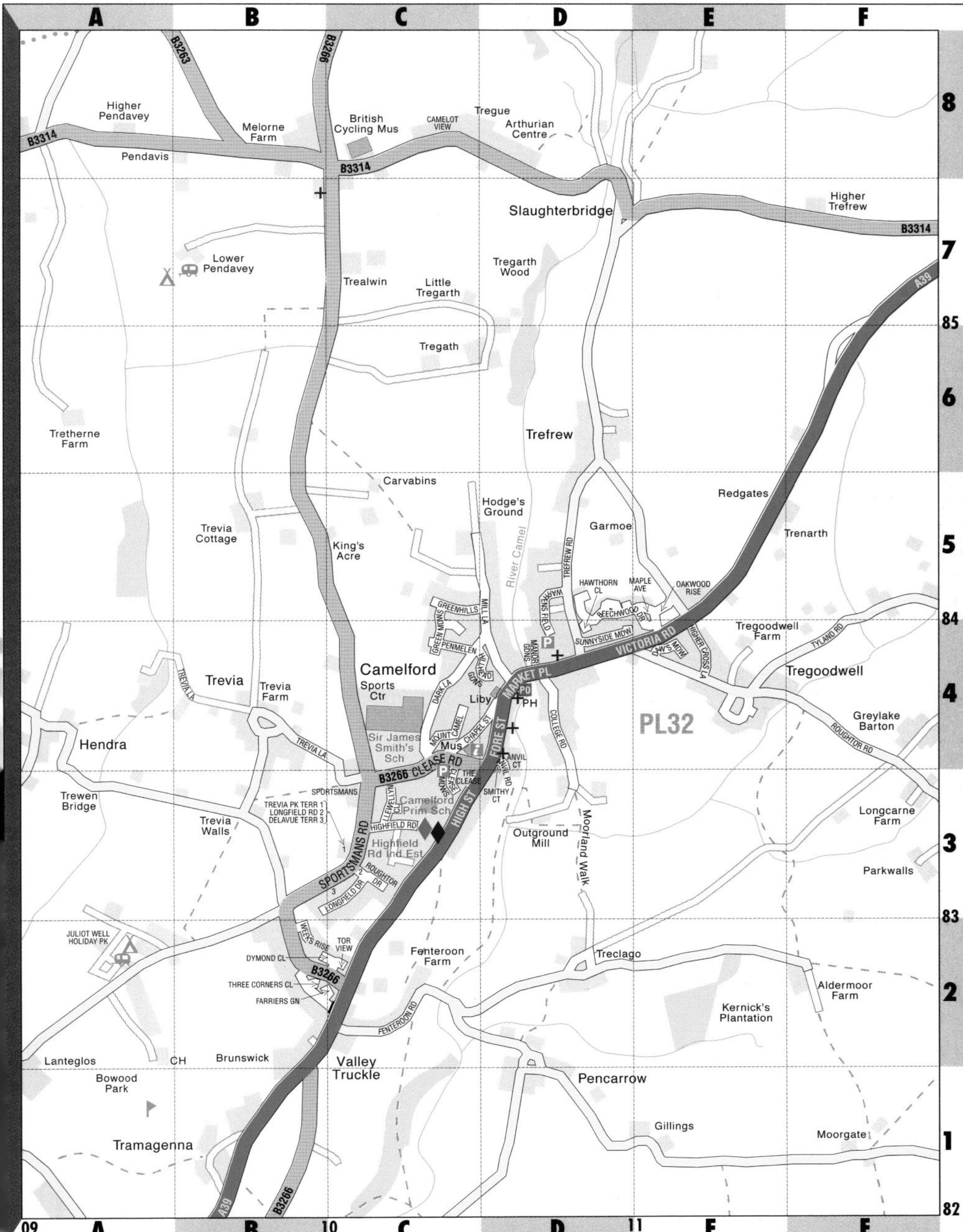

14
24
15

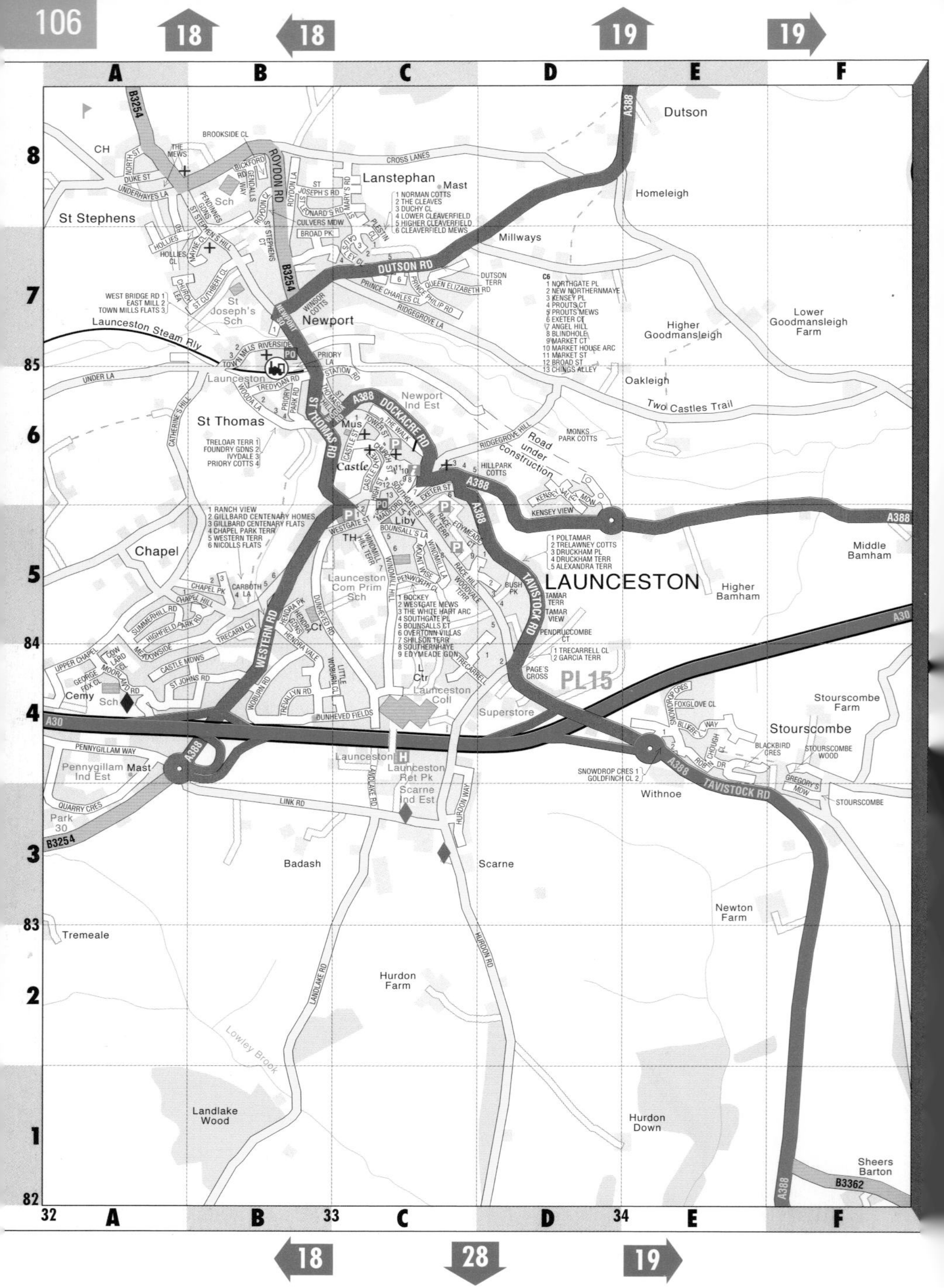

18
18
19
19
A
B
C
D
E
F
8
7
85
6
5
84
4
3
83
2
1
82
32
33
34
Dutson
A388
B3254
CH
BROOKSIDE CL
THE MEWS
NORTH ST
DUKE ST
UNDERHAYES LA
ROYDON RD
ROYDON LA
CROSS LANES
Lanstephan
Mast
Homeleigh
St Stephens
Sch
BICKFORD RD
GENDALLS WAY
PENDINNES GDNS
ST STEPHEN'S HILL
ST JOSEPH'S RD
ST LEONARD'S RD
CULVERS MDW
BROAD PK
1 NORMAN COTTS
2 THE CLEAVES
3 DUCHY CL
4 LOWER CLEAVERFIELD
5 HIGHER CLEAVERFIELD
6 CLEAVERFIELD MEWS
Millways
HOLLIES
HOLLIES CL
MAYNE CL
ST STEPHENS CT
DUTSON RD
QUEEN ELIZABETH RD
PRINCE PHILIP RD
PRINCE CHARLES CL
RIDGEGROVE LA
DUTSON TERR
C6
1 NORTHGATE PL
2 NEW NORTHERNMAYE
3 KENSEY PL
4 PROUTS CT
5 PROUTS MEWS
6 EXETER CT
7 ANGEL HILL
8 BLINDHOLE
9 MARKET CT
10 MARKET HOUSE ARC
11 MARKET ST
12 BROAD ST
13 CHINGS ALLEY
Higher Goodmansleigh
Lower Goodmansleigh Farm
WEST BRIDGE RD 1
EAST MILL 2
TOWN MILLS FLATS 3
CHURCH LEA
ST CUTHBERT CL
St Joseph's Sch
NEWPORT SQ
WINSOR COTTS
Newport
Launceston Steam Rly
TOWN MILLS
RIVERSIDE
PO
PRIORY LA
STATION RD
UNDER LA
Launceston
TREDYDAN RD
WOODA LA
PRIORY PARK RD
Oakleigh
Two Castles Trail
ST THOMAS RD
A388
DOCKACRE RD
Newport Ind Est
St Thomas
CATHERINE'S HILL
Mus
THE WALK
TOWER ST
CASTLE ST
Castle
CHURCH ST
RIDGEGROVE HILL
Road under construction
MONKS PARK COTTS
HILLPARK COTTS
TRELOAR TERR 1
FOUNDRY GDNS 2
IVYDALE 3
PRIORY COTTS 4
KENSEY VALE
MDW
KENSEY VIEW
EXETER ST
SOUTHGATE ST
MADFORD LA
WESTGATE ST
BOUNSALL'S LA
RACE HILL TERR
EDYMEADE CT
P
TH
Liby
A388
1 RANCH VIEW
2 GILLBARD CENTENARY HOMES
3 GILLBARD CENTENARY FLATS
4 CHAPEL PARK TERR
5 WESTERN TERR
6 NICOLLS FLATS
1 POLTAMAR
2 TRELAWNEY COTTS
3 DRUCKHAM PL
4 DRUCKHAM TERR
5 ALEXANDRA TERR
Middle Bamham
Chapel
WINDMILL HILL TERR
WINDMILL HILL
MOUNT WISE
WINDMILL LA
RACE HILL
WOODVALE TERR
BUSH PK
LAUNCESTON
Higher Bamham
CARBOTH LA
CHAPEL PK
CHAPEL HILL
Launceston Com Prim Sch
PENWORTH CL
TAMAR TERR
TAMAR VIEW
TAVISTOCK RD
A30
SUMMERHILL RD
HIGHFIELD PARK RD
TRECARN CL
MEADOWSIDE
WESTERN RD
HENDRA PK
HENDRA CL
DUNHEVED RD
Ct
1 BOCKEY
2 WESTGATE MEWS
3 THE WHITE HART ARC
4 SOUTHGATE PL
5 BOUNSALLS CT
6 OVERTONN VILLAS
7 SHILSON TERR
8 SOUTHERNHAYE
9 EDYMEADE GDN
PENDRUCCOMBE CT
1 TRECARRELL CL
2 GARCIA TERR
UPPER CHAPEL
COW LARD CL
GEORGE FOX CL
MOORLAND RD
CASTLE MDWS
ST JOHNS RD
HENDRA VALE
WOBURN CL
LITTLE WOBURN CL
L Ctr
TRECARRELL
PAGE'S CROSS
PL15
Cemy
Sch
WOBURN RD
TREVALYN RD
Launceston Coll
DUNHEVED FIELDS
Superstore
SNOWDROP CRES
FOXGLOVE CL
BLUEBELL WAY
CHOUGH CL
ROBIN DR
BLACKBIRD CRES
Stourscombe Farm
Stourscombe
STOURSCOMBE WOOD
A30
PENNYGILLAM WAY
Pennygillam Ind Est
Mast
Launceston
H
Launceston Ret Pk
Scarne Ind Est
SNOWDROP CRES 1
GOLDFINCH CL 2
Withnoe
TAVISTOCK RD
GREGORY'S MDW
STOURSCOMBE
QUARRY CRES
Park 30
B3254
LINK RD
LANDLAKE RD
HURDON WAY
Badash
Scarne
Tremeale
Newton Farm
HURDON RD
Hurdon Farm
LANDLAKE RD
Lowley Brook
Landlake Wood
Hurdon Down
Sheers Barton
B3362
A388
A
B
C
D
E
F
18
28
19

20 21 21

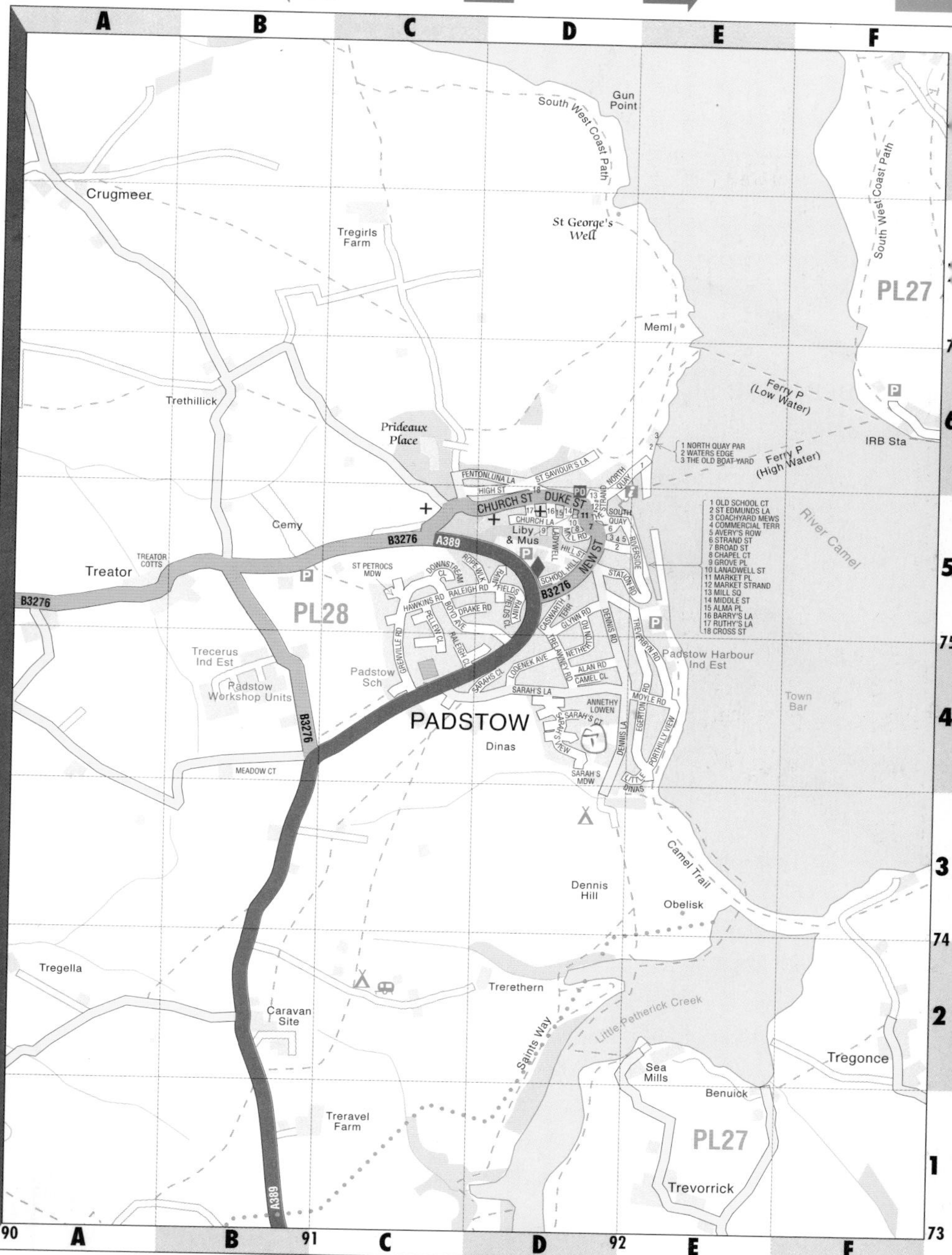

32 32 32

B5
1 COMMISSIONERS RD
2 EDDYSTONE TERR
3 EDDYSTONE PL
4 MOLESWORTH CT
5 CHAPEL LA
6 FOUNDRY ST
7 CLARENCE TERR
8 RIVERSDALE PL
9 POLMEAR CT
10 POLMORLA MEWS
11 BELMONT CT
12 BROOKDALE CT
13 ORCHARD WLK

33 22 34

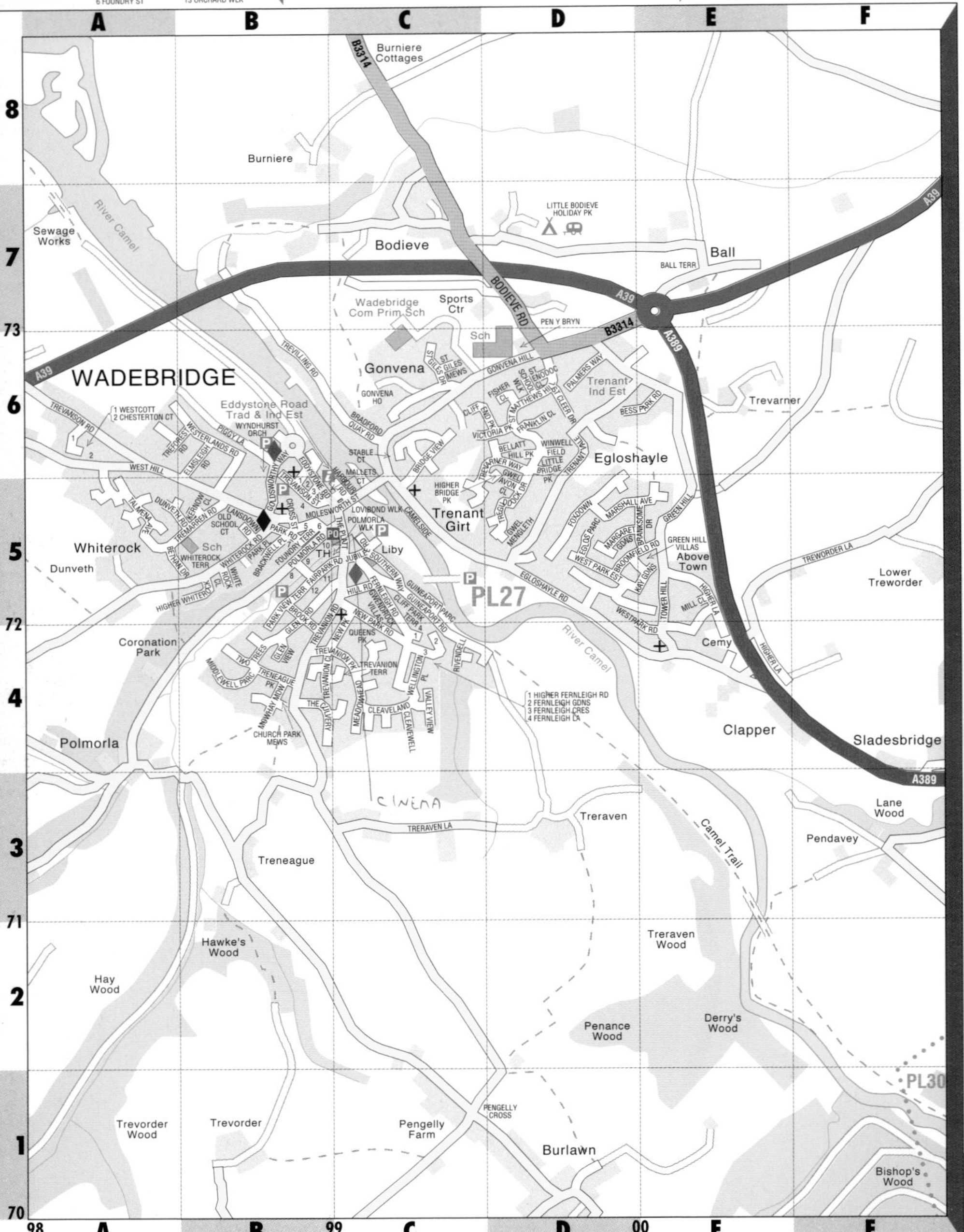

33 33 34

34 34 35 35

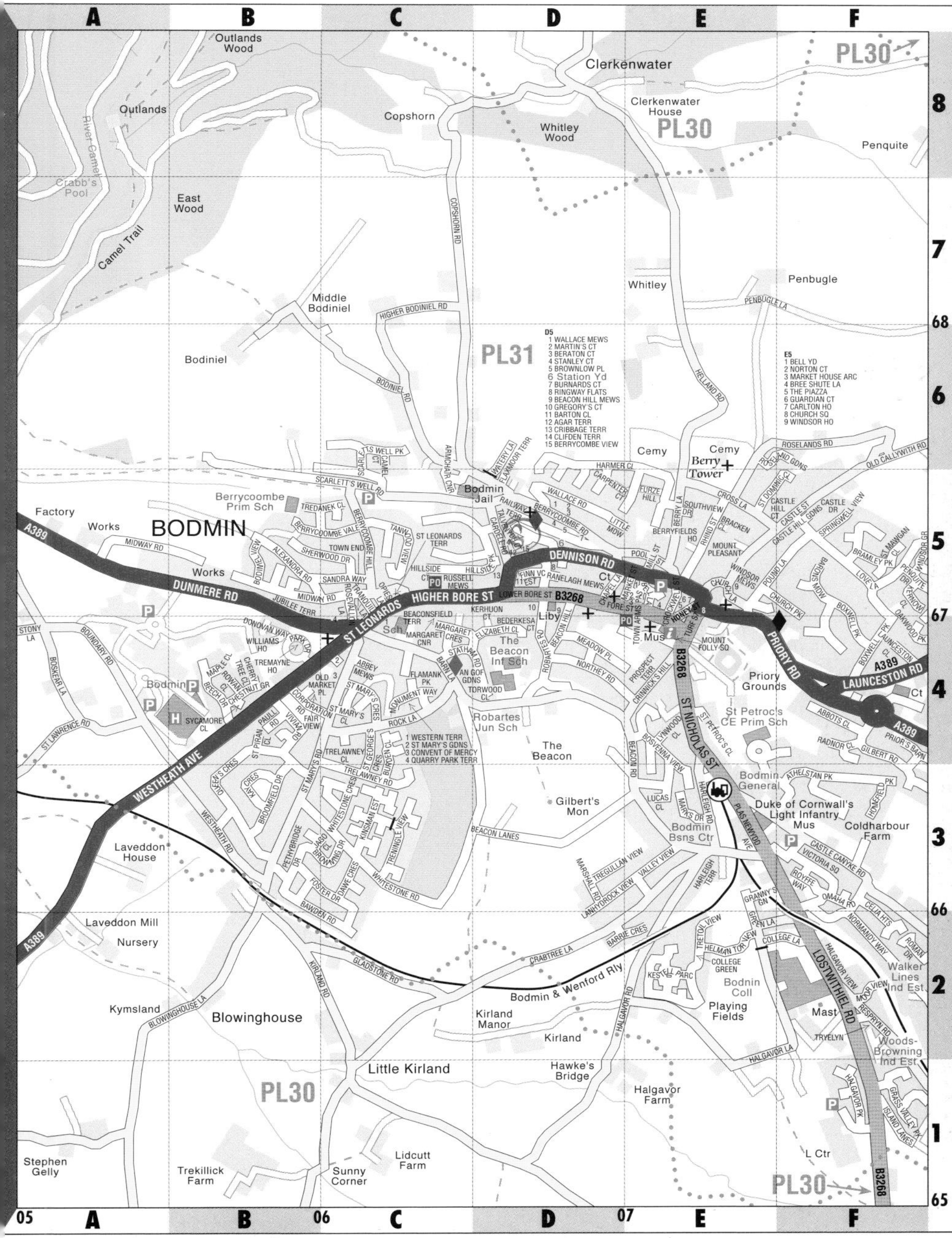

47 48 48

43 43 44

43 43 44

44
44

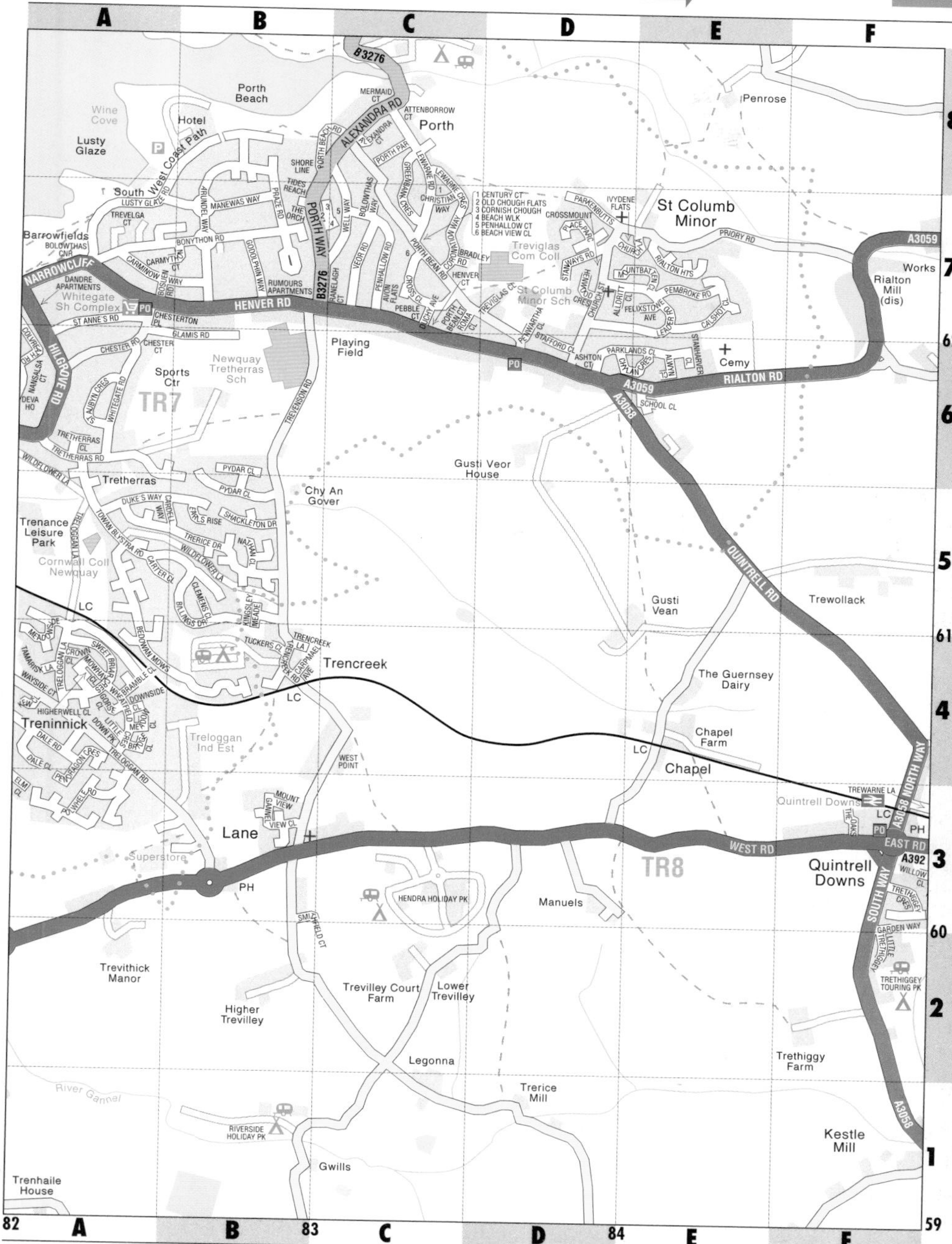
A
B
C
D
E
F
Porth Beach
Wine Cove
Lusty Glaze
Hotel
South West Coast Path
Barrowfields
Porth
Penrose
St Columb Minor
B3276
ALEXANDRA RD
MERMAID CT
ATTENBORROW CT
PORTH WAY
HENVER RD
NARROWCLIFF
HILGROVE RD
Whitegate Sh Complex
PO
ST ANNE'S RD
CHESTERTON PL
GLAMIS RD
CHESTER RD
Sports Ctr
Newquay Tretherras Sch
Playing Field
TR7
Treviglas Com Coll
St Columb Minor Sch
PRIORY RD
A3059
Works
Rialton Mill (dis)
RIALTON RD
Cemy
A3058
SCHOOL CL
1 CENTURY CT
2 OLD CHOUGH FLATS
3 CORNISH CHOUGH
4 BEACH WLK
5 PENHALLOW CT
6 BEACH VIEW CL
Tretherras
Trenance Leisure Park
Cornwall Coll Newquay
Gusti Veor House
Chy An Gover
QUINTRELL RD
Gusti Vean
Trewollack
Trencreek
The Guernsey Dairy
Chapel Farm
Chapel
LC
Treninnick
Treloggan Ind Est
WEST POINT
Lane
Superstore
PH
WEST RD
TR8
Quintrell Downs
NORTH WAY
SOUTH WAY
EAST RD
A392
TREWARNE LA
HENDRA HOLIDAY PK
Manuels
Trevithick Manor
Higher Trevilley
Trevilley Court Farm
Lower Trevilley
Legonna
Trerice Mill
Trethiggy Farm
TRETHIGGEY TOURING PK
Kestle Mill
River Gannel
RIVERSIDE HOLIDAY PK
Gwills
Trenhaile House
8
7
62
6
5
61
4
3
60
2
1
82
83
84
59

44
44

48 48 49 49

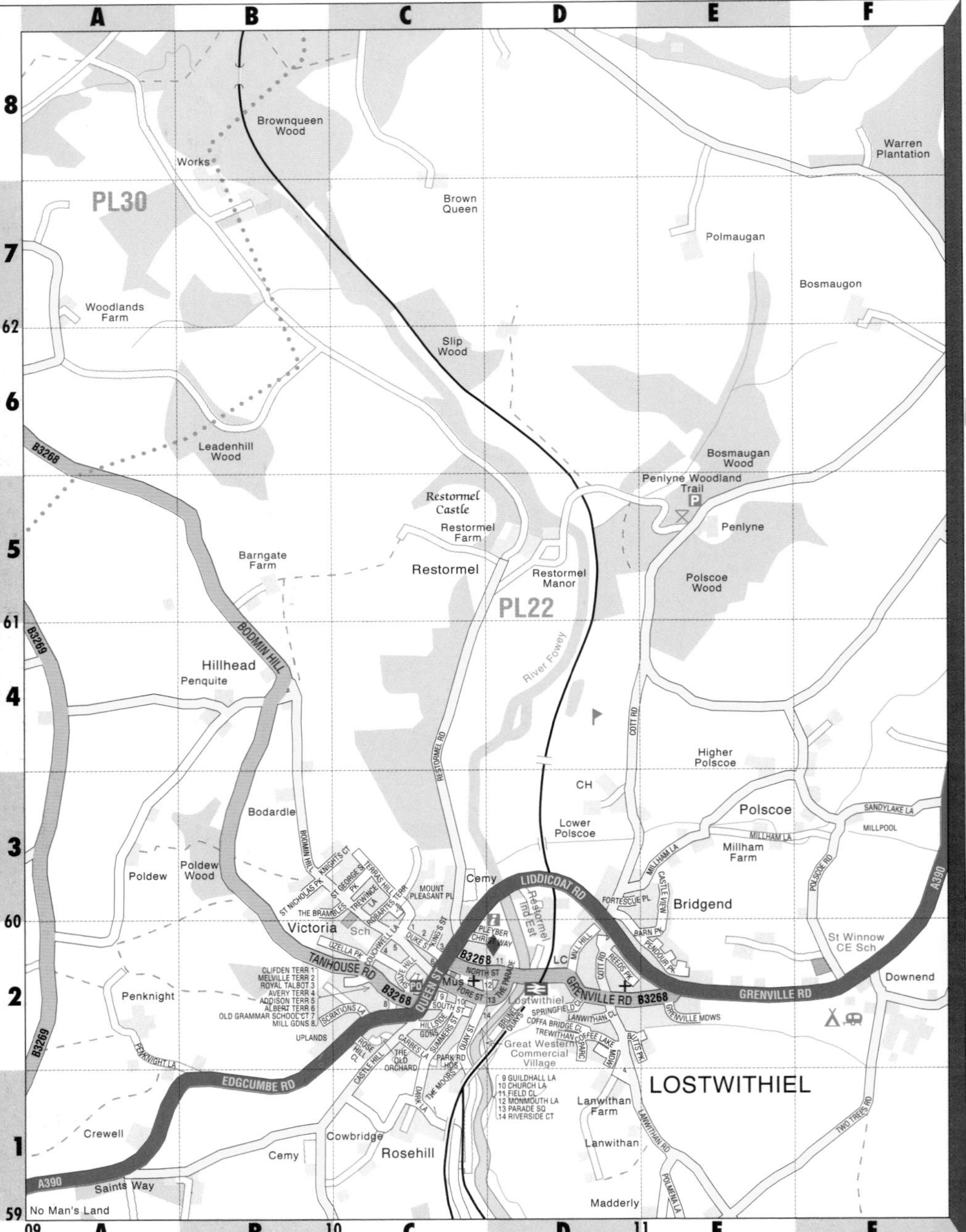
A
B
C
D
E
F
8
7
62
6
5
61
4
3
60
2
1
59
09
10
11
Brownqueen Wood
Works
PL30
Brown Queen
Polmaugan
Warren Plantation
Bosmaugon
Woodlands Farm
Slip Wood
Leadenhill Wood
B3268
Bosmaugan Wood
Penlyne Woodland Trail
Restormel Castle
Restormel Farm
Penlyne
Barngate Farm
Restormel
Restormel Manor
Polscoe Wood
PL22
B3269
BODMIN HILL
River Fowey
Hillhead
Penquite
COTT RD
RESTORMEL RD
Higher Polscoe
CH
Bodardle
Lower Polscoe
Polscoe
SANDYLAKE LA
MILLPOOL
MILLHAM LA
Millham Farm
Poldew
Poldew Wood
BODMIN HILL
KNIGHTS CT
ST GEORGE'S PK
TERRAS HILL
TREWINCE LA
ROBARTES TERR
MOUNT PLEASANT PL
Cemy
LIDDICOAT RD
Restormel Ind Est
FORTESCUE PL
CASTLE VIEW
Bridgend
POLSCOE RD
A390
ST NICHOLAS PK
THE BRAMBLES
Victoria
Sch
UZELLA PK
COUCHWELL LA
DUKE ST
KING'S ST
PLEYBER
CHRISTWAY
MILL HILL
COTT RD
REEDS PK
BARN PK
PENDOUR PK
St Winnow CE Sch
TANHOUSE RD
B3268
NORTH ST
THE PARADE
LC
Downend
CLIFDEN TERR 1
MELVILLE TERR 2
ROYAL TALBOT 3
AVERY TERR 4
ADDISON TERR 5
ALBERT TERR 6
OLD GRAMMAR SCHOOL CT 7
MILL GDNS 8
PO
QUEEN ST
Mus
FORE ST
Lostwithiel
GRENVILLE RD
B3268
GRENVILLE RD
Penknight
SCRATIONS LA
SOUTH ST
BRUNEL QUAYS
SPRINGFIELD
LANWITHAN CL
GRENVILLE MDWS
UPLANDS
HILLSIDE GDNS
SUMMERS ST
QUAY ST
COFFA BRIDGE CL
TREWITHAN PARC
COFFEE LAKE MDW
BUTTS PK
ROSE HILL CL
CASTLE HILL
CARBES LA
THE OLD ORCHARD
PARK RD HOS
Great Western Commercial Village
PENKNIGHT LA
EDGCUMBE RD
DARK LA
THE MOORS
9 GUILDHALL LA
10 CHURCH LA
11 FIELD CL
12 MONMOUTH LA
13 PARADE SQ
14 RIVERSIDE CT
Lanwithan Farm
LOSTWITHIEL
LANWITHAN RD
TWO TREES RD
Crewell
Cowbridge
Cemy
Rosehill
Lanwithan
A390
Saints Way
POLMENA LA
Madderly
No Man's Land

37 51 38 51

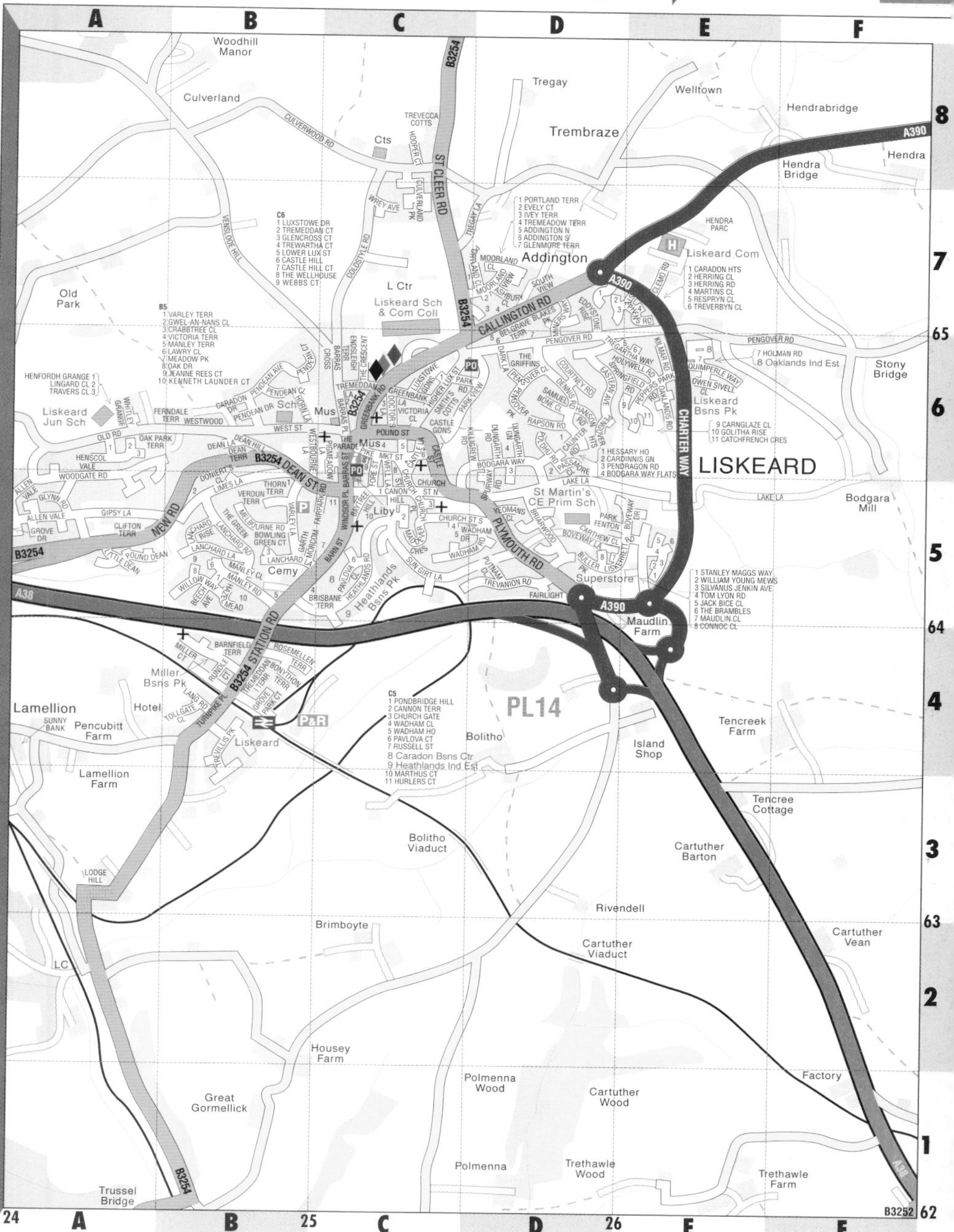

51 51 51

59 59

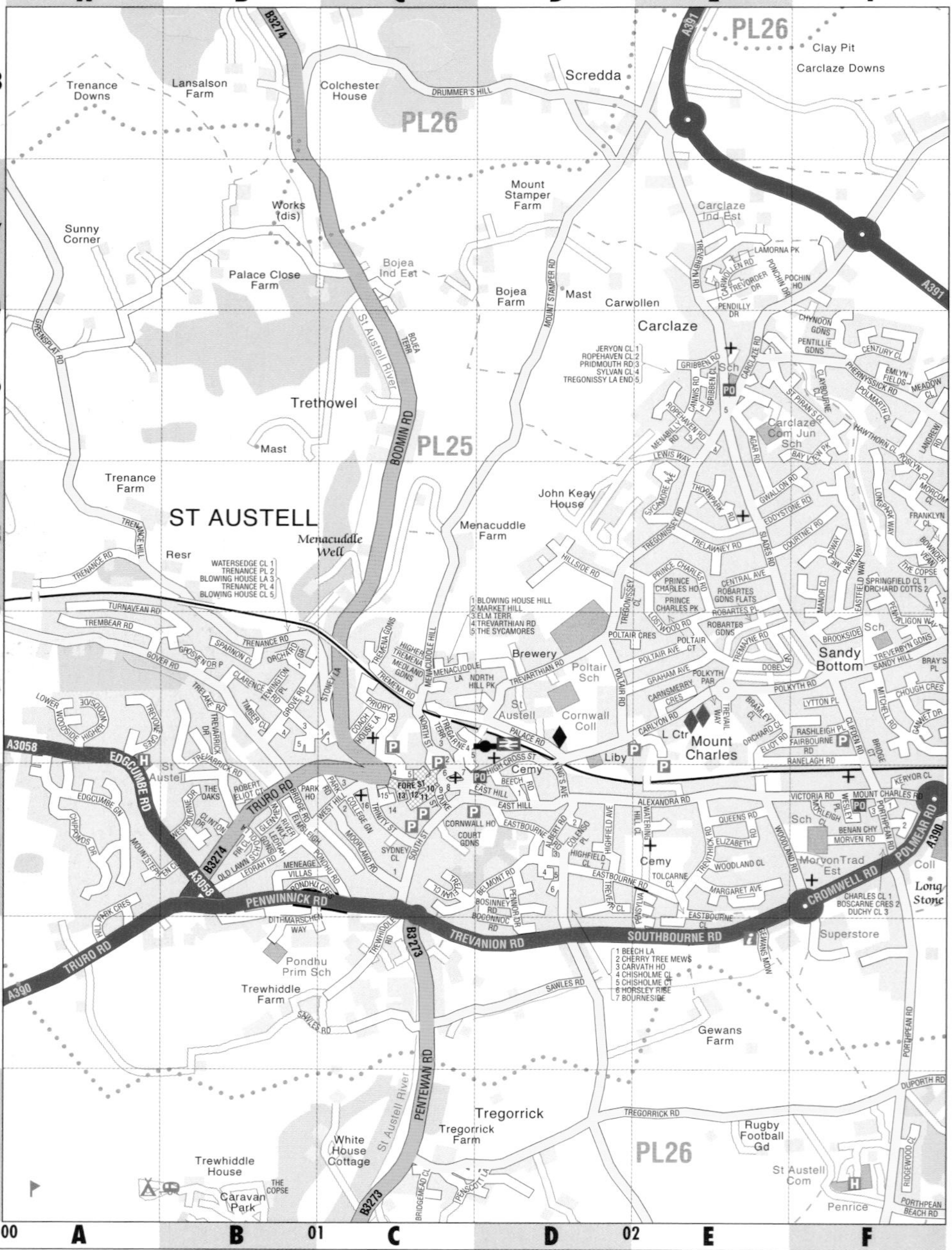

A B C D E F

C3
1 MOORLAND CT
2 GRENVILLE CT
3 SAVOY BLDG
4 GRANT'S WLK
5 BIDDICK'S CT
6 MARKET ST
7 CROSS LA
8 CHURCH ST
9 VICTORIA PL
10 VICARAGE HILL
11 OLD VICARAGE PL
12 CHANDOS PL
13 AYLMER PL
14 AYLMER SQ
15 BURTON HO
16 WEST HILL CT

59 59

59 60 60

A5
1 CARRICKOWEL CRES
2 ROSLYN CL
3 GLEN-DALE CL
4 COURTLANDS CRES

60 60

60
61
61

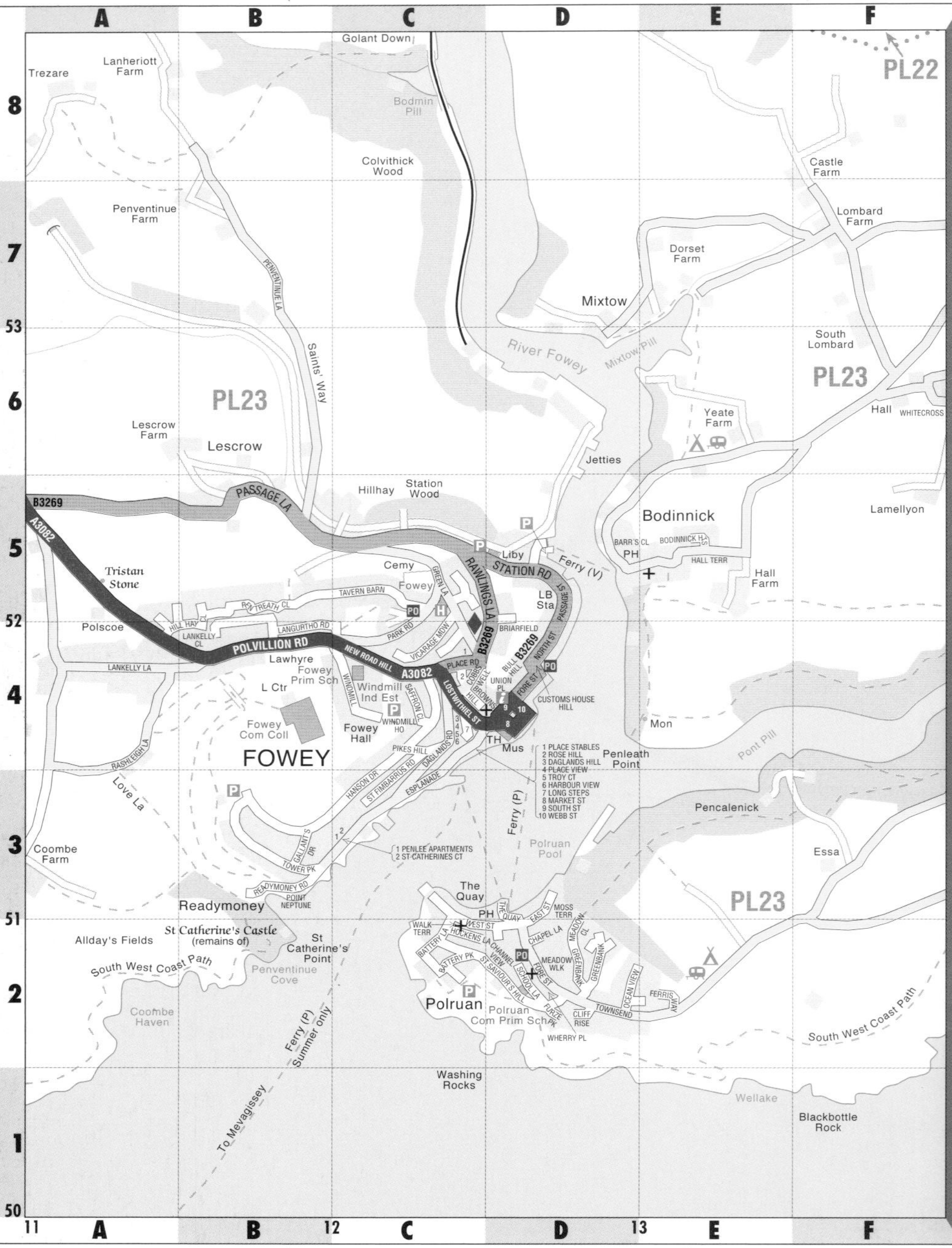
A
B
C
D
E
F
8
7
53
6
5
52
4
3
51
2
1
50
11
12
13
Golant Down
Trezare
Lanheriott Farm
Bodmin Pill
PL22
Colvithick Wood
Castle Farm
Penventinue Farm
Lombard Farm
Dorset Farm
PENVENTINUE LA
Mixtow
Saints' Way
River Fowey
Mixtow Pill
South Lombard
PL23
PL23
Yeate Farm
Hall
WHITECROSS
Lescrow Farm
Lescrow
Jetties
Hillhay
Station Wood
Bodinnick
Lamellyon
B3269
PASSAGE LA
A3082
BARR'S CL
BODINNICK H S
PH
HALL TERR
Liby
Ferry (V)
Hall Farm
Tristan Stone
Cemy
STATION RD
RAWLINGS LA
Fowey
TAVERN BARN
PEN TREATH CL
GREEN LA
LB Sta
PASSAGE ST
HILL HAY CL
PO
H
Polscoe
LANKELLY CL
LANGURTHO RD
PARK RD
BRIARFIELD
VICARAGE MDW
B3269
B3269
NORTH ST
POLVILLION RD
NEW ROAD HILL
PLACE RD
BULL HILL
PO
LANKELLY LA
Lawhyre
Fowey Prim Sch
A3082
COBBS WELL
UNION PL
FORE ST
L Ctr
WINDMILL
Windmill Ind Est
SAFFRON CL
LOSTWITHIEL ST
BROWNS HILL
CUSTOMS HOUSE HILL
WINDMILL HO
Mon
Fowey Com Coll
Fowey Hall
TH
Mus
1 PLACE STABLES
2 ROSE HILL
3 DAGLANDS HILL
4 PLACE VIEW
5 TROY CT
6 HARBOUR VIEW
7 LONG STEPS
8 MARKET ST
9 SOUTH ST
10 WEBB ST
Penleath Point
Pont Pill
RASHLEIGH LA
PIKES HILL
FOWEY
DAGLANDS RD
Love La
HANSON DR
ST FIMBARRUS RD
ESPLANADE
Ferry (P)
Pencalenick
Coombe Farm
GALLANT'S DR
1 PENLEE APARTMENTS
2 ST CATHERINES CT
Polruan Pool
Essa
TOWER PK
READYMONEY RD
The Quay
PL23
POINT NEPTUNE
Readymoney
PH
THE QUAY
EAST ST
MOSS TERR
WALK TERR
WEST ST
St Catherine's Castle (remains of)
Allday's Fields
St Catherine's Point
HOCKENS LA
CHAPEL LA
MEADOW CL
BATTERY LA
CHANNEL VIEW
PO
MEADOW WLK
GREENBANK
BATTERY PK
ST SAVIOUR'S HILL
SCHOOL LA
FORE ST
South West Coast Path
Penventinue Cove
OCEAN VIEW
FERRIS WAY
Polruan
Polruan Com Prim Sch
FURZE PK
CLIFF RISE
TOWNSEND
Coombe Haven
WHERRY PL
South West Coast Path
Ferry (P) Summer only
Washing Rocks
To Mevagissey
Wellake
Blackbottle Rock

60
61

63 63 63

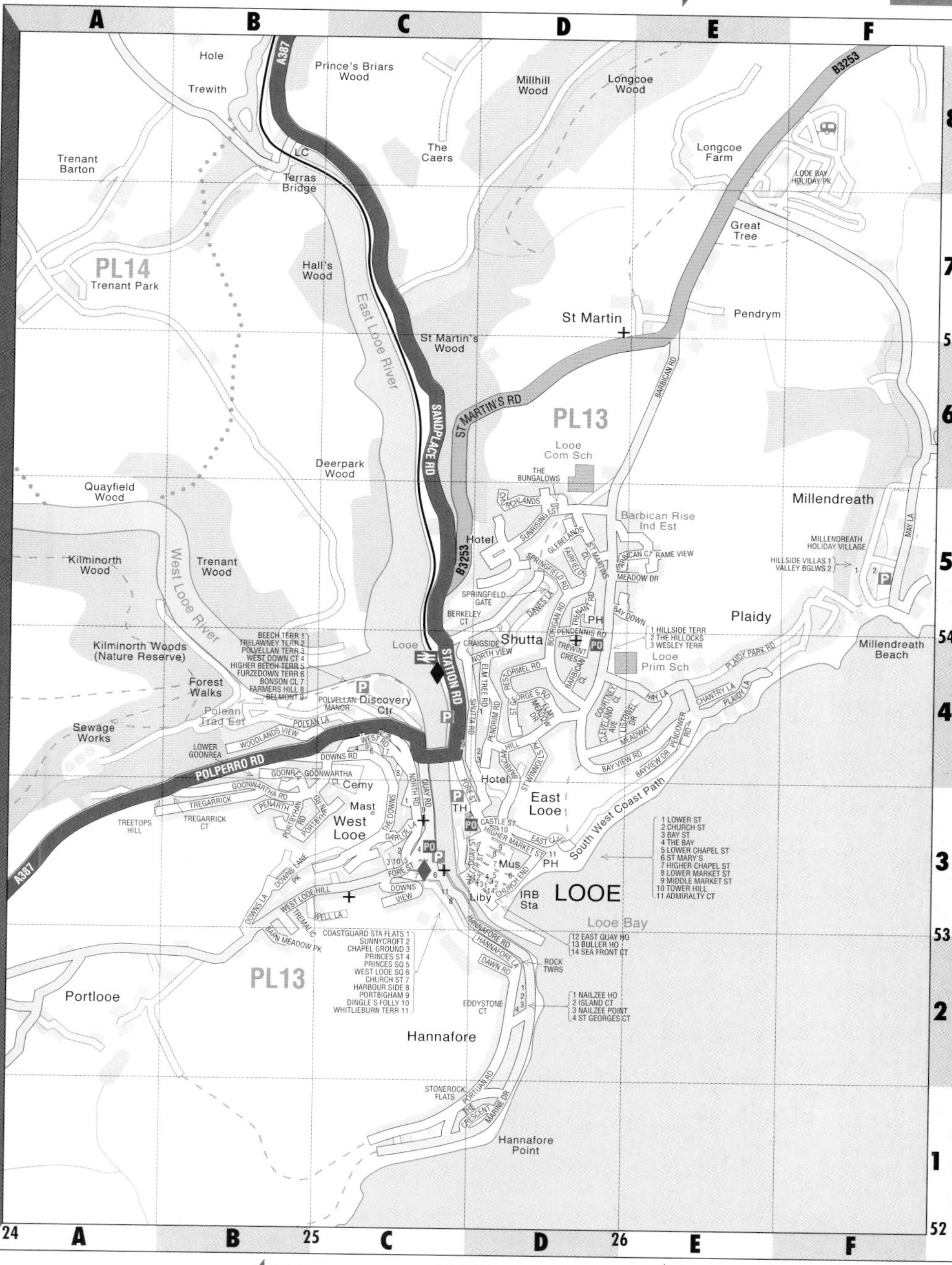

63 63 63

53
40

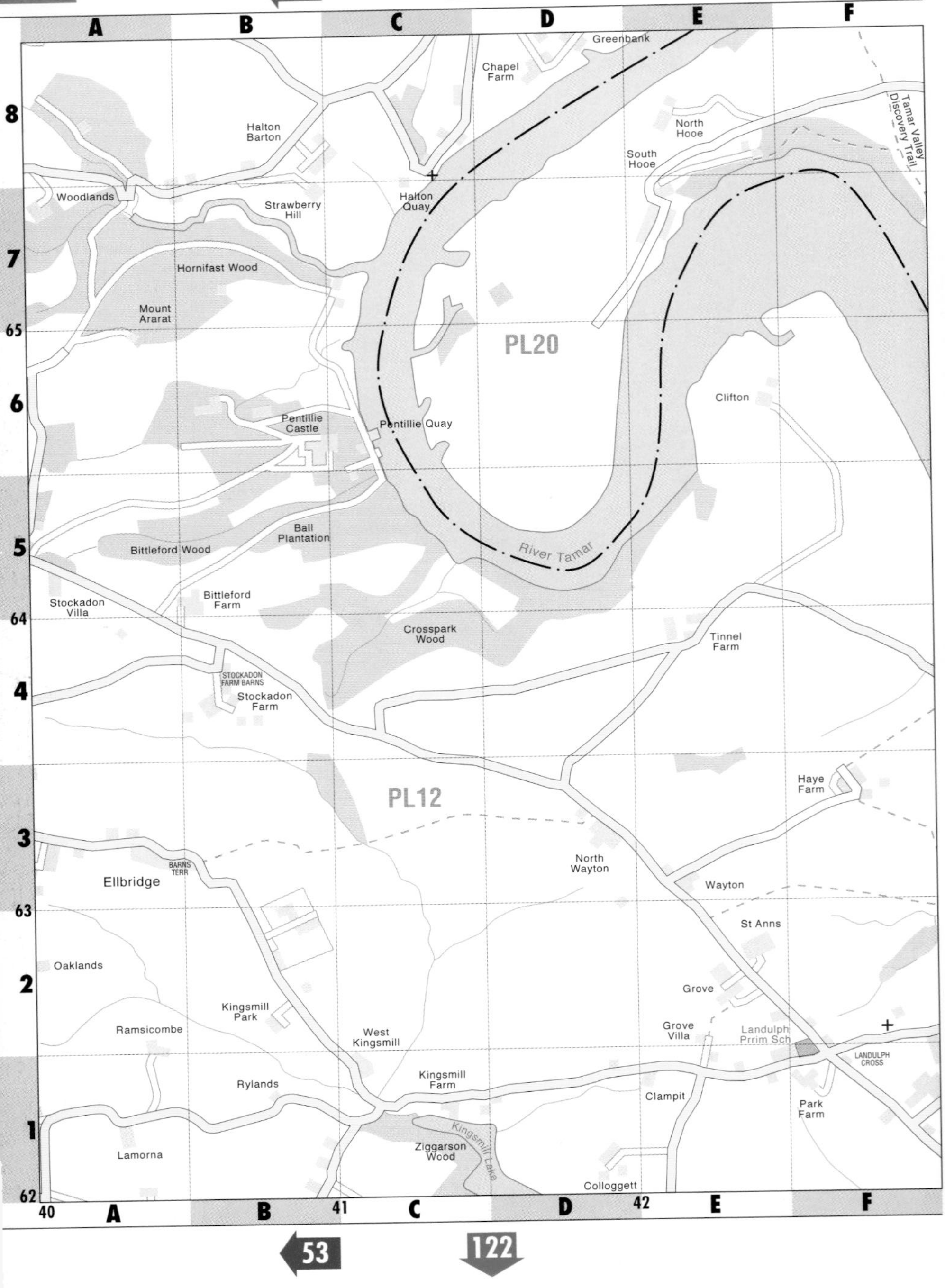
A
B
C
D
E
F
8
7
65
6
5
64
4
3
63
2
1
62
40
41
42
Greenbank
Chapel Farm
Halton Barton
North Hooe
South Hooe
Tamar Valley Discovery Trail
Woodlands
Strawberry Hill
Halton Quay
Hornifast Wood
Mount Ararat
PL20
Clifton
Pentillie Castle
Pentillie Quay
Ball Plantation
Bittleford Wood
River Tamar
Stockadon Villa
Bittleford Farm
Crosspark Wood
Tinnel Farm
STOCKADON FARM BARNS
Stockadon Farm
Haye Farm
PL12
BARNS TERR
North Wayton
Ellbridge
Wayton
St Anns
Oaklands
Grove
Kingsmill Park
Grove Villa
Landulph Prrim Sch
Ramsicombe
West Kingsmill
LANDULPH CROSS
Kingsmill Farm
Rylands
Clampit
Park Farm
Kingsmill Lake
Ziggarson Wood
Lamorna
Colloggett

53
122

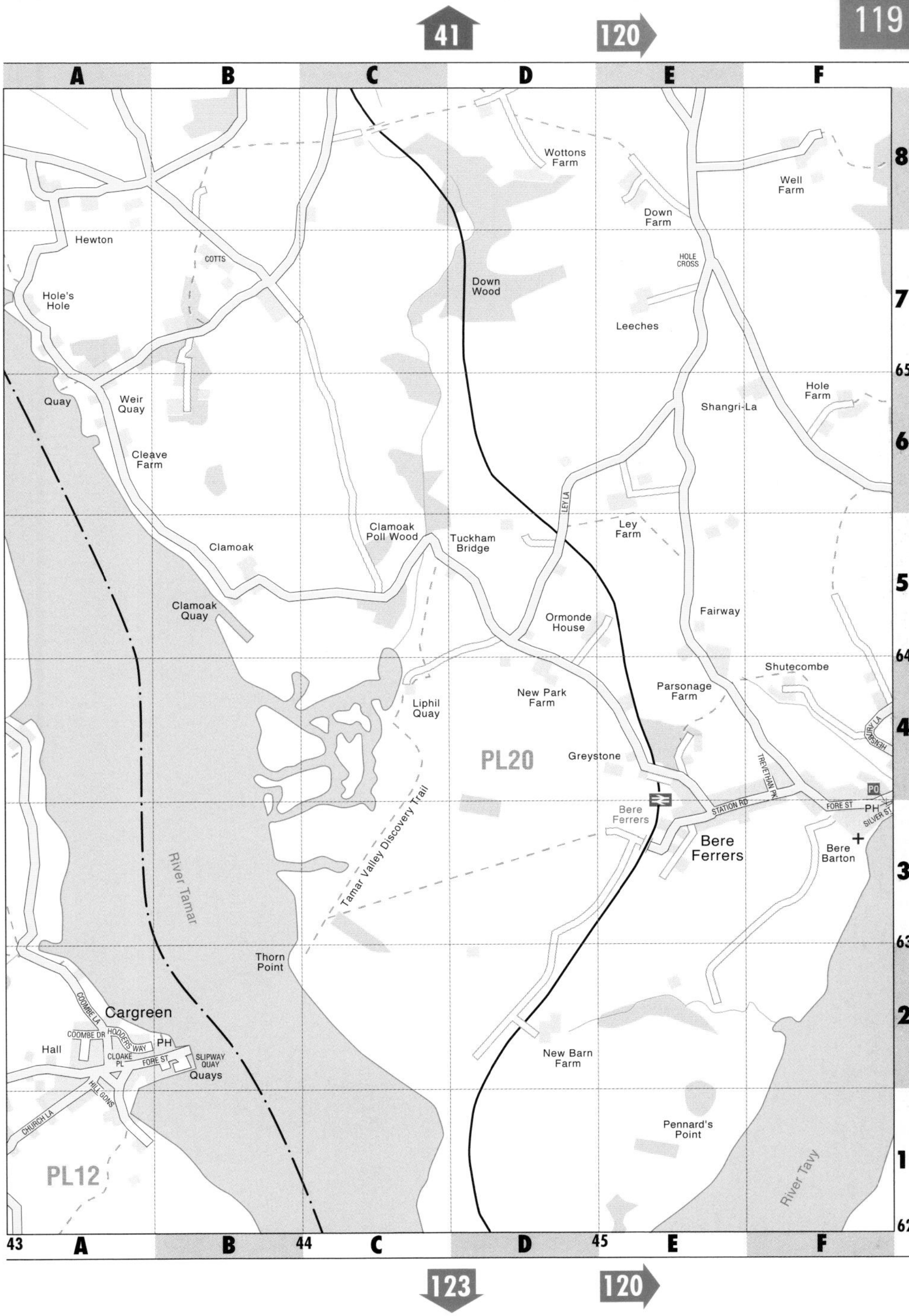
41
120
A
B
C
D
E
F
8
7
65
6
5
64
4
3
63
2
1
62
43
44
45
Wottons Farm
Well Farm
Down Farm
Hewton
COTTS
HOLE CROSS
Down Wood
Hole's Hole
Leeches
Quay
Weir Quay
Hole Farm
Shangri-La
Cleave Farm
LEY LA
Ley Farm
Clamoak Poll Wood
Tuckham Bridge
Clamoak
Fairway
Clamoak Quay
Ormonde House
Shutecombe
New Park Farm
Parsonage Farm
Liphil Quay
PL20
Greystone
HENSBURY LA
TREVETHAN PK
PO
Tamar Valley Discovery Trail
STATION RD
FORE ST
PH
SILVER ST
Bere Ferrers
Bere Ferrers
Bere Barton
River Tamar
Thorn Point
Cargreen
COOMBE LA
COOMBE DR
HOOPERS WAY
PH
Hall
CLOAKE PL
FORE ST
SLIPWAY QUAY
Quays
New Barn Farm
HILL GDNS
CHURCH LA
Pennard's Point
PL12
River Tavy
123
120

119
41

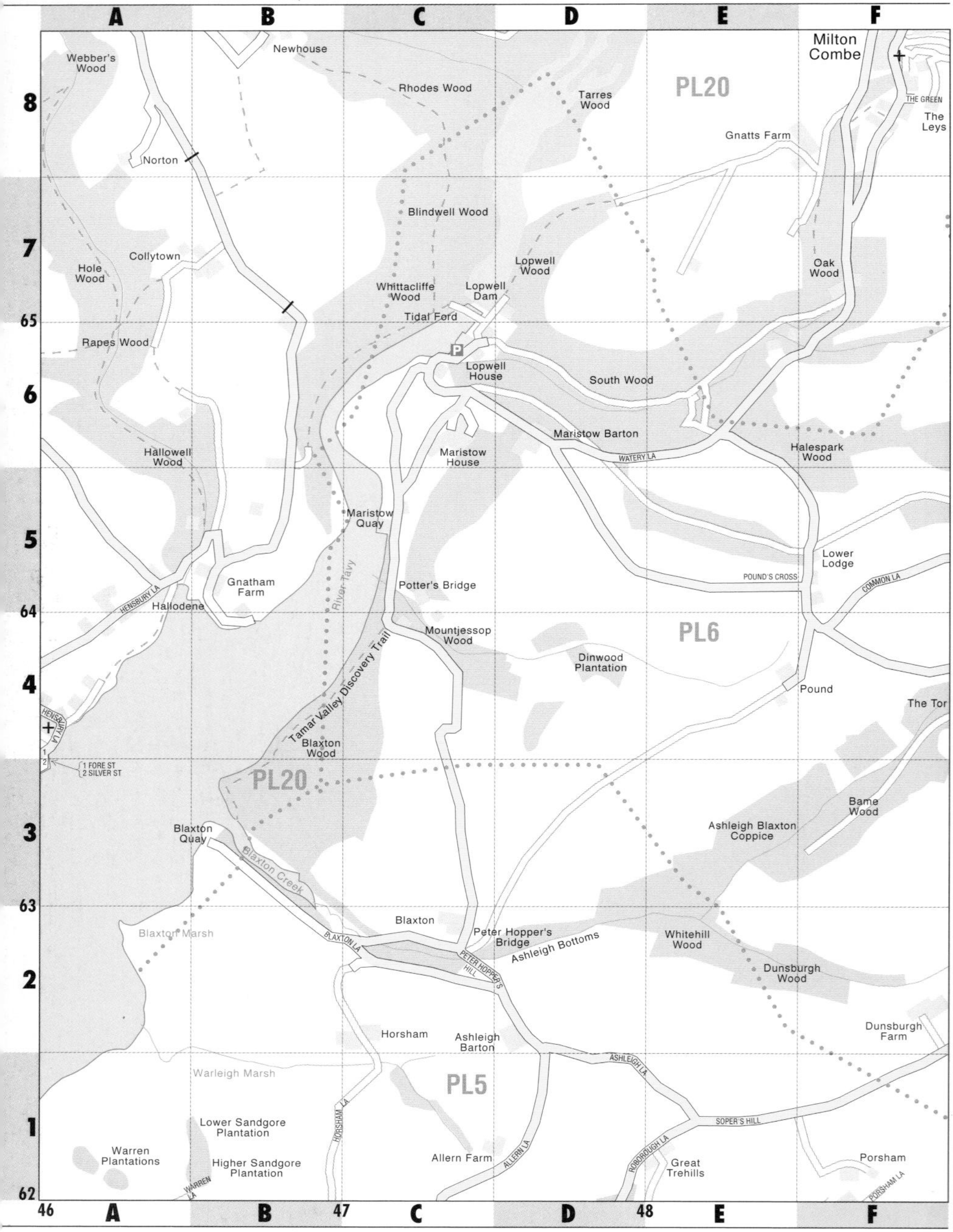

119
124

42

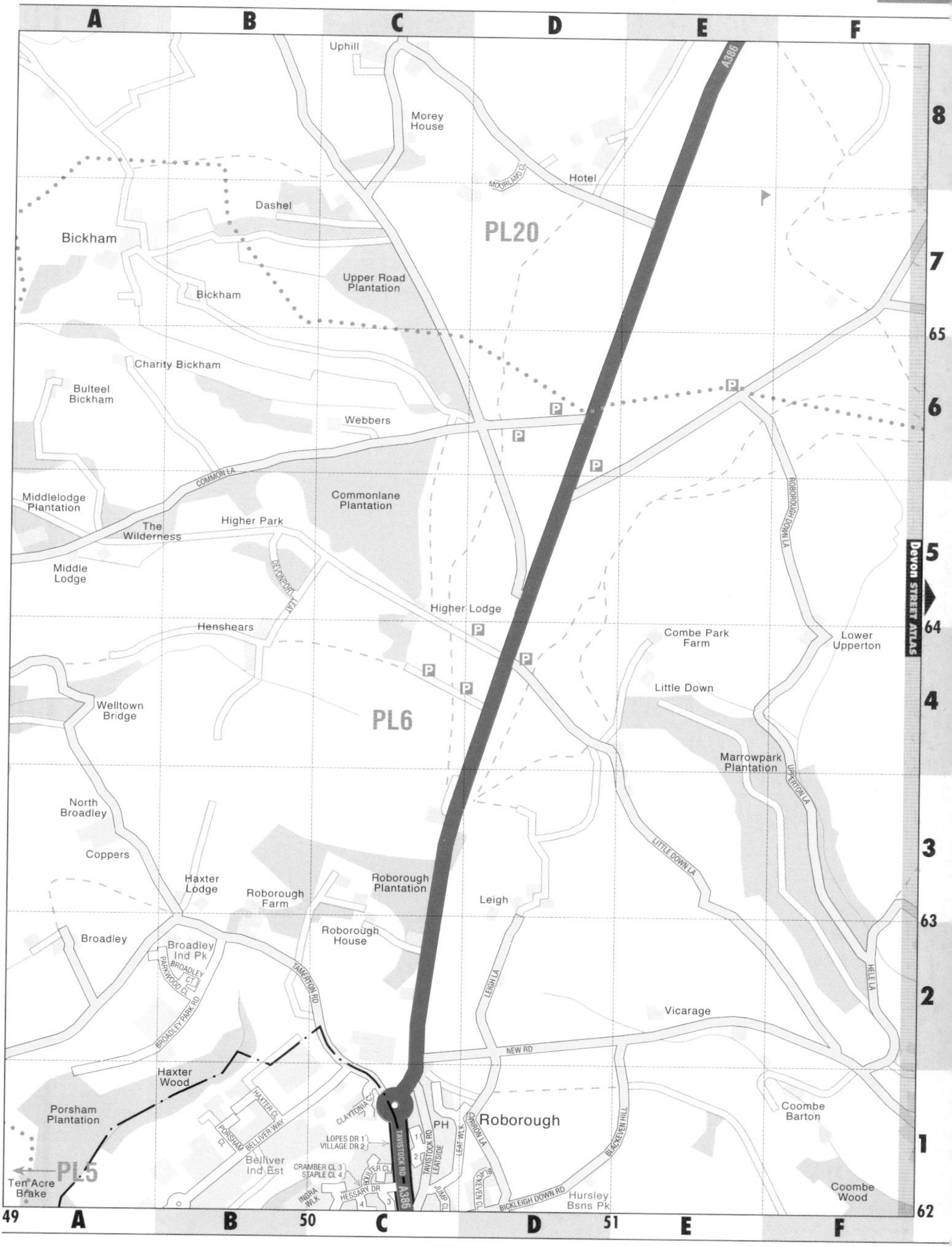
A
B
C
D
E
F
8
7
65
6
5
64
4
3
63
2
1
62
49
50
51
Devon STREET ATLAS
Uphill
Morey House
Hotel
MOORLAND CL
A386
Dashel
Bickham
PL20
Upper Road Plantation
Bickham
Charity Bickham
Bulteel Bickham
Webbers
COMMON LA
Middlelodge Plantation
Commonlane Plantation
The Wilderness
Higher Park
Middle Lodge
DEVONPORT LEAT
Higher Lodge
Henshears
Combe Park Farm
Lower Upperton
ROBOROUGH DOWN LA
Little Down
Welltown Bridge
PL6
Marrowpark Plantation
UPPERTON LA
North Broadley
LITTLE DOWN LA
Coppers
Haxter Lodge
Roborough Farm
Roborough Plantation
Leigh
Broadley
Broadley Ind Pk
BROADLEY CT
PARKWOOD CL
Roborough House
TAMERTON RD
LEIGH LA
HELE LA
BROADLEY PARK RD
Vicarage
NEW RD
Haxter Wood
Porsham Plantation
HAXTER CL
CLAYTONIA CL
PH
Roborough
Coombe Barton
PORSHAM CL
BELLIVER WAY
LOPES DR 1
VILLAGE DR 2
TAVISTOCK RD
LEATSIDE
LEAT WLK
CARRON LA
BLACKEVEN HILL
Belliver Ind Est
PL5
Ten Acre Brake
CRAMBER CL 3
STAPLE CL 4
BOULTER CL
HESSARY DR
INGRA WLK
JUMP CL
BICKLEIGH DOWN RD
Hursley Bsns Pk
Coombe Wood

125

53
118

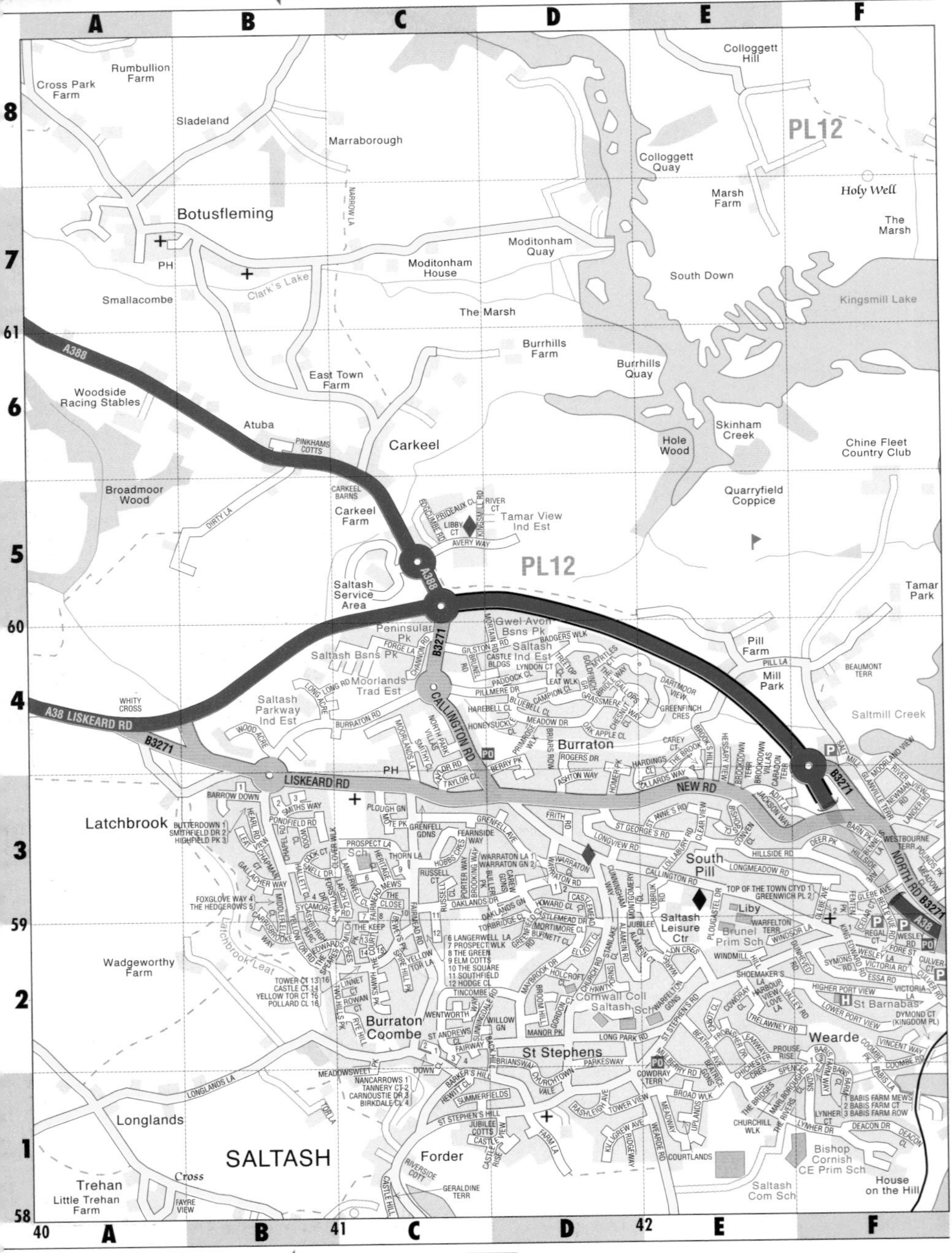
A
B
C
D
E
F
8
7
61
6
5
60
4
3
59
2
1
58
40
41
42
Rumbullion Farm
Cross Park Farm
Sladeland
Marraborough
Colloggett Hill
PL12
Colloggett Quay
Marsh Farm
Holy Well
The Marsh
Botusfleming
PH
Moditonham Quay
Moditonham House
Clark's Lake
Smallacombe
South Down
Kingsmill Lake
The Marsh
NARROW LA
Burrhills Farm
Burrhills Quay
A388
Woodside Racing Stables
East Town Farm
Atuba
PINKHAMS COTTS
Carkeel
Hole Wood
Skinham Creek
Chine Fleet Country Club
Broadmoor Wood
CARKEEL BARNS
Carkeel Farm
Quarryfield Coppice
DIRTY LA
Tamar View Ind Est
AVERY WAY
PL12
Saltash Service Area
Tamar Park
Peninsular Pk
Gwel Avon Bsns Pk
Saltash Ind Est
Saltash Bsns Pk
Moorlands Trad Est
Pill Farm
PILL LA
Mill Park
BEAUMONT TERR
WHITY CROSS
A38 LISKEARD RD
Saltash Parkway Ind Est
CALLINGTON RD
Burraton
Saltmill Creek
B3271
LISKEARD RD
NEW RD
PH
Latchbrook
South Pill
NORTH RD
B3271
Liby
Saltash Leisure Ctr
Brunel Prim Sch
A38
Latchbrook Leat
Wadgeworthy Farm
Cornwall Coll Saltash
Sch
St Barnabas
Burraton Coombe
St Stephens
Wearde
LONGLANDS LA
Longlands
Bishop Cornish CE Prim Sch
SALTASH
Forder
Cross
Trehan
Little Trehan Farm
Saltash Com Sch
House on the Hill

53
126

119
124

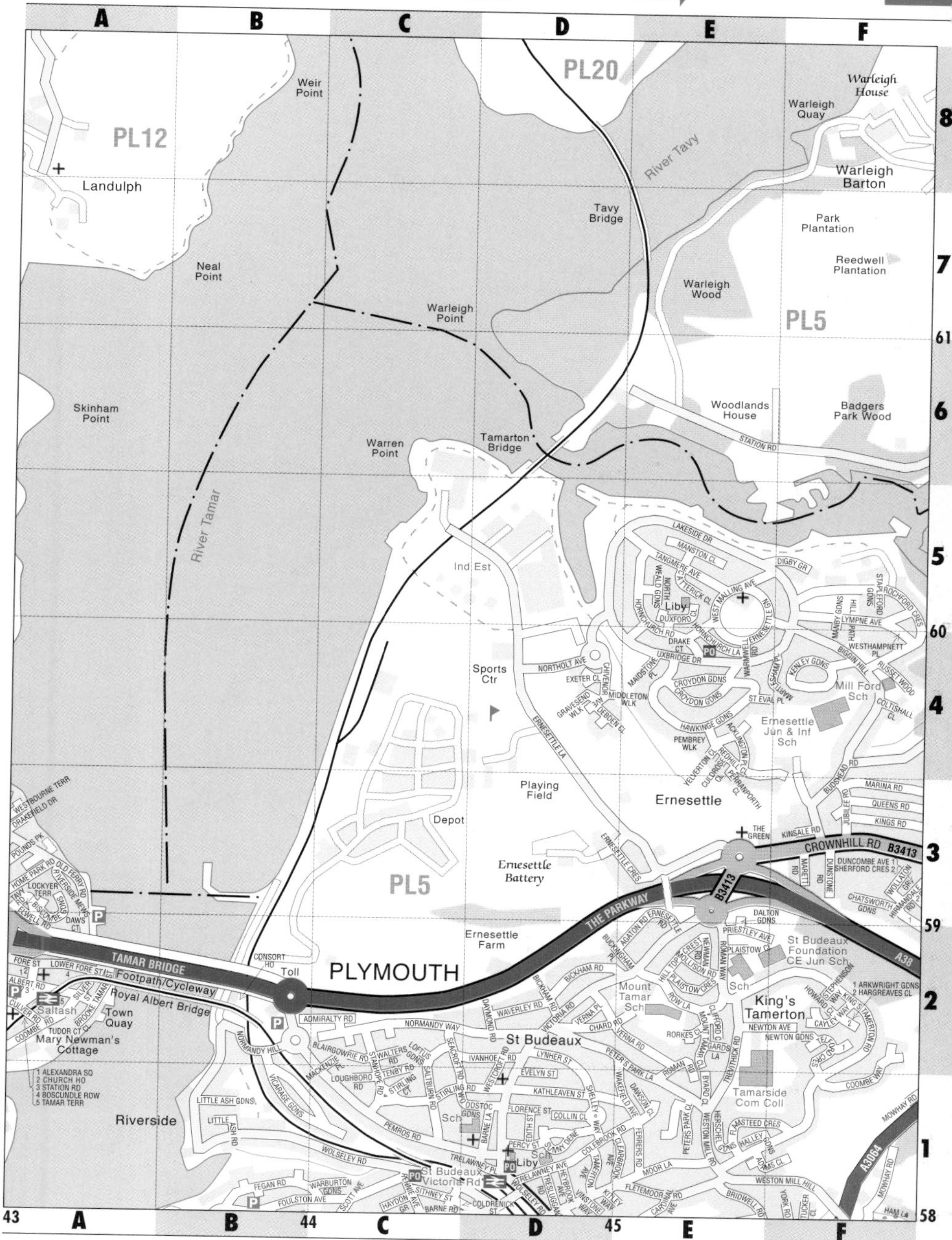

127
124

123
120

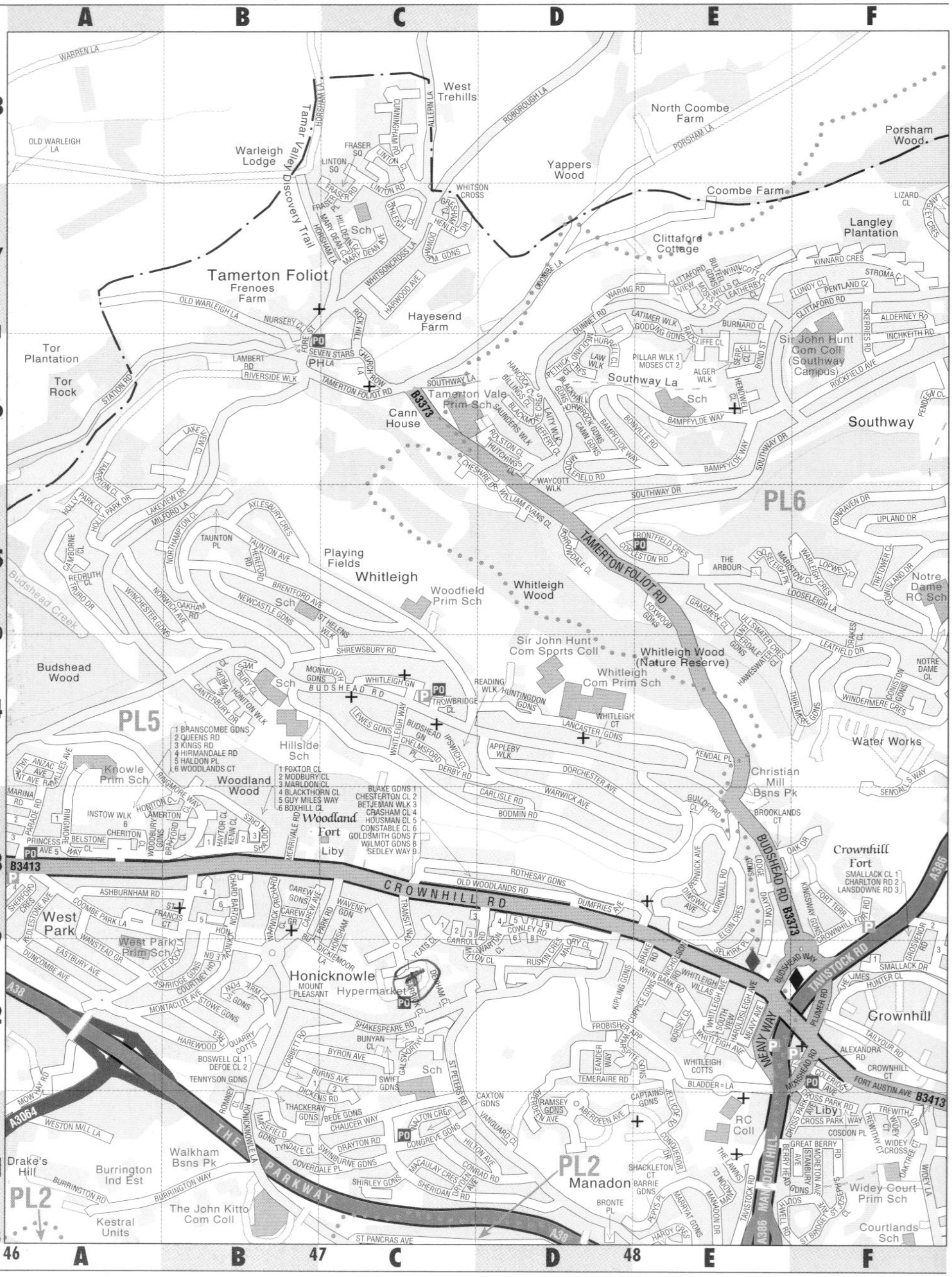
A
B
C
D
E
F
8
7
61
6
5
60
4
3
59
2
1
58
46
47
48
WARREN LA
OLD WARLEIGH LA
Warleigh Lodge
Tamar Valley Discovery Trail
HORSHAM LA
CUNNINGHAM RD
ALLERN LA
West Trehills
ROBOROUGH LA
North Coombe Farm
PORSHAM LA
Porsham Wood
Yappers Wood
WHITSON CROSS
Coombe Farm
LIZARD CL
Langley Plantation
Clittaford Cottage
KINNARD CRES
STROMA CL
PENTLAND CL
LUNDY CL
CLITTAFORD RD
ALDERNEY RD
INCHKEITH RD
Sir John Hunt Com Coll (Southway Campus)
ROCKFIELD AVE
Tamerton Foliot
Frenoes Farm
OLD WARLEIGH LA
NURSERY CL
WHITSONCROSS LA
HARWOOD AVE
Hayesend Farm
COOMBE LA
WARING RD
DUNNET RD
LATIMER WLK
GODDING GDNS
RATCLIFFE CL
BURNARD CL
BOND ST
Tor Plantation
Tor Rock
STATION RD
LAMBERT RD
RIVERSIDE WLK
SEVEN STARS LA
PH
CHURCH ROW LA
TAMERTON FOLIOT RD
SOUTHWAY LA
B3373
Tamerton Vale Prim Sch
Cann House
Southway La
Sch
PILLAR WLK
MOSES CT
ALGER WLK
BAMPFYLDE WAY
Southway
PENDEEN CL
LAKE VIEW CL
HOLLY PARK CL
HOLLY PARK DR
LAKEVIEW DR
MILFORD LA
CHESHIRE DR
WILLIAM EVANS CL
WAYCOTT WLK
MAYFIELD RD
SOUTHWAY DR
PL6
DUNRAVEN DR
UPLAND DR
AYLESBURY CRES
NORTHAMPTON CL
TAUNTON PL
TAUNTON AVE
Playing Fields
Whitleigh
TAMERTON FOLIOT RD
FRONTFIELD CRES
COLLESTON RD
THE ARBOUR
LOPWELL CL
TRETOWER CL
Notre Dame RC Sch
Budshead Creek
CAMBORNE CL
REDRUTH CL
TRURO DR
WINCHESTER GDNS
NORWICH AVE
OAKHAM RD
HEREFORD RD
BRENTFORD AVE
NEWCASTLE GDNS
Sch
ST HELENS WLK
Woodfield Prim Sch
Whitleigh Wood
FOXWOOD GDNS
GRASMERE CL
ULLSWATER CRES
LOOSELEIGH LA
LEATFIELD DR
NOTRE DAME CL
SHREWSBURY RD
Budshead Wood
Sir John Hunt Com Sports Coll
Whitleigh Wood (Nature Reserve)
Whitleigh Com Prim Sch
HAWESWATER CL
CONISTON GDNS
WINDERMERE CRES
MONMOUTH GDNS
WHITLEIGH GN
BUDSHEAD RD
PO
TROWBRIDGE CL
READING WLK
HUNTINGDON GDNS
CANTERBURY DR
HONITON WLK
PL5
LEWES GDNS
WHITLEIGH WAY
BUDSHEAD GN
IPSWICH CL
WHITLEIGH CT
LANCASTER GDNS
THIRLMERE GDNS
Water Works
1 BRANSCOMBE GDNS
2 QUEENS RD
3 KINGS RD
4 HIRMANDALE RD
5 HALDON PL
6 WOODLANDS CT
Hillside Sch
CHELMSFORD PL
APPLEBY WLK
DERBY RD
DORCHESTER AVE
KENDAL PL
Christian Mill Bsns Pk
SENDALLS WAY
ANZAC AVE
Knowle Prim Sch
1 FOXTOR CL
2 MODBURY CL
3 MARLDON CL
4 BLACKTHORN CL
5 GUY MILES WAY
6 BOXHILL CL
Woodland Wood
CARLISLE RD
WARWICK AVE
GUILDFORD CL
MARINA RD
PARADE RD
RINGMORE WAY
INSTOW WLK
HONITON CL
LAMERTON CL
BLAKE GDNS 1
CHESTERTON CL 2
BETJEMAN WLK 3
CRASHAM CL 4
HOUSMAN CL 5
CONSTABLE CL 6
GOLDSMITH GDNS 7
WILMOT GDNS 8
SEDLEY WAY 9
Woodland Fort
BODMIN RD
BROOKLANDS CT
BUDSHEAD RD
Crownhill Fort
PRINCESS AVE
BELSTONE CL
CHERITON CL
MERRIVALE RD
Liby
B3413
ROTHESAY GDNS
OLD WOODLANDS RD
CROWNHILL RD
DUMFRIES AVE
BERWICK AVE
KIRKWALL RD
SMALLACK CL 1
CHARLTON RD 2
LANSDOWNE RD 3
A386
ASHBURNHAM RD
CHARD BARTON
CAREW GDNS
CAREW AVE
WAVENEY GDN
TRANSIT WAY
DINGWALL AVE
ELGIN CRES
B3373
KINGSWAY GDNS
FORT TERR
CROWNHILL FORT RD
West Park
COOMBE PARK LA
ST FRANCIS CT
HORSHAM LA
CARROLL RD
COWLEY RD
SELKIRK PL
BUDSHEAD WAY
TAVISTOCK RD
GROSVENOR RD
West Park Prim Sch
WANSTEAD GR
EASTBURY AVE
DUNCOMBE AVE
LITTLE DOCK LA
DICKIEMOOR LA
YEATS CL
RUSKIN CRES
BRAKE RD
WHIN BANK RD
WHITLEIGH VILLAS
SMALLACK DR
HUNTER CL
Honicknowle
MOUNT PLEASANT
Hypermarket
KIPLING GDNS
COPPICE GDNS
HAROLDSLEIGH AVE
MEAVY AVE
PLUMER RD
A38
ASHRIDGE GDNS
COURTNEY RD
STOWE GDNS
MONTACUTE AVE
SHAKESPEARE RD
Crownhill
FROBISHER APP
MEAVY WAY
TAILYOUR RD
HAREWOOD CRES
QUARRY COTTS
BUNYAN CL
GALSWORTHY CL
BYRON AVE
LEANDER WAY
WHITLEIGH AVE
ALEXANDRA RD
BOSWELL CL 1
DEFOE CL 2
TENNYSON GDNS
BURNS AVE
Sch
TEMERAIRE RD
WHITLEIGH COTTS
BLADDER LA
CROWNHILL CT
MORSHEAD RD
COLERIDGE AVE
FORT AUSTIN AVE
B3413
MOWHAY RD
DICKENS RD
SWIFT GDNS
CAXTON GDNS
RAMSEY GDNS
ABERDEEN AVE
CAPTAINS GDNS
CROSS PARK RD
Liby
TREWITHY CL
CROSS PARK WAY
COSDON PL
A3064
WESTON MILL LA
THACKERAY GDNS
BEDE GDNS
CHAUCER WAY
NALTON CRES
CONGREVE GDNS
VANGUARD CL
RC Coll
WIDEY CROSS
TREMATON CT
MASEFIELD GDNS
TYNDALE CL
DRAYTON RD
HILTON AVE
CONQUEROR DR
THE LAWNS
GREAT BERRY RD
MORTON AVE
STANBURY AVE
Drake's Hill
Walkham Bsns Pk
Burrington Ind Est
THE PARKWAY
COVERDALE PL
SWINBURNE GDNS
MACAULAY CRES
CONRAD RD
PL2
Manadon
SHACKLETON CT
BARRIE GDNS
MANADON HILL
BERRY HEAD GDNS
OAKTREE CT
WIDEY LA
BURRINGTON RD
BURRINGTON WAY
SHIRLEY GDNS
SHERIDAN RD
DRYDEN AVE
BRONTE PL
PEPYS PL
MARRYAT GDNS
MANADON DR
TAVISTOCK RD
Widey Court Prim Sch
PL2
Kestral Units
The John Kitto Com Coll
A38
ST PANCRAS AVE
HARDY CRES
A386
ST BRIDGET AVE
Courtlands Sch

121

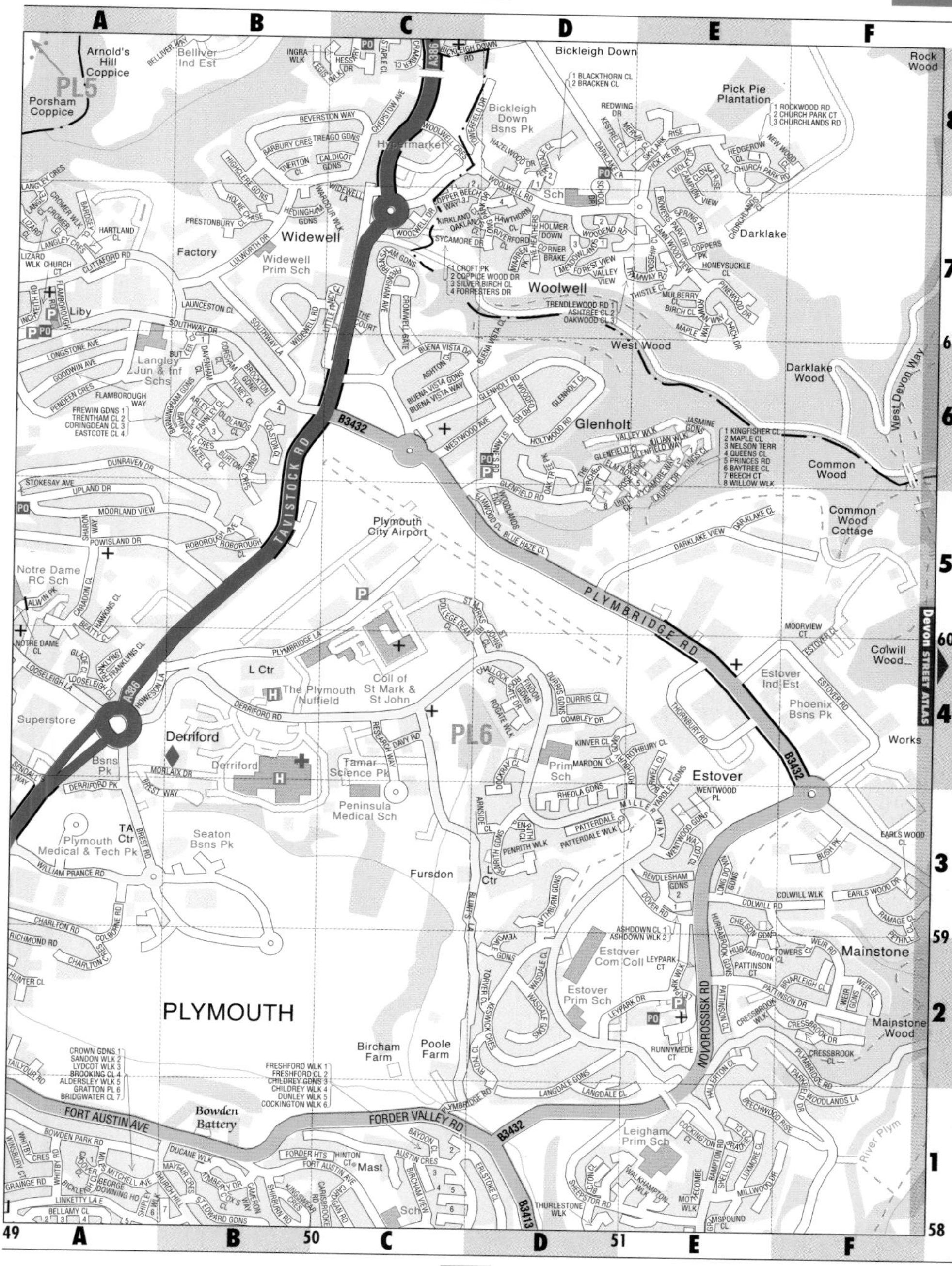
A
B
C
D
E
F
8
7
61
6
5
60
4
3
59
2
1
58
49
50
51
Arnold's Hill Coppice
Porsham Coppice
PL5
Belliver Ind Est
Bickleigh Down
Rock Wood
Pick Pie Plantation
Bickleigh Down Bsns Pk
Hypermarket
Widewell
Widewell Prim Sch
Factory
Liby
Langley Jun & Inf Schs
Woolwell
West Wood
Darklake
Darklake Wood
West Devon Way
Glenholt
Common Wood
Common Wood Cottage
Plymouth City Airport
Notre Dame RC Sch
TAVISTOCK RD
A386
B3432
PLYMBRIDGE RD
Colwill Wood
Estover Ind Est
Phoenix Bsns Pk
Works
Coll of St Mark & St John
The Plymouth Nuffield
L Ctr
Superstore
Derriford
Bsns Pk
Tamar Science Pk
Peninsula Medical Sch
PL6
Prim Sch
Estover
Plymouth Medical & Tech Pk
TA Ctr
Seaton Bsns Pk
Fursdon
Estover Com Coll
Estover Prim Sch
Mainstone
Mainstone Wood
PLYMOUTH
Bircham Farm
Poole Farm
NOVOROSSISK RD
Bowden Battery
FORT AUSTIN AVE
FORDER VALLEY RD
B3413
Leigham Prim Sch
Mast
Sch
River Plym
Devon STREET ATLAS
1 BLACKTHORN CL
2 BRACKEN CL
1 ROCKWOOD RD
2 CHURCH PARK CT
3 CHURCHLANDS RD
1 CROFT PK
2 COPPICE WOOD DR
3 SILVER BIRCH CL
4 FORRESTERS DR
TRENDLEWOOD RD 1
ASHTREE CL 2
OAKWOOD CL 3
FREWIN GDNS 1
TRENTHAM CL 2
CORINGDEAN CL 3
EASTCOTE CL 4
1 KINGFISHER CL
2 MAPLE CL
3 NELSON TERR
4 QUEENS CL
5 PRINCES RD
6 BAYTREE CL
7 BEECH CT
8 WILLOW WLK
CROWN GDNS 1
SANDON WLK 2
LYDCOT WLK 3
BROOKING CL 4
ALDERSLEY WLK 5
GRATTON PL 6
BRIDGWATER CL 7
FRESHFORD WLK 1
FRESHFORD CL 2
CHILDREY GDNS 3
CHILDREY WLK 4
DUNLEY WLK 5
COCKINGTON WLK 6
ASHDOWN CL 1
ASHDOWN WLK 2

129

65
122

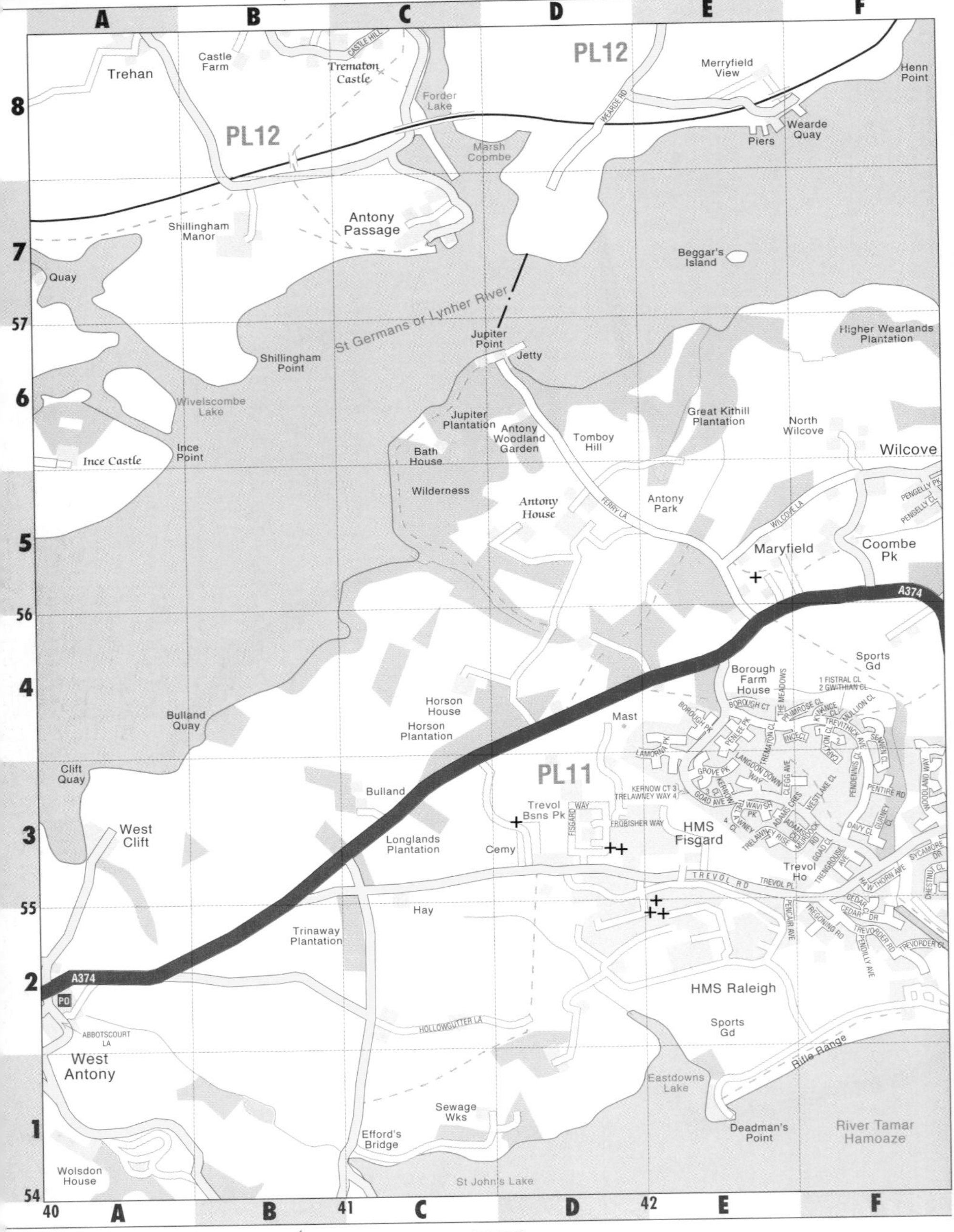
A
B
C
D
E
F
8
7
57
6
5
56
4
3
55
2
1
54
40
41
42
Trehan
Castle Farm
Tremation Castle
CASTLE HILL
Forder Lake
PL12
Merryfield View
Henn Point
WEARDE RD
Wearde Quay
Piers
PL12
Marsh Coombe
Shillingham Manor
Antony Passage
Beggar's Island
Quay
St Germans or Lynher River
Jupiter Point
Jetty
Higher Wearlands Plantation
Shillingham Point
Wivelscombe Lake
Jupiter Plantation
Antony Woodland Garden
Tomboy Hill
Great Kithill Plantation
North Wilcove
Wilcove
Ince Point
Ince Castle
Bath House
Wilderness
Antony House
FERRY LA
Antony Park
WILCOVE LA
PENGELLY PK
PENGELLY CL
Maryfield
Coombe Pk
A374
Sports Gd
Borough Farm House
THE MEADOWS
BOROUGH CT
1 FISTRAL CL
2 GWITHIAN CL
MULLION CL
Horson House
Horson Plantation
Bulland Quay
Mast
BOROUGH PK
PRIMROSE CL
TREVITHICK AVE
SENNEN CL
PENLEE PK
TREMATON CL
INCE CL
LAMORNA PK
LANGDON DOWN WAY
PENDENNIS CL
PENTIRE RD
WOODLAND WAY
PL11
GROVE PK
KERNOW CL
CLEGG AVE
WESTLAKE CL
Clift Quay
Bulland
KERNOW CT 3
TRELAWNEY WAY 4
GOAD AVE
WAVISH PK
ADAMS CRES
Trevol Bsns Pk
FISGARD WAY
FROBISHER WAY
HMS Fisgard
MURDOCK RD
GURNEY CL
DAVY CL
West Clift
Longlands Plantation
Cemy
TRELAWNEY RISE
GOAD CL
TRENGROUSE AVE
Trevol Ho
HAWTHORN AVE
SYCAMORE DR
CHESTNUT CL
TREVOL RD
TREVOL PL
CEDAR CL
CEDAR DR
Hay
PENCAIR AVE
TREGONING RD
TREVORDER RD
TREVORDER CL
PENDILLY AVE
Trinaway Plantation
A374
PO
HMS Raleigh
HOLLOWGUTTER LA
ABBOTSCOURT LA
Sports Gd
Rifle Range
West Antony
Eastdowns Lake
Sewage Wks
Deadman's Point
River Tamar Hamoaze
Efford's Bridge
Wolsdon House
St John's Lake

65
132

123

128

F5
1 NEPEAN ST
2 ADELAIDE ST
3 BRUNEL TERR
4 EPWORTH TERR
5 SUSSEX TERR
6 RAILWAY COTTS
7 YORK TERR
8 ST MAWES TERR

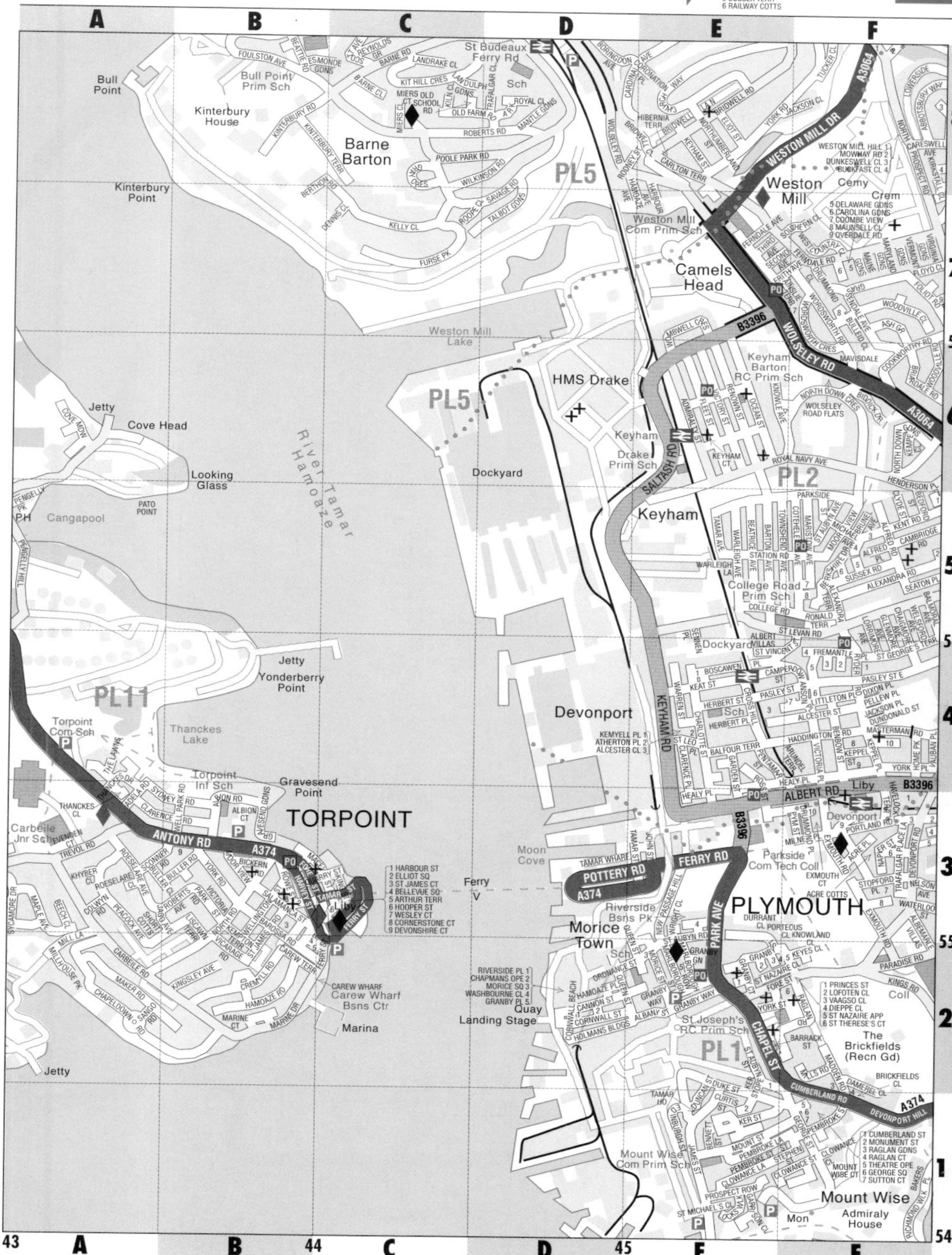

133

F3
1 CLARENDON HO
2 GARFIELD TERR
3 TRAFALGAR PL
4 THE MEWS
5 NELSON GDNS

128

6 BEYROUT PL
7 ST MICHAEL'S CT
8 ST MICHAEL'S TERR
9 PORTLAND CT
10 MOLYNEAUX PL

F4
1 ST GEORGES CT
2 HORNBY ST
3 PHILLIMORE ST
4 FREMANTLE GDNS
5 FAIRFAX TERR
6 HARGOOD TERR
7 HARRISON ST
8 KEPPEL TERR
9 HEALY CT
10 BRUNSWICK PL

A5
1 MELVILLE PL
2 Wolseley Bsns Pk
3 AUCKLAND RD
4 HALEY BARTON
5 GREATLANDS PL
6 WADHAM TERR
7 CRANTOCK TERR

127
124

E6
1 BRENT KNOLL RD
2 LUDLOW RD
3 SWAINDALE RD
4 TYTHING WLK
5 GLENHURST RD
6 VENN CL

F4
1 GROSVENOR COTTS
2 HILLSBOROUGH
3 PEARSON AVE
4 PENLEE PL
5 PENROSE VILLAS
6 CROZIER RD

7 MARINA TERR
8 KENSINGTON PL

F6
1 RESERVOIR LA
2 PEARN COTTS
3 BRANDRETH RD
4 GLENEAGLE AVE

5 GLENEAGLE VILLAS
6 HENDERS CNR
7 ROSEVEAN HO
8 ROSEVEAN CT
9 MANNAMEAD CT
10 FOSBROOKE CT

A3
1 UNDERHILL VILLAS
2 OSBORNE VILLAS
3 EDGCUMBE CT
4 NELSON GDNS
5 COLLINGWOOD VILLAS
6 PAVILAND GRANGE
7 FITZROY TERR

A4
1 WESLEY PL
2 MASTERMAN RD
3 DUCKWORTH ST
4 DUNDAS ST
5 BROMLEY PL
6 BROMLEY HO
7 LEESIDE CT
8 BELMONT CT
9 Stoke Damerel Bsns Ctr

127

A4
10 SOMERSET COTTS
11 SOMERSET PLACE LA
12 PARK PLACE LA

134

E4
1 HERMITAGE CT
2 WARLEIGH RD
3 ROCHESTER RD
4 CHESTER PL
5 ALEXANDRA PL
6 CONNAUGHT LA

For full street detail of the highlighted area see pages 148 and 149.

125
130

C7
1 BRAMBLE WLK
2 BOWHAYS WLK
3 BRISMAR WLK
4 MOORFIELD AVE
5 BEAUDYN WLK
6 BEESTON WLK

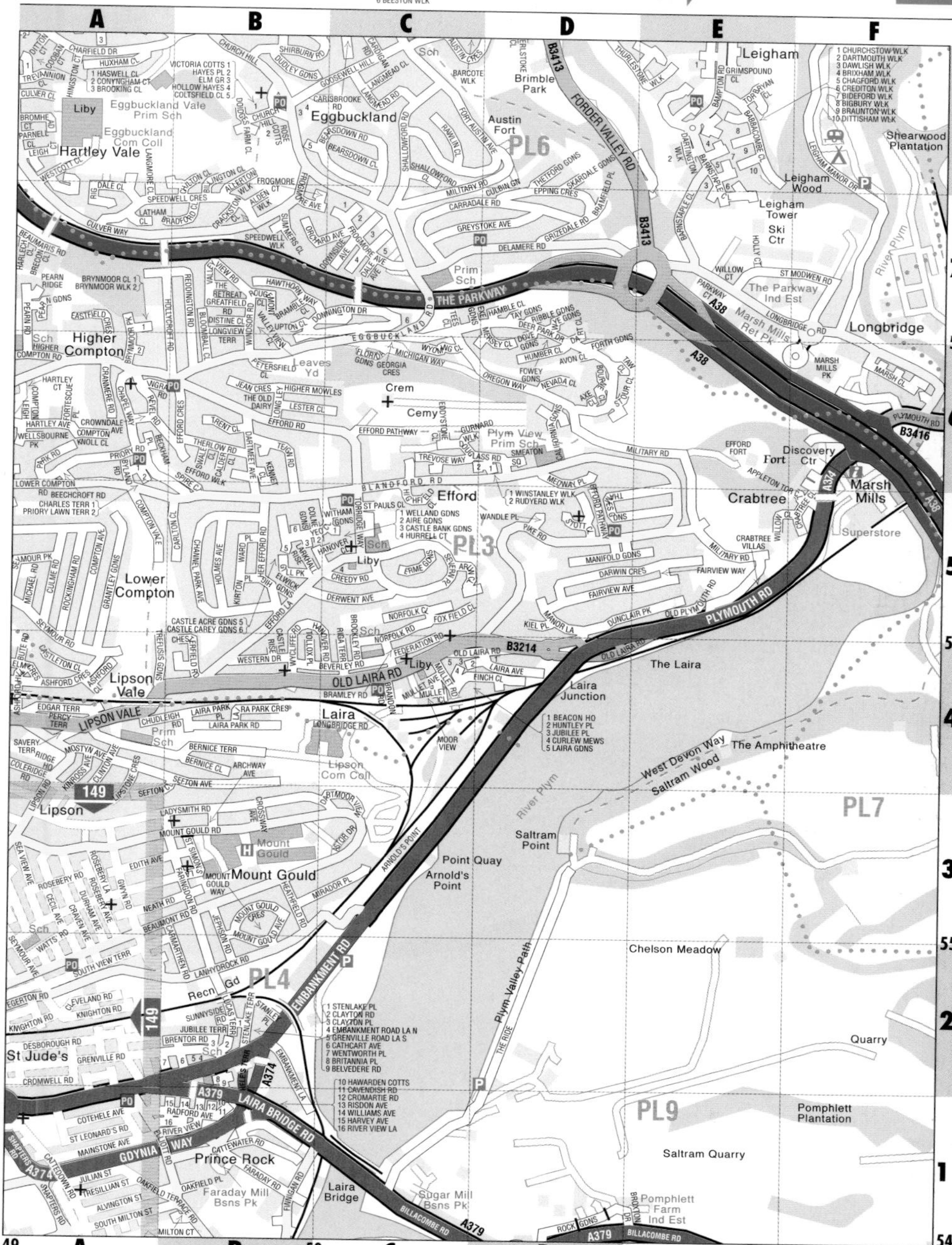
A
B
C
D
E
F
8
7
57
6
5
56
4
3
55
2
1
54
49
50
51
Leigham
Eggbuckland
Hartley Vale
Brimble Park
Austin Fort
PL6
Leigham Wood
Leigham Tower
Ski Ctr
Shearwood Plantation
The Parkway Ind Est
Marsh Mills Ret Pk
Longbridge
Higher Compton
Leaves Yd
Crem
Cemy
Plym View Prim Sch
Efford
Efford Fort
Discovery Ctr
Crabtree
Marsh Mills
Superstore
PL3
Lower Compton
Lipson Vale
Laira
Laira Junction
The Laira
The Amphitheatre
West Devon Way
Saltram Wood
PL7
Lipson
Lipson Com Coll
Mount Gould
Saltram Point
Point Quay
Arnold's Point
Chelson Meadow
PL4
Recn Gd
St Jude's
Prince Rock
Faraday Mill Bsns Pk
Laira Bridge
Sugar Mill Bsns Pk
Pomphlett Farm Ind Est
Saltram Quarry
Pomphlett Plantation
Quarry
PL9
Plym Valley Path
THE PARKWAY
A38
B3413
FORDER VALLEY RD
PLYMOUTH RD
B3416
A374
B3214
OLD LAIRA RD
LIPSON VALE
EMBANKMENT RD
LAIRA BRIDGE RD
A379
GDYNIA WAY
BILLACOMBE RD
1 CHURCHSTOW WLK
2 DARTMOUTH WLK
3 DAWLISH WLK
4 BRIXHAM WLK
5 CHAGFORD WLK
6 CREDITON WLK
7 BIDEFORD WLK
8 BIGBURY WLK
9 BRAUNTON WLK
10 DITTISHAM WLK
1 BEACON HO
2 HUNTLEY PL
3 JUBILEE PL
4 CURLEW MEWS
5 LAIRA GDNS
1 STENLAKE PL
2 CLAYTON RD
3 CLAYTON PL
4 EMBANKMENT ROAD LA N
5 GRENVILLE ROAD LA S
6 CATHCART AVE
7 WENTWORTH PL
8 BRITANNIA PL
9 BELVEDERE RD
10 HAWARDEN COTTS
11 CAVENDISH RD
12 CROMARTIE RD
13 RISDON AVE
14 WILLIAMS AVE
15 HARVEY AVE
16 RIVER VIEW LA
1 WELLAND GDNS
2 AIRE GDNS
3 CASTLE BANK GDNS
4 HURRELL CT
1 WINSTANLEY WLK
2 RUDYERD WLK
1 HASWELL CL
2 CONYNGHAM CT
3 BROOKING CL
VICTORIA COTTS 1
HAYES PL 2
ELM GR 3
HOLLOW HAYES 4
COLTSFIELD CL 5
CASTLE ACRE GDNS 5
CASTLE CAREY GDNS 6
CHARLES TERR 1
PRIORY LAWN TERR 2
BRYNMOOR CL 1
BRYNMOOR WLK 2
149

For full street detail of the highlighted area see page 149.

135
130

129

E7
1 PERSEVERANCE COTTS
2 BLANCHARD PL

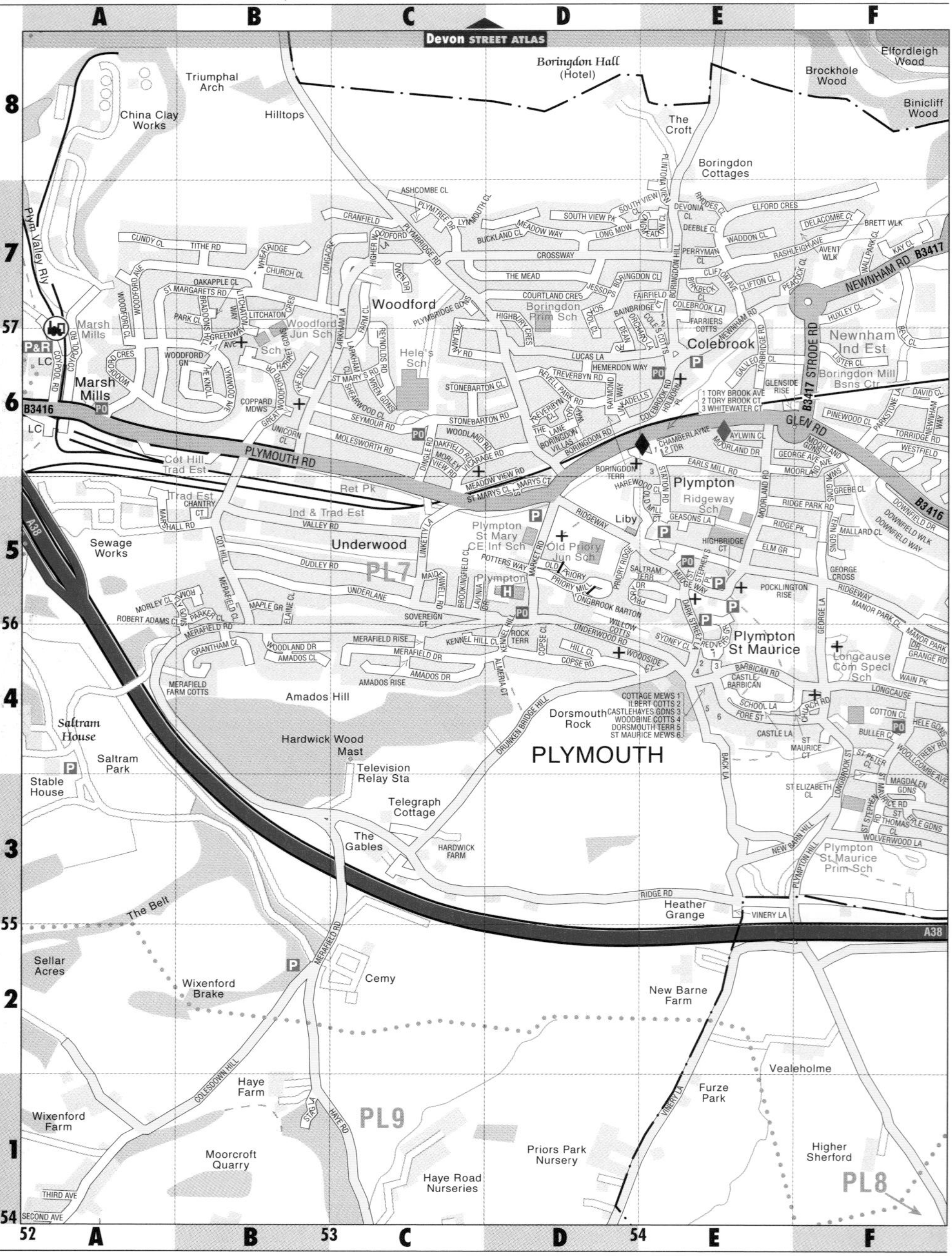

129

136

B5
1 CALEDONIA CL
2 ELDER CL
3 MAGNOLIA CL
4 TURBILL GDNS
5 PAYNTER WLK

C5
1 EIGHT ACRE CL
2 LAWN CL
3 ORCHARD CL
4 GREAT PARK CL
5 LONG TERRACE CL
6 CYPRESS CL
7 CAMPION CL
8 RODDICK WAY
9 BRANSON CT

65
126

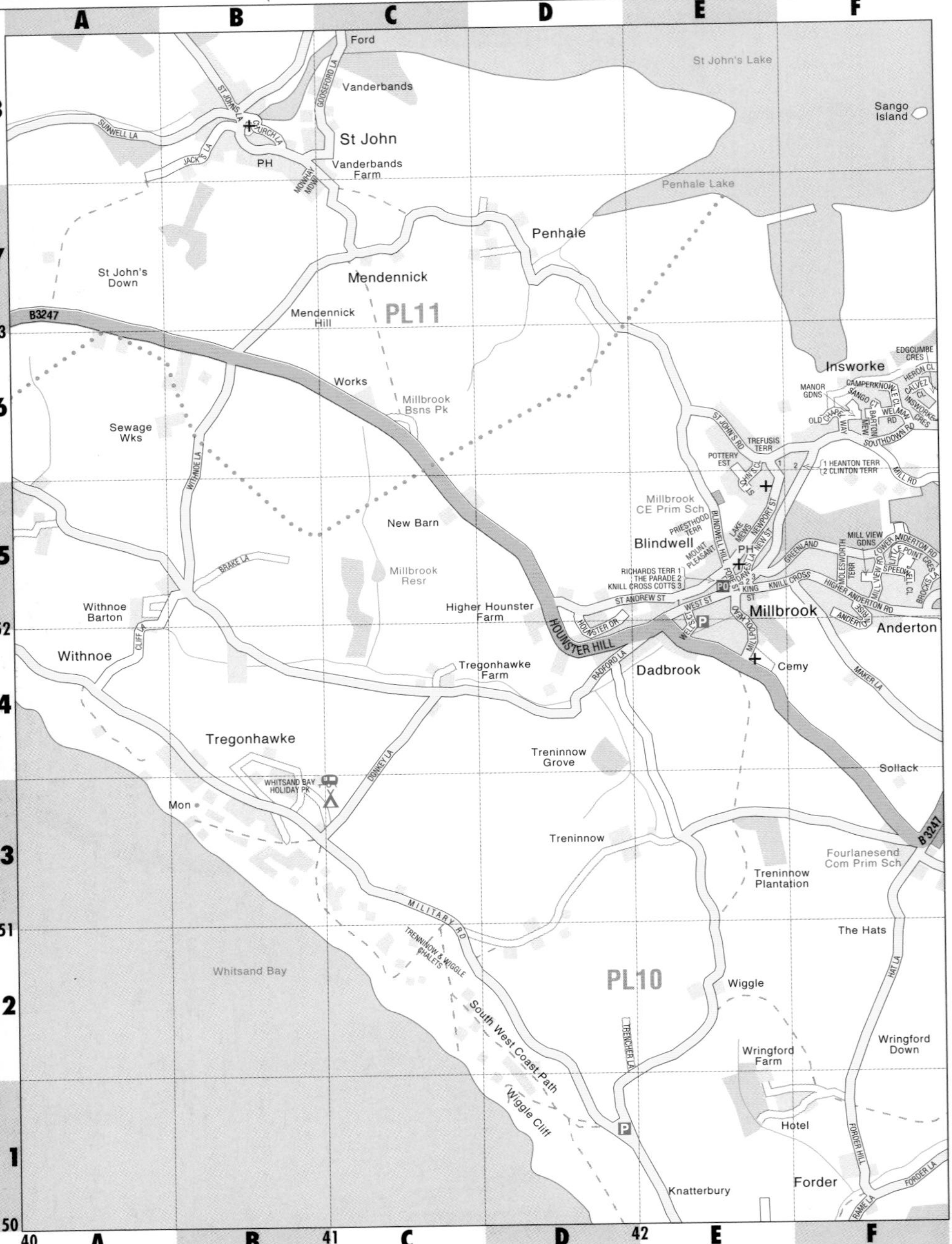
Ford
St John's Lake
Vanderbands
Sango Island
St John
Vanderbands Farm
PH
Penhale Lake
Penhale
St John's Down
Mendennick
Mendennick Hill
PL11
B3247
Works
Millbrook Bsns Pk
Insworke
Sewage Wks
Millbrook CE Prim Sch
New Barn
Blindwell
Millbrook Resr
Withnoe Barton
Higher Hounster Farm
Millbrook
Anderton
Withnoe
Tregonhawke Farm
Dadbrook
Cemy
Tregonhawke
Treninnow Grove
Sollack
WHITSAND BAY HOLIDAY PK
Mon
Treninnow
Fourlanesend Com Prim Sch
Treninnow Plantation
The Hats
Whitsand Bay
PL10
Wiggle
South West Coast Path
Wringford Farm
Wringford Down
Wiggle Cliff
Hotel
Forder
Knatterbury
HOUNSTER HILL
MILITARY RD
WITHNOE LA
DONKEY LA
RADFORD LA
TRENCHER LA
HAT LA
FORDER HILL
MAKER LA
ST ANDREW ST
WEST ST
KING ST
MILLPOOL HEAD
BLINDWELL HILL
NEW ST
NEWPORT ST
LAKE MEWS
GREENLAND
MILL VIEW GDNS
HIGHER ANDERTON RD
RICHARDS TERR 1
THE PARADE 2
KNILL CROSS COTTS 3
PRIESTHOOD TERR
MOUNT PLEASANT
POTTERY EST
TREFUSIS TERR
1 HEANTON TERR
2 CLINTON TERR
MILL RD
MANOR GDNS
EDGCUMBE CRES
HERON CL
SOUTHDOWN RD
SUNWELL LA
JACK'S LA
CHURCH LA
ST JOHNS LA
GOOSEFORD LA
BRAKE LA
CLIFF LA
TRENINNOW & WIGGLE CHALETS
FORDER LA
RAME LA

127
134
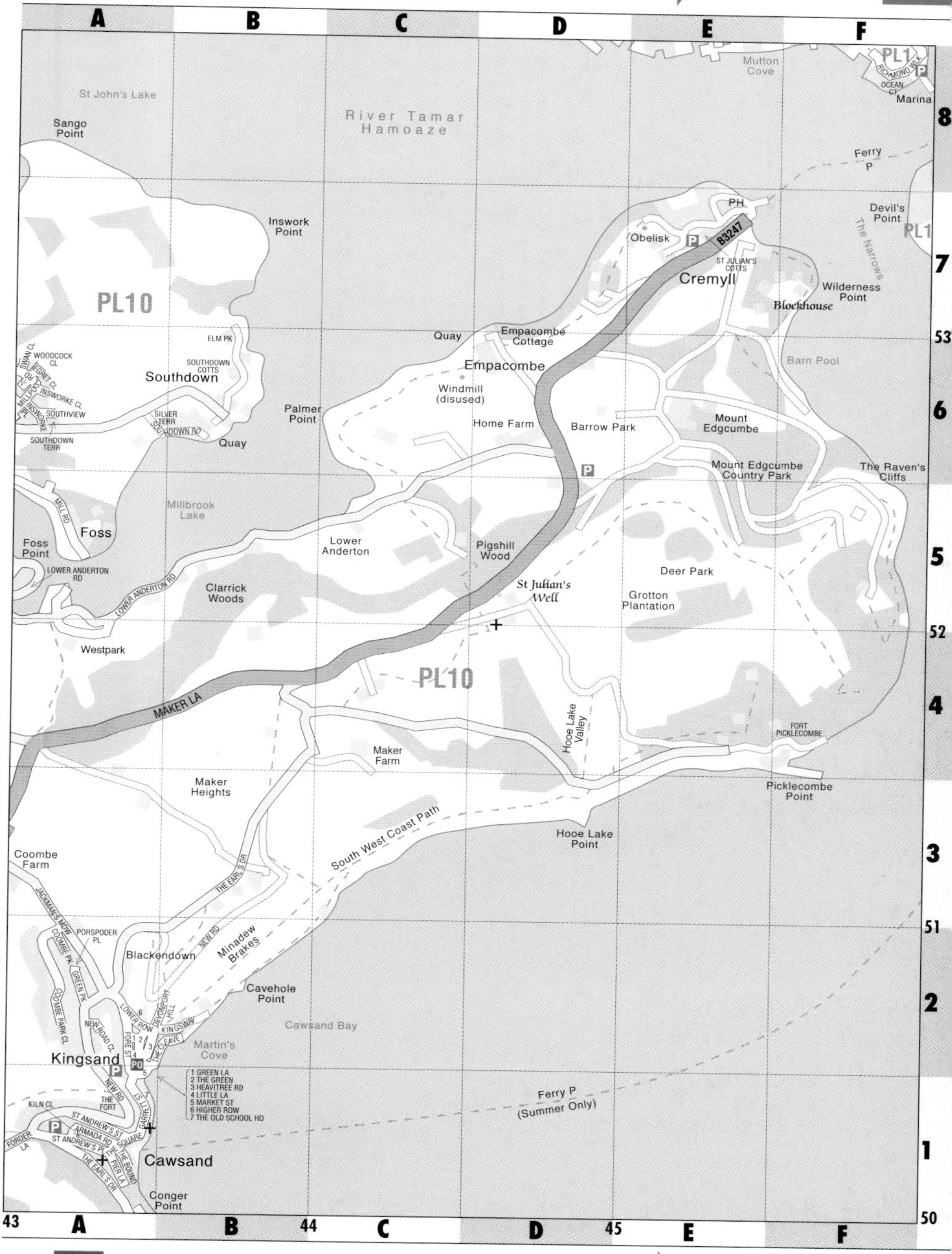
A
B
C
D
E
F
St John's Lake
Sango Point
River Tamar Hamoaze
Mutton Cove
PL1
RICHMOND WLK
OCEAN CT
Marina
8
Ferry P
Devil's Point
PL1
The Narrows
PH
Inswork Point
Obelisk
B3247
ST JULIAN'S COTTS
Cremyll
7
Wilderness Point
Blockhouse
PL10
ELM PK
Quay
Empacombe Cottage
53
WOODCOCK CL
SWAN CL
EGRET CL
MILLPOOL RD
INSWORKE CL
SOUTHDOWN COTTS
Southdown
Empacombe
Barn Pool
Windmill (disused)
SOUTHVIEW
SILVER TERR
SOUTHDOWN RD
SOUTHDOWN TERR
Palmer Point
Home Farm
Barrow Park
Mount Edgcumbe
6
Quay
Mount Edgcumbe Country Park
The Raven's Cliffs
MILL RD
Millbrook Lake
Foss
Lower Anderton
Pigshill Wood
Foss Point
5
LOWER ANDERTON RD
Deer Park
Clarrick Woods
St Julian's Well
Grotton Plantation
52
Westpark
PL10
MAKER LA
4
Hooe Lake Valley
FORT PICKLECOMBE
Maker Farm
Maker Heights
Picklecombe Point
South West Coast Path
Hooe Lake Point
Coombe Farm
3
THE EARL'S DR
JACKMAN'S MDW
COOMBE PK
PORSPODER PL
51
NEW RD
Blackendown
Minadew Brakes
GREEN PK
COOMBE PARK CL
Cavehole Point
2
LOWER ROW
DEVONPORT HILL
KINGSWAY
NEW ROAD CL
FORE ST
THE CLEAVE
Cawsand Bay
Martin's Cove
Kingsand
PO
1 GREEN LA
2 THE GREEN
3 HEAVITREE RD
4 LITTLE LA
5 MARKET ST
6 HIGHER ROW
7 THE OLD SCHOOL HO
NEW RD
Ferry P (Summer Only)
KILN CL
THE FORT
GARRETT ST
ST ANDREW'S ST
ARMADA RD
THE SQUARE
FORDER LA
ST ANDREW'S PL
PIER LA
THE BOUND
1
THE EARL'S DR
Cawsand
Conger Point
43
44
45
50
64
134

133
128
For full street detail of the highlighted area see pages 148 and 149.

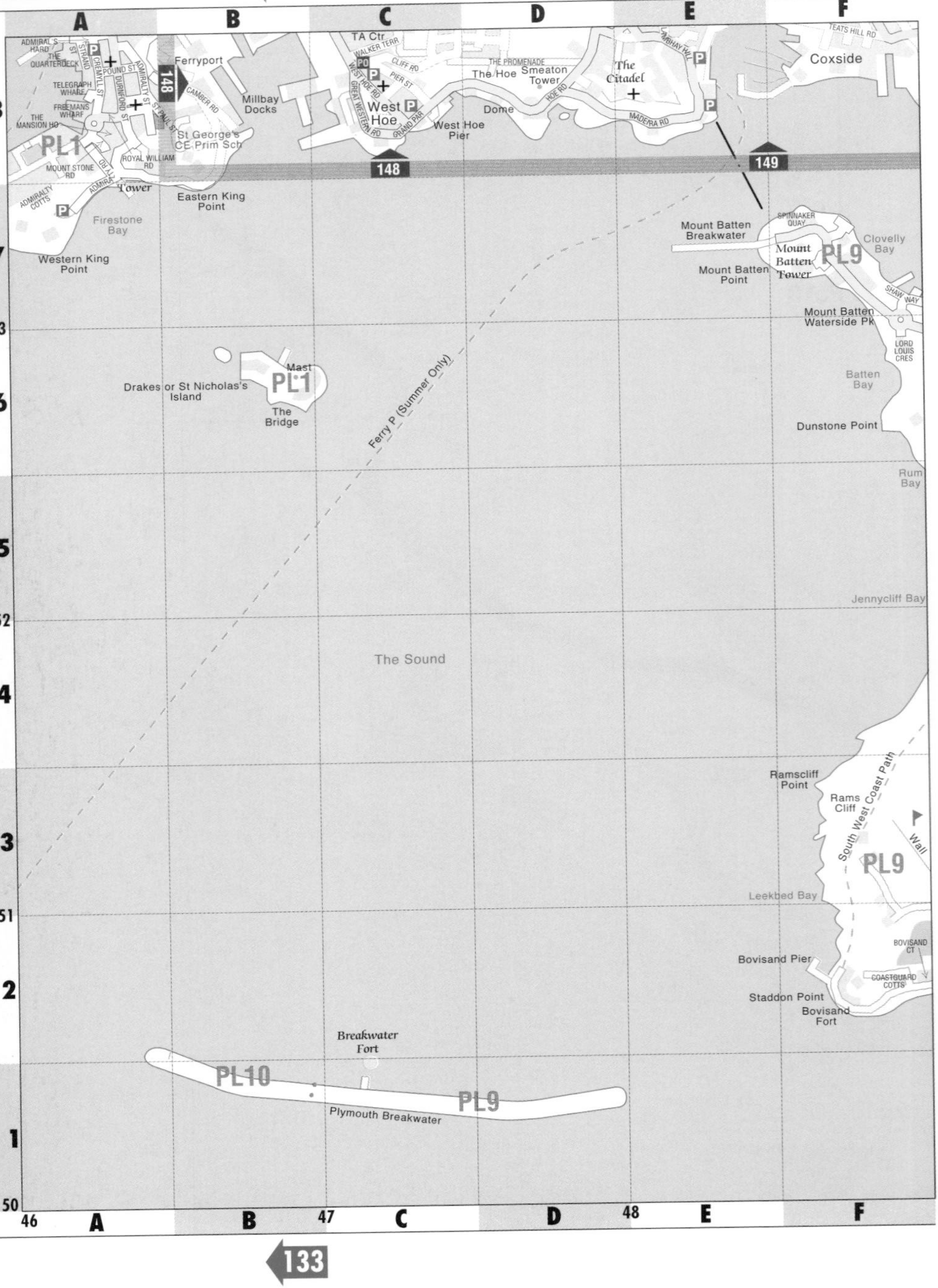

133

For full street detail of the highlighted area see page 149.

129

136

F5
1 CHALLGOOD CL
2 ORCHARDTON TERR

F7
1 THE DUKES RYDE
2 MAPLE CT
3 MAGNOLIA CT
4 HORN LANE FLATS
5 SELKIRK HO

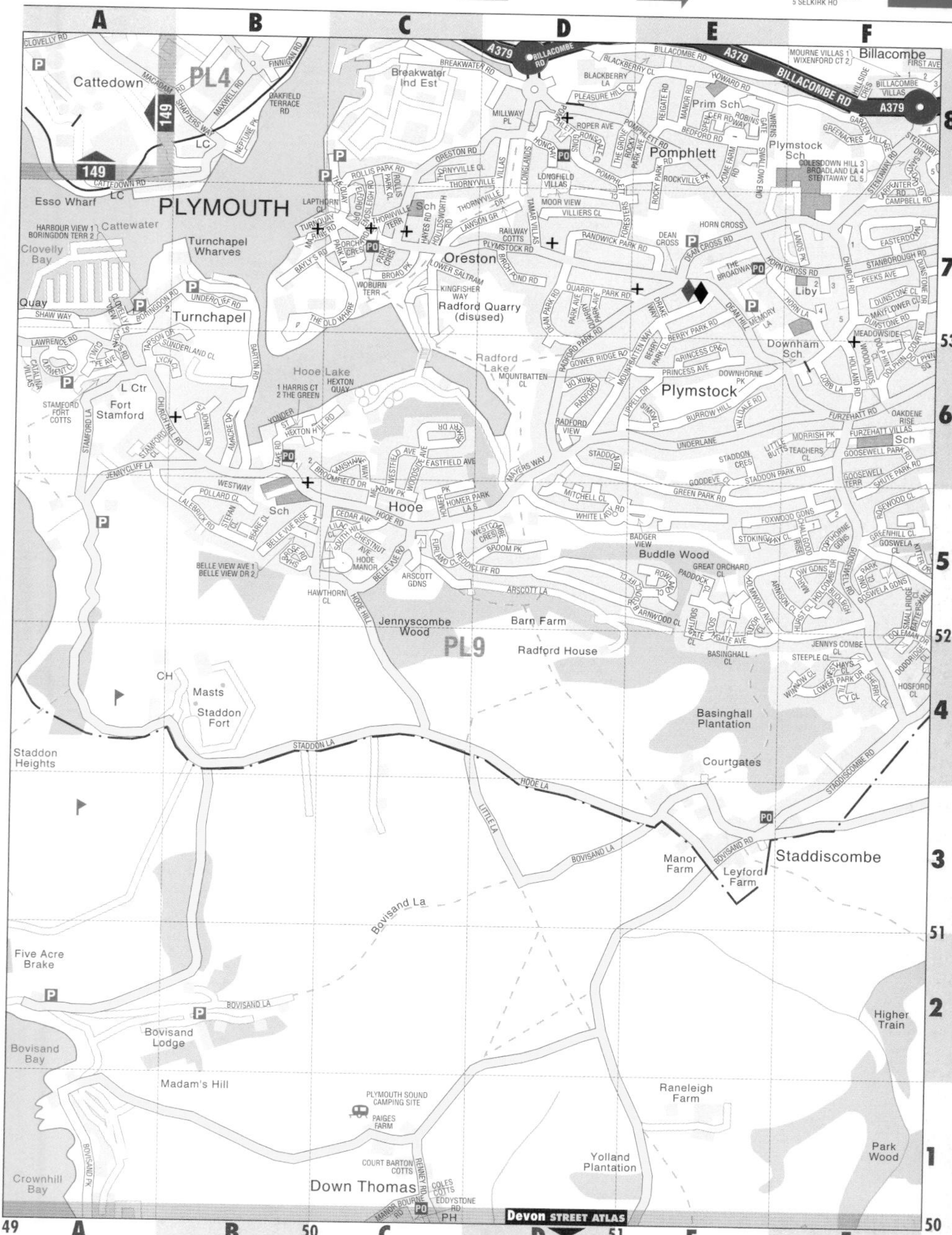

136

135
130

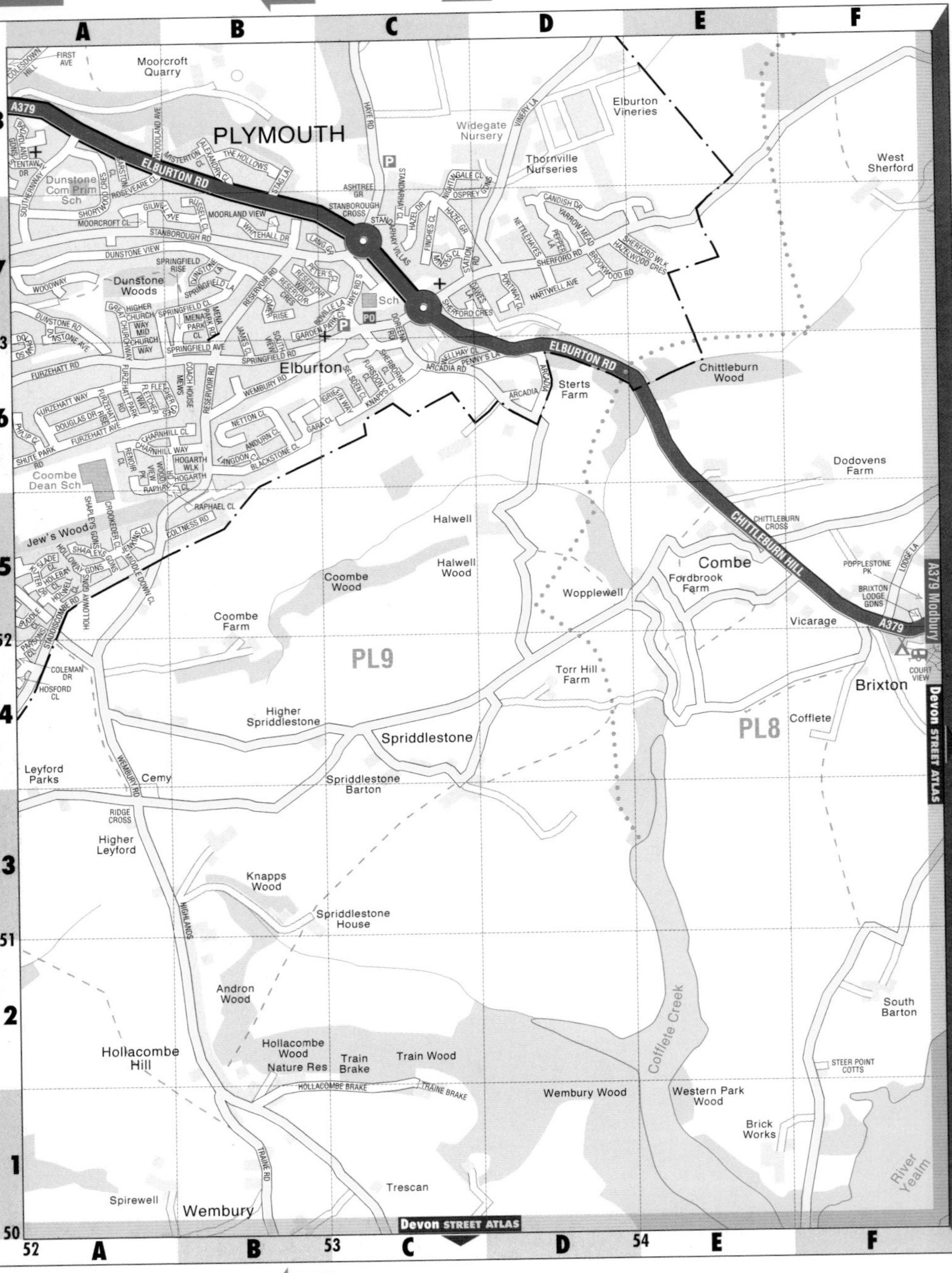
A
B
C
D
E
F
8
7
53
6
5
52
4
3
51
2
1
50
52
53
54
PLYMOUTH
A379
ELBURTON RD
Moorcroft
Quarry
Dunstone
Com Prim
Sch
Dunstone
Woods
Elburton
Widegate
Nursery
Elburton
Vineries
Thornville
Nurseries
West
Sherford
Chittleburn
Wood
Sterts
Farm
Coombe
Dean Sch
Jew's Wood
Halwell
Halwell
Wood
Coombe
Wood
Coombe
Farm
Dodovens
Farm
CHITTLEBURN HILL
Combe
Fordbrook
Farm
Wopplewell
Vicarage
A379 Modbury
Brixton
PL9
Torr Hill
Farm
Higher
Spriddlestone
Spriddlestone
Coffleté
PL8
Leyford
Parks
Cemy
Spriddlestone
Barton
RIDGE
CROSS
Higher
Leyford
Knapps
Wood
Spriddlestone
House
HIGHLANDS
Andron
Wood
Cofflete Creek
South
Barton
Hollacombe
Hill
Hollacombe
Wood
Nature Res
Train
Brake
Train Wood
HOLLACOMBE BRAKE
TRAINE BRAKE
Wembury Wood
Western Park
Wood
STEER POINT
COTTS
Brick
Works
TRAINE RD
Trescan
River
Yealm
Spirewell
Wembury
Devon STREET ATLAS

135

69

C5
1 SANDHURST TERR
2 CORNWALL TERR
3 TREHAVERNE TERR
4 ST MARY'S TERR
5 HENDRA CL

70

D5
1 BENSON HO
2 BENSON GDNS
3 ST CLEMENT'S TERR
4 MITCHELL HILL TERR
5 PROSPECT PL
6 SOLAR ROW

70

D5
7 PARKINS TERR
8 MIDDLE ROSEWIN ROW
9 LOWER ROSEWIN ROW
10 EAST ROSEWIN ROW
11 MITCHELL CT
12 CHURCH WLK
13 BELMONT VILLAS

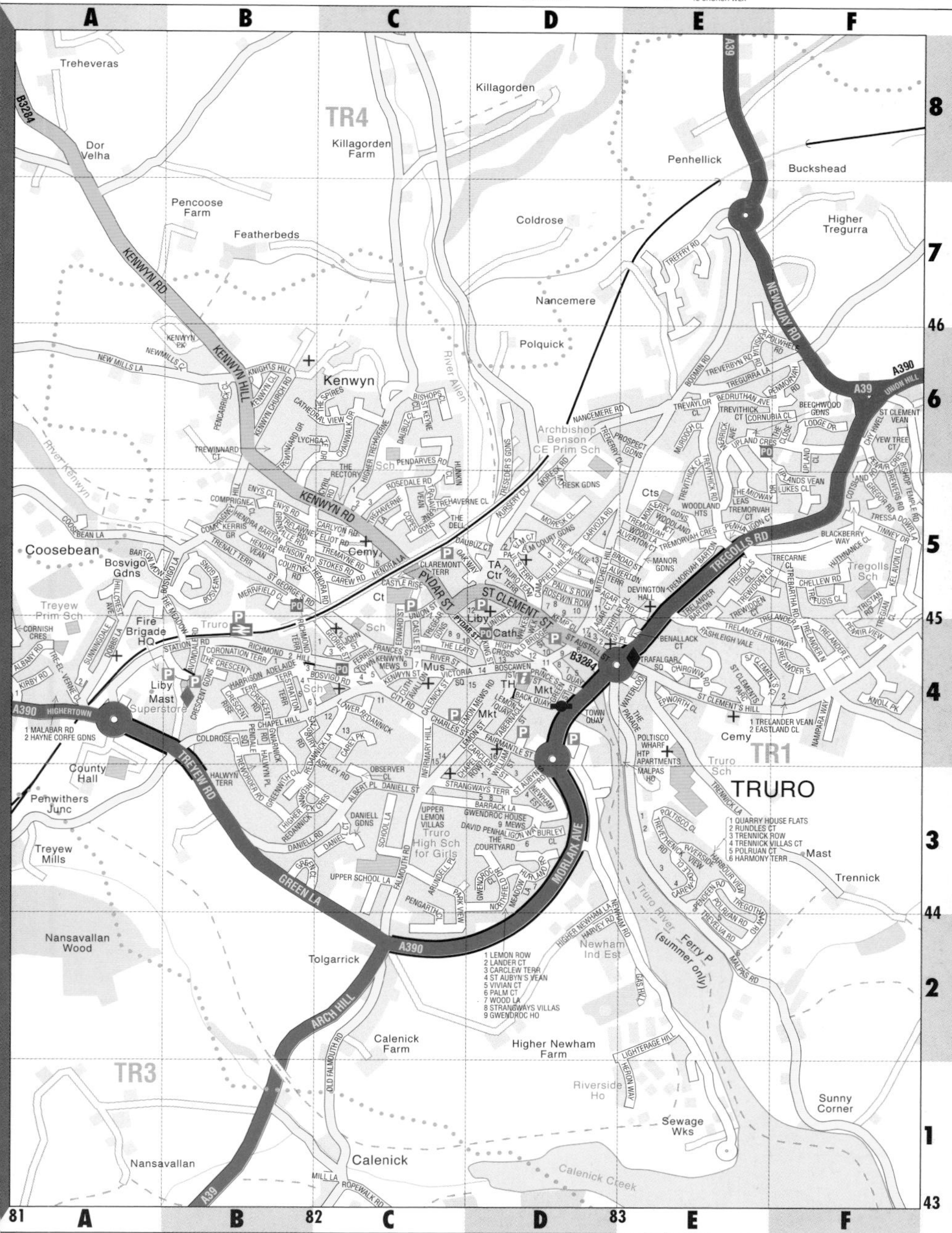

B4
1 CLIFTON GDNS
2 ALEXANDRA TERR
3 RICHMOND PL
4 PARKVEDRAS TERR
5 PARKVEDRAS HO
6 DEREHAM TERR

C4
1 CARVEDRAS CT
2 WELLINGTON TERR
3 ANDREW PL
4 ST DOMINIC SQ
5 ST DOMINIC ST
6 THOMAS JOHNSON CT
7 LITTLE CASTLE ST
8 PYDAR MEWS
9 COOMBES LA

69

C4
10 NALDER'S CT
11 CARLYON CL
12 CULROY FLATS
13 ROBARTES CT
14 SOUTHLEIGH MEWS
15 SOUTHLEIGH HO

70

D4
1 BAYNARDS CL
2 ST PIRANS CL
3 SALMON ROW
4 CLIFT CT
5 ENYS QUAY
6 SUNLEY ORFORD HO
7 LOWEN CT
8 QUAY MEWS
9 NEW BRIDGE ST

70

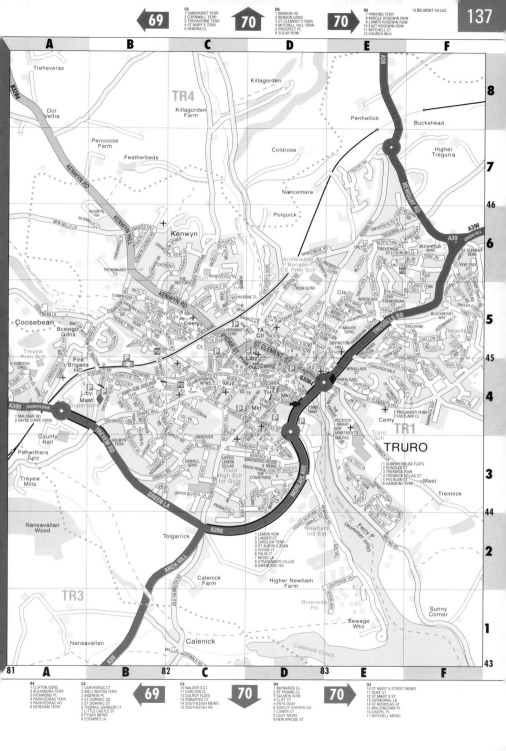

D4
10 ST MARY'S STREET MEWS
11 DUKE ST
12 ST MARY'S ST
13 CATHEDRAL LA
14 ST NICHOLAS ST
15 WALSINGHAM PL
16 CHAPEL PL
17 MITCHELL MEWS

66
67

F7
1 PENGERON AVE
2 PENROSE CT
3 ROSEMULLION GDNS
4 RESWYTHEN WLK
5 Wheal Agar
6 The Setons

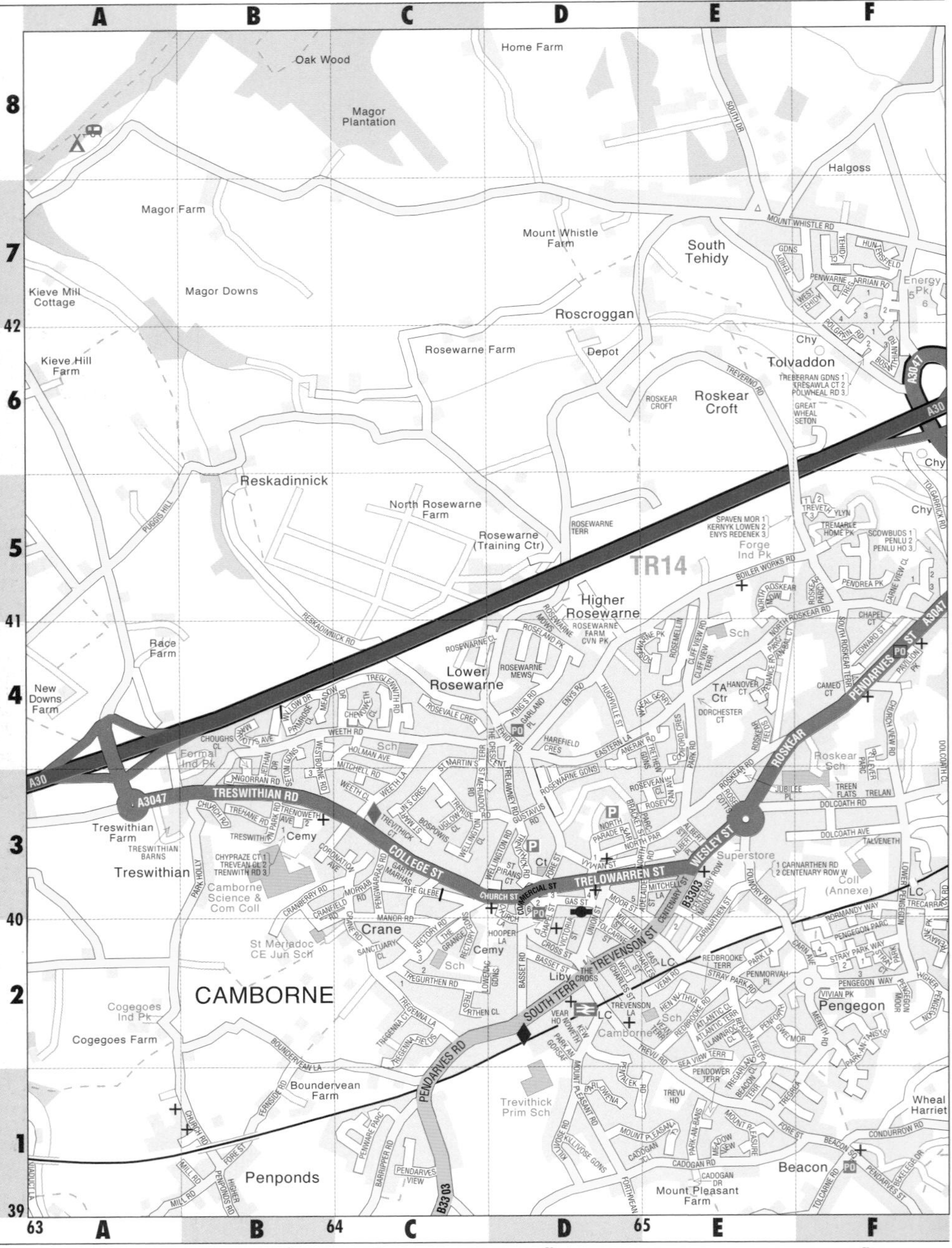

79
79

C2
1 BETHANY HOMES
2 ST MARTIN'S CL
3 SANDFIELD CRES

D3
1 ROSEWARNE RD
2 GURNEY'S LA
3 COMMERCIAL SQ
4 NEW CONNECTION ST
5 GODOLPHIN CT
6 GURNETS MEWS

F2
1 ROCK CL
2 PARC VENTON CL
3 GWEL ERYON
4 CLOS TREVITHICK

67
140

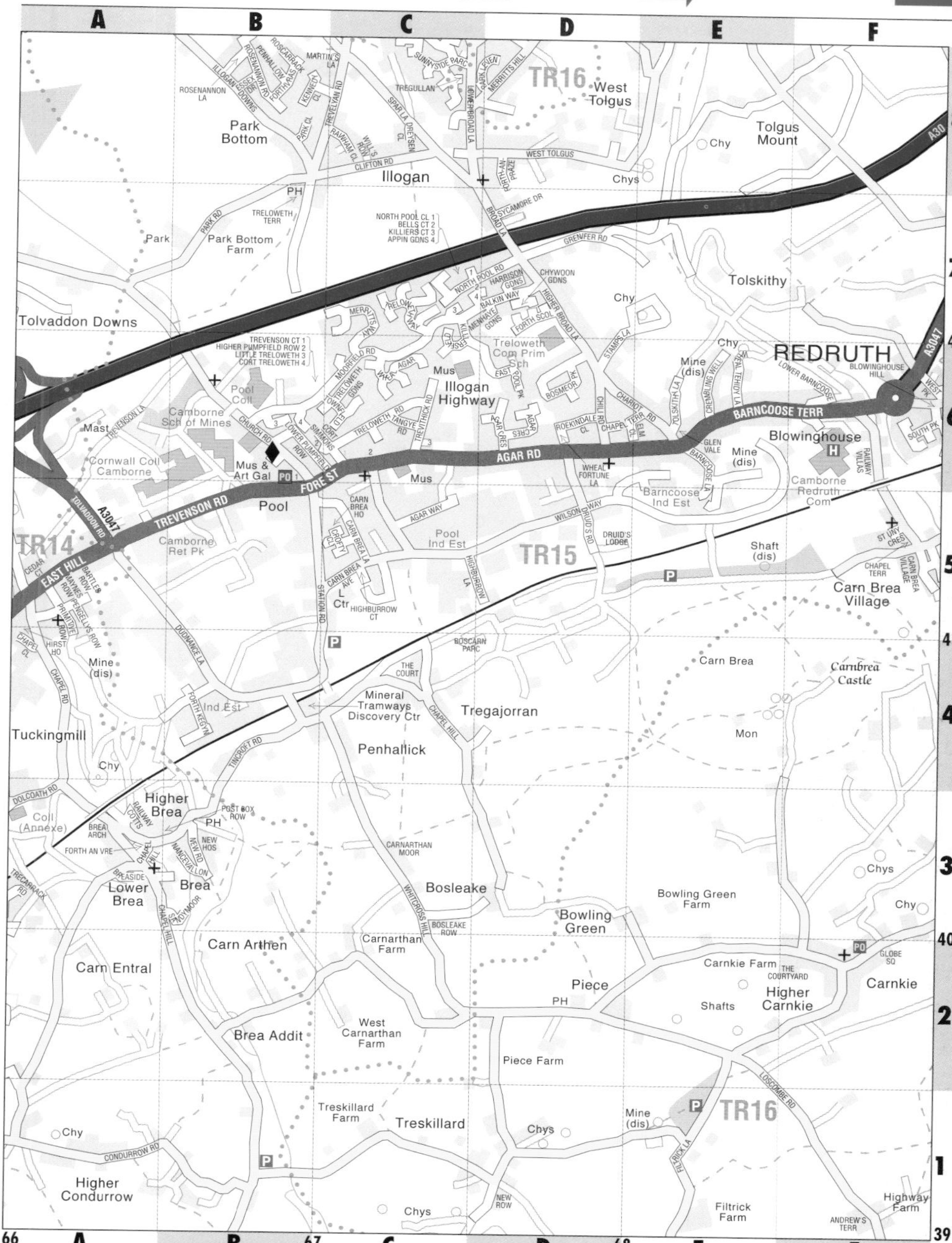

79
80
80

C6
1 POLGARTH
2 AGAR CT
3 TREVITHICK CT

B5
1 STANLEY TERR
2 CHAPEL ROW
3 BALMORAL PL
4 BALMORAL TERR
5 FOUNDRY ROW
6 TREVENNER MEWS
7 MARKET STRAND
8 TREVENNER HO
9 CHAPEL CT
10 LEGGOS CT

67

C5
1 CARDREW LA
2 HILLSIDE TERR
3 GLADSTONE TERR
4 PAULLS ROW
5 JENKINS TERR
6 MIDDLETONS ROW
7 SIDNEY TERR
8 ROSEACRE DR

68

68

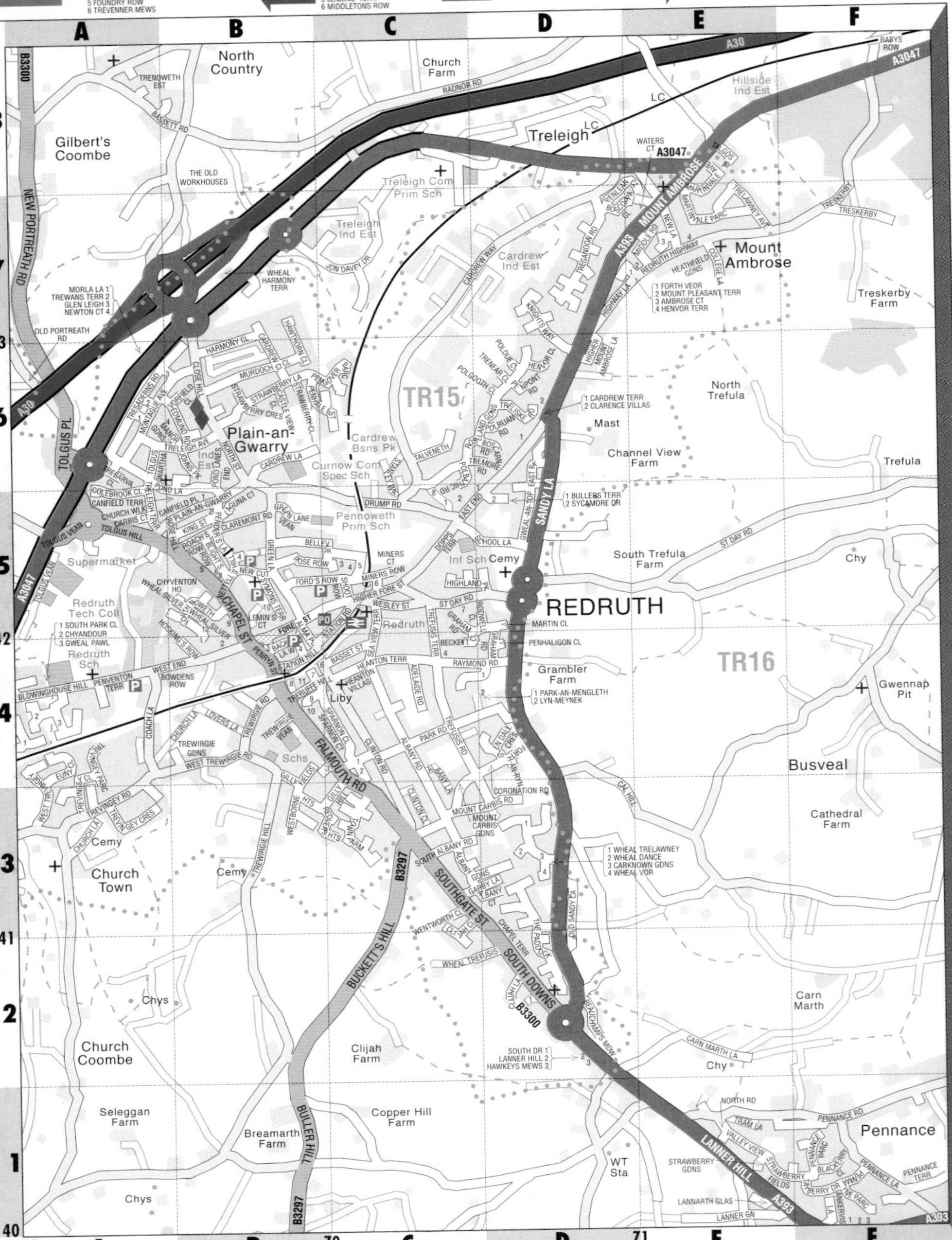

139

B4
1 SILVER CT
2 WEST END CT
3 CROSS ST
4 CLINTON PAS
5 MARKET WAY
6 BOND ST
7 SUNNYSIDE
8 GAS LA
9 TRERUFFE TERR
10 NANSCOTHAN
11 MARTIN HO
12 CAPTAINS CT

C4
1 SPARNON HILL
2 SPARNON TERR
3 LITTLE GILLY HILL
4 CHANNEL VIEW TERR

80

80

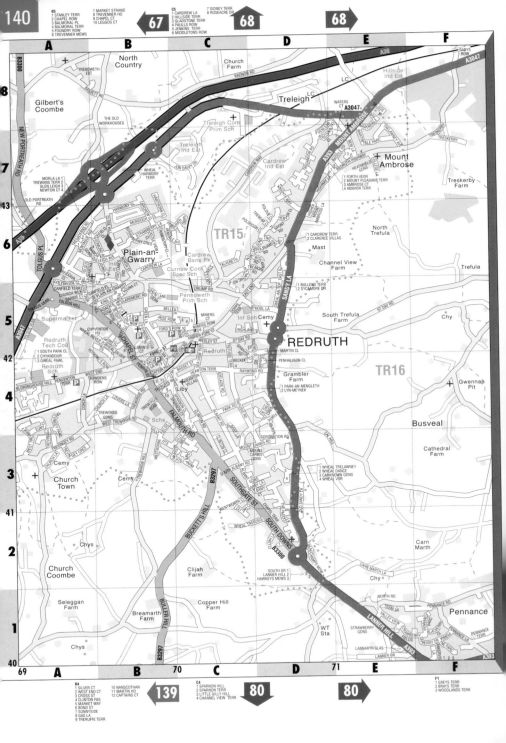

F1
1 GREYS TERR
2 BRAYS TERR
3 WOODLANDS TERR

77
77

A5
1 AYR CT
2 TREGARTHEN
3 SOUTHFIELDS PL
4 WINDSOR TERR
5 BULLANS TERR
6 TRERICE RD
7 CARNELLS RD
8 NANJIVEY PL
9 NANJIVEY TERR
10 BOSTENNACK PL
11 BOSTENNACK TERR
12 PEARCE'S LA
13 MIDDLE STENNACK COTTS
14 STENNACK GDNS
15 SANDOWS LA
16 ROSEWALL COTTS
17 ROSEWALL TERR
18 FERN GLEN
19 LITTLE-IN-SIGHT

B5
1 ST ANDREW'S ST
2 REDFERN CT
3 STREET-AN-POL
4 TREGENNA PL
5 GABRIEL ST
6 BEDFORD PL
7 WESLEY PL
8 WINDSOR HILL
9 DRILLFIELD LA

77

B5
10 ALMA TERR
11 TRENWITH TERR
12 NORTH TERR
13 UMFULLA PL
14 TRENWITH PL
15 DOVE ST
16 TREGENNA HILL
17 STREET-AN-GARROW
18 SKIDDEN HILL

77

B5
19 FERN LEE TERR
20 SEA VIEW TERR
21 ALBERT PL
22 PADNOVER TERR
23 PORTHMINSTER TERR
24 PETES PL
25 CARRACK WIDDEN
26 ALBERT TERR
27 HARLEQUINS

77

B5
28 ROSEMORRAN
29 TALLAND CT
30 STONES CT

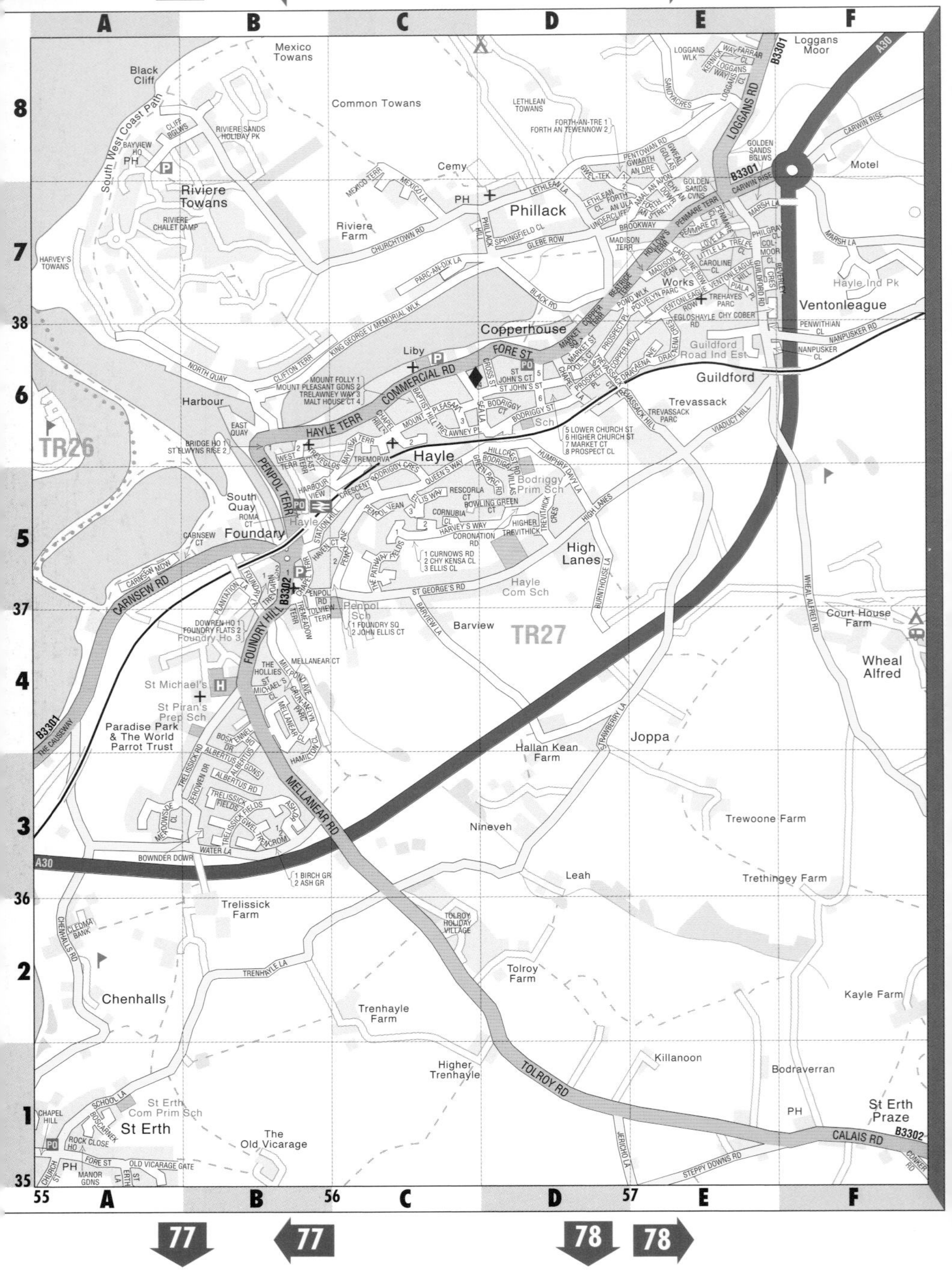
77
77
78
78
Mexico Towans
Black Cliff
Common Towans
South West Coast Path
Riviere Sands Holiday Pk
Riviere Towans
Riviere Chalet Camp
Harvey's Towans
Lethlean Towans
Loggans Moor
Loggans Rd
B3301
A30
Carwin Rise
Golden Sands Bglws
Motel
Cemy
Phillack
Riviere Farm
Churchtown Rd
Glebe Row
Works
Ventonleague
Hayle Ind Pk
Copperhouse
Guildford
Guildford Road Ind Est
Liby
Fore St
Commercial Rd
Hayle Terr
Harbour
North Quay
East Quay
TR26
Penpol Terr
Hayle
South Quay
Foundary
Carnsew Rd
Trevassack
Bodriggy Prim Sch
High Lanes
Hayle Com Sch
St George's Rd
Barview
TR27
Foundry Hill
B3302
Penpol Sch
Court House Farm
Wheal Alfred
Wheal Alfred Rd
St Michael's
St Piran's Prep Sch
Paradise Park & The World Parrot Trust
Joppa
Hallan Kean Farm
B3301
The Causeway
Mellanear Rd
Nineveh
Trewoone Farm
A30
Leah
Trethingey Farm
Trelissick Farm
Tolroy Holiday Village
Tolroy Farm
Chenhalls
Trenhayle Farm
Kayle Farm
Higher Trenhayle
Killanoon
Bodraverran
Tolroy Rd
St Erth Com Prim Sch
St Erth
St Erth Praze
Calais Rd
The Old Vicarage
Steppy Downs Rd
A
B
C
D
E
F
8
7
38
6
5
37
4
3
36
2
1
35
55
56
57
77
77
78
78

C7
1 ROSCADGHILL PARC
2 HEABROOK PARC
3 NICHOLAS PARC
4 MYTHYON CT
5 HEA COTTS
6 HAIG PL
88

7 POLTAIR TERR
8 BROOKWARD TERR
9 HOLLY TERR
10 CARMEN SQ
11 WESLEY ST
12 SYLVERTON PL
13 JAMAICA TERR
88

14 JAMAICA PL
15 PLEASANT PL
16 NEVADA PL
17 MELBOURNE TERR
D5
1 GREENBANK
2 HAWKINS CT
88

3 TREVEAN GDNS
4 ALVERTON TERR
5 STANFORD CL
6 WEETHES COTTS
7 ALVERNE BLDGS
8 CARMINOWE CRES

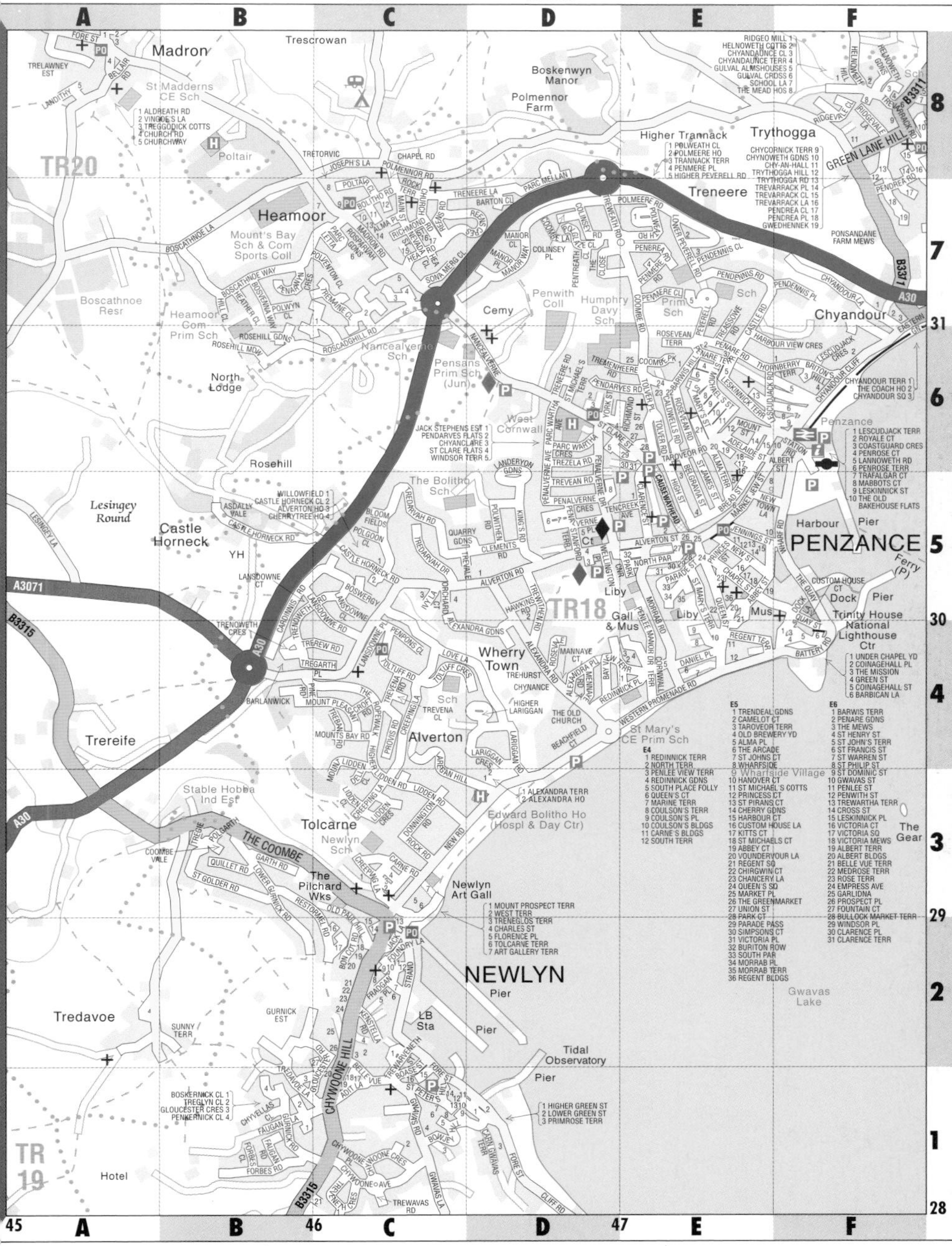

C1
1 TREVENETH PL
2 TREWINCE TERR
3 HIGHER GWAVAS RD
4 GWAVAS BGLWS
5 BOWJEY TERR
6 SEA VIEW TERR
7 LYN TERR
8 MEADOW VILLAS
9 BOWJEY CT
10 NAVY INN CT
11 HARBOUR LIGHTS
12 EBENEZER PL
13 EDEN TERR
14 EDEN GDNS
15 CHURCH ST
16 FRANWILL TERR
17 PARC VILLAS
18 PARK RD
19 PARC TERR
20 JUBILEE BGLWS
21 BOUNDARY CL
88

C2
1 NORTH CNR
2 MALT HOUSE GDNS
3 THE MALT HOUSE
4 ANTOINE CL
5 WESLEY PL
6 STRICKLAND COTTS
7 GWAVAS QUAY
8 FARMERS MDW
9 CHAPEL ST
88

10 ORCHARD PL
11 ORCHARD HO
12 THE FRADGAN
13 THE BRIDGE HO
14 CLIFTON HILL
15 CLIFTON TERR
16 PENGWEL
17 BARLANDHU
18 BON VILLAS
19 HIGHFIELDS
88

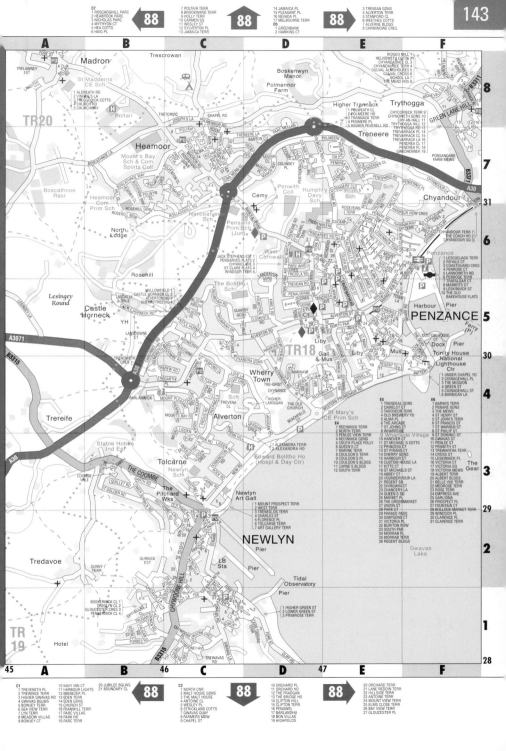

20 ORCHARD TERR
21 LANE REDDIN TERR
22 HILLSIDE TERR
23 ANTOINE TERR
24 MOUNT VIEW TERR
25 ELMS CLOSE TERR
26 BAY VIEW TERR
27 GLOUCESTER PL

81
81

C7
1 HARRIS CT
2 SLADES LA
3 BENNETTS COTTS
4 RUSSELL WAY
5 SARACEN HO
6 BANK COTTS

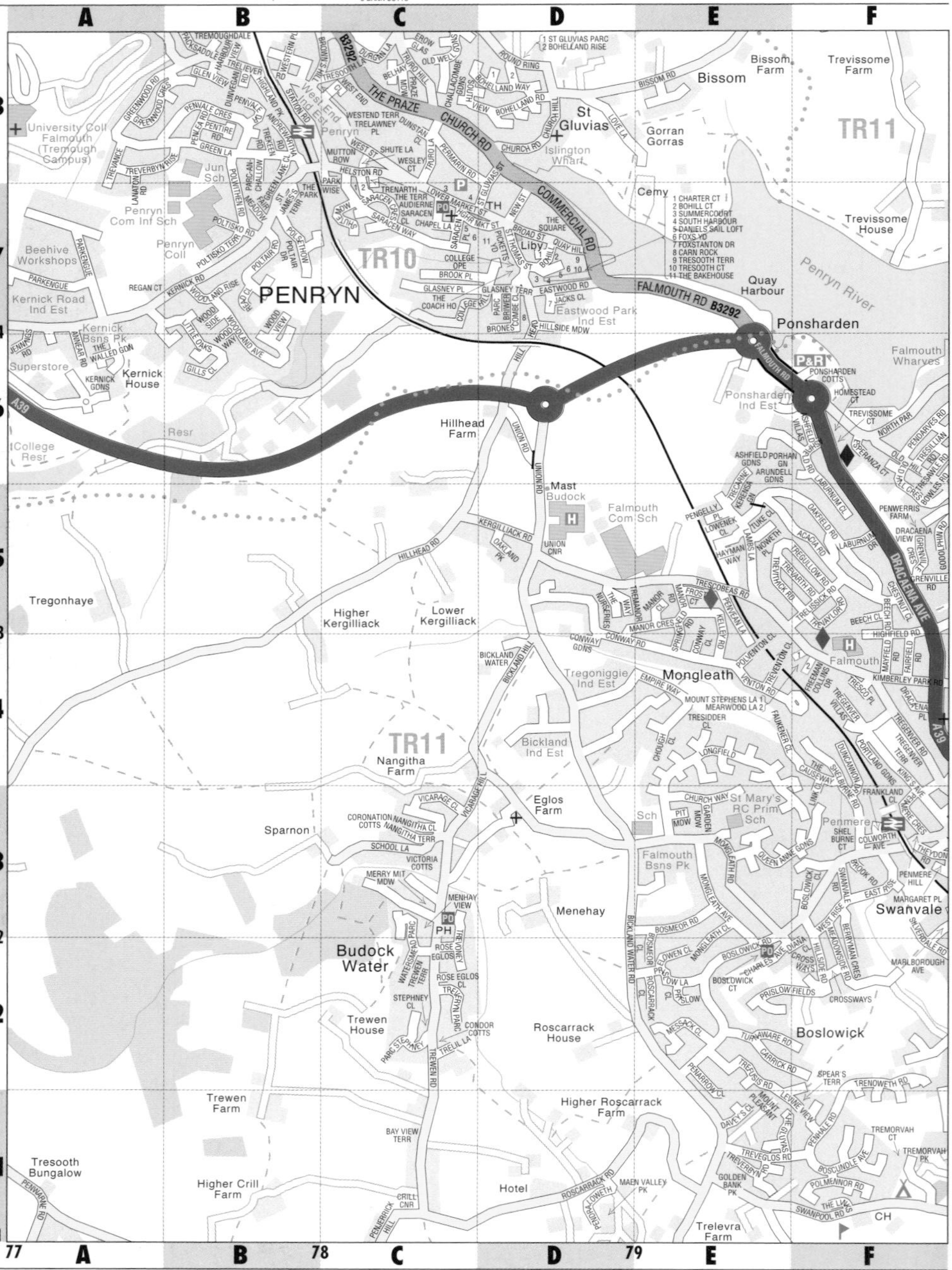

93
93

A4
1 CHY NAMPARA
2 TREVETHAN GDNS
3 BERKELEY PATH
4 BERKELEY MEWS
5 HENRY SCOTT TUKE HO
6 BROOK CT
7 ST JOHN'S CT
8 PENVALE CT
9 KILLIGREW PL
10 LISTER HILL
11 NEW WINDSOR TERR
12 HAWKINS WAY
13 RALEIGH PL
14 CLIFTON PL
15 CLIFTON TERR
16 CLIFTON CRES

A5
1 CLAREMONT COTTS
2 TREVETHAN CT
3 CLAREMONT TERR
4 LAMBERT TERR
5 BEACON TERR
6 POLWHAVERAL TERR
7 PELLEW CL
8 LANGTON TERR
9 FROBISHER TERR
10 PENWERRIS TERR
11 BASSET PL
12 DUNSTANVILLE TERR

82
82

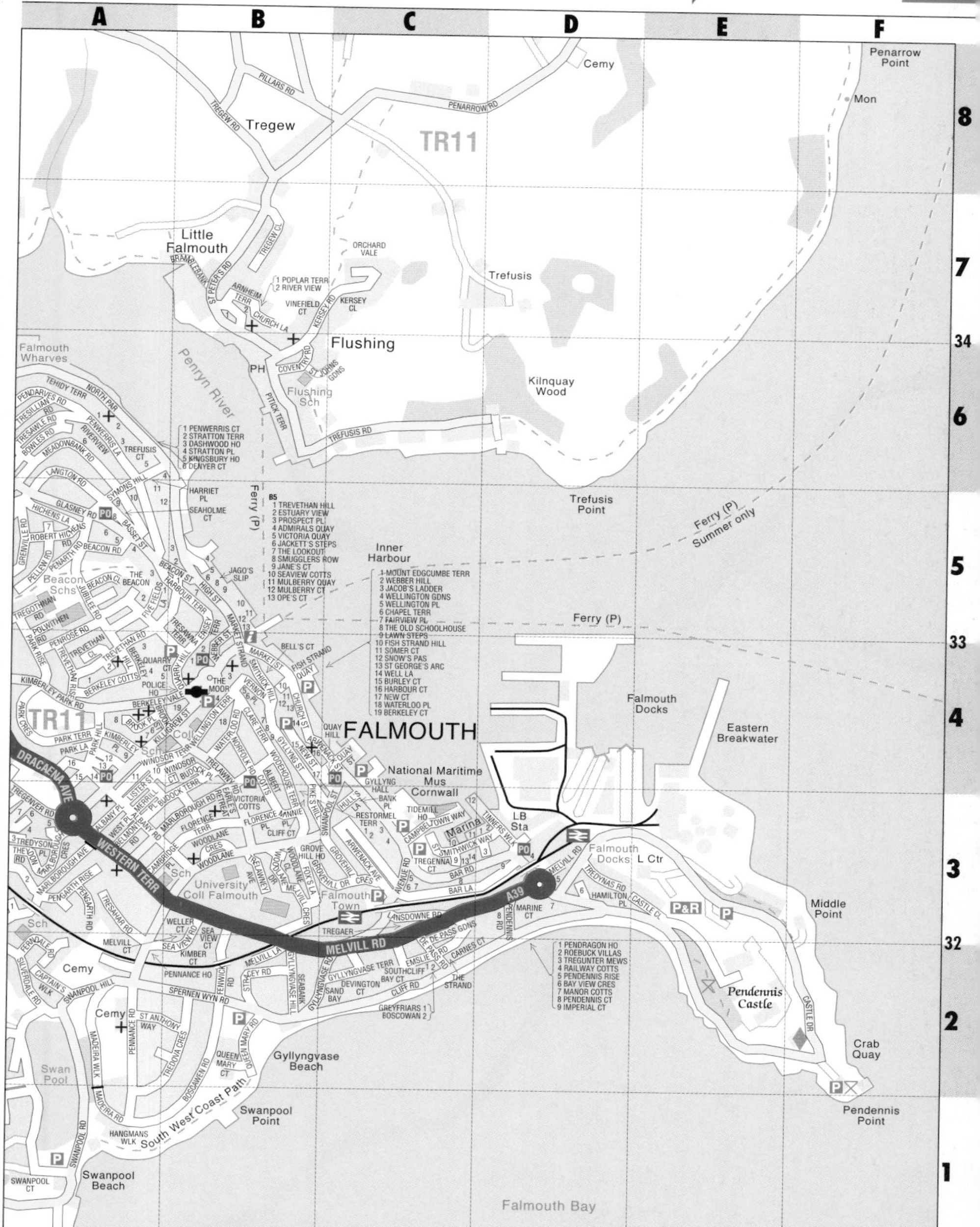

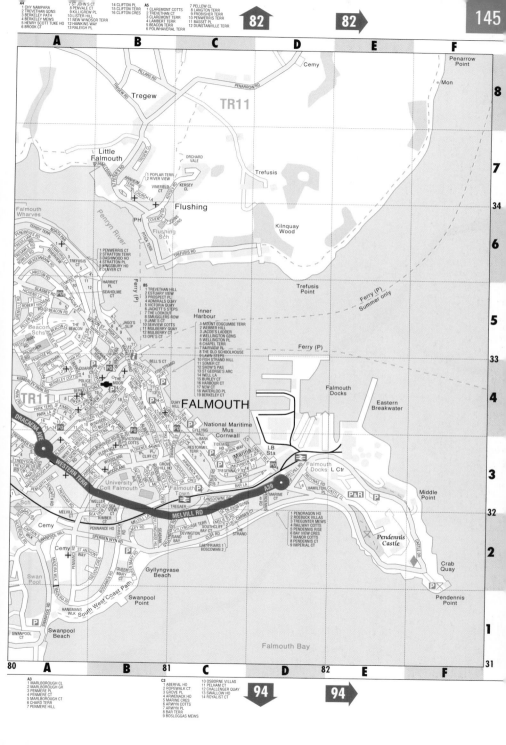

A3
1 MARLBOROUGH CL
2 MARLBOROUGH GR
3 PENMERE PL
4 PENMERE CT
5 MARLBOROUGH CT
6 CHARD TERR
7 PENMERE HILL

C3
1 ABERFAL HO
2 ROPEWALK CT
3 GROVE PL
4 ARWENACK HO
5 MARINE CRES
6 ARWYN COTTS
7 ARWYN PL
8 BAR TERR
9 BOSLOGGAS MEWS
10 OSBORNE VILLAS
11 PELHAM CT
12 CHALLENGER QUAY
13 SWALLOW HO
14 ROYALIST CT

94
94

91 91 92

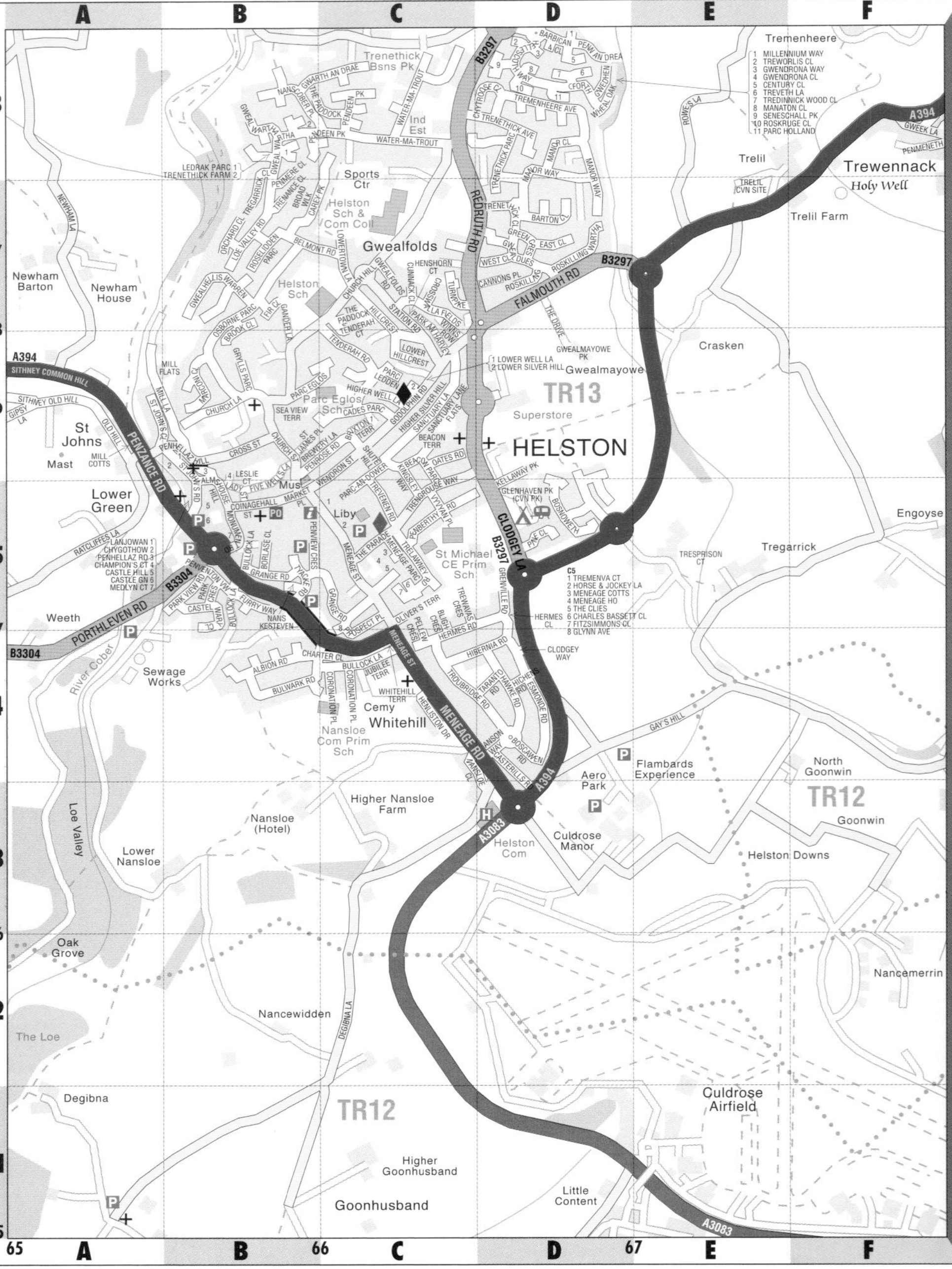

98 98 99 99

30 30

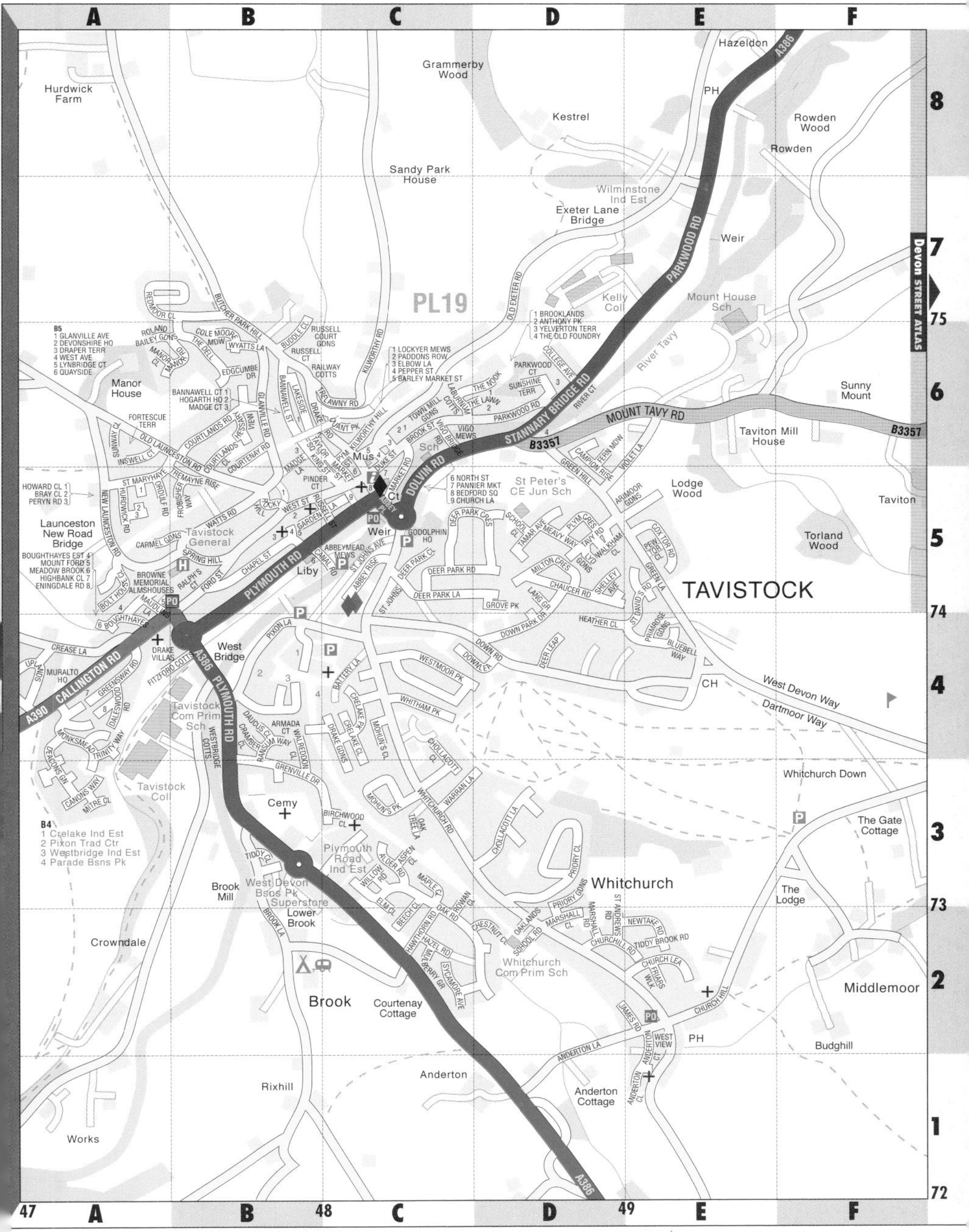

41 41 42 42

128

128

One-way Streets

House numbers 1 59 HIGH ST

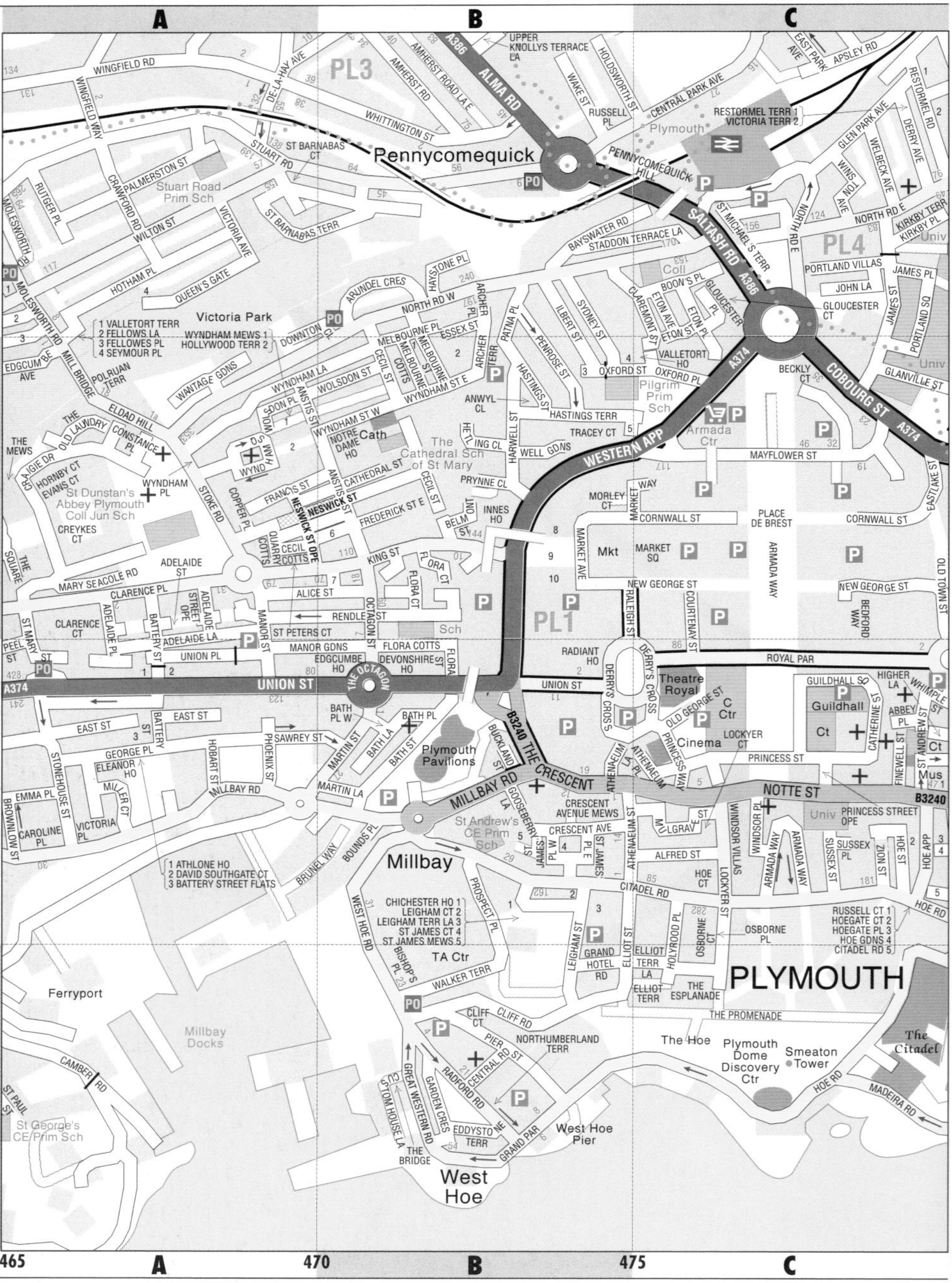

B3
1 ANSON HO
2 MELBOURNE GN
3 ETON TERR
4 OXFORD TERR
5 CAMBRIDGE LA W
6 FREDERICK ST W
7 ALICE LA
8 HARWELL CT
9 FRANKFORT GATE
10 COLIN CAMPBELL CT

134

134

Scale: 3½ inches to 1 mile
0 110 yards 220 yards
0 125 m 250 m

128 129 129

A4
1 ABINGDON RD
2 ENDSLEIGH GDNS
3 SHAFTESBURY CT
4 The Old Tannery Bsns Pk
5 WINIFRED BAKER CT

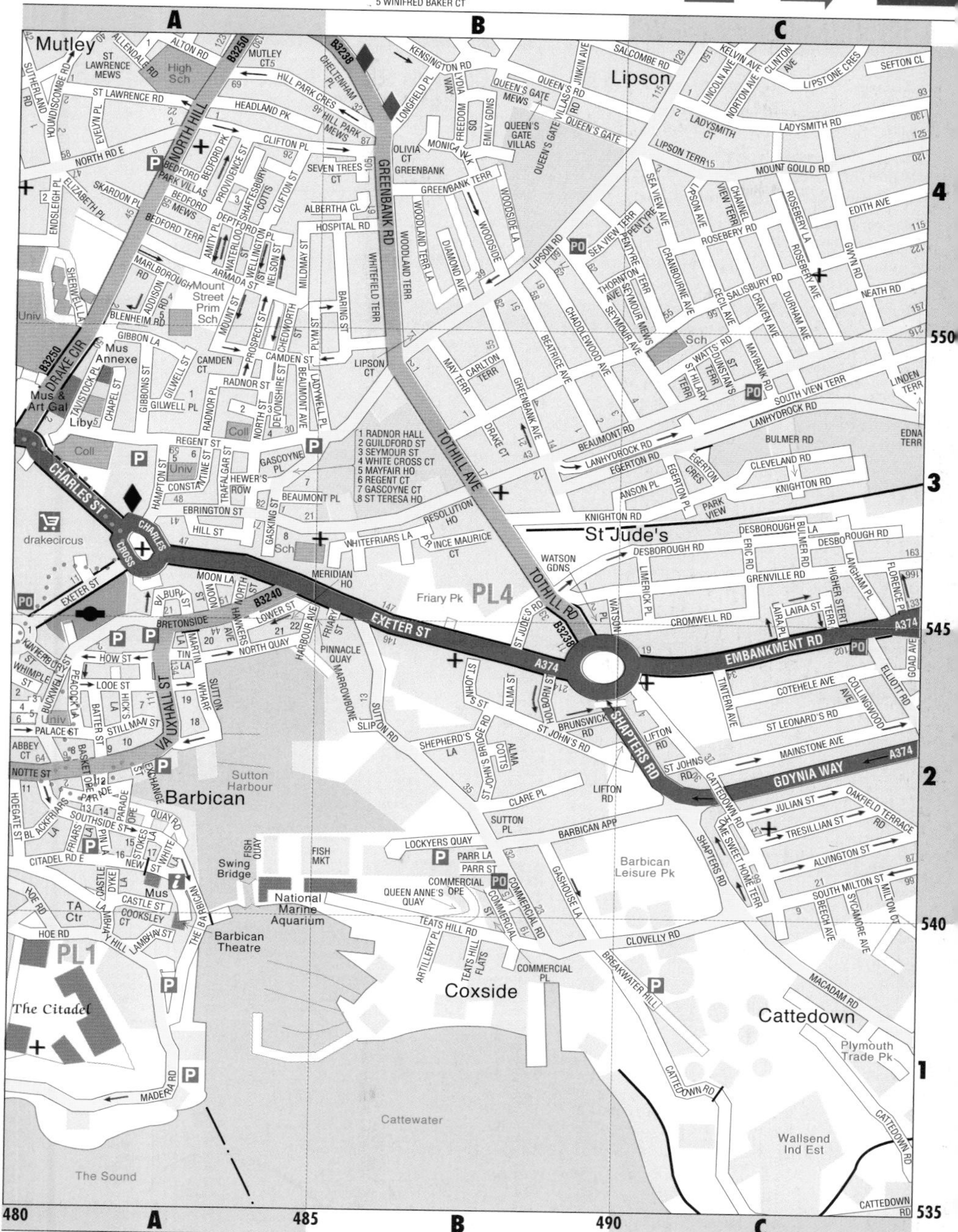

134 135 135

A2
1 ST ANDREWS CROSS
2 ELIZABETH CT
3 HIGH ST
4 HIGHER LA
5 EASTLAKE HO
6 LOWER LA
7 STILLMAN CT
8 WOOLSTER CT
9 BROCK HO
10 VAUXHALL CT
11 ELSPETH SITTERS HO
12 BARBICAN CT
13 CITADEL OPE
14 SOUTHSIDE OPE
15 MITRE CT
16 HANOVER CT
17 JOHN SPARKE HO
18 DOLPHIN HO
19 VAUXHALL STREET FLATS
20 DISCOVERY WHARF
21 BEAUFORT HO
22 SUTTON MEWS

Index

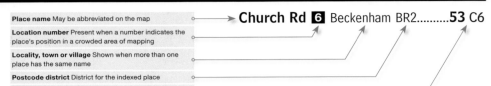

Place name May be abbreviated on the map → **Church Rd 6 Beckenham BR2..........53 C6**

Location number Present when a number indicates the place's position in a crowded area of mapping

Locality, town or village Shown when more than one place has the same name

Postcode district District for the indexed place

Page and grid square Page number and grid reference for the standard mapping

Public and commercial buildings are highlighted in magenta Places of interest are highlighted in blue with a star★

Abbreviations used in the index

Acad	**Academy**	Comm	**Common**	Gd	**Ground**	L	**Leisure**	Prom	**Promenade**
App	**Approach**	Cott	**Cottage**	Gdn	**Garden**	La	**Lane**	Rd	**Road**
Arc	**Arcade**	Cres	**Crescent**	Gn	**Green**	Liby	**Library**	Recn	**Recreation**
Ave	**Avenue**	Cswy	**Causeway**	Gr	**Grove**	Mdw	**Meadow**	Ret	**Retail**
Bglw	**Bungalow**	Ct	**Court**	H	**Hall**	Meml	**Memorial**	Sh	**Shopping**
Bldg	**Building**	Ctr	**Centre**	Ho	**House**	Mkt	**Market**	Sq	**Square**
Bsns, Bus	**Business**	Ctry	**Country**	Hospl	**Hospital**	Mus	**Museum**	St	**Street**
Bvd	**Boulevard**	Cty	**County**	HQ	**Headquarters**	Orch	**Orchard**	Sta	**Station**
Cath	**Cathedral**	Dr	**Drive**	Hts	**Heights**	Pal	**Palace**	Terr	**Terrace**
Cir	**Circus**	Dro	**Drove**	Ind	**Industrial**	Par	**Parade**	TH	**Town Hall**
Cl	**Close**	Ed	**Education**	Inst	**Institute**	Pas	**Passage**	Univ	**University**
Cnr	**Corner**	Emb	**Embankment**	Int	**International**	Pk	**Park**	Wk, Wlk	**Walk**
Coll	**College**	Est	**Estate**	Intc	**Interchange**	Pl	**Place**	Wr	**Water**
Com	**Community**	Ex	**Exhibition**	Junc	**Junction**	Prec	**Precinct**	Yd	**Yard**

Index of localities, towns and villages

A

Addington..........113 D7
Albaston..........40 E5
Alfardisworthy..........5 E6
Altarnun..........26 C8
Alverton..........143 C4
Amalebra..........76 F3
Amalveor..........76 E4
Anderton..........132 F4
Angarrack..........78 C5
Antony..........65 E5
Ashton..........90 E3

B

Badgall..........17 C5
Badharlick..........17 E5
Bakesdown..........7 D3
Baldhu..........69 C1
Ball..........108 E7
Balnoon..........77 A5
Balwest..........90 D5
Bangors..........6 F2
Barbican..........149 A2
Barcelona..........62 E4
Bareppa..........93 D4
Barkla Shop..........54 E1
Barne Barton..........127 C8
Barripper..........79 B5
Bathpool..........27 C1
Beacon..........138 F1
Bealsmill..........28 E3
Beeny..........9 E3
Belowda..........46 D4
Bennacott..........12 E2
Bere Alston..........41 B1
Bere Ferrers..........119 E3
Berepper..........98 F5
Berriowbridge..........27 B2
Besoughan..........45 A3
Bethel..........115 A5
Bickham..........121 A7
Billacombe..........135 F8
Billacott..........12 B1
Biscovey..........60 B4
Bishop's Quay..........99 F8
Bissoe..........81 D8
Bissom..........144 E8
Black Cross..........45 E3
Black Rock..........79 D1
Blackwater..........68 D5
Blindwell..........132 E5
Blisland..........35 D8
Blowinghouse
Bodmin..........109 B2
Redruth..........139 F6
Blue Anchor..........57 D8
Bodelva..........115 F8
Bodieve..........108 C7
Bodilly..........91 F7
Bodinnick..........116 E5
Bodmin..........109 B5
Bodwen..........47 E3
Bohetherick..........40 F2
Bohortha..........95 C5
Bolenowe..........79 F5
Bolingey..........55 B4
Bolitho..........79 F1
Bolventor..........25 E3
Boquio..........91 F8
Borea..........76 F2
Boscadjack..........91 F6
Boscarne..........34 C2
Boscastle..........9 C1
Boscoppa..........115 A6
Boscreege..........90 C5
Boskednan..........76 A1
Boskenna..........97 C4
Bosleake..........139 C3
Boslowick..........144 F2
Bosporthennis..........75 F3
Bossiney..........14 D8
Boswednack..........76 A4
Boswinger..........85 B5
Botallack..........86 E7
Bottoms..........96 E5
Botusfleming..........122 B7
Bowling Green
Bugle..........47 E1
Redruth..........139 D3
Boyton..........13 B2
Braddock..........49 F5
Bradford..........24 D2
Brane..........87 C3
Bray Shop..........28 B1
Brazacott..........12 B2
Brea..........139 B3
Brea Addit..........139 B2
Breage..........90 F3
Brent..........62 E2
Bridge..........67 E5
Bridgend..........112 E3
Bridgerule..........8 A6
Bridges..........59 F8
Bridgetown..........19 B8
Brighton..........57 D5
Brixton..........136 F4
Broadlane..........90 E5
Brocton..........34 A3
Brook..........147 B2
Brunnion..........77 A3
Buckland Monachorum..........42 A3
Bude..........104 E6
Budock Water..........144 C2
Bugle..........47 D1
Burhos..........79 F2
Burlawn..........108 D1
Burraton..........122 D4
Burraton Coombe..........122 C2
Bursdon..........3 B6
Busveal..........140 F4
Buttsbear Cross..........7 F7

C

Cadgwith..........103 B4
Calenick..........137 C1
Callestick..........55 C1
Callington..........39 E5
Calloose..........78 D2
Calstock..........41 A3
Camborne..........138 B2
Cambrose..........67 F6
Camelford..........105 C4
Camels Head..........127 E7
Cannalidgey..........32 E4
Canonstown..........77 C2
Canworthy Water..........11 D2
Caradon Town..........38 E6
Carbis..........47 A2
Carbis Bay..........141 D3
Carclaze..........114 E6
Cardinham..........35 E3
Carfury..........76 A1
Cargreen..........119 A2
Carharrack..........80 F8
Carkeel..........122 C6
Carleen..........90 F5
Carlidnack..........93 E4
Carloggas
Foxhole..........58 C5
Penwithick..........59 D7
St Mawgan..........45 A8
Carluddon..........59 D6
Carlyon Bay..........115 E3
Carn Arthen..........139 B2
Carn Brea Village..........139 F5
Carne
St Dennis..........46 C1
Veryan..........83 F5
Carn Entral..........139 A2
Carnhell Green..........78 F4
Carnhot..........68 F4
Carnkie..........139 F2
Carnkief..........55 D3
Carnon Downs..........82 A7
Carn Towan..........96 C7
Carnyorth..........86 F8
Carpalla..........58 D4
Carthew..........59 B6
Carwynnen..........79 D4
Carzise..........78 D1
Castallack..........97 F6
Castle Gate..........76 F1
Castle Horneck..........143 B5
Catchall..........97 D8
Cattedown..........149 C1
Cawsand..........133 B1
Chacewater..........68 F3
Chaddlewood..........131 B6
Chapel
Launceston..........106 A5
Quintrell Downs..........111 E4
Chapel Town..........57 B6
Chaple Amble..........22 D2
Chapman's Well..........13 E4
Charlestown..........115 B2
Chenhalls..........142 A2
Chillaton..........29 F8
Chilsworthy..........40 E7
Churchbridge..........50 F1
Church Combe..........140 A2
Church Cove..........103 A2
Churchtown
Bridgerule..........8 B6
Camborne..........67 E5
Lanivet..........47 E7
St Breward..........24 B4
Church Town..........140 A3
Chyandour..........143 F7
Chy-an-Gweal..........141 B2
Chycoose..........82 A6
Chynhale..........91 C5
Clapper..........108 E4
Cleers..........46 E1
Clerkenwater..........109 D8
Cliff..........61 B6
Clifford..........3 F8
Clowance Wood..........79 A1
Clubworthy..........12 C3
Coad's Green..........27 D4
Cocks..........55 B3
Cockwells..........77 C1
Colan..........44 F4
Cold Northcoot..........16 F5
Coldvreath..........46 F1
Colebrook..........130 E6
Combe..........136 E5
Come-to-Good..........82 B7
Comford..........80 F6
Common Moor..........37 F4
Condon's Shop..........27 B5
Connor Downs..........78 D5
Constantine..........92 E3
Constantine Bay..........20 D1
Cooksland..........35 B2
Coombe
Camborne..........66 F3
Perranarworthal..........81 B8
Playing Place..........82 D8
St Stephen..........58 B2
Coosebean..........137 A5
Coppathorne..........7 A3
Copperhouse..........142 D6
Copthorne..........12 B3
Coswinsawsin..........79 A5
Coverack..........101 C1
Coverack Bridges..........91 E5
Coxford..........10 D7
Cox Hill..........68 F2
Coxpark..........40 D7
Coxside..........149 B1
Crabtree..........129 E5
Crackington Haven..........10 B7
Crafthole..........65 B5
Crane..........138 C2
Crantock..........43 D3
Crapstone..........42 B2
Crean..........96 F5
Creed..........72 A6
Creegbrawse..........68 F2
Crelly..........91 F7
Cremyll..........133 E7
Crimp..........3 A2
Cripplesease..........77 A3
Croanford..........34 C6
Crofthandy..........68 E1
Croft Mitchell..........79 E4
Crossgate..........19 A7
Cross Lanes..........99 C4
Crosstown..........2 B1
Crowan..........79 C1
Crowlas..........89 C8
Crownhill..........124 F2
Crowntown..........91 B5
Crows-an-wra..........96 F8
Crow's Nest..........38 B4
Crugmeer..........107 A7
Crumplehorn..........62 D2
Cubert..........55 D8
Curgurrell..........83 C4

Currian Vale 58 D8
Curry Lane 12 E4
Cury 99 B4
Cusgarne 81 B7
Cusveorth Coombes 69 B2
Cuttivett 53 B5

D

Dadbrook 132 E4
Darite 38 B4
Darracott 2 D4
Davidstow 16 A6
Daw's House 18 E1
Delabole 14 D3
Demelza 46 E6
Derriford 125 B4
Derril 8 D6
Deveral 78 D2
Devonport 127 D4
Devoran 81 F6
Dinworthy 3 F2
Dizzard 6 B1
Dobwalls 50 E8
Docton 2 F8
Doublebois 50 C8
Dousland 42 F3
Downderry 64 C5
Downgate
- Kelly Bray 40 A7
- Pensilva 38 D5

Downinney 11 B1
Down Thomas 135 C1
Drawbridge 49 F8
Drift 87 F3
Drym 91 A8
Duloe 51 A1
Dunmere 34 D2
Dunsley 38 C6
Dunterton 28 F6
Duporth 115 A1
Durgan 93 D2
Dutson 106 E8

E

Eastcott 3 A3
East Looe 117 D3
East Panson 13 F3
East Portholland 84 E5
East Taphouse 50 B6
East Youlstone 3 C2
Edistone 2 F8
Efford 129 C5
Eggbeare 19 A7
Eggbuckland 129 C8
Egloskerry 18 A5
Egoshayle 108 D6
Elburton 136 B6
Elmscott 2 E8
Empacombe 133 D6
Enniscaven 46 D2
Ernesettle 123 E3
Estover 125 E4

F

Fairy Cross 49 B5
Falmouth 145 C4
Farms Common 79 F1
Fentonadle 24 A5
Feock 82 C5
Fernsplatt 81 C8
Fiddlers Green 56 B5
Fletchersbridge 48 F8
Flexbury 104 E6
Flushing
- Manaccan 101 B8
- Penryn 145 C6

Fonston 11 C2
Ford 128 A5
Forder
- Cawsand 132 F1
- Saltash 122 C1

Ford Park 128 D4
Forge 68 A4
Forrabury 9 C2
Foss 133 A5
Foundary 142 B5
Four Lanes 80 A5
Fowey 116 B4
Foxhole 58 D5
Fraddam 78 D1
Fraddon 45 E1
Freathy 65 E3
Frogpool 81 C7
Frogwell 39 D3

G

Gam 24 A4
Gang 38 F3
Garras 99 D6
Gatherley 19 E1
Gear 99 F7
Georgia 76 E3
Germoe 90 C4
Germoe Cross Roads 90 C3
Gerrans 83 B2
Gilbert's Coombe 140 A8
Gillan 101 C8
Glenholt 125 D6
Gloweth 69 E3
Gluvian 45 E7
Godolphin Cross 90 E6
Godrevy Towans 66 B3
Golant 61 A5
Golberdon 39 C6
Goldsithney 89 D5
Gollawater 55 A1
Gonamena 38 B5
Gonvena 108 C6
Goonbell 68 D8
Goon Gumpas 68 F1
Goonhavern 55 E4
Goonhusband 146 C1
Goonown 54 D1
Goonvrea 68 B8
Gooseham 2 E3
Gorran Churchtown 73 B1
Gorran Haven 85 D5
Gorran High Lanes 72 F2
Gothers 46 D1
Gover Valley 59 A4
Grampound 72 B7
Grampound Road 57 E1
Great Bosullow 87 D8
Green Bottom 69 B4
Greensplat 59 A6
Grenofen 42 A6
Grimscott 5 A2
Grumbla 87 C4
Guildford 142 E6
Gulval 88 E6
Gulworthy 41 B8
Gunnislake 40 F5
Gunwalloe 98 E5
Gwallon 89 C6
Gwavas 91 D4
Gwealfolds 146 C7
Gweek 92 C1
Gwennap 80 F7
Gwinear 78 D4
Gwithian 66 B2
Gwithian Towans 66 A2

H

Halamanning 90 A6
Hale Mills 69 A1
Halgabron 14 E7
Hallew 47 C2
Hallivick 58 A4
Hallworthy 16 D6
Halsetown 77 A5
Halvosso 93 A8
Halwin 92 B8
Ham 128 A8
Hannafore 117 C2
Harcourt 82 B4
Hardisworthy 2 D7
Harlyn 20 D2
Harrowbarrow 40 D5
Hartley 128 E7
Hartley Vale 129 A8
Hatt 53 E4
Haye 39 D4
Hayle 142 C6
Heamoor 143 B7
Hele 13 C2
Helebridge 7 A6
Helford 93 B1
Helford Passage 93 C2
Helland 35 A5
Hellandbridge 34 F6
Hellesveor 77 A7
Helston 146 D6
Helstone 24 B8
Hemerdon 131 D7
Henaford 2 F5
Hendra
- Bodmin 46 F7
- Camelford 105 A4
- Mullion 102 F7
- St Dennis 58 C8

Henford 13 F5
Henwood 38 B8
Herniss 80 F1
Herodsfoot 50 E3
Hessenford 64 C8
Hewas Water 72 D8
Higher Bal 54 B2
Higher Boscaswell 75 A1
Higher Brea 139 B3
Higher Carnkie 139 F2
Highercliff 63 B8
Higher Compton 129 A6
Higher Condurrow 139 A1
Higher Crackington 10 C6
Higher Downs 89 F5
Higher Larrick 27 E5
Higher Porthpean 59 D1
Higher Rosewarne 138 D5
Higher Tolcarne 45 B8
Highertown
- Camelford 24 E8
- Truro 69 F3

Higher Trewince 44 E6
Highlanes 32 B7
High Lanes 142 D5
High Street 58 D4
Hill 10 B5
Hingston Down 40 B6
Holestrow 102 E2
Hollacombe Hill 136 A2
Holmbush 115 B4
Holywell 43 B2
Honicknowle 124 B2
Hooe 135 C5
Horningtops 51 E3
Horrabridge 42 C5
Horsebridge 29 C1
Horsedowns 78 F1
Huddisford 3 F6

I

Idless 70 B6
Illogan 67 E4
Illogan Highway 139 C6
Indian Queens 45 E1
Insworke 132 F6

J

Jacobstow 11 B6
Jewel's Cross 7 F6
Jolly's Bottom 69 A4
Joppa
- Hayle 142 E4
- St Just 87 A4

K

Kehelland 66 F2
Kelly 29 B8
Kelly Bray 39 F6
Kelynack 86 F4
Kennards House 18 B2
Kenneggy 90 A3
Kenneggy Downs 90 B4
Kents 10 F6
Kenwyn 137 C6
Kerris 97 E8
Kerrow Moor 59 D8
Kestle 73 A4
Kestle Mill 111 F1
Keybridge 35 B8
Keyham 127 E5
Kilkhampton 5 A6
Killatown 37 B1
Killivose 79 C5
Kingbeare 27 A1
Kingsand 133 A2
King's Tamerton 123 F2
Knightsmill 23 F7
Kuggar 103 B6

L

Ladock 57 C1
Lady Nance 44 F3
Laira 129 C4
Lake 42 E3
Lamanva 93 C6
Lambourne 55 B2
Lamellion 113 A4
Lamerton 30 B3
Lamorick 47 E7
Lamorna 97 E5
Lamorran 83 C8
Lana 13 D7
Landrake 53 B3
Landreyne 27 C2
Landulph 123 A7
Lane 111 B3
Laneast 17 B2
Lanescot 60 D6
Langdon 11 C3
Langore 18 D5
Lanivet 47 F6
Lanjeth 58 E3
Lanjew 46 F7
Lank 24 B2
Lanlivery 48 C1
Lanner 80 D6
Lanreath 62 B7
Lansallos 62 A2
Lanstephan 106 C8
Lanteglos 14 F1
Lanteglos Highway 61 E4
Latchley 40 D8
Launceston 106 D5
Lawhitton 19 C1
Leburnick 28 D8
Leedstown 78 E1
Leigham 129 E8
Lelant 77 E4
Lelant Downs 77 D2
Lerryn 61 D8
Lescrow 116 B6
Lesnewth 10 A1
Levalsa Meor 73 B8
Lewannick 27 B7
Ley 36 E1
Lezant 28 B6
Lifton 19 F3
Liftondown 19 D4
Linkinhorne 39 B8
Lipson 149 C4
Lipson Vale 129 A4
Liskeard 113 E6
Little Bosullow 75 D1
Little Brynn 46 E5
Little Comfort 28 C7
Little Falmouth 145 B7
Little Kirland 109 C1
Little Petherick 32 C6
Little Prideaux 60 B7
Lizard 102 F2
Lockengate 47 E4
London Apprentice 59 B1
Longbridge 129 F7
Longcross 29 F6
Longdowns 81 A1
Longlands 122 A1
Longrock 88 F6
Longstone
- Carbis Bay 141 E1
- St Mabyn 34 F8

Looe 117 D3
Lostwithiel 112 E1
Lovaton 42 F1
Lower Bodinnar 87 E7
Lower Boscaswell 74 F2
Lower Brea 139 A3
Lower Clicker 51 F4
Lower Compton 129 A5
Lower Green 146 A5
Lower Ninnes 76 B1
Lower Porthpean 59 E1
Lower Prospidnick 91 C6
Lower Rose 55 D5
Lower Rosewarne 138 C4
Lowertown
- Helston 91 E4
- Lostwithiel 48 A4

Lower Trebullett 28 A4
Luckett 40 B8
Ludgvan 89 A7
Luffincott 13 C5
Lutsford 3 A6
Luxulyan 48 A1
Lynstone 104 D3

M

Mabe Burnthouse 93 C8
Maders 39 D6
Madron 143 B8
Maenporth 93 F4
Maer 104 D8
Mainstone 125 F2
Malpas 70 D2
Manaccan 101 A8
Manadon 124 D1
Mannamead 128 F5
Manor Parsley 68 B5
Marazion 89 B6
Marhamchurch 7 B6
Marshgate 10 C2
Marsh Mills 130 A6
Mawgan 99 D7
Mawgan Porth 31 B2
Mawla 68 B4
Mawnan 93 E2
Mawnan Smith 93 E3
Maxworthy 12 A3
Mayon 96 B6
Mead 2 D4
Meadwell 29 C8
Meavy 42 F2
Meddon 3 C4
Melbur 57 F5
Mellingey 32 D6
Menadarva 66 E2
Menagissey 68 C5
Mendennick 132 C7
Menheniot 52 A5
Merrifield 7 F4
Merrymeet 38 C1
Merther 70 F3
Merther Lane 70 F1
Metherell 40 D4
Mevagissey 73 D3
Michaelstow 24 A5
Middle Crackington 10 B6
Middle Greadow 48 B1
Middlehill 38 D3
Middlemoor 147 F2
Middlewood 27 B2
Milcombe 62 F6
Millbay 148 B2
Millbrook 132 E5
Millendreath 117 F5
Millhill 30 B1
Millook 6 D2
Millpool
- Cardinham 35 F5
- Praa Sands 90 B5

Milltown
- Cardinham 35 E3
- Lostwithiel 60 F8

Milton Abbot 29 D6
Milton Combe 120 F8
Milton Green 29 D5
Mingoose 68 C7
Minions 38 B6
Mitchell 56 F5
Mithian 54 F1
Mithian Downs 68 F8
Mixtow 116 D7
Molinnis 47 C2
Mongleath 144 E4
Moortown
- Tavistock 42 D8
- Tetcott 13 C7

Morice Town 127 D3
Mornick 39 B7
Morvah 75 C2
Morval 63 D7
Morwellham 41 B4
Morwenstow 2 B2
Mount
- Cardinham 36 B2
- Cubert 55 C7

Mount Ambrose 140 E7
Mount Charles 114 E4
Mount Gould 129 B3
Mount Hawke 68 C6
Mountjoy 45 A3
Mount Lane 13 E6
Mount Wise 127 F1
Mousehole 88 D1
Muchlarnick 62 E7
Mulfra 76 B1
Mullion 99 A1
Mutley 128 F4
Myler Churchtown 82 C2
Mylor Bridge 82 A3

N

Nancegollan 91 C7
Nancemellin 66 D1
Nancledra 76 F2
Nanpean 58 D7
Nansladron 73 B7
Nanstallon 34 C1
Nantithet 99 B5
Narkurs 64 D6
Navarino 18 B8
Nethercott 13 E7
Netherton 38 D7
Newbridge
- Callington 39 D2
- Penzance 87 E6
- Truro 69 F3

New Downs
- St Agnes 54 B2
- St Just 86 E6

Newlyn 143 D2
Newmill
- Penzance 76 B1
- Poundstock 7 A1

New Polzeath 21 E6
Newport 106 B7
Newquay 110 E7
Newtown
- Coad's Green 27 D5
- Praa Sands 90 B4

Newtown-in-St Martin 100 E6
Ninnis Bridge 77 B2
No Man's Land 63 E7
Noonvares 90 E7
Norris Green 40 E4
North Beer 12 F3
North Brentor 30 E8
North Corner 101 C2
Northcott
- Bude 4 C3
- St Giles on the Heath 13 D3

North Country 140 B8
North Darley 38 D8
North Hill 27 B3
Northmoor 3 F3
North Petherwin 18 A8
North Prospect 128 A6
North Tamerton 12 F8
Numphra 87 A4

O

Old Kea 82 E8
Oreston 135 C7
Otterham 10 D1
Otterham Station 16 A8
Ottery 30 A2

P

Padstow 107 C4
Palmersbridge 25 F4
Pancrasweek 8 C8
Pantersbridge 36 D3
Par 60 C4
Paramoor 72 E8
Parc Erissey 68 A3
Park Bottom 139 B8
Parkfield 39 A2
Parnacott 8 E8
Paul 88 C2
Paul's Green 90 E8
Paynter's Lane End 67 E4
Pelynt 62 D5
Penbeagle 141 A4
Penberth 97 A3
Pencarrow 105 D1
Pencuke 10 D5
Pendeen 75 A1
Pendoggett 23 A6
Pendrift 24 B1
Penelewey 82 C7
Pengegon 138 F2
Pengelly 14 E2
Pengold 10 A5
Penhale
- Indian Queens 57 D8
- Millbrook 132 D7
- Mullion 99 D1

Penhallick 139 C4
Penhallow 55 B2
Penhalvean 80 C4
Penmarth 80 C2
Penmayne 21 E3
Pennance 140 F1
Pennycomequick 148 B4
Pennycross 128 C8
Pennytinney 23 A4
Penpethy 14 F5
Penpillick 60 D7
Penpol 82 B6

Penpoll 61 D5
Penponds 138 B1
Penpont 24 A1
Penrose
  St Breward 24 A3
  St Eval 31 E5
Penryn 144 B7
Pensilva 38 E5
Penstraze 69 A4
Pentewan 73 C6
Pentire 43 D4
Penwartha Coombe 55 B3
Penweathers 69 F2
Penwithick 59 E7
Penzance 143 F5
Percuil 83 A1
Perranarworthal 81 D6
Perrancoombe 55 A3
Perran Downs 89 E5
Perranporth 55 B5
Perranuthnoe 89 D4
Perranwell
  Goonhavern 55 C3
  Perranarworthal 81 C6
Perranzabuloe 55 B3
Peter's Finger 19 C7
Peterville 54 D1
Petherwin Gate 18 B7
Peverell 128 D6
Phillack 142 D7
Philleigh 83 B6
Piece 139 D2
Pillaton 53 B6
Pillatonmill 53 B6
Pipers Pool 17 F3
Pityme 21 F3
Plaidy 117 E5
Plain-an-Gwarry 140 B6
Playing Place 82 B8
Plushabridge 38 F7
Plymouth 148 C1
Plympton 130 E5
Plympton St Maurice 130 E4
Plymstock 135 E6
Point 82 B5
Polbathic 64 F8
Polborder 53 D7
Polbrock 34 A4
Polgigga 96 D4
Polgooth 59 A1
Polkerris 60 E3
Polladras 90 F5
Polmassick 72 E4
Polmear 60 E4
Polmorla 108 A4
Polpeor 77 B3
Polperro 62 E1
Polruan 116 C2
Polscoe 112 E3
Poltesco 103 B5
Polyphant 17 F1
Polzeath 21 E5
Pomphlett 135 E8
Poniou 76 A5
Ponsanooth 81 B5
Ponsharden 144 E7
Ponsongath 103 E7
Pont 61 D3
Pool 139 B5
Porkellis 92 B8
Porteath 22 A6
Port Gaverne 22 E7
Porth 111 C8
Porthallow
  Looe 62 F2
  St Keverne 101 D6
Porthcothan 31 C6
Porthcurno 96 E3
Porthilly 21 D2
Porth Kea 70 B1
Porthleven 98 B8
Porthmeor 75 F4
Porth Navas 93 B2
Porthoustock 101 E4
Porthtowan 68 A6
Portington 29 E3
Port Isaac 22 D8
Portloe 84 B3
Portlooe 117 A2
Portmellon 73 C3
Port Quin 22 B7
Portreath 67 C6
Portscatho 83 B2
Portwrinkle 65 B4
Poughill 4 D2
Poundstock 6 E2
Praa Sands 90 C3
Praze-an-Beeble 79 C2
Prince Rock 129 B1
Probus 71 C6
Pyworthy 8 E5

Q

Quethiock 52 C7
Quintrell Downs 44 E3
Quither 30 A8
Quoit 45 F4

R

Rame
  Cawsand 64 B2
  Stithians 92 E8
Readymoney 116 B3
Reawla 78 E3
Redmonsford 3 F2
Red Post 7 F8
Redruth 140 D5
Rejerrah 55 F7
Releath 91 E8
Relubbus 90 A7
Rescassa 72 F1
Rescorla 59 D8
Reskadinnick 138 B5
Reskivers 71 F3
Restormel 112 C5
Restronguet Passage 82 A4
Resugga Green 59 D7
Rezare 28 E4
Rilla Mill 38 E8
Rinsey 90 D2
Riverside 123 A1
Riviere Towans 142 B7
Roborough 121 D1
Roche 46 F3
Rock 21 D2
Rockhead 14 E3
Roscroggan 138 D7
Rose 55 C5
Rose-an-Grouse 77 D2
Rosecare 10 D6
Rosedinnick 45 E8
Rosehill
  Goonhavern 55 D5
  Lostwithiel 112 C1
Roseland 51 E6
Rosemelling 59 F8
Rosemergy 75 D3
Rosenannon 33 A1
Roserrow 21 E5
Rosevean 47 D1
Rosevear 99 C7
Rosevine 83 B3
Rosewarne 78 F3
Roseworthy
  Camborne 78 F6
  Shortlanesend 69 E6
Roseworthy Barton 78 F6
Roskear Croft 138 E6
Rosudgeon 89 F4
Row 24 B3
Ruan High Lanes 83 E6
Ruan Lanihorne 83 E8
Ruan Major 102 F6
Ruan Minor 103 B5
Ruddlemoor 59 B6
Rumford 32 A5
Rushford 30 A3
Ruthernbridge 34 A1
Ruthvoes 45 F3

S

St Agnes 54 D1
St Agnes Beacon 54 B1
St Allen 56 B1
St Ann's Chapel 40 E6
St Anthony 95 B5
St Anthony-in-Meneage 101 C8
St Austell 114 B5
St Blazey 60 B5
St Blazey Gate 115 F6
St Breock 33 C6
St Breward 24 B3
St Budeaux 123 D2
St Buryan 97 B6
St Cleer 37 F2
St Clement 70 D2
St Clether 17 A3
St Columb Major 45 E6
St Columb Minor 111 E7
St Columb Road 45 D2
St Day 68 E1
St Dennis 58 C8
St Dominick 40 D3
St Endellion 22 D5
St Enoder 57 B7
St Erme 70 E8
St Erney 53 B2
St Erth 142 A1
St Erth Praze 142 F1
St Eval 31 F3
St Ewe 72 E5
St Gennys 10 C8
St Germans 65 A8
St Giles on the Heath 13 E1
St Gluvias 144 D8
St Hilary 89 E6
St Issey 32 E6
St Ive 38 F2
St Ive Cross 39 A1
St Ives 141 C6
St Jidgey 32 F4
St John 132 C8
St Johns 146 A6
St Jude's 149 B3
St Just 86 E6
St Just In Roseland 82 F2
St Keverne 101 C4
St Kew 23 A4
St Kew Highway 23 A2
St Keyne 51 A3
St Lawrence 34 D1
St Levan 96 D3
St Mabyn 34 C8
St Martin
  Looe 117 D7
  Mawgan 100 D6
St Mawes 95 B6
St Mawgan 45 A8
St Mellion 53 E8
St Mellion Pk 53 C8
St Merryn 31 F8
St Mewan 59 A2
St Michael Caerhays 72 D1
St Michael Penkevil 70 F1
St Minver 22 A4
St Neot 36 F2
St Newlyn East 56 C7
St Pinnock 50 D6
St Ruan 103 A4
St Stephen 58 B4
St Stephens
  Launceston 106 A8
  Saltash 122 D2
St Teath 23 E7
St Thomas 106 B6
St Tudy 23 E3
St Veep 61 C6
St Wenn 46 D7
St Winnow 61 A8
Salem 68 F3
Saltash 122 B1
Sampford Spiney 42 E7
Sancreed 87 E4
Sandplace 63 C7
Sandy Bottom 114 F4
Saveock 69 B3
Scarcewater 57 E5
Scorrier 68 D3
Scredda 114 D8
Seaton 64 B5
Sellan 87 E5
Sennen 96 B6
Sennen Cove 96 B7
Seworgan 92 C6
Sheffield 97 F7
Sheviock 65 B6
Shop
  Morwenstow 2 D1
  St Merryn 31 E8
Shortlanesend 69 F6
Shutta 117 D4
Silverwell 68 F7
Sithney 91 B3
Sithney Common 91 C3
Sithney Green 91 C4
Skinners Bottom 68 D5
Sladesbridge 34 A6
Slaughterbridge 105 D7
Southcott 11 A6
Southdown 133 B6
South Hill 39 C7
South Hole 2 D7
South Petherwin 27 E8
South Pill 122 E3
South Tehidy 138 E7
Southway 124 F6
South Wheatley 11 F3
Sparkwell 131 F8
Sparnon 96 F5
Sparnon Gate 67 F4
Splatt
  Rock 21 E3
  Warbstow Cross 17 B7
Spriddlestone 136 C4
Staddiscombe 135 F3
Start 77 E3
Stenalees 59 B8
Stennack 79 D4
Stepaside 58 B5
Stibb 4 D5
Sticker 58 F1
Stithians 80 F3
Stoke 128 A3
Stoke Climsland 28 E1
Stonehouse 128 A1
Stoptide 21 E2
Stourscombe 106 F4
Stowford 5 E8
Stratton 4 E1
Summercourt 57 C7
Swanvale 144 F3
Sydenham Damerel 29 D2

T

Talland 62 F2
Talskiddy 45 E8
Tamerton Foliot 124 B7
Tavistock 147 E5
Temple 36 B8
Tencreek 63 A3
Terras 58 A4
Tetcott 13 C7
The Beacon 10 F6
Thorne Moor 19 F8
Three Burrows 68 F5
Three Hammers 17 C6
Threemilestone 69 D4
Threewaters 34 C1
Thurdon 5 D5
Tideford 52 F2
Tintagel 14 D7
Titson 7 D4
Todpool 68 F2
Tolborough 25 E4
Tolcarne
  Camborne 79 D5
  Newlyn 143 C3
Toldish 45 F2
Tolgus Mount 139 E8
Tolskithy 139 E7
Tolvaddon 138 F6
Tolvaddon Downs 139 A7
Torpoint 127 C3
Tosberry 3 B8
Towan Cross 68 B7
Towednack 76 E5
Townlake 29 C1
Townshend 90 D7
Traboe 100 E4
Tramagenna 105 A1
Trannack 91 D5
Treal 103 A6
Treath 93 C1
Treator 107 A5
Trebarber 44 F5
Trebartha 27 A4
Trebarvah 89 E4
Trebarwith 14 C5
Trebeath 17 F6
Trebetherick 21 D4
Trebudannon 45 C4
Trebullett 28 A5
Treburgett 23 D6
Treburley 28 C4
Treburrick 31 D5
Trebyan 48 C6
Trecrogo 27 E7
Tredavoe 143 A2
Tredethy 34 F6
Tredinnick
  Looe 63 A8
  Penzance 76 A1
  St Issey 32 D5
Tredown 2 E5
Tredrizzick 21 F4
Treen
  Porthcurno 96 F3
  Zennor 75 F4
Treesmill 60 D6
Trefanny Hill 62 D8
Trefofda 24 A8
Trefrew 105 D6
Trefrize 27 E3
Tregadillett 18 C2
Tregajorran 139 D4
Tregamere 45 F7
Tregarland 63 C8
Tregarlandbridge 63 B8
Tregarrick Mill 62 D7
Tregaswith 45 C5
Tregatta 14 C6
Tregavarras 85 A5
Tregeare 17 D5
Tregellist 22 E4
Tregeseal 86 F7
Tregew 145 B8
Tregiskey 73 C5
Tregole 6 E1
Tregolls 80 F3
Tregonce 107 F2
Tregonetha 46 C6
Tregonhawke 132 B4
Tregonna 32 C7
Tregony 71 F4
Tregoodwell 105 F4
Tregorrick 114 D1
Tregoss 46 D3
Tregreenwell 23 F7
Tregrehan Mills 115 D6
Tregune 10 F4
Tregunna 33 B8
Tregurrian 44 E8
Tregustick 33 D1
Trehan 122 A1
Trehunist 52 C6
Trekeivesteps 37 E4
Trekenner 28 B5
Trekenning 45 D5
Treknow 14 C5
Trelan 100 E1
Trelash 10 F1
Treleigh 140 D8
Trelew 82 B2
Treligga 14 C3
Trelights 22 C6
Trelill 23 C5
Treliver 46 E8
Trelyon 141 B3
Tremail 16 B5
Tremar 38 A2
Trematon 53 E2
Tremayne 79 C2
Trembraze 113 D8
Tremethick Cross 88 A5
Tremollett 27 D2
Tremore 47 C7
Trenance
  Newquay 110 E5
  Roche 46 F7
  St Issey 32 D5
  Tregurrian 31 C2
Trenant 37 C3
Trenant Girt 108 C5
Trenarren 73 E7
Trencreek 111 C4
Trencrom 77 B3
Trendeal 57 C3
Trenear 92 A6
Treneere 143 E7
Treneglos 16 F7
Trenerth 78 D2
Trenewan 62 A4
Trengale 37 C2
Trengune 11 A4
Treninnick 111 A4
Trenoweth 93 B8
Trenwheal 90 F7
Trequite 23 B3
Trerise 103 A7
Trerulefoot 52 D2
Tresarrett 35 B8
Tresawle 71 C5
Trescowe 90 B5
Tresillian 70 F5
Tresinney 24 C8
Treskillard 139 C1
Treskinnick Cross 6 F1
Treslothan 79 D4
Tresowes Green 90 D4
Tresowes Hill 90 E4
Tresparrett 10 B2
Tresparrett Posts 10 C4
Treswithian 138 A3
Trethellan 110 C6
Trethevey 14 F8
Trethewey 96 E4
Trethosa 58 A5
Trethowel 114 C6
Trethurgy 59 F6
Trevadlock 27 A6
Trevail 43 D1
Trevalga 9 B1
Trevance 32 E6
Trevanger 21 F4
Trevanson 33 C7
Trevarnon 78 D6
Trevarren 45 E3
Trevarrian 31 C1
Trevarrick 72 F2
Trevarth 80 E7
Treveighan 23 F6
Trevellas 54 F2
Trevelmond 50 D6
Trevemper 110 E2
Treven 14 C6
Trevenning 23 F5
Treverbyn
  Penwithick 59 C7
  St Cleer 37 B2
Treverva 93 B6
Trevescan 96 B5
Trevethoe 77 D3
Trevia 105 B4
Treviades 93 A3
Trevigro 39 C4
Trevilla 82 C6
Trevilson 56 D6
Treviscoe 58 B7
Trevollard 53 D1
Trevone 20 E2
Trevorrick 107 E1
Trevowhan 75 C2
Trew 90 F4
Trewalder 14 E1
Trewarmett 14 D5
Trewassa 15 F5
Trewellard 86 F8
Trewen 17 E2
Trewennack 146 F8
Trewennan 23 E8
Trewetha 22 E7
Trewethern 22 E3
Trewey 76 B5
Trewidland 51 C2
Trewint 10 F8
Trewithian 83 B4
Trewold 9 E1
Trewoodloe 39 B6
Trewoon
  Mullion 99 B2
  St Austell 59 A3
Treworga 83 D7
Treworlas 83 D5
Trewornan 22 C1
Treworrick 37 E3
Treworthal 83 C5
Trezaise 47 A2
Trispen 56 D1
Troan 57 C8
Troon 79 E5
Truro 137 E3
Truscott 18 D4
Truthan 56 C2
Truthwall
  Marazion 89 D7
  St Just 86 E7
Trythogga 143 F8
Tubbs Mill 72 D2
Tuckermarsh 41 B2
Tuckingmill
  Camborne 139 A4
  St Breward 24 B4
Turfdown 48 E8
Turnchapel 135 B7
Tutwell 29 A2
Twelveheads 69 B1
Two Burrows 68 E5
Tywardreath 60 E5

U

Underwood 130 C5
United Downs 81 A8
Upcott 2 F4
Upton
  Bude 104 C2
  Upton Cross 38 C7
Upton Cross 38 D6
Upton Towans 78 B6

V

Valley Truckle 105 C2
Vellanoweth 89 A8
Venterdon 28 D2
Ventongimps 55 C2
Ventonleague 142 F7
Veryan 83 F6
Veryan Green 83 F7

Victoria
Lostwithiel 112 B2
Roche 46 F4
Vogue 68 D1

W

Wadebridge 108 A6
Wainhouse Corner 10 E6
Walkhampton 42 D4
Wall 78 E3
Wanson 6 F3
Warbstow 11 B1
Warbstow Cross 11 B2
Warleggan 36 C4
Warleigh Barton 123 F8
Washaway 34 C4
Watergate 24 E8
Waterloo 35 D7
Wearde 122 F2
Week Green 11 E8
Week St Mary 11 E8
Welcombe 2 D5
Welsford 3 C8
Wembury 136 B1
Wendron 91 F6
Wenfordbridge 24 A2
Wenmouth
Cross 37 A3
Werrington 18 F6
West Blackdown 30 F8
West Curry 12 D4
Westdowns 14 C1
West Hoe 148 B1
West Looe 117 C3
Weston Mill 127 E8
West Panson 13 D2
West Park 124 A3
West Pentire 43 C3
West
Portholland 84 D5
West Taphouse 49 E6
West Tolgus 139 D8
West Watergate 62 E4
West Youlstone 3 B2
Wheal Alfred 142 F4
Wheal Busy 68 F3
Wheal Frances 55 D3
Wheal Rose 68 C3
Wheal Vor 91 A5
Wherry Town 143 D4
Whipsiderry 44 C6
Whitchurch 147 D3
Whitecross
Crowlas 77 C1
Wadebridge 33 B7
White Cross
Mullion 99 B4
St Columb Road 45 C2
Whitehill 146 C4
Whitemoor 58 E8
Whiterock 108 A5
Whitewell 23 D7
Whitleigh 124 C5
Whitstone 7 F1
Widegates 63 F8
Widemouth Bay 6 F5
Widewell 125 B7
Wilminstone 30 F3
Windmill 20 F1
Witheven 11 D3
Withiel 47 A8
Withielgoose Mills 47 C8
Withnoe 132 A4
Woodford
Plymouth 130 C7
Shop 4 D8
Woolley 3 A3
Woolston 38 E3
Woolwell 125 D7
Wringsdown 18 E6

Y

Yelverton 42 D3
Yeolmbridge 18 F6

Index of streets, hospitals, industrial estates, railway stations, schools, shopping centres, universities and places of interest

A

Abbey Cl PL20 . . . 42 B2
Abbey Ct
19 Penzance TR18 . . . 143 E5
Plymouth PL1 . . . 149 A2
Abbey Hill TR26 . . . 77 E3
Abbey Mdw TR26 . . . 77 E4
Abbeymead Mews PL19 . 147 C5
Abbey Mews PL31 . . . 109 C4
Abbey Pl
Plymouth PL1 . . . 148 C2
Tavistock PL19 . . . 147 C5
Abbey Rise PL19 . . . 147 C5
Abbey St TR18 . . . 143 E5
Abbotsbury Way PL2 . . . 127 F8
Abbots Cl PL31 . . . 109 F4
Abbotscourt La PL11 . . . 126 A2
Abbotsfield Cl PL19 . . . 41 D8
Abbotsfield Cres PL19 . . . 41 D8
Abbotts Rd PL3 . . . 128 E6
Aberdeen Ave PL5 . . . 124 D1
Aberdeen Cl PL24 . . . 60 B6
Aberfal Ho 1 TR11 . . . 145 C3
Abingdon Rd 1 PL4 . . . 149 A4
Abney Cres PL6 . . . 125 B6
Abscott La PL9 . . . 135 C5
Acacia Rd TR11 . . . 144 F5
Academy Terr 30 TR26 . . . 141 B6
Acklington Pl PL5 . . . 123 E4
Acland Cl EX23 . . . 104 E7
Acland Gdns TR7 . . . 110 D6
Acorn Dr PL25 . . . 115 A3
Acre Cotts PL1 . . . 127 F3
Acre Pl PL1 . . . 127 F3
Adams Cl
Plymouth PL5 . . . 123 F1
Torpoint PL11 . . . 126 F3
Adams Cres PL11 . . . 126 E3
Adams Row TR16 . . . 68 D3
Addington N PL14 . . . 113 D6
Addington S PL14 . . . 113 D6
Addison Rd PL4 . . . 149 A4
Addison Terr PL22 . . . 112 C2
Adelaide La PL1 . . . 148 A2
Adelaide Pl PL1 . . . 148 A3
Adelaide Rd TR15 . . . 140 C4
Adelaide St
Camborne TR14 . . . 138 E3
Penzance TR18 . . . 143 E6
2 Plymouth, Ford PL2 . . . 127 F5
Plymouth PL1 . . . 148 A3
Adelaide Street Ope PL1 148 A3
Adelaide Terr TR1 . . . 137 B4
Adela Rd PL11 . . . 127 A3
Adit La
Newlyn TR18 . . . 143 C1
Saltash PL12 . . . 122 E3
Adits The PL18 . . . 41 A3
Admiral's Hard PL1 . . . 134 A8
Admirals Quay 4 TR11 . . . 145 B5
Admiralty Cotts PL1 . . . 134 A7
Admiralty Ct PL13 . . . 117 D3
Admiralty Rd
Plymouth, Millbay PL1 . . . 134 A8
Plymouth, St Budeaux PL5. 123 C2
Admiralty St
Plymouth, Keyham PL2 . . . 127 E6
Plymouth, Millbay PL1 . . . 134 A8
Admiralty Terr TR2 . . . 83 B2
African Row TR14 . . . 79 B5
Agar Cres TR15 . . . 139 D6
Agar Ct
2 Camborne TR15 . . . 139 C6
Truro TR1 . . . 137 D5
Agar Mdws 11 TR3 . . . 81 F7
Agar Rd
Camborne TR15 . . . 139 D6
Newquay TR7 . . . 110 E5
St Austell PL25 . . . 114 E6
Truro TR1 . . . 137 E5
Agar Terr 12 PL31 . . . 109 D5
Agar Way TR15 . . . 139 C5
Agaton Rd PL5 . . . 123 E3
Agnes Cl EX23 . . . 104 F4
Ainslie Terr PL2 . . . 127 E7
Aire Gdns PL3 . . . 129 B5
Alamein Ct PL12 . . . 122 E2
Alamein Rd PL12 . . . 122 D2
Alan Harvey Cl 14 TR26 . . . 77 A6
Alan Rd PL28 . . . 107 D4
Alansmere Ct TR2 . . . 57 A1
Alanta Flats TR7 . . . 110 B5
Albany Cl TR5 . . . 68 D8
Albany Ct
4 Newquay TR7 . . . 110 F6
Redruth TR15 . . . 140 D3
Albany Gdns TR15 . . . 140 C3
Albany La TR15 . . . 140 C4
Albany Pl TR11 . . . 145 A3
Albany Rd
Falmouth TR11 . . . 145 A3
5 Newquay TR7 . . . 110 F6
Redruth TR15 . . . 140 C4
Truro TR1 . . . 137 A4
Albany St PL1 . . . 127 E2
Albany Terr TR26 . . . 141 B4
Albemarle Villas PL1 . . . 127 F3
Albert Bldgs 20 TR18 . . . 143 E6
Albert Cotts TR11 . . . 145 B4
Albertha Cl PL4 . . . 149 B4
Albert Pl
Camborne TR14 . . . 138 E3
21 St Ives TR26 . . . 141 B5
Truro TR1 . . . 137 C3
Albert Rd
Plymouth PL2 . . . 127 F3
Saltash PL12 . . . 123 A2
St Austell PL25 . . . 114 D3
St Ives TR26 . . . 141 B5
Albert St
Camborne TR14 . . . 138 E3
Penzance TR18 . . . 143 F6
Albert Terr
Gunnislake PL18 . . . 40 F5
Lostwithiel PL22 . . . 112 C2
19 Penzance TR18 . . . 143 E6
26 St Ives TR26 . . . 141 B5
Albertus Dr TR27 . . . 142 B3
Albertus Gdns TR27 . . . 142 B3
Albertus Rd TR27 . . . 142 B3
Albert Villas PL2 . . . 127 E4
Albion Ct PL11 . . . 127 B3
Albion Dr PL2 . . . 128 B7
Albion Rd
Helston TR13 . . . 146 B4
Torpoint PL11 . . . 127 B3
Albion Row TR16 . . . 80 F8
Alcester Cl PL2 . . . 127 E4
Alcester St PL2 . . . 127 F4
Alden Wlk PL6 . . . 129 B7
Aldercombe La EX23 . . . 5 A6
Alderney Rd PL6 . . . 124 F7
Alder Rd PL19 . . . 147 C3
Aldersley Wlk PL6 . . . 125 A1
Aldreath Cl TR20 . . . 88 B7
Aldreath Rd TR20 . . . 88 B7
Alexander Ct
14 Carnon Downs TR3 . . . 81 F7
Gorran Haven PL26 . . . 85 D5
Alexandra Cl
5 Illogan TR16 . . . 67 E4
Plymouth PL9 . . . 136 B8
St Ives TR26 . . . 77 A7
Alexandra Ct TR7 . . . 111 C8
Alexandra Dr PL20 . . . 41 C1
Alexandra Gdns TR18 . . . 143 D4
Alexandra Ho TR18 . . . 143 D3
Alexandra Pl
Penzance TR18 . . . 143 D4
5 Plymouth PL4 . . . 128 E4
St Ives TR26 . . . 77 A7
Alexandra Rd
Bodmin PL31 . . . 109 B5
Illogan TR16 . . . 67 D4
Newquay TR7 . . . 111 C8
Penzance TR18 . . . 143 D4
Plymouth, Crownhill PL6 . . . 124 F2
Plymouth, Ford PL2 . . . 127 F5
Plymouth, Mutley PL4 . . . 128 F4
St Austell PL25 . . . 114 E3
St Ives TR26 . . . 77 A7
Alexandra Sq PL12 . . . 123 A2
Alexandra Terr
Mount Hawke TR4 . . . 68 C6
Penzance TR18 . . . 143 D3
Plymouth PL2 . . . 127 F5
St Ives TR26 . . . 141 A5
Tremar PL14 . . . 38 A4
2 Truro TR1 . . . 137 B4
Alford Cl EX23 . . . 104 F5
Alfred Pl PL2 . . . 127 F5
Alfred Rd PL2 . . . 127 F5
Alfred St PL1 . . . 148 C2
Alger Wlk PL6 . . . 124 E6
Alice La 7 PL1 . . . 148 B3
Alice St PL1 . . . 148 A3
Alldritt Cl TR7 . . . 111 D7
Allenby Rd PL2 . . . 128 A6
Allendale PL26 . . . 58 E8
Allendale Rd PL4 . . . 149 A4
Allen Pk PL30 . . . 23 B2
Allen Vale PL14 . . . 113 A5
Allern La PL5 . . . 120 D1
Allerton Wlk PL6 . . . 129 B7
Alley Hill PL20 . . . 42 A1
Alleyn Gdns PL3 . . . 128 E8
Allium Ct TR4 . . . 70 D8
All Saints Pk PL18 . . . 40 E5
Alma Cl TR5 . . . 68 D8
Alma Cotts PL4 . . . 149 B2
Alma Pl
Heamoor TR18 . . . 143 C7
Newquay TR7 . . . 110 D6
Padstow PL28 . . . 107 D5
5 Penzance TR18 . . . 143 E5
Redruth TR15 . . . 140 B5
Alma Rd
Plymouth PL3 . . . 128 C4
Truro TR1 . . . 69 F3
Alma St PL4 . . . 149 B2
Alma Terr
Carharrack TR16 . . . 80 F8
Gunnislake PL18 . . . 41 A6
Penzance TR18 . . . 143 E5
10 St Ives TR26 . . . 141 B5
Almeria Ct PL7 . . . 130 D4
Almond Dr PL7 . . . 131 B6
Almshouse Hill TR13 . . . 146 B5
Altarnun Com Prim Sch PL15 . . . 26 C7
Alton Pl PL4 . . . 128 E4
Alton Rd PL4 . . . 149 A4
Alverne Bldgs 7 TR18 . . 143 D5
Alverton Com Prim Sch TR18 . . . 143 C4
Alverton Ct TR1 . . . 137 E5
Alverton Ho TR18 . . . 143 C5
Alverton Rd TR18 . . . 143 D5
Alverton St TR18 . . . 143 E5
Alverton Terr
4 Penzance TR18 . . . 143 D5
Truro TR1 . . . 137 D5
Alvington St PL4 . . . 149 C2
Alwin Pk PL6 . . . 125 A5
Alwyn Cl TR7 . . . 111 E6
Amacre Dr PL9 . . . 135 B6
Amados Cl PL7 . . . 130 B4
Amados Dr PL7 . . . 130 C4
Amados Rise PL7 . . . 130 C4
Amal An Avon TR27 . . . 142 E7
Amanda Way PL14 . . . 38 E4
Amble Rd 26 PL17 . . . 39 F4
Ambrose Ct TR15 . . . 140 E7
Amelia Cl TR2 . . . 71 C6
Amherst Rd PL3 . . . 148 B4
Amherst Road La E PL3 . . 148 B4
Amity Pl PL4 . . . 149 A4
Anderton Cl PL19 . . . 147 E1
Anderton Ct PL19 . . . 147 E2
Anderton La PL19 . . . 147 D2
Anderton Rise PL10 . . . 132 F4
Andrewartha Rd TR10 . . . 144 B8
Andrew Pl 3 TR1 . . . 137 C4
Andrew's Terr TR16 . . . 139 F1
Andrews Way PL12 . . . 53 E5
Andurn Cl PL9 . . . 136 B6
Aneray Rd TR14 . . . 138 D4
Angarrack La TR27 . . . 78 D5
Angarrack Mews TR27 . . . 78 C5
Angavran Mdw TR8 . . . 55 D8
Angel Hill 7 PL15 . . . 106 C6
An Gof Gdns PL31 . . . 109 C4
Angwin Ave 4 TR5 . . . 54 C1
Anjardyn Pl PL24 . . . 60 C5
Ankervis La TR16 . . . 140 F1
Annear Rd TR10 . . . 144 A6
Ann's Pl PL3 . . . 128 A4
Anson Ho 1 PL1 . . . 148 B3
Anson Pl
Plymouth, Devonport PL2 . . . 127 F4
Plymouth, St Jude's PL4 . . 149 C3
Anson Rd PL27 . . . 31 F3
Anson Way TR13 . . . 146 D4
Anstis St
Plymouth PL1 . . . 148 A3
Plymouth PL1 . . . 148 B3
Anthony Cl EX23 . . . 4 C3
Anthony Lowen PL28 . . . 107 D4
Anthony Pk PL19 . . . 147 D6
Anthony Rd TR7 . . . 110 E4
Antoine Cl 4 TR18 . . . 143 C2
Antoine Terr 23 TR18 . . . 143 C2
Antony CE Sch PL11 . . . 65 E5
Antony Gdns PL2 . . . 128 C8
Antony Hill PL11 . . . 65 E5
Antony House* PL11 . . . 126 D5
Antony Rd PL11 . . . 127 B3
Antony Woodland Gdn* PL11 . . . 126 D6
Antron Hill TR10 . . . 81 B1
Antron La TR10 . . . 93 C8
Antron Way TR10 . . . 93 C8
Anvil Ct
Camelford PL32 . . . 105 D3
Venterdon PL17 . . . 28 D1
Anvil Rd PL32 . . . 105 D4
An Vownder Goth TR13 . . . 91 B7
Anwyl Cl PL1 . . . 148 B3
Anzac Ave PL5 . . . 124 A4
Appin Gdns TR15 . . . 139 C7
Appleby Wlk PL5 . . . 124 D4
Appleton Tor Cl PL3 . . . 129 F5
Appletree La PL25 . . . 115 D3
Apsley Rd PL4 . . . 128 D4
Arbour The PL6 . . . 124 E5
Arcade The 6 TR18 . . . 143 E5
Arcadia PL9 . . . 136 D6
Arcadia Rd PL9 . . . 136 C6
Archbishop Benson CE Prim Sch TR1 . . . 137 D6
Archer Pl PL1 . . . 148 B4
Archer Terr PL1 . . . 148 B3
Arch Hill TR1 . . . 137 C2
Arch La TR27 . . . 77 D1
Archway Ave PL4 . . . 129 B3
Arden Gr PL2 . . . 128 C8
Arena Cres PL25 . . . 115 B4
Argal & College Water Park* TR10, TR11 . . . 93 C7
Argal View TR10 . . . 93 B6
Arimoor Gdns PL19 . . . 147 E5
Ark Royal Cl PL5 . . . 127 D8
Arkwright Gdns PL5 . . . 123 F2
Arley Cl PL6 . . . 125 B6
Arlington Rd PL4 . . . 128 F4
Armada Ct PL19 . . . 147 B4
Armada Ctr PL1 . . . 148 C3
Armada Rd PL10 . . . 133 A1
Armada St PL4 . . . 149 A4
Armada Way
Plymouth PL1 . . . 148 C2
Plymouth PL1 . . . 148 C3
Armchair Cnr PL31 . . . 109 C5
Arnheim Terr TR11 . . . 145 B7
Arnison Cl PL9 . . . 135 F5
Arnold's Point PL4 . . . 129 C3
Arnside Cl PL6 . . . 125 D3
Arrallas Barns TR2 . . . 57 B4
Arscott Gdns PL9 . . . 135 C5
Arscott La PL9 . . . 135 D5
Art Gallery Terr TR18 . . . 143 C3
Arthurian Centre The* PL32 . . . 105 D8
Arthur Terr PL11 . . . 127 B2
Artillery Pl PL4 . . . 149 B1
Arun Cl PL3 . . . 129 C5
Arundel Cres PL1 . . . 148 B4
Arundel Ct TR27 . . . 78 D6
Arundell Cl PL16 . . . 19 F4
Arundell Gdns
Falmouth TR11 . . . 144 E6
Lifton PL16 . . . 19 F4
Arundell Pl TR1 . . . 137 C3
Arundel Pk TR27 . . . 78 D6
Arundel Terr
Bude EX23 . . . 104 D4
Plymouth PL2 . . . 127 F4
Arundel Way
Connor Downs TR27 . . . 78 D6
Newquay TR7 . . . 111 B7
Arundle Cl PL26 . . . 58 C8
Arwenack Ave TR11 . . . 145 C3
Arwenack Ho 4 TR11 . . . 145 C3
Arwenack St TR11 . . . 145 C4
Arworthal Mdws TR3 . . . 81 D6
Arwyn Cotts 6 TR11 . . . 145 C3
Arwyn Pl 7 TR11 . . . 145 C3
Asdally Vale TR18 . . . 143 B5
Ashburgh Parc PL12 . . . 122 B3
Ashburnham Rd PL5 . . . 124 A3
Ashbury Cl PL14 . . . 113 D7
Ash Cl
16 Par PL24 . . . 60 B4
7 Yelverton PL20 . . . 42 C3
Ashcombe Cl PL7 . . . 130 C7
Ashdown Cl
Plymouth PL6 . . . 125 E3
Sticker PL26 . . . 58 E1
Ashdown Wlk PL6 . . . 125 E3
Ash Dr TR27 . . . 142 B3
Ashery Dr PL9 . . . 135 C6
Ashfield Gdns TR11 . . . 144 E6
Ashfield Rd TR11 . . . 144 F6
Ashfield Villas TR11 . . . 144 F6
Ashford Cl PL3 . . . 129 A4
Ashford Cres PL3 . . . 129 A4
Ashford Hill PL4 . . . 129 A4
Ashford Rd PL4 . . . 128 F4
Ash Gr
Hayle TR27 . . . 142 B3
Par PL24 . . . 60 B4
Plymouth PL2 . . . 127 F7
Ashleigh Cl PL5 . . . 124 C7
Ashleigh La PL5 . . . 120 D1
Ashleigh Way
Plymouth PL7 . . . 131 C4
Probus TR2 . . . 71 D6
Ashley Cl 9 PL26 . . . 59 D7
Ashley Rd
Shortlanesend TR4 . . . 69 F6
Truro TR1 . . . 137 C4
Ashmead TR2 . . . 57 E1
Ashridge Gdns PL5 . . . 124 B2
Ashton Cl PL6 . . . 125 C6
Ashton Ct TR7 . . . 111 D6
Ashton Way PL12 . . . 122 D3
Ashton Wlk EX23 . . . 6 F5
Ashtree Cl PL6 . . . 125 D7
Ashtree Gr PL9 . . . 136 C8
Ash Vale PL16 . . . 19 F4
Ashwood Cl PL7 . . . 131 B5
Ashwood Park Rd PL7 . . . 131 C6
Aspen Cl PL19 . . . 147 C3
Aspen Gdns PL7 . . . 131 B5
Astor Dr PL4 . . . 129 C3
Astwood Developments PL13 . . . 63 F8
Athelstan Pk PL31 . . . 109 F3
Athenaeum La PL1 . . . 148 B2
Athenaeum Pl PL1 . . . 148 C2
Athenaeum St PL1 . . . 148 B2
Atherton Pl PL2 . . . 127 E4
Athlone Ho PL1 . . . 148 A2
Atlanta PL28 . . . 20 E2
Atlantic Cl
Camborne TR14 . . . 138 E2
Treknow PL34 . . . 14 C5
Widemouth Bay EX23 . . . 6 F5
Atlantic Coast Cvn Pk TR27 . . . 66 B1
Atlantic Cres TR19 . . . 96 C7
Atlantic Mews
New Polzeath PL27 . . . 21 D6
8 St Agnes TR5 . . . 54 D1
Atlantic Rd
Delabole PL33 . . . 14 D2
Newquay TR7 . . . 110 C6
Tintagel PL34 . . . 14 C7
Atlantic Terr
Camborne TR14 . . . 138 E2
New Polzeath PL27 . . . 21 D6
Atlantic Terr *continued*
43 St Ives TR26 . . . 141 B6
Trevone PL28 . . . 20 E2
Atlantic Way
Porthtowan TR4 . . . 68 A6
4 Tintagel PL34 . . . 14 C7
Attenborrow Ct TR7 . . . 111 C8
Attery View PL15 . . . 18 E6
Atwell Farm Cvn Pk PL30 . 48 A1
Auckland Rd 3 PL2 . . . 128 A5
Audierne TR10 . . . 144 C7
Austin Ave PL2 . . . 128 A6
Austin Cres PL6 . . . 125 C1
Austin Farm Prim Sch PL6 . . . 129 C7
Automobilia Motor Mus* PL26 . . . 58 A4
Ava PL26 . . . 73 C4
Avallen Cl TR11 . . . 82 A3
Avent Wlk PL7 . . . 130 F7
Avenue Rd TR11 . . . 145 C3
Avenue The
St Hilary TR20 . . . 89 F6
Truro TR1 . . . 137 D5
Avery's Row PL28 . . . 107 D5
Avery Terr PL22 . . . 112 C2
Avery Way PL12 . . . 122 C5
Avon Cl
Plymouth PL3 . . . 129 D6
St Austell PL25 . . . 115 A5
Avondale Rd TR1 . . . 137 B4
Avon Flats TR7 . . . 111 C7
Avrack Cl TR19 . . . 87 F3
Axe Cl PL3 . . . 129 D6
Axford Hill PL17 . . . 39 F2
Axtown La PL20 . . . 42 C2
Aycliffe Gdns PL7 . . . 131 A3
Aylesbury Cres PL5 . . . 124 B5
Aylmer Pl 13 PL25 . . . 114 C3
Aylmer Sq 14 PL25 . . . 114 C3
Aylwin Cl PL7 . . . 130 E6
Ayr Ct 1 TR26 . . . 141 A5
Ayreville Rd PL2 . . . 128 B7
Ayr La TR26 . . . 141 B6
Ayr Terr TR26 . . . 141 A6
Aysshton Gdns 15 PL17 . . . 39 F4

B

Babbacombe Cl PL6 . . . 129 E8
Baber Cl PL12 . . . 40 C2
Baber Ct PL12 . . . 40 D2
Babis Farm Cl PL12 . . . 122 F1
Babis Farm Ct PL12 . . . 122 F1
Babis Farm Mews PL12 . . 122 F2
Babis Farm Row PL12 . . . 122 F1
Babis Farm Way PL12 . . . 122 F2
Babis La PL12 . . . 122 F1
Baby Beach La PL27 . . . 21 D6
Back Hill
Port Isaac PL29 . . . 22 D7
Saltash PL12 . . . 122 D2
Back La
Angarrack TR27 . . . 78 C5
Callington PL17 . . . 39 F4
Marazion TR17 . . . 89 B5
Plymouth PL7 . . . 130 E4
St Erth TR27 . . . 77 D2
17 St Ives TR26 . . . 141 B6
Tintagel PL34 . . . 14 D7
Tregony TR2 . . . 71 F4
Veryan TR2 . . . 83 F6
Back La W TR15 . . . 140 B4
Back Quay TR1 . . . 137 D4
Back Rd PL18 . . . 41 A3
Back Rd E 7 TR26 . . . 141 B6
Back Rd W TR26 . . . 141 B6
Back St 42 TR26 . . . 141 B6
Badger's Cross TR20 . . . 88 E8
Badgers Wlk PL12 . . . 122 D4
Badger View PL9 . . . 135 E5
Bagbury Rd EX23 . . . 104 E3
Bag La
Polbathic PL12 . . . 64 F8
St Germans PL12 . . . 65 A8
Bahavella Dr TR26 . . . 141 B4
Bailey Gdns EX22 . . . 8 A5
Baileys La 20 TR26 . . . 141 B6
Bailey Terr EX22 . . . 8 A5
Bainbridge Ave PL3 . . . 128 F7
Bainbridge Ct PL7 . . . 130 E7
Baines Hill TR16 . . . 67 C6
Bakehouse La 12 PL17 . . . 39 E4
Bakehouse The TR10 . . . 144 D7
Bake Lane End PL12 . . . 52 D1
Bakers Cl PL7 . . . 131 C5
Bakers Ct TR7 . . . 110 E6
Bakers Gn PL25 . . . 115 B4
Bakers Pl PL1 . . . 127 F1
Bakers Row TR13 . . . 90 F3
Balcoath TR16 . . . 68 D1
Baldhu Row TR 20 . . . 76 F2
Balfield Rd 15 TR13 . . . 98 C8
Balfour Terr PL2 . . . 127 E4
Bal-Jinjy Cl 19 PL24 . . . 60 B4
Balkin Way TR15 . . . 139 D7
Ballard Cl TR16 . . . 80 B5
Ballard Est TR16 . . . 80 B5
Ball Terr PL27 . . . 108 E7
Balmoral Ave PL2 . . . 127 F5
Balmoral Pl 3 TR15 . . . 140 B5

Balmoral Terr 4 TR15 140 B5
Balnoon Flats TR26 77 A4
Bal Rd TR13 91 E4
Bambry Cl TR20 89 E5
Bampfylde Way PL6 124 D6
Bampfylde Way
Goldsithney TR20 89 F5
Plymouth PL6 124 E6
Bampton Rd PL6 125 E1
Band House La PL26 59 C7
Bangors Est EX23 6 F2
Bangors Rd PL15 18 E2
Bank Cotts 6 TR10 144 C7
Bank Pl TR11 145 C3
Bank Sq TR19 86 F6
Bank St
Newquay TR7 110 D6
St Columb Major TR9 45 E6
Bannawell Ct PL19 147 B6
Bannawell St PL19 147 B6
Banns Rd TR4 68 C6
Baptist Hill TR27 142 C6
Baptist St PL17 41 A3
Bara Pl PL17 39 F6
Barbara Hepworth Mus & Sculpture Gdn* TR26 141 B6
Barbican App PL4 149 B2
Barbican Cl
Helston TR13 146 D8
Looe PL13 117 D4
Barbican Ct
Looe PL13 117 D5
12 Plymouth PL4 149 A2
Barbican Hill PL13 117 D4
Barbican La TR18 143 F4
Barbican Leisure Pk PL4 149 C2
Barbican Rd
Looe PL13 117 E6
Plymouth PL7 130 E4
Barbican Rise Ind Est PL13 117 E5
Barbican The PL1 149 A2
Barbican Theatre PL1 149 A1
Barbican Way TR13 91 E4
Barbury Cres PL6 125 B8
Barcote Wlk PL6 129 C8
Bardsey Cl PL6 125 A7
Baring St PL4 149 B4
Barker's Hill PL12 122 C1
Barkhouse La PL25 115 B2
Bar La
Connor Downs TR27 78 C6
Falmouth TR11 145 C3
Barlandhu 17 TR18 143 C2
Barlanwick TR18 143 B4
Barley Market St PL19 147 C6
Barlowena TR14 138 D1
Barlow Gdns PL2 128 B7
Bar Mdws TR1 70 D2
Barnaloft 13 TR26 141 B6
Barn Cl
Plymouth PL7 131 D4
Wainhouse Corner EX23 10 F6
Barncoose Ind Est TR15 139 E5
Barncoose La TR15 139 E6
Barncoose Terr TR15 139 E6
Barn Crtyd TR27 78 D6
Barndale Cres PL6 125 B6
Barne Barton Prim Sch PL5 127 D8
Barne Cl PL5 127 C8
Barnecut Cl 6 PL14 38 A3
Barne La PL5 123 D1
Barne Rd PL5 127 C8
Barnfield Dr PL7 131 C5
Barnfield Gdns TR18 88 E6
Barnfield Pk EX23 4 E1
Barnfield Terr
3 Indian Queens TR9 45 E1
Liskeard PL14 113 B4
Barn Hill
Cadgwith TR12 103 B4
Polbathic PL12 64 F8
Tideford PL12 52 F1
Barningham Gdns PL6 125 B6
Barn La
Bodmin PL31 109 C4
18 St Columb Major TR9 45 E6
Barn Meadow Pk PL13 117 B2
Barnoon Hill TR26 141 B6
Barnoon Terr 29 TR26 141 B6
Barn Park La PL31 35 B2
Barnpark Rd PL35 9 C1
Barn Park Rd PL3 128 D6
Barn Pk
Lostwithiel PL22 112 E2
Saltash PL12 122 F3
Barn St PL14 113 C5
Barnstaple Cl PL6 129 E7
Barns Terr PL12 118 A3
Barnwood Cl PL9 135 E5
Baron Ct PL15 17 D5
Barons Mdw PL31 109 F5
Barons Rd PL20 42 E3
Barossa Rd PL11 127 B3
Barrack La TR1 137 D3
Barrack Pl PL1 128 A1
Barrack's La TR16 68 E1
Barrack St PL1 127 E2
Barras Cross PL14 113 C6
Barras Pl PL14 113 C6
Barras St PL14 113 C6
Bar Rd
Falmouth TR11 145 C3
Mawnan Smith TR11 93 C2
Barrepta Cl TR26 141 D1
Barrie Cres PL31 109 E2
Barripper Rd
Camborne TR14 138 C1
Penponds TR14 79 C5
Barrow Down PL12 122 B3
Barr's Cl PL23 116 D5
Barry's La PL28 107 D5
Bar Terr 8 TR11 145 C3
Bartholomew Rd PL2 128 B5
Bartles Cl TR12 99 D7
Bartles Ind Est TR15 140 B6
Bartles Row TR14 139 A5
Barton Ave PL2 127 E5
Barton Cl
11 Bodmin PL31 109 D5
Heamoor TR18 143 D7
Helston TR13 146 D7
Landrake PL12 53 C3
Plymouth PL7 131 C5
Barton Ct PL26 58 A7
Barton La TR9 45 D1
Barton Mdw
Pelynt PL13 62 D6
Truro TR1 137 A5
Barton Mdws PL12 53 B7
Barton Mews
Landrake PL12 53 C3
Millbrook PL10 132 F6
Barton Rd
Plymouth PL9 135 B6
St Dennis PL26 58 A7
Barton The PL29 22 D6
Barview La TR27 142 C4
Barwis Hill TR18 143 E6
Barwis Terr 1 TR18 143 E6
Basinghall Cl PL9 135 E5
Basket Ope PL4 149 A2
Basset Rd TR14 138 D2
Basset St
Camborne TR14 138 D2
Falmouth TR11 145 A5
Redruth TR15 140 C4
Bassett Cl PL26 47 A1
Bassett Pl 11 TR11 145 A5
Bassett Rd
Illogan TR16 67 E4
Redruth TR15 140 B8
Bassett Terr TR16 67 D6
Bastville EX22 11 E8
Bath La PL1 148 B2
Bath Pl PL1 148 B2
Bath Pl W PL1 148 B2
Bath St PL1 148 B2
Battershall Cl PL9 135 F5
Batter St PL4 149 A2
Battery Hill TR16 67 C6
Battery La
Polruan PL23 116 C2
Tavistock PL19 147 C4
Battery Mill La TR27 77 E1
Battery Pk PL23 116 C2
Battery Rd TR18 143 F4
Battery St PL1 148 A2
Battery Street Flats PL1 148 A2
Battery Terr PL26 73 C3
Battery The TR7 110 D7
Battisford Pk PL7 131 E3
Bawden Rd PL31 109 B3
Bay Apartments TR7 110 A6
Bay Ct TR11 145 C2
Baydon Cl PL6 125 C1
Bay Down PL13 117 D5
Bayly's Rd PL9 135 B7
Baynards Cl 1 TR1 137 D4
Baynes Cl 3 PL14 38 A3
Bay Rd PL28 20 F2
Bay St PL13 117 D3
Bayswater Rd PL1 148 B4
Bay The PL13 117 D3
Baytree Cl PL6 125 D6
Bay Tree Cotts 3 EX23 4 D1
Baytree Gdns PL2 128 A7
Baytree Hill PL14 113 C5
Bayview 11 PL24 60 C4
Bay View Cres TR11 145 D3
Bayview Dr PL13 117 E4
Bayview Ho TR27 142 A8
Bay View Pk PL25 114 F6
Bay View Rd PL13 117 D4
Bay View Terr
Budock Water TR11 144 C1
Hayle TR27 142 C6
26 Newlyn TR18 143 C2
Newquay TR7 110 E5
Penzance TR18 143 D4
13 Porthleven TR13 98 B8
Bay Villas TR20 88 F6
Beach Ct TR26 141 C6
Beachfield Ave TR7 110 D6
Beachfield Ct TR18 143 D4
Beach Hill PL11 64 C4
Beach La 12 TR6 55 A5
Beach Rd
Carbis Bay TR26 141 D2
Crantock TR8 43 D3
Mevagissey PL26 73 C4
Newquay TR7 110 D6
Perranporth TR6 55 A5
Porthtowan TR4 68 A6
St Austell PL25 115 D3
St Ives TR26 141 A6
Trevone PL28 20 F2
Beachside Ct TR4 68 A6
Beachside L Pk TR27 78 A6
Beach View Cl TR7 111 C7
Beachview Flats TR4 68 A6
Beach Wlk TR7 111 C7
Beacon Cl
Falmouth TR11 145 A5
Beacon Cl *continued*
St Austell PL25 115 A5
Beacon Com Jun Sch TR11 145 A5
Beacon Cross PL26 72 F4
Beacon Down Ave PL2 128 B7
Beacon Dr TR5 54 B1
Beacon Est TR20 87 D4
Beacon Farm TR5 54 C1
Beaconfield Rd PL2 128 B7
Beacon Fields TR14 138 E2
Beacon Hill PL31 109 D4
Beacon Hill Mews 9 PL31 109 D5
Beacon Ho PL3 129 D4
Beacon Inf Sch TR11 145 A5
Beacon Inf Sch The PL31 109 D4
Beacon Lanes PL31 109 D3
Beacon Parc TR13 146 C6
Beacon Park Rd PL2 128 B7
Beacon Pk
Boyton PL15 13 A2
Pelynt PL13 62 D5
Beacon Rd
Bodmin PL31 109 E3
Falmouth TR11 145 A5
Foxhole PL26 58 D5
Marazion TR17 89 B5
Newquay TR7 110 D7
Porthleven TR13 98 B8
St Agnes TR5 54 C1
Summercourt TR8 57 B7
Beacons PL13 62 E5
Beaconsfield Pl 2 TR5 54 C1
Beaconsfield Terr PL31 109 C5
Beaconside
Foxhole PL26 58 D5
Summercourt TR8 57 B7
Beacon Sq TR14 138 F1
Beacon St TR11 145 B5
Beacon Terr
Camborne TR14 138 E1
5 Falmouth TR11 145 A5
Foxhole PL26 58 D5
Helston TR13 146 C6
Lizard TR12 102 F2
Beacon The TR11 145 A5
Beacon View TR4 55 B2
Beacon View Pk 23 TR16 67 E4
Bealswood Cl PL18 41 A6
Bealswood Rd PL18 41 A6
Beam Rd PL26 47 C1
Beam Terr PL26 47 B1
Beam Villas PL30 47 D5
Beare Cl PL9 135 B5
Bearsdown Cl PL6 129 C8
Bearsdown Rd PL6 129 C8
Bears Terr TR16 80 E7
Beatrice Ave
Plymouth, Keyham PL2 127 E5
Plymouth, St Jude's PL4 149 B3
Saltash PL12 122 E2
Beatrice Gdns PL12 122 E1
Beatrice Rd PL31 48 D8
Beatrice Terr TR27 142 D7
Beattie Rd PL5 127 B8
Beatty Cl PL6 125 A4
Beauchamp Cres PL2 128 C7
Beauchamp Rd PL2 128 C7
Beauchamps Mdw TR15 140 D2
Beaudyn Wlk 5 PL6 129 C7
Beaufighter Ave PL27 31 F3
Beaufort Ave 8 PL27 31 F3
Beaufort Ho 21 PL4 149 A2
Beauly Cl PL7 131 A5
Beaumaris Gdns PL3 128 F8
Beaumaris Rd PL3 128 F7
Beaumont Ave PL4 149 A3
Beaumont Pl PL4 149 A3
Beaumont Rd PL4 149 B3
Beaumont St PL2 128 A5
Beaumont Terr PL12 122 F4
Beck Adams PL12 53 C3
Beckett Cl TR15 140 C4
Beckford Cl PL7 131 A5
Beckham Pl PL3 129 A6
Beckly Ct PL1 148 C3
Bede Gdns PL5 124 C1
Bede Haven Cl EX23 104 E4
Bederkesa Ct PL31 109 D4
Bedford Cl PL18 40 F6
Bedford Mews PL4 149 A4
Bedford Park Villas PL4 149 A4
Bedford Pk
10 Bere Alston PL20 41 B1
Plymouth PL4 149 A4
Bedford Pl
6 Bere Alston PL20 41 B1
6 St Ives TR26 141 B5
Bedford Rd
Horrabridge PL20 42 C4
Plymouth PL9 135 E8
St Ives TR26 141 B5
Bedford Sq PL19 147 C5
Bedford St
Bere Alston PL20 41 B1
Plymouth PL2 127 F5
Bedford Terr PL4 149 A4
Bedford Units PL18 40 F5
Bedford Villas 7 PL20 41 B1
Bedford Way PL1 148 C3
Bedowan Mdws TR7 111 A4
Bedruthan Ave TR1 137 E6
Bedruthan Steps* PL27 31 B4
Beech Ave
Liskeard PL14 113 B5
Plymouth PL4 149 C2
Beech Cl
Falmouth TR11 144 F5
Tavistock PL19 147 C2
Torpoint PL11 127 A3
Beechcombers TR8 44 D7
Beechcroft Rd
Plymouth, Lower Compton PL3 129 A6
Plymouth, North Prospect PL2 128 B7
Beech Ct PL6 125 D5
Beech Dr
Bodmin PL31 109 B4
Lewannick PL15 27 A6
4 St Columb Major TR9 45 D6
Beeches The 9 PL14 38 E4
Beechfield Ave PL20 42 D3
Beechfield Gr PL3 128 E6
Beech Hall Flats 19 TR2 95 A6
Beeching Pk PL17 39 F6
Beech La PL25 114 D3
Beech Rd
17 Callington PL17 39 F4
Falmouth TR11 144 F5
St Austell PL25 114 D3
Beech Terr PL13 117 C4
Beechwood Ave PL4 128 D4
Beechwood Cross PL7 131 F7
Beechwood Dr PL32 105 D5
Beechwood Gdns TR1 137 E6
Beechwood Rise PL6 125 E1
Beechwood Terr PL4 128 D4
Beechwood Way PL7 131 D5
Beehive Workshops TR10 144 A7
Beeston Wlk 6 PL6 129 C7
Behenna Dr TR1 69 F3
Bekelege Dr TR14 138 F1
Belair Rd PL2 128 C7
Belair Villas PL2 128 C7
Belerion Rd TR16 67 C5
Belgrave La PL4 128 F4
Belgrave Rd PL4 128 F4
Belgrave Terr PL14 113 D6
Belgravia St TR18 143 E5
Belhay TR10 144 C8
Bellair Rd TR20 143 A8
Bellair Terr 38 TR26 141 B6
Bellamy Cl PL6 125 A1
Bellatt PL27 108 D6
Bella Vista Gdns TR10 81 E2
Bell Cl PL7 130 F6
Belle Acre Cl PL3 128 F6
Bellever Parc TR14 138 F4
Bellevue TR15 140 C5
Belle Vue
Bude EX23 104 D6
Newlyn TR18 143 C1
Belle Vue Ave
Bude EX23 104 D6
Plymouth PL9 135 B5
Bellevue Cotts TR10 81 E2
Belle Vue Dr PL9 135 B5
Belle Vue La EX23 104 D6
Belle Vue Rd
Plymouth PL9 135 C5
Saltash PL12 122 F2
Belle Vue Rise PL9 135 B5
Bellevue Sq PL11 127 B2
Bellevue Terr TR3 81 D6
Belle Vue Terr
Gunnislake PL18 41 A6
21 Penzance TR18 143 E6
Bell Hill PL26 85 C5
Belliers La TR26 141 B5
Bellingham Cres PL7 131 C4
Belliver Ind Est PL6 121 B1
Belliver Way PL6 121 B1
Bell La
Bodmin PL31 109 E5
Lanner TR16 80 D6
Bells Ct TR15 139 C7
Bell's Ct TR11 145 B4
Bell's Hill TR11 82 A3
Bell Veor TR16 80 E6
Bell Yd 1 PL31 109 E5
Belmont PL13 117 C4
Belmont Cl PL33 14 D2
Belmont Ct
8 Plymouth PL3 128 A4
11 Wadebridge PL27 108 B5
Belmont Mews PL14 38 D4
Belmont Pk PL14 38 D4
Belmont Pl
Newquay TR7 110 D7
Plymouth PL3 128 A4
St Ives TR26 141 A6
Belmont Rd
Falmouth TR11 145 A3
Helston TR13 146 B7
St Austell PL25 114 D3
Belmont St
Plymouth PL1 148 B3
8 Tywardreath PL24 60 D5
Belmont Terr
Devoran TR3 81 F6
St Ives TR26 141 A6
Belmont Villas 13 TR1 137 D5
Belstone Cl PL5 124 A3
Belvedere La TR20 89 F5
Belvedere Rd PL4 129 B2
Belyars Ct TR26 141 B4
Belyars La TR26 141 B4
Benallack Ct TR1 137 E4
Benan Chy PL25 114 F3
Benbow St PL2 127 F4
Bencoolen Rd EX23 104 D5
Beneathway PL14 50 E7
Bennets La PL12 122 F3
Bennetts Cotts 3 TR10 144 C7
Bennett St PL1 127 E1
Benny Halt Sta* TR8 56 C8
Benson Gdns 2 TR1 137 D5
Benson Ho 1 TR1 137 D5
Benson Rd TR1 137 B5
Bentley Dr 5 EX23 4 D1
Beramic Cl TR27 78 D6
Beraton Ct 3 PL31 109 D5
Bere Alston Prim Sch PL20 41 B1
Bere Alston Sta PL20 41 B2
Bere Ferrers Sta PL20 119 E3
Berepper Cross TR12 98 E5
Beresford St PL2 128 A4
Berkeley Cl EX23 4 D1
Berkeley Cotts TR11 145 A4
Berkeley Ct
Falmouth TR11 145 B4
Looe PL13 117 C5
Berkeley Hill TR11 145 A4
Berkeley Mews 4 TR11 145 A4
Berkeley Path 3 TR11 145 A4
Berkeley Vale TR11 145 A4
Berkshire Dr PL2 127 F5
Bernice Cl PL4 129 B4
Bernice Terr PL4 129 B4
Berries Ave EX23 104 E4
Berries Mount EX23 104 F4
Berrow Park Rd PL3 128 E6
Berrycombe View 15 PL31 109 D5
Berrycoombe Hill PL31 109 C5
Berrycoombe Prim Sch PL31 109 B5
Berrycoombe Rd PL31 109 D5
Berrycoombe Vale PL31 109 C5
Berryfields Ho PL31 109 E5
Berry Head Gdns PL6 124 E1
Berryhill PL30 47 C6
Berry La PL31 109 E5
Berryman Cres TR11 144 F3
Berry Park Cl PL9 135 E6
Berry Park Rd PL9 135 E7
Berry Pk PL12 122 D4
Berry Rd TR7 110 E6
Berthon Rd PL5 127 C8
Berveth Cl TR3 69 D3
Berwick Ave PL5 124 E3
Bess Park Rd PL27 108 E6
Bethan Dr PL27 108 B5
Bethany Homes 1 TR14 138 C2
Bethany Pl TR19 86 F6
Bethel Rd PL25 115 A4
Bethesda Pl 10 TR26 141 B6
Betjeman Wlk PL5 124 C3
Beverley Cres TR27 142 E7
Beverley Rd PL3 129 C4
Beverston Way PL6 125 B8
Beweys Pk PL12 122 C2
Beyrout Pl 6 PL1 127 F3
Bezant Pl TR7 110 B5
Bickern Rd PL11 127 B3
Bickford Cres TR13 91 B1
Bickford Rd PL15 106 B8
Bickham Park Rd PL3 128 D7
Bickham Rd PL5 123 D2
Bickland Hill TR11 144 D4
Bickland Ind Est TR11 144 D4
Bickland Water Rd TR11 144 D2
Bickland Wlk TR11 144 D4
Bickleigh Cl PL6 125 A1
Bickleigh Down Bsns Pk PL6 125 D8
Bickleigh Down CE Prim Sch PL6 125 D7
Bickleigh Down Rd PL6 121 D1
Bicton Cl PL6 125 D1
Biddick Dr PL2 127 F6
Biddick's Ct 5 PL25 114 C3
Bideford Mews 13 EX23 4 E1
Bideford Wlk PL6 129 E8
Bigbury Wlk PL6 129 E8
Biggin Hill PL5 123 F4
Big Gn PL13 62 D1
Bilbury St PL4 149 A3
Billacombe Rd PL9 129 E1
Billacombe Villas PL9 135 F8
Billings Cl PL6 124 D6
Billings Dr TR7 111 B5
Billington Cl PL6 129 B7
Bindown Ct PL13 63 E8
Binhamy Cl EX23 104 F4
Binhamy Rd EX23 7 B8
Binkham Hill PL20 42 D3
Bircham View PL6 125 C1
Birch Cl PL6 125 E7
Birches The PL6 125 D6
Birchfield Ave PL2 128 B6
Birch Gr TR27 142 B3
Birchill PL30 47 C6
Birch Pond Rd PL9 135 D7
Birchwood Cl PL19 147 C3
Birchwood Gdns PL7 131 A7
Birkbeck Cl PL7 130 E7
Birkdale Cl PL12 122 C2
Biscombe Gdns PL12 123 A2
Biscombes La 8 PL17 39 E4
Biscovey Jun & Inf Schs PL24 60 B4
Biscovey Rd PL24 115 F5
Bishop Bronescombe CE Sch PL25 115 B5

Bishop Cornish CE Prim Sch PL12 122 F1
Bishop's CE Prim Sch The TR7 110 F4
Bishops Cl
Saltash PL12 122 E3
Truro TR1 137 C6
Bishops Ct TR9 45 E6
Bishop's Hill Rd PL27 21 D6
Bishop's Pl PL1 148 B1
Bishop's Rd TR26 141 B5
Bishop Temple Rd TR1 137 F6
Bissom Rd TR10, TR11 81 F2
Blackberry Cl PL9 135 E8
Blackberry La PL9 135 E8
Blackberry Way TR1 137 F5
Blackbird Cres PL15 106 E4
Blackbrook Cl PL20 42 E4
Blackerry Cl TR16 140 F1
Blackeven Cl PL6 121 D1
Blackeven Hill PL6 121 E1
Blackfriars La PL1 149 A2
Blackhall Gdns PL6 124 D6
Blackmore Cres PL6 124 D6
Black Rd TR27 142 D7
Blacksmith La TR27 78 D6
Blackstone Cl PL9 136 B6
Blackthorn Cl
Plymouth, Honicknowle PL5 124 B3
Plymouth, Woolwell PL6 125 D8
Blackwater Com Prim Sch TR4 68 E5
Bladder La PL5 124 E2
Blagdon Cross EX21 13 F7
Blagdon Lodge Cross EX21 13 F8
Blairgowrie Rd PL5 123 C2
Blake Gdns PL5 124 C3
Blakes Pk PL14 113 D7
Blanchard Pl 2 PL7 130 E7
Blanchdown Dr PL18 40 F7
Blanchminster Rd EX23 104 E5
Blandford Rd PL3 129 C6
Blatchborough Cross EX22 3 E1
Blaxton La PL5 120 C2
Blenheim Rd PL4 149 A4
Bligh Cres TR13 146 C5
Blight's Row TR15 140 B5
Blindhole 8 PL15 106 C6
Blind La PL11 64 D6
Blindwell Hill PL10 132 E5
Blisland Com Prim Sch PL30 35 D7
Blissoe Rd TR3 81 F7
Bloomball Cl PL3 129 B6
Bloom Fields TR18 143 C5
Blowing House Cl PL25 114 B4
Blowinghouse Hill TR15 140 A4
Blowing House Hill
Crowlas TR20 89 B8
Hayle TR20 77 A1
St Austell PL25 114 C4
Blowinghouse La PL30 109 B2
Blowing House La PL25 114 B4
Bluebell Cl PL12 122 D4
Bluebell Way
Launceston PL15 106 E4
Tavistock PL19 147 E4
Blue Haze Cl PL6 125 D5
Blue Reef Aquarium* TR7 110 D6
Blunt's La PL6 125 C3
Boaden Cl PL12 53 E5
Boase St TR18 143 C1
Bobs Rd PL24 60 B4
Bochym Hill TR12 99 C3
Boconnic La PL20 42 D3
Boconnoc Ave PL17 39 F3
Boconnoc Rd PL25 114 D2
Bodelva Rd PL24 115 E8
Bodgara Way PL14 113 D6
Bodgara Way Flats PL14 113 D6
Bodieve Rd PL27 108 D7
Bodinar Rd TR10 81 D2
Bodiniel Rd PL31 109 C6
Bodiniel View PL31 109 B5
Bodinnar Cl TR20 87 E6
Bodinnar La TR20 87 E6
Bodinnick Hts PL23 116 E5
Bodinnick Parc PL30 23 E3
Bodinnick Rd PL30 23 E3
Bodmin Bsns Ctr PL31 109 E3
Bodmin Bsns Pk PL31 35 B2
Bodmin Coll PL31 109 F2
Bodmin General Sta* PL31 109 E3
Bodmin Hill PL22 112 B4
Bodmin Hospl PL31 109 B4
Bodmin Jail* PL31 109 D5
Bodmin Parkway Sta PL30 49 A7
Bodmin Rd
Plymouth PL5 124 D3
St Austell PL25 114 C6
Truro TR1 137 E6
Bodmin Ret Pk PL31 35 B1
Bodmin Town Mus* PL31 109 E4
Bodmin & Wenford Rly* PL30, PL31 109 D2
Bodrigan Rd PL13 117 D5
Bodriggy Cres TR27 142 C5
Bodriggy Ct TR27 142 D6
Bodriggy Prim Sch
Hayle TR27 142 D5
Hayle TR27 142 D6
Bodriggy St TR27 142 D6
Bodriggy Villas TR27 142 D6
Body's Ct PL18 40 F6
Bohelland Rd TR10 144 D8
Bohelland Rise TR10 144 D8
Bohelland Way TR10 144 D8
Bohella Rd 20 TR2 95 A6
Bohill TR10 144 D7
Bohill Ct TR10 144 D7
Boiler Works Rd TR14 138 E5
Bojea Ind Est PL25 114 C7
Bojea Terr PL25 114 C6
Bojewyan Stennack TR19 75 B1
Bokenna Cross PL14 37 C1
Boldventure Ave PL25 115 B5
Boldventure Cl PL25 115 B5
Boldventure Rd PL25 115 B5
Bolenna La TR6 55 A4
Bolenowe Terr TR14 79 F4
Bolingey Chapel Flats TR6 55 B4
Bolingey Rd TR6 55 A4
Bolitho Rd TR18 143 C7
Bolitho Sch The TR18 143 C5
Bollowal Pl TR19 86 E6
Bolowthas Cnr TR7 111 A7
Bolowthas Way TR7 111 C7
Bolster Cl 8 TR5 54 C1
Boltern Rd TR17 89 C5
Bolt House Cl PL19 147 A5
Bolventor La PL13 63 E8
Bonallack La TR12 92 D1
Bon Cot Rd TR18 143 C2
Bond St
Plymouth PL6 124 E6
6 Redruth TR15 140 B4
Bone Cellar Row TR2 70 F5
Bone Mill Rd TR6 55 B4
Bones La PL12 52 E4
Bonson Cl PL13 117 C4
Bon Villas 18 TR18 143 C2
Bonville Rd PL6 124 E6
Bonython Cl TR11 82 A3
Bonython Dr TR2 72 A7
Bonython Rd TR7 111 B7
Bonython Terr PL14 113 B4
Boon's Pl PL1 148 C4
Borgwitha TR16 80 B5
Boringdon Ave PL5 127 D8
Boringdon Cl PL7 130 D7
Boringdon Hill PL7 130 E7
Boringdon Mill Bsns Ctr PL7 130 F6
Boringdon Prim Sch PL7 130 D7
Boringdon Rd
Plymouth, Plympton PL7 130 D6
Plymouth, Turnchapel PL9 135 A7
Boringdon Terr
Plymouth, Plympton PL7 130 D6
Plymouth, Turnchapel PL9 135 A7
Boringdon Villas PL7 130 D6
Borlase Cl TR13 146 B5
Borough Cross EX22 7 F5
Borough Ct PL11 126 E4
Borough Pk PL11 126 E4
Borrowdale Cl PL6 124 D5
Bosawna Cl TR16 68 E1
Boscarn Cl TR14 79 B5
Boscarne Cres PL25 114 F3
Boscarne Junction Sta* PL30 34 D2
Boscarnek TR27 142 A1
Boscarne View PL30 34 D2
Boscarn Parc TR15 139 C4
Boscarn Rd TR15 140 D6
Boscastle Com Prim Sch PL35 9 C1
Boscastle Gdns PL2 128 C8
Boscastle Visitor Ctr* PL35 9 D2
Boscaswell Downs TR19 75 A1
Boscaswell Est TR19 74 F1
Boscaswell Rd TR19 75 A1
Boscaswell Terr TR19 75 A1
Boscathnoe La TR18 143 B7
Boscathnoe Way TR18 143 B7
Boscawen Ct 17 TR6 55 A4
Boscawen Gdns 11 TR6 55 A4
Boscawen Pk PL26 58 B8
Boscawen Pl PL2 127 E4
Boscawen Rd
7 Chacewater TR4 69 A3
Falmouth TR11 145 B2
Helston TR13 146 D4
Perranporth TR6 55 A4
St Dennis PL26 58 C8
Boscawen St TR1 137 D4
Boscean Cl TR14 79 E4
Boscoppa Cl TR15 140 D7
Boscoppa Rd
St Austell, Bethel PL25 115 A5
St Austell, Boscoppa PL25 115 B5
Boscowan TR11 145 C2
Boscreege Cvn Site TR13 90 D5
Boscundle Ave TR11 144 F1
Boscundle Cl PL25 115 D5
Boscundle Row PL12 123 A2
Bosence Rd TR27 90 C7
Bosillion La TR2 72 A7
Bosinney Rd PL25 114 D3
Bosinver La PL26 59 A1
Boskear La PL31 109 A4
Boskenna Cross TR19 97 C5
Boskennal Barton TR19 97 B6
Boskennal La TR19 97 B6
Boskenna Rd TR16 80 A5
Boskennel Dr TR27 142 B4
Boskenwyn Com Prim Sch TR13 92 B3
Boskenza Ct TR26 141 C2
Boskernick Cl TR18 143 B1
Boskernow TR12 100 D6
Boskerris Cres TR26 141 D2
Boskerris Mews TR26 141 D1
Boskerris Rd TR26 141 D2
Boslandew Hill TR19 88 C2
Bosleake Row TR15 139 C3
Bosloggas Mews 9 TR11 145 C3
Boslowick Cl TR11 144 F3
Boslowick Ct TR11 144 E2
Boslowick Rd TR11 144 E2
Bosmeor Cl TR11 144 E2
Bosmeor Pk TR15 139 D6
Bosmeor Rd TR11 144 E3
Bosnoweth
Helston TR13 146 D5
Probus TR2 71 D6
Bosollow Vean TR20 87 D8
Bosorne Cl TR19 86 E6
Bosorne Rd TR19 86 E6
Bosorne St TR19 86 E6
Bosorne Terr TR19 86 E6
Bosparva La
Leedstown TR27 78 F2
Praze-an-Beeble TR14 79 A3
Bospolvans Rd 2 TR9 45 D6
Bospowis TR14 138 C3
Bossiney Rd PL34 14 D7
Bostennack Pl 10 TR26 141 A5
Bostennack Terr 11 TR26 141 A5
Bosuen Rd TR7 111 A7
Bos Vean TR12 102 F2
Bosvean Gdns
11 Illogan TR16 67 E4
Truro TR1 137 B5
Bosvean Rd TR4 69 F6
Bosvenna View PL31 109 E4
Bosvenna Way TR18 143 B7
Bosvenning Pl TR20 87 E6
Bosvigo Gdns* TR1 137 A5
Bosvigo La TR1 137 B5
Bosvigo Rd TR1 137 C4
Bosvigo Sch TR1 137 C4
Boswedden Pl TR19 86 E6
Boswedden Rd TR19 86 E6
Boswell Cl PL5 124 B2
Boswergy TR18 143 C5
Boswithian Rd TR14 138 F6
Bosworgey Cl 3 TR9 45 D6
Bosworgy Rd TR20, TR27 90 B8
Botallack La TR19 86 E7
Botetoe Hill TR14 79 C4
Botetoe Rd TR14 79 B4
Botha Rd 1 PL27 31 F3
Bothwicks Rd TR7 110 E6
Boughthayes Est PL19 147 A5
Boulden Cl PL7 131 C5
Boulter Cl PL6 121 C1
Boundary Cl 21 TR18 143 C1
Boundary Dr EX23 7 B6
Boundary Rd
Bodmin PL31 109 A4
Dousland PL20 42 E3
Bounders La TR6 55 B4
Bounder Treath TR12 101 C1
Boundervean La TR14 138 B2
Bounds Cross EX22 8 B4
Bounds Pl PL1 148 B2
Bound The PL10 133 A1
Bounsalls Ct PL15 106 C5
Bounsall's La PL15 106 C5
Bourne Cl PL3 129 D6
Bourneside PL25 114 D3
Boveway Dr PL14 113 E5
Boveway La PL14 113 D5
Boville La PL9 136 C7
Bovisand Ct PL9 134 F2
Bovisand La
Down Thomas PL9 135 B2
Staddiscombe PL9 135 D3
Bovisand Pk PL9 135 A1
Bovisand Rd PL9 135 E3
Bowden 14 EX23 4 D1
Bowden Park Rd PL6 125 A1
Bowdens Row TR15 140 A4
Bowers Park Dr PL6 125 E7
Bowers Rd PL2 128 B5
Bowglas Cl TR20 89 A8
Bowhays Wlk 2 PL6 129 C7
Bowjey Ct 9 TR18 143 C1
Bowjey Hill TR18 143 C1
Bowjey Terr 5 TR18 143 C1
Bow La EX23 4 D2
Bowles Rd TR11 145 A6
Bowling Gn
Menheniot PL14 51 F5
34 St Ives TR26 141 B6
Bowling Gn Terr 35 TR26 141 B6
Bowling Gn The TR2 82 F2
Bowling Green Ct
Hayle TR27 142 D5
Liskeard PL14 113 B5
Bowling Green Rd TR11 92 F3
Bownder Dowr TR27 142 B3
Bownder Vean PL25 115 A5
Bowood Pk
Delabole PL33 14 F1
Helstone PL32 24 B8
Boxhill Cl PL5 124 B3
Boxhill Gdns PL2 128 C8
Box's Shop EX23 7 A4
Boxwell Pk PL31 109 F4
Boyd Ave PL28 107 C5
Boyton Com Prim Sch PL15 13 A3
Bracken Cl
Bodmin PL31 109 E5
Plymouth PL6 125 D8
Brackenside PL13 62 D1
Bracken Terr TR7 110 E5
Brackwell Pl PL27 108 B5
Braddock CE Prim Sch
East Taphouse PL14 50 B6
Lostwithiel PL22 49 D6
Braddock Cl PL26 58 D6
Braddons Hill PL7 130 B7
Bradfield Cl PL6 125 E1
Bradford Cl PL6 129 B7
Bradford Quay Rd PL27 108 C6
Bradley Rd
Newquay TR7 111 C7
Plymouth PL4 128 F4
Bradridge Ct PL15 13 A4
Braemar Cl PL7 131 C4
Braeside Pk PL14 50 E8
Braggs Hill PL15 13 B3
Brake La PL10 132 B5
Brake Rd PL5 124 E2
Brake The PL14 37 F4
Bramblebank TR11 145 B7
Bramble Cl
Newquay TR7 111 A4
Plymouth PL3 129 B7
Widemouth Bay EX23 6 F5
Bramble Hill EX23 104 E5
Brambles The
Liskeard PL14 113 E5
Lostwithiel PL22 112 C3
Bramble Wlk 1 PL6 129 C7
Bramfield Pl PL6 129 D7
Bramley Cl PL25 114 E4
Bramley Pk PL31 109 F5
Bramley Rd PL3 129 C4
Brancker Rd PL2 128 C6
Brandon Rd PL3 129 C4
Brandon Wlk EX23 6 F5
Brandreth Rd 3 PL3 128 F6
Brandy La TR20 89 F4
Branksome Dr PL27 108 E5
Brannel Sch PL26 58 B3
Branscombe Gdns PL5 124 A3
Branson Ct 9 PL7 131 C5
Branson Pk PL19 42 A6
Branwell La TR18 88 E6
Braunton Wlk PL6 129 E8
Bray Cl PL19 147 A5
Brayford Cl PL5 124 B3
Bray's Pl PL25 114 F4
Brays Terr 2 TR16 140 F1
Brazacott Cross PL15 12 B2
Brea Arch TR14 139 A3
Bread St TR18 143 E5
Breage CE Sch TR13 90 F3
Break My Neck La TR20 88 B8
Breakwater Hill PL4 149 C1
Breakwater Ind Est PL9 135 C8
Breakwater Rd
Bude EX23 104 D5
Plymouth PL9 135 C8
Brean Down Cl PL3 128 E6
Brean Down Rd PL3 128 E7
Brea Rd PL27 21 D2
Breaside TR14 139 A3
Brecon Cl
Plymouth PL3 129 A7
1 St Agnes TR5 54 C1
Bree Shute La 4 PL31 109 E5
Brentford Ave PL5 124 B5
Brent Knoll Rd 1 PL3 128 E6
Brenton Rd PL11 64 B5
Brentons Pk PL29 22 D6
Brentor Rd
Mary Tavy PL19 30 F6
Plymouth PL4 129 B2
Brent Tor* PL19 30 D7
Brentwartha PL13 62 E2
Brest Rd PL6 125 A3
Brest Way PL6 125 A3
Bretonside PL4 149 A2
Brett Wlk PL7 130 F7
Brewartha TR2 57 E1
Brewers Cl PL30 47 F6
Brewers Hill PL26 58 C8
Brewers Rd TR1 137 F5
Brewery Hill TR26 77 E4
Brewery La TR13 146 B6
Briansway PL12 122 D2
Briardale Rd PL2 127 F6
Briarfield PL23 116 D4
Briarleigh Cl PL6 125 F2
Briar Rd
Bude EX23 104 E4
Plymouth PL3 128 F7
Briars Row PL12 122 D4
Briars Ryn PL12 53 B7
Briar Tor PL20 42 D3
Briarwood PL14 113 D5
Brickfields Cl PL1 127 F1
Brickworks Hill TR16 68 D1
Bridals La PL13 62 E2
Bridge TR9 45 E7
Bridge Cl TR7 111 A4
Bridge Ct PL25 114 F4
Bridge Hill
Illogan TR16 67 E5
St Columb Major TR9 45 E6
Bridge Ho
Delabole PL33 14 E2
Hayle TR27 142 B6
Bridge Ho The 13 TR18 143 C2
Bridge La PL12 53 A3
Bridgemead Cl PL26 114 C1
Bridgemoor Cross EX22 8 C6
Bridge Pk EX22 8 A5
Bridge Rd
Goonhavern TR4 55 D4
Illogan TR16 67 E4
Seaton PL11 64 B5
St Austell PL25 114 B3
Tideford PL12 52 F2
Bridge Row TR16 67 E5
Bridgerule CE Prim Sch EX22 8 A5
Bridgerule Ind Est EX22 7 F4
Bridge St
Par PL24 60 B6
7 Stratton EX23 4 D1
Bridges The PL12 122 E1
Bridge The PL1 148 B1
Bridge View PL27 108 C6
Bridge Wlk 2 PL35 9 C2
Bridgwater Cl PL6 125 B1
Bridle Cl PL7 131 B7
Bridle Way
Quintrell Downs TR8 44 E3
Saltash PL12 122 D4
Bridwell Cl PL5 127 E8
Bridwell La N PL5 127 E8
Bridwell Rd PL5 127 E8
Brillwater Rd TR11 92 E4
Brimford Cross EX22 3 D4
Brimhill Cl PL7 131 B3
Brisbane Terr PL14 113 C5
Brismar Wlk 3 PL6 129 C7
Briston Orch PL12 53 E7
Britannia Pl PL4 129 B2
British Cycling Mus* PL32 105 C8
British Rd TR5 54 D1
Briton's Hill TR18 143 F6
Brixham Wlk PL6 129 E8
Brixton Lodge Gdns PL8 136 F5
Brixton Terr TR13 146 C6
Broad Cl EX22 11 E7
Broadclose Hill EX23 104 E5
Broad La
Illogan TR15 139 D7
Trematon PL12 53 E2
Broadland Gdns PL9 136 A8
Broadland La PL9 135 F8
Broadlands Cl PL7 131 A3
Broadley Ct PL6 121 B2
Broadley Ind Pk PL6 121 B2
Broadley Park Rd PL6 121 B2
Broad Mead PL17 39 E5
Broad Park Rd
Bere Alston PL20 41 B2
Plymouth PL3 128 D6
Broad Pk
Launceston PL15 106 B7
Plymouth PL9 135 C7
St Keyne PL14 51 B3
Broadshell Cross EX22 8 E5
Broads La TR11 81 F3
Broad St
12 Launceston PL15 106 C6
Lifton PL16 19 F4
Newquay TR7 110 D6
Padstow PL28 107 D5
Penryn TR10 144 D7
7 St Columb Major TR9 45 E6
Truro TR1 137 E5
Broads Yd PL11 64 C5
Broadview PL19 30 A6
Broad View TR4 56 D1
Broadway The PL9 135 E7
Broad Wlk
Helston TR13 146 B7
Saltash PL12 122 E1
Brock Ho 9 PL4 149 A2
Brocklands Adventure Pk* EX23 5 A6
Brockley Rd PL3 129 C4
Brocks La PL10 132 F5
Brockstone Rd PL25 115 A5
Brockton Gdns PL6 125 B6
Bromfield Cres TR2 57 E1
Bromhead Ct PL6 129 A8
Bromley Ho 6 PL2 128 A4
Bromley Pl 5 PL2 128 A4
Bronescombe Cl TR10 144 D7
Bronte Pl PL5 124 D1
Brook Cl
Helston TR13 146 B7
Plymouth PL7 131 A3
Brook Ct 6 TR11 145 A4
Brookdale Ct 12 PL27 108 B5
Brookdown Terr PL12 122 E3
Brookdown Villas PL12 122 E3
Brook Dr EX23 104 E7
Brooke Cl PL12 123 A2
Brookfield Cl
Lanjeth PL26 58 E3
Plymouth PL7 131 B5
Brooking Cl PL6 129 A8
Brookingfield Cl PL7 130 C5
Brooking Way PL12 122 C3
Brook La PL19 147 B2
Brooklands
New Polzeath PL27 21 D6
Tavistock PL19 147 D6
Brooklands Ct PL6 124 E3
Brooklyn Flats 18 TR2 95 A6
Brooklyn Terr 17 TR2 95 A6

Brook Pl
Falmouth TR11 145 A4
Penryn TR10 144 C7
Brook Rd
Falmouth TR11 144 F3
Wadebridge PL27 108 B5
Brooks PL22 49 E3
Brookside
Chacewater TR4 68 F3
St Austell PL25 114 F4
Brookside Cl PL15 106 B8
Brook St
Falmouth TR11 145 A4
17 Mousehole TR19 88 C1
Tavistock PL19 147 C6
Brook The PL12 122 E4
Brookward Terr 8 TR18 143 C7
Brookway TR27 142 E7
Brookwood Rd PL9 136 D7
Broomfield Dr
Bodmin PL31 109 B3
Plymouth PL9 135 C5
Broomfield Rd PL27 108 D5
Broom Hill PL12 122 D2
Broomhill Cross EX22 5 E3
Broomhill La EX23 4 D2
Broom Pk PL9 135 D5
Broughton Cl PL3 128 F7
Browne Memorial Almshouses PL19 147 A5
Browning Cl 14 TR9 45 D6
Browning Dr PL31 109 C3
Browning Rd PL2 128 A5
Brownlow Pl 5 PL31 109 D5
Brownlow St PL1 148 A2
Browns Hill PL23 116 C4
Brown's Hill TR10 144 C8
Broxton Dr PL9 129 E1
Brunel Ave PL2 127 F5
Brunel Prim Sch PL12 122 E2
Brunel Quays PL22 112 D2
Brunel Rd PL12 122 C4
Brunel Terr 3 PL2 127 F5
Brunel Way PL1 148 A2
Brunswick Pl 10 PL2 127 F4
Brunswick Rd PL4 149 B2
Brush End TR26 77 E4
Brynmoor Cl PL3 129 A7
Brynmoor Pk PL3 129 A6
Brynmoor Wlk PL3 129 A6
Bryny Cl PL30 23 E7
Buckett's Hill TR15 140 C2
Buckeys La TR2 95 B6
Buckfast Cl PL2 128 A8
Buckingham Nip TR4 68 F3
Buckingham Pl PL5 123 E2
Buckingham's Cl TR8 56 B7
Buckingham Terr TR16 68 D1
Buckland Abbey★ PL20 41 F1
Buckland Cl PL7 130 D7
Buckland St PL1 148 B2
Buckland Terr PL20 42 C2
Bucklawren Rd PL13 63 E7
Bucklers Ho PL25 115 B4
Bucklers La PL25 115 B4
Buckler Village (Mobile Homes Pk) PL25 115 B4
Buckwell St PL1, PL4 149 A2
Buctor Pk PL19 41 D8
Buddle Cl
Plymouth PL9 136 A5
Tavistock PL19 147 B6
Budehaven Com Sch EX23 104 F5
Bude Ind Est EX23 104 F4
Bude Inf Sch EX23 104 E5
Bude Jun Sch EX23 104 E5
Budemeadows Cvn Site EX23 7 A4
Bude-Stratton Bsns Pk EX23 7 B8
Bude-Stratton Mus★ EX23 104 D5
Budge Mdws PL15 28 C4
Budleigh Cl PL9 135 F5
Budnic Est TR6 55 B5
Budnic Hill TR6 55 B5
Budock Hospl TR11 144 D5
Budock Pl TR11 145 B4
Budock Terr TR11 145 B3
Budock Vean La TR11 93 B2
Budshead Gn PL5 124 C4
Budshead Rd PL5 124 C4
Budshead Way PL5 124 E2
Buena Vista Cl PL6 125 D6
Buena Vista Dr PL6 125 C6
Buena Vista Gdns PL6 125 C6
Buena Vista Way PL6 125 C6
Bugle Rural Workshops PL26 47 C1
Bugle Sch PL26 47 C1
Bugle Sta PL26 47 C2
Buildings The TR20 89 A6
Bullan's La TR26 141 A5
Bullans Terr 5 TR26 141 A5
Bulleid Cl PL2 127 F7
Bulleid Way EX23 104 E4
Buller Cl
Plymouth PL7 130 F4
Torpoint PL11 127 A3
Buller Hill TR16 80 B6
Buller Ho PL13 117 D3
Buller Pk
Liskeard PL14 113 D5
Saltash PL12 122 D3
Buller Rd PL11 127 B3
Buller St PL13 117 C3
Bullers Terr TR15 140 D5
Bull Hill PL23 116 D4
Bullock La
Helston, Lower Green TR13 146 B5
Helston, Whitehill TR13 146 C4
Bullock Market Terr 28 TR18 143 E6
Bull Point Prim Sch PL5 127 B8
Bulmer Rd PL4 149 C3
Bulteel Gdns PL6 124 E7
Bulwark Rd TR13 146 B4
Bungalows The
Looe PL13 117 D6
Tintagel PL34 14 D7
Bunkers Hill
22 St Ives TR26 141 B6
Townshend TR27 90 C8
Bunyan Cl PL5 124 C2
Burden Cl PL31 109 C4
Burgess Cl EX23 4 D2
Burhos Row TR13 79 F1
Buriton Row 32 TR18 143 E5
Burleigh La PL3 128 D7
Burleigh Manor PL3 128 D7
Burleigh Park Rd PL3 128 D6
Burley Cl TR1 137 D3
Burley Ct TR11 145 B4
Burnard Cl PL6 124 E7
Burnards Ct 7 PL31 109 D5
Burnett Cl PL12 122 D2
Burnett Rd PL6 128 F8
Burnham Park Rd PL3 128 D6
Burniston Cl PL7 131 A3
Burnistone Cl PL7 131 A3
Burn La PL19 30 E8
Burns Ave PL5 124 C2
Burns View PL11 65 B5
Burnthouse PL14 37 C1
Burnthouse Cotts TR10 81 C1
Burnthouse La TR27 142 D5
Burn View EX23 104 D6
Burnwithian Terr TR16 68 D1
Burraton Com Prim Sch PL12 122 C3
Burraton Rd PL12 122 C4
Burrator Rd PL20 42 E3
Burrington Ind Est PL5 124 A1
Burrington Rd PL5 124 A1
Burrington Way PL5 124 B1
Burrow Hill PL9 135 E6
Burrows The TR26 141 A5
Bursdon Moor Cross EX39 3 B7
Burthallan La TR26 77 A7
Burton Cl PL6 125 B6
Burton Ho 15 PL25 114 C3
Burwell Cl PL6 125 E4
Bury Cl PL15 11 B1
Bush Hill PL14 36 F2
Bush Pk
Launceston PL15 106 D5
Plymouth PL6 125 F3
Butcher Park Hill PL19 147 B7
Bute Rd PL4 129 A4
Butler Cl PL6 125 B6
Butney Cnr TR14 66 E3
Butson Pk TR5 68 D8
Butterdown PL12 122 B3
Buttlegate PL11 64 D5
Butt Park Rd PL5 124 B3
Butts La PL35 9 D1
Butts Pk PL22 112 D2
Butts The
St Newlyn East TR8 56 B7
Tintagel PL34 14 D7
Byard Cl PL5 123 E1
Byland Rd PL3 129 A6
Byron Ave PL5 124 C2

C

Cabot Cl PL12 122 E2
Cades Parc TR13 146 C6
Cadoc Cl PL28 20 E1
Cadogan Cl TR14 138 E1
Cadogan Dr TR14 138 E1
Cadogan Rd TR14 138 E1
Cadover Cl PL6 125 A1
Caernarvon Gdns PL2 128 B7
Caernarvon Lodge TR7 110 D5
Calais Rd TR27 78 C2
Calartha Rd TR19 75 A1
Calartha Terr TR19 75 A1
Calder Cl PL3 129 B6
Caldicot Gdns PL6 125 C8
Caldwells Rd TR18 143 E6
Caledonia Cl 1 PL7 131 B5
Calenick St TR1 137 C4
Cal Hill TR16 140 D3
California Gdns
Plymouth PL3 129 D6
Portscatho TR2 83 B2
Callington Com Coll PL17 39 F5
Callington Mus★ PL17 39 E4
Callington Prim Sch PL17 39 E4
Callington Rd
Harrowbarrow PL17 40 C4
Liskeard PL14 113 D7
Saltash PL12 122 E3
Tavistock PL19 147 A4
Calloose Farm Cvn Pk TR27 78 D2
Calloose La E TR27 78 D1
Calloose La W TR27 78 D1
Callywith Gate Ind Est PL31 35 B2
Calshot Cl TR7 111 E7
Calstock Com Prim Sch PL18 41 A3
Calstock Rd PL18 41 A6
Calstock Sta PL17 41 A3
Calvez Cl PL10 132 F6
Camaret Dr TR26 141 B4
Cambeak PL35 9 C1
Cambeak Cl EX23 10 C6
Camber Rd PL1 148 A1
Camborne Cl PL5 124 A5
Camborne Geological Mus & Art Gal★ TR15 139 B6
Camborne Redruth Com Hospl TR15 139 F6
Camborne Ret Pk TR15 139 B5
Camborne Sch of Mines TR15 139 B6
Camborne Science & Com Coll TR14 138 B3
Camborne Sta TR14 138 D2
Cambridge La W 5 PL1 148 B3
Cambridge Pl TR11 145 A3
Cambridge Rd PL2 127 F5
Camden Ct PL4 149 A3
Camden St PL4 149 A3
Camel Cl PL28 107 D4
Camel Ct PL30 109 C6
Camelford Com Prim Sch PL32 105 C3
Camelot Ct 2 TR18 143 E5
Camelot View PL32 105 C8
Camelside PL27 108 C5
Camel Valley Vineyard★ PL30 34 B2
Cameo Ct TR14 138 F4
Cameron Cl EX23 104 D7
Cameron Way PL6 125 B1
Camilla Terr PL2 128 D7
Campbell Rd PL9 135 F7
Campbeltown Way TR11 145 C3
Camp Cross PL15 19 F7
Camperdown St PL2 127 F4
Camperknowle Cl PL10 132 F6
Campfield Hill TR1 137 D5
Camp Hall Rd TR8 43 B1
Campion Cl
7 Plymouth PL7 131 C5
Saltash PL12 122 D4
Campion Rise PL19 147 D6
Campion View PL6 125 E8
Camullas Way TR7 110 A5
Canal Rd PL19 147 B5
Candish Dr PL9 136 D7
Canefields Ave PL7 131 B3
Canfield Pl TR15 140 A5
Canfield Terr TR15 140 A5
Canhaye Cl PL7 131 A3
Cannamanning Rd 3 PL26 59 D7
Canna Park Sta★ PL15 18 D3
Cann Gdns PL6 124 D6
Cannis Rd PL25 114 E6
Cannon Hill PL14 113 C5
Cannons Pl TR13 146 D7
Cannon St PL1 127 D2
Cannon Terr 2 PL14 113 C5
Cann Wood View PL6 125 E7
Canons Way PL19 147 A3
Canterbury Dr PL5 124 B4
Cantillion Cl PL27 21 E3
Canton PL26 85 D5
Canyke Rd PL31 48 D8
Cape Cl TR19 86 E6
Cape Cornwall Rd TR19 86 E6
Cape Cornwall Sch TR19 86 E6
Cape Cornwall St TR19 86 E6
Cape Terr TR19 86 E6
Cape Trelew TR19 86 E6
Captains Gdns PL5 124 E1
Captains Ho PL26 73 C3
Captain's Wlk TR11 145 A2
Caradon Bsns Ctr 8 PL14 113 C5
Caradon Cl
9 Callington PL17 39 E4
1 Pensilva PL14 38 E4
Plymouth PL6 125 A5
Caradon Ct 2 PL20 42 C4
Caradon Dr PL14 113 B6
Caradon Hts
Liskeard PL14 113 D7
Tremar PL14 38 B4
Caradon Terr PL12 122 E3
Caradon View PL14 37 F3
Carbeile Jnr Sch PL11 127 A3
Carbeile Rd PL11 127 A2
Carbes La PL22 112 C2
Carbis Bay Holiday Pk TR26 77 C4
Carbis Bay Sta TR26 141 D2
Carbis Beach Apartments TR26 141 D2
Carbis Ct TR15 140 A5
Carboth La PL15 106 B5
Carclaze Com Inf Sch PL25 114 E6
Carclaze Com Jun Sch PL25 114 E6
Carclaze Ind Est PL25 114 E7
Carclaze Rd PL25 114 E6
Carclew Ave TR7 110 E6
Carclew Rd TR11 81 F4
Carclew St TR1 137 D3
Carclew Terr
Devoran TR3 81 F6
Truro TR1 137 D3
Cardell Rd PL31 109 D5
Cardell Way TR7 111 A5
Cardiff Cl PL7 131 B4
Cardigan Rd PL6 125 C1
Cardinal Ave PL5 127 D8
Cardinham Sch PL30 35 F3
Cardinham Woods Forest Walks★ PL30 35 C1
Cardinnis Gn PL14 113 D6
Cardinnis Rd TR18 143 B5
Cardrew Bsns Pk TR15 140 C6
Cardrew Cl TR15 140 B6
Cardrew Ind Est TR15 140 D7
Cardrew La 1 TR15 140 C5
Cardrew Terr TR15 140 D6
Cardrew Way TR15 140 D7
Cardwen Est PL13 62 C6
Careswell Ave PL2 127 F8
Carew Ave PL5 124 B3
Carew Cl
Crafthole PL11 65 B5
St Day TR16 68 E1
Carew Gdns
Plymouth PL5 124 B3
Saltash PL12 122 D3
Carew Gr PL5 124 B3
Carew-Pole Cl TR1 137 E3
Carew Rd
St Day TR16 68 D1
Truro TR1 137 C5
Carew Terr PL11 127 B2
Carew Wharf PL11 127 C2
Carew Wharf Bsns Ctr PL11 127 C2
Carey Ct PL12 122 E3
Carey Pk
Helston TR13 146 B7
Polperro PL13 62 E2
Truro TR1 137 C4
Cargoll Rd TR8 56 B7
Cargwyn PL26 59 D6
Carisbrooke Rd PL6 125 C1
Carkeek's Cl PL26 58 B3
Carkeel Barns PL12 122 C5
Carland Cross TR8 56 D4
Carlidnack Cl TR11 93 D3
Carlidnack La TR11 93 D4
Carlidnack Rd TR11 93 E4
Carlisle Rd PL5 124 D3
Carloggas Cl TR8 45 A8
Carloggas Farm TR8 45 A8
Carloggas Gr 6 TR9 45 D6
Carloggas Way 10 TR9 45 D6
Carlton Cl PL3 129 B5
Carlton Ho 7 PL31 109 E5
Carlton Terr
Plymouth, Lipson PL4 149 B3
Plymouth, Weston Mill PL5 127 E8
Carlton Vills PL12 53 E4
Carlyon Cl
Threemilestone TR3 69 D3
Torpoint PL11 126 F4
11 Truro TR1 137 C4
Carlyon Ct TR3 82 B8
Carlyon Ho TR1 69 E4
Carlyon Rd
Playing Place TR3 82 B8
St Austell PL25 114 E4
Truro TR1 137 C5
Carmarthen Rd PL4 129 B2
Carmel Gdns PL19 147 A5
Carmen Sq 10 TR18 143 C7
Carminow Cross PL30 48 D8
Carminowe Cres 8 TR18 143 D5
Carminow Rd PL31 48 D8
Carminow Road Ind Est 5 PL31 48 D8
Carminow Way TR7 111 A7
Carmython Ct TR7 111 B7
Carnarthan Moor TR15 139 C3
Carnarthen Rd TR14 138 E3
Carnarthen St TR14 138 E2
Carn Ave TR14 138 F2
Carn Bargus PL26 58 E8
Carn Bosavern TR19 86 F6
Carn Bosavern Cl TR19 86 F6
Carn Brea Ave TR15 139 C5
Carn Brea Ho TR15 139 C5
Carn Brea La TR15 139 C5
Carn Brea Village TR15 139 F5
Carn Cl TR27 78 E1
Carncrows Rd TR26 141 C6
Carncrows St TR26 141 C6
Carne Cross PL24 59 F7
Carne Ct PL26 58 C8
Carnedon PL14 38 C7
Carnego La TR8 57 B6
Carne Hill
St Dennis PL26 46 C1
Trewoon PL25 58 F4
Carnellis Rd 7 TR26 141 A5
Carne Mdws TR2 70 F5
Carne Rd TR18 143 C3
Carne's Bldgs 11 TR18 143 E4
Carnes Ct TR11 145 C2
Carne's Flats PL24 60 B5
Carneton Cl TR8 43 D3
Carn Euny Settlement★ TR20 87 C3
Carne View Cl TR14 138 F5
Carne View Rd TR2 71 D6
Carnglaze Caverns★ PL14 36 F1
Carnglaze Cl PL14 113 E6
Carn Gloose Rd TR19 86 D6
Carn Gwavas Terr TR18 143 D1
Carnhell Rd TR14, TR27 78 F4
Carninney La TR26 141 C1
Carnkief Cnr TR4 55 D4
Carn Marth La TR16 140 E2
Carnock Rd PL2 128 D8
Carnon Cres 13 TR3 81 F7
Carnon Terr TR3 81 F6
Carnoustie Dr PL12 122 C2
Carn Rock TR10 144 D7
Carn Ros TR19 74 F1
Carnsew Cl TR10 81 C1
Carnsew Cres TR10 81 C1
Carnsew Ct TR27 142 B5
Carnsew Mdw TR27 142 A5
Carnsew Rd TR27 142 A5
Carnsmerry PL26 47 C1
Carnsmerry Cres PL25 114 E4
Carnstabba Rd 13 TR26 77 A6
Carntiscoe Workshops TR27 77 C2
Carn Todden TR19 88 D1
Carn View TR16 80 F6
Carn View Terr TR19 75 A1
Carnyorth Hill TR19 86 F8
Carnyorth Terr TR19 86 F8
Carolina Gdns PL2 127 F7
Caroline Cl TR27 142 E7
Caroline Pl PL1 148 A2
Caroline Row TR27 142 E7
Carpalla Rd PL26 58 D5
Carpalla Terr PL26 58 D5
Carpenter Cl PL31 109 D5
Carpenter Rd PL9 135 F8
Carpmael Ave TR8 111 B4
Carracawn Cross PL12 64 D8
Carrack Dhu 37 TR26 141 B6
Carrack Dhu Est 36 TR26 141 B6
Carrack Gladden TR26 141 D2
Carrack Widden 25 TR26 141 B5
Carradale Rd PL6 129 C7
Carrallack Mews TR19 86 E6
Carrallack Terr TR19 86 E5
Carriage Ho The TR3 69 F1
Carriage Parc TR4 55 D4
Carrickowel Cres 1 PL25 115 A5
Carrick Rd TR11 144 E2
Carrick Way TR2 95 A6
Carrine Rd TR1 69 F3
Carrisbrooke Way PL12 122 B2
Carrnown Gdns TR15 140 D3
Carroll Rd PL5 124 C2
Carron La PL6 121 D1
Carsize La TR27 78 E1
Carter Cl TR7 111 A5
Carteret Rd EX23 104 E5
Carthew Cl
Liskeard PL14 113 D5
St Ives TR26 141 A6
Carthew Ct TR26 141 A6
Carthew La
Four Lanes TR13 80 A3
Praze-an-Beeble TR13 79 F2
Carthew Terr TR26 141 A6
Carthew Way TR26 141 A6
Carvath Ho PL25 114 D3
Carvedras Ct 1 TR1 137 C4
Carvossa Est TR20 89 B8
Carvoza Rd TR1 137 D5
Carvynick Cotts TR8 57 A7
Carwinard Cl TR27 78 C5
Carwinion Gdn★ TR11 93 E3
Carwinion Rd TR11 93 E3
Carwin La TR27 78 C5
Carwin Rise
Angarrack TR27 78 C5
Hayle TR27 142 E7
Carwollen Rd PL25 114 E7
Carworgie Ct 10 TR9 45 E2
Carworgie Manor TR8 45 D3
Carworgie Way 7 TR9 45 E2
Carwynnen Cl TR14 79 B3
Casey La PL13 62 D5
Castel Wary Cl TR13 146 B5
Casterills Rd TR13 146 D4
Castle Acre Gdns PL3 129 B5
Castle Bank Gdns PL3 129 B5
Castle Barbican PL7 130 E4
Castle Bldgs PL12 122 D4
Castle Canyke Rd PL31 109 F3
Castle Carey Gdns PL3 129 B5
Castle Cl TR11 145 E3
Castle Ct
Praa Sands TR20 90 C3
Saltash PL12 122 C2
Castle Dr
Bodmin PL31 109 F5
Falmouth TR11 145 F2
Praa Sands TR20 90 B3
St Mawes TR2 94 F5
Castle Dyke PL15 106 C6
Castle Dyke La PL1 149 A2
Castle Gdns PL14 113 C6
Castle Gn TR13 146 B5
Castlehayes Gdns PL7 130 E4
Castle Hill
Helston TR13 146 B5
6 Liskeard PL14 113 C6
Lostwithiel PL22 112 C2
Saltash PL12 122 C1
Castle Hill Ct
Bodmin PL31 109 E5
7 Liskeard PL14 113 C6
Castle Hill Gdns PL31 109 F5
Castle Horneck Cl TR18 143 C5
Castle Horneck Rd TR18 143 C5
Castle Hts 3 PL34 14 C7
Castle La
Liskeard PL14 113 C6

Castle La *continued*
Plymouth PL7 .... 130 E4
Castle Mdws
Launceston PL15 .... 106 A4
2 St Agnes TR5 .... 54 D1
Castlemead Cl PL12 ..... 122 D3
Castlemead Dr PL12 .... 122 D3
Castle Meadows Ct 3
TR5 .... 54 D1
Castle Rd
Longrock TR20 .... 88 F8
Ludgvan TR20 .... 89 A8
Penzance TR18 .... 143 E7
Tintagel PL34 .... 14 C7
Castle Rise
Plymouth PL3 .... 129 B4
Saltash PL12 .... 122 D1
Truro TR1 .... 137 C5
Castle St
Bodmin PL31 .... 109 F5
Launceston PL15 .... 106 C6
Liskeard PL14 .... 113 C6
Looe PL13 .... 117 D3
Plymouth PL1 .... 149 A2
Truro TR1 .... 137 C4
Castleton Cl PL3 .... 129 A4
Castle View
Longrock TR20 .... 88 F6
Lostwithiel PL22 .... 112 E3
Saltash PL12 .... 122 D1
Tintagel PL34 .... 14 C7
Castle View Cl TR15 ..... 140 B6
Castle View Pk TR11 ...... 93 D3
Caswarth Terr PL28 ..... 107 D5
Catalina Row PL27 .... 31 F3
Catalina Villas PL9 ...... 135 A6
Catchfrench Cres PL14 ... 113 E6
Cathcart Ave PL4 .... 129 B2
Cathebedron Rd
Carnhell Green TR14 ...... 78 F4
Praze-an-Beeble TR14 ..... 79 A3
Cathedral Church of the Blessed Virgin Mary*
TR1 .... 137 D4
Cathedral La 13 TR1 .... 137 D4
Cathedral School of St Mary
The PL1 .... 148 B3
Cathedral St PL1 .... 148 B3
Cathedral View TR1 ..... 137 C6
Catherine Cl EX23 ...... 104 F4
Catherine Pk PL13 .... 62 E5
Catherine's Hill PL15 .... 106 A6
Catherine St PL1 .... 148 C2
Cath of St Mary & St
Boniface PL1 .... 148 B3
Cattedown Rd PL4 ...... 149 C1
Catterick Cl PL5 .... 123 E5
Cattewater Rd PL4 ...... 129 B1
Caudledown La PL26 ...... 59 C8
Caunter Rd PL14 .... 113 D6
Causeland Sta PL14 .... 51 B2
Causewayhead TR18 ..... 143 E5
Causeway The
Falmouth TR11 .... 144 F4
Hayle TR27 .... 142 A4
Causley Cl PL15 .... 106 C7
Cavendish Rd PL4 .... 129 B1
Caxton Gdns PL5 .... 124 C1
Cayforth Flats TR16 ...... 67 C6
Cayley Way PL5 .... 123 F2
Cecil Ave PL4 .... 149 C4
Cecil Cotts PL1 .... 148 A3
Cecil St PL1 .... 148 B3
Cedar Ave PL9 .... 135 C5
Cedar Cl
21 Callington PL17 .... 39 F4
Torpoint PL11 .... 126 F2
Cedarcroft Rd PL2 ...... 128 B7
Cedar Ct
Camborne TR14 .... 139 A5
Saltash PL12 .... 122 F2
Cedar Dr PL11 .... 126 F2
Cedar Gr EX23 .... 104 E7
Cedar House Flats TR26 ... 77 E4
Celandine Gdns PL7 .... 131 C5
Celia Hts PL31 .... 109 F2
Celtic Rd PL17 .... 39 F4
Cemetery Rd PL18 .... 40 F5
Centenary Row Middle
TR14 .... 138 E3
Centenary Row W TR14 .. 138 E2
Centenary St TR14 ...... 138 E3
Central Ave PL25 .... 114 E5
Central Cl PL26 .... 58 B4
Central Park Ave PL4 ... 148 C4
Central Rd
Holywell TR8 .... 43 B1
Plymouth PL1 .... 148 B1
Central Sq TR7 .... 110 D6
Central Treviscoe PL26 .... 58 A7
Century Cl
Helston TR13 .... 146 D8
St Austell PL25 .... 114 F6
Century Ct TR7 .... 111 C7
Century La TR2 .... 83 F6
Century Sq 7 PL14 .... 38 E4
Ceres Ct EX23 .... 104 E4
Chacewater Com Prim Sch
TR4 .... 69 A3
Chacewater Hill TR4 ...... 69 A3
Chaddlewood Ave PL4 ... 149 B3
Chaddlewood Cl PL7 .... 131 A4
Chaddlewood Ho PL7 ... 131 B5
Chaddlewood Inf Sch
PL7 .... 131 A5
Chaddlewood Jun Sch
PL7 .... 131 A5
Chagford Wlk PL6 ...... 129 E8
Chainwalk Dr TR1 ...... 137 C6
Chalets The TR18 .... 88 E6
Chalet The PL11 .... 64 C4
Challacombe Gdns TR10 144 C8
Challenger Quay 12
TR11 .... 145 C3
Challgood Cl 1 PL9 ..... 135 F5
Challgood Rise PL9 ..... 135 F5
Challis Ave TR8 .... 45 A8
Challock Cl PL6 .... 125 D4
Chamberlayne Dr PL7 .... 130 E6
Champion's Ct TR13 .... 146 B6
Chancery Cl TR4 .... 70 D8
Chancery La 23 TR18 .... 143 E5
Chandlers Wlk PL25 .... 115 A3
Chandos Pl 12 PL25 ..... 114 C3
Channel Park Ave PL3 ... 129 B5
Channel View
Polruan PL23 .... 116 D2
St Ives TR26 .... 141 A6
Channel View Terr
Plymouth PL4 .... 149 C4
4 Redruth TR15 .... 140 C4
Channon Rd PL12 .... 122 C4
Chantry Ct PL7 .... 130 B5
Chantry La PL13 .... 117 E4
Chantry Pk 18 PL17 ...... 39 E4
Chapel Cl
Camborne, Kehelland
TR14 .... 66 F1
Camborne, Tuckingmill
TR14 .... 139 A4
Coad's Green PL15 .... 27 D3
Connor Downs TR27 ...... 78 D6
Crantock TR8 .... 110 A3
Gunnislake PL18 .... 40 E5
4 Horrabridge PL20 ...... 42 C4
St Just In R TR2 .... 82 F2
Chapel Cnr EX22 .... 8 A5
Chapel Cotts EX23 .... 4 C8
Chapel Cres TR4 .... 56 A2
Chapel Ct
Camborne TR14 .... 138 F4
Padstow PL28 .... 107 D5
9 Redruth TR15 .... 140 B5
Chapeldown Rd PL11 .... 127 A2
Chapel Farm TR14 .... 79 E5
Chapel Field PL25 ...... 115 B5
Chapel Gn PL26 .... 59 A1
Chapel Ground PL13 .... 117 C3
Chapel Hill
Camborne, Brea TR14 .... 139 A3
Camborne, Tregajorran
TR15 .... 139 C4
Gweek TR12 .... 92 C2
Hayle TR27 .... 142 C6
Lanner TR16 .... 80 D6
Launceston PL15 .... 106 B5
Newquay TR7 .... 110 D6
Perranporth TR6 .... 55 B4
Polgooth PL26 .... 59 A1
Ponsanooth TR3 .... 81 B4
Porthtowan TR4 .... 68 A5
Redruth TR16 .... 68 A4
St Erth TR27 .... 142 A1
Sticker PL26 .... 58 F1
Truro TR1 .... 137 B4
Chapel La
Bodmin PL31 .... 109 D5
Goldsithney TR20 .... 89 F5
Hayle TR27 .... 142 D6
Horrabridge PL20 .... 42 C4
Lizard TR12 .... 102 F2
Penryn TR10 .... 144 C7
Polruan PL23 .... 116 D2
St Austell PL25 .... 115 C6
St Mabyn PL30 .... 34 D8
St Teath PL30 .... 23 F6
5 Wadebridge PL27 ..... 108 B5
Chapel Mdw
Buckland Monachorum
PL20 .... 41 F3
Perranarworthal TR3 ...... 81 D6
Chapel Park Terr PL15 .. 106 B5
Chapel Pk PL15 .... 106 B5
Chapel Pl
Pillaton PL12 .... 53 B7
16 Truro TR1 .... 137 D4
Chapel Point La PL26 ..... 73 C2
Chapel Rd
Camborne TR14 .... 139 A4
Foxhole PL26 .... 58 D5
Heamoor TR18 .... 143 C8
Indian Queens TR9 .... 45 E1
Leedstown TR27 .... 78 E1
2 Par PL24 .... 60 C4
Roche PL26 .... 46 F3
Saltash PL12 .... 122 B3
St Just TR19 .... 86 E6
St Tudy PL30 .... 23 E3
Chapel Row
Praze-an-Beeble TR14 ..... 79 B2
2 Redruth TR15 .... 140 B5
Tremar PL14 .... 38 A3
Truro TR1 .... 137 D4
Widegates PL13 .... 63 F8
Chapel Sq
Crowlas TR20 .... 89 B8
Mevagissey PL26 .... 73 C3
Troon TR14 .... 79 E5
Chapel St
4 Bere Alston PL20 ...... 41 B1
4 Callington PL17 .... 39 F4
Camborne TR14 .... 138 D2
Camelford PL32 .... 105 C4
Chapel St *continued*
Grimscott EX23 .... 5 B2
Gunnislake PL18 .... 40 F6
Lifton PL16 .... 19 F4
Marazion TR17 .... 89 B5
Mevagissey PL26 .... 73 C3
21 Mousehole TR19 .... 88 C1
9 Newlyn TR18 .... 143 C2
Penzance TR18 .... 143 E5
Plymouth, Mount Wise PL1 . 127 E2
Plymouth PL4 .... 149 A3
Probus TR2 .... 71 C6
Redruth TR15 .... 140 B5
St Day TR16 .... 68 D1
St Ives TR26 .... 141 B5
St Just TR19 .... 86 E6
Tavistock PL19 .... 147 B5
Chapel Terr
Camborne TR15 .... 139 D6
Devoran TR3 .... 81 F6
Falmouth TR11 .... 145 B4
Hayle TR27 .... 142 B5
Par PL24 .... 60 B6
9 Porthleven TR13 .... 98 B8
Portreath TR16 .... 67 C6
Redruth, Carn Brea Village
TR15 .... 139 F5
Redruth TR15 .... 140 D2
Ruan Minor TR12 .... 103 A5
St Day TR16 .... 68 E1
10 St Mawes TR2 .... 95 A6
Trewellard TR19 .... 86 F8
Chapel Town Cl TR11 ..... 93 D4
Chapel Way PL3 .... 129 A6
Chapman Ct PL12 .... 122 B3
Chapmans Ope PL1 ..... 127 D2
Charaton Cross PL14 ...... 38 F4
Chard Barton PL5 ...... 124 B3
Chard Rd PL5 .... 123 D2
Chard Terr 6 TR11 ..... 145 A3
Charfield Dr PL6 .... 129 A8
Chariot Rd TR15 .... 139 E6
Charles Ave TR11 ...... 144 E2
Charles Bassett Cl 6
TR13 .... 146 C5
Charles Cl PL25 .... 114 F3
Charles Cross PL4 ...... 149 A3
Charles St
Bugle PL26 .... 47 C1
Newlyn TR18 .... 143 C3
Plymouth PL1 .... 149 A3
Truro TR1 .... 137 C4
Charles Terr PL3 .... 129 A6
Charlestown Prim Sch
PL25 .... 115 C3
Charlestown Rd PL25 .... 115 B3
Charlestown Shipwreck, Rescue & Heritage Ctr*
PL25 .... 115 B2
Charlotte Cl TR4 .... 68 C6
Charlotte St PL2 .... 127 E4
Charlton Cres PL6 ...... 125 A2
Charlton Rd PL6 .... 125 A3
Charnhill Cl PL9 .... 136 A6
Charnhill Way PL9 ...... 136 A6
Charter Cl TR13 .... 146 C4
Charter Ct TR10 .... 144 D7
Charter Way PL14 ...... 113 E6
Chateau Cl PL26 .... 46 D1
Chatsworth Gdns PL5 ... 123 F3
Chatsworth Way PL25 ... 115 C2
Chaucer Prim Sch PL5 ... 124 C2
Chaucer Rd PL19 .... 147 D5
Chaucer Way PL5 .... 124 C1
Chawleigh Cl PL18 .... 40 F5
Chedworth St PL4 ...... 149 A3
Chegwin Gdns TR7 ...... 110 E5
Chegwins Hill PL26 .... 58 D5
Chegwyn Gdns 6 TR5 ..... 54 C1
Chegwyns PL26 .... 58 D5
Chelfham Senior Sch
PL20 .... 40 F3
Chellean Vean TR4 .... 81 C7
Chellew Rd TR1 .... 137 F5
Chelmer Cl PL7 .... 131 A5
Chelmsford Pl PL5 ...... 124 C4
Chelson Gdns PL6 ...... 125 E3
Cheltenham Pl
Newquay TR7 .... 110 D6
Plymouth PL4 .... 149 B4
Cheney Mill Farm Park*
TR27 .... 77 E1
Chenhalls Cl TR27 .... 77 E2
Chenhalls Rd TR27 ..... 142 A2
Chenoweth Cl TR14 ..... 138 C4
Chepstow Ave PL6 ...... 125 C8
Chequetts Cl 10 PL17 ..... 39 E4
Cheriton Cl PL5 .... 124 A3
Cherrill Gdns EX23 ..... 104 E7
Cherrington TR7 .... 110 B5
Cherry Cross EX22 .... 12 B7
Cherry Gdns 14 TR18 .... 143 E5
Cherry Pk PL7 .... 131 A3
Cherry Tree Cl PL31 .... 109 B4
Cherrytree Ho TR18 .... 143 C5
Cherry Tree La PL7 ..... 131 A4
Cherry Tree Mews PL25 . 114 D3
Cheshire Dr PL6 .... 124 D6
Chesnut Cl PL12 .... 122 D4
Chester Ct TR7 .... 111 A6
Chesterfield Rd PL3 .... 129 B4
Chester Pl 4 PL4 .... 128 E4
Chester Rd TR7 .... 111 A6
Chesterton Cl PL5 ...... 124 C3
Chesterton Ct PL27 .... 108 A6
Chesterton Pl TR7 ...... 111 A7
Chestnut Ave PL9 ...... 135 C5
Chestnut Cl
Callington PL17 .... 40 A4
Falmouth TR11 .... 144 F5
Lamerton PL19 .... 30 A4
St Tudy PL30 .... 23 E3
Tavistock PL19 .... 147 D2
Torpoint PL11 .... 126 F3
Chestnut Gr PL31 ...... 109 B4
Chestnut Rd PL3 .... 128 D7
Chestnut Terr PL19 ...... 30 A4
Cheviot Rd TR7 .... 110 E4
Chichester Cl PL26 .... 58 E5
Chichester Cres
Newquay TR7 .... 110 F4
Saltash PL12 .... 122 E1
Chichester Ct PL20 .... 42 C4
Chichester Ho PL1 ...... 148 B2
Childrey Gdns PL6 ..... 125 C1
Childrey Wlk PL6 .... 125 C1
Chili Rd TR15 .... 139 D6
Chilton Cl PL6 .... 129 B7
Chings Alley 13 PL15 .... 106 C6
Chipponds Dr PL25 .... 114 A3
Chirgwin Ct 22 TR18 .... 143 E5
Chirgwin Rd TR1 .... 137 E4
Chisholme Cl PL25 ..... 114 D3
Chisholme Ct PL25 ..... 114 D3
Chittleburn Cross PL8 ... 136 E5
Chittleburn Hill PL8 .... 136 E5
Chivenor Ave PL5 ...... 123 D4
Chiverton Cl TR20 .... 89 F4
Chiverton Cross
Blackwater TR4 .... 68 F5
Rosudgeon TR20 .... 89 F4
Chiverton Greenacres
TR5 .... 68 D8
Chiverton Way TR20 ...... 89 F4
Chollacott Cl PL19 ..... 147 C4
Chollacott La PL19 ..... 147 D3
Chough Cl
Falmouth TR11 .... 144 E4
Launceston PL15 .... 106 E4
Chough Cres PL25 ...... 114 F4
Choughs Cl TR14 .... 138 B3
Christa Ct PL14 .... 38 D7
Christian Mill Bsns Pk
PL6 .... 124 E4
Christian Way TR7 ...... 111 C7
Chubb Dr PL3 .... 128 B4
Chudleigh Rd PL4 ...... 129 A4
Chun Castle* TR20 .... 87 C8
Church Cl
Blisland PL30 .... 35 D8
Lelant TR26 .... 77 E4
Plymouth PL7 .... 130 B7
Trispen TR4 .... 56 D1
Church Cove Rd TR12 ... 103 A2
Church Ct PL6 .... 125 A7
Church End PL13 ...... 117 D3
Churchfield Cl TR20 ...... 89 A8
Churchfield Pl PL24 ...... 60 B5
Churchfields Rd TR8 ..... 55 D8
Church Gate 3 PL14 .... 113 C5
Church Hill
Calstock PL18 .... 41 A3
Chacewater TR4 .... 68 F2
Golant PL23 .... 61 B6
Helston TR13 .... 146 C7
Herodsfoot PL14 .... 50 E3
Hessenford PL11, PL12 .... 64 B8
Ludgvan TR20 .... 89 A8
Milton Combe PL20 ...... 41 F1
Penryn TR10 .... 144 D8
5 Pensilva PL14 .... 38 E4
Plymouth PL6 .... 125 B1
Port Isaac PL29 .... 22 D7
St Day TR16 .... 68 E1
Sticker PL26 .... 58 F1
7 St Mawes TR2 .... 95 A6
Tavistock PL19 .... 147 E2
Tintagel PL34 .... 14 C7
Church Hill Rd PL9 ..... 135 A6
Church Ho PL12 .... 123 A2
Churchill Rd PL19 ..... 147 D2
Churchill Way
10 Penwithick PL26 .... 59 D7
Plymouth PL3 .... 128 E6
Churchill Wlk PL12 ..... 122 E1
Church La
Bodmin PL31 .... 109 E5
Bude EX23 .... 104 D5
Calstock PL18 .... 41 A3
Camborne TR14 .... 138 D3
Cargreen PL12 .... 119 A1
Flushing TR11 .... 145 B7
Helston TR13 .... 146 B6
Lelant TR26 .... 77 E4
Lostwithiel PL22 .... 112 C2
Mevagissey PL26 .... 73 C4
Padstow PL28 .... 107 D5
Redruth TR15 .... 140 A3
St Columb Minor TR7 .... 111 E7
St John PL11 .... 132 B8
Tavistock PL19 .... 147 C5
Churchlands PL13 ...... 117 D5
Churchlands Cl PL6 ..... 125 E7
Churchlands Rd PL6 .... 125 E8
Church Lea
Launceston PL15 .... 106 A7
Tavistock PL19 .... 147 E2
Church Mews
Stithians TR3 .... 80 F3
Week St Mary EX22 ...... 11 E8
Church Park Ct PL6 .... 125 E8
Church Park Mews PL27 . 108 B4
Church Park Rd
Crackington Haven EX23 ... 10 C6
Plymouth PL6 .... 125 E8
Church Path EX23 ...... 104 C5
Church Pk
Bodmin PL31 .... 109 F5
Horrabridge PL20 .... 42 C4
Lerryn PL22 .... 61 D8
St Mellion PL12 .... 53 D8
Church Pl
Liskeard PL14 .... 113 C5
18 St Ives TR26 .... 141 B6
Church Rd
Camborne TR15 .... 139 B6
Cury TR12 .... 99 A4
Four Lanes TR16 .... 80 A5
Heamoor TR18 .... 143 C7
Illogan TR16 .... 67 E4
Lanivet PL30 .... 47 E7
Lelant TR26 .... 77 E4
Mabe Burnthouse TR10 .... 93 C8
Madron TR20 .... 143 A8
Mount Hawke TR4 .... 68 C6
Mylor Bridge TR11 .... 82 B2
Pendeen TR19 .... 75 A1
Penponds TR14 .... 138 B1
Penryn TR10 .... 144 C8
Perranarworthal TR3 ...... 81 D5
Plymouth, Plympton PL7 .. 130 F4
Plymouth, Plymstock PL9 . 135 F7
Saltash PL12 .... 122 D2
Shortlanesend TR4 .... 69 F6
St Austell PL25 .... 115 B3
St Dennis PL26 .... 46 C1
Stithians TR3 .... 80 F4
St Tudy PL30 .... 23 E3
Tideford PL12 .... 52 F2
Church Row
Carharrack TR16 .... 80 F8
Lanner TR16 .... 80 D6
3 Porthleven TR13 .... 98 B8
Sheviock PL11 .... 65 C6
Church Row La PL5 .... 124 C6
Church St N PL14 ...... 113 C5
Church St S PL14 ...... 113 C5
Church Sq
8 Bodmin PL31 .... 109 E5
Constantine TR11 .... 92 F4
St Just TR19 .... 86 F6
4 Stratton EX23 .... 4 E1
Church St
Callington PL17 .... 39 E4
Calstock PL18 .... 41 A3
Camborne TR14 .... 138 D3
Carharrack TR16 .... 80 F8
Falmouth TR11 .... 145 B4
Gorran Haven PL26 ...... 85 D5
Helston TR13 .... 146 B6
Landrake PL12 .... 53 C3
Launceston PL15 .... 106 C6
Liskeard PL14 .... 113 C5
Looe, East Looe PL13 .... 117 D3
Looe, West Looe PL13 .... 117 C3
Mevagissey PL26 .... 73 C3
15 Newlyn TR18 .... 143 C1
Padstow PL28 .... 107 D5
Par PL24 .... 60 B5
Plymouth PL3 .... 128 A4
Poughill EX23 .... 4 D2
8 St Austell PL25 ...... 114 C3
St Columb Minor TR7 .... 111 D7
St Day TR16 .... 68 E1
St Erth TR27 .... 142 A1
St Germans PL12 .... 65 A8
St Just TR19 .... 86 F6
5 Stratton EX23 .... 4 E1
Tywardreath PL24 .... 60 D5
Churchstow Wlk PL6 .... 129 E8
Church Terr
Devoran TR3 .... 81 F6
Grampound Road TR2 ..... 57 E1
St Kew PL30 .... 23 A3
Churchtown
Cardinham PL30 .... 35 F3
Gwinear TR27 .... 78 D4
7 Mullion TR12 .... 99 A2
5 St Agnes TR5 .... 54 C1
St Minver PL27 .... 22 A4
St Newlyn East TR8 ...... 56 B7
Church Town Cotts TR3 .. 81 D5
Churchtown Mdws PL26 ... 58 B4
Churchtown Mews PL30 ... 35 C8
Churchtown Rd
Gwithian TR27 .... 66 B2
Illogan TR16 .... 67 E5
Phillack TR27 .... 142 C7
Portscatho TR2 .... 83 B2
St Stephen PL26 .... 58 B4
Churchtown Terr PL27 .... 32 D6
Churchtown Vale PL12 .. 122 D1
Church View
St Cleer PL14 .... 37 F3
St Dominick PL12 .... 40 D2
St Neot PL14 .... 36 F2
Treburley PL15 .... 28 B5
Walkhampton PL20 ...... 42 E4
Church View Rd
Camborne TR14 .... 138 F4
Probus TR2 .... 71 D6
Churchway
Madron TR20 .... 143 A8
11 Marazion TR17 .... 89 C5
Church Way
Falmouth TR11 .... 144 E3
Plymouth PL5 .... 127 E8
St Clether PL15 .... 17 B2
Church Wlk
Redruth TR15 .... 140 A5
South Petherwin PL15 .... 27 E8
12 Truro TR1 .... 137 D5
Chute La PL26 .... 85 D5

Cotsland Rd TR1 .... 137 F5
Cotswold Ave PL26 .... 58 E1
Cotswold Cl PL26 .... 58 E1
Cottage Gdns PL15 .... 27 B7
Cottage Mews PL7 .... 130 E4
Cotton Cl PL7 .... 130 F4
Cott Rd
Lostwithiel PL22 .... 112 D2
Lostwithiel, Polscoe PL22 . 112 D4
Cotts PL20 .... 119 B7
Cot Wood TR3 .... 81 B4
Couchwell La PL22 .... 112 C2
Coulson's Bldgs 10 TR18 . 143 E4
Coulson's Pl 9 TR18 .... 143 E4
Coulson's Terr 8 TR18 ... 143 E4
Coulthard Dr TR13 .... 91 A3
Countess Bridge La TR27 .. 90 A8
Count House La TR26 .... 141 C2
County Cl PL7 .... 131 A5
County Rd EX23 .... 104 E2
Court Barton Cotts PL9 . 135 C1
Court Barton Mews PL19 .. 30 B4
Courtenay Rd PL19 .... 147 B6
Courtenay St PL1 .... 148 C3
Courtfield Rd PL3 .... 128 F5
Court Gdns PL25 .... 114 C3
Courtland Cres PL7 .... 130 D7
Courtlands PL12 .... 122 E1
Courtlands Cl PL19 .... 147 B6
Courtlands Cres 4 PL25 115 A5
Courtlands Rd PL19 .... 147 B6
Courtlands Sch PL6 .... 124 F1
Court Mdw PL13 .... 62 B7
Courtney Cl PL13 .... 117 D4
Courtney Ho PL5 .... 124 B2
Courtney Rd
Liskeard PL14 .... 113 D6
St Austell PL25 .... 114 F5
Truro TR1 .... 137 B5
Court The
Camborne TR15 .... 139 C4
Plymouth PL6 .... 125 C7
Saltash PL12 .... 122 C2
Court View PL8 .... 136 F4
Courtyard Cotts TR4 .... 70 C6
Courtyard The
Redruth TR16 .... 139 F2
Truro TR1 .... 137 D3
Cove Hill
Perranarworthal TR3 .... 81 D5
Sennen Cove TR19 .... 96 B7
Cove Mdw PL11 .... 127 A6
Coventry Rd TR11 .... 145 B6
Coverack Com Prim Sch
TR12 .... 101 C1
Cove Rd TR19 .... 96 C7
Coverdale Pl PL5 .... 124 C1
Cowdray Cl PL12 .... 122 E2
Cowdray Terr PL12 .... 122 E1
Cow Lard Cl PL15 .... 106 A4
Cowley Rd PL5 .... 124 D3
Cowling Gdns PL14 .... 51 F6
Cowling Rd 2 TR3 .... 81 F7
Cox Park Terr PL18 .... 40 C6
Cox's Cl PL6 .... 125 B1
Coxs Mdw EX22 .... 13 C7
Cox Tor Cl 6 PL20 .... 42 C3
Cox Tor Rd PL19 .... 147 E5
Coypool Rd PL7 .... 130 A6
Crabbs Cl PL15 .... 13 F1
Crabbtree Cl 3 PL14 .... 113 B5
Crabtree Cl PL3 .... 129 F5
Crabtree La PL30, PL31 .. 109 D2
Crabtree Villas PL3 .... 129 E5
Crackston Cl PL6 .... 129 B7
Craigie Dr PL1 .... 148 A3
Craigmore Ave PL2 .... 127 F5
Craigside PL13 .... 117 D4
Cramber Cl
Roborough PL6 .... 125 C8
Tavistock PL19 .... 147 B4
Cranberry Rd TR14 .... 138 B3
Cranbourne Ave PL4 .... 149 C4
Crane Rd TR14 .... 138 C2
Cranfield PL7 .... 130 C7
Cranfield Rd TR14 .... 138 B3
Cranmere Rd PL3 .... 129 A6
Crantock St TR7 .... 110 D6
Crantock Terr 7 PL2 .... 128 A5
Crapstone Terr PL20 .... 42 B2
Crashaw Cl PL5 .... 124 D3
Craven Ave PL4 .... 149 C4
Crawford Rd PL1 .... 148 A4
Creakavose PL26 .... 58 B4
Creakavose Pk PL26 .... 58 A4
Crealy Adventure Park
(Cornwall)* PL27 .... 32 D4
Crease La PL19 .... 147 A4
Creathorne Rd EX23 .... 104 E7
Creaz - An - Bre PL26 .... 58 D5
Crediton Wlk PL6 .... 129 E8
Creed La TR2 .... 72 A7
Creedy Rd PL3 .... 129 C5
Creekside View TR2 .... 70 F4
Creeping La
Newlyn TR18 .... 143 C3
Penzance TR18 .... 143 C4
Crelake Cl PL19 .... 147 C4
Crelake Ind Est 1 PL19 .. 147 B4
Crelake Pk PL19 .... 147 C4
Crellow Fields TR3 .... 80 F3
Crellow Hill TR3 .... 80 F3
Crellow La TR3 .... 80 F3
Crellow Terr TR3 .... 80 F3
Crellow Vale TR3 .... 80 F3
Crembling Well TR15 .... 139 E6
Cremyll Rd PL11 .... 127 B2
Cremyll St PL1 .... 134 A8
Crescent Ave PL1 .... 148 B2
Crescent Avenue Mews
PL1 .... 148 B2
Crescent Cl
Hayle TR27 .... 142 C5
Widemouth Bay EX23 .... 6 F5
Crescent Gdns TR1 .... 137 B4
Crescent Pl TR19 .... 74 F1
Crescent Rd
Bugle PL26 .... 47 C1
Truro TR1 .... 137 B4
Crescent Rise
Constantine Bay PL28 .... 20 C1
Truro TR1 .... 137 B4
Crescent The
Bude EX23 .... 104 D5
Camborne TR14 .... 138 D4
Carbis Bay TR26 .... 77 C4
Common Moor PL14 .... 37 F4
Crapstone PL20 .... 42 B3
Gunnislake PL18 .... 41 A6
Landrake PL12 .... 53 C3
Lifton PL16 .... 19 F4
Liskeard PL14 .... 113 C6
Looe PL13 .... 117 D1
Newquay TR7 .... 110 E6
Plymouth PL1 .... 148 B2
Porthleven TR13 .... 91 B1
St Ives TR26 .... 77 A7
St Mabyn PL30 .... 34 D8
Truro TR1 .... 137 B4
Widemouth Bay EX23 .... 6 F5
Cressbrook Cl PL6 .... 125 F2
Cressbrook Dr PL6 .... 125 F2
Cressbrook Wlk PL6 .... 125 E2
Cres The PL25 .... 115 B5
Cresthill Rd PL2 .... 128 B7
Creswell Terr TR19 .... 86 F7
Creykes Ct PL1 .... 148 A3
Cribbage Terr 13 PL31 ... 109 D5
Cricketers Hollow PL27 ... 21 E3
Cricket Pk EX23 .... 7 B6
Crift Cotts PL14 .... 51 F7
Crift La PL12 .... 64 F8
Criggan Mill Cvn Pk
TR12 .... 102 C7
Crill Cnr TR11 .... 144 C1
Crinnick's Hill PL31 .... 109 E4
Crinnis Cl PL25 .... 115 E3
Crinnis Rd PL25 .... 115 B3
Crinnis Wood PL25 .... 115 E3
Crinnis Wood Ave PL25 . 115 D3
Crocker's Row PL18 .... 41 A6
Crockers Way PL15 .... 13 F1
Crockwell St PL31 .... 109 E5
Croft Comm TR14 .... 79 E5
Croftlands PL27 .... 21 E3
Croft Parc TR12 .... 102 F2
Croft Pk PL6 .... 125 C7
Croft Rd TR18 .... 143 C4
Croft Row TR16 .... 80 F8
Crofty Cl TR15 .... 139 C5
Cromartie Rd PL4 .... 129 B1
Cromer Cl PL6 .... 125 A7
Cromer Wlk PL6 .... 125 A7
Cromwell Gate PL6 .... 125 C7
Cromwell Rd
Plymouth PL4 .... 149 C3
St Austell PL25 .... 114 F3
Crookeder Cl PL9 .... 136 A5
Crookedor La PL11 .... 65 D5
Crooklets EX23 .... 104 C7
Crooklets Rd EX23 .... 104 D6
Cross PL30 .... 47 F1
Cross Cl TR7 .... 111 C7
Cross Comm TR12 .... 102 F2
Cross Gn PL15 .... 19 F7
Cross Hill PL2 .... 127 E4
Cross La
Bodmin PL31 .... 109 E5
7 St Austell PL25 .... 114 C3
Cross Lanes
Chacewater TR4 .... 69 B1
Cross Lanes TR12 .... 99 C4
Launceston PL15 .... 106 C8
Stratton EX23 .... 4 F1
Crossmount TR7 .... 111 D7
Cross Park Ave PL6 .... 124 F1
Cross Park Rd PL6 .... 124 F1
Cross Park Terr PL26 .... 73 C4
Cross Park Way PL6 .... 124 F1
Cross Pk
Buckland Monachorum
PL20 .... 42 A3
Crafthole PL11 .... 65 B5
Crossroads Camping Site
TR8 .... 43 D1
Cross St
Camborne TR14 .... 138 D2
Hayle TR27 .... 142 D6
Helston TR13 .... 146 B6
Padstow PL28 .... 107 D5
14 Penzance TR18 .... 143 E6
3 Redruth TR15 .... 140 B4
Wadebridge PL27 .... 108 B5
Cross Terr PL18 .... 40 F5
Cross The
Camborne TR14 .... 138 D2
St Dominick PL12 .... 40 D2
St Newlyn East TR8 .... 56 B7
Crosswalla Fields TR13 . 146 C7
Crosswater EX23 .... 2 C1
Crossway PL7 .... 130 D7
Crossway Ave PL4 .... 129 B3
Crossways TR11 .... 144 F2
Crowan Prim Sch TR14 .... 79 C2
Crowlas Ind Est TR20 .... 89 B8
Crown Cl TR7 .... 111 A4
Crown Cres TR8 .... 56 B7
Crowndale Ave PL3 .... 129 A6
Crown Gdns PL6 .... 125 A1
Crownhill Ct PL6 .... 124 F2
Crownhill Fort* PL6 .... 124 F3
Crownhill Fort Rd PL6 .... 124 F3
Crownhill Rd PL5 .... 124 C3
Crown Rd PL26 .... 58 D8
Crown Terr PL26 .... 58 D8
Crow Pk PL3 .... 128 F5
Crows-An-Eglos 5 TR26 .. 77 A6
Croydon Gdns PL5 .... 123 E4
Crozier Rd 6 PL4 .... 128 F4
Crun-Melyn Parc TR27 .... 142 B4
Crusoe Flats 48 TR26 .... 141 B6
Cryben TR12 .... 92 C1
Crylla Valley Cvn & Camping
Pk PL12 .... 53 D3
Cryon View TR1 .... 69 E3
Cubert Sch TR8 .... 43 D1
Cuby Cl TR2 .... 72 A3
Cuby Rd TR2 .... 71 F4
Cuckoo La TR20 .... 77 A3
Cuddenbeake Terr PL12 .... 65 B8
Cuffe Rd PL3 .... 128 C4
Culbin Gn PL6 .... 129 D7
Culdrose Airfield TR12 .... 146 E1
Culdrose Cl PL5 .... 123 E4
Cullen View TR2 .... 71 C6
Culme Rd PL3 .... 129 A5
Cul-Rian PL26 .... 58 D7
Culroy Flats 12 TR1 .... 137 C4
Culver Cl PL6 .... 129 A8
Culver Ct PL12 .... 122 F2
Culverland Pk PL14 .... 113 C7
Culver Rd PL12 .... 122 F2
Culvers Mdw PL15 .... 106 B8
Culver Way PL6 .... 129 A7
Culverwood Cl PL7 .... 131 C6
Culverwood Rd PL14 .... 113 B8
Culvery The PL27 .... 108 B4
Cumberland Rd PL1 .... 127 F1
Cumberland St PL1 .... 127 E2
Cumble Tor La PL12 .... 53 D2
Cundy Cl PL7 .... 130 A7
Cundy's La PL26 .... 58 D4
Cunliffe Ave PL9 .... 135 A6
Cunnack Cl TR13 .... 146 C7
Cunningham Pk TR10 .... 81 C1
Cunningham Rd PL5 .... 124 C8
Cunningham Way PL12 .. 122 D3
Curlew Cl TR7 .... 110 B5
Curlew Mews PL3 .... 129 C4
Curlew Pk Ind Est TR4 .... 69 C3
Curlews TR8 .... 43 B1
Curnow Com Spec Sch
TR15 .... 140 B6
Curnows Rd TR27 .... 142 C5
Currian Hill PL26 .... 58 D8
Currian Rd PL26 .... 58 D7
Curtis St PL1 .... 127 E1
Curtis VC Cl TR8 .... 56 B7
Cury CE Prim Sch TR12 ... 99 A4
Cusgarne Com Prim Sch
TR4 .... 81 C7
Cusgarne Hill TR4, TR16 .... 81 B8
Custom House Ct TR18 ... 143 F5
Custom House La
16 Penzance TR18 .... 143 E5
Plymouth PL1 .... 148 B1
Customs House Hill
PL23 .... 116 D4
Cutcrew La PL12 .... 52 E3
Cuth Avallon TR1 .... 137 C4
Cutmere Hill PL12 .... 52 D3
Cutmere La PL12 .... 52 D3
Cuxhaven Way TR20 .... 88 F6
Cuxton Mdws PL20 .... 41 F3
Cypress Ave PL25 .... 115 F4
Cypress Cl 6 PL7 .... 131 C5
Cyril Rd TR1 .... 137 C5

D

Dabryn Way PL26 .... 58 B4
Daglands Hill PL23 .... 116 C4
Daglands Rd PL23 .... 116 C4
Dairyland Farm World*
TR8 .... 44 F1
Daisymount Dr PL28 .... 31 F7
Dale Ave PL6 .... 129 C7
Dale Cl TR7 .... 111 A4
Dale Gdns PL4 .... 128 D4
Dale Rd
Newquay TR7 .... 111 A4
Plymouth PL4 .... 128 D4
Daleswood Rd PL19 .... 147 A4
Dalton Gdns PL5 .... 123 E3
Damerel Cl PL1 .... 127 F2
Dandre Apartments TR7 . 111 A7
Dane Rd TR7 .... 110 D7
Daniel Cl PL25 .... 115 A4
Daniell Ct TR1 .... 137 C3
Daniell Gdns TR1 .... 137 C3
Daniell Rd TR1 .... 137 B3
Daniell St TR1 .... 137 C3
Daniel Pl TR18 .... 143 E4
Daniels La PL25 .... 115 B4
Daniels Sail Loft TR10 ... 144 D7
Danmore Cl PL34 .... 14 C7
Danum Dr PL7 .... 131 B3
Daphne Du Maurier's
Smugglers at Jamaica Inn
Mus* PL15 .... 25 E3
Darite Prim Sch PL14 .... 38 A4
Darkey La PL16 .... 19 F4
Dark La
Camelford PL32 .... 105 C4
Liskeard PL14 .... 113 D6
Lostwithiel PL22 .... 112 C1
Darklake Cl PL6 .... 125 E5
Darklake La PL6 .... 125 D8
Darklake View PL6 .... 125 E5
Dark Street La PL7 .... 130 E4
Darlington Rd TR20 .... 88 F6
Darloe La PL13 .... 117 C3
Darracott Hill EX39 .... 2 E4
Dart Cl
Plymouth PL3 .... 129 D7
St Giles on t H PL15 .... 13 F1
Dartington Wlk PL6 .... 129 E8
Dartmeet Ave PL3 .... 129 B6
Dartmoor View
Plymouth PL4 .... 129 C3
Saltash PL12 .... 122 E4
Dartmouth Wlk PL6 .... 129 E8
Darwin Cres PL3 .... 129 D5
Dashwood Ho TR11 .... 145 A6
Daubuz Cl TR1 .... 137 C6
Daubuz Ct TR1 .... 137 D5
Daucus Cl PL19 .... 147 B4
Davenham Cl PL6 .... 125 B6
Davey's Cl TR11 .... 144 E1
David Cl PL7 .... 130 F6
David Penhaligon Way
TR1 .... 137 D3
David Southgate Ct PL1 . 148 A2
Davy Cl
Torpoint PL11 .... 126 F3
Tremar PL14 .... 38 A3
Davy Rd PL6 .... 125 C4
Davys Row PL14 .... 37 E4
Dawe Cres PL31 .... 109 C3
Dawes Cl PL14 .... 50 E7
Dawes La
Looe PL13 .... 117 D5
Millbrook PL10 .... 132 E5
Plymouth PL9 .... 136 D7
Dawlish Wlk PL6 .... 129 E8
Dawney Terr PL11 .... 65 B5
Dawn Rd PL13 .... 117 D2
Daws Ct PL12 .... 123 A2
Daw's Mdw PL32 .... 105 E4
Dawson Cl PL5 .... 123 E1
Daymer La PL27 .... 21 D4
Daymond Rd PL5 .... 123 D2
Dayton Cl PL6 .... 124 E3
Deacon Dr PL12 .... 122 F1
Deacons Gn PL19 .... 147 A3
Dean Cross PL9 .... 135 E7
Dean Cross Rd PL9 .... 135 E7
Dean Hill
Liskeard PL14 .... 113 B6
Plymouth PL9 .... 135 E7
Dean La PL14 .... 113 B6
Dean Park Rd PL9 .... 135 D7
Dean Rd PL7 .... 130 D6
Dean St PL14 .... 113 B5
Dean Terr PL14 .... 113 B6
Debden Cl PL5 .... 123 D4
Deeble Cl
Plymouth PL7 .... 130 E7
Threemilestone TR3 .... 69 C3
Deeble Dr 20 PL24 .... 60 B4
Deep La PL7 .... 131 C3
Deer Leap PL19 .... 147 D4
Deer Park Cl PL19 .... 147 C5
Deer Park Cres PL19 .... 147 C5
Deer Park Dr PL3 .... 129 D7
Deerpark Forest Trail*
PL14 .... 50 C3
Deer Park La PL19 .... 147 C5
Deer Park Rd PL19 .... 147 C5
Deer Pk
Newquay TR7 .... 110 D6
Saltash PL12 .... 122 F3
Defoe Cl PL5 .... 124 C1
Degibna La TR12, TR13 ... 146 C2
Delabole Com Prim Sch
PL33 .... 14 D2
Delacombe Cl PL7 .... 130 F7
De-La-Hay Ave PL3 .... 148 A4
Delamere Holiday Bglws
PL33 .... 14 D2
Delamere Rd PL6 .... 129 D7
Delavue Terr PL32 .... 105 C3
Delaware Com Prim Sch
PL18 .... 40 F5
Delaware Cotts PL18 .... 40 F6
Delaware Ct PL18 .... 40 F5
Delaware Gdns PL2 .... 127 F7
Delaware Rd PL18 .... 40 F6
Dell Cl TR18 .... 143 C3
Dell Mdw PL15 .... 18 B8
Dell The
Plymouth PL7 .... 130 B6
Tavistock PL19 .... 147 B6
Truro TR1 .... 137 C5
Denas Water TR2 .... 71 A5
Dengie Cl PL7 .... 131 B5
Denham Cl PL5 .... 124 C2
Dennis Cl PL5 .... 127 C7
Dennis Gdns PL15 .... 18 C2
Dennis La PL28 .... 107 D4
Dennison Ave PL25 .... 115 A4
Dennison Rd PL31 .... 109 D5
Dennis Rd
Liskeard PL14 .... 113 D6
Padstow PL28 .... 107 D5
Dennybowl La
Tideford PL12 .... 52 E3
Tideford PL12 .... 52 F2
Denyer Ct TR11 .... 145 A6
Denys View TR9 .... 45 F2
De Pass Gdns TR11 .... 145 C3
De Pass Rd TR11 .... 145 C2
Deptford Pl PL4 .... 149 A4
Derby Rd PL5 .... 124 C4
Derby's La PL26 .... 85 C5
Dereham Terr 6 TR1 .... 137 B4
Derowen Dr TR27 .... 142 B3
Derriford Bsns Pk PL6 .. 125 A4
Derriford Hospl PL6 .... 125 B4
Derriford Pk PL6 .... 125 A3
Derriford Rd PL6 .... 125 B4
Derriton Rd EX22 .... 8 F6
Derry Ave PL4 .... 148 C4
Derry's Cross PL1 .... 148 B2
Derwent Ave PL3 .... 129 C5
Desborough La PL4 .... 149 C3
Desborough Rd PL4 .... 149 C3
Deva Ho TR7 .... 111 A6
Deveral Rd TR27 .... 78 D2
Deveron Cl PL7 .... 131 A5
Devington Ct TR11 .... 145 C2
Devington Hall TR1 .... 137 E5
Deviock Hill PL11 .... 64 C5
Devonia Cl PL7 .... 130 E7
Devonport High Sch for Boys
PL1 .... 128 A2
Devonport High Sch for Girls
PL2 .... 128 C6
Devonport Hill
Kingsand PL10 .... 133 A2
Plymouth PL1 .... 127 F1
Devonport Leat PL6 .... 121 B5
Devonport Rd PL3 .... 127 F3
Devonport Sta PL1 .... 127 F3
Devonshire Ct PL11 .... 127 B3
Devonshire Ho
Plymouth PL1 .... 148 B2
2 Tavistock PL19 .... 147 B5
Devonshire St PL4 .... 149 A3
Devon Terr PL3 .... 128 E5
Devon Tors PL20 .... 42 D3
Devon Tors Rd 9 PL20 .... 42 C3
Devoran La TR3 .... 81 F6
Devoran Sch TR3 .... 81 F6
Diamond Ave PL4 .... 149 B4
Diana Cl TR11 .... 144 E2
Dickens Rd PL5 .... 124 B1
Dickiemoor La PL5 .... 124 C2
Dickna St PL15 .... 13 F1
Dicky La TR3 .... 82 D6
Diddies La EX23 .... 4 E1
Diddies Rd EX23 .... 4 E1
Dieppe Cl PL1 .... 127 F2
Digby Gr PL5 .... 123 F5
Digey Flats 49 TR26 .... 141 B6
Digey The 25 TR26 .... 141 B6
Diggory's Field 4 PL14 ... 38 A3
Dinas Ct PL11 .... 64 C5
Dinas Rd 1 TR9 .... 45 D6
Dingle Cl PL17 .... 28 D1
Dingle Rd
Plymouth, North Prospect
PL2 .... 128 A6
Plymouth, Plympton PL7 .. 130 C6
Dingles Cl TR3 .... 81 B4
Dingle's Folly PL13 .... 117 C3
Dingwall Ave PL5 .... 124 E3
Dipper Cl EX23 .... 5 A6
Dipper La EX23 .... 5 A7
Dirty La PL12 .... 122 B5
Discovery Wharf 20 PL4 . 149 A2
Distine Cl PL3 .... 129 B7
Dithmarschen Way PL25 . 114 B2
Dittisham Wlk PL6 .... 129 E8
Ditton Ct PL6 .... 129 A8
Dixon Pl PL2 .... 127 F4
Dobbin Cl PL28 .... 20 F2
Dobbin La PL28 .... 20 F2
Dobbin Rd PL28 .... 20 F2
Dobbs La TR1 .... 137 A4
Dobell Rd PL25 .... 114 E4
Dobwalls Com Prim Sch
PL14 .... 50 E7
Dobwalls Family Adventure
Park* PL14 .... 50 E8
Dockacre Rd PL15 .... 106 C6
Dockey PL15 .... 106 C5
Dock La TR18 .... 143 F5
Dockray Cl PL6 .... 125 D4
Dockyard PL2 .... 127 E4
Doctors Hill
8 Boscastle PL35 .... 9 C1
5 St Keverne TR12 .... 101 C4
Doctors La PL12 .... 65 A8
Doctor's La PL14 .... 113 C6
Doddridge Cl PL9 .... 135 F4
Dodson's Gap TR12 .... 99 B7
Doidges Farm Cl PL6 .... 129 B8
Dola La TR20 .... 89 E5
Dolbeare Pk (Cvn Pk)
PL12 .... 53 B4
Dolcoath Ave TR14 .... 138 F3
Dolcoath Cl TR14 .... 138 F3
Dolcoath Rd TR14 .... 138 F3
Dolgey Post PL27 .... 32 A4
Dolphin Cl PL9 .... 135 F6
Dolphin Court Rd PL9 .... 135 F6
Dolphin Ho 18 PL4 .... 149 A2
Dolphin Sq PL9 .... 135 F6
Dolphin St PL29 .... 22 D7
Dolvin Rd PL19 .... 147 C5
Domellick Cnr PL26 .... 46 B1
Domellick Hill PL26 .... 46 B1
Doniert's Cl PL14 .... 113 B5
Donkey La
Millbrook PL10 .... 132 C4

Donkey La *continued*
Portwrinkle PL11 65 A4
Donkey Pk PL28 31 F8
Donnington Dr PL3 129 C7
Donnington Rd TR18 143 C3
Donovan Way PL31 109 B4
Dopps Terr TR15 140 C5
Dorchester Ave PL5 124 D4
Dorchester Ct TR14 138 E4
Doreena Rd PL9 136 C7
Dormy Ave PL3 128 F5
Dorset Pk PL15 13 A2
Dorsmouth Terr PL7 130 E4
Doublebois Ind Est PL14 50 D7
Doubletrees PL24 60 B4
Doubletrees Ct 2 PL24 60 B4
Doubletrees Sch PL24 60 B4
Douglas Cl PL26 47 A3
Douglas Dr PL9 136 A6
Douglass Rd PL3 129 C6
Doulton Rd PL25 115 A4
Dousland Ho PL20 42 E3
Dousland Rd PL20 42 D3
Dousland Terr PL20 42 E3
Dovedale Rd PL2 128 A7
Dove Gdns PL3 129 D7
Dover Rd PL6 125 E3
Dove St 15 TR26 141 B5
Dower's Terr TR16 80 B5
Down Cl PL12 122 C2
Downfield Dr PL7 130 F5
Downfield Way PL7 130 F5
Downfield Wlk PL7 130 F5
Downgate Gdns PL2 128 D8
Downham Gdns PL5 124 C7
Downham Sch PL9 135 F7
Downhorne Pk PL9 135 F6
Downlea PL19 147 D4
Down Park Dr PL19 147 D4
Down Parks EX23 5 B7
Down Rd
Plymouth PL7 131 C5
Tavistock PL19 147 D4
Downs Cl PL26 58 C8
Downs Hill PL23 61 B5
Downside Ave PL6 129 C7
Downside Cl TR7 111 A4
Downs La PL13 117 B3
Downs Lane Pk PL13 117 B3
Downs Rd PL13 117 C4
Downs The PL13 117 C3
Downstream Cl PL28 107 C5
Downs View
Bude EX23 104 D7
Looe PL13 117 C3
Down The PL20 41 C1
Downton Cl PL1 148 A4
Dowren Ho TR27 142 B5
Dozmere TR3 82 C5
Dozmere Cl TR3 82 C5
Dracaena Ave
Falmouth TR11 144 F5
Hayle TR27 142 E6
Dracaena Cres TR27 142 E6
Dracaena Pl TR11 144 F4
Dracaena View TR11 144 F5
Drake Cir PL1, PL4 149 A3
drakecircus Sh Ctr PL1 149 A3
Drake Ct
Plymouth, Ernesettle PL5 123 E4
Plymouth, St Jude's PL4 149 B3
Drakefield Dr PL12 123 A3
Drake Gdns PL19 147 C4
Drake Prim Sch PL2 127 E6
Drake Rd
Padstow PL28 107 C5
Tavistock PL19 147 C6
Drakes Cl PL6 124 F4
Drake's Pk 3 PL20 41 B1
Drake Villas PL19 147 A4
Drakewalls Gdns PL18 40 F5
Drakewalls Pl PL18 40 F5
Drake Way PL9 135 E7
Drang The TR9 45 E1
Drannack La TR27 78 D4
Draper Terr 3 PL19 147 B5
Drax Gdns PL6 128 E8
Draycott Terr TR26 141 C4
Drayton Rd PL5 124 C1
Dreysen Cl TR15 139 C8
Drift Cl TR20 87 F3
Drift La PL14 49 C7
Drillfield La 9 TR26 141 B5
Drinnick Terr PL26 58 D6
Drive The
Helston TR13 146 D7
Plymouth PL3 128 E7
Driving La PL24 60 C6
Drogeada Cl PL15 27 D3
Droskyn Castle 19 TR6 55 A5
Droskyn Cl 22 TR6 55 A5
Droskyn House Villas TR6 55 A5
Droskyn Way TR6 55 A5
Druckham Pl PL15 106 D5
Druckham Terr PL15 106 D5
Druid's Lodge TR15 139 D5
Druid's Rd TR15 139 D5
Drummer's Hill PL26 114 C8
Drummond Cl PL2 127 F7
Drummond Pl PL1 127 F3
Drump Rd TR15 140 C5
Drunken Bridge Hill PL7 130 D4
Dryburgh Cres PL2 128 A8
Dryden Ave PL5 124 C1
Drym La
Leedstown TR14 78 F1
Nancegollan TR14 91 A8
Drym Rd TR13 91 B7
Dualstone Cross EX22 8 D3
Ducane Wlk PL6 125 B1
Duchy Ave TR7 111 C7
Duchy Cl
Launceston PL15 106 C7
St Austell PL25 114 F3
Duchy Coll
St Breock PL27 33 C7
Stoke Climsland PL17 28 D1
Duchy Cotts PL17 28 D1
Duchy Hospl TR1 69 E4
Duchy Terr
Minions PL14 38 B6
Upton Cross PL14 38 D7
Duck La PL12 53 E2
Duck St 9 TR19 88 C1
Duckworth St 3 PL2 128 A4
Ducky La PL12 53 C3
Ducky Row PL17 40 D4
Dudley Gdns PL6 129 B8
Dudley Rd PL7 130 B5
Dudman Rd TR1 69 F3
Dudnance La TR15 139 B4
Duke of Cornwall's Light Infantry Mus* PL31 109 F3
Duke's Ct PL26 46 F3
Dukes Dr PL19 41 B4
Dukes Ryde The 1 PL9 135 F7
Duke St
Launceston PL15 106 A8
Lostwithiel PL22 112 C2
Padstow PL28 107 D5
Plymouth PL1 127 E2
St Austell PL25 114 C3
Tavistock PL19 147 C6
11 Truro TR1 137 D4
Duke's Way TR7 111 A5
Duloe CE Jun & Inf Sch PL14 51 A1
Duloe Gdns PL2 128 C8
Dumbarton Terr 7 TR19 88 C1
Dumfries Ave PL5 124 D3
Duncannon Dr TR11 144 F4
Duncan St PL1 127 E1
Dunclair Pk PL3 129 D5
Duncombe Ave PL5 124 A2
Dundas St 4 PL2 128 A4
Dunders Hill PL27 21 D5
Dundonald St PL2 127 F4
Dungarth Gn PL14 113 D6
Dungarth Rd PL14 113 D6
Dunhead View PL15 28 B6
Dunheved Fields PL15 106 C4
Dunheved Rd
Launceston PL15 106 C5
Saltash PL12 122 F2
Dunkeswell Cl PL2 127 F8
Dunley Wlk PL6 125 C1
Dunmere Cl 1 PL24 60 C4
Dunmere Rd PL31 109 B5
Dunnet Rd PL6 124 D7
Dunn St 10 PL35 9 C1
Dunraven Dr PL6 125 A6
Dunsdon Cross EX22 5 F3
Dunstable Cl PL26 58 D6
Dunstan Cl TR10 144 C8
Dunstan La PL12 40 A1
Dunstanville Terr 12 TR11 145 A5
Dunster Cl PL7 131 C4
Dunston Cl PL26 58 C8
Dunstone Ave PL9 136 A7
Dunstone Cl PL9 135 F7
Dunstone Com Prim Sch PL9 136 A8
Dunstone Dr PL9 135 F7
Dunstone La PL9 136 B7
Dunstone Rd
Plymouth, Plymstock PL9 135 F7
Plymouth, St Budeaux PL5 123 F3
Dunstone View PL9 136 A7
Duntz Hill PL16 19 F4
Dunvegan Rd TR10 144 B8
Dunveth Rd PL27 108 A5
Dupath La PL17 40 A4
Duporth Bay PL26 115 A1
Duporth Holiday Village PL26 115 A1
Duporth Rd PL25, PL26 115 A2
Dural Cross EX22 3 E3
Durban Rd PL3 128 D5
Durgan Crossroads TR11 93 D3
Durgan La TR10 144 C8
Durham Ave PL4 149 C4
Durley Dene TR26 77 E4
Durnford St PL1 128 A1
Durnford Street Ope PL1 128 A1
Durning Rd TR5 54 C1
Durrant Cl PL1 127 E3
Durris Cl PL6 125 D4
Durris Gdns PL6 125 D4
Durston Rd EX23 104 E7
Durwent Cl PL9 135 A6
Dutson Rd PL15 106 C7
Dutson Terr PL15 106 C7
Dux Cross EX22 8 C6
Duxford Cl PL5 123 E5
Dye House Cotts PL14 36 F2
Dymond Cl PL32 105 B2
Dymond Ct (Kingdom Pl) PL12 122 F2
Dynas-la Rd TR26 141 B4
Dynevor Cl PL3 128 F7

E

Eagle Rd PL7 131 C4
Earle's Retreat TR11 145 B3
Earl's Acre PL3 128 C4
Earl's Dr The
Cawsand PL10 133 A1
Kingsand PL10 133 B3
Earls Mill Rd PL7 130 E6
Earls Rise TR7 111 B5
Earls Wood Cl PL6 125 F3
Earls Wood Dr PL6 125 F3
Eastbourne Cl PL25 114 E3
Eastbourne Rd PL25 114 D3
East Bridge 4 TR4 69 A3
Eastbury Ave PL5 124 A2
East Camps Bay PL11 64 D4
East Charles St TR14 138 E2
East Cl TR13 146 D7
East Cliff PL13 117 D3
Eastcliff Ave TR4 68 A7
Eastcliff Avenue No 2 TR4 68 A7
Eastcliffe Rd PL24 60 C5
East Cliff La TR17 89 C5
Eastcote Cl PL6 125 B6
Eastcott Cross EX23 3 A2
Eastella Rd PL20 42 D2
East End TR15 140 C5
Easterdown Cl PL9 135 F7
Eastern Ave PL14 113 D6
Eastern Gn
Gulval TR18 88 E6
Penzance TR18 143 F7
Eastern Green Pk TR18 88 E6
Eastern La TR14 138 D4
Eastern Wood Rd PL7 131 D4
East Fairholme Rd EX23 104 F7
Eastfield Ave PL9 135 C6
Eastfield Cres PL3 129 A6
Eastfield Way PL25 114 F5
East Hill
Camborne TR14 139 A5
St Austell PL25 114 D3
Eastlake Ho 5 PL1 149 A2
Eastlake St PL4 148 C3
Eastland Cl TR1 137 F4
East Mill PL15 106 B7
East Park Ave PL4 148 C4
East Pk
Pensilva PL14 38 D4
Redruth TR15 140 D6
East Pool Pk TR15 139 D6
East Quay TR27 142 B6
East Quay Ho PL13 117 D3
East Rd
Kilkhampton EX23 5 A6
Menheniot PL14 52 A5
Quintrell Downs TR8 44 E3
Stithians TR3 80 F3
East Rise TR11 144 F3
East Rosewin Row 10 TR1 137 D5
East St
Newquay TR7 110 E6
Plymouth PL1 148 A2
Polruan PL23 116 D3
1 St Columb Major TR9 45 E6
East Terr TR27 142 B6
East View PL14 51 F5
East Wharf PL26 73 C3
Eastwood Park Ind Est TR10 144 D7
Eastwood Rd TR10 144 D7
East Youlstone Cross EX23 3 C2
Ebenezer Pl 12 TR18 143 C1
Ebrington St PL4 149 A3
Eddystone Cl PL3 129 C6
Eddystone Ct PL13 117 D2
Eddystone Pl 3 PL27 108 B5
Eddystone Rd
Down Thomas PL9 135 C1
St Austell PL25 114 E5
Wadebridge PL27 108 B6
Eddystone Rise PL14 113 D7
Eddystone Road Trad & Ind Est PL27 108 B6
Eddystone Terr
Plymouth PL1 148 B1
2 Wadebridge PL27 108 B5
Eden Cl 11 PL24 60 B4
Eden Gdns 14 TR18 143 C1
Eden Project The* PL24, PL26 115 D8
Edenside PL3 128 F6
Eden Terr 13 TR18 143 C1
Edgar Rd
Jacobstow EX23 11 A6
Wainhouse Corner EX23 10 F6
Edgar Terr PL4 129 A4
Edgcumbe Ave
Newquay TR7 110 F5
Plymouth PL1 148 A3
Edgcumbe Cl PL18 41 A6
Edgcumbe Cres PL10 132 F6
Edgcumbe Ct 3 PL3 128 A3
Edgcumbe Dr PL19 147 B6
Edgcumbe Gdns TR7 110 F6
Edgcumbe Gn PL25 114 A3
Edgcumbe Ho PL1 148 B2
Edgcumbe Park Rd PL3 128 D6
Edgcumbe Rd
Lostwithiel PL22 112 B1
Roche PL26 46 F3
Saltash PL12 122 C5
St Austell PL25 114 A3
St Dominick PL12 40 D2
Edgcumbe St PL1 128 A1
Edgcumbe Terr
Milton Abbot PL19 29 C6
1 Par PL24 60 B4
Edgecombe Way PL18 40 E5
Edgecumbe Terr 14 PL20 41 B1
Edgemoor Cl PL14 38 A3
Edinburgh Cl PL25 115 C3
Edinburgh St PL1 127 E1
Edith Ave PL4 149 C4
Edith St PL5 123 D1
Edmonton PL27 33 B7
Edmund Rd TR15 140 B6
Edna Terr PL4 149 C3
Ednovean La TR20 89 E4
Edward Bolitho Ho (Hospl & Day Ctr) TR18 143 D3
Edward Hain Hospl TR26 141 B5
Edwards Cl PL7 131 B4
Edwards Cres PL12 122 C2
Edwards Dr PL7 131 B5
Edwards Rd
Devoran TR3 81 F6
St Giles on t H PL15 13 F1
Edward St
Camborne TR14 138 F4
Truro TR1 137 C4
Edymeade Ct PL15 106 C5
Edymeade Gdn PL15 106 C5
Effingham Cres PL3 128 D7
Efford Cres PL3 129 B6
Efford Down Pk EX23 104 C5
Efford Farm Bsns Pk EX23 104 C4
Efford Farm Cotts EX23 104 C4
Efford Fort PL3 129 E6
Efford La PL3 129 B5
Efford Pathway
Plymouth PL3 129 C6
Plymouth PL3 129 D5
Efford Rd PL3 129 B6
Efford Wlk PL3 129 B6
Egan's Way PL33 14 D2
Egerton Cres PL4 149 C3
Egerton Pl PL4 149 C3
Egerton Rd
Padstow PL28 107 E4
Plymouth PL4 149 C3
Eggbuckland Com Coll PL6 129 A8
Eggbuckland Rd PL3 129 C7
Eggbuckland Vale Prim Sch PL6 129 A8
Eglos Ct PL30 23 E7
Egloshayle Rd
Hayle TR27 142 E6
Wadebridge PL27 108 D5
Egloskerry Sch PL15 18 A5
Eglos Mdw TR11 82 A3
Eglos Parc
Mullion TR12 99 A2
Wadebridge PL27 108 D5
Eglos Rd
Ludgvan TR20 89 A7
Shortlanesend TR4 69 F6
St Erme TR4 70 D8
Eglos View 2 PL35 9 C1
Egret Cl PL10 133 A6
Eider Wlk TR27 77 E3
Eight Acre Cl 1 PL7 131 C5
Elaine Cl PL7 130 B5
Elbow La PL19 147 C6
Elburton Prim Sch PL9 136 C7
Elburton Rd PL9 136 B8
Eldad Hill PL1 148 A3
Elder Cl 2 PL7 131 B5
Elderfield Cl 7 PL24 60 D5
Eleanor Ho PL1 148 A2
Elerkey Cl TR2 83 F6
Elerkey La TR2 83 F6
Elford Cres PL7 130 E7
Elford Dr PL9 135 C7
Elford Pk PL20 42 D2
Elgin Cres PL5 124 E3
Elim Ct PL3 128 E5
Elim Terr PL3 128 E5
Eliot Cl PL15 18 C2
Eliot Ct TR7 110 F6
Eliot Dr PL12 65 B8
Eliot Gdns TR7 110 F6
Eliot Rd
St Austell PL25 114 E4
Truro TR1 137 C5
Eliot St PL5 127 E8
Elizabethan House (Mus) The* PL1 149 A2
Elizabeth Cl
Bodmin PL31 109 D4
Threemilestone TR3 69 C3
Elizabeth Ct
Bugle PL26 47 C1
2 Plymouth PL1 149 A2
Elizabeth Pl PL4 149 A4
Elizabeth Rd
Bude EX23 104 F5
St Austell PL25 114 E3
Elizabeth Terr TR17 89 B5
Ellen Cl TR4 68 C6
Ellenglaze Ct TR8 55 D8
Ellenglaze La TR8 55 D8
Ellenglaze Mdw TR8 55 D8
Elliot Sq PL11 127 B3
Elliot St PL1 148 B1
Elliott Cl PL12 122 D2
Elliot Terr PL1 148 C1
Elliot Terrace La PL1 148 C1
Elliott Rd PL4 129 B1
Ellis Cl TR27 142 C5
Elliston Gdns 3 TR13 98 C8
Ellis Way TR27 142 C5
Elm Cl
Callington PL17 39 F4
Camborne TR15 139 D6
Newquay TR7 110 F4
Tavistock PL19 147 C3
Elm Cotts PL12 122 C3
Elm Court Gdns TR1 137 D5
Elm Cres PL3, PL4 129 A4
Elm Croft PL2 128 B7
Elm Ct TR1 137 D5
Elm Dr
Bude EX23 104 F5
8 St Columb Major TR9 45 D6
Elmgate Crossways PL12 65 E8
Elm Gr
Feock TR3 82 C5
Plymouth, Eggbuckland PL6 129 B8
Plymouth, Plympton PL7 130 E5
Elm Grove Cotts TR10 93 C6
Elmlea EX23 104 F5
Elm Mdw TR3 82 C5
Elm Meadow Dr PL13 117 D4
Elm Pk PL10 133 B6
Elm Rd
Plymouth, Glenholt PL6 125 D6
Plymouth, Mannamead PL4 128 F4
Elms Close Terr 25 TR18 143 C2
Elmsleigh PL25 114 B3
Elmsleigh Rd PL27 108 B6
Elms The
Perranuthnoe TR20 89 D4
Plymouth PL3 128 A3
Elm Terr
8 Mullion TR12 99 A2
1 Plymouth PL3 128 F5
St Austell PL25 114 C4
Elm Tree Rd PL13 117 D4
Elmwood Cl PL6 125 D5
Elowen Cl TR11 144 E2
Elphinstone Rd PL2 128 C7
Elspeth Sitters Ho 11 PL4 149 A2
Elwell Rd PL12 123 A2
Elwick Gdns PL3 129 B5
Embankment La PL4 129 B2
Embankment Rd PL4 129 B2
Embankment Road La N PL4 129 B2
Emily Gdns PL4 149 B4
Emlyn Fields PL25 114 F6
Emma Pl PL1 128 A1
Emma Place Ope PL1 128 A1
Empire Way TR11 144 E4
Empress Ave 24 TR18 143 E6
Emslie Rd TR11 145 C2
Endsleigh Dr PL15, PL19 28 F5
Endsleigh Gdns
Milton Abbot PL19 29 B5
2 Plymouth PL4 149 A4
Endsleigh Park Rd PL3 128 D6
Endsleigh Pk EX23 7 B6
Endsleigh Pl PL4 149 A4
Endsleigh Rd PL9 135 C7
Endsleigh Terr PL14 113 C6
Eningdale Rd PL19 147 A4
Ennerdale Gdns PL6 124 E5
Ennis Cl TR4 56 D1
Ennor's Rd TR7 110 D6
Enys Cl
Carbis Bay TR26 141 D1
Truro TR1 137 B5
Enys Cotts TR19 75 A2
Enys Quay 5 TR1 137 D4
Enys Rd
Camborne TR14 138 D4
Truro TR1 137 B5
Enys Redenek TR14 138 F5
Epping Cres PL6 129 D7
Epworth Cl TR1 137 E4
Epworth Terr 4 PL2 127 F5
Erdiston Ct EX23 104 D6
Ergue-Gaberic Way EX23 104 D5
Eric Rd
Calstock PL18 41 B3
Plymouth PL4 149 C3
Erisey Terr TR11 145 B4
Erith Ave PL2 127 E7
Erle Gdns PL7 130 F3
Erlstoke Cl PL6 125 D1
Erme Gdns PL3 129 C5
Ermington Terr PL4 128 E4
Ernesettle Com Prim Sch PL5 123 F4
Ernesettle Cres PL5 123 E3
Ernesettle Gn PL5 123 E4
Ernesettle La PL5 123 D4
Ernesettle Rd PL5 123 E3
Erow Glas TR10 144 C8
Esmonde Gdns PL5 127 B8
Esmond Rd TR13 146 D4
Esperanza Ct TR11 144 F6
Esplanade PL23 116 C3
Esplanade Rd TR7 110 A6
Esplanade The PL1 148 C1
Essa Rd PL12 122 F2
Essex Dr TR15 139 B8
Essex St PL1 148 B4
Eston Cl TR10 93 C8
Estover Cl PL6 125 F5
Estover Com Coll PL6 125 D2
Estover Ind Est PL6 125 E4

Estover Prim Sch PL6 125 D2
Estover Rd PL6 125 F4
Estuary View
2 Falmouth TR11 145 B5
Lelant TR26 77 E3
Newquay TR7 110 D5
Eton Ave PL1 148 C4
Eton Pl PL1 148 C4
Eton St PL1 148 C4
Eton Terr 3 PL1 148 B3
Euny Cl TR15 140 A4
Eureka Vale 7 TR6 55 A5
Europa Ct TR8 31 C2
Evans Ct PL1 148 A3
Evans Pl PL2 128 B5
Evans Way TR20 90 C4
Evea Cl TR1 69 F3
Evely Ct PL14 113 D7
Evelyn Pl PL4 149 A4
Evelyn St PL5 123 D1
Evenden Ct PL11 127 A3
Example Cross PL15 27 B6
Exchange St PL1 149 A2
Exe Gdns PL3 129 C7
Exeter Cl PL5 123 D4
Exeter Ct 6 PL15 106 C6
Exeter St
Launceston PL15 106 C6
Plymouth, Barbican PL4 149 A3
Plymouth, St Jude's PL4 149 B2
Exmouth Ct PL1 127 F3
Exmouth Rd PL1 127 F3
Explorer Ct PL2 128 B5

F

Factory Cotts PL14 51 F5
Fairbourne Rd PL25 114 F4
Fair Cross TR2 72 C6
Fairfax Rd TR2 70 F5
Fairfax Terr 5 PL2 127 F4
Fairfield
Plymouth PL7 130 E7
St Germans PL12 65 A8
Fair Field TR20 89 B8
Fairfield Ave PL2 128 C7
Fairfield Cl
Lelant TR26 77 E4
St Austell PL25 115 A4
Fairfield Pk PL15 26 C7
Fairfield Rd
Bude EX23 104 E5
Falmouth TR11 144 F4
Fairfields PL13 117 D5
Fairlight PL14 113 D5
Fairmantle St TR1 137 D4
Fairmead Cl PL12 53 E4
Fairmead Mews PL12 122 C3
Fairmeadow TR10 144 B7
Fairmead Rd PL12 122 C2
Fairpark Rd
Liskeard PL14 113 C5
Wadebridge PL27 108 B5
Fair Park View TR8 56 F5
Fair St TR9 45 E6
Fair View
Bodmin PL31 109 B4
Lanivet PL26 47 E4
Fairview Ave PL3 129 D5
Fairview Pk 5 TR9 45 E2
Fairview Pl TR11 145 B4
Fairview Terr TR7 110 E6
Fair View Terr TR4 55 D8
Fairview Way PL3 129 E5
Fairway
Saltash PL12 122 C2
St Austell PL25 115 D3
Fairways The PL30 48 C7
Fairway The TR11 93 C2
Falcon Terr EX23 104 D5
Falmouth Bsns Pk TR11 144 E3
Falmouth Com Sch
TR11 144 D5
Falmouth Docks Sta
TR11 145 D3
Falmouth Hospl TR11 144 F4
Falmouth Marine Sch
TR11 145 B4
Falmouth Pl TR19 86 F8
Falmouth Rd
Helston TR13 146 D7
Penryn TR10 144 E7
Redruth TR15 140 C4
Truro TR1 137 C3
Falmouth Town (The Dell)
Sta TR11 145 C3
Falmouth Wharves TR11 145 A6
Fanshawe Way PL9 135 C6
Faraday Mill Bsns Pk
PL4 129 B1
Faraday Rd PL4 129 B1
Farfield Pl TR7 110 B5
Faringdon Rd PL4 129 B3
Farm Cl PL7 130 C7
Farmers Cl PL14 50 B6
Farmers Ct TR20 89 B8
Farmers Hill PL13 117 C4
Farmer's La PL14 50 B6
Farmers Mdw 8 TR18 143 C2
Farm La
Plymouth PL5 124 B2
Saltash PL12 122 D1
Farm Town TR15 140 C3
Farnley Cl PL6 125 B6
Farrar Cl TR27 142 E8
Farriers Cotts PL7 130 E7
Farriers Gn PL32 105 B2
Farriers The PL19 30 A3
Faugan La TR18 143 B1
Faugan Rd TR18 143 B1
Faukener Cl TR11 144 E4
Fayre View PL12 122 B1
Fearnside Way PL12 122 C3
Federation Rd PL3 129 C4
Fegan Rd PL5 123 B1
Feliskirk La TR17 89 B6
Felixstowe Ave TR7 111 E7
Fellowes Pl PL1 128 A2
Fellows La PL1 148 A4
Fenten Pk PL12 122 F3
Fenteroon Rd PL32 105 C2
Fentonluna La PL28 107 D6
Fenwick Rd TR11 145 B2
Fern Cl PL7 131 C5
Ferndale Ave PL2 127 F7
Ferndale Cl PL6 125 D8
Ferndale Rd
Falmouth TR11 145 A2
Plymouth PL2 127 F7
Ferndale Terr PL14 113 B6
Fern Glen 18 TR26 141 A5
Fernhill Rd TR7 110 D6
Fern Lee Terr 19 TR26 141 B5
Fernleigh Cres PL27 108 C4
Fernleigh Gdns PL27 108 C4
Fernleigh La PL27 108 C4
Fernleigh Rd
Plymouth PL3 128 F5
Wadebridge PL27 108 C5
Fernleigh Terr
Gunnislake PL18 40 E5
Nanpean PL26 58 C6
Fern Mdw PL19 147 D6
Fernside Pk PL14 38 A3
Fernside Rd TR14 138 B1
Ferrers Rd PL5 123 E1
Ferretts Cross EX23 11 A6
Ferris Town TR1 137 C4
Ferris Way PL23 116 E2
Ferry La PL11 126 D5
Ferry Rd PL1 127 E3
Ferry St PL11 127 C3
Festival Villas TR3 69 D3
Feversham Cl PL7 131 B6
Field Cl PL22 112 D2
Field Pl TR11 93 D3
Field The TR 20 76 F2
Fifield Ho PL26 58 B4
Fillace La 10 PL20 42 C4
Fillace Pk PL20 42 C4
Filtrick La TR16 139 E1
Finch Cl PL3 129 D4
Finches Cl PL9 136 C7
Findon Gdns PL6 125 D4
Finewell St PL1 148 C2
Finnigan Rd PL4 129 B1
Finn VC Est PL31 109 D5
Finnygook La PL11 65 A4
Fir Cl
Goonhavern TR4 55 D4
Helston TR13 146 B7
St Austell PL25 114 B3
Fir Cres PL26 58 D5
Fircroft Rd PL2 128 B7
Firebeacon Cross EX39 2 F7
Fir Gr 8 TR3 81 F7
Firsleigh Pk PL26 46 F3
First Ave
Plymouth, Billacombe
PL9 135 F8
Plymouth, Stoke PL1 128 A2
Firs The PL26 58 E8
Fisgard Way PL11 126 D3
Fisher Cl PL27 108 D6
Fisher Rd PL2 128 A5
Fish Mkt PL4 149 B2
Fish Quay PL4 149 A2
Fish St 9 TR26 141 B6
Fish Strand Hill TR11 145 B4
Fish Strand Quay TR11 145 B4
Fistral Cl PL11 126 F4
Fistral Cres TR7 110 A5
Fistral Ct TR7 110 A5
Fistral Sands Apartments
TR7 110 D7
Fitzford Cotts PL19 147 B4
Fitzroy Rd PL1 128 A3
Fitzroy Terr 7 PL1 128 A3
Fitzsimmons Cl 7 TR13 146 C5
Five Fields La TR11 145 A5
Five Wells La TR13 146 B5
Flamank Pk PL31 109 C4
Flambards Experience*
TR13 146 E4
Flamborough Rd PL6 125 A7
Flamborough Way PL6 125 A6
Flamsteed Cres PL5 123 E1
Flaxmoor Terr PL31 109 D5
Fleet St PL2 127 E6
Fletcher Cres PL9 136 B6
Fletcher Way PL9 136 A6
Fletemoor Rd PL5 123 E1
Flexbury Ave EX23 104 E7
Flexbury Mews EX23 104 E7
Flexbury Park Ct EX23 104 E7
Flexbury Park Rd EX23 104 E6
Flexbury Pk EX23 104 E7
Flora Cotts PL1 148 B2
Flora Ct PL1 148 B3
Flora St PL1 148 B2
Florence Hill PL17 39 F5
Florence Pl
Falmouth TR11 145 B3
Newlyn TR18 143 C3
Plymouth PL4 149 C3
Florence Rd PL17 39 F5
Florence Road Bsns Pk
PL17 39 F6
Florence Road Ind Est
PL17 39 F6
Florence St PL5 123 D1
Florence Terr TR11 145 B3
Florida Gdns PL3 129 C6
Floyd Cl PL2 127 F7
Flushing Sch TR11 145 B6
Folders La PL30 23 F6
Foliot Ave PL2 128 A6
Foliot Rd PL2 128 A6
Folkstone Cl PL26 58 E6
Forbes Cl TR18 143 B1
Forbes Rd TR18 143 B1
Ford PL22 49 E3
Forder Hill PL10 132 F1
Forder Hts PL6 125 B1
Forder La PL10 132 F1
Forder Valley Rd PL6 129 D8
Ford Hill PL2 128 A5
Ford Park La PL4 128 E4
Ford Park Rd PL4 128 D4
Ford Prim Sch PL2 128 A5
Fords Hill TR12 100 D7
Ford's Row TR15 140 B5
Ford St PL19 147 B5
Foredown Pk PL14 38 C3
Fore St
Ashton TR13 90 E3
Barripper TR14 79 B5
Bere Alston PL20 41 B1
Bere Ferrers PL20 119 F3
Bodmin PL31 109 D5
Boscastle PL35 9 C1
Bugle PL26 47 C1
6 Callington PL17 39 E4
Calstock PL18 41 A3
Camborne TR15 139 B6
Camelford PL32 105 D4
Cargreen PL12 119 A2
Carharrack TR16 80 F8
Chacewater TR4 69 A3
Constantine TR11 92 F4
Crumplehorn PL13 62 D1
Fowey PL23 116 D4
Golant PL23 61 B5
Goldsithney TR20 89 E5
Grampound Road TR2 57 E1
Grampound TR2 72 A7
Gunnislake PL18 40 F5
Gunnislake PL18 41 A6
Hayle TR27 142 D6
Herodsfoot PL14 50 E3
Kingsand PL10 133 A2
Lelant TR26 77 E4
Lerryn PL22 61 C7
Lifton PL16 19 F4
Liskeard PL14 113 C6
Looe PL13 117 C3
Lostwithiel PL22 112 C2
Madron TR20 88 B7
Marazion TR17 89 C5
Mevagissey PL26 73 C3
Millbrook PL10 132 E5
Milton Abbot PL19 29 C6
Mount Hawke TR4 68 C6
13 Mousehole TR19 88 C1
Nanpean PL26 58 D7
Newlyn TR18 143 C1
Newquay TR7 110 D6
Par PL24 60 B5
Penponds TR14 138 B1
Pensilva PL14 38 E4
Plymouth, Devonport PL1 127 F2
Plymouth, Plympton PL7 130 E4
Plymouth, Tamerton Foliot
PL5 124 B6
Polgooth PL26 59 A1
Polruan PL23 116 D2
4 Porthleven TR13 98 B8
Port Isaac PL29 22 D7
Praze-an-Beeble TR14 79 B2
Probus TR2 71 C6
Redruth TR15 140 B5
Roche PL26 46 F2
Saltash PL12 122 F2
St Austell PL25 114 C3
St Cleer PL14 37 F3
St Columb Major TR9 45 E6
St Day TR16 68 D1
St Dennis PL26 58 C8
St Erth TR27 142 A1
St Germans PL12 65 A8
Sticker PL26 58 E1
St Ives TR26 141 B6
St Just TR19 86 F6
7 Stratton EX23 4 E1
St Stephen PL26 58 B4
St Teath PL30 23 E7
Tintagel PL34 14 C7
Torpoint PL11 127 B3
Tregony TR2 71 F3
Troon TR14 79 E5
9 Tywardreath PL24 60 D5
Forest Ave PL2 128 C7
Foresters Rd PL9 135 D7
Forest Hos TR4 70 D8
Forest View PL6 125 D7
Forge Gdns EX23 6 F1
Forge Ind Pk TR14 138 E5
Forge La PL12 122 C4
Forge The TR3 82 A7
Forge Way TR4 69 F6
Forlaze Rd PL27 21 D2
Formal Ind Pk TR14 138 B4
Forrabury Hill 5 PL35 9 C1
Forreglos Dr 10 TR17 89 C5
Forresters Dr PL6 125 D7
Forsythia Dr PL12 122 C3
Fort Austin Ave PL6 125 C1
Fortescue Cl PL26 58 D6
Fortescue Pl
Lostwithiel PL22 112 D3
Plymouth PL3 129 A6
Fortescue Terr PL19 147 A6
Forth An Cos TR3 81 B4
Forth-an-Eglas TR16 68 D1
Forth-an-Nance TR16 67 C6
Forth-An-Praze
Illogan TR15 139 D8
St Day TR16 68 D1
Forth-An-Ryn TR15 140 D4
Forth An Streth TR27 142 E7
Forth An Tewennow
TR27 142 D7
Forth-An-Tre TR27 142 D7
Forth An Ula TR27 142 E7
Forth An Vre TR14 139 A3
Forth Coth TR3 82 A7
Forthcrom TR12 92 C1
Forth Dall 21 TR16 67 E4
Forth Gdns PL3 129 D6
Forth Gwedhen TR13 146 D8
Forth Kegyn TR15 139 B4
Forthnoweth TR15 140 B5
Forth Noweth 4 TR3 81 F7
Forth Scol
Camborne TR15 139 D7
6 Porthleven TR13 98 C8
Forthvean
Camborne TR14 138 D1
Portreath TR16 67 C5
Forth Vean TR13 90 E6
Forthvean Cres TR4 68 A6
Forthvean Rd TR4, TR16 67 F7
Forth Veor TR15 140 E7
Forthvras TR15 139 B8
Fort Picklecombe PL10 133 F4
Fort Terr PL6 124 F3
Fort The PL10 133 A1
Fosbrooke Ct 10 PL3 128 F6
Foster Dr PL31 109 C3
Fosters La PL34 14 C7
Fosters Way EX23 104 F6
Foulston Ave PL5 127 B8
Foundry Flats TR27 142 B5
Foundry Gdns PL15 106 B6
Foundry Hill
Hayle TR27 142 B4
Stithians TR3 80 F3
Foundry Ho TR27 142 B5
Foundry La
Hayle TR27 142 B5
Newlyn TR18 143 C2
Foundry Rd TR14 138 E3
Foundry Row
Marhamchurch EX23 7 B6
5 Redruth TR15 140 B5
Foundry Sq TR27 142 B5
Foundry St 6 PL27 108 B5
Foundry Terr PL27 108 B5
Fountain Ct 27 TR18 143 E6
Fountains Cres PL2 128 C8
Four Acres Rd TR2 83 F6
Fourgates Est PL14 51 F5
Four Lanes' End TR19 97 F6
Fourlanesend Com Prim Sch
PL10 132 F3
Four Turnings PL23 60 F3
Fowey Com Coll PL23 116 B4
Fowey Cres 27 PL17 39 F4
Fowey Gdns PL3 129 D6
Fowey Hospl PL23 116 C5
Fowey Mus* PL23 116 D4
Fowey Prim Sch PL23 116 C4
Fowlfield Row TR13 90 F3
Foxdown PL27 108 D5
Foxes Field TR18 88 E6
Foxes La 5 TR19 88 C1
Foxes Row TR16 80 E8
Fox Field Cl PL3 129 C5
Foxglove Cl PL15 106 E4
Foxglove Cres PL28 31 F7
Foxglove Way PL12 122 B3
Foxhole La PL26 85 D5
Foxhole Prim Sch PL26 58 D5
Fox's La TR11 145 B3
Foxstanton Dr TR10 144 D7
Foxs Yd TR10 144 D7
Foxtor Cl PL5 124 B3
Foxwood Gdns
Plymouth, Plymstock PL9 135 F5
Plymouth, Southway PL6 124 E5
Foyle Cl PL7 131 A5
Fraddam Rd TR27 78 D1
Fradgan Pl TR18 143 C2
Fradgan The 12 TR18 143 C2
Frances St TR1 137 C4
Francis La PL27 21 D5
Francis Rd PL27 21 D5
Francis St PL1 148 A3
Frankfort Gate 9 PL1 148 B3
Frankland Cl TR11 144 F3
Franklin Cl PL27 108 D6
Franklyn Cl PL25 114 F5
Franklyns' PL6 125 A4
Franklyns Cl PL6 125 A4
Franwill Terr 16 TR18 143 C1
Fraser Pl PL5 124 C7
Fraser Rd PL5 124 C7
Fraser Sq PL5 124 C7
Frederick St E PL1 148 B3
Frederick St W 6 PL1 148 B3
Fredington Gr PL2 128 B6
Freedom Sq PL4 149 B4
Freeman Collins Dr
TR11 144 F4
Freemans Wharf PL1 134 A8
Fremantle Gdns 4 PL2 127 F4
Fremantle Pl PL2 127 F4
Frenchman's La PL12 53 C4
Frensham Ave PL6 125 C7
Frensham Gdns PL6 125 C7
Freshbrook Cl TR18 88 E6
Freshford Cl PL6 125 C1
Freshford Wlk PL6 125 C1
Freshwater La TR2 95 B6
Frewin Gdns PL6 125 B6
Friar's La TR12 102 F6
Friars' La PL1 149 A2
Friar's La TR12 103 B5
Friars Wlk PL19 147 E2
Friary Pk PL4 149 B3
Friary St PL4 149 B3
Frith Rd PL12 122 D3
Frobisher App PL5 124 D2
Frobisher Dr PL12 122 E2
Frobisher Terr 9 TR11 145 A5
Frobisher Way
Tavistock PL19 147 B5
Torpoint PL11 126 D3
Frog La TR2 71 F3
Frogmore Ave
Plymouth PL6 129 B7
Plymouth PL6 129 C7
Frogmore Ct PL6 129 B7
Frogwell Rd PL17 39 E4
Frome Cl PL7 131 A4
Frontfield Cres PL6 124 E5
Front Rd PL11 64 C4
Frost Ct TR11 144 E5
Fuggoe Croft TR26 141 C3
Fuggoe La TR26 141 C2
Fullaford Rd PL17 40 A4
Fuller Rd TR6 55 A5
Fullerton Rd PL2 128 A5
Fuller-Tre Cl PL26 46 F3
Furland Cl PL9 135 C5
Furneaux Ave PL2 128 B5
Furneaux Rd PL2 128 B6
Furry Way TR13 146 B5
Fursdon Cl PL9 136 C6
Furse Pk PL5 127 C7
Furzeacre Cl PL7 131 A7
Furze Cross EX22 8 B5
Furzedown Terr PL13 117 C4
Furze Gdns EX23 2 D1
Furzehatt Ave PL9 136 A6
Furzehatt Park Rd PL9 136 A6
Furzehatt Rd PL9 135 F6
Furzehatt Rise PL9 136 A6
Furzehatt Villas PL9 135 F6
Furzehatt Way PL9 136 A6
Furze Hill PL31 109 E5
Furzehill Rd PL4 128 F4
Furze Pk
Polruan PL23 116 D2
St Issey PL27 32 D5
Trelights PL29 22 D6

G

Gabriel St 5 TR26 141 B5
Gaia Energy Ctr The*
PL32 14 F4
Gainsborough Ct TR7 110 D5
Gainsborough Ho PL19 147 B6
Gainsborough Park Cvn Pk
PL26 58 E6
Gains Cross EX22 5 F3
Galileo Cl PL7 130 E6
Gallacher Way PL12 122 B3
Galland Rd TR1 69 F4
Gallant's Dr PL23 116 B3
Galleon Ct TR7 110 D4
Galleries The 46 TR26 141 B6
Gallery La
Landrake PL12 53 A1
St Germans PL12 65 A8
Galligan Cl TR19 97 A6
Galligan La TR19 97 A6
Gallops The PL12 122 D4
Galsworthy Cl PL5 124 C2
Galva Rd PL7 131 C8
Gander La TR13 146 B6
Ganges Cl TR11 82 C2
Ganges Rd PL2 128 A5
Ganna Park Rd PL3 128 D6
Gannel Rd TR7 110 E4
Gannel View Cl TR8 111 B3
Gannet Dr PL25 114 F4
Gara Cl PL9 136 B6
Garby La TR15 140 C3
Garcia Terr PL15 106 D4
Garden Cl PL7 131 D5
Garden Cres PL1 148 B1
Gardeners Way PL27 32 E6
Garden House The* PL20 42 A3
Garden La PL19 147 B5
Garden Mdw TR11 144 E3
Garden Park Cl PL9 136 C7
Garden St PL2 127 E4
Garden Village PL9 135 F8
Garden Way TR8 111 F3
Gards La PL5 123 E2
Garfield Terr PL1, PL3 128 A3
Garland Pl TR14 138 D4

Garlidna 25 TR18 143 E6
Garras Com Prim Sch TR12 99 D7
Garrett St PL10 133 A1
Garrick Cl PL5 124 C2
Garris Cotts TR20 88 E8
Garrison Cl PL1 127 E1
Garro La TR12 99 A1
Garston Cl PL9 136 A8
Garth-An-Creet TR26 77 A7
Garth Marhas TR14 138 C3
Garth Morcom PL14 113 B5
Garth Rd TR18 143 B3
Gascoyne Ct PL4 149 A3
Gascoyne Pl PL4 149 A3
Gas Hill TR1 137 E2
Gashouse La PL4 149 B2
Gasking St PL4 149 A3
Gas La 8 TR15 140 B4
Gas St TR14 138 D3
Gateway Ct TR27 77 E2
Gatewynyack TR12 101 C1
Gavercoombe Pk 2 PL34 14 C7
Gay's Hill TR12, TR13 146 E4
Gays La PL12 65 A8
Gdynia Way PL4 149 C2
Gear Hill
Madron TR20 88 C8
Mawgan TR12 99 E8
Gear La TR20 88 B8
Gears La
Goldsithney TR17, TR20 89 D6
Goldsithney TR20 89 E5
Geasons La PL7 130 E5
Geevor Cotts TR19 86 F8
Geevor Tin Mine* TR19 74 F1
Geevor Tin Mine Mus* TR19 74 F1
Geffery Cl PL12 53 C3
Gendalls Way PL15 106 B8
Gennys Cl PL18 40 E6
George Ave PL7 130 F6
George Cross PL7 130 F5
George Downing Ho PL6 125 A1
George Fox Cl PL15 106 A4
George La PL7 130 F5
George Pl
Callington PL17 39 E4
Plymouth PL1 148 A2
Georges La PL11 65 C6
Georges Paddock PL15 27 B3
George Sq PL1 127 F1
George St
Plymouth PL1 127 F1
Truro TR1 137 C4
Georgia Cres PL3 129 C6
Geraldine Terr PL12 122 C1
Germoe Com Prim Sch TR20 90 C4
Gerrans Cl PL25 115 B5
Gerrans Hill TR2 83 B2
Gerrans Sch TR2 83 B1
Gerrans Sq TR2 83 B2
Gewans Mdw PL25 114 E2
Ghost Hill TR12 99 A1
Gibbon La PL4 149 A3
Gibbons Fields 9 TR12 99 A2
Gibbons St PL4 149 A3
Gibbs La PL35 9 C1
Gibraltar Terr 6 TR2 95 A6
Gibralter Sq 6 EX23 4 E1
Gibson Way TR13 91 B1
Gifford Pl PL3 128 D4
Gifford Terrace Rd PL3 128 E5
Gig La TR3 82 A7
Gilbert Cl PL26 58 B4
Gilbert Ct PL7 131 B6
Gilbert La PL2 128 C5
Gilbert Rd PL31 109 F4
Gill-An-Creet TR26 77 A7
Gillbard Centenary Flats PL15 106 B5
Gillbard Centenary Homes PL15 106 B5
Gilley La PL26 73 A4
Gill Pk PL3 129 B5
Gills Cl TR10 144 B6
Gilly Fields TR15 140 B3
Gilly Gabben Ind Est TR12 99 B7
Gilly Hill
Cury TR12 99 B5
Redruth TR15 140 C3
Gilly La TR26 77 C1
Gilston Rd PL12 122 D4
Gilwell Ave PL9 136 B7
Gilwell Pl PL4 149 A3
Gilwell St PL4 149 A3
Gipsy La
Liskeard PL14 113 A5
Sithney TR13 91 C2
Gitchell La
Crowlas TR20 89 C8
St Erth TR26 77 C1
Glade Cl PL6 125 A4
Glade The
Crapstone PL20 42 B2
St Minver PL27 22 A3
Gladstone Rd PL30 109 C2
Gladstone Terr
Longrock TR20 88 F6
3 Redruth TR15 140 C5
Gladwell Gdns 10 EX23 4 D1
Glamis Rd TR7 111 B6
Glantis Cres TR9 45 E2
Glanville Ave 1 PL19 147 B5
Glanville Rd PL19 147 B6
Glanville St PL1, PL4 148 C3
Glanville Terr PL12 122 F3
Glasney Pl TR10 144 C7
Glasney Rd TR11 145 A5
Glasney Terr TR10 144 D7
Glebe Ave PL12 122 F3
Glebe Cl
Mawgan TR12 99 D7
Pelynt PL13 62 D5
6 St Columb Major TR9 45 E6
Glebe Cres PL27 32 D6
Glebe Dr PL26 46 F3
Glebe Est PL14 38 F2
Glebelands
Callington PL17 39 E5
Looe PL13 117 D5
Glebe Mdw PL17 39 E5
Glebe Parc PL30 23 E3
Glebe Pl TR12 103 B5
Glebe Row TR27 142 D7
Glebe Terr
Constantine TR11 92 F4
Ruan Minor TR12 103 B5
Glebe The
Camborne TR14 138 C3
Cubert TR8 55 D8
St Mellion PL12 53 D8
Tregony TR2 71 F4
Week St Mary EX22 11 E8
Glenavon Rd PL3 128 E5
Glenburn Cl PL3 128 E7
Glencross Ct 3 PL14 113 C6
Glen-Dale Cl 3 PL25 115 A5
Glendale Cres TR4 68 C6
Glen Dale Cres TR15 140 D4
Glen-Dale Cres PL25 115 A5
Glendale Terr PL26 58 E3
Glendower Rd PL3 128 D5
Glendurgan Gdns* TR11 93 D2
Gleneagle Ave 4 PL3 128 F6
Gleneagle Rd PL3 128 F6
Gleneagle Villas 5 PL3 128 F6
Glenfeadon Terr TR16 67 C6
Glenfield Cl PL6 125 D6
Glenfield Rd PL6 125 D5
Glenfield Way PL6 125 E6
Glenhaven Pk (Cvn Pk) TR13 146 D5
Glenholt Cl PL6 125 D6
Glenholt Rd PL6 125 D6
Glenhurst Rd 5 PL3 128 E6
Glen Leigh TR15 140 A6
Glenleigh Pk PL26 58 E1
Glenmoor La TR12 99 A1
Glenmore Ave PL2 127 F5
Glenmore Terr
Liskeard PL14 113 D6
Mabe Burnthouse TR10 81 A1
Glennaven Cl PL7 131 C6
Glen Park Ave PL4 148 C4
Glen Park Prim Sch PL7 131 B5
Glen Pk PL14 38 D4
Glen Rd
Plymouth, Mannamead PL3 128 F5
Plymouth, Plympton PL7 130 F6
Wadebridge PL27 108 B5
Glenside Rise PL7 130 E6
Glenthorne Rd TR3 69 C3
Glentor Rd PL3 128 E7
Glentowan Rd PL26 73 C6
Glen Vale TR15 139 E6
Glenview PL25 114 B3
Glen View
Callington PL17 39 E5
Penryn TR10 144 B8
Tywardreath PL24 60 D5
Wadebridge PL27 108 B4
Glenwood Rd PL3 128 E6
Globerdon Rd PL14 38 E4
Globe Sq TR16 139 F2
Globe Vale Cvn Pk TR16 68 B3
Gloucester Ave PL25 115 C3
Gloucester Cres TR18 143 B1
Gloucester Ct PL1 148 C4
Gloucester Pl
27 Newlyn TR18 143 C2
Plymouth PL1 148 C4
Gloucester Rd TR18 143 C2
Gloweth View TR1 69 E3
Gloweth Villas TR1 69 E3
Gluyas The TR11 144 E1
Glynn Ave 8 TR13 146 C5
Glynn Rd
Liskeard PL14 113 A5
Padstow PL28 107 D5
Glyn Way TR3 69 D3
Goad Ave
Plymouth PL4 149 C2
Torpoint PL11 126 E3
Goad Cl PL11 126 F3
Godding Gdns PL6 124 E6
Godolphin Ave TR17 89 B5
Godolphin Cl TR17 89 B6
Godolphin Cres TR13 90 E6
Godolphin Ct 5 TR14 138 D3
Godolphin Dr TR17 89 B5
Godolphin Ho
Godolphin Cross TR13 90 E6
Tavistock PL19 147 C5
Godolphin Pk 11 PL17 39 E4
Godolphin Pl TR17 89 B5
Godolphin Prim Sch TR13 90 E6
Godolphin Rd
Falmouth TR11 144 F5
Helston TR13 146 C6
Longrock TR20 88 F6
Godolphin Terr TR17 89 B5
Godolphin Way TR7 111 B7
Godrevy Ct TR26 141 D2
Godrevy Ho TR1 69 E4
Godrevy Pk (Cvn Pk) TR27 66 B1
Godrevy Terr 28 TR26 141 B6
Goldbank Bglws PL30 34 C2
Golden Bank Pk TR11 144 E1
Golden Sands 11 TR6 55 A5
Golden Sands Bglws TR27 142 E7
Golden Sands Cvns TR27 142 E7
Goldfinch Cl PL15 106 E4
Goldfinch Gr PL12 122 D4
Goldmartin Cl TR11 93 D3
Goldmartin Sq TR11 93 D3
Goldsmith Gdns PL5 124 D3
Goldsworthy Way PL27 108 B5
Golf House Rd EX23 104 D6
Golf Terr TR7 110 C6
Golf View TR14 79 B2
Golitha Falls* PL14 37 D3
Golitha Rise PL14 113 E6
Golva Cl TR13 91 E4
Gonvena Hill PL27 108 D6
Gonvena Ho PL27 108 C6
Goodeve Cl PL9 135 E6
Goodmans La PL14 38 D4
Goodwin Ave PL6 125 A6
Goodwin Cres PL2 128 A6
Goonabarn Cotts PL26 58 C5
Goonavean Pk PL26 58 D5
Goongumpas La TR16 68 E1
Goonhavern Ind Est TR4 55 D4
Goonhavern Prim Sch TR4 55 D4
Goonhilly Cl TR4 55 D4
Goonhilly Earth Station* TR12 99 F4
Goonlaze Terr
St Agnes TR5 54 D1
Stithians TR3 80 D4
Goonown La TR5 54 D1
Goonown Rd
Goonbell TR5 68 D8
St Agnes TR5 54 D1
Goonrea PL13 117 B4
Goonvrea TR3 81 D5
Goonvrea Cl TR7 110 F4
Goonvrea Ct TR7 110 F4
Goonvrea Rd TR5 54 C1
Goonwartha Cl PL13 117 C4
Goonwartha Rd PL13 117 B3
Gooseberry La
Pensilva PL14 38 E4
Plymouth PL1 148 B2
Gooseford La PL11 132 C8
Goosewell Hill PL6 129 C8
Goosewell Park Rd PL9 135 F6
Goosewell Prim Sch PL9 135 F6
Goosewell Rd PL9 135 F5
Goosewell Terr PL9 135 F6
Gordon Ct PL12 122 D2
Gordon Pl 8 TR9 45 E6
Gordons Cl TR3 80 F3
Gordon Terr PL4 128 E4
Gorran Sch PL26 85 B5
Gorse Cl TR7 111 A4
Gorsey Cl PL5 124 E2
Gorvin Cross EX39 3 E6
Goswela Cl PL9 135 F5
Goswela Gdns PL9 135 F5
Gotch Gdns PL14 50 B6
Gothers Hill PL26 46 D1
Gothers Rd
St Dennis, Gothers PL26 46 D1
St Dennis, Hendra PL26 58 C8
Goudges La PL26 58 E8
Gounce The 14 TR6 55 A5
Gover Cl TR4 68 C6
Gover La TR7 110 D6
Gover Rd PL25 114 B4
Goverseth Cvn Pk PL26 58 D6
Goverseth Hill PL26 58 D6
Goverseth Rd PL26 58 D6
Goverseth Terr PL26 58 D6
Gower Ridge Rd PL9 135 D6
Goyne's Field TR4 68 A7
Gracca Terr PL26 47 C1
Grade-Ruan CE Sch TR12 103 B5
Grafton Rd PL4 128 E4
Graham Ave PL25 114 E4
Graham Rd
Redruth TR15 140 C5
Redruth TR15 140 D4
Grainge Rd PL6 125 A1
Grampound Road Ind Est TR2 57 E1
Grampound Road Village CE Sch TR2 57 E1
Grampound-with-Creed CE Sch TR2 72 A7
Granby Ct PL1 127 E2
Granby Gn PL1 127 E2
Granby Pl PL1 127 E2
Granby St PL1 127 E2
Granby Way PL1 127 E2
Grand Hotel Rd PL1 148 B1
Grand Par PL1 148 B1
Grange Rd
Helston TR13 146 B5
Plymouth PL7 131 A4
Yelverton PL20 42 C3
Grange The TR14 138 C2
Granite Way PL17 39 F4
Grannery Ct EX23 104 D5
Granny's Gn PL31 109 E3
Granny's La TR6 55 A4
Grantham Cl PL7 130 B4
Grantley Gdns PL3 129 A5
Grant's Ct PL25 114 C3
Grant's Wlk 4 PL25 114 C3
Granville Terr EX23 104 D5
Grasmere Cl PL6 124 E5
Grasmere La PL14 38 B5
Grassendale Ave PL2 127 F7
Grass La PL2 128 C6
Grassmere Way PL12 122 D4
Grass Valley Pk PL31 109 F1
Gratton Cross PL20 42 D2
Gratton La PL20 42 D2
Gratton Pl PL6 125 A1
Gravesend Gdns PL11 127 B3
Gravesend Wlk PL5 123 D4
Graybridge Rd PL20 42 C4
Gray Cres PL5 127 C8
Great Berry Rd PL6 124 F1
Great Charles Cl PL26 58 B4
Great Churchway PL9 136 A7
Greatfield Rd PL3 129 B7
Greatlands Cres PL2 128 A6
Greatlands Pl 5 PL2 128 A5
Great Mdw PL14 36 F2
Great Mills Ind Parc PL25 115 E4
Great Mis Tor Cl 5 PL20 42 C3
Great Orchard Cl PL9 135 E5
Great Park Cl 4 PL7 131 C5
Great Western Commercial Village PL22 112 D2
Great Western Rd PL1 148 B1
Great Wheal Seton TR14 138 F6
Greatwood TR11 82 C3
Great Woodford Dr PL7 130 B6
Grebe Cl PL7 130 F5
Greeb Way TR20 89 D4
Green Acre PL15 28 A5
Greenacres
Bodmin PL30 34 C2
Plymouth PL9 135 F8
Greenbank
Connor Downs TR27 78 D6
1 Penzance TR18 143 D5
Plymouth PL4 149 B4
Polruan PL23 116 D2
Greenbank Ave PL4 149 B3
Greenbank Cl TR2 57 E1
Greenbank Cres TR7 111 C7
Greenbank La PL14 113 C6
Greenbank Rd
Devoran TR3 81 F6
Liskeard PL14 113 C6
Plymouth PL4 149 B4
Greenbanks Ct PL27 21 E2
Greenbanks Rd PL27 21 E2
Greenbank Terr
1 Callington PL17 39 F4
Plymouth PL4 149 B4
Yelverton PL20 42 D3
Green Cl
Feock TR3 82 C5
Truro TR1 137 B3
Green Cres TR13 146 D7
Greendale Rd PL2 128 A7
Green Field Cl TR12 102 F2
Greenfield Rd PL12 122 D2
Greenfields Cl TR11 93 D3
Greenfield Terr TR16 67 D6
Greenfinch Cres PL12 122 E4
Green Hill
Lamerton PL19 30 A3
St Martin TR12 100 D6
Tavistock PL19 147 D5
Wadebridge PL27 108 E5
Greenhill Cl PL9 135 F5
Greenhills PL32 105 C5
Green Hill Terr TR12 100 D6
Green Hill Villas PL27 108 E5
Green La
Bodmin PL31 109 F2
Boscastle PL35 9 C1
Crantock TR8 43 D3
Fowey PL23 116 C5
Gwithian TR27 66 B2
Kingsand PL10 133 A2
Lelant TR26 77 E4
Lizard TR12 103 A2
Marazion TR17 89 B6
Penryn TR10 144 B8
Porthleven TR13 91 B1
Portreath TR16 67 C6
Redruth, Plain-an-Gwarry TR15 140 B5
Redruth, Wheal Rose TR16 68 C4
Rock PL27 21 D2
Tavistock PL19 147 E5
Truro TR1 137 B3
Veryan TR2 83 F6
Yelverton PL20 42 C1
Greenland PL10 132 F5
Greenlands Est PL19 147 D5
Green Lane Cl TR10 144 B8
Green Lane Hill TR18 143 F8
Green Lane Vean TR15 140 B5
Green La The TR27 77 F1
Green La W TR17 89 B6
Greenlees Dr PL7 131 B3
Greenmarket The 26 TR18 143 E5
Green Mdws PL32 105 C4
Green Parc Rd TR27 142 D5
Green Park Ave PL4 128 D4
Green Park Rd PL9 135 E5
Green Pk PL10 133 A2
Greensplat Rd PL25 114 A6
Green St
Penzance TR18 143 F4
Truro TR1 137 D4
Greens The TR19 96 C7
Greensway Rd PL19 147 A4
Green The
Bridgerule EX22 8 A5
Carnon Downs TR3 82 A5
5 Horrabridge PL20 42 C5
Kingsand PL10 133 A2
Liskeard PL14 113 B5
Meavy PL20 42 F2
Milton Combe PL20 120 F8
Nancegollan TR13 91 B7
Plymouth, Ernesettle PL5 123 E3
Plymouth, Hooe PL9 135 B6
Probus TR2 71 C6
Saltash PL12 122 C3
St Buryan TR19 97 A6
St Martin TR12 100 D6
6 Trewoon PL25 59 A3
Greenway Ave PL7 130 B6
Greenway Cl 2 PL20 42 C5
Greenwich Pl PL12 122 F3
Greenwith Cl TR1 137 B3
Greenwith Cres TR3 81 D6
Greenwith Hill TR3 81 D6
Greenwith Rd TR3 81 D6
Greenwood Cres TR10 144 A8
Greenwood Park Cl PL7 131 B6
Greenwood Park Rd PL7 131 B6
Greenwood Rd TR10 144 A8
Gregor Rd TR1 137 F5
Gregory's Ct 10 PL31 109 D5
Gregory's Mdw PL15 106 F3
Grenfell Ave PL12 122 D3
Grenfell Gdns PL12 122 C3
Grenfell St 19 TR19 88 C1
Grenifer Rd TR15 139 D7
Grenna La TR3 81 D7
Grenofen Cl PL19 42 A6
Grenville Cl PL17 39 F4
Grenville Cres TR11 144 F5
Grenville Ct
Plymouth PL7 131 C6
2 St Austell PL25 114 C3
Grenville Dr
6 St Agnes TR5 54 D1
Tavistock PL19 147 B3
Grenville Gdns TR14 79 E5
Grenville Mdws PL22 112 E2
Grenville Pk PL20 42 D2
Grenville Rd
Falmouth TR11 145 A5
Helston TR13 146 D5
Lostwithiel PL22 112 D2
Padstow PL28 107 C4
Plymouth PL4 149 C3
Truro TR1 137 B5
Grenville Road La S PL4 129 B2
Grenville Wlk PL13 62 D2
Gresham Cl
Newquay TR7 110 F4
Plymouth PL5 124 C7
Greyfriars TR11 145 C2
Greys Terr 1 TR16 140 F1
Greystoke Ave PL6 129 D7
Greystone Ave PL26 58 E5
Gribbas Cl TR3 80 F3
Gribbas Cnr TR3 80 F3
Gribben Cl PL25 114 E6
Gribben Rd PL25 114 E6
Gribbon Way PL24 60 C4
Griffins The PL14 113 D6
Griffin Way PL9 136 C6
Griggs Cl PL7 131 B4
Griggs Hill TR27 77 E3
Grimscott Est EX23 5 B2
Grimspound Cl PL6 129 E8
Grimstone Terr PL20 42 B2
Grist La TR27 78 C5
Grizedale Rd PL6 129 D7
Grose Hill Cres 11 PL26 59 D7
Grose Mdws PL26 58 B8
Grosvenor Ave TR7 110 E6
Grosvenor Cotts 1 PL4 128 F4
Grosvenor Pl PL25 114 B4
Grosvenor Rd PL6 124 F2
Grove Cotts TR2 57 C1
Grove Dr 4 PL14 51 A7
Grove Hill
Mawnan Smith TR11 93 D3
St Mawes TR2 95 A6
Grovehill Cres TR11 145 C3
Grovehill Dr TR11 145 C3
Grovehill Ho TR11 145 B3
Grove La TR20 89 F5
Grove Park Ct PL14 113 B4
Grove Pk
Par PL24 60 C6
Tavistock PL19 147 D5
Torpoint PL11 126 E3
Grove Pl
3 Falmouth TR11 145 C3
Padstow PL28 107 D5
Grove Rd
Par PL24 115 F6
St Austell PL25 114 B4
Grove The
Plymouth, Plymstock PL9 135 D8
Plymouth, Stoke PL3 128 A4
Grovewood Ct TR9 45 E1
Grylls Parc TR13 146 B6
Grylls Pk PL13 62 A7

Guardian Ct 6 PL31 ... 109 E5
Gue The 2 TR13 ... 98 C8
Guildford Cl
Foxhole PL26 ... 58 D6
Plymouth PL5 ... 124 E3
Guildford Rd TR27 ... 142 E7
Guildford Road Ind Est
TR27 ... 142 E6
Guildford St PL4 ... 149 A3
Guildhall La PL22 ... 112 C2
Guildhall Sq PL1 ... 148 C2
Guineaport Parc PL27 ... 108 C5
Guineaport Rd PL27 ... 108 C5
Guipavas Rd PL17 ... 39 F4
Gulland Rd PL27 ... 21 D6
Gull Rock TR7 ... 110 A5
Gully's La PL26 ... 58 B8
Gulval Almshouses TR18 ... 143 F8
Gulval Com Prim Sch
TR18 ... 88 E6
Gulval Cross TR18 ... 143 F8
Gulworthy Cotts PL19 ... 41 B7
Gulworthy Cross PL19 ... 41 B7
Gulworthy Prim Sch PL19 ... 41 B7
Gun Hill Rd TR8 ... 43 B1
Gunnislake Prim Sch
PL18 ... 40 F6
Gunnislake Rural Workshops
PL18 ... 40 F6
Gunnislake Sta PL18 ... 40 F5
Gunpool La 9 PL35 ... 9 C1
Gunver PL28 ... 31 F7
Gunwennap PL32 ... 10 B2
Gurlyn Hill TR20 ... 90 A7
Gurnard Wlk PL3 ... 129 C6
Gurney Cl
Bude EX23 ... 104 E7
Torpoint PL11 ... 126 F3
Gurney's La 2 TR14 ... 138 D3
Gurneys Mews 6 TR14 ... 138 D3
Gurnick Est TR18 ... 143 B2
Gurnick Rd TR18 ... 143 B1
Gurnick St 24 TR19 ... 88 C1
Gustavus Rd TR14 ... 138 D3
Gustory Rd TR8 ... 43 D3
Guy Miles Way PL5 ... 124 B3
Gwallon La TR17 ... 89 C6
Gwallon Rd PL25 ... 114 E5
Gwarnick Rd TR1 ... 137 B4
Gwarth An Drae TR13 ... 146 C8
Gwarth An Dre TR27 ... 142 E8
Gwavas Bglws 4 TR18 ... 143 C1
Gwavas La TR18 ... 88 C2
Gwavas Quay 7 TR18 ... 143 C2
Gwavas Rd TR18 ... 143 C1
Gwavas St 10 TR18 ... 143 E6
Gweal-An-Top TR15 ... 140 D5
Gweal-an-Top Inf Sch
TR15 ... 140 C5
Gweal Darras TR10 ... 81 C1
Gwealdues TR13 ... 146 D7
Gwealfolds Rd TR13 ... 146 C7
Gweal Gollas TR27 ... 142 E8
Gwealhellis Warren
TR13 ... 146 B7
Gwealmayowe Pk TR13 ... 146 D6
Gweal Pawl TR15 ... 140 A4
Gweal Wartha TR13 ... 146 B8
Gwedhennek TR18 ... 143 F7
Gweek Dr
Gweek TR12 ... 92 C1
Mawgan TR12 ... 99 D8
Gweek La TR13 ... 92 A3
Gwel An Garrek 2 TR12 ... 99 A1
Gwel-an-mor
1 Marazion TR17 ... 89 C5
St Austell PL25 ... 115 A5
Trenance TR8 ... 31 C2
Gwel-an-mor Apartments
TR26 ... 141 C4
Gwelanmor Cl TR26 ... 141 D2
Gwelanmor Rd TR26 ... 141 D2
Gwel-An-Nans Cl 2
PL14 ... 113 B5
Gwel-An-Scol TR3 ... 82 C5
Gwel An Wheal TR26 ... 141 A4
Gwel An Wheal Cres
TR26 ... 141 A4
Gwel Avon Bsns Pk PL12 ... 122 D4
Gwelavon Cl PL27 ... 108 D5
Gwelenys Rd 3 TR19 ... 88 C1
Gwel Eryon 3 TR14 ... 138 F2
Gwel Gwarthe TR16 ... 68 C3
Gwell-An-Nans TR2 ... 71 C6
Gwel Lewern TR18 ... 88 E6
Gwel Marten Flats TR26 ... 141 E2
Gwelmeneth Pk 8 PL14 ... 38 A3
Gwel Mengleth PL27 ... 108 D5
Gwelmor TR14 ... 138 E2
Gwel-Mor TR19 ... 75 A1
Gwel-Tek TR27 ... 142 D8
Gwel Trencrom TR27 ... 142 B3
Gwendra La PL26 ... 58 E8
Gwendroc Cl TR1 ... 137 D3
Gwendroc Ho TR1 ... 137 D3
Gwendroc House Mews
TR1 ... 137 D3
Gwendrock Villas PL27 ... 108 C5
Gwendrona Cl TR13 ... 146 D8
Gwendrona Way TR13 ... 146 D8
Gwennap Pit* TR16 ... 140 F4
Gwindra Ind Est PL26 ... 58 C3
Gwindra Rd PL26 ... 58 B4
Gwinear Com Prim Sch
TR27 ... 78 E4
Gwinear La TR27 ... 78 E4
Gwinear Rd TR27 ... 78 E5
Gwithian Cl PL11 ... 126 F4
Gwithian Rd TR27 ... 78 D6
Gwithian Sands Chalet Pk
TR27 ... 66 B1
Gwyn Rd PL4 ... 149 C4
Gwythian Way TR6 ... 55 A4
Gyllyng Hall TR11 ... 145 B3
Gyllyng St TR11 ... 145 B4
Gyllyngvase Hill TR11 ... 145 B2
Gyllyngvase Rd TR11 ... 145 C2
Gyllyngvase Terr TR11 ... 145 C2
Gypsy La PL33 ... 14 C1

H

Haddington Rd PL2 ... 127 F4
Haddon Way PL25 ... 115 D3
Haddy's Row PL14 ... 39 A2
Haig Pl 6 TR18 ... 143 C7
Hain Wlk TR26 ... 141 C4
Halbullock View TR1 ... 69 E3
Halcyon Ct PL2 ... 128 A6
Halcyon Rd PL2 ... 128 A6
Haldon Pl PL5 ... 124 A3
Haley Barton 4 PL2 ... 128 A5
Halgavor La PL31 ... 109 E2
Halgavor Pk PL31 ... 109 F1
Halgavor Rd PL30, PL31 ... 109 D2
Halgavor View PL31 ... 109 F2
Halifax Rd PL27 ... 31 F3
Halimote Rd PL26 ... 58 C8
Hallane Rd PL25 ... 115 A6
Hallan Vean TR19 ... 96 A6
Hallaze Rd PL26 ... 59 D7
Hallerton Cl PL6 ... 125 E2
Hallett Cl PL12 ... 122 B3
Hallett Way EX23 ... 104 F7
Hallew Rd PL26 ... 58 C7
Halley Gdns PL5 ... 123 E1
Halloon Ave 9 TR9 ... 45 E2
Hall Rd PL26 ... 58 C8
Hall Terr PL23 ... 116 E5
Halt Rd
Goonhavern TR4 ... 55 D4
St Newlyn East TR8 ... 56 B7
Halvarras Pk TR3 ... 82 B8
Halvarras Rd TR3 ... 82 B8
Halveor Cl 5 TR9 ... 45 E6
Halveor Ct TR6 ... 55 B5
Halveor La TR9 ... 45 D6
Halwin La TR13 ... 92 B8
Halwin Sch TR13 ... 92 C8
Halwyn Cl 12 TR3 ... 81 F7
Halwyn Hill TR8 ... 110 A3
Halwyn Pl TR1 ... 137 B4
Halwyn Rd TR8 ... 110 A3
Halwyn Terr TR1 ... 137 B3
Hamble Cl PL3 ... 129 D7
Ham Cl PL2 ... 128 B8
Ham Dr PL2 ... 128 B8
Ham Gn PL2 ... 128 A7
Ham Green Ct PL2 ... 128 A7
Ham Green La PL2 ... 128 A7
Ham Ho PL2 ... 128 A8
Hamilton Cl TR27 ... 142 B4
Hamilton Gdns PL4 ... 128 D4
Hamilton Pl TR11 ... 145 D3
Ham La PL2 ... 128 A8
Hammill's Cl 13 TR13 ... 98 C8
Hammills Dr 12 TR13 ... 98 C8
Hamoaze Ave PL5 ... 127 D8
Hamoaze Pl PL1 ... 127 D2
Hamoaze Rd PL11 ... 127 B2
Hampton Cl TR7 ... 110 D6
Hampton St PL4 ... 149 A3
Hancock Cl PL6 ... 124 D6
Hancock La 14 TR2 ... 95 A6
Hangmans Wlk TR11 ... 145 A1
Hannaford Rd PL16 ... 19 F3
Hannafore PL13 ... 117 C3
Hannafore La PL13 ... 117 D2
Hannafore Rd PL13 ... 117 D2
Hanover Cl
17 Perranporth TR6 ... 55 A5
Plymouth PL3 ... 129 B5
Hanover Ct
Camborne TR14 ... 138 E4
10 Penzance TR18 ... 143 E5
16 Plymouth PL1 ... 149 A2
Hanover Ho EX23 ... 4 D4
Hanover Pk TR9 ... 45 F2
Hanover Rd PL3 ... 129 C4
Hanson Dr PL23 ... 116 C3
Hanson Rd PL14 ... 113 D6
Harbour Ave
Plymouth, Camels Head
PL5 ... 127 E8
Plymouth PL4 ... 149 A2
Harbour Ct
Falmouth TR11 ... 145 B4
15 Penzance TR18 ... 143 E5
Portreath TR16 ... 67 C6
Harbour Ct Flats TR2 ... 83 B2
Harbour Lights 11 TR18 ... 143 C1
Harbour Mews TR19 ... 96 B7
Harbour Rd
Par PL24 ... 60 C4
Porthleven TR13 ... 98 B8
Wadebridge PL27 ... 108 C5
Harbourside 12 TR13 ... 98 B8
Harbour Side PL13 ... 117 C3
Harbour St PL11 ... 127 B3
Harbour Terr
Falmouth TR11 ... 145 B5
Portreath TR16 ... 67 C6
Harbour View
Fowey PL23 ... 116 C4
Hayle TR27 ... 142 B5
Marazion TR17 ... 89 B5
Penryn TR10 ... 144 B8
Plymouth PL9 ... 135 A7
5 Porthleven TR13 ... 98 B8
Saltash PL12 ... 122 E2
Truro TR1 ... 137 E3
Harbour View Cres TR18 ... 143 E6
Harcourt Cl TR1 ... 69 F3
Hardings Cl PL12 ... 122 E3
Hardisworthy Cross EX39 ... 2 E7
Hardwick Farm PL7 ... 130 C3
Hardy Cres PL5 ... 124 E1
Hardy Ho TR3 ... 80 F3
Harebell Cl PL12 ... 122 D4
Harefield Cres TR14 ... 138 D4
Hareston Cl PL7 ... 131 B5
Harewood Cl PL7 ... 130 E5
Harewood Cres PL5 ... 124 B2
Harewood Rd PL18 ... 41 A3
Hargood Terr 6 PL2 ... 127 F4
Hargreaves Cl PL5 ... 123 F2
Harlech Cl PL3 ... 129 A7
Harleigh Rd PL31 ... 109 E3
Harleigh Terr PL31 ... 109 E3
Harlequins 27 TR26 ... 141 B5
Harlyn Barton PL28 ... 20 D2
Harlyn Cotts PL28 ... 20 D2
Harlyn Rd PL28 ... 20 D1
Harmer Cl PL31 ... 109 D6
Harmony Cl
Redruth TR15 ... 140 B6
Roche PL26 ... 46 F3
Harmony Mdw PL26 ... 46 F3
Harmony Rd PL26 ... 46 F3
Harmony Terr
4 Illogan TR16 ... 67 E4
Truro TR1 ... 137 E2
Harnorlen Rd PL2 ... 128 D7
Haroldsleigh Ave PL5 ... 124 E2
Harriet Gdns PL7 ... 130 B6
Harriet Pl TR11 ... 145 A5
Harris Cl PL17 ... 39 F6
Harris Ct
1 Penryn TR10 ... 144 C7
Plymouth PL9 ... 135 B6
Harrison Gdns TR15 ... 139 D7
Harrison St 7 PL2 ... 127 F4
Harrison Terr TR1 ... 137 B4
Harriss Hill TR3 ... 82 A7
Harrowbarrow Sch PL17 ... 40 D4
Harrowbeer La PL20 ... 42 C3
Hartland Cl PL6 ... 125 A7
Hartland Forest Golf &
Leisure Parc EX39 ... 3 E6
Hartland Rd PL29 ... 22 E7
Hartland Terr EX23 ... 104 D6
Hartley Ave PL3 ... 129 A6
Hartley Ct PL3 ... 129 A6
Hartley Park Gdns PL3 ... 128 F6
Hartley Rd PL3 ... 128 E6
Hartmeade PL14 ... 52 A5
Hartwell Ave PL9 ... 136 D7
Harvenna Cl TR9 ... 45 E1
Harvest Moon TR7 ... 110 D7
Harvey Ave PL4 ... 129 B1
Harvey Rd TR1 ... 137 D2
Harvey St PL11 ... 127 B3
Harvey's Towans TR27 ... 142 A7
Harvey's Way TR27 ... 142 C5
Harwell Ct 8 PL1 ... 148 B3
Harwell St PL1 ... 148 B3
Harwood Ave PL5 ... 124 C7
Hastings St PL1 ... 148 B3
Hastings Terr PL1 ... 148 B3
Haswell Cl PL6 ... 129 A8
Hatch's Hill TR27 ... 78 C5
Hatfield Cres TR7 ... 110 B5
Hat La PL10 ... 132 F2
Havelock Terr PL2 ... 127 F3
Haven Ct TR27 ... 142 C5
Haven Pk PL14 ... 39 A2
Haven Rd EX23 ... 10 C6
Havett Cl PL14 ... 50 E8
Havett Rd PL14 ... 50 E8
Hawarden Cotts PL4 ... 129 B1
Haweswater Cl PL6 ... 124 E4
Hawke Cl TR7 ... 110 D6
Hawkens Way 9 TR9 ... 45 D6
Hawke Rd TR13 ... 146 D4
Hawkers Ave PL4 ... 149 A2
Hawkers La PL3 ... 128 E5
Hawkeys Mews TR15 ... 140 D2
Hawkinge Gdns PL5 ... 123 E4
Hawkins Cl PL6 ... 125 A5
Hawkins Ct 2 TR18 ... 143 D5
Hawkins Rd
Newquay TR7 ... 110 E5
Padstow PL28 ... 107 C5
Penzance TR18 ... 143 D5
Hawkins Way 12 TR11 ... 145 A4
Hawks Pk PL12 ... 122 C2
Hawk's Tor Dr PL15 ... 27 B7
Hawthorn Ave
Bude EX23 ... 104 E4
Torpoint PL11 ... 126 F3
Hawthorn Cl
Bude EX23 ... 104 E4
Camelford PL32 ... 105 D4
Plymouth, Hooe PL9 ... 135 C5
Plymouth, Woolwell PL6 ... 125 D7
Redruth TR15 ... 140 B6
St Austell PL25 ... 114 F6
7 St Columb Major TR9 ... 45 D6
Hawthorn Gr PL2 ... 128 C7
Hawthorn Rd PL19 ... 147 C2
Hawthorns PL12 ... 122 D2
Hawthorn Way
Plymouth PL3 ... 129 B7
Threemilestone TR3 ... 69 C3
Haxter Cl PL6 ... 121 B1
Haydon Gr PL5 ... 123 C1
Haydown Cl PL30 ... 24 B4
Haye La PL17 ... 39 E5
Haye Rd
Callington PL17 ... 39 D4
Plymouth PL7, PL9 ... 130 C1
Haye Rd S PL9 ... 136 C7
Hayes Pl PL6 ... 129 B8
Hayes Rd PL9 ... 135 C7
Hay La
Looe PL13 ... 117 E4
Sheviock PL11 ... 65 B6
Hayle Com Sch TR27 ... 142 D5
Hayle Ind Pk TR27 ... 142 F7
Hayle Rd TR27 ... 78 C1
Hayle Sta TR27 ... 142 B5
Hayle Terr TR27 ... 142 C6
Hayman Way TR11 ... 144 E5
Hayne Corfe Gdns TR1 ... 137 A4
Haystone Pl PL1 ... 148 B4
Haytor Cl PL5 ... 124 B3
Hazel Cl
Plymouth PL6 ... 125 B6
St Austell PL25 ... 115 A6
Hazel Dr PL9 ... 136 C7
Hazel Gr
Plymouth PL9 ... 136 C7
Yelverton PL20 ... 42 D3
Hazelmead PL14 ... 113 B5
Hazelmere Dr PL25 ... 115 B4
Hazel Rd PL19 ... 147 C2
Hazelwood Cres PL9 ... 136 D7
Hazelwood Dr PL6 ... 125 D8
Hazelwood Rd PL17 ... 39 F4
Heabrook Parc 2 TR18 ... 143 C7
Hea Cl TR18 ... 143 C7
Hea Cotts 5 TR18 ... 143 C7
Head La TR5 ... 68 D8
Headland Cl TR26 ... 141 E2
Headland Cotts
Coverack TR12 ... 103 H7
Newquay TR7 ... 110 C8
Headland Ct TR26 ... 141 E2
Headland Pk PL4 ... 149 A4
Headland Point TR7 ... 110 C7
Headland Rd
Carbis Bay TR26 ... 141 E2
Newquay TR7 ... 110 C7
Headlands The TR6 ... 55 A5
Headleigh Rd TR7 ... 110 F5
Headon Cross EX23 ... 11 A5
Healy Ct 9 PL2 ... 127 F4
Healy Pl PL2 ... 127 F4
Heamoor Com Prim Sch
TR18 ... 143 B6
Heanton Terr
Millbrook PL10 ... 132 E6
Redruth TR15 ... 140 C4
Heanton Villas TR15 ... 140 C4
Hea Rd TR18 ... 143 C7
Hearl Rd PL12 ... 122 B3
Heatherbell Gdns TR26 ... 141 E1
Heather Cl
Heamoor TR18 ... 143 B7
Tavistock PL19 ... 147 D4
Heather La TR27 ... 77 D2
Heather Mdw TR9 ... 45 E1
Heathers The
Foxhole PL26 ... 58 E5
Plymouth PL6 ... 125 D7
Heather Vean TR3 ... 69 D4
Heather Way TR20 ... 89 F4
Heathfield Gdns TR15 ... 140 E7
Heathfield Pk PL20 ... 42 D3
Heathfield Rd PL4 ... 129 B3
Heathlands Bsns Pk
PL14 ... 113 C5
Heathlands Ind Est 9
PL14 ... 113 C5
Heathlands Rd PL14 ... 113 C5
Heath Terr PL18 ... 40 F5
Heavitree Rd PL10 ... 133 A2
Hedgerow Cl PL6 ... 125 E8
Hedgerows The PL12 ... 122 B3
Hedingham Cl PL7 ... 131 C4
Hedingham Gdns PL6 ... 125 B7
Helca Dr TR26 ... 141 C3
Helebridge Rd EX23 ... 7 B6
Hele Cross PL15 ... 13 E3
Hele Gdns PL7 ... 131 A4
Hele La PL6 ... 121 F2
Helena Ct 7 PL26 ... 59 D7
Hele Rd EX23 ... 7 A6
Hele's Sch PL7 ... 130 C6
Hele's Terr PL4 ... 129 B2
Heligan Ho PL26 ... 73 A5
Helland Rd PL31 ... 109 E6
Hellescoth Way TR13 ... 146 D8
Hellescott Rd PL15 ... 18 B7
Hellesvean 2 TR26 ... 77 A6
Hellesvean Cl 3 TR26 ... 77 A6
Hellesvoer Cvn & Camping
Site TR26 ... 141 A6
Helleur Cl 4 PL24 ... 60 B4
Helman Tor View PL31 ... 109 E2
Helnoweth Cotts TR18 ... 143 F8
Helnoweth Gdns TR18 ... 143 F8
Helnoweth Hill TR18 ... 143 F8
Helscott Rd EX23 ... 7 A6
Helston Com Hospl
TR13 ... 146 D3
Helston Folk Mus*
TR13 ... 146 B5
Helston Rd TR10 ... 144 C8
Helston Sch TR13 ... 146 B7
Helston Sch & Com Coll
TR13 ... 146 C7
Hembal Cl 5 PL25 ... 59 A3
Hembal La PL25 ... 59 A3
Hembal Rd 4 PL25 ... 59 A3
Hemerdon House* PL7 ... 131 E7
Hemerdon Hts PL7 ... 131 A6
Hemerdon La PL7 ... 131 C8
Hemerdon Way PL7 ... 130 D6
Hendergulling PL13 ... 62 F4
Henders Cnr 6 PL3 ... 128 F6
Henderson Pl PL2 ... 127 F6
Hendra Barton TR1 ... 137 B5
Hendra Cl
Ashton TR13 ... 90 E3
Stithians TR3 ... 80 E4
5 Truro TR1 ... 137 C5
Hendra Gdns PL15 ... 106 B5
Hendra Holiday Pk TR8 ... 111 C3
Hendra La
Ashton TR13 ... 90 D2
Truro TR1 ... 137 C5
Hendra Parc PL14 ... 113 E7
Hendra Pk PL15 ... 106 B5
Hendra Prazey PL26 ... 58 B8
Hendra Rd
St Dennis PL26 ... 58 C8
Stithians TR3 ... 80 E4
Truro TR1 ... 137 C5
Hendras Ct TR26 ... 141 E2
Hendras Parc TR26 ... 141 D2
Hendra Terr TR3 ... 80 E4
Hendra Tor View PL15 ... 26 C7
Hendra Vale PL15 ... 106 B4
Hendra Vean
Carbis Bay TR26 ... 141 E1
Truro TR1 ... 137 B5
Hendrawna La TR6 ... 55 B4
Hendwell Cl PL6 ... 124 E6
Henfor Cl 12 TR17 ... 89 C5
Henfordh Grange PL14 ... 113 A6
Henfor Mews 6 TR17 ... 89 C5
Henfor Terr 13 TR17 ... 89 C5
Hengar La PL30 ... 23 F3
Henley Cl TR4 ... 68 C6
Henley Cres TR4 ... 68 C6
Henley Dr
Mount Hawke TR4 ... 68 C6
Plymouth PL5 ... 124 C7
Henliston Dr TR13 ... 146 C4
Henry Scott Tuke Ho 5
TR11 ... 145 A4
Hensbury La PL20 ... 119 F4
Henscol TR16 ... 80 D6
Henscol Praze TR16 ... 80 D6
Henscol Vale PL14 ... 113 A6
Henshorn Ct TR13 ... 146 C7
Hental 3 TR6 ... 55 A4
Hentervene Cvn & Camping
Pk EX23 ... 10 C5
Henver Cl TR27 ... 78 E3
Henver Ct TR7 ... 111 C7
Henver Gdns TR27 ... 78 E3
Henver La TR4 ... 56 A3
Henver Rd TR7 ... 111 B7
Henvor Cl TR15 ... 140 D6
Henvor Terr TR15 ... 140 E7
Henwood Cres TR7 ... 111 D7
Hen Wythva TR14 ... 138 E2
Herbert Pl PL2 ... 127 E4
Herbert St PL2 ... 127 E4
Hereford Rd PL5 ... 124 B5
Heritage Cl PL12 ... 122 C3
Herland Hill TR27 ... 78 D4
Herland Rd TR13 ... 90 E6
Hermes Cl TR13 ... 146 D5
Hermes Rd TR13 ... 146 C4
Hermitage Ct 1 PL4 ... 128 E4
Hermitage Rd
Plymouth PL3 ... 128 E5
Roche PL26 ... 46 F3
Heron Cl
Millbrook PL10 ... 132 F6
Tresillian TR2 ... 70 F5
Herons Ct 13 TR6 ... 55 A5
Heron Way TR1 ... 137 E1
Herring Cl PL14 ... 113 D7
Herring Rd PL14 ... 113 D7
Herschel Gdns PL5 ... 123 E1
Hersham Cross EX23 ... 5 B2
Hertland Wlk PL2 ... 128 A7
Hessary Dr PL6 ... 121 C1
Hessary Ho PL14 ... 113 D6
Hessary View
Saltash PL12 ... 122 E4
Tavistock PL19 ... 147 B6
Hessenford Rd PL13, PL11 ... 64 B6
Hetling Cl PL1 ... 148 B3
Hewer's Row PL4 ... 149 A3
Hewitt Cl PL12 ... 122 C1
Hexham Pl PL2 ... 128 A8
Hexton Hill Rd PL9 ... 135 B6
Hexton Quay PL9 ... 135 C6
Heybrook Ave PL5 ... 123 D1
Heybrook Mews TR7 ... 110 D6
Hibernia Rd TR13 ... 146 D4
Hibernia Terr PL5 ... 127 E8
Hichens La TR11 ... 145 A5
Hichens Rd TR13 ... 146 D4
Hickory Dr PL7 ... 131 B5
Hicks Cl TR2 ... 71 C6
Hick's La PL4 ... 149 A2
Hidden Valley Adventure
Pk* PL15 ... 18 A3
High Atlantic TR8 ... 44 C6
Highbank Cl PL19 ... 147 A4

Highbridge Ct PL7 130 E5
Highburrow 24 TR13 98 C8
Highburrow Ct TR15 139 C5
Highburrow La TR15 139 C5
Highbury PL17 38 E8
Highbury Cres PL7 130 D7
Highclere Gdns PL6 125 B8
Highcliffe PL27 21 D5
High Cross
Lanivet PL30 47 F5
Porth Navas TR11 93 A4
12 St Columb Major TR9 45 D6
Truro TR1 137 D4
High Cross St PL25 114 D4
Higher Albion Row TR16 80 F8
Higher Anderton Rd
PL10 132 F5
Higher Beech Terr PL13 117 C4
Higher Bodiniel Rd PL31 109 C7
Higher Bojewyan TR19 75 B1
Higher Bolenna 14 TR6 55 A4
Higher Bore St PL31 109 C5
Higher Boskerris TR26 141 D1
Higher Bridge Pk PL27 108 D5
Higher Broad La TR15 139 D7
Higher Bugle
Bugle PL26 47 C1
Stenalees PL26 59 C8
Higher Burrow Cl TR26 141 A4
Higher Chapel St PL13 117 D3
Higher Church St TR27 142 D6
Higher Churchway PL9 136 A7
Higher Cleaverfield
PL15 106 C7
Higher Compton Rd PL3 128 F6
Higher Cotts TR2 57 C1
Higher Croft Parc TR12 102 F2
Higher Cross La PL32 105 E4
Higher Daws La PL15 18 E2
Higher East St 9 TR9 45 E6
Higher Efford Rd PL3 129 B5
Higher Elms PL27 21 F3
Higher Fernleigh Rd
PL27 108 C4
Higher Fore St
Marazion TR17 89 C5
Redruth TR15 140 C5
Higher Glen Pk PL14 38 D4
Higher Goongumpas La
TR16 68 F1
Higher Green St TR18 143 D1
Higher Grumbla TR20 87 C4
Higher Gwavas Rd 3
TR18 143 C1
Higher Kelly PL18 41 A3
Higher La
Ashton TR13 90 E3
Mawgan TR12 99 D7
Plymouth PL1 148 C2
Wadebridge PL27 108 E4
Wadebridge PL27 108 E5
Higher Lariggan TR18 143 D4
Higher Lavorrick PL26 73 C4
Higher Lidden Rd TR18 143 C3
Higher Lux St PL14 113 C6
Higher Market St
Looe PL13 117 D3
Penryn TR10 144 C7
Higher Mdw PL14 50 E7
Higher Medrose PL33 14 E3
Higher Middle Hill PL14 38 D4
Highermoor Cross EX22 5 E1
Higher Mount Ambrose La
TR15 140 D6
Higher Mowles PL3 129 B6
Higher Newham La TR1 137 D2
Higher Park Cl PL7 131 B3
Higher Park Stenak TR16 80 F8
Higher Pengegon TR14 138 F2
Higher Penponds Rd
TR14 79 B5
Higher Peverell Rd TR18 143 E7
Higher Polsue Way TR2 70 F5
Higher Port View PL12 122 F2
Higher Pumpfield Row
TR15 139 B6
Higher Railway Terr TR16 80 F8
Higher Rd
Breage TR13 90 F3
Pensilva PL14 38 D4
Higher Redannick TR1 137 B3
Higher Row
Ashton TR13 90 E3
Kingsand PL10 133 A2
Higher Silver Hill TR13 146 C6
Higher Stennack TR26 141 A5
Higher Stert Terr PL4 149 C3
Higher Tamar Terr PL18 41 A7
Higher Terr TR3 81 B4
Higher Tower Rd TR7 110 C6
Highertown
Portscatho TR2 83 B2
Truro TR1 69 F3
Highertown Pk PL12 53 C3
Higher Trebyan Bsns Pk
PL30 48 C6
Higher Tregenna Rd
TR26 141 B3
Higher Trehaverne TR1 137 C6
Higher Tremena PL25 114 C4
Higher Tresavean Terr
TR16 80 E6
Higher Trevithick TR27 142 D5
Higher Trevorian Barns
TR19 97 B7
Higher Trewidden Rd
TR26 141 B4
Higher Trezaise PL26 47 A1
Higher Tristram PL27 21 D5
Higher Vicarage La 7
TR12 99 A1
Higherwell Cl TR7 111 A4
Higher Well La TR13 146 C6
Higher Well Pk PL26 73 C3
Higher West End PL26 73 C6
Higher Whiterock PL27 108 B5
Higher Woodford La
PL7 130 C7
Higher Woodside PL25 114 A4
Highfield Ave
St Austell PL25 114 D3
13 St Columb Major TR9 45 D6
Highfield Cl
Plymouth PL3 129 C5
St Austell PL25 114 D3
Highfield Ct 9 TR5 54 D1
Highfield Est 3 PL14 38 E4
Highfield Park Rd PL15 106 A5
Highfield Pk PL12 122 B3
Highfield Prim Sch PL3 129 C5
Highfield Rd
Camelford PL32 105 C3
Falmouth TR11 144 F4
Mount Hawke TR4 68 C6
Highfield Rd Ind Est
PL32 105 C3
Highfields 19 TR18 143 C2
Highgate Hill 1 TR9 45 E1
Highglen Dr PL7 131 B7
Highgrove PL15 27 A6
Highland Pk
Penryn TR10 144 B8
Redruth TR15 140 C5
Highlands PL9 136 B3
High Lanes
Cubert TR8 55 E8
Hayle TR27 142 D5
High Pk PL12 52 F6
High St
Boscastle PL35 9 D1
Camelford PL32 105 C3
Chacewater TR4 68 F3
Delabole PL33 14 D3
Falmouth TR11 145 B5
Launceston PL15 106 C6
Padstow PL28 107 D5
Penzance TR18 143 E5
3 Plymouth PL1 149 A2
Plymouth, Stonehouse PL1 128 A2
Probus TR2 71 C6
St Ives TR26 141 B6
St Keverne TR12 101 C4
High Street Ind Est PL26 58 D3
High Street Prim Sch
PL1 128 A2
High Street & Waterloo
Street Flats PL1 128 A1
Hightrip La PL17 39 F7
High Trip La PL17 40 A8
Highview TR4 68 E5
Highview Cl PL14 38 A2
Highview Cres TR4 68 E5
Highway PL14 50 B6
Highway La TR15 140 D7
Highwood Pk PL14 50 E7
Higman Cl PL14 50 E7
Hilgrove Rd TR7 111 A6
Hill Church TR4 68 F2
Hill Cl
Heamoor TR18 143 B7
Plymouth PL7 130 D4
St Breward PL30 24 B3
Hillcrest
Helston TR13 146 C7
Shortlanesend TR4 69 F6
Hill Crest PL3 128 E5
Hillcrest Ave TR1 137 A5
Hillcrest Cl
Plymouth PL7 131 A5
14 St Columb Major TR9 45 E6
Hillcrest Dr PL7 131 A4
Hillcrest Rd TR27 142 D6
Hilldale Rd PL9 135 E6
Hilldean Cl PL5 124 C7
Hill Gdns PL12 119 A2
Hill Hay Cl PL23 116 A4
Hillhead TR2 95 A6
Hill Head TR10 144 D6
Hillhead Gdns PL32 105 D4
Hillhead Rd TR11 144 C5
Hill La PL3 128 F7
Hillocks The PL13 117 D4
Hillpark Cotts PL15 106 D6
Hill Park Cres
Plymouth PL4 149 A4
St Austell PL25 114 A2
Hill Park Mews PL4 149 B4
Hill Path PL5 123 F5
Hill Pk PL27 108 D6
Hill Rd PL27 108 C5
Hillsborough 2 PL4 128 F4
Hillsborough Cross EX22 8 D7
Hillsdale Bglws TR13 90 F5
Hillsdunne Rd PL3 128 E6
Hillside
Grampound Road TR2 57 E1
Lanivet PL30 47 E7
Portreath TR16 67 C6
St Austell PL25 115 B3
Trewellard TR19 86 F8
Hillside Ave
Par PL24 60 B4
Plymouth PL4 128 D4
Saltash PL12 122 F3
Hillside Cl PL20 41 F3
Hillside Cres PL9 135 F8
Hillside Ct
Angarrack TR27 78 C5
Bodmin PL31 109 C5
Hillside Gdns PL22 112 C2
Hillside Ind Est TR16 140 E8
Hillside Mdw TR10 144 D7
Hillside Mdws PL26 58 D5
Hillside Parc TR20 88 B7
Hillside Pk PL31 109 D5
Hillside Rd
Falmouth TR11 144 F2
Saltash PL12 122 E3
St Austell PL25 114 D5
Hillside Sch PL5 124 B4
Hillside Terr
Carharrack TR16 80 E8
Downderry PL11 64 C5
Looe PL13 117 D4
22 Newlyn TR18 143 C2
2 Redruth TR15 140 C5
Hillside Villas PL13 117 F5
Hillson Cl PL29 22 E7
Hill St
Padstow PL28 107 D5
Plymouth PL4 149 A3
Hillsview PL13 62 D2
Hill Top Crest PL5 123 E2
Hill View PL20 41 F3
Hilton Ave PL5 124 D1
Hilton Rd EX23 7 B6
Hingston Ct PL6 129 A8
Hinton Ct PL6 125 C1
Hirmandale Rd PL5 123 F3
Hirst Ho TR14 139 A4
Hobart St PL1 148 A2
Hobbacott La EX23 7 B6
Hobbs Cres PL12 122 C3
Hockens La PL23 116 C2
Hockings Ho PL14 37 F3
Hodders Way PL12 119 A2
Hodge Cl PL12 122 C2
Hoe App PL1 148 C2
Hoe Ct PL1 148 C2
Hoegate Ct PL1 148 C2
Hoegate Pl PL1 148 C2
Hoegate St PL1 149 A2
Hoe Gdns PL1 148 C2
Hoe Rd PL1 148 C1
Hoe St PL1 148 C2
Hoe The PL1 148 C1
Hogarth Cl PL9 136 B6
Hogarth Ho PL19 147 B6
Hogarth Wlk PL9 136 B6
Holborn Pl PL7 130 E6
Holborn St PL4 149 B2
Holcombe Dr PL9 135 F5
Holcroft Cl PL12 122 D2
Holdsworth St PL4 148 B4
Holebay Cl PL9 136 A5
Hole Cross PL20 119 E7
Hollabury Rd EX23 104 F7
Hollacombe Brake PL9 136 C1
Holland Rd
Plymouth, Chaddlewood
PL7 131 D5
Plymouth, Peverell PL3 128 E6
Plymouth, Plymstock PL9 135 F6
Widegates PL13 63 E7
Hollies Cl PL15 106 B7
Hollies Rd PL15 106 A7
Hollies The TR27 142 B4
Hollong Pk PL11 65 E5
Holloway Gdns PL9 136 A5
Hollowell Ho 1 PL35 9 C2
Hollowgutter La PL11 126 C2
Hollow Hayes PL6 129 B8
Hollow's Terr TR27 142 E7
Hollows The PL9 136 B8
Holly Cl TR3 69 C3
Hollycroft Rd PL3 129 A7
Holly Ct PL6 129 E7
Holly Park Cl PL5 124 A5
Holly Park Dr PL5 124 A5
Holly Terr 9 TR18 143 C7
Hollywell Bay Fun Pk*
TR8 43 C1
Hollywood Terr PL1 148 A3
Holman Ave TR14 138 C4
Holman Ct PL2 128 C8
Holman Rd PL14 113 E6
Holmans Bldgs PL1 127 D2
Holmans Mdw PL15 19 C1
Holman's Pl 1 TR13 98 C8
Holman's Terr TR16 80 B5
Holmbush Arch Rd PL25 115 B3
Holmbush Hill PL17 39 F7
Holmbush Ind Est PL25 115 B4
Holmbush Rd PL25 115 C4
Holmer Down PL6 125 D7
Holmes Ave PL3 129 B5
Holmwood Ave PL9 135 E5
Holne Chase PL6 125 B7
Holnicote Rd EX23 104 E5
Holt Cres TR7 110 D5
Holtwood Rd PL6 125 D6
Holwell Cl PL9 136 A5
Holy Cross RC Prim Sch
PL4 149 A3
Holyrood Pl PL1 148 C2
Holyway Cross PL15 18 A1
Holywell Ct TR3 82 B8
Holywell Rd
Cubert TR8 55 D8
Holywell TR8 43 C1
Liskeard PL14 113 E6
Newquay TR7 110 F6
Playing Place TR3 82 B8
Home Farm Rd PL9 135 E8
Homefield Pk PL31 109 F3
Home Park Ave PL3 128 E6
Home Park (Plymouth Argyle
Fc) PL2 128 C5
Home Park Rd PL12 123 A3
Home Pk
Landrake PL12 53 C3
Plymouth PL2 127 F4
Homer Park La S PL9 135 C5
Homer Park Rd PL28 20 F2
Homer Pk
Plymouth PL9 135 C5
Saltash PL12 122 D3
Homer Rise PL9 136 B7
Homer Water Pk PL26 58 B4
Homestead Ct TR11 144 F6
Home Sweet Home Terr
PL4 149 C2
Homeyard Homes The
TR2 83 F6
Honcray PL9 135 D8
Honey's Hill PL30 47 E7
Honey St PL31 109 E4
Honeysuckle Cl
Plymouth PL6 125 E7
Saltash PL12 122 D4
Honicknowle PL5 124 B2
Honicknowle Gn PL5 124 B2
Honicknowle La PL5 124 B1
Honicombe Cnr PL17 40 E5
Honicombe Manor Holiday
Village PL17 40 E5
Honicombe Pk PL17 40 E5
Honiton Cl PL5 124 B3
Honiton Wlk PL5 124 B4
Hood Hill TR14 79 A6
Hooe Hill PL9 135 C5
Hooe La PL9 135 D3
Hooe Manor PL9 135 C5
Hooe Prim Sch PL9 135 B5
Hooe Rd PL9 135 C5
Hooksbury Ave PL7 131 B3
Hooper Ct PL14 113 C8
Hooper La TR14 138 D2
Hoopers Cl PL12 53 C3
Hoopers La PL18 40 F6
Hooper St PL11 127 C3
Hope Terr TR7 110 D6
Hopton Cl PL6 128 F8
Hornapark Cl PL16 19 F3
Hornbrook Gdns PL6 124 D6
Hornby Ct PL1 148 A3
Hornby St 2 PL2 127 F4
Hornchurch La PL5 123 E4
Hornchurch Rd PL5 123 E5
Horn Cross PL9 135 E7
Horn Cross Rd PL9 135 F7
Hornick Hill PL26 58 E4
Horn La
Liskeard PL14 113 B6
Plymouth PL9 135 F7
Horn Lane Flats 4 PL9 135 F7
Horrabridge Com Prim Sch
PL20 42 C4
Horse & Jockey La 2
TR13 146 C5
Horsepool La PL11 65 B6
Horsepool Rd
Connor Downs TR27 78 E6
Sheviock PL11 65 B6
Horseshoe Cl PL26 47 A3
Horsewhim Dr PL17 39 E6
Horse Whim Dr PL25 115 B5
Horsham La
Plymouth, Honicknowle
PL5 124 C2
Plymouth, Tamerton Foliot
PL5 124 C7
Horsley Rise PL25 114 D3
Horswell Cl PL7 131 B5
Horton Cross EX22 3 F3
Hosford Cl PL9 136 A4
Hosken's Mdw TR19 97 A6
Hosking's Row TR15 140 B4
Hospital Rd
Plymouth PL4 149 B4
Stratton EX23 4 D1
Hotham Pl PL1 148 A4
Houldsworth Rd PL9 135 C7
Houndiscombe Rd PL4 128 E4
Hounster Dr PL10 132 D4
Hounster Hill PL10 132 D4
Housel Bay Rd TR12 102 F2
Housman Cl PL5 124 D3
Howard Cl
Plymouth PL5 123 F2
Saltash PL12 122 D3
Tavistock PL19 147 A5
Howard La EX23 7 C8
Howard Rd PL9 135 E8
Howards Way EX23 104 D5
Howe Downs TR14 79 A2
Howell's Rd 10 EX23 4 E1
Howeson La PL6 125 A4
How St PL4 149 A2
HTP Apartments TR1 137 E4
Hudson Cross EX22 5 E4
Hudson Rd PL27 31 F3
Hughville St TR14 138 D4
Hugus Rd TR3 69 D3
Hull's La TR11 145 C3
Humber Cl PL3 129 D6
Humphrey's Cl PL14 37 F3
Humphry Davy La TR27 142 D5
Humphry Davy Sch TR18 143 E6
Hungerford Rd PL2 128 B5
Hunkin Cl TR1 137 C5
Hunter Cl PL6 124 F2
Huntersfield TR14 138 F7
Hunters's Oak PL20 41 D2
Huntfield Gdns 15 EX23 4 E1
Huntingdon Gdns PL5 124 D4
Huntley Pl PL3 129 C4
Hunts Crossing Sta*
PL15 18 E4
Hurdon Rd PL15 106 D2
Hurdon Way PL15 106 C3
Hurdwick Rd PL19 147 A5
Hurland Rd TR1 137 D3
Hurlers The* PL14 38 A6
Hurrabrook Cl PL6 125 E2
Hurrabrook Gdns PL6 125 E2
Hurrell Cl PL6 124 D6
Hurrell Ct PL3 129 C5
Hursley Bsns Pk PL6 121 D1
Hurst Cl PL9 135 F5
Hustyns PL27 33 D3
Hutchings Cl PL6 124 D6
Huthnance Cl TR1 137 F5
Hutton Hts TR1 69 F3
Huxham Cl PL6 129 A8
Huxley Cl PL7 130 F7
Hyde Park Jun & Inf Schs
PL3 128 E5
Hyde Park Rd PL3 128 E5

I

Idless La TR4 69 F6
Idless Wood Forest Walk*
TR4 70 B6
Ilbert Cotts PL7 130 E4
Ilbert St PL1 148 B4
Illogan Downs TR15 139 B8
Illogan Pk 8 TR16 67 E4
Illogan Sch TR16 67 D5
Imperial Ct TR11 145 D3
Ince Cl PL11 126 F4
Inchkeith Rd PL6 124 F7
Indian Queens Com Prim Sch
TR9 45 E1
Indian Queens Ind Est
TR9 45 F2
Industrial Est The TR6 55 B4
Infirmary Hill TR1 137 C4
Ingra Rd PL3 129 A6
Ingra Tor Cl 2 PL20 42 C3
Ingra Wlk PL6 125 B8
Innes Ho PL1 148 B3
Inney Cl PL17 39 F4
Inny Vale Holiday Village
PL32 16 A5
Inow Terr TR11 93 A2
Institute Hill TR13 98 B8
Instow Wlk PL5 124 A3
Inswell Ct PL19 147 A6
Insworke Cl PL10 133 A6
Insworke Cres PL10 132 F6
Insworke Pl PL10 133 A6
Inverdene PL3 128 D5
Ipswich Cl PL5 124 C4
Iron Mine La PL20 42 E3
Isacombe Oaks PL17 39 F6
Island Cres TR7 110 E6
Island Ct PL13 117 D2
Island Lanes PL31 109 F1
Island Point TR8 44 C6
Island Rd 4 TR26 141 B6
Island Sq 8 TR26 141 B6
Islington Wharf TR10 144 D8
Ivanhoe 6 TR7 110 F6
Ivanhoe Rd PL5 123 D2
Ivey Terr PL14 113 D7
Ivy Cotts PL18 40 F6
Ivydale PL15 106 B6
Ivydale Rd PL4 128 F4
Ivydene Flats TR7 111 D7
Ivy La TR18 143 C5
Ivyleaf Holiday Pk EX23 4 F3

J

Jack Bice Cl PL14 113 E5
Jackett's Steps 6 TR11 145 B5
Jack La TR18 143 C2
Jackman's Mdw PL10 133 A3
Jacks Cl TR10 144 D7
Jack's La PL11 132 B8
Jackson Cl PL5 127 F8
Jackson Pl PL2 127 F4
Jackson Way PL12 122 E3
Jack Stephens Est TR18 143 D6
Jacob's Ladder TR11 145 B4
Jacobstow Com Prim Sch
EX23 11 A6
Jago Ave PL11 127 B3
Jago Cl PL31 109 B3
Jago's Slip TR11 145 B5
Jake's La 1 TR4 69 A3
Jamaica Pl 14 TR18 143 C7
Jamaica Terr 13 TR18 143 C7
James Cl PL9 136 B6
James Pl
Plymouth PL4 148 C4
Truro TR1 137 D4
James Rd PL19 147 E2
James's Cross EX23 2 C2
James St
Plymouth, Mount Wise
PL1 127 E1
Plymouth PL4 148 C4

Jane's Ct 9 TR11 . . . . 145 B5
Jasmine Gdns
Plymouth, Chaddlewood PL7 . . . . 131 B5
Plymouth, Glenholt PL6 . . . . 125 E6
Jasmine Way PL28 . . . . 31 F7
Jasper Parc PL14 . . . . 37 F3
Jays Cross PL15 . . . . 19 C6
Jean Cres PL3 . . . . 129 B6
Jeanne Rees Ct 9 PL14 . . 113 B5
Jedburgh Cres PL2 . . . . . 128 A8
Jeffery Cl PL6 . . . . 124 D6
Jelbert Way TR18 . . . . 88 E6
Jellicoe Rd PL5 . . . . 124 E1
Jenkins Cl PL9 . . . . 136 A5
Jenkins Ct TR7 . . . . 110 E6
Jenkins Terr 5 TR15 . . . . 140 C5
Jenner Parc TR9 . . . . 45 D6
Jennings Rd TR10 . . . . 144 A6
Jennings St TR18 . . . . 143 E5
Jenns Cross EX22 . . . . 5 F7
Jennycliff La PL9 . . . . 135 A6
Jennys Combe Cl PL9 . . . . 135 F4
Jephson Rd PL4 . . . . 129 B3
Jericho La TR27 . . . . 142 D1
Jeryon Cl PL25 . . . . 114 E6
Jessops PL7 . . . . 130 D7
Jethan Dr TR14 . . . . 138 B4
Jetty St PL26 . . . . 73 C3
Jewell's Terr TR16 . . . . 80 B5
Jinkin Ave PL4 . . . . 149 B4
John Ellis Ct TR27 . . . . . . 142 C5
John Kitto Com Coll The PL5 . . . . 124 B1
John La PL4 . . . . 148 C4
John's Cnr TR20 . . . . 89 F5
Johnson Cl 2 PL20 . . . . 41 B1
Johnson Pk PL18 . . . . 41 A3
John Sparke Ho 17 PL1 . . 149 A2
Johns Pk TR15 . . . . 140 B6
John St
Plymouth PL1 . . . . 127 E3
Truro TR1 . . . . 137 C4
Jon Davey Dr TR16 . . . . . . 140 C7
Jopes Cl 2 PL14 . . . . 38 A3
Jordan La PL20 . . . . 42 C5
Jorys Mdw PL30 . . . . 23 E3
Joseph's Ct 27 TR6 . . . . . . 55 A5
Joseph's La TR18 . . . . 143 C8
Jubilee Bglws 20 TR18 . . 143 C1
Jubilee Cl
Cubert TR4 . . . . 55 D8
Duloe PL14 . . . . 51 A1
Kilkhampton EX23 . . . . 5 A6
Saltash PL12 . . . . 122 D2
Jubilee Cotts
Landrake PL12 . . . . 53 C3
Saltash PL12 . . . . 122 C1
Jubilee Ct 15 TR26 . . . . . . 77 A6
Jubilee Hill PL13 . . . . 62 D5
Jubilee Mdw PL25 . . . . . . 115 C5
Jubilee Pl
Camborne TR14 . . . . 138 E3
Plymouth PL3 . . . . 129 C4
Jubilee Rd
Falmouth TR11 . . . . 145 A5
Pensilva PL14 . . . . 38 D4
Plymouth PL5 . . . . 123 F3
Threemilestone TR3 . . . . 69 C3
Wadebridge PL27 . . . . 108 C5
Jubilee St TR7 . . . . 110 D6
Jubilee Terr
Bodmin PL31 . . . . 109 B5
Goonhavern TR4 . . . . 55 D5
Helston TR13 . . . . 146 C4
Plymouth PL4 . . . . 129 B2
Julian St PL4 . . . . 149 C2
Julian Wlk PL6 . . . . 125 E6
Juliot Well Holiday Pk PL32 . . . . 105 A2
Jump Cl PL6 . . . . 121 C1
Juniper Way PL7 . . . . 131 B5

K

Kailem Cl TR9 . . . . 45 D5
Karenza Ct TR26 . . . . 141 E2
Kathleaven St PL5 . . . . . . 123 D1
Kay Cl PL7 . . . . 130 F7
Kay Cres PL31 . . . . 109 B3
Kay Gdns PL27 . . . . 108 E5
Kays Mews 7 PL34 . . . . 14 C7
Kea Com Prim Sch TR3 . . . 70 A1
Keason Est PL14 . . . . 39 A2
Keason Hill PL14 . . . . 53 C8
Keast Cl 2 TR9 . . . . 45 E1
Keat St PL2 . . . . 127 E4
Kedlestone Ave PL5 . . . . . . 124 A3
Keeble Pk TR3 . . . . 81 E6
Keep The PL12 . . . . 122 C2
Kehelland Village Sch TR14 . . . . 66 F1
Keigwen Pl TR19 . . . . 88 C1
Kel Avon Cl TR1 . . . . 137 F5
Kellaway Pk TR13 . . . . 146 D6
Kelley Rd TR11 . . . . 144 E5
Kelliwith TR3 . . . . 82 B6
Kellow Hill PL13 . . . . 62 D2
Kellow Pk PL11 . . . . 65 A7
Kellow Rd PL26 . . . . 58 C8
Kelly Cl PL5 . . . . 127 C7
Kelly Coll PL19 . . . . 147 D7
Kelly Pk PL30 . . . . 34 C8
Kelvin Ave PL4 . . . . 149 C4
Kelwyn Ct TR26 . . . . 141 C2
Kemp Cl TR1 . . . . 137 D4
Kempe Cl PL2 . . . . 127 F6
Kemp's Cl 7 TR5 . . . . 54 C1
Kempton Terr PL11 . . . . 127 B2
Kemyell Pl PL2 . . . . 127 E4
Kendal Gn TR2 . . . . 57 C1
Kendal Pl PL5 . . . . 124 E4
Kenidjack Cl TR26 . . . . 141 E1
Kenilworth Rd PL2 . . . . 128 B7
Kenilworth Way PL26 . . . . . . 58 E5
Kenley Gdns PL5 . . . . 123 F4
Kenmare Dr PL7 . . . . 131 A5
Kennall Pk TR3 . . . . 81 B4
Kennall Vale TR3 . . . . 81 B4
Kennall Vale Sch TR3 . . . . . . 81 B4
Kenna Pk TR1 . . . . 69 F3
Kenn Cl PL5 . . . . 124 B3
Kennedy Cl TR15 . . . . 139 B8
Kennel Hill PL7 . . . . 130 D4
Kennel Hill Cl PL7 . . . . . . 130 C4
Kennerley Terr 16 TR2 . . . . 95 A6
Kennet Cl PL3 . . . . 129 B6
Kenneth Launder Ct 10 PL14 . . . . 113 B5
Kensa Way TR27 . . . . 78 E6
Kensey Pl 3 PL15 . . . . . . 106 C6
Kensey Valley Mdw PL15 . . . . 106 D6
Kensey View PL15 . . . . 106 D5
Kensington Pl 8 PL4 . . . . . 128 F4
Kensington Rd PL4 . . . . . . 149 B4
Kenstella Rd TR18 . . . . 143 C2
Kent Ave PL25 . . . . 115 D3
Kent Cl PL26 . . . . 58 C8
Kent Rd PL2 . . . . 127 F5
Kenwyn Church Rd TR1 . . 137 B6
Kenwyn Cl
Bude EX23 . . . . 104 D7
Truro TR1 . . . . 137 B6
Kenwyn Hill TR1 . . . . 137 B6
Kenwyn Mews TR1 . . . . . . 137 C4
Kenwyn Pk
St Kew Highway PL30 . . . . . . 23 B2
Truro TR1 . . . . 137 B6
Kenwyn Rd
Truro TR1 . . . . 137 C5
Truro TR4, TR1 . . . . 137 A7
Kenwyn St TR1 . . . . 137 C4
Kenython La TR19 . . . . 86 F7
Keppel Pl PL2 . . . . 127 F4
Keppel St PL2 . . . . 127 F4
Keppel Terr 8 PL2 . . . . 127 F4
Kerensa Gdns TR5 . . . . 68 D8
Kerensa Gn TR11 . . . . 144 E5
Kergilliack Rd TR11 . . . . . 144 D5
Kerhuon Ct PL31 . . . . 109 D5
Kerley Gr TR1 . . . . 69 F3
Kerley Hill TR4 . . . . 69 A3
Kerley Vale TR4 . . . . 69 A3
Kernick Bsns Pk TR10 . . . 144 A6
Kernick Gdns TR10 . . . . . . 144 A6
Kernick Rd TR10 . . . . 144 B7
Kernick Road Ind Est TR10 . . . . 144 A7
Kernick Way TR27 . . . . 142 E8
Kernow Cl
Bodmin PL31 . . . . 109 F5
Torpoint PL11 . . . . 126 E3
Wadebridge PL27 . . . . 108 B5
Kernow Cres EX23 . . . . 104 E4
Kernow Ct
Newquay TR7 . . . . 110 E6
Torpoint PL11 . . . . 126 E3
Kernow Mill* PL12 . . . . 52 E1
Kernyk Lowen TR14 . . . . . . 138 F5
Kerris Gr TR1 . . . . 137 B5
Ker St Ope PL1 . . . . 127 E2
Kersbrook Cross PL17 . . . . . 27 F2
Kersey Cl TR11 . . . . 145 C7
Kersey Rd TR11 . . . . 145 B7
Ker St PL1 . . . . 127 E1
Keryor Cl PL25 . . . . 114 F3
Kestell Parc PL31 . . . . 109 E2
Kestle Dr TR1 . . . . 69 F3
Kestral Units PL5 . . . . 124 A1
Kestral Way 10 TR16 . . . . . . 67 E4
Kestrel Cl
Plymouth PL6 . . . . 125 D8
7 Porthleven TR13 . . . . 98 B8
Keswick Cres PL6 . . . . 125 D2
Keveral Gdns PL11 . . . . 64 B5
Keveral La PL11 . . . . 64 B5
Kew Cl TR7 . . . . 111 A4
Kew Noweth TR14 . . . . 138 D2
Kew Pendra TR19 . . . . 97 A6
Kew Pendra Cl TR19 . . . . . . 97 A6
Kew Vean TR26 . . . . 141 C3
Keyes Cl PL1 . . . . 127 F2
Keyham Barton RC Prim Sch PL2 . . . . 127 E6
Keyham Ct PL2 . . . . 127 E6
Keyham Rd PL2 . . . . 127 E4
Keyham St PL5 . . . . 127 E8
Keyham Sta PL2 . . . . 127 E6
Khyber Cl PL11 . . . . 127 A3
Kibbiscombe Terr PL14 . . . . 63 A8
Kidwelly Cl PL7 . . . . 131 C4
Kiel Pl PL3 . . . . 129 D5
Kilhallon PL24 . . . . 60 C5
Kilhallon Woodlands PL24 . . . . 60 C5
Kilkhampton Jun & Inf Sch EX23 . . . . 5 A6
Killarney Springs Leisure Pk* EX23 . . . . 3 B1
Killatree Cross EX22 . . . . 8 F7
Killerton Rd EX23 . . . . 104 E5
Killicourt TR3 . . . . 82 A7
Killiers Ct TR15 . . . . 139 C7
Killiersfield TR15 . . . . 139 C6
Killigrew Ave PL12 . . . . . . 122 D1
Killigrew Gdns TR4 . . . . . . 70 D8
Killigrew Pl 9 TR11 . . . . . . 145 A4
Killigrew Rd PL14 . . . . 113 D6
Killigrew St TR11 . . . . 145 A4
Killivose Gdns TR14 . . . . . . 138 D1
Killivose Rd TR14 . . . . 138 D1
Killyvarder Way PL25 . . . . 115 B6
Kilmar Cl PL14 . . . . 37 F3
Kilmar Rd PL14 . . . . 113 E6
Kilmar Way PL14 . . . . 37 F3
Kilminorth Woods (Nature Reserve)* PL13 . . . . 117 A4
Kilna La PL12 . . . . 53 A2
Kiln Cl
Cawsand PL10 . . . . 133 A1
Mevagissey PL26 . . . . 73 C4
Plymouth PL5 . . . . 127 C8
Kiln Mdws TR12 . . . . 92 C1
Kilworthy Hill PL19 . . . . . . 147 C6
Kilworthy Rd PL19 . . . . 147 C6
Kimber Ct TR11 . . . . 145 B2
Kimberley Ct TR7 . . . . 110 D6
Kimberley Foster Cl PL11 . 65 B5
Kimberley Park Rd TR11 145 A4
Kimberley Pk PL14 . . . . 38 A3
Kimberley Pl TR11 . . . . 145 A4
Kimberly Cl TR7 . . . . 110 D6
Kimberly Dr PL6 . . . . 125 B1
Kiming EX23 . . . . 104 E4
King Arthurs Terr 5 PL34 . 14 C7
King Charles Prim Sch TR11 . . . . 145 A3
King Edward Cres TR7 . . 110 D7
King Edward Rd PL12 . . . . 122 F2
Kingfisher Cl PL6 . . . . 125 E6
Kingfisher Dr PL25 . . . . . . 115 A4
Kingfisher Way PL9 . . . . . 135 C7
King George V Memorial Wlk TR27 . . . . 142 C6
King's Ave
Falmouth TR11 . . . . 144 F4
St Austell PL25 . . . . 114 D3
Kingsbury Ho TR11 . . . . . . 145 A6
Kings Cl PL6 . . . . 125 E6
Kings Cross EX39 . . . . 2 E5
Kings Ct PL1 . . . . 128 A3
King's Hill EX23 . . . . 104 E3
Kings Hill Cl EX23 . . . . . . 104 E4
King's Hill Ind Est EX23 . . 104 F3
Kings Hill Mdw EX23 . . . . . 104 E3
Kingsland Gardens Cl PL3 . . . . 128 E6
Kingsley Ave PL11 . . . . 127 B2
Kingsley Cl TR1 . . . . 69 E3
Kingsley Cove TR4 . . . . 68 A7
Kingsley Ct TR9 . . . . 57 E8
Kingsley Meade TR8 . . . . . 111 B5
Kingsley Rd PL4 . . . . 128 E4
Kingsley Terr TR16 . . . . . . 67 C6
Kingsley Way TR13 . . . . . . 146 C5
Kingsmill Rd PL12 . . . . . . 122 C5
Kings Pippin PL26 . . . . 58 E5
Kings Rd
Marazion TR17 . . . . 89 B5
Plymouth, Devonport PL1 . . 127 F2
Plymouth, West Park PL5 . . 123 F3
4 St Mawes TR2 . . . . 95 A6
King's Rd
Camborne TR14 . . . . 138 D4
Penzance TR18 . . . . 143 D5
Plymouth PL1 . . . . 128 A2
Kings Sch PL3 . . . . 128 E6
King's St PL22 . . . . 112 C2
King St
Bude EX23 . . . . 104 E5
Gunnislake PL18 . . . . 41 A6
Millbrook PL10 . . . . 132 E5
Newquay TR7 . . . . 110 D6
Plymouth PL1 . . . . 148 B3
Redruth TR15 . . . . 140 B5
Tavistock PL19 . . . . 147 B6
Torpoint PL11 . . . . 127 C3
Truro TR1 . . . . 137 D4
King's Tamerton Rd PL5 . . 123 F2
Kingston Cl PL7 . . . . 131 A5
Kingston Dr PL7 . . . . 131 B5
Kingston Rd PL17 . . . . 28 E1
Kingsway PL10 . . . . 133 B2
Kingsway Gdns PL6 . . . . . . 124 F3
Kingswear Cres PL6 . . . . . 125 B1
King's Wood* PL26 . . . . 73 B7
Kingswood Est PL14 . . . . . . 38 C1
Kingswood Park Ave PL3 . . . . 128 D6
Kingswood Rd PL18 . . . . . . 41 A6
Kinnard Cres PL6 . . . . 124 F7
Kinross Ave PL4 . . . . 129 A4
Kinsale Rd PL5 . . . . 123 F3
Kinsman Est PL31 . . . . 109 C3
Kinterbury Rd PL5 . . . . . . 127 B8
Kinterbury St PL1 . . . . 149 A2
Kinterbury Terr PL5 . . . . . 127 B8
Kinver Cl PL6 . . . . 125 D4
Kipling Gdns PL5 . . . . 124 D2
Kirby Rd TR1 . . . . 137 A4
Kirkby Pl PL4 . . . . 148 C4
Kirkby Terr PL4 . . . . 148 C4
Kirkdale Gdns PL2 . . . . . . 128 B7
Kirkella Rd PL20 . . . . 42 D2
Kirkland Cl PL6 . . . . 125 C7
Kirkstall Cl PL2 . . . . 128 A8
Kirkwall Rd PL5 . . . . 124 E3
Kirland Bower PL30 . . . . . . 48 B7
Kirland Rd PL30 . . . . 109 B2
Kirton Pl PL3 . . . . 129 B5
Kit Hill Cres PL5 . . . . 127 C8
Kit Hill Ctry Pk* PL17 . . . . 40 A6
Kitley Way PL5 . . . . 123 D1
Kitter Dr PL9 . . . . 136 A5
Kittiwake Cl TR27 . . . . 77 E3
Kitts Ct 17 TR18 . . . . 143 E5
Kleinfontein Terr PL14 . . . . 38 D4
Knapmedown PL15 . . . . 11 B1
Knapps Cl PL9 . . . . 136 C6
Knave-Go-By TR14 . . . . 79 D5
Kneele Gdns PL3 . . . . 128 E8
Knighton Rd PL4 . . . . 149 C3
Knighton Terr 3 PL20 . . . . 42 C5
Knightor Cl PL26 . . . . 59 E6
Knights Cl 1 PL34 . . . . 14 C7
Knights Ct PL22 . . . . 112 B3
Knights Hill TR1 . . . . 137 B6
Knight's Mdws TR3 . . . . 81 F7
Knights Way TR15 . . . . 140 D7
Knill Cl TR26 . . . . 141 C2
Knill Cross PL10 . . . . 132 E5
Knill Cross Cotts PL10 . . . 132 E5
Knoll Pk TR1 . . . . 137 F4
Knoll The PL7 . . . . 130 B6
Knowland Cl PL1 . . . . 127 F3
Knowle Ave PL2 . . . . 127 E6
Knowle Prim Sch PL5 . . . 124 A4
Knowle Terr PL20 . . . . 42 E4
Koth Karrji PL30 . . . . 23 E7
Kyl Cober Parc PL17 . . . . . 28 E1
Kynance Cl PL11 . . . . 126 F4
Kynance Ho TR1 . . . . 69 E4
Kynance Terr TR12 . . . . . . 102 F2

L

Labernum Terr EX23 . . . . 5 A6
Laburnum Cl TR11 . . . . 144 F5
Laburnum Cotts PL19 . . . . 147 C6
Laburnum Dr TR11 . . . . 144 F5
Lacey Cl TR14 . . . . 79 E5
Ladock CE Sch TR2 . . . . . . 57 C2
Ladock Rd
Ladock TR2 . . . . 57 C1
Probus TR2 . . . . 71 C7
Ladycross PL15 . . . . 18 F7
Lady Modifords CE Prim Sch PL20 . . . . 42 E4
Ladysmith Ct PL4 . . . . 149 C4
Ladysmith Rd PL4 . . . . 129 B3
Lady St TR13 . . . . 146 B5
Ladywell PL28 . . . . 107 D5
Ladywell Pl PL4 . . . . 149 B3
Laflouder Fields TR12 . . . . 99 A2
Laflouder La TR12 . . . . 99 A2
Lafrowda Cl TR19 . . . . 86 E6
Lafrowda Terr TR19 . . . . . . 86 F6
Laguna Ct TR15 . . . . 140 B5
Laira Ave PL3 . . . . 129 D4
Laira Bridge Rd PL4 . . . . . 129 B1
Laira Gdns PL3 . . . . 129 C4
Laira Green Prim Sch PL3 . . . . 129 C4
Laira Park Cres PL4 . . . . . . 129 B4
Laira Park Pl PL4 . . . . 129 B4
Laira Park Rd PL4 . . . . 129 B4
Laira Pl PL4 . . . . 149 C2
Laira St PL4 . . . . 149 C3
Laity La TR26 . . . . 77 C4
Laity Rd TR14 . . . . 79 E4
Laity Wlk PL6 . . . . 124 D6
Lake La
Dousland PL20 . . . . 42 E3
Liskeard PL14 . . . . 113 D5
Lake Mews PL10 . . . . 132 E5
Lake Rd PL9 . . . . 135 B6
Lakeside PL19 . . . . 147 B6
Lakeside Dr PL5 . . . . 123 E5
Lake View PL12 . . . . 53 C8
Lake View Cl PL5 . . . . 124 B6
Lakeview Dr PL5 . . . . 124 B5
Lalebrick Rd PL9 . . . . 135 B5
Lamanva Cl 16 TR16 . . . . . . 67 E4
Lamanva Rd 17 TR16 . . . . . . 67 E4
Lambert Rd PL5 . . . . 124 B6
Lambert Terr 4 TR11 . . . . 145 A5
Lambhay Hill PL1 . . . . 149 A1
Lambhay St PL1 . . . . 149 A1
Lambourne Ave 7 TR5 . . . . 54 D1
Lamb Pk 5 PL24 . . . . 60 C4
Lambs La TR11 . . . . 144 E5
Lamellyn Dr TR1 . . . . 69 F3
Lamellyn Rd PL24 . . . . 60 B4
Lamerhooe Cross PL19 . . . . 29 C1
Lamerhooe Dr
Horsebridge PL19 . . . . 29 C1
Luckett PL19 . . . . 40 C8
Lamerton Cl PL5 . . . . 124 B3
Lametton Gn PL14 . . . . 51 B4
Lamledra Hill PL26 . . . . . . 85 D5
Lamorak Cl PL26 . . . . 73 B3
Lamorna Ct TR16 . . . . 67 D6
Lamorna Dr 11 PL17 . . . . . 39 F4
Lamorna Parc 12 PL17 . . . . 39 F4
Lamorna Pk
St Austell PL25 . . . . 114 E7
Torpoint PL11 . . . . 126 E4
Lamorne Cl 4 TR6 . . . . 55 A4
Lampen Rd PL14 . . . . 36 F2
Lampen Terr PL14 . . . . 36 F2
Lana Cotts EX22 . . . . 13 C7
Lanadwell St PL28 . . . . . . 107 D5
Lanaton Rd TR10 . . . . 144 A8
Lancamshire La TR20 . . . . . 89 F5
Lancaster Cres PL27 . . . . . 31 F3
Lancaster Gdns PL5 . . . . . 124 D4
Lanchard La PL14 . . . . 113 B5
Lanchard Rd PL14 . . . . 113 B5
Lanchard Rise PL14 . . . . . . 113 B5
Landaviddy La PL13 . . . . . . 62 D2
Lander Ct TR1 . . . . 137 D3
Lander Rd PL12 . . . . 122 F3
Landeryon Gdns TR18 . . . . 143 D5
Landithy TR20 . . . . 143 A8
Landlake Cross PL15 . . . . . 28 A8
Landlake Rd PL15 . . . . 106 B2
Landrake Cl PL5 . . . . 127 C8
Landreath Pl PL24 . . . . 60 B5
Landrew Rd PL25 . . . . 114 F6
Lands End Rd TR19 . . . . . . 97 A6
Land's End (St Just) Aerodrome TR19 . . . . 86 F3
Lands Pk PL9 . . . . 135 F7
Landulph Cross PL12 . . . . 118 F1
Landulph Gdns PL5 . . . . . 127 C8
Landulph Prim Sch PL12 . 118 F1
Lane End Cross PL19 . . . . . 29 D2
Lanepark La EX39 . . . . 2 D5
Lane Reddin Terr 21 TR18 . . . . 143 C2
Lane The PL7 . . . . 130 D6
Langage Cross PL7 . . . . . . 131 F6
Langage Ind Est PL7 . . . . . 131 D4
Langage Pk PL7 . . . . 131 C4
Langage Science Pk PL7 . . . . 131 D5
Langarth Cl TR3 . . . . 69 D4
Langdale Cl PL6 . . . . 125 D1
Langdale Gdns PL6 . . . . . . 125 D1
Langdon Cross PL15 . . . . . . 18 D8
Langdon Ct PL9 . . . . 136 B6
Langdon Down Way PL11 . . . . 126 E3
Langerwell Cl PL12 . . . . . . 122 C3
Langerwell La PL12 . . . . . . 122 C3
Langfords Mdw 4 PL35 . . . . 9 C1
Lang Gdns PL18 . . . . 41 A3
Lang Gr
Plymouth PL9 . . . . 136 C7
Tavistock PL19 . . . . 147 D5
Langham Pl PL4 . . . . 149 C3
Langhill Rd PL3 . . . . 128 D5
Langley Cl PL6 . . . . 125 A7
Langley Cres PL6 . . . . 124 F7
Langley Jun & Inf Schs PL6 . . . . 125 A6
Langman Ct 13 PL20 . . . . . . 41 B1
Langmead Cl PL6 . . . . 129 C8
Langmead Rd PL6 . . . . 129 C8
Langmore Cl PL6 . . . . 129 A7
Langorran Rd TR14 . . . . . . 138 B3
Lang Rd PL14 . . . . 113 B4
Langreek Bglws PL13 . . . . . 62 C2
Langreek Rd PL13 . . . . 62 C2
Langstone Rd PL2 . . . . 128 C7
Langstone Terr PL2 . . . . . . 128 C7
Langton Rd
Falmouth TR11 . . . . 145 A6
8 Yelverton PL20 . . . . 42 C3
Langton Terr 8 TR11 . . . . 145 A5
Langurroc Rd TR8 . . . . 110 A3
Langurtho Rd PL23 . . . . . . 116 B4
Langweath Est TR12 . . . . . . 99 D7
Langweath Gdns TR27 . . . . . 77 E3
Langweath La TR12 . . . . 99 D7
Langwedh TR16 . . . . 67 D4
Lanhenvor Ave TR7 . . . . . . 110 E5
Lanherne Ave TR8 . . . . 45 A8
Lanheverne Parc 4 TR12 . . . . 101 C4
Lanhydrock Ho & Gdns* PL30 . . . . 48 D6
Lanhydrock Rd PL4 . . . . . . 129 B2
Lanhydrock View PL31 . . 109 D3
Lanivet Com Prim Sch PL30 . . . . 47 E7
Lanjowan TR13 . . . . 146 B6
Lankelly Cl PL23 . . . . 116 B4
Lankelly La PL23 . . . . 116 A4
Lanlivery Com Prim Sch PL30 . . . . 48 D2
Lanlovie Mdw TR8 . . . . 55 D8
Lanmoor Est TR16 . . . . 80 D6
Lannarth Glas TR16 . . . . . . 140 E1
Lanner Gn TR16 . . . . 140 E1
Lanner Hill
Redruth, Pennance TR16 . . . 140 E1
Redruth TR15 . . . . 140 D2
Lanner Moor Terr TR16 . . . . 80 E6
Lanner Prim Sch TR16 . . . . 80 D6
Lanner Sq TR16 . . . . 80 D6
Lannoweth Rd TR18 . . . . . . 143 F6
Lanoweth TR10 . . . . 81 D2
Lanreath CE Prim Sch PL13 . . . . 62 A8
Lanreath Farm & Folk Mus* PL13 . . . . 62 B8
Lansallos St PL13 . . . . 62 D1
Lansdown Cl EX23 . . . . . . 104 D5
Lansdowne TR26 . . . . 141 B4
Lansdowne Cl TR18 . . . . . . 143 C5
Lansdowne Ct TR18 . . . . . . 143 B5
Lansdowne Pk TR16 . . . . . . 68 C3
Lansdowne Pl TR18 . . . . . . 143 C4
Lansdowne Rd
Callington PL17 . . . . 39 E4
Falmouth TR11 . . . . 145 C3
Penzance TR18 . . . . 143 C5
Plymouth PL6 . . . . 124 F2
Lansdown Rd
Bude EX23 . . . . 104 D5
Wadebridge PL27 . . . . 108 B5
Lantallack Cross PL12 . . . . 53 A3
Lanuthnoe Est TR27 . . . . . . 77 F1

Lanwithan Cl PL22 112 D2
Lanwithan Rd PL22 112 E1
Lanxon Cres PL30 48 C2
Lanyon Ct PL14 37 F3
Lanyon Rd TR3 82 B8
Lappa Valley Steam Railway* TR8 56 C7
Lapthorn Cl PL9 135 C7
Larch Cl PL12 122 C3
Larch Dr PL6 125 E7
Larcombe Rd PL25 115 A6
Laregan Hill TR18 143 C3
Lariggan Cres TR18 143 D4
Lariggan Rd TR18 143 D4
Larkfield Cl PL26 58 E5
Larkhall Rise PL3 129 B5
Larkham Cl PL7 130 C6
Larkham La PL7 130 C6
Lark Hill PL2 128 A6
Latham Cl PL6 129 A7
Latimer Cl PL7 131 B5
Latimer Wlk PL6 124 E7
Launcells Cross EX23 5 B1
Launceston Castle* PL15 106 C6
Launceston Cl
Bodmin PL31 109 F4
Plymouth PL6 125 B7
Launceston Coll PL15 106 C4
Launceston Com Prim Sch PL15 106 C5
Launceston Hospl PL15 106 C4
Launceston Rd
Bodmin PL31 35 B1
Kelly Bray PL17 39 E6
Launceston Ret Pk PL15 106 C4
Launceston Sta* PL15 106 B6
Launceston Steam Rly* PL15 18 E3
Laura Cl PL34 14 D7
Laura Dr PL25 115 A5
Laurel Ct PL2 128 A7
Laurel Dene PL2 128 A7
Laurel Dr PL6 125 E5
Laurel Rd PL2 128 A7
Laurels The PL18 40 E6
La Vague TR3 82 C5
Lavington Cl PL7 131 B5
Lavinia Dr PL7 130 C5
Lavorrick Orchs PL26 73 C4
Lawn Cl 2 PL7 131 C5
Lawn Steps TR11 145 B4
Lawns The
Plymouth PL5 124 E1
Torpoint PL11 127 A4
Lawn The
Par PL24 60 B5
Tavistock PL19 147 D6
Lawrence House Mus* PL15 106 C6
Lawrence Rd
Plymouth PL9 135 A6
St Agnes TR5 54 C1
Lawry Cl 6 PL14 113 B5
Lawson Gr PL9 135 C7
Lawton Cl TR7 110 B5
Law Wlk PL6 124 D6
Leader Rd TR7 111 E7
Leafield PL31 35 B2
Leander Way PL5 124 D2
Leanway PL12 122 E2
Leap Pk TR3 69 C3
Leas The TR1 137 E5
Leat Cl PL20 42 E3
Leatfield PL26 73 C3
Leatfield Dr PL6 124 F4
Leatherby Cl PL6 124 E7
Leather Tor Cl 4 PL20 42 C3
Leat Rd
Lifton PL16 19 F3
Pendeen TR19 75 A1
Leatside PL6 121 C1
Leats The TR1 137 C4
Leat The 9 EX23 4 E1
Leat View PL12 122 B3
Leat Wlk
Plymouth PL3 128 E6
Roborough PL6 121 D1
Saltash PL12 122 D4
Leaves Yd PL3 129 B7
Lea Way EX23 104 F6
Leburnick Cross PL15 28 D8
Ledgate La PL7 131 F8
Ledra Cl TR12 103 A4
Ledrah Gdns PL25 114 B3
Ledrah Rd PL25 114 B3
Ledrak Parc TR13 146 B8
Leedstown Com Prim Sch TR27 78 E1
Leeside Ct 7 PL2 128 A4
Lefra Orch TR19 97 B6
Legendry Land's End* TR19 96 A5
Leggos Ct 10 TR15 140 B5
Legion La 3 PL24 60 D5
Legis Wlk PL6 125 B8
Leigham Ct PL1 148 B2
Leigham Manor Dr PL6 129 F8
Leigham Prim Sch PL6 125 E1
Leigham St PL1 148 B1
Leigham Terrace La PL1 148 B2
Leigh Ct PL6 129 A8
Leigh La
Hatt PL12 53 D6
Roborough PL6 121 D2
Leighton Rd PL3 128 F8
Lelant Mdws TR26 77 E4
Lelant Saltings Sta TR26 77 E3
Lelant Sta TR26 77 E4
Lemellen Gdns PL30 23 B2
Lemin Parc TR27 78 E3
Lemin's Ct TR15 140 B5
Lemon Hill TR11 82 A3
Lemon Hill Gdns TR11 82 A3
Lemon Mews Rd TR1 137 D4
Lemon Quay TR1 137 D4
Lemon Row TR1 137 D3
Lemon St
St Keverne TR12 101 D4
Truro TR1 137 D4
Lemon Terr TR4 81 D8
Lender La 5 TR12 99 A2
Lendewedneck Com Prim Sch TR12 102 F2
Lendra La PL17 39 D4
Lerryn CE Prim Sch PL22 61 D8
Lerryn View PL22 61 C8
Lerwick Rd PL27 31 F3
Lescudjack Cres TR18 143 F6
Lescudjack Rd TR18 143 E6
Lescudjack Terr TR18 143 F6
Lesingey La TR20 88 A5
Leskinnick Pl 15 TR18 143 E6
Leskinnick St TR18 143 E6
Leskinnick Terr TR18 143 E6
Leslie Ct TR13 146 B6
Lesnewth 18 PL24 60 B4
Lester Cl PL3 129 B6
Lestraynes La TR10 92 E8
Lethlean Cl TR27 142 D7
Lethlean La TR27 142 D7
Lethlean Towans TR27 142 D8
Levant Beam Engine* TR19 74 E1
Levant Cl TR19 86 F8
Levant Rd TR19 86 F8
Leven Cotts EX23 104 D5
Leverlake Rd EX23 6 F4
Levine View TR11 144 E1
Lewannick Cl PL15 27 B7
Lewannick Com Prim Sch PL15 27 B7
Lewannick Rd TR8 43 D1
Lewarne Cres TR7 111 C7
Lewarne Rd TR7 111 C8
Lewes Gdns PL5 124 C4
Lewis Way PL25 114 E6
Lewman Cl TR2 71 C6
Lewman Rd TR2 71 C6
Leworthy Cross EX22 8 E4
Ley La PL20 119 D6
Leypark Ct PL6 125 E2
Leypark Dr PL6 125 E2
Leypark Wlk PL6 125 E2
Leys La TR17 89 B5
Libby Ct PL12 122 C5
Liberator Row 4 PL27 31 F3
Lidden Cl TR18 143 C3
Lidden Cres TR18 143 C3
Lidden Rd TR18 143 C3
Liddicoat Rd PL22 112 D3
Liddle Way PL7 131 B6
Lifeboat Hill 32 TR26 141 B6
Lifton Com Prim Sch PL16 19 F4
Liftondown Cross PL16 19 D4
Lifton Rd PL4 149 C2
Lighterage Hill TR1 137 E2
Lighthouse Hill TR16 67 C6
Lighthouse La PL26 85 C5
Lighthouse Rd TR12 102 F2
Lilac Cl PL9 135 C5
Lily Way PL28 31 F7
Limerick Pl PL4 149 C3
Limes La PL14 113 B5
Limes The PL6 124 F2
Limetree Rd PL3 128 D7
Lime Tree Way PL15 27 D4
Lincoln Ave PL4 149 C4
Lincoln Row 6 PL27 31 F3
Linden Ave TR7 110 E5
Linden Cres TR7 110 E5
Linden Terr PL4 149 C3
Lingard Cl PL14 113 A6
Lingfield Ave PL26 58 E1
Linhay Cl PL25 115 D6
Linkadells PL7 130 D6
Link Cl TR11 144 F4
Linketty La PL7 130 C5
Linketty La E PL6 125 A1
Linketty La W PL6 128 F8
Link Rd PL15 106 B3
Links The
Falmouth TR11 144 F1
Praa Sands TR20 90 C4
Links View EX23 104 F6
Linley Cl TR3 69 D3
Linnet Ct PL12 122 C2
Linton Cl PL5 124 C8
Linton La EX39 2 E5
Linton Rd PL5 124 C7
Linton Sq PL5 124 C8
Lippell Dr PL9 135 E6
Lipson Ave PL4 149 C4
Lipson Com Coll PL4 129 C4
Lipson Ct PL4 149 B3
Lipson Rd PL4 149 B4
Lipson Terr PL4 149 C4
Lipson Vale PL4 129 A4
Lipson Vale Prim Sch PL4 129 A4
Lipstone Cres PL4 149 C4
Lisbon Terr TR19 97 A6
Liscawn Terr PL11 127 B3
Liscombe Cl PL18 41 A7
Lishaperhill Cross EX22 5 E2
Liskeard Bsns Pk PL14 113 E6
Liskeard Com Hospl PL14 113 E7
Liskeard & District Mus* PL14 113 C6
Liskeard Hill PL14 36 F2
Liskeard Inf Sch PL14 113 B6
Liskeard Jun Sch PL14 113 A6
Liskeard Rd
Callington PL17 39 E4
Saltash PL12 122 B3
Trematon PL12 53 E3
Liskeard Sch & Com Coll PL14 113 C7
Liskeard Sta PL14 113 B4
Liskeard Town Mus* PL14 113 C6
Liskerrett Rd PL14 113 D5
Liskey TR6 55 A4
Liskey Hill TR6 55 A4
Liskey Hill Cres 1 TR6 55 A4
Liskey Tourist Pk TR3 69 C4
Lisson Gr PL4 128 F4
Lister Cl PL7 130 F6
Lister Hill 10 TR11 145 A4
Lister St TR11 145 A3
Listowel Dr PL13 117 D4
Listry Rd TR7 110 E5
Litchaton Cres PL7 130 B7
Litchaton Way PL7 130 B7
Litchfield Cl PL7 131 B6
Little Ash Gdns PL5 123 B1
Little Ash Rd PL5 123 B1
Little Bodieve Holiday Pk PL27 108 D7
Little Bridge Cross EX22 8 A5
Littlebridge Mdw EX22 8 A5
Little Bridge Pk PL27 108 D6
Little Butts PL9 135 E6
Little Castle St 7 TR1 137 C4
Little Dean PL14 113 A5
Little Dinas PL28 107 E4
Little Dock La PL5 124 B2
Little Down La PL6 121 E3
Little Down Pk TR7 111 A4
Little Fancy Cl PL6 125 C7
Little Gilly Hill 3 TR15 140 C4
Little Gregwartha TR16 80 A5
Little-in-sight 19 TR26 141 A5
Little La
Hayle TR27 142 E7
Kingsand PL10 133 A2
Staddiscombe PL9 135 D3
Little Laney PL13 62 D1
Little Mdw
Bodmin PL31 109 D5
Pyworthy EX22 8 E5
Little Mill La TR27 77 E2
Little Oaks TR10 144 B6
Little Orch PL12 53 C3
Little Point Cres PL10 132 F5
Little Stark Cl PL26 58 B4
Littleton Pl PL2 127 F4
Little Trelower Pk PL26 58 F1
Little Treloweth TR15 139 B6
Little Trelyn PL27 21 E2
Little Trethewey Est TR19 96 E4
Little Trethiggey TR8 111 F2
Little Treverrow PL27 21 E2
Little Western Rly* TR7 110 F5
Little Woburn Cl PL15 106 C4
Littlewood Cl PL7 131 A4
Lizard Cl PL6 124 F7
Lizard Head La TR12 102 E2
Lizard Lighthouse TR12 102 F1
Lizard Nature Reserve The* TR12 100 F2
Lizard Wlk PL6 125 A7
Llawnroc Cl TR14 138 E2
Llewellyn Cl PL32 105 C3
Lloyds Rd TR12 103 A2
Loatmead Cross EX22 3 E3
Lockeridge Rd PL20 41 B1
Lockington Ave PL3 128 F7
Locks Wlk PL1 127 E1
Lockyer Ct PL1 148 C2
Lockyer Mews PL19 147 C6
Lockyer Rd PL3 128 E5
Lockyers Quay PL4 149 B2
Lockyer St PL1 148 C2
Lockyer Terr PL12 123 A3
Lodenek Ave PL28 107 D4
Lodge Dr TR1 137 F6
Lodge Gdns PL6 124 E3
Lodge Hill PL14 113 A3
Lodge La PL8 136 F5
Lodge Way TR9 45 F2
Loe Bar Rd TR13 98 C8
Loe Valley Rd TR13 146 B7
Lofoten Cl PL1 127 E2
Loftus Gdns PL5 123 C2
Logans Ct TR26 141 D2
Loggans Cl TR27 142 E8
Loggans Rd
Hayle TR27 78 B6
Phillack TR27 142 E8
Loggans Way TR27 142 E8
Loggans Wlk TR27 142 E8
Lollabury Rd PL12 122 E3
Lomond Hall TR26 141 D1
Longacre
Harrowbarrow PL17 40 C4
Plymouth PL7 130 B7
Long Acre PL12 122 B4
Long-A-Row Cl EX23 10 C6
Long Barn The TR20 89 D8
Longbridge Cl PL6 129 F6
Longbridge Rd
Plymouth, Laira PL3 129 C4
Plymouth, Longbridge PL6 129 E7
Longbrook Barton PL7 130 D5
Longbrook St PL7 130 F4
Longcause PL7 130 F4
Longcause Com Specl Sch PL7 130 F4
Longcoombe La PL13 62 D3
Long Cross PL29 22 C6
Longcross Victorian Gardens* PL29 22 C6
Long Down Gdns PL6 125 E3
Longdowns Trad Est TR10 81 A1
Longfield TR11 144 E4
Longfield Cl 25 PL17 39 F4
Longfield Dr PL32 105 C3
Longfield Pl PL4 149 B4
Longfield Rd PL32 105 C3
Longfield Villas PL9 135 D8
Longhouse La PL27 21 E3
Long La
High Street PL26 58 C4
Ludgvan TR20 89 A7
St Erth TR20, TR27 89 E8
Longlands PL9 135 D8
Longlands La PL12 122 B1
Long Lanes TR20 89 F7
Long Ley PL3 129 B6
Longman's La 3 PL17 39 E4
Long Mdw PL7 130 D7
Longmeadow Cl PL7 130 E7
Longmeadow Rd PL12 122 E3
Long Moor TR12 103 A5
Long Orch PL20 41 B1
Long Park Cl PL9 135 F5
Longpark Dr EX23 6 F5
Long Park Dr PL6 125 D7
Long Park Rd PL12 122 D2
Longpark Way PL25 114 F5
Long Pk PL15 18 D2
Long Rd PL12 122 B4
Longrock Bsns Pk TR20 88 F6
Longrock Ind Est TR20 88 F6
Long Row TR19 97 F7
Long Rowden PL3 128 E6
Long Steps PL23 116 C4
Longstone Ave PL6 125 A6
Longstone Cl TR26 141 E1
Longstone Hill TR26 141 E1
Long Terrace Cl 5 PL7 131 C5
Longview Rd PL12 122 D3
Longview Terr PL3 129 B7
Longwood Cl PL7 131 A4
Longwool Mdw EX23 7 B6
Looe Bay Holiday Pk PL13 117 F8
Looe Com Sch PL13 117 D6
Looe Hill
Looe PL13 63 F5
Seaton PL13, PL11 64 A5
Looe Prim Sch PL13 117 D4
Looe St PL4 149 A2
Looe Sta PL13 117 C4
Lookout The 7 TR11 145 B5
Looseleigh Cl PL6 125 A4
Looseleigh La PL6 124 F5
Looseleigh Pk PL6 124 E5
Lopes Dr PL6 121 C1
Lopes Rd
Dousland PL20 42 E3
Plymouth PL2 128 B6
Lopwell Cl PL6 124 F5
Lord Louis Cres PL9 134 F6
Lords Mdw TR2 71 F3
Lorrimore Ave PL2 127 F5
Loscombe Ct TR16 80 A5
Loscombe La TR16 80 A5
Loscombe Rd TR16 139 E1
Lost Gdns of Heligan The* PL26 73 B5
Lostwithiel Mus* PL22 112 C2
Lostwithiel Rd PL30, PL31 48 C7
Lostwithiel Sch PL22 112 C2
Lostwithiel St PL23 116 C4
Lostwithiel Sta PL22 112 D2
Lostwood Rd PL25 114 E4
Lotherton Cl PL7 131 B3
Loughboro Rd PL5 123 C1
Love La
Bodmin PL31 109 F5
Hayle TR27 142 E7
Mousehole TR19 88 C1
Penryn TR10 144 D8
Penzance TR18 143 C4
Saltash PL12 122 E2
24 St Ives TR26 141 B6
Lovell Rd PL3 128 F6
Lovely La PL12 65 A8
Loveny Cl PL14 36 F2
Loveny Rd PL14 36 F2
Lovibond Wlk PL27 108 C5
Lowenac Cres TR27 78 E6
Lowenac Gdns TR14 138 C2
Lowen Ct 7 TR1 137 D4
Lowenek Cl TR11 144 E5
Lowenna Manor PL27 21 E3
Lowen Way TR3 69 C3
Lower Anderton Rd PL10 132 F5
Lower Barncoose TR15 139 F6
Lower Biteford Cross EX39 3 E6
Lower Bore St PL31 109 D5
Lower Boscaswell Parc TR19 74 F1
Lower Broad La TR15, TR16 139 C8
Lower Cardrew La TR15 140 B6
Lower Castle Rd TR2 95 A5
Lower Chapel St PL13 117 D3
Lower Church St TR27 142 D6
Lower Cleaverfield PL15 106 C7
Lower Clicker Rd PL14 51 F4
Lower Compton Rd PL3 128 F5
Lower Coronation Terr 9 PL17 39 F4
Lower Eastcliff TR4 68 A7
Lower Elms PL27 21 F3
Lower Fairfield PL12 65 A8
Lower Farm Rd PL7 131 A4
Lower Fore St PL12 123 A2
Lower Glen Pk PL14 38 D4
Lower Goongumpas La TR16 68 F1
Lower Goonrea PL13 117 B4
Lower Greenbanks PL27 21 E2
Lower Green St TR18 143 D1
Lower Gurnick Rd TR18 143 B3
Lower Hill TR13 146 C6
Lower Hillcrest
Helston TR13 146 C6
9 Perranporth TR6 55 A4
Lower Hillside PL14 50 B6
Lower Hugus Rd TR3 69 C3
Lower Kelly PL18 41 A3
Lower La
Mawgan TR12 99 D7
6 Plymouth PL1 149 A2
Lower Lux St 5 PL14 113 C6
Lower Market St
Looe PL13 117 D3
Penryn TR10 144 C7
Lower Mdw 5 TR4 69 A3
Lower Merritts Hill 22 TR16 67 E4
Lower Middle Hill PL14 38 E4
Lower Molinnis PL26 47 D2
Lower Parc TR12 92 C2
Lower Park Dr PL9 135 F4
Lower Pengegon TR14 138 F3
Lower Peverell Rd TR18 143 E7
Lower Pk TR2 70 F5
Lower Polstain Rd TR3 69 D3
Lower Port View PL12 122 F2
Lower Pumpfield Row TR15 139 B6
Lower Rd PL11 64 C4
Lower Redannick TR1 137 C4
Lower Ridings PL7 131 B7
Lower Rosewin Row 9 TR1 137 D5
Lower Row PL10 133 A2
Lower Rowes Terr PL26 58 D5
Lower Saltram PL9 135 C7
Lower Sheffield TR19 97 F7
Lowerside PL2 128 A8
Lower Sq EX22 11 E8
Lower St
Looe PL13 117 D3
Plymouth PL4 149 A3
Lower Tamar Terr PL18 41 A7
Lower Terr TR3 81 B4
Lower Town PL17 28 E1
Lowertown Cl PL12 53 C3
Lowertown La TR13 146 C7
Lower Tregongeeves PL26 59 A1
Lower Tywarnhayle 18 TR6 55 A5
Lower Well La TR13 146 C6
Lower Well Pk PL26 73 C3
Lower Wesley Terr PL14 38 D4
Lower Woodside PL25 114 A4
Lowery Cross PL20 42 F4
Low Lee Rd TR19 88 D1
Lowley Rd PL15 18 E2
Lucas Cl PL31 109 E3
Lucas La PL7 130 D6
Lucas Terr PL4 129 B2
Lucknow Rd PL31 48 D8
Lucknow Rd S 3 PL31 48 D8
Ludgvan Com Prim Sch TR20 89 B8
Ludlow Rd 2 PL3 128 E6
Luffman Cl PL13 62 D6
Lugger The TR2 83 B2
Lukes Cl TR1 137 F5
Luke's La TR20 89 F6
Lulworth Dr PL6 125 B7
Lundtnant Cvn Site PL27 21 E6
Lundy Cl PL6 124 F7
Lundy Dr EX23 10 C6
Lundy Rd PL29 22 E7
Lusart Dr TR12 102 F2
Lusty Glaze Rd TR7 111 A7
Lutsford Cross EX39 3 A6
Lutyens Fold PL19 29 C6
Luxmore Cl PL6 125 E1
Luxon Dr TR7 110 F4
Luxstowe Dr 1 PL14 113 C6
Luxstowe Gdns PL14 113 C6
Luxulyan Rd PL24 115 F7
Luxulyan Sch PL30 48 A1
Luxulyan Sta PL30 47 F1
Lych Cl PL9 135 A6
Lychgate Dr TR1 137 C6
Lydcott Cl PL13 63 F8
Lydcott Cres PL13 63 F8
Lydcot Wlk PL6 125 A1
Lydford Park Rd PL3 128 D5
Lyd Gdns PL19 147 D5
Lydia Way PL4 149 B4
Lympne Ave PL5 123 F5
Lynbridge Ct 5 PL19 147 B5

Lyndhurst Ave PL25 115 A4
Lyndhurst Cl PL2 128 C6
Lyndhurst Rd PL2 128 C6
Lyndon Ct PL12 122 D4
Lyndrick Rd PL3 128 E7
Lynes Cotts 2 PL14 51 A7
Lynher Cl PL15 27 B3
Lynher Ct PL12 122 F1
Lynher Dr PL12 122 F1
Lynher St PL5 123 D2
Lynher View PL17 38 E8
Lynher Way
28 Callington PL17 39 F4
North Hill PL15 27 A4
Lyn-Meynek TR15 140 D4
Lynmouth Cl PL7 130 C7
Lynstone Cotts EX23 104 D3
Lynstone Rd EX23 104 D4
Lyn Terr 7 TR18 143 C1
Lynwood Ave PL7 130 B6
Lynwood Cl PL31 109 E4
Lynwood Cotts 1 TR19 88 C1
Lynwood Flats TR13 91 A1
Lyons Rd PL25 115 B4
Lytton Pl PL25 114 F4

M

Mabbots Ct TR18 143 F6
Mabe Com Prim Sch TR10 81 C1
Mabena Cl PL30 34 C8
MacAdam Rd PL4 149 C1
MacAulay Cres PL5 124 C1
Macey St PL11 127 C3
Mackenzie Pl PL5 123 C2
McLean Dr PL26 58 D5
Madden Rd PL1 127 F2
Maddever Cres PL14 113 C5
Maddock Cl PL7 131 A4
Maddock Dr PL7 131 B4
Maddocks Cross EX22 3 F2
Madeira Dr EX23 6 F5
Madeira Rd
Falmouth TR11 145 A1
Plymouth PL1 149 A1
Madeira Villas 1 PL20 42 C5
Madeira Wlk TR11 145 A2
Madford La PL15 106 C5
Madge Ct PL19 147 B6
Madge La PL19 147 B6
Madison Terr TR27 142 E7
Madison Vean TR27 142 E7
Madron Rd TR18 143 C7
Maenporth Est TR11 93 E4
Maenporth Rd TR11 93 E4
Maen Valley Pk TR11 93 E5
Maer Down Rd EX23 104 C7
Maer La EX23 104 D8
Magdalen Gdns PL7 130 F3
Magnificent Music Machines Mus* PL14 51 C3
Magnolia Cl 3 PL7 131 B5
Magnolia Ct 3 PL9 135 F7
Magor Ave TR14 79 E5
Maida Vale Terr PL4 128 F4
Maiden St 1 EX23 4 E1
Maidenwell Rd PL7 130 C5
Maidstone Pl PL5 123 E4
Maine Gdns PL2 127 F7
Main Rd
Crumplehorn PL13 62 D2
Downderry PL11 64 C5
Main St TR18 143 C7
Mainstone Ave PL4 149 C2
Maitland Dr PL3 128 F8
Maker La PL10 133 B4
Maker Rd PL11 127 A2
Maker View PL3 128 B4
Malabar Ho TR1 69 F3
Malabar Rd TR1 69 F3
Mallard Cl PL7 130 F5
Mallets Ct PL27 108 C6
Malmesbury Cl PL2 128 B8
Malory Cl PL5 124 D2
Malpas Ho TR1 137 E4
Malpas Rd TR1 137 E2
Malt House Ct TR27 142 D6
Malt House Gdns 2 TR18 143 C2
Malthouse La TR17 89 C5
Malt House The 3 TR18 143 C2
Manaccan Prim Sch TR12 101 A8
Manadon Cl PL5 124 E1
Manadon Dr PL5 124 E1
Manadon Hill PL5, PL6 124 E1
Manadon Vale Prim Sch PL5 128 E8
Manaton Cl TR13 146 D8
Manby Gdns PL5 123 F5
Mandalay Villas 8 TR9 45 E1
Mandeley Cl PL33 14 D2
Manely Way PL17 40 C4
Manewas Way TR7 111 B7
Manfield Way PL25 115 C4
Manifold Gdns PL3 129 D5
Manley Cl PL14 113 B5
Manley Rd PL14 113 B5
Manley Terr 5 PL14 113 B5
Mannamead Ave PL3 128 F5
Mannamead Ct 9 PL3 128 F6
Mannamead Rd PL3 128 F6
Man Of War View TR12 102 F2
Manor Bourne Rd PL9 135 C1
Manor Cl
Blisland PL30 35 D8
Crackington Haven EX23 10 C6
Falmouth TR11 144 E5
Heamoor TR18 143 D7
Helston TR13 146 D8
St Austell PL25 114 F5
Tavistock PL19 147 A6
Manor Cotts TR11 145 D3
Manor Cres TR11 144 E5
Manor Ct 1 TR2 95 A6
Manor Dr TR26 141 C3
Manor Farm PL20 42 E3
Manor Farm Cl 7 TR20 89 E5
Manor Gdns
Camelford PL32 105 D4
Horrabridge PL20 42 B4
Millbrook PL10 132 F6
Plymouth PL1 148 B2
Redruth TR15 140 B6
St Erth TR27 142 A1
Truro TR1 137 E5
Manor La PL3 129 D5
Manor Park Cl PL7 130 F5
Manor Park Dr PL7 131 A4
Manor Pk
Dousland PL20 42 E3
Duloe PL14 51 A1
Saltash PL12 122 D2
Manor Pl TR18 143 D7
Manor Rd
Bude EX23 104 E4
Camborne TR14 138 C2
Carharrack TR16 80 E8
Falmouth TR11 144 E5
Newquay TR7 110 D6
Plymouth PL9 135 E8
Tavistock PL19 147 B6
Manor St PL1 148 A3
Manor View PL24 60 B4
Manor Way
Heamoor TR18 143 D7
Helston TR13 146 D8
Manse Rd 6 TR3 81 F7
Mansion Ho The PL1 134 A8
Manson Pl PL26 58 C8
Manston Cl PL5 123 E5
Mantle Gdns PL5 127 D8
Maple Ave
Camelford PL32 105 E5
Torpoint PL11 127 A3
Maple Cl
Bodmin PL31 109 B4
23 Callington PL17 39 F4
Plymouth PL6 125 E6
5 St Columb Major TR9 45 D6
St Dennis PL26 58 B8
Tavistock PL19 147 C3
Maple Ct 2 PL9 135 F7
Maple Gr
Plymouth, Mutley PL4 128 D4
Plymouth, Plympton PL7 130 B5
Maple Way PL6 125 E7
Marazion Mus* TR17 89 B5
Marazion Sch TR17 89 C5
Marchant's Cross PL20 42 F1
Marchant's Way PL20 42 F2
Marconi Centre Mus The* TR13 98 F2
Marconi Cl TR13 146 B6
Marcus Hill TR7 110 E6
Marcwheal 6 TR19 88 C1
Mardon Cl PL6 125 D4
Marett Rd PL5 123 F3
Margaret Ave PL25 114 E3
Margaret Cnr PL31 109 C4
Margaret Cres PL31 109 C4
Margaret Gdns PL27 108 D5
Margaret Pk PL3 128 E8
Margaret Pl TR11 144 F3
Margaret's La PL29 22 D7
Margate La PL30 35 C1
Marhamchurch CE Prim Sch EX23 7 B6
Maria's La TR19 96 B7
Maribou Ct PL28 31 F7
Marina Ct TR16 67 C5
Marina Rd PL5 123 F3
Marina Terr 7 PL4 128 F4
Marine Cres 5 TR11 145 C3
Marine Ct
Falmouth TR11 145 D3
26 Perranporth TR6 55 A5
Torpoint PL11 127 B2
Marine Dr
Looe PL13 117 D1
Torpoint PL11 127 B2
Widemouth Bay EX23 6 E5
Marine Par TR2 95 A5
Marine Rd PL9 135 B7
Marine Terr
Boscastle PL35 9 C2
7 Penzance TR18 143 E4
Maristow Ave PL2 127 F5
Maristow Cl PL6 124 F5
Maritime Mus* TR18 143 E5
Market Ave PL1 148 B3
Market Cl PL1 128 A1
Market Ct
Hayle TR27 142 D6
9 Launceston PL15 106 C6
Market Hill PL25 114 C4
Market House Arc
3 Bodmin PL31 109 E5
10 Launceston PL15 106 C6
Market Inn PL24 60 B5
Market Jew St TR18 143 E5
Market Pl
Camelford PL32 105 D4
Helston TR13 146 B5
Marazion TR17 89 B5
Padstow PL28 107 D5
25 Penzance TR18 143 E5
St Columb Major TR9 45 E6
33 St Ives TR26 141 B6
Week St Mary EX22 11 E8
Market Rd
Plymouth PL7 130 D5
Tavistock PL19 147 C5
Market Sq
19 Callington PL17 39 E4
Hayle TR27 142 D6
Plymouth PL1 148 C3
St Day TR16 68 D1
St Just TR19 86 F6
Market St
Bodmin PL31 109 E5
Devoran TR3 81 F6
Falmouth TR11 145 B4
Fowey PL23 116 D4
Hayle TR27 142 D6
Kingsand PL10 133 A1
11 Launceston PL15 106 C6
Liskeard PL14 113 C6
Plymouth PL1 128 A1
6 St Austell PL25 114 C3
St Just TR19 86 F6
3 Stratton EX23 4 E1
Tavistock PL19 147 C5
Market Strand
Falmouth TR11 145 B4
Padstow PL28 107 D5
7 Redruth TR15 140 B5
31 St Ives TR26 141 B6
Market Way
Plymouth PL1 148 C3
5 Redruth TR15 140 B4
Marks Dr PL31 109 E3
Mark's Way TR7 110 D4
Markwell La PL12 53 C1
Marlborough Ave TR11 145 A3
Marlborough Cl
1 Falmouth TR11 145 A3
Saltash PL12 122 F1
Marlborough Cres TR11 145 A3
Marlborough Ct 5 TR11 145 A3
Marlborough Gr 2 TR11 145 A3
Marlborough Prim Sch PL1 127 E2
Marlborough Rd
Falmouth TR11 145 B3
Plymouth PL4 149 A4
Marlborough Row PL1 127 E2
Marlborough Sch TR11 145 A3
Marlborough St PL1 127 E2
Marlborough Way PL26 58 E1
Marldon Cl PL5 124 B3
Marlow Cres PL16 29 F8
Marlow Gdns PL9 135 F5
Marriotts Ave TR14 138 B4
Marrowbone Slip PL4 149 B2
Marryat Gdns PL5 124 E1
Marshall Ave PL27 108 D5
Marshall Cl
Roche PL26 46 F3
Tavistock PL19 147 D2
Marshallen Rd TR4 68 C6
Marshall Rd
Bodmin, Nanstallon PL30 34 C2
Bodmin PL31 109 D3
Plymouth PL7 130 A5
Tavistock PL19 147 D2
Marshalls Way PL29 22 D6
Marsh Cl PL6 129 F6
Marshfield View PL11 64 B5
Marsh La
Angarrack TR27 142 F7
Calstock PL18 41 A3
Hayle TR27 142 E7
Marshlands PL27 34 A6
Marsh Mills PL6 129 F7
Marsh Mills Pk PL6 129 F6
Marsh Mills Ret Pk PL6 129 E7
Marsh Mills Sta* PL7 130 A7
Marthus Ct 10 PL14 113 C5
Martin Cl TR15 140 D5
Martin Ho 11 TR15 140 B4
Martin La
Plymouth, Barbican PL4 149 A2
Plymouth, Millbay PL1 148 B2
Martins Cl PL14 113 E7
Martin's Ct 2 PL31 109 D5
Martin's La TR15 139 C8
Martin Sq 6 PL17 39 F4
Martin St PL1 148 B2
Martinvale Ave TR15 140 E7
Martinvale Parc TR15 140 E7
Martlesham Pl PL5 123 F4
Martyn's Cl TR4 55 D4
Mary Dean Ave PL5 124 C7
Mary Dean Cl PL5 124 C7
Mary Dean's CE Prim Sch PL5 124 C7
Maryland Gdns PL2 127 F7
Mary Moon Cl PL12 53 B7
Mary Newman's Cottage* PL12 123 A2
Mary Seacole Rd PL1 148 A3
Marythorne Rd 15 PL20 41 B1
Masefield Gdns PL5 124 B1
Masons Row PL18 40 F6
Masterman Rd PL2 127 F4
Matela Cl 10 TR13 98 C8
Matthews Way PL14 51 F6
Maudlin Cl PL14 113 D5
Maudlins La PL19 147 A5
Maunsell Cl PL2 127 F7
Mavisdale PL2 127 F6
Mawes Ct PL18 40 D5
Mawgan TR12 99 D6
Mawgan Cross TR12 99 D7
Mawgan-in-Pydar Com Prim Sch TR8 45 A8
Mawgan Vu TR9 57 E8
Mawnan CE Prim Sch TR11 93 D3
Maxwell Rd PL4 135 B8
Maxworthy Cross PL15 12 B4
Maybank Rd PL4 149 C3
Maybrook Dr PL12 122 D2
Mayers Way PL9 135 D6
Mayfair Cres PL6 125 B1
Mayfair Ho PL4 149 A3
Mayfield Cl
Bodmin PL31 35 B2
Port Isaac PL29 22 D7
St Austell PL25 115 A4
Mayfield Cres TR7 110 E5
Mayfield Dr
Port Isaac PL29 22 E7
Roche PL26 47 A3
Mayfield Rd
Falmouth TR11 144 F4
Newquay TR7 110 E5
Port Isaac PL29 22 D7
Mayflower Cl
19 Bere Alston PL20 41 B1
Plymouth PL9 135 F7
Mayflower Dr PL2 128 B5
Mayflower St PL1 148 C3
May Gdns TR16 80 D6
May La PL13 117 F5
Maymear Terr PL30 23 E3
Mayna Parc PL15 18 B8
Maynarde Cl PL7 131 B5
Maynard Pk PL20 41 B1
Mayne Cl PL15 106 B7
Maynes Row TR14 139 A5
Mayon Farm TR19 96 B6
Mayon Green Cres TR19 96 B7
May Terr PL4 149 B3
Mead Cnr EX39 2 D4
Meadfoot Terr 2 PL4 128 F5
Mead Hos The TR18 143 F8
Meadowbank TR11 82 A3
Meadowbank Rd TR11 145 A6
Meadow Brook PL19 147 A4
Meadow Cl
Gloweth TR1 69 E3
Newquay TR7 111 A4
Plymouth PL7 131 D4
Polruan PL23 116 D2
Saltash PL12 122 F3
St Austell PL25 114 F6
St Stephen PL26 58 B4
Meadow Ct
Mevagissey PL26 73 C3
Padstow PL28 107 B4
Stithians TR3 80 E4
St Mabyn PL30 34 C8
Meadow Dr
Bude EX23 104 F6
Camborne TR14 138 C4
Looe PL13 117 D5
Par PL24 115 F5
Saltash PL12 122 D4
Meadowfield Pl PL7 131 B3
Meadow Flats 27 TR26 141 B6
Meadowhead PL27 108 C4
Meadow La TR1 137 D3
Meadowlands PL6 125 D7
Meadow Pk
7 Liskeard PL14 113 B5
Plymouth PL9 135 C5
Trewoon PL25 59 A3
Meadow Pl PL31 109 D4
Meadow Plash PL30 35 C8
Meadow Rd PL13 62 A7
Meadow Rise
Foxhole PL26 58 D6
1 Penwithick PL26 59 D7
Plymouth PL7 131 A4
12 St Columb Major TR9 45 E6
Meadowside
Launceston PL15 106 A4
Lewannick PL15 27 A6
Newquay TR7 111 A4
Plymouth PL9 135 F7
St Austell PL25 115 C6
Whitstone EX22 12 B8
Meadowside Cl
Hayle TR27 142 A3
St Kew Highway PL30 23 B2
Meadowside Rd TR11 144 F2
Meadow St PL26 73 C3
Meadows The
St Dennis PL26 58 C8
St Dominick PL12 40 D2
St Teath PL30 23 E7
Torpoint PL11 126 E4
Meadowsweet Pk PL12 122 C2
Meadow Terr PL14 37 F3
Meadow The
Illogan TR16 67 D4
Polgooth PL26 59 A1
47 St Ives TR26 141 B6
Truro TR1 137 B5
Meadow View
Camborne TR14 138 E1
8 Goldsithney TR20 89 E5
St Minver PL27 21 F3
Meadow View Rd PL7 130 D5
Meadow Villas 8 TR18 143 C1
Meadow Way
Plymouth PL7 130 D7
St Issey PL27 32 E6
Meadow Wlk PL23 116 D2
Mead The PL7 130 D7
Meadway
Looe PL13 117 E4
Saltash PL12 122 E1
St Austell PL25 114 F5
Mearwood La TR11 144 F4
Meaver Rd TR12 99 B1
Meavy Ave PL5 124 E2
Meavy Bourne PL20 42 D2
Meavy CE Prim Sch PL20 42 F2
Meavy La PL20 42 D2
Meavy Villas PL20 42 D2
Meavy Way
Plymouth PL5 124 E2
Tavistock PL19 147 D5
Meddon Cross
Edistone EX39 3 C5
Welcombe EX39 3 C4
Medland Cres PL6 124 D6
Medland Gdns PL25 114 C4
Medlyn Ct TR13 146 B5
Medrose St PL33 14 E3
Medrose Terr 22 TR18 143 E6
Medrow PL15 27 A8
Medway Pl PL3 129 D6
Melbourne Cotts PL1 148 B3
Melbourne Gn 2 PL1 148 B3
Melbourne Pl PL1 148 B4
Melbourne Rd PL14 113 B5
Melbourne St PL1 148 B3
Melbourne Terr 17 TR18 143 C7
Mellanear Cl TR27 142 B4
Mellanear Ct TR27 142 B4
Mellanear Rd TR27 142 B3
Mellanvrane La TR7 110 F4
Melliars Way EX23 104 F6
Melrose Ave PL2 128 C8
Melrose Terr 6 TR9 45 E1
Melvill Cres TR11 145 B3
Melvill Ct TR11 145 B2
Melville Pl 1 PL2 128 A5
Melville Rd
Plymouth PL2 128 A5
Threemilestone TR3 69 D3
Melville Terr PL22 112 C2
Melville Terrace La PL2 128 A5
Melvill La TR11 145 B2
Melvill Rd TR11 145 C2
Memory La PL9 135 E7
Menabilly Cl PL17 39 E3
Menabilly Rd PL25 114 E6
Menacuddle Hill PL25 114 C4
Menacuddle La PL25 114 C4
Menadue Ct TR27 78 E3
Menage St TR13 146 C5
Menague PL27 21 E3
Menakarne TR16 80 F8
Menallack Cheese Farm* TR10 93 A6
Mena Park Cl PL9 136 B7
Mena Park Rd PL9 136 B7
Meneage Cotts 3 TR13 146 C5
Meneage Ho 4 TR13 146 C5
Meneage Parc TR13 146 C5
Meneage Rd TR13 146 C4
Meneage St TR13 146 C5
Meneage Villas PL25 114 B3
Menear Rd PL25 115 A6
Menefreda Way PL27 22 A4
Meneth TR12 92 C1
Meneth Rd TR14 138 F2
Menhaye Gdns TR15 139 D7
Menhay View TR11 144 C3
Menheniot Cres PL15 18 D5
Menheniot Prim Sch PL14 52 A5
Menheniot Sta PL14 51 F4
Menhinick Cl PL12 53 C3
Menhyr Dr TR26 141 C2
Menna La TR2 57 E5
Mennaye Ct TR18 143 D4
Mennaye Rd TR18 143 D4
Merafield Cl PL7 130 B5
Merafield Dr PL7 130 C4
Merafield Farm Cotts PL7 130 B4
Merafield Rd PL7 130 B4
Merafield Rise PL7 130 C4
Merbein Cotts TR8 44 E8
Merchants House (Mus)* PL1 148 C2
Merchants Quay PL15 18 E2
Meredith Rd PL2 128 C6
Meres Valley TR12 99 A2
Meridian Ho PL4 149 A3
Merlin Cl PL6 125 E8
Merlins Way PL34 14 D7
Mermaid Ct TR7 111 C8
Merrick Ave TR1 137 E6
Merrifield Cl TR1 137 B5
Merrifield Cross EX22 7 F4
Merrill Pl TR11 145 A3
Merritts Hill TR16 67 E4
Merritts Way TR15 139 C7
Merrivale Rd
Plymouth, Ham PL2 128 B7
Plymouth, Honicknowle PL5 124 B3
Merrivale View Rd PL20 42 E3
Merrose Cvn Site TR2 83 B4
Merry Mit Mdw TR11 144 C3
Mersey Cl PL3 129 D6
Merther Cl TR13 91 B3
Messack Cl TR11 144 E2

Metha Pk TR8 56 C7
Metha Rd TR8 56 C7
Methleigh Bottoms TR13 91 A1
Methleigh Parc TR13 91 A1
Mevagissey Aquarium* PL26 73 C3
Mevagissey Com Prim Sch PL26 73 C4
Mevagissey Ho TR1 69 E4
Mevagissey Mus* PL26 73 C3
Mews Ct PL14 51 F6
Mews The
Launceston PL15 106 A8
Par PL24 60 B5
3 Penzance TR18 143 E6
Plymouth, Devonport PL1 128 A3
Plymouth, Stonehouse PL1 148 A3
Mexico La TR27 142 C7
Mexico Terr TR27 142 C8
Michael Rd PL3 129 A5
Michaelstow Holiday Village PL30 23 F5
Michell Ave TR7 110 E6
Michell Ct TR7 110 D6
Michigan Way PL3 129 C6
Mid Churchway PL9 136 A7
Mid Cornwall Bsns Ctr PL25 115 E4
Middle Down Cl PL9 136 A5
Middlefield Rd PL6 124 D6
Middlefield Cl PL12 122 B2
Middlegates 5 TR5 54 D1
Middle Market St PL13 117 D3
Middle Rd TR15 140 E7
Middle Rosewin Row 8 TR1 137 D5
Middle Row TR13 90 E3
Middle St
Padstow PL28 107 D5
Port Isaac PL29 22 D7
Middle Stennack Cotts 13 TR26 141 A5
Middleton Cres TR7 110 F4
Middletons Row 6 TR15 140 C5
Middleton Wlk PL5 123 D4
Middleway PL24 60 B5
Middlewell Parc PL27 108 B4
Middle Wharf PL26 73 C3
Midella Rd PL20 42 D2
Mid Moor PL14 38 B6
Midway Dr TR1 137 E5
Midway Rd PL31 109 A5
Miers Cl PL5 127 C8
Miers Ct PL5 127 C8
Milch Pk PL12 122 C2
Mildmay St PL4 149 A4
Mile End TR12 102 F4
Milehouse Rd PL2 128 A5
Miles Mitchell Ave PL6 125 A1
Milestone Ct TR3 69 D4
Milford La PL5 124 B5
Military Rd
Millbrook PL10 132 C3
Plymouth PL3 129 E6
Rame PL10 64 C2
St Mawes TR2 95 B4
Milladon La PL12 64 D8
Mill Ball Hill EX23 10 B7
Millbank Mdw TR27 78 E1
Millbay Rd PL1 148 A2
Mill Bridge PL1 148 A3
Millbrook Bsns Ctr PL11 132 C6
Millbrook CE Prim Sch PL10 132 E5
Mill Cl
Porthleven TR13 91 A1
Wadebridge PL27 108 E5
Mill Cotts TR13 146 A6
Millendreath Holiday Village PL13 117 F5
Millenium Appartments TR10 81 D2
Millennium Way TR13 146 D8
Miller Bsns Pk PL14 113 B4
Miller Ct
Liskeard PL14 113 B4
Plymouth PL1 148 A2
Miller Way PL6 125 E3
Millet Cl TR17 89 D5
Millfield TR18 88 E6
Mill Flats TR13 146 B6
Mill Ford Sch PL5 123 F4
Mill Gdns PL22 112 C2
Millham La PL22 112 E3
Mill Hill
Crumplehorn PL13 62 D1
Lelant TR27 77 E3
Lostwithiel PL22 112 D2
St Just In R TR2 82 F3
Mill Hill Cotts PL19 30 B1
Millhouse Pk PL11 127 A2
Mill La
Camelford PL32 105 D5
Coad's Green PL15 27 C1
Grampound TR2 72 A7
Helston TR13 146 B6
20 Mousehole TR19 88 C1
Porthleven TR13 91 A1
St Breward PL30 24 B3
St Germans PL12 65 A8
Torpoint PL11 127 A2
Tregony TR2 71 F3
Truro TR3 137 C1
Millpond Ave TR27 142 B4
Millpool
Lostwithiel PL22 112 F3
Rilla Mill PL14 38 E8
Mill Pool 15 TR19 88 C1
Millpool Head PL10 132 E4
Millpool Rd PL10 133 A6
Mill Rd
Millbrook PL10 133 A5
Padstow PL28 107 D5
Penponds TR14 79 B5
Perranporth TR6 55 B4
Tideford PL12 52 F2
Mill Rd Est PL12 52 F2
Mill Sq PL28 107 D5
Mills Rd PL1 127 F2
Mills' St TR16 68 E1
Mill St PL31 109 E5
Milltown Gdns PL15 18 E6
Mill View Gdns PL10 132 F5
Mill View Rd PL10 132 F5
Millway Pl PL9 135 D8
Millwood Dr PL6 125 E1
Milne Pl PL1 127 F3
Milton Abbot Sch PL19 29 D5
Milton Cl PL5 124 D2
Milton Cres PL19 147 D5
Milton Ct
Plymouth, Cattedown PL4 149 C2
Plymouth, Prince Rock PL4 129 B1
Minack Theatre* TR19 96 E2
Mine Hill PL14 51 F6
Mine La PL30 47 E7
Mineral Tramways Discovery Ctr* TR15 139 B4
Miners Ct
Perranporth TR6 55 A4
Redruth TR15 140 C5
Miners Row TR15 140 C5
Miners Way PL14 113 D7
Minerva Cl PL7 131 A6
Minions Heritage Ctr* PL14 38 B6
Minions Row PL14 38 B6
Minnie Pl TR11 145 B3
Minorca La PL26 47 D2
Minses Cl PL9 136 C7
Minster Ave EX23 104 F4
Minster Mdw TR12 101 A8
Minster Terr TR12 101 A8
Minton Cl PL25 115 A4
Mirador Pl PL4 129 C3
Mission The TR18 143 F4
Misterton Cl PL9 136 B8
Mitchell Cl
Lizard TR12 102 F2
Plymouth PL9 135 D5
Mitchell Ct 11 TR1 137 D5
Mitchell Hill TR1 137 D5
Mitchell Hill Terr 4 TR1 137 D5
Mitchell La
Camborne TR14 138 E3
Mitchell TR8 56 E5
Mitchell Mews 17 TR1 137 D4
Mitchell Rd
Camborne TR14 138 C3
St Austell PL25 114 F4
Mitchell's Boatyard PL26 73 C2
Mitchells Cnr 24 TR6 55 A5
Mithian Sch TR5 54 E1
Mitre Cl PL19 147 A3
Mitre Ct 15 PL1 149 A2
Modbury Cl PL5 124 B3
Modus La PL26 58 E1
Modyford Wlk PL20 41 F3
Mohun's Cl PL19 147 C4
Mohun's Pk PL19 147 C3
Molenick La PL12 52 E3
Molesworth Ct 4 PL27 108 B5
Molesworth Rd
Plymouth, Plympton PL7 130 C6
Plymouth, Stoke PL1, PL3 128 A3
Molesworth St
Tintagel PL34 14 C7
Wadebridge PL27 108 B5
Molesworth Terr PL10 132 F5
Molinnis PL26 47 C2
Molinnis Rd PL26 47 C2
Mollison Rd PL5 123 E2
Molyneaux Pl 10 PL1 127 F3
Monastery Cl TR12 101 D4
Mongleath Ave TR11 144 E3
Mongleath Cl TR11 144 E3
Mongleath Rd TR11 144 E3
Monica Wlk PL4 149 B4
Monkey Sanctuary The* PL13 63 F5
Monks Hill PL15 28 C4
Monksmead PL19 147 A4
Monks Park Cotts PL15 106 D6
Monmouth Gdns PL5 124 C4
Monmouth La PL22 112 D2
Montacute Ave PL5 124 B2
Montague Ave TR15 140 A6
Monterey Cl EX23 104 E4
Monterey Gdns TR1 137 E5
Montgomery Cl PL12 122 D3
Montgomery Rd 2 PL26 59 D7
Montpelier Com Prim Sch PL2 128 B6
Montpelier Rd PL2 128 C7
Monument Rd TR13 146 B5
Monument St PL1 127 E1
Monument Way PL31 109 C4
Moon La PL4 149 A3
Moonrakers TR26 141 D2
Moonsfield 5 PL17 39 F4
Moon St PL4 149 A3
Moorcroft Cl PL9 136 A7
Moor Cross EX22 8 D3
Moor Cross Cotts EX23 4 C3
Moorfield PL16 19 F4
Moorfield Ave 4 PL6 129 C7
Moorfield Rd
Camborne TR15 139 C6
St Giles on t H PL15 13 F1
Moor La PL5 123 E1
Moorland Ave PL7 130 F6
Moorland Cl
Liskeard PL14 113 D7
Pendeen TR19 74 F1
Yelverton PL20 121 D8
Moorland Ct
1 St Austell PL25 114 C3
Yelverton PL20 42 C2
Moorland Dr PL7 130 E6
Moorland Gdns PL7 130 F6
Moorland Rd
Indian Queens TR9 45 F2
Launceston PL15 106 A4
Plymouth PL7 130 E5
St Austell PL25 114 C3
Tywardreath PL24 60 C4
Moorland Road Ind Est TR9 45 F2
Moorlands La PL12 122 C4
Moorlands Trad Est PL12 122 C4
Moorland View
Golberdon PL17 39 B6
Liskeard PL14 113 D7
Plymouth, Derriford PL6 125 A5
Plymouth, Plymstock PL9 136 B7
Saltash PL12 122 F4
Moorland Way PL18 40 F5
Moorlan Mdws PL26 47 A3
Moor Parc TR12 100 D6
Moor St TR14 138 D3
Moors The PL22 112 C1
Moorswater Ind Est PL14 51 A7
Moor The TR11 145 B4
Moor View
Bodmin PL31 109 F2
Plymouth, Keyham PL2 127 F5
Plymouth, Laira PL3 129 C4
Plymouth PL9 135 D7
Torpoint PL11 127 B3
Moorview Ct PL6 125 F5
Moorview Terr PL14 38 D7
Moor View Terr
Plymouth PL4 128 E4
Yelverton PL20 42 D2
Morcom Cl PL25 115 A5
Moresk Cl TR1 137 D5
Moresk Gdns TR1 137 D5
Moresk Rd TR1 137 D5
Moreton Ave PL6 124 F1
Morice Sq PL1 127 E2
Morice St PL1 127 E2
Morice Town Prim Sch PL2 127 E4
Morlaix Ave TR1 137 D3
Morlaix Dr PL6 125 B4
Morla La TR15 140 A6
Morleigh Cl PL25 114 F3
Morley Cl PL7 130 A5
Morley Ct PL1 148 B3
Morley Dr PL20 42 A2
Morley View Rd PL7 130 C6
Morrab Ct 8 TR7 110 F6
Morrab Pl 34 TR18 143 E5
Morrab Rd
Camborne TR14 138 C3
Penzance TR18 143 E5
Morrab Terr 35 TR18 143 E5
Morris Gdns TR7 110 D4
Morrish Pk PL9 135 F6
Morshead Rd PL6 124 F2
Mortain Rd PL12 122 D4
Mortimore Cl PL12 122 D2
Morvan Trad Est PL25 114 F3
Morven Rd PL25 114 F3
Morview Rd PL13 63 F8
Morwell Gdns PL2 128 A6
Morwellham Quay* PL19 41 B4
Morwenna Gdns TR6 55 B5
Morwenna Rd EX23 2 D1
Morwenna Terr EX23 104 D6
Morweth Cotts PL11 64 C5
Morweth Ct PL11 64 C5
Moses Cl PL6 124 E7
Moses Ct PL6 124 E7
Mosquito Cres 3 PL27 31 F3
Moss Side Ind Est PL17 39 F4
Moss Terr PL23 116 D3
Mostyn Ave PL4 129 A4
Mote Pk PL12 122 C3
Mothecombe Wlk PL6 125 E1
Moulton Cl PL7 131 B5
Moulton Wlk PL7 131 B4
Mount Agar Rd TR3 81 F7
Mount Ambrose TR15 140 E7
Mountbatten Cl
Plymouth PL9 135 D6
St Columb Minor TR7 111 E7
Mountbatten Rd 5 PL26 59 D7
Mount Batten Waterside Pk* PL9 134 F7
Mountbatten Way PL9 135 E6
Mount Bennett Rd 5 PL24 60 D5
Mount Bennett Terr 4 PL24 60 D5
Mount Camel PL32 105 C4
Mount Carbis Gdns TR15 140 C3
Mount Carbis Rd TR15 140 D3
Mount Charles Jun & Inf Sch PL25 114 F3
Mount Charles Rd PL25 114 F3
Mount Cres PL24 60 C4
Mount Edgcumbe Country Pk* PL10 133 E6
Mount Edgcumbe Terr TR11 145 B4
Mountfield Terr 6 PL24 60 C4
Mount Folly TR27 142 C6
Mount Folly Sq PL31 109 E4
Mount Ford PL19 147 A5
Mount George Rd TR3 82 B7
Mount Gould Ave PL4 129 B2
Mount Gould Cres PL4 129 B3
Mount Gould Hospl PL4 129 B3
Mount Gould Rd PL4 129 B3
Mount Gould Way PL4 129 B3
Mount Hawke Chalet Pk TR4 68 B6
Mount Hawke Com Prim Sch TR4 68 C6
Mount Ho PL11 64 C5
Mount House Sch PL19 147 E7
Mountlea Dr 9 PL24 60 C4
Mount Lidden TR18 143 C4
Mount Pleasant
Bodmin PL31 109 E5
Boscastle PL35 9 D1
Falmouth TR11 144 E1
Hayle TR27 142 C6
Lelant TR26 77 E3
Millbrook PL10 132 E5
Newlyn TR18 143 C4
Par PL24 60 B6
Plymouth PL5 124 B2
39 St Ives TR26 141 B6
Mount Pleasant Cl TR14 138 E1
Mount Pleasant Gdns TR27 142 C6
Mount Pleasant Pl PL22 112 C3
Mount Pleasant Rd
Camborne TR14 138 D1
11 Porthleven TR13 98 B8
Threemilestone TR3 69 D3
Mount Pleasant Terr
Mousehole TR19 88 C1
Redruth TR15 140 E7
Mount Pleasure TR14 138 E1
Mount Prospect Terr TR18 143 C3
Mount Rd PL24 60 C4
Mount's Bay Holiday Flats TR18 88 E6
Mounts Bay Rd TR18 143 C4
Mount's Bay Sch & Com Sports Coll TR18 143 B7
Mounts Bay Terr TR13 90 E3
Mount's Bay Terr 21 TR13 98 C8
Mount's Rd 20 TR13 98 C8
Mount St
Mevagissey PL26 73 C3
Penzance TR18 143 E6
Plymouth, Mount Wise PL1 127 E1
Plymouth, Mutley PL4 149 A4
Mount Stamper Rd PL25 114 D7
Mountstephen Cl PL25 114 B3
Mount Stephens La TR11 144 F4
Mount Stone Rd PL1 134 A8
Mount Street Prim Sch PL4 149 A4
Mount Tamar Cl PL5 123 E2
Mount Tamar Sch PL5 123 E2
Mount Tavy Rd PL19 147 E6
Mount Terr 9 PL24 60 B4
Mount View
Lane TR8 111 B3
Madron TR20 88 A7
Mount View Cotts TR20 89 A7
Mount View Terr
5 Marazion TR17 89 C5
24 Newlyn TR18 143 C2
Mount Whistle Rd TR14 138 F7
Mount Wise
Launceston PL15 106 C5
Newquay TR7 110 D5
Mount Wise Com Prim Sch PL1 127 E1
Mount Wise Cotts TR7 110 E5
Mount Wise Ct PL1 127 F1
Mount Zion 52 TR26 141 B6
Mourne Villas PL9 135 F8
Mousehole Com Prim Sch TR19 88 C1
Mousehole La TR19 88 C1
Mowbray Mews PL32 10 B2
Mowhay Cl TR7 111 A4
Mowhay Cotts PL26 85 C5
Mowhay La 1 PL17 39 E4
Mowhay Mdw
St John PL11 132 B8
Wadebridge PL27 108 B4
Mowhay Rd
Plymouth PL5 123 F1
Plymouth PL5 124 A2
Mowie The 13 TR9 45 E2
Moyle Rd PL28 107 E4
Mudges Terr PL18 41 A6
Mudge Way PL7 130 E5
Mulberry Cl PL6 125 E7
Mulberry Ct 12 TR11 145 B5
Mulberry Gr PL19 147 C2
Mulberry Quay 11 TR11 145 B5
Mulberry Rd PL12 122 E1
Mulgrave St PL1 148 C2
Mullet Ave PL3 129 C4
Mullet Cl PL3 129 C4
Mullet Rd PL3 129 C4
Mullion Cl PL11 126 F4
Mullion Com Prim Sch TR12 99 A1
Mullion Cove TR12 102 B7
Mullion Cove Bglws TR12 98 F1
Mullion Rural Workshops TR12 99 A1
Mullion Sch TR12 99 B1
Mundys Field TR12 103 A5
Muralto Ho PL19 147 A4
Murdoch Cl
Redruth TR15 140 B6
Truro TR1 137 E6
Murdock Rd PL11 126 F3
Murray Villas TR19 86 E6
Murtons Terr TR16 80 E7
Mus of Witchcraft* PL35 9 C2
Mutley Ct PL4 149 A4
Mutley Plain PL4 128 E4
Mutley Plain La PL4 128 E4
Mutley Rd PL3 128 E5
Mutton Hill TR27 78 D6
Mutton Row TR10 144 C8
Mylor Cl PL2 128 D8
Mylor Com Prim Sch TR11 82 A3
My Lords Rd TR9 57 E8
Myrtle Cl PL20 42 E3
Myrtle Ct PL26 73 C3
Myrtles Ct PL12 122 D4
Myrtleville PL2 128 A6
Mythyon Ct 4 TR18 143 C7

N

Nailzee Ho PL13 117 D2
Nailzee Point PL13 117 D2
Nalder's Ct 10 TR1 137 C4
Nampara Cl TR26 141 E2
Nampara Ct 7 TR6 55 A4
Nampara Way TR1 137 F4
Nancarrows PL12 122 C2
Nancealverne TR18 143 D6
Nancealverne Sch TR20 143 C6
Nancedden Farm TR20 89 A8
Nancegollan Ind Est TR13 91 B7
Nancemere Rd TR1 137 D6
Nancevallon TR14 139 B3
Nancherrow Hill TR19 86 F6
Nancherrow Row TR19 86 F6
Nancledra Sch TR 26 76 F3
Nangitha Cl TR11 144 C3
Nangitha Terr TR11 144 C3
Nanhayes Row TR8 56 B7
Nanjivey Pl 8 TR26 141 A5
Nanjivey Terr 9 TR26 141 A5
Nanpean Com Prim Sch PL26 58 D6
Nanpusker Cl TR27 142 E6
Nanpusker Rd TR27 78 C4
Nansalsa Ct TR7 111 A6
Nansavallon Rd TR1 69 F3
Nanscober Pl TR13 146 B8
Nanscothan 10 TR15 140 B4
Nans Kestenen TR13 146 B5
Nansloe Cl TR13 146 D4
Nansloe Com Prim Sch TR13 146 C4
Nansmellyon Rd TR12 99 A1
Nanstallon Com Prim Sch PL30 34 C1
Nanterrow La TR27 66 D1
Nanturras Parc TR20 89 F5
Nanturras Row TR20 89 E5
Napier St PL1 127 F3
Napier Terr PL4 128 E4
Narkurs Cross PL11 64 D7
Narrowcliff TR7 111 A7
Narrow La
Botusfleming PL12 122 C7
Summercourt TR8 57 C8
Nash Cl PL7 131 A5
Nathan Cl TR7 111 B5
National Marine Aquarium* PL4 149 A2
National Maritime Mus (Cornwall)* TR11 145 C3
National Seal Sanctuary The* TR12 92 C1
National Seal Sanctuary Visitor Ctr* TR12 92 C1
Navy Inn Ct 10 TR18 143 C1
Neal Cl PL7 131 B4
Neath Rd PL4 149 C4
Neeham Rd TR8 56 B7
Nelson Ave PL1 127 F3
Nelson Gdns 5 PL1 127 F3
Nelson St PL4 149 A4
Nelson Terr PL6 125 E6
Nepean St 1 PL2 127 F3
Neptune Ave PL27 31 F3
Neptune Pk PL9 135 B8
Neswick St PL1 148 B3
Neswick Street Ope PL1 148 A3
Nethercott Cross EX21 13 F7
Netherton Est PL20 42 A3
Netherton Rd PL28 107 D4
Nettell's Hill TR15 140 B5
Nettlehayes PL9 136 D7
Netton Cl PL9 136 B6
Nevada Cl PL3 129 D6
Nevada Pl 16 TR18 143 C7
Nevada St TR18 143 C7
Nevada Villas 8 PL24 60 C4
Newacott Cross EX22 7 F5

New Barn Hill PL7 130 F3
New Bglws PL30 36 B3
Newbridge Hill PL18 41 A6
Newbridge La TR1, TR3 69 F3
New Bridge St 9 TR1 137 D4
Newbridge Way TR1 69 F3
Newbury Cl PL5 124 B4
Newcastle Gdns PL5 124 B5
New Connection St 4 TR14 138 D3
New Cotts
Gunnislake PL18 41 A6
Kilkhampton EX23 5 A6
New Ct TR11 145 B4
New Cut TR15 140 B5
New Dairy La TR17 89 B6
New George St PL1 148 C3
Newham Est TR1 137 D3
Newham Ind Est TR1 137 D2
Newham La
Helston TR13 146 A7
Lostwithiel PL22 49 A1
Newham Rd TR1 137 E2
New Hill Est TR2 72 A7
New Hos TR14 139 B3
Newhouses PL17 38 E8
New La TR15 140 E7
New Launceston Rd PL19 147 A5
Newlyn Art Gall* TR18 143 C3
Newlyn Rd TR19 97 B6
Newlyn Sch TR18 143 C3
Newman Rd
Plymouth PL5 123 E2
Saltash PL12 122 F3
Newmills Cl TR1 137 B6
New Mills Farm Pk* PL15 18 D4
New Mills La TR1, TR4 137 A6
Newmills Sta* PL15 18 D4
New Molinnis PL26 47 C2
Newnham Ind Est PL7 130 F6
Newnham Rd PL7 130 F7
Newnham Way PL7 130 F6
New Northernmaye 2 PL15 106 C6
New Park Rd
Plymouth PL7 131 A4
Wadebridge PL27 108 C5
New Passage Hill PL1 127 E3
New Pk
Horrabridge PL20 42 C4
Wadebridge PL27 108 C4
Newport
Callington PL17 39 E4
St Germans PL12 65 A8
Newport Cl 8 PL17 39 F4
Newport Ind Est PL15 106 C6
New Portreath Rd
Illogan TR16 67 F5
Redruth TR16 140 A7
Newport Sq PL15 106 B7
Newport St
Millbrook PL10 132 E5
Plymouth PL1 128 A1
Newport Terr 3 PL17 39 F4
Newquay Airport TR8 44 F8
Newquay Hospl TR7 110 F5
Newquay Jun Sch TR7 110 F6
Newquay Rd
Goonhavern TR4 55 D4
St Columb Major TR9 45 D6
Truro TR1 137 F7
Newquay Sta TR7 110 F6
Newquay Tretherras Sch TR7 111 B6
New Rd
Barripper TR14 79 B5
Bere Alston PL20 41 B2
Boscastle PL35 9 C2
Cadgwith TR12 103 A4
Callington PL17 39 E4
Camborne TR14 139 B3
Cawsand PL10 133 A1
Kingsand PL10 133 B2
Lifton PL16 19 F4
Liskeard PL14 113 B5
Newlyn TR18 143 C3
Perranporth TR6 55 B4
Port Isaac PL29 22 D7
Roborough PL6 121 D2
Saltash PL12 122 E3
St Columb Major TR9 45 E6
St Hilary TR20 89 F6
Stithians TR3 80 F3
St Just TR19 86 F6
Stratton EX23 4 D1
Summercourt TR8 57 D7
Tregony TR2 71 F3
Troon TR14 79 E4
New Road Cl PL10 133 A2
New Road Hill PL23 116 C4
New Road Terr PL12 53 C3
New Row
Gweek TR12 92 C1
Mylor Bridge TR11 82 A3
Nancledra TR 20 76 F2
Redruth TR16 139 D1
Summercourt TR8 57 B6
New St
Bugle PL26 47 C1
Falmouth TR11 145 B4
Millbrook PL10 132 E5
Padstow PL28 107 D5
Penryn TR10 144 D7
New St *continued*
Penzance TR18 143 E5
Plymouth PL1 149 A2
Troon TR14 79 E4
Newtake Rd PL19 147 E2
Newton Ave PL5 123 E2
Newton Ct
Dobwalls PL14 50 E8
Redruth TR15 140 B6
Newton Farm Cotts PL13 62 E3
Newton Gdns PL5 123 F2
Newton Pk 13 TR2 95 A6
Newton Rd
St Mawes TR2 95 A6
Troon TR14 79 E5
Newton's Margate Ind Est PL31 35 B1
Newtown PL23 60 F3
Newtown La TR17, TR20 89 A7
New Town La TR18 143 E5
New Windsor Terr 11 TR11 145 A4
New Wood Cl PL6 125 E8
New Zealand Ho PL3 128 B4
Nicholas Ave TR16 80 A5
Nicholas Mdw PL17 40 E4
Nicholas Parc 3 TR18 143 C7
Nicholson Rd PL5 124 E2
Nicolls Flats PL15 106 B5
Nightingale Cl PL9 136 C8
Nine Oaks PL20 42 F3
No Go By Hill TR19 86 F7
No Mans' Land Rd TR11 93 D5
Nook The PL19 147 D6
Norfolk Cl PL3 129 C5
Norfolk Rd
Falmouth TR11 145 B4
Plymouth PL3 129 C4
Norman Cotts PL15 106 C7
Normandy Hill PL5 123 B2
Normandy Way
Bodmin PL31 109 F2
Camborne TR14 138 F3
Plymouth PL5 123 C2
Norman's Way PL30 23 E3
Northampton Cl PL5 124 B5
North Cl EX23 5 A6
North Cliff 12 TR19 88 C1
North Cnr 1 TR18 143 C2
North Cornwall Mus & Gall* PL32 105 C4
Northcott Mouth Rd EX23 104 F8
North Dimson PL18 40 F6
North Down Cres PL2 127 F6
North Down Gdns PL2 127 F6
North Down Rd PL2 128 B6
Northesk St PL2 128 A4
Northey Cl TR4 69 F6
Northey Rd PL31 109 D4
Northfield Cl TR16 68 E1
Northfield Dr TR1 137 D3
Northgate Pl 1 PL15 106 C6
North Grange Ind Est TR3 81 F6
North Hill
Blackwater TR4 68 E5
Carharrack TR16 80 F8
Chacewater TR4 68 F3
Plymouth PL4 149 A4
North Hill Pk PL25 114 D4
North Moor Cross EX22 3 F3
Northolt Ave PL5 123 D4
North Orchard Ct 1 TR20 89 E5
North Par
Camborne TR14 138 E3
Falmouth TR11 145 A6
Penzance TR18 143 E5
Portscatho TR2 83 B2
North Parade Rear TR14 138 D3
North Park Villas PL12 122 C4
North Petherwin Ind Est PL15 18 A8
North Petherwin Prim Sch PL15 12 B1
North Pl 15 TR26 141 B6
North Pool Cl TR15 139 C7
North Pool Rd TR15 139 C7
North Prospect Prim Sch PL2 128 A7
North Prospect Rd PL2 128 A6
North Quay
Hayle TR27 142 B6
Padstow PL28 107 D6
Plymouth PL4 149 A2
North Quay Hill TR7 110 D7
North Quay Par PL28 107 E6
North Rd
Camborne TR14 138 D3
Goldsithney TR20 89 E5
Landrake PL12 53 C3
Lifton PL16 19 F4
Looe PL13 117 C3
Pentewan PL26 73 C6
Redruth TR16 140 E1
Saltash PL12 122 F3
St Teath PL30 23 E7
Torpoint PL11 127 B3
Whitemoor PL26 58 E8
Yelverton PL20 42 C3
North Rd E PL4 148 C4
North Rd W PL1 148 B4
North Roskear Mdw TR14 138 E5
North Roskear Rd TR14 138 F5
North Row TR19 86 F6
North St
Fowey PL23 116 D4
Launceston PL15 106 A8
North St *continued*
Lostwithiel PL22 112 C2
Marazion TR17 89 B5
14 Mousehole TR19 88 C1
Plymouth PL4 149 A3
Redruth TR15 140 B6
St Austell PL25 114 C4
Tavistock PL19 147 C5
Tywardreath PL24 60 D5
North Terr
2 Penzance TR18 143 E4
12 St Ives TR26 141 B5
Whitemoor PL26 58 E8
Northumberland St PL5 127 E8
Northumberland Terr PL1 148 B1
North View PL13 117 D4
North Way TR8 111 F4
North Weald Gdns PL5 123 E5
Norton Ave PL4 149 C4
Norton Ct 2 PL31 109 E5
Norwich Ave PL5 124 B5
Notre Dame Cl PL6 124 F5
Notre Dame Ho PL1 148 B3
Notre Dame RC Sch PL6 124 F5
Notter Mill Holiday Village PL12 53 D4
Notte St PL1 148 C2
Novorossisk Rd PL6 125 E2
Noweth Pl TR11 144 E5
Nunnery Hill PL26 72 F7
Nurseries The TR11 144 D5
Nursery Cl
Plymouth PL5 124 B7
Truro TR1 137 D5
11 Tywardreath PL24 60 D5
Nut La TR27 77 E3
Nut Tree Hill PL12 65 B8

O

Oakapple Cl PL7 130 B7
Oak Apple Cl PL12 122 D4
Oak Ave PL12 40 A1
Oakcroft Rd PL2 128 B6
Oakdene Rise PL9 135 F6
Oakdene Villas 7 TR9 45 E1
Oak Dr
8 Liskeard PL14 113 B5
Plymouth PL6 124 F3
Oakey Orch PL17 40 D4
Oakfield PL15 27 D3
Oakfield Cl PL7 131 C6
Oakfield Pl PL4 129 B1
Oakfield Rd
Falmouth TR11 144 F5
Plymouth PL7 130 C6
Oakfield Terrace Rd PL4 129 B1
Oak Ford PL30 48 C7
Oakham Rd PL5 124 B5
Oakhill PL30 47 C6
Oak La
Truro TR1 69 E4
Whitstone EX22 7 F1
Oakland Pk TR11 144 D5
Oaklands PL19 147 D2
Oaklands Bsns Pk PL13 63 D8
Oaklands Cl PL6 125 C7
Oaklands Dr PL12 122 C3
Oaklands Gn PL12 122 D3
Oaklands Ind Est PL14 113 E6
Oaklands Rd PL14 113 E6
Oakleigh Terr TR7 110 F6
Oak Park Terr PL14 113 A6
Oak Pk PL30 23 E3
Oak Rd PL19 147 C2
Oakridge PL12 53 C7
Oak Ridge PL16 19 F4
Oaks The
Quintrell Downs TR8 111 F3
St Austell PL25 114 B3
Oak Tree Cl PL25 115 B3
Oaktree Ct PL6 124 F1
Oak Tree La PL19 147 C3
Oak Tree Pk PL6 125 D6
Oak Vale TR2 72 A7
Oak Way TR1 137 D5
Oakwood Cl PL6 125 D7
Oakwood Pk PL31 109 F4
Oakwood Rise PL32 105 E5
Oates Rd
Helston TR13 146 C6
Marazion TR17 89 C5
Plymouth PL2 128 B5
Observer Cl TR1 137 C3
Ocean Cres 22 TR13 98 C8
Ocean Ct
Plymouth PL1 133 F8
Porthtowan TR4 68 A7
Ocean St PL2 127 E6
Ocean View
Indian Queens TR9 45 E1
Polruan PL23 116 D2
Porthleven TR13 98 B8
Ocean View Rd EX23 104 D7
Ocean View Terr TR26 141 A6
Octagon St PL1 148 B3
Octagon The PL1 148 B2
Okehampton Cl PL7 131 B4
Old Bakehouse Flats The TR18 143 F6
Old Barn Ct TR7 110 D4
Old Barns The TR14 66 F2
Old Boat Yard The PL28 107 E6
Old Boys School TR16 67 E5
Old Brewery Yd 4 TR18 143 E5
Old Bridge St TR1 137 D4
Old Butchers Shop The TR20 89 B8
Old Cable La TR19 96 E3
Old Callywith Rd PL31 35 B2
Old Canal Cl EX23 7 B6
Old Carnon Hill TR3 81 F6
Old Chapel The TR4 68 F5
Old Chapel Way PL10 132 F6
Old Chough Flats TR7 111 B7
Old Church Rd TR11 93 E2
Old Church The TR18 143 D4
Old Coach Rd
Lanivet PL26, PL30 47 D6
Playing Place TR3 82 B8
Truro TR3 70 A1
Old Coastguard Cotts PL11 65 A4
Old Coastguard Row TR19 96 B7
Old Corn Mill The TR12 92 C1
Old Dairy The
Plymouth PL3 129 B6
Sancreed TR20 87 E4
Old Drovers Way EX23 4 E1
Old English Ind Est PL20 42 E3
Old Exeter Rd PL19 147 D7
Old Falmouth Rd TR1 137 C1
Old Farm Rd PL5 127 C8
Old Ferry Rd PL12 123 A3
Old Foundry Cl TR19 86 F6
Old Foundry The
Menheniot PL14 51 E6
Tavistock PL19 147 D6
Old George St PL1 148 C2
Old Grammar School Ct PL22 112 C2
Old Greystone Hill PL15, PL19 28 F6
Old Guildhall Mus* PL13 117 D3
Old Hill
Falmouth TR11 144 F6
Grampound TR2 72 A7
Helston TR13 146 A6
Old Hill Cres TR11 144 F5
Old La PL26 46 F3
Old Laira Rd PL3 129 C4
Oldlands Cl PL6 125 B6
Old Launceston Rd PL19 147 B6
Old Laundry The PL1 148 A3
Old Lawn School La PL25 114 B3
Old Market Pl PL31 109 C4
Old Mill Cl PL15 27 B3
Old Mill Ct PL7 130 E5
Old Mill Herbary The* PL30 34 F6
Old Mill La
Camborne TR14 78 F6
Penponds TR14 79 A6
Old Mill The
3 Boscastle PL35 9 C2
Lerryn PL22 61 D8
Old Mine La PL18 40 E6
Old Nursery Cl TR13 91 A1
Old Orchard Cl EX23 7 B6
Old Orchard The PL22 112 C2
Old Park Rd PL3 128 D6
Old Paul Hill TR18 143 C2
Old Plymouth Rd PL3 129 E5
Old Portreath Rd
Illogan TR16 67 F5
Redruth TR15 67 F4
Old Post Office* PL34 14 C7
Old Post Office Hill 8 EX23 4 E1
Old Pound PL26 58 E6
Old Priory PL7 130 D5
Old Priory Jun Sch PL7 130 D5
Old Quarry Rd PL20 42 A3
Old Quay La PL12 65 B8
Old Rd
Boscastle PL35 9 C2
Liskeard PL14 113 A6
Old Rectory Dr TR9 45 E6
Old Rectory Mews Cvn Pk TR9 45 D6
Old Roselyon Cres PL24 60 B5
Old Roselyon Rd PL24 60 C4
Old Sandy La TR16 140 D3
Old School Cl PL27 21 F3
Old School Ct
Padstow PL28 107 D5
Wadebridge PL27 108 B5
Old School Ho The PL10 133 A1
Old Schoolhouse The TR11 145 B4
Old School La PL30 34 D4
Old School Rd PL5 127 C8
Old School The 10 TR5 54 D1
Old Smithy Cl 4 TR17 89 C5
Old Smithy Cotts EX39 2 E4
Old Station Rd
Horrabridge PL20 42 C4
1 Liskeard PL14 51 A7
Old Station The PL20 42 B4
Old Tannery Bsns Pk The 4 PL4 149 A4
Old Town Hall The PL24 60 B5
Old Town St PL1 148 C3
Old Tram Rd TR3 82 A5
Old Vicarage Cl TR3 80 F4
Old Vicarage Gate TR27 142 A1
Old Vicarage Pl 11 PL25 114 C3
Old Vicarage The TR 26 76 E5
Old Warleigh La PL5 124 B7
Old Well Gdns TR10 144 C8
Old Wharf The PL9 135 C7
Old Woodlands Rd PL5 124 D3
Old Workhouses The TR15 140 B8
Oliver Ct PL12 40 A1
Oliver's Terr TR13 146 C5
Olive Villas TR3 81 F6
Olivey Pl TR11 82 A3
Olivia Ct PL4 149 B4
Omaha Rd PL31 109 F3
Onslow Rd PL2 128 C7
Ope's Ct 13 TR11 145 B5
Opies La PL31 109 C5
Opie's Row TR16 80 B5
Opie's Terr TR16 80 A5
Orange La TR26 141 A6
Orchard Ave PL6 129 B7
Orchard Cl
Helston TR13 146 B7
3 Plymouth PL7 131 C5
Poughill EX23 4 D2
St Austell PL25 114 E4
St Giles on t H PL15 13 F1
St Mellion PL12 53 C8
Tavistock PL19 41 D8
Tideford PL12 52 F2
Truro TR1 69 F3
Orchard Cotts
Lamerton PL19 30 B3
St Austell PL25 114 F5
Orchard Cres PL9 135 C7
Orchard Ct
Lamerton PL19 30 A3
Penzance TR18 143 C5
Orchard Gr PL25 114 B4
Orchard Ho 11 TR18 143 C2
Orchard La
Helford TR12 93 B1
Plymouth PL7 130 E6
Orchard Pk PL26 47 C2
Orchard Pl 10 TR18 143 C2
Orchard Rd PL2 128 B7
Orchard Terr 20 TR18 143 C2
Orchard The
Gunnislake PL18 41 A6
Lerryn PL22 61 D8
Newquay TR7 111 B7
North Petherwin PL15 18 B8
St Erth TR27 77 E2
Orchardton Terr 2 PL9 135 F5
Orchard Vale TR11 145 C7
Orchard Way 6 TR20 89 E5
Orchard Wlk 13 PL27 108 B5
Ordnance St PL1 127 E2
Ordulf Rd PL19 147 A5
Oregon Way PL3 129 D6
Oreston Prim Sch PL9 135 C7
Oreston Rd PL9 135 C8
Orion Dr PL27 31 F3
Osborne Ct PL1 148 C2
Osborne Parc TR13 146 B7
Osborne Pl PL1 148 C2
Osborne Rd PL3 128 A3
Osborne Villas
10 Falmouth TR11 145 C3
2 Plymouth PL3 128 A3
Osprey Gdns PL9 136 C7
Otterham Com Prim Sch PL32 10 C2
Otterham Pk PL32 16 A8
Ottery Cotts PL19 30 A2
Ottery Park Ind Est PL19 30 A2
Outland Rd PL2 128 C7
Overcliff PL29 22 D8
Overdale Rd PL2 128 A7
Overton Gdns 3 PL3 128 F5
Overtonn Villas PL15 106 C5
Owen Dr PL7 130 C7
Owen Sivell Cl PL14 113 E6
Oxford Ave PL3 128 E5
Oxford Gdns PL3 128 E5
Oxford Pl PL1 148 C3
Oxford St PL1 148 B3
Oxford Terr 4 PL1 148 B3
Oxland Rd TR16 67 E5

P

Paardeburg Rd 2 PL31 48 D8
Packet La TR20 89 F5
Packington St PL2 128 A4
Packsaddle TR10 81 D2
Packsaddle Cl TR10 81 D2
Paddock Cl
Plymouth PL9 135 E5
Saltash PL12 122 D4
Paddock The
Helston TR13 146 C7
Helston TR13 146 C8
Redruth TR15 140 D2
Sticker PL26 58 E1
Paddons Row PL19 147 C6
Padnover Terr 22 TR26 141 B5
Padstow Harbour Ind Est PL28 107 E4
Padstow Mus* PL28 107 D5
Padstow Sch PL28 107 C4
Padstow Workshop Units PL28 107 B4
Page's Cross PL15 106 D4
Paiges Farm PL9 135 C1
Painton Water EX39 3 A8
Palace Rd PL25 114 D4
Palace St PL1 149 A2
Palm Ct TR1 137 D3
Palmers Terr PL34 14 C6
Palmerston St PL1 148 A4
Palmers Way PL27 108 D6

Pannier La TR26 141 C2
Pannier Mkt PL19 147 C5
Panson Cross PL15 13 E3
Parade PL1 149 A2
Parade Bsns Pk 4 PL19 147 B4
Parade Hill TR19 88 D1
Parade Ope PL1 149 A2
Parade Pass 29 TR18 143 E5
Parade Rd PL5 124 A3
Parade Sq PL22 112 D2
Parade St TR18 143 E5
Parade The
Helston TR13 146 C5
Liskeard PL14 113 C6
Lostwithiel PL22 112 D2
Millbrook PL10 132 E5
Milton Abbot PL19 29 C6
Mousehole TR19 88 D1
Truro TR1 137 E4
Paradise Park & The World Parrot Trust* TR27 142 A4
Paradise Pk EX22 7 F1
Paradise Pl PL1 128 A2
Paradise Rd
Boscastle PL35 9 C1
Plymouth PL1 128 A2
Parc-Abnac TR20 88 B2
Parc-An-Bal Ct TR14 138 E4
Parc-An-Bre Dr PL26 58 C8
Parc-an-Cady Est TR19 97 A6
Parc-An-Challow TR10 144 B8
Parc-An-Creet TR26 77 A7
Parc-An-Dillon Rd TR2 83 B2
Parc-An-Dix La TR27 142 C7
Parc-An-Dower TR13 146 C6
Parcandowr TR2 57 E1
Parc-An-Forth 6 TR26 77 A6
Parc An Gate TR19 88 C1
Parc-An-Gwarry 7 TR3 81 F7
Parc-An-Ithan TR12 102 F2
Parc-An-Maen 11 TR13 98 C8
Parc An Manns TR11 93 D3
Parc-An-Peath TR19 97 A6
Parc-An-Stamps 4 TR26 77 A6
Parc An Yorth TR19 86 F8
Parc-Askell Cl TR12 98 E5
Parc Bean Terr TR26 141 A6
Parc Behan Ct TR2 83 F6
Parc Bowen TR13 92 A3
Parc-Bracket St TR14 138 D3
Parc Brawse TR12 102 F2
Parc Briwer TR10 144 D7
Parc Eglos
Helston TR13 146 B6
St Merryn PL28 31 F8
Parc Eglos Sch TR13 146 C6
Parc Enys TR12 99 B4
Parc Erissey Ind Est TR16 68 A3
Parc Fer Cl EX23 4 E1
Parc Godrevy TR7 110 C5
Parc Holland TR13 146 D8
Parc Ledden TR13 146 C6
Parc Letta TR18 143 C7
Parc Mellan TR18 143 D7
Parc Merys TR2 83 B2
Parc Monga Rd TR11 92 F3
Parc Morrep TR20 90 B3
Parc-n-Drea Cvn Pk TR12 99 B4
Parc Owles TR26 141 D2
Parc Peneglos TR11 82 A3
Parc Pennkarn PL33 14 E3
Parc Rowan TR9 57 E8
Parc Shady TR26 77 C1
Parc Stephney TR11 144 C2
Parc Terr 19 TR18 143 C1
Parc Trenance PL28 31 F7
Parc Trethias PL28 31 F7
Parc Vean PL30 34 C1
Parc Venton Cl 2 TR14 138 F2
Parc Villas 17 TR18 143 C1
Parc Wartha Ave TR18 143 D6
Parc Wartha Cres TR18 143 D6
Par Gn PL24 60 C4
Pargolla Rd TR7 110 F6
Park 30 PL15 106 A3
Parka Cl 12 TR9 45 E2
Park-An-Bans TR14 138 E1
Parkancreeg 9 TR3 81 F7
Park An Gonwyn TR26 141 E2
Park An Gorsaf TR14 138 D2
Park An Harvey TR13 146 C6
Park-an-Mengleth TR15 140 D4
Park-An-Pyth TR19 75 A1
Park-An-Tansys TR14 138 F2
Parka Rd
Indian Queens TR9 45 E1
8 St Columb Road TR9 45 E2
Park Ave
Plymouth, Devonport PL1 127 E3
Plymouth, Plymstock PL9 135 D7
St Ives TR26 141 B5
Park Cl
Illogan TR15 139 B8
Nancegollan TR13 91 B7
Plymouth PL7 130 B7
Park Cnr TR18 143 E5
Park Cres
Falmouth TR11 145 A4
Helston TR13 146 B5
Plymouth PL9 135 C7
Ponsanooth TR3 81 B4
Park Ct
Chillaton PL16 29 F8
28 Penzance TR18 143 E5
Park Dr PL31 109 B4
Parkenbutts TR7 111 D7
Parkengear Vean TR2 71 D6
Parkengue TR10 144 A7
Parkenhead La PL28 20 F2
Park Enskellaw 6 TR12 99 A2
Park-en-Vine PL27 32 D6
Parker Cl PL7 130 B5
Parker Rd PL2 128 B6
Parker's Gn PL18 40 F6
Parkesway PL12 122 D2
Park Fenton PL14 113 D5
Parkfield Dr PL6 125 F1
Park Gwyn PL26 58 B4
Park Hill TR11 145 A4
Park Ho PL25 114 B3
Park Holly TR14 138 B3
Parkins Terr 7 TR1 137 D5
Park La
8 Bere Alston PL20 41 B1
Bugle PL26 47 C1
Camborne TR14 138 E2
Falmouth TR11 145 A4
Plymouth PL9 135 C7
Parklands PL26 58 C7
Parklands Cl TR7 111 D6
Park Leder TR16 68 C3
Park Leven TR16 139 C8
Park Lowen TR26 141 C2
Parknoweth TR12 99 A4
Parknoweth Cl TR8 56 B6
Park Pl
Grampound Road TR2 57 E1
Wadebridge PL27 108 B5
Park Place La 12 PL3 128 A4
Park Rd
Camborne TR14 138 E4
Fowey PL23 116 C4
Illogan TR15 139 B7
Lifton PL16 19 F3
Liskeard PL14 113 C6
18 Newlyn TR18 143 C1
Plymouth PL3 129 A6
Ponsanooth TR3 81 B4
Redruth TR15 140 C4
St Austell PL25 114 C3
St Dominick PL12 40 D2
Torpoint PL11 127 B3
Wadebridge PL27 108 B5
Whitemoor PL26 58 E8
Park Rd Hos PL22 112 C2
Park Rise TR11 145 A4
Parkryn Rd 4 TR19 88 C1
Parkside PL2 127 F5
Parkside Com Tech Coll PL1 127 E3
Park St PL3 128 A4
Park Stenak TR16 80 F8
Parkstone La PL7 130 F6
Park Street Ope PL3 128 A4
Park Terr
Falmouth TR11 145 A4
Truro TR1 70 D1
Park The
Penryn TR10 144 B7
Tregony TR2 71 F4
Parkvedras Ho 5 TR1 137 B4
Parkvedras Terr 4 TR1 137 B4
Parkventon PL26 47 C2
Park View
Lifton PL16 19 F4
Liskeard PL14 113 C6
Perranarworthal TR3 81 E6
Plymouth PL4 149 C3
Summercourt TR8 57 B7
Truro TR1 137 C3
Parkview Apartments TR7 110 F5
Park View Cl TR3 82 A7
Park View Rd TR13 146 B5
Park View Terr PL27 108 B5
Park Villas TR3 81 B4
Park Way PL25 114 F5
Parkway Ct PL6 129 E7
Parkway Ind Est The PL6 129 E7
Parkway The PL3, PL5, PL6 124 B1
Park Wise TR10 144 C8
Parkwood Cl PL6 121 B2
Parkwood Ct PL19 147 D6
Parkwood Rd
Tavistock PL19 147 D6
Tavistock PL19 147 E7
Park Wood Rise PL16 19 F4
Parkwoon Cl PL26 46 F3
Par La PL24 60 B4
Par Moor Rd
Par PL24, PL25 60 B3
St Austell PL24, PL25 115 F4
Parnell Cl PL6 129 A8
Parr La PL4 149 B2
Parr St PL4 149 B2
Parsonage Ct PL16 19 F4
Parsons Cl PL9 136 A4
Parsons Gn PL17 39 E6
Par Sta PL24 60 C5
Partwayes PL19 30 A3
Pascoe Cl TR3 69 D4
Pasley St E PL2 127 F4
Pasley St PL2 127 E4
Passage Hill TR11 82 A3
Passage La PL23 116 B5
Passage St PL23 116 D5
Passmore Cl
Blackwater TR4 68 E5
Liskeard PL14 113 D6
Pathfields EX23 104 E5
Pathway Fields The TR27 142 C5
Patna Pl PL1 148 B4
Pato Point PL11 127 A5
Patterdale Cl PL6 125 D3
Patterdale Wlk PL6 125 D3
Pattinson Cl PL6 125 E2
Pattinson Ct PL6 125 E2
Pattinson Dr PL6 125 F2
Paull Rd PL31 109 B4
Paulls Row 4 TR15 140 C5
Paul's Row TR1 137 D5
Paul's Terr TR1 137 D5
Paviland Grange 6 PL1 128 A3
Pavilion Pk TR14 138 F4
Pavlova Cl PL14 113 C5
Pavlova Ct 6 PL14 113 C5
Paynter's Cross PL12 53 E7
Paynter's Cross Cotts PL12 53 E7
Paynters La TR16 67 E4
Paynter's Lane End Est TR16 67 D4
Paynter Wlk 5 PL7 131 B5
Peacock Ave PL11 127 A3
Peacock Cl PL7 130 F7
Peacock La PL4 149 A2
Pearce's La 12 TR26 141 A5
Pearce's Row 3 PL24 60 C4
Pearn Cotts 2 PL3 128 F6
Pearn Gdns PL3 129 A7
Pearn Rd PL3 129 A7
Pearn Ridge PL3 129 A7
Pearson Ave 3 PL4 128 F4
Pearson Rd PL4 128 F4
Pebble Ct TR7 111 C7
Pedlars Cl PL15 18 B8
Pedna Carne Mobile Home Pk TR9 57 E8
Pednandrea TR19 86 E6
Pedn-mên-du TR19 96 A7
Pedn-Moran TR2 95 B6
Pednolva Wlk TR26 141 B5
Pedn-y-ke 1 TR12 99 A1
Peek Moor Cross EX22 13 E4
Peeks Ave PL9 135 F7
Peel St PL1 128 A1
Peguarra Cl PL28 20 E1
Peguarra Ct PL28 20 E1
Pelean Cross TR3 81 B5
Pelham Ct 11 TR11 145 C3
Pellew Cl
7 Falmouth TR11 145 A5
Padstow PL28 107 C5
Pellew Cres TR13 146 C4
Pellew Pl PL2 127 F4
Pellew Rd TR11 145 A5
Pellor Fields TR13 90 F3
Pelynt Prim Sch PL13 62 D6
Pembrey Wlk PL5 123 E4
Pembroke Cl 7 PL24 60 C4
Pembroke La PL1 127 E1
Pembroke Rd TR7 111 E7
Pembroke St
Plymouth PL1 127 E1
Plymouth PL1 127 F1
Pemros Rd PL5 123 C1
Penair Cres TR1 137 F6
Penair Sch TR1 70 D4
Penair View TR1 137 F4
Penally Ct PL35 9 D2
Penally Hill PL35 9 D2
Penally Terr PL35 9 C2
Penalverne Ave TR18 143 D5
Penalverne Cres TR18 143 D5
Penalverne Dr TR18 143 D5
Penalverne Pl TR18 143 D5
Penameyne Ct 5 TR26 141 B6
Pen-An-Gwel TR26 141 A4
Penare Gdns 2 TR18 143 E6
Penare Rd TR18 143 E6
Penare Terr TR18 143 E6
Penarrow Cl TR11 144 E2
Penarrow Rd TR11 145 C8
Penarth PL13 117 B3
Penarth Rd TR11 145 A5
Penarwyn Cres TR18 143 B7
Penarwyn Rd PL24 60 B4
Penarwyn Woods 6 PL24 60 B4
Penbeagle Cl 17 TR26 77 A6
Penbeagle Cres 8 TR26 77 A6
Penbeagle Ind Est TR26 77 A6
Penbeagle La TR26 77 A6
Penbeagle Terr 7 TR26 77 A6
Penbeagle Way TR26 141 A4
Penberthy Cross TR27 89 F7
Penberthy Rd
Helston TR13 146 C5
Portreath TR16 67 D6
Penbothidno TR11 92 F3
Pen Brea Cl TR2 95 B6
Penbrea Rd TR18 143 E7
Penbugle La PL31 109 E7
Pencair Ave PL11 126 E2
Pencalenick Sch TR1 70 E4
Pencantol TR4 81 C7
Pencarn Parc TR16 80 A5
Pencarrick Cl TR1 137 B6
Pencarrow* PL30 34 D6
Pencarrow Cl PL17 39 E3
Pencarrow Rd 18 TR16 67 E4
Pencavo Hill PL12 53 A3
Pencoys Prim Sch TR16 80 A5
Pencreber Rd 3 PL20 42 C4
Pendale Sq TR1 137 B4
Pendarves
St Merryn PL28 31 F7
Tresillian TR2 70 F5
Pendarves Flats TR18 143 D6
Pendarves Rd
Camborne TR14 138 C1
Pendarves Rd *continued*
Falmouth TR11 144 F6
Penzance TR18 143 D6
Truro TR1 137 C6
Pendarves St
Camborne, Beacon TR14 138 F1
Troon TR14 79 E4
Pendarves View TR14 138 C1
Pendean Ave PL14 113 B6
Pendean Cl PL14 113 B6
Pendean Ct PL14 113 B6
Pendean Dr PL14 113 B6
Pendeen Cl
Plymouth PL6 124 F6
Threemilestone TR3 69 D3
Pendeen Cres
Plymouth PL6 125 A6
Threemilestone TR3 69 D3
Pendeen Ho TR1 69 E4
Pendeen Lighthouse Mus* TR19 75 A1
Pendeen Pk TR13 146 C8
Pendeen Pl TR7 110 F6
Pendeen Prim Sch TR19 75 A1
Pendeen Rd
Porthleven TR13 91 B1
Threemilestone TR3 69 D3
Truro TR1 137 E3
Pendennis Castle* TR11 145 E2
Pendennis Cl
Penzance TR18 143 E7
Plymouth PL3 128 F8
Torpoint PL11 126 F3
Pendennis Ct TR11 145 D3
Pendennis Pl TR18 143 F7
Pendennis Rd
Falmouth TR11 145 D3
Looe PL13 117 D5
Penzance TR18 143 E7
Pendennis Rise TR11 145 D3
Pender's La TR15 140 B5
Pendilly Ave PL11 126 F2
Pendilly Dr PL25 114 E7
Pendinnes Gdns PL15 106 B8
Pendour Pk PL22 112 E2
Pendower Ct TR2 83 D5
Pendower Rd
Looe PL13 117 E4
Veryan TR2 83 F6
Pendower Terr TR14 138 E1
Pendragon Cres TR7 111 A4
Pendragon Ho TR11 145 D3
Pendragon Rd PL14 113 D6
Pendra Loweth TR11 144 D1
Pendray Gdns PL14 50 E7
Pendrea Cl TR18 143 F7
Pendrea Pk TR14 138 F5
Pendrea Pl TR18 143 F7
Pendrea Rd TR18 143 F7
Pendrea Wood TR1 69 F3
Pendrim Rd PL13 117 D4
Pendruccombe Ct PL15 106 D5
Pen-Eglos 8 TR2 95 A6
Penforth TR14 138 E2
Pengannel Cl TR7 110 D4
Pengarrock Hill TR12 101 D5
Pengarth 1 TR5 54 D1
Pengarth Cl TR1 137 C2
Pengarth Rd TR11 145 A3
Pengarth Rise TR11 145 A3
Pengegon Moor TR14 138 F2
Pengegon Parc TR14 138 F2
Pengegon Way TR14 138 F2
Pengelly
24 Callington PL17 39 F4
Delabole PL33 14 E2
Pengelly Cl PL11 126 F5
Pengelly Cross
Godolphin Cross TR27 90 F7
Wadebridge PL27 108 C1
Pengelly Hill PL11 127 A5
Pengelly Pk PL11 126 F5
Pengelly Pl TR11 144 E5
Pengellys Row TR14 139 A5
Pengelly Way TR3 69 D3
Pengeron Ave 1 TR14 138 F7
Pengersick Est TR20 90 C3
Pengersick La TR20 90 C3
Pengersick Parc TR20 90 C3
Pengliddon PL27 33 B7
Pengover Cl PL14 113 D6
Pengover Gn PL14 51 E8
Pengover Hts PL14 113 D6
Pengover Parc TR15 140 C6
Pengover Pk PL14 113 D6
Pengover Rd PL14 113 E6
Pengrowyn PL26 59 D6
Pengwarras Rd TR14 138 C3
Pengwel 16 TR18 143 C2
Penhale 1 TR6 55 A5
Penhale Cl PL14 37 F3
Penhale Cotts TR3 82 D6
Penhale Est TR15 140 B6
Penhale Gdns TR9 57 D8
Penhale Mdw PL14 37 F3
Penhale Rd
Barripper TR14 79 A4
Carnhell Green TR14 78 F4
Falmouth TR11 144 F1
Penwithick PL26 59 D7
Penhaligon Cl TR15 140 D4
Penhaligon Ct TR1 137 E5
Penhaligon Way PL25 114 F4
Penhall La TR4 68 C6
Penhallow TR15 139 B8
Penhallow Cl
Mount Hawke TR4 68 C6
Veryan TR2 83 C5
Penhallow Ct TR7 111 C7
Penhallow Parc PL33 14 D2
Penhallow Rd TR7 111 C7
Penhalls Way TR3 82 B8
Penhalt Farm Holiday Pk EX23 6 E3
Penhaven Cl TR8 56 B7
Penhaven Ct TR7 110 E6
Penhellaz Hill TR13 146 B6
Penhellaz Rd TR13 146 B6
Penhole Cl PL15 27 D3
Penina Ave TR7 110 F4
Peninsula Medical Sch PL6 125 C3
Peninsular Pk PL12 122 C4
Penjerrick Gdns* TR11 93 D5
Penjerrick Hill
Budock Water TR11 144 C1
Falmouth TR11 93 E5
Penkenna Cl EX23 10 C6
Penkernick Cl TR18 143 B1
Penkernick Way TR9 45 E6
Penknight La PL22 112 A2
Penlean Cl TR15 140 D7
Penlea Rd TR10 144 B8
Penlee Apartments PL23 116 C3
Penlee Cl
13 Callington PL17 39 F4
Praa Sands TR20 90 C3
Tregony TR2 71 F4
Penlee Cotts PL10 64 C2
Penlee Cvn Site TR19 88 D1
Penlee Gdns PL3 128 A4
Penlee Ho TR1 69 E4
Penlee House Gall & Mus* TR18 143 E5
Penlee Manor Dr TR18 143 E4
Penlee Pk PL11 126 E4
Penlee Pl 4 PL4 128 F4
Penlee Rd PL3 128 A4
Penlee St 11 TR18 143 E6
Penlee View Terr 3 TR18 143 E4
Penlee Villas TR3 82 B8
Penlee Way PL3 128 B4
Penlu TR14 138 F5
Penlu Ho TR14 138 F5
Penluke Cl TR16 80 A5
Penlyne Woodland Trail* PL22 112 E5
Penmare Cl TR27 142 E7
Penmare Ct TR27 142 E7
Penmare Terr TR27 142 E7
Penmayne Parc TR16 140 F1
Penmayne Villas PL27 21 E3
Penmead Rd PL33 14 E2
Penmelen PL32 105 C4
Penmeneth TR13 146 F8
Penmenner Est 7 TR12 101 C4
Penmenner Rd TR12 102 F2
Penmere Cl
Helston TR13 146 B7
Penzance TR18 143 E7
Penmere Cres TR11 144 F3
Penmere Ct 4 TR11 145 A3
Penmere Dr TR7 110 C5
Penmere Hill 7 TR11 145 A3
Penmere Pl
3 Falmouth TR11 145 A3
Penzance TR18 143 E7
Penmere Rd
Penzance TR18 143 E7
St Austell PL25 115 A4
Penmere Sta TR11 144 F3
Penmerrin Ct TR7 110 E5
Penmeva View PL26 73 C3
Penmorvah TR11 82 A2
Penmorvah Pl TR14 138 E2
Penmorvah Rd TR1 137 F6
Pennance Hill TR11 93 F5
Pennance Ho TR11 145 A2
Pennance La TR16 140 F1
Pennance Parc TR16 140 F1
Pennance Rd
Falmouth TR11 145 A2
Lanner TR16 80 E7
Redruth TR16 140 F1
Pennance Terr TR16 140 F1
Penn An Drea TR13 146 D8
Pennant Farm PL29 22 E6
Pennard Villas PL27 33 B5
Pennor Dr PL25 114 D3
Pennoweth Prim Sch TR15 140 C5
Pennycomequick Hill PL1, PL3 148 B4
Pennycross Cl PL2 128 D8
Pennycross Park Rd PL2 128 C7
Pennycross Prim Sch PL2 128 C8
Pennygillam Ind Est PL15 106 A4
Pennygillam Way PL15 18 E2
Pennys La PL24 115 F5
Penny's La PL9 136 D6
Penoweth TR11 82 A2
Penpol Ave TR27 142 C5
Penpol Hill
Crantock TR8 110 B4
Devoran TR3 82 B6
Penpol Rd TR27 142 B5
Penpol Sch TR27 142 C5
Penpol Terr TR27 142 B5
Penpol Vean TR27 142 C5
Penponds Rd TR13 91 A1

Penponds Sch TR14 .... 79 B5
Penpons Cl TR18 .... 143 C4
Penpont Rd TR15 .... 140 D6
Penpont View PL15 .... 26 C7
Pen Porth Ave TR26 .... 77 A7
Penquite Dr PL31 .... 109 F5
Penrice Com Coll PL25 .. 115 A3
Penrice Hospl (Maternity & Gastric) PL26 .... 114 F1
Penrice Parc PL25 .... 115 A3
Penrith Cl PL6 .... 125 D3
Penrith Gdns PL6 .... 125 D3
Penrith Wlk PL6 .... 125 D3
Penrose Ct
Penzance TR18 .... 143 F6
2 South Tehidy TR14 .... 138 F7
Penrose Parc TR13 .... 91 B1
Penrose Rd
Falmouth TR11 .... 145 A4
Helston TR13 .... 146 C6
Penrose St PL1 .... 148 B3
Penrose Terr TR18 .... 143 F6
Penrose Villas 5 PL4 .... 128 F4
Penrose Walks* TR12, TR13 .... 98 D8
Penruan La TR2 .... 95 B6
Penryn Coll TR10 .... 144 B7
Penryn Com Inf Sch TR10 .... 144 B7
Penryn Jun Sch TR10 .... 144 B8
Penryn St TR15 .... 140 B4
Penryn Sta TR10 .... 144 B8
Pensans Prim Sch (Inf) TR18 .... 143 E7
Pensans Prim Sch (Jun) TR18 .... 143 D6
Penscombe Cross PL15 ... 28 C6
Penscott La PL26 .... 114 C1
Pensilva TR6 .... 55 A4
Pensilva Prim Sch PL14 .... 38 E5
Pensilva Rd TR1 .... 137 E6
Pensilva Rural Workshops PL14 .... 38 E4
Penstowe Pk Holiday Village EX23 .... 4 F6
Penstowe Rd EX23 .... 5 A6
Penstrasse Pl 1 PL24 .... 60 D5
Penstraze Bsns Ctr TR4 ... 69 A5
Penstraze La PL26 .... 47 A4
Pensylva PL25 .... 114 E3
Pentalek Rd TR14 .... 138 D1
Pentamar St PL2 .... 127 E4
Pentargon Rd 1 PL35 .... 9 C1
Pentewan Hill PL26 .... 73 D6
Pentewan Rd PL25, PL26 ... 59 C1
Pentidna La TR27 .... 66 B2
Pentillie PL26 .... 73 C4
Pentillie Cres PL4 .... 128 D4
Pentillie Gdns
14 Callington PL17 .... 39 E4
St Austell PL25 .... 114 F6
Pentillie Rd
Bere Alston PL20 .... 41 B1
Plymouth PL4 .... 128 E4
Pentillie Way PL26 .... 73 C4
Pentire Ave TR7 .... 110 A5
Pentire Cres TR7 .... 110 B5
Pentire Ct TR7 .... 110 B6
Pentire Gn TR8 .... 43 D3
Pentire Hts TR7 .... 110 A5
Pentire Rd
Newquay TR7 .... 110 C5
Penryn TR10 .... 144 B8
Torpoint PL11 .... 126 F3
Pentland Cl PL6 .... 124 F7
Pen Tor PL30 .... 35 C8
Pentor Ct PL30 .... 35 C8
Pentour 3 PL24 .... 60 B4
Pentowan Ct TR26 .... 141 E2
Pentowan Rd TR27 .... 142 E8
Pentreath Cl
Fowey PL23 .... 116 B5
Lanner TR16 .... 80 E7
Penzance TR18 .... 143 D7
Pentreath La
Lizard TR12 .... 102 F2
Praa Sands TR20 .... 90 B3
Pentreath Terr TR16 .... 80 E7
Pentre Ct EX23 .... 4 D4
Pentrevah Ct TR7 .... 110 D6
Pentrevah Rd 8 PL26 .... 59 D7
Pen-Tye TR27 .... 78 E3
Pentyre Ct PL4 .... 149 C4
Pentyre Terr PL4 .... 149 C4
Penvale 4 PL14 .... 38 E4
Penvale Cl TR14 .... 79 B5
Penvale Cres TR10 .... 144 B8
Penvale Ct 8 TR11 .... 145 A4
Penvale Dr TR10 .... 144 B8
Penvean Cl TR10 .... 93 C8
Penvean La TR11 .... 144 E5
Penvenen 2 TR6 .... 55 A5
Penventinnie La TR1 .... 69 E4
Penventinue La PL23 .... 116 B7
Penventon Terr
Four Lanes TR16 .... 80 B6
Redruth TR15 .... 140 A4
Penventon View TR13 .... 146 B5
Penview Cres TR13 .... 146 B5
Penvorder Cotts PL30 .... 24 B2
Penvorder La PL30 .... 24 B2
Penware Parc TR14 .... 138 C1
Penwarne Cl TR14 .... 138 F7
Penwarne La PL26 .... 73 C3
Penwarne Rd TR11 .... 93 D5
Penwartha TR12 .... 101 B2
Penwartha Cl
Constantine TR11 .... 92 F3
St Columb Minor TR7 .... 111 D7
Penwartha Ct TR11 .... 92 F3
Penwartha Rd
15 Illogan TR16 .... 67 E4
Perranporth TR6 .... 55 B4
Penwartha Vean 14 TR16 .. 67 E4
Penwerris Ct TR11 .... 145 A6
Penwerris Farm TR11 .... 144 F5
Penwerris La TR11 .... 145 A6
Penwerris Rd TR1 .... 69 F3
Penwerris Rise TR20 .... 90 B3
Penwerris Terr 10 TR11 .. 145 A5
Penwethers La TR1 .... 69 F3
Penwinnick Cl 9 TR5 .... 54 C1
Penwinnick Parc 4 TR5 .. 54 D1
Penwinnick Rd
St Agnes TR5 .... 68 D8
St Austell PL25 .... 114 B3
Penwith Bsns Ctr TR20 .... 88 F6
Penwith Cl TR26 .... 141 A4
Penwith Coll TR18 .... 143 D7
Penwithhick Rd PL26 .... 59 D7
Penwithian Cl TR27 .... 142 E6
Penwithick Pk 6 PL26 .... 59 D7
Penwith Rd TR26 .... 141 A4
Penwith St 12 TR18 .... 143 E6
Penworth Cl PL15 .... 106 C5
Penwyth TR12 .... 92 C1
Pen y Bryn PL27 .... 108 D6
Penzance Rd
Helston TR13 .... 146 A6
St Buryan TR19 .... 97 C7
Pepo La TR2 .... 72 A7
Pepper Cl PL12 .... 40 C2
Pepper La PL9 .... 136 D7
Peppers Ct PL12 .... 40 C2
Peppers Hill Cl PL15 .... 18 F7
Peppers Park Rd PL14 .... 113 E6
Pepper St PL19 .... 147 C6
Pepys Pl PL5 .... 124 E1
Percuil View TR2 .... 95 B6
Percy Davy Cl TR6 .... 55 A5
Percy St PL5 .... 123 D1
Percy Terr PL4 .... 129 A4
Pergolla Ct 9 TR7 .... 110 F6
Perhaver Pk PL26 .... 85 D5
Perhaver Way PL26 .... 85 D5
Periwinkle Dr PL7 .... 131 C5
Per Kithen TR12 .... 102 F2
Permarin Rd TR10 .... 144 C8
Perran-ar-worthal Com Prim Sch TR3 .... 81 D6
Perran Cl TR3 .... 81 F6
Perrancombe Garden Ct TR6 .... 55 A4
Perran Crossroads TR20 ... 89 E5
Perranporth Cl PL5 .... 123 E4
Perranporth Com Prim Sch TR6 .... 55 A4
Perran Sands Holiday Ctr TR6 .... 55 B6
Perran View Holiday Pk TR5 .... 54 E2
Perranwell Rd TR4 .... 55 D4
Perranwell Sta TR3 .... 81 E6
Perranzabuloe Mus* TR6 .55 A5
Perryman Cl PL7 .... 130 E7
Perseverance Cotts 1 PL7 .... 130 E7
Peryn Rd PL19 .... 147 A5
Peter Hopper's Hill PL5 . 120 C2
Peter's Cl PL9 .... 136 C7
Petersfield Cl PL3 .... 129 B6
Peters Hill PL26 .... 58 E4
Peters Park Cl PL5 .... 123 E1
Peter's Park La PL5 .... 123 E1
Peters Row TR19 .... 75 A1
Petes Pl 24 TR26 .... 141 B5
Petherick Creek Holiday Bglws PL27 .... 32 C7
Petherick Rd EX23 .... 104 E7
Pethericks Mill EX23 .... 104 E4
Pethick Cl PL6 .... 124 D6
Pethill Cl PL6 .... 125 F2
Pethybridge Dr PL31 .... 109 B3
Peverell Park Rd PL3 ... 128 D6
Peverell Rd
Penzance TR18 .... 143 E7
7 Porthleven TR13 .... 98 C8
Peverell Terr
Plymouth PL3 .... 128 D5
Porthleven TR13 .... 98 B8
Pew Tor Cl
Tavistock PL19 .... 147 E5
3 Yelverton PL20 .... 42 C3
Phernyssick Rd PL25 .... 114 F6
Philgray Cl TR27 .... 142 E7
Philip Cl PL9 .... 136 A6
Philip Gdns PL9 .... 135 F6
Phillack Hill TR27 .... 142 D7
Phillimore St 3 PL2 .... 127 F4
Phoenix Bsns Pk PL6 .... 125 F4
Phoenix Cl 8 PL20 .... 42 C4
Phoenix St PL1 .... 148 A2
Piala Pl TR27 .... 142 E7
Piazza 14 TR26 .... 141 B6
Piazza The 5 PL31 .... 109 E5
Pickard Way EX23 .... 104 D7
Pickering Villas TR4 .... 69 A3
Picketts Yd TR10 .... 144 D7
Pick Pie Dr PL6 .... 125 E8
Pier La PL10 .... 133 A1
Pier St PL1 .... 148 B1
Pigmeadow La PL14 .... 113 C6
Pike Rd PL3 .... 129 D5
Pikes Hill PL23 .... 116 C4
Pike's Hill TR11 .... 145 B3
Pike St PL14 .... 113 C6
Pilchard Works The* TR18 .... 143 C3
Pilgrim Cl PL2 .... 128 B6
Pilgrim Ct 11 PL20 .... 41 B1
Pilgrim Dr PL20 .... 41 B1
Pilgrim Prim Sch PL1 .... 148 B3
Pilgrims Way TR27 .... 78 C1
Pillars Cl TR8 .... 56 F5
Pillars Rd
Flushing TR11 .... 145 B8
Mylor Bridge TR11 .... 82 A2
Pillar Wlk PL6 .... 124 F7
Pill La PL12 .... 122 E4
Pillmere Dr PL12 .... 122 D4
Pilot Cotts PL28 .... 21 B4
Pinch Hill EX23 .... 7 B7
Pinder Ct PL19 .... 147 B5
Pine Cl TR13 .... 146 D5
Pine Ct
Par PL24 .... 115 F6
Perranarworthal TR3 .... 81 D6
Pine Green Cvn Pk PL14 .. 50 C7
Pine Lodge Gdns* PL25. 115 D4
Pine Rd TR18 .... 143 B4
Pine Trees Camp Site* TR12 .... 99 F5
Pine View
Gunnislake PL18 .... 41 A6
St Dennis PL26 .... 46 D1
Pinewood Cl PL7 .... 130 F6
Pinewood Dr PL6 .... 125 E7
Pinewood Flats PL27 .... 21 D5
Pinkhams Cotts PL12 .... 122 B6
Pink Moors TR16 .... 68 D1
Pin La PL1 .... 149 A2
Pinnacle Quay PL4 .... 149 B2
Pinsla Garden & Nursery* PL30 .... 35 E1
Pinslow Cross PL15 .... 19 C8
Pintail Ave TR27 .... 77 E3
Pipers Cl PL15 .... 18 E2
Piran Hts EX23 .... 104 C2
Pitick Terr TR11 .... 145 B6
Pitland Cnr PL19 .... 30 D4
Pit Mdw TR11 .... 144 E3
Pits La PL10 .... 64 B2
Pityme PL27 .... 21 F3
Pityme Bsns Ctr PL27 .... 21 F3
Pityme Farm Rd PL27 .... 21 F3
Pityme Ind Est PL27 .... 21 F3
Pixon La PL19 .... 147 B4
Pixon Trad Ctr 2 PL19 ... 147 B4
Place de Brest PL1 .... 148 C3
Place Parc TR7 .... 111 D7
Place Rd PL23 .... 116 C4
Place Stables PL23 .... 116 C4
Place View PL23 .... 116 C4
Place View Rd 15 TR2 .... 95 A6
Plaidy La PL13 .... 117 E4
Plaidy Park Rd PL13 .... 117 E4
Plain-An-Gwarry TR15 .... 140 B5
Plaistow Cl PL5 .... 123 E2
Plaistow Cres PL5 .... 123 E2
Plaistow Hill Inf Sch PL5 123 E2
Planet Pk PL33 .... 14 D2
Plantation La TR27 .... 142 B5
Plas Newydd Ave PL31 .... 109 E3
Platt The PL27 .... 108 C5
Playingfield La TR7 .... 110 D5
Pleasant Pl 15 TR18 .... 143 C7
Pleasant Terr TR19 .... 86 E6
Pleasure Hill Cl PL9 .... 135 D8
Plestin Cl PL15 .... 106 C7
Pleyber Christ Way PL22 112 C2
Pleydon Cl PL13 .... 62 E2
Plintona View PL7 .... 130 E7
Plougastel Dr PL12 .... 122 E3
Plough Ct TR10 .... 81 C2
Plough Gn PL12 .... 122 C3
Plumer Rd PL6 .... 124 F2
Plymbridge Gdns PL7 .... 130 C7
Plymbridge La PL6 .... 125 B4
Plymbridge Rd
Plymouth, Eggbuckland PL6 .... 125 C1
Plymouth, Estover PL6 .... 125 E5
Plymouth, Mainstone PL6 .. 125 F2
Plymouth, Plympton PL7 .. 130 C7
Plym Cres PL19 .... 147 D5
Plymouth City Airport PL6 .... 125 C5
Plymouth Coll PL4 .... 128 E4
Plymouth Coll Inf Sch PL3 .... 128 F5
Plymouth Coll of Art & Design PL4 .... 149 A3
Plymouth Coll of Art & Design (Sutton Annexe) PL4 .... 149 A3
Plymouth Coll of F Ed PL1 .... 128 A2
Plymouth Coll of F Ed (Annexe) PL1 .... 148 C4
Plymouth Coll Prep Sch PL3 .... 128 E6
Plymouth Discovery Ctr* PL3 .... 129 F6
Plymouth Dome Discovery Ctr* PL1 .... 148 C1
Plymouth High Sch for Girls PL4 .... 149 A4
Plymouth Medical & Tech Pk PL6 .... 125 A3
Plymouth Nuffield Hospl The PL6 .... 125 B4
Plymouth Pavilions PL1 .. 148 B2
Plymouth Rd
Liskeard PL14 .... 113 D5
Plymouth PL7 .... 130 B6
Tavistock PL19 .... 147 B4
Plymouth Road Ind Est PL19 .... 147 C3
Plymouth Ski Ctr* PL6 .. 129 E7
Plymouth Sound Camping Site PL9 .... 135 C1
Plymouth Sta PL4 .... 148 C4
Plymouth Trade Pk PL4 . 149 C1
Plympton Hill PL7 .... 130 F3
Plympton Hospl PL7 .... 130 D5
Plympton St Mary CE Inf Sch PL7 .... 130 D5
Plympton St Maurice Prim Sch PL7 .... 130 F3
Plym St PL4 .... 149 A3
Plymstock Rd PL9 .... 135 D7
Plymstock Sch PL9 .... 135 F8
Plymtree Dr PL7 .... 130 C7
Plym Valley Rly* PL7 ... 130 A7
Plym View Prim Sch PL3 .... 129 D6
Poad's Trust PL14 .... 51 F5
Pochin Ho PL25 .... 114 F7
Pocklington Rise PL7 .... 130 E5
Pocohontas Cres 4 TR9 ... 45 E1
Pode Dr PL7 .... 131 B4
Point Curlew Country Holiday Est PL28 .... 31 F6
Point Neptune PL23 .... 116 B3
Point Rd TR3 .... 82 A6
Polapit Tamar PL15 .... 19 A8
Polbathic Rd TR15 .... 140 C6
Polbreen Ave TR5 .... 54 C1
Polbreen La TR5 .... 54 C1
Poldark Gdns 7 PL24 .... 60 B4
Poldark Mine Heritage Complex* TR13 .... 92 A6
Poldark Rd 12 TR16 .... 67 E4
Poldhu Cl TR26 .... 141 D1
Poldhu Rd
Liskeard PL14 .... 113 D6
Mullion TR12 .... 99 A2
Poldice La TR16 .... 68 E1
Poldice Terr TR16 .... 68 E1
Poldrea PL24 .... 60 D5
Poldrissick Hill PL12 .... 53 C2
Poldrissick La PL12 .... 53 C2
Poldue Cl TR15 .... 140 D6
Polean La PL13 .... 117 B4
Polean Trad Est PL13 .... 117 B4
Polecoverack La TR12 .... 101 C1
Polgarth
1 Camborne TR15 .... 139 C6
Newlyn TR18 .... 143 B3
Polgarth Cl TR26 .... 141 D1
Polgaver Ho PL25 .... 115 E3
Polgine Cl TR14 .... 79 E5
Polgine La TR14 .... 79 E5
Polglase Wlk TR4 .... 70 D8
Polglaze Cl TR18 .... 143 D7
Polglist PL26 .... 58 D5
Polgoon Cl TR18 .... 143 C5
Polgooth Cl TR15 .... 140 D6
Polgover Way 5 PL24 .... 60 B4
Polgrain Rd TR14 .... 138 F6
Polgrean Pl PL24 .... 60 B5
Polhigey Terr TR16 .... 80 C2
Polhorman La TR12 .... 99 A2
Police Ho TR11 .... 145 B4
Polisken Way TR4 .... 56 D1
Polkerris Pk PL24 .... 60 C4
Polkerris Rd TR16 .... 80 F8
Polkirt Hill
Gorran Haven PL26 .... 73 B1
Mevagissey PL26 .... 73 C3
Polkirt Hts PL26 .... 73 C3
Polkyth Par PL25 .... 114 E4
Polkyth Rd PL25 .... 114 F4
Pollard Cl
Plymouth PL9 .... 135 B5
Saltash PL12 .... 122 B2
Pollard Rd 7 PL17 .... 39 F4
Pollards Cl
Goonhavern TR4 .... 55 D4
Pensilva PL14 .... 38 E4
Pollards Way PL12 .... 122 E3
Polmark Dr PL28 .... 20 D2
Polmarth Cl PL25 .... 114 F6
Polmassick Vineyard* PL26 .... 72 E4
Polmear Ct 9 PL27 .... 108 B5
Polmear Hill PL24 .... 60 E4
Polmear Parc PL24 .... 60 D4
Polmear Rd
St Austell PL25 .... 114 F3
Tywardreath PL24 .... 60 D4
Polmeere Ho TR18 .... 143 E7
Polmeere Rd TR18 .... 143 E7
Polmena La PL22 .... 112 E1
Polmennor Dr TR26 .... 141 D1
Polmennor Rd
Falmouth TR11 .... 144 F1
Heamoor TR18 .... 143 C8
Polmenor Downs N TR14, TR27 .... 78 F5
Polmenor Downs S TR14 .. 78 F4
Polmeor Cl TR26 .... 141 D1
Polmewan Flats PL26 .... 59 A1
Polmorla Mews 10 PL27 ... 108 B5
Polmorla Rd PL27 .... 108 B5
Polmorla Wlk PL27 .... 108 C5
Polmor Rd TR20 .... 89 B8
Polpeor Row TR27 .... 77 A3
Polperro Heritage Mus* PL13 .... 62 E2
Polperro Model Village* PL13 .... 62 D1
Polperro Prim Sch PL13 ... 62 E2
Polperro Rd PL13 .... 117 B4
Polpey La PL24 .... 60 D5
Polruan Cl TR26 .... 77 C4
Polruan Com Prim Sch PL23 .... 116 D2
Polruan Ct TR1 .... 137 E2
Polruan Rd
Redruth TR15 .... 140 D6
Truro TR1 .... 137 E2
Polruan Terr PL1 .... 148 A3
Polscoe Rd PL22 .... 112 F3
Polsethow TR10 .... 144 B7
Polstain Cres TR3 .... 69 D3
Polstain Rd TR3 .... 69 D3
Polstain Villas TR3 .... 69 D3
Polsue Way TR2 .... 70 F5
Poltair Ave PL25 .... 114 E4
Poltair Cl TR18 .... 143 C7
Poltair Cres PL25 .... 114 D4
Poltair Ct PL25 .... 114 E4
Poltair Dr TR10 .... 144 B7
Poltair Hospl TR20 .... 143 B8
Poltair Rd
Penryn TR10 .... 144 B7
St Austell PL25 .... 114 D4
Poltair Sch PL25 .... 114 D4
Poltair Terr 7 TR18 .... 143 C7
Poltamar PL15 .... 106 D5
Poltesco La TR12 .... 103 B5
Poltisco Cl TR1 .... 137 E3
Poltisco Wharf TR1 .... 137 E4
Poltisko Rd TR10 .... 144 B7
Poltisko Terr TR10 .... 144 B7
Poltreen Cl TR26 .... 141 D1
Polurrian Rd TR12 .... 99 A1
Polvarth Est TR2 .... 95 B6
Polvarth Rd TR2 .... 95 A6
Polvean Cross PL14 .... 51 A1
Polvean Terr PL14 .... 51 A1
Polvella Cl TR7 .... 110 B5
Polvellan Manor PL13 ... 117 C4
Polvellan Terr PL13 .... 117 C4
Polvelyn Parc TR27 .... 142 E7
Polventon Cl
Falmouth TR11 .... 144 E4
Heamoor TR18 .... 143 C7
Polventon Parc 6 TR12 . 101 C4
Polvillion Rd PL23 .... 116 B4
Polweath Cl TR18 .... 143 E7
Polweath Rd TR18 .... 143 E7
Polwhaveral Terr 6 TR11 .... 145 A5
Polwheal Rd TR14 .... 138 F6
Polwhele House Sch TR4 .. 70 C6
Polwhele Rd
Newquay TR7 .... 111 A3
Truro TR1 .... 137 F6
Polwithen Ct TR26 .... 141 C2
Polwithen Dr TR26 .... 141 C1
Polwithen Gdns TR26 .... 141 C1
Polwithen Rd
Falmouth TR11 .... 145 A4
Penryn TR10 .... 144 B7
Penzance TR18 .... 143 D5
Polwrath Terr PL14 .... 38 A3
Polwyn Cl TR18 .... 143 B7
Polyear Cl PL26 .... 59 A1
Polyne Cotts PL13 .... 62 F3
Polzeath Ct PL27 .... 21 D6
Polzeath Gdns PL2 .... 128 D8
Pomphlett Cl PL9 .... 135 D8
Pomphlett Farm Ind Est PL9 .... 129 E1
Pomphlett Gdns PL9 .... 135 D8
Pomphlett Prim Sch PL9 135 E8
Pomphlett Rd PL9 .... 135 E8
Ponchin Dr PL25 .... 114 E7
Pondbridge Hill 1 PL14 113 C5
Pondfield Rd PL12 .... 122 B3
Pondhu Cres PL25 .... 114 B3
Pondhu Prim Sch PL25 ... 114 B2
Pondhu Rd PL25 .... 114 C3
Pond La TR15 .... 140 A6
Pond Lanes End TR15 .... 140 B6
Ponds Hill TR19 .... 75 B1
Pond View Terr PL26 .... 58 D5
Pond Wlk TR27 .... 142 D7
Poniou La TR20 .... 88 F6
Poniou Rd TR20 .... 88 F6
Poniou Way TR20 .... 88 F6
Ponsandane Farm Mews TR18 .... 143 F7
Ponsharden Cotts TR11 .. 144 F6
Ponsharden Ind Est TR11 .... 144 E6
Ponsmere Ct 9 TR6 .... 55 A5
Ponsmere Rd TR6 .... 55 A5
Ponsonby Rd PL3 .... 128 B4
Ponstantual Hill TR12 .... 99 D7
Ponsvale TR3 .... 81 B4
Pontsmill Rd PL24 .... 60 C6
Pool Bsns & Enterprise Coll TR15 .... 139 B6
Poole Park Rd PL5 .... 127 C8
Pool Hall PL14 .... 51 F5
Pool Ind Est TR15 .... 139 C5
Pool's Ct TR27 .... 142 D6
Pool St PL31 .... 109 E5
Poplar Cl PL7 .... 131 B5
Poplars Ct 16 TR6 .... 55 A5
Poplar Terr TR11 .... 145 B7
Popplestone Pk PL8 .... 136 F5
Porcupine Rd PL24 .... 60 C6

Pordenack Cl TR26 141 E2
Porfell Animal Land* PL14 50 A2
Porhan Gn TR11 144 E6
Pork St TR12 100 D6
Porsham Cl PL6 121 B1
Porsham La PL5 124 E8
Porspoder Pl PL10 133 A2
Portbigham PL13 117 C3
Portbyhan Rd PL13 117 C3
Porteath Bee Ctr* PL27 22 A6
Porteous Cl PL1 127 F3
Porter Way PL12 122 C3
Porth Beach Rd TR7 111 B8
Porth Bean Ct TR7 111 C7
Porth Bean Rd TR7 111 C7
Porthcollum La TR27 78 A1
Porthcurno Telegraph Mus* TR19 96 E3
Portheast Cl PL26 85 C5
Portheast Way PL26 85 C5
Porthellow Vineyard* TR12 101 D5
Portherras Cross TR19 75 A1
Portherras Terr TR19 75 A1
Portherras Villas TR19 75 A1
Porthgwidden TR3 82 C4
Porthgwidden Studios TR26 141 C6
Porthia Cl TR26 141 A4
Porthia Cres TR26 141 A4
Porthia Rd 12 TR26 77 A6
Porthilly Cvn Site PL27 21 D2
Porthilly La PL27 21 D2
Porthilly View PL28 107 E4
Porthkerris Water Sports Ctr* TR12 101 E5
Porthleven Rd TR13 146 A5
Porthleven Sch TR13 91 B1
Porthmellon Gdns PL17 39 F4
Porthmeor Ct 51 TR26 141 B6
Porthmeor Hill TR26 141 A6
Porthmeor Rd
St Austell PL25 115 B3
6 St Ives TR26 141 B6
Porthmeor Sq 21 TR26 141 B6
Porthmeor Studios 50 TR26 141 B6
Porthminster Terr 23 TR26 141 B5
Porth Par TR7 111 C8
Porthpean Beach Rd PL26 59 E1
Porthpean Rd PL25, PL26 114 F2
Porthrepta Rd TR26 141 E1
Porth Sawle Flats TR2 83 B2
Porth View TR2 95 B6
Porth Way TR7 111 B7
Port Isaac Com Prim Sch PL29 22 E7
Port La PL15 27 B2
Portland Cl PL14 113 D7
Portland Ct 9 PL1 127 F3
Portland Gdns TR11 144 F4
Portland Pl 23 TR19 88 C1
Portland Rd PL1 127 F3
Portland Sq PL4 148 C4
Portland Terr PL14 113 C7
Portland Villas PL4 148 C4
Portmellon Pk PL26 73 C3
Portreath Com Prim Sch TR16 67 D6
Portuan Rd PL13 117 D1
Portway Cl PL9 136 D7
Posses La TR18 88 E6
Possession La PL12 53 C3
Post Box Row TR14 139 B3
Post Office Row PL26 58 D7
Potters La PL35 9 C1
Potters Way PL7 130 D5
Pottery Est PL10 132 E6
Pottery Rd PL1 127 D3
Poughill Rd EX23 104 F7
Poultney Cl PL7 131 A5
Pounda PL14 51 B4
Pound Dean PL14 113 A5
Poundfield Cl 2 EX23 4 D1
Poundfield Hill 1 EX23 4 D1
Poundfield La EX23 4 D1
Pound Hill PL12 53 C3
Pound La
Bodmin PL31 109 E5
Stoke Climsland PL17 28 E1
Threemilestone TR3 69 E1
Pound Pk PL14 51 F5
Pound Rd PL20 42 B3
Pound's Cross PL6 120 E5
Pounds Park Rd
1 Bere Alston PL20 41 B1
Plymouth PL3 128 D7
Pounds Pk PL12 122 F3
Pound St
Liskeard PL14 113 C6
Plymouth PL1 134 A8
Poundstock Cl PL30 35 F3
Powderham Rd PL3 128 F7
Powis Gdns PL5 124 B2
Powisland Dr PL6 125 A5
Praa Sands Holiday Village TR20 90 B3
Praed Pl TR26 77 E4
Praed's La TR17 89 C5
Pras Coth TR16 68 C3
Praze-An-Creet TR26 77 A7
Praze-An-Cronor TR9 45 E5
Prazegooth La TR12 103 A4
Praze Mdw TR10 144 C8
Praze Rd
Leedstown TR27 78 E1
Praze Rd *continued*
Newquay TR7 111 B7
Porthleven TR13 91 B1
Praze-an-Beeble TR14 79 A2
Praze The TR10 144 C8
Predannack Rd 4 TR12 99 A1
Preeze Cross PL30 35 E6
Prestonbury Cl PL6 125 B7
Prevenna Rd 2 TR19 88 C1
Prideaux Cl PL12 122 C5
Prideaux Place* PL28 107 C6
Prideaux Rd PL24 60 B6
Pridham La PL2 128 D7
Pridmouth Rd PL25 114 E6
Priestacott Pk EX23 5 A6
Priesthood Terr PL10 132 E5
Priestley Ave PL5 123 E2
Primitive Row TR14 139 A5
Primrose Cl
Camborne TR14 138 B4
9 Goldsithney TR20 89 E5
Roche PL26 47 A3
Torpoint PL11 126 E4
Primrose Cotts TR2 71 C6
Primrose Ct TR26 141 B4
Primrose Dr PL28 31 F7
Primrose Gdns
Illogan TR16 67 D4
Tavistock PL19 147 E4
Primrose Hill TR20 89 E5
Primrose La 4 TR20 89 E5
Primrose Rd EX23 104 F5
Primrose Terr
Newlyn TR18 143 D1
Portreath TR16 67 D6
Tresillian TR2 70 F5
Primrose Valley TR26 141 C4
Primrose Way PL15 27 A6
Primrose Wlk PL12 122 D4
Prince Charles Cl PL15 106 C7
Prince Charles Ho PL25 114 E5
Prince Charles Pk PL25 114 E5
Prince Charles Rd PL25 114 E5
Prince Maurice Ct PL4 149 B3
Prince Maurice Rd PL4 128 F4
Prince of Wales Quarry Trail* PL34 14 E5
Prince Philip Rd PL15 106 C7
Prince Rock Prim Sch PL4 129 B2
Princes Rd PL6 125 E6
Princes Rd PL14 38 B6
Princess Ave
Plymouth, Plymstock PL9 135 E6
Plymouth, West Park PL5 124 A3
Princess Cres PL9 135 E6
Princess Ct 12 TR18 143 E5
Princess Parc TR9 45 E1
Princes Sq PL13 117 C3
Princess Rd PL14 38 E4
Princess St
Plymouth PL1 148 C2
St Just TR19 86 E6
Princess Street Ope PL1 148 C2
Princes St
Bude EX23 104 D6
Looe PL13 117 C3
Penzance TR18 143 E5
Plymouth PL1 127 E2
Prince's St TR1 137 D4
Princess Terr 8 PL14 38 E4
Princess Villas PL17 28 B1
Princess Way PL1 148 C2
Prior's Barn PL31 109 F4
Priors Cl 10 TR26 77 A6
Priors Row TR13 90 E3
Priory Cl
Par PL24 60 C5
Tavistock PL19 147 D3
Priory Cotts PL15 106 B6
Priory Dr PL7 130 D5
Priory Gdns PL19 147 D3
Priory La PL15 106 B7
Priory Lawn Terr PL3 129 A6
Priory Mill PL7 130 D5
Priory Park Rd PL15 106 B6
Priory Rd
Bodmin PL31 109 F4
Plymouth PL3 129 A6
St Austell PL25 114 C4
St Columb Minor TR7, TR8 111 E7
Priory Ridge PL7 130 D5
Prislow Cl TR11 144 E2
Prislow Fields TR11 144 E2
Prislow La TR11 144 E2
Probus Com Prim Sch TR2 71 C6
Probus Gdns* TR2 71 D6
Promenade The PL1 148 C1
Prospect Bldgs TR7 110 E6
Prospect Cl TR27 142 D6
Prospect Gdns TR1 137 E6
Prospect La PL12 122 C3
Prospect Pl
Ashton TR13 90 E3
3 Falmouth TR11 145 B5
Hayle TR27 142 D6
Helston TR13 146 C5
Mevagissey PL26 73 C4
26 Penzance TR18 143 E6
Plymouth PL1 148 B2
8 Porthleven TR13 98 B8
5 Truro TR1 137 D5
Prospect Row
Ashton TR13 90 E3
Plymouth PL1 127 E1
Prospect St PL4 149 A3
Prospect Terr
Bodmin PL31 109 E4
Gunnislake PL18 41 A6
Gunnislake, St Ann's Chapel PL18 40 E5
Mevagissey PL26 73 C4
Prospect Wlk PL12 122 C3
Prosper Cl PL26 47 A2
Prosper Hill TR27 66 B1
Prosper Rd PL26 47 A2
Prouse Cres PL2 128 C8
Prouse Rise PL12 122 E2
Prouts Ct 4 PL15 106 C6
Prout's La TR27 78 D6
Prouts Mews 5 PL15 106 C6
Prouts Way PL15 18 C2
Providence Pl
Calstock PL18 41 A3
Plymouth PL1 128 A3
Providence St PL4 149 A4
Provis Rd TR18 143 C4
Prynne Cl PL1 148 B3
Puckator La PL14 38 A2
Puggis Hill TR14 138 A5
Pulla Cross TR4 81 B6
Putnam Cl PL14 113 D5
Pydar Cl TR7 111 B5
Pydar Mews 8 TR1 137 C4
Pydar St TR1 137 C5
Pym St
Plymouth PL1 127 F3
Tavistock PL19 147 C6
Pyramid Cl PL25 58 F4
Pyworthy CE Prim Sch EX22 8 E5

Q

Quakers Rd TR4, TR3 81 B6
Quant Pk PL19 147 C6
Quarry Cl EX23 104 E7
Quarry Cnr PL20 41 C2
Quarry Cotts
Plymouth, Honicknowle PL5 124 B2
Plymouth PL1 148 A3
Quarry Cres PL15 106 A3
Quarry Ct TR11 145 B4
Quarryfield Camping Site TR8 110 A4
Quarry Gdns TR18 143 D5
Quarry Hill
Falmouth TR11 145 B4
Gulval TR18 88 E7
Quarry House Flats TR1 137 E3
Quarry La
Gunnislake PL18 40 F6
Landrake PL12 53 D3
Launceston PL15 18 E2
Sheffield TR19 97 F7
St Germans PL12 65 A8
Quarrymans Cotts PL27 33 B7
Quarry Park Ave PL9 135 D7
Quarry Park Rd
Newquay TR7 110 F5
Plymouth, Peverell PL3 128 D5
Plymouth, Plymstock PL9 135 D7
Quarry Park Terr PL31 109 C4
Quarry Rd
Pensilva PL14 38 E4
Perranporth TR6 55 B4
Quarry St
St Germans PL12 65 A8
Torpoint PL11 127 C3
Quarterdeck The PL1 134 A8
Quay Hill
Falmouth TR11 145 C4
Penryn TR10 144 D7
Quay La PL12 53 D1
Quay Mews 8 TR1 137 D4
Quay Rd
Crumplehorn PL13 62 D1
Devoran TR3 81 F6
Landrake PL12 53 A2
Looe PL13 117 C3
Mylor Bridge TR11 82 B4
Plymouth PL1 149 A2
St Agnes TR5 54 D2
St Austell PL25 115 B2
St Germans PL12 65 B8
Tideford PL12 52 F2
Quayside 6 PL19 147 B5
Quay St
Falmouth TR11 145 C4
Looe PL13 117 C3
Lostwithiel PL22 112 C2
11 Mousehole TR19 88 C1
Penzance TR18 143 F4
St Ives TR26 141 C6
Truro TR1 137 D4
Quay The
Pentewan PL26 73 C6
Penzance TR18 143 F5
Plymouth PL9 135 C7
Polruan PL23 116 D3
Portscatho TR2 83 B2
St Germans PL12 65 B8
St Mawes TR2 95 A6
Queen Anne Gdns TR11 144 E3
Queen Anne's Quay PL4 149 B2
Queen Elizabeth Rd PL15 106 C7
Queen Mary Ct TR11 145 B2
Queen Mary Rd TR11 145 B2
Queens Cl
5 Indian Queens TR9 45 E1
Plymouth PL6 125 E6
Queen's Cres PL31 109 B3
Queen's Ct 6 TR18 143 E4
Queen's Gate
Plymouth, Lipson PL4 149 B4
Plymouth, Stoke PL3 148 A4
Queen's Gate Mews PL4 149 B4
Queen's Gate Villas PL4 149 B4
Queen's Gate Villas Rd PL4 149 B4
Queens Pk PL27 108 C4
Queens Rd
Plymouth PL5 123 F3
St Austell PL25 114 E3
Queen's Rd PL4 149 B4
Queen's Sq 24 TR18 143 E5
Queen St
Bude EX23 104 D6
Goldsithney TR20 89 E5
Lostwithiel PL22 112 C2
Penzance TR18 143 E5
Plymouth PL1 127 D2
St Just TR19 86 E6
Queen's Way
2 Goldsithney TR20 89 E5
Hayle TR27 142 C5
Queen Terr PL17 40 C4
Quenchwell Rd TR3 81 F7
Quethiock Prim Sch PL14 52 C7
Quillet Rd TR18 143 B3
Quilver Cl PL26 85 D5
Quimperle Way PL14 113 E6
Quintrell Cl TR8 44 E3
Quintrell Downs Sta TR8 111 F3
Quintrell Gdns TR8 44 E3
Quintrell Rd TR7, TR8 111 E5

R

Rabys Row TR16 140 F8
Race Hill
Launceston PL15 106 C5
Truro TR4 81 C8
Race Hill Terr PL15 106 C5
Rachel's Way 17 TR9 45 E6
Radcliffe Cl PL6 124 E6
Radford Ave PL4 129 B1
Radford La PL10 132 D4
Radford Park Dr PL9 135 D6
Radford Park Rd PL9 135 D6
Radford Rd PL1 148 B1
Radford View PL9 135 D6
Radiant Ho PL1 148 B2
Radland Cross PL12 40 C3
Radnor Cl PL31 109 F4
Radnor Hall PL4 149 A3
Radnor Pl PL4 149 A3
Radnor Rd
Redruth, North Country TR16 140 C8
Redruth, Scorrier TR16 68 D3
Radnor St PL4 149 A3
Raginnis Hill 25 TR19 88 C1
Raglan Ct PL1 127 F2
Raglan Gdns PL1 127 F2
Raglan Rd PL1 127 F2
Railway Cotts
Camborne TR14 139 A3
Falmouth TR11 145 D3
6 Plymouth, Ford PL2 127 F5
Plymouth, Plymstock PL9 135 D7
Tavistock PL19 147 B6
Railway Cres PL14 38 A4
Railway Terr
Bodmin PL31 109 D5
Carharrack TR16 80 F8
Railway Villas TR15 139 F6
Rainham Cl TR15 139 C8
Rainyfields PL28 107 D5
Rainy Fields Cl PL28 107 D5
Raleigh Cl PL28 107 C4
Raleigh Ct PL7 131 B6
Raleigh Pl 13 TR11 145 A4
Raleigh Rd PL28 107 C5
Raleigh St PL1 148 B3
Ralph's Ct PL19 147 B5
Ramage Cl PL6 125 F3
Rame Croft TR10 80 E1
Ramehead Cotts PL10 64 B1
Ramehead La PL10 64 B1
Rame La
Cawsand PL10 132 F1
Rame PL10 64 B2
Rame Terr TR10 80 E1
Rame View PL13 117 E5
Ramillies Ave PL5 124 A4
Ramoth Way TR6 55 B5
Ramsey Gdns PL5 124 D1
Ranch View PL15 106 A5
Randwick Park Rd PL9 135 D7
Ranelagh Ct TR7 111 C7
Ranelagh Mews PL31 109 D5
Ranelagh Rd PL25 114 F4
Ransum Way PL19 147 B4
Raphael Cl PL9 136 B5
Raphael Dr PL9 136 A6
Raphael Rd PL13 62 C1
Rapson Rd PL14 113 D6
Rashleigh Ave
Plymouth PL7 130 F7
Saltash PL12 122 D1
Rashleigh Ct PL25 115 C3
Rashleigh La PL23 116 A4
Rashleigh Mews PL25 115 A3
Rashleigh Pl PL25 114 F4
Rashleigh Vale TR1 137 E4
Ratcliffes La TR13 146 A5
Rattle St PL26 85 D5
Rawley Ct TR7 110 E5
Rawley La TR7 110 E5
Rawlin Cl PL6 129 C8
Rawlings La PL23 116 D5
Raymond Rd TR15 140 C4
Raymond Way PL7 130 D6
Raynham Rd PL3 128 B4
Read Cl TR10 144 B7
Reading Wlk PL5 124 C4
Readymoney Rd PL23 116 B3
Reawla La TR27 78 E3
Rebecca Cl PL24 60 B6
Recreation Rd PL2 128 C7
Recreation Road Ind Est PL2 128 C7
Rectory Gdns
Camborne TR14 138 C2
Lanreath PL13 62 B8
St Stephen PL26 58 B4
Rectory Rd
Camborne TR14 138 C2
Lanivet PL30 47 F6
Plymouth PL1 128 A2
St Buryan TR19 97 B6
St Dennis PL26 46 B1
St Stephen PL26 58 B4
Rectory The TR1 137 C5
Redannack 2 TR12 99 A2
Redannack N 1 TR12 99 A2
Redannick Cres TR1 137 B3
Redannick La TR1 137 B4
Redbrooke Rd TR14 138 E2
Redbrooke Terr TR14 138 E2
Reddicliff Cl PL9 135 E5
Reddicliff Rd PL9 135 D5
Reddington Rd PL3 129 B7
Redfern Ct 2 TR26 141 B5
Redhill Cl PL5 123 E4
Redinnick Gdns 4 TR18 143 E4
Redinnick Pl TR18 143 D4
Redinnick Terr 1 TR18 143 E4
Red La
Bugle PL26 47 C2
Rosudgeon TR20 89 F5
Redmoor Cl
Kelly Bray PL17 39 E6
Tavistock PL19 147 A7
Redmoor Rd PL17 39 E6
Redruth Cl PL5 124 A5
Redruth Highway TR15 140 E7
Redruth Rd TR13 146 D7
Redruth Sch TR15 140 A4
Redruth Sta TR15 140 C5
Redruth Tech Coll TR15 140 A5
Redvale Rd PL30 23 E3
Redvers Gr PL7 130 E4
Redvers Hts TR15 140 B3
Redwing Dr PL6 125 D8
Redwood Cl EX23 104 E5
Redwood Dr PL7 131 B5
Redwood Gr EX23 104 E5
Reeds Pk PL22 112 D2
Reeds Way TR7 110 D5
Reen Hill TR6 55 B4
Reen La TR6 55 B5
Reens Cres TR18 143 D7
Reens Rd TR18 143 C7
Reeves Cl TR13 91 B1
Regal Ct PL12 122 F2
Regan Ct TR10 144 A7
Regency Ho PL25 115 E3
Regent Bldgs 36 TR18 143 E5
Regent Ct PL4 149 A3
Regent Sq 21 TR18 143 E5
Regent St PL4 149 A3
Regent Terr
Penzance TR18 143 E4
St Just TR19 86 E6
Reigate Rd PL9 135 E8
Relistian La TR27 78 E3
Relistian Pk TR27 78 E3
Relubbus Hill TR20 90 A6
Relubbus La TR20 90 A6
Rendlesham Gdns PL6 125 E3
Rendle St
Delabole PL33 14 E3
Plymouth PL1 148 B3
Renney Rd PL9 135 C1
Rennie Ave PL5 123 C1
Renoir Cl PL9 136 A6
Renown St PL2 127 E6
Reperry Cross PL30 47 E6
Reppersfield Row TR13 90 F3
Rescorla Ct TR27 142 C5
Research Way PL6 125 C4
Reservoir Cres PL9 136 B7
Reservoir La 1 PL3 128 F6
Reservoir Rd
Plymouth, Hartley PL3 128 F6
Plymouth, Plymstock PL9 136 B7
Reservoir Way PL9 136 B7
Reskadinnick Rd TR14 138 B4
Resolution Ho PL4 149 B3
Respryn Cl PL14 113 D6
Respryn Rd PL31 48 D8
Restormel Castle* PL22 112 C5
Restormel Ind Est PL22 112 D2
Restormel Rd
Looe PL13 117 D4
Lostwithiel PL22 112 C4
Newlyn TR18 143 C3
Plymouth PL4 148 C4
Restormel Terr
Falmouth TR11 145 B3
Plymouth PL4 148 C4

Restronguet Hill TR11 82 B4
Resugga Green Residential Homes Pk PL26 59 D7
Reswythen Wlk 4 TR14 138 F7
Retallack Gdns 3 TR20 89 E5
Retallick Mdws PL25 115 B5
Retanna Cvn Pk TR13 92 D7
Retanning La PL26 58 E1
Retreat The
8 Chacewater TR4 69 A3
Plymouth PL3 129 B7
St Columb Major TR9 45 E6
Revell Park Rd PL7 130 D6
Revel Rd PL3 129 A6
Reynolds Gr PL5 127 C8
Reynolds Rd PL7 130 C6
Rheola Gdns PL6 125 D3
Rhind St PL31 109 E5
Rhodes Cl PL7 130 E7
Rhubarb Hill TR8 43 B1
Rhude Cross EX23 5 B3
Rialton Hts TR7 111 E7
Rialton Rd TR7, TR8 111 E6
Ribble Gdns PL3 129 D7
Rice La PL26 85 C5
Richard Lander Sch TR1 69 F3
Richards Cres TR1 69 F3
Richards La TR16 67 E4
Richards Row PL3 128 F7
Richards Terr PL10 132 E5
Richmond Hill TR1 137 B4
Richmond Pl
40 St Ives TR26 141 B6
3 Truro TR1 137 B4
Richmond Rd
Pelynt PL13 62 D6
Plymouth PL6 125 A2
Richmond St
Heamoor TR18 143 C7
Penzance TR18 143 E6
Richmond Terr
Buckland Monachorum PL20 41 F3
Truro TR1 137 B4
Richmond Way TR26 141 D1
Richmond Wlk PL1 127 F1
Ricketts Rd PL26 59 A1
Rick Mdw PL15 18 E6
Ride The PL7, PL9 129 D2
Ridge Cross PL9 136 A3
Ridgegrove Hill PL15 106 D6
Ridgegrove La PL15 106 C7
Ridge Ho PL4 129 A4
Ridgeo Mill TR18 143 F8
Ridge Park Ave PL4 128 D4
Ridge Park Rd PL7 130 F5
Ridge Pk PL7 130 E5
Ridge Rd PL7 130 E3
Ridgevale Cl TR18 143 F8
Ridgevale La TR18 143 F8
Ridgeway
28 Perranporth TR6 55 A5
Plymouth, Plympton PL7 130 D5
Plymouth, Plympton St Maurice PL7 130 F5
Probus TR2 71 C6
Saltash PL12 122 D1
Ridgeway Sch PL7 130 E5
Ridgewell Terr TR9 57 E8
Ridgewood Cl PL26 114 F1
Riga Terr PL3 129 C4
Rigdale Cl PL6 129 A7
Ringmore Way PL5 124 B3
Ringway Flats 8 PL31 109 D5
Ringwell Valley Holiday Pk TR3 81 F7
Rinsey La TR13 90 D2
Risdon Ave PL4 129 B1
Rivendell PL27 108 C4
River Ct
Saltash PL12 122 D5
Tavistock PL19 147 D6
Riverford Cl PL6 125 D7
Riversdale Pl 8 PL27 108 B5
Riverside
Angarrack TR27 78 C4
3 Chacewater TR4 69 A3
Lanivet PL30 47 E7
Launceston PL15 106 B7
Lelant TR26 77 E4
Padstow PL28 107 E5
Riverside Ave TR7 110 A5
Riverside Bsns Pk PL1 127 E3
Riverside Cl 1 PL20 42 C4
Riverside Cott PL12 122 C1
Riverside Cres TR7 110 A5
Riverside Ct PL22 112 C2
Riverside Ho TR1 137 D1
Riverside Holiday Pk TR8 111 B1
Riverside Mews
Angarrack TR27 78 C5
Saltash PL12 123 A3
Riverside Pl PL1 127 D2
Riverside View TR1 137 E3
Riverside Wlk PL5 124 B6
River St
Mevagissey PL26 73 C3
Portscatho TR2 83 B2
Truro TR1 137 C4
Rivers The PL12 122 E1
Riverview TR11 145 A6
River View
Flushing TR11 145 B7
Gunnislake PL18 40 E5
River View *continued*
Lerryn PL22 61 C7
Plymouth PL4 129 B1
Saltash PL12 122 F3
Tresillian TR2 70 E4
River View La PL4 129 B1
River Wlk PL25 114 B3
Riviera Apartments TR26 141 D2
Riviera Est TR1 70 D1
Riviera La TR2 95 A6
Riviere Chalet Camp TR27 142 A7
Riviere Sands Holiday Park TR27 142 B8
Riviere Towans TR27 142 B7
Roach's Ct TR26 141 E1
Roach's Row TR15 140 B5
Robartes Ct 13 TR1 137 C4
Robartes Gardens Flats PL25 114 E4
Robartes Gdns PL25 114 E4
Robartes Jun Sch PL31 109 D4
Robartes Pl PL25 114 E5
Robartes Rd
Bodmin PL31 109 D4
Newquay TR7 110 F5
St Dennis PL26 58 C8
Robartes Terr
3 Illogan TR16 67 E4
Lostwithiel PL22 112 C3
Robert Adams Cl PL7 130 B5
Robert Eliot Ct PL25 114 B3
Robert Hichens Rd TR11 145 A5
Roberts Ave PL11 127 B3
Roberts Rd PL5 127 D8
Robin Dr PL15 106 E4
Robins Cl 13 PL24 60 B4
Robins Way PL9 135 E8
Roborough Ave PL6 125 B5
Roborough Cl PL6 125 B5
Roborough Down La PL6 121 F5
Roborough La PL5 124 D8
Robyns Cl PL7 131 B5
Roche Com Prim Sch PL26 46 F2
Roche Rd
Bugle PL26 47 C2
Stenalees PL26 59 C7
Roche Rural Workshops PL26 47 A4
Roche Sta PL26 47 A4
Rochester Rd 3 PL4 128 E4
Rochford Cres PL5 123 F5
Rock Cl 1 TR14 138 F2
Rock Close Ho TR27 142 A1
Rockfield Ave PL6 124 F6
Rock Gdns PL9 129 D1
Rockhaven Gdns PL27 21 F3
Rockhead St PL33 14 E3
Rock Hill PL5 124 C7
Rockingham Rd PL3 129 A5
Rock La PL31 109 C4
Rock Rd
Newlyn TR18 143 C3
St Minver PL27 21 E2
Rock Terr
Heamoor TR18 143 C7
Plymouth PL7 130 D4
Rock Twrs PL13 117 D2
Rock View Parc PL26 47 A3
Rock Villas PL27 21 D2
Rockville Pk PL9 135 E8
Rockwood Rd PL6 125 E8
Rocky Hill PL19 147 B5
Rocky La
Praa Sands TR20 90 C6
St Agnes TR5 54 C2
Veryan TR2 83 D5
Rocky Park Ave PL9 135 E8
Rocky Park Rd PL9 135 E8
Rodda Cl PL18 41 A7
Rodda's Rd TR4 68 C6
Roddick Way 8 PL7 131 C5
Rodings The PL14 51 F5
Rodney St PL5 127 D8
Rodwell Cl TR15 140 D5
Rodwill Cl TR27 78 E1
Roebuck Villas TR11 145 D3
Roekindale Cl TR15 139 D6
Roeselare Ave PL11 127 A3
Roeselare Cl PL11 127 A3
Rogate Dr PL6 125 D4
Rogate Wlk PL6 125 D4
Rogers Dr PL12 122 D4
Roland Bailey Gdns PL19 147 A6
Rollis Park Cl PL9 135 C8
Rollis Park Rd PL9 135 C8
Rolston Cl PL6 124 D6
Roma Cl TR7 111 C7
Roma Ct TR27 142 B5
Roman Bridge PL13 62 D1
Roman Dr PL31 109 F2
Roman Rd PL5 123 E2
Roman Way PL5 123 E2
Romilly Gdns PL7 130 B5
Romney Cl PL5 124 B1
Ronald Terr PL2 127 F5
Ronsdale Cl PL9 135 D8
Roope Cl PL5 127 C7
Ropehaven Cl PL25 114 E6
Ropehaven Rd PL25 114 E6
Roper Ave PL9 135 D8
Ropewalk Ct 2 TR11 145 C3
Ropewalk Rd TR3 137 C1
Ropewalk The TR18 143 C4
Rope Wlk
Mount Hawke TR4 68 C6
Padstow PL28 107 D5
Rope Wlk The
3 St Ives TR26 141 B6
9 St Mawes TR2 95 A6
Rorkes Cl PL5 123 E2
Roscadghill Parc 1 TR18 143 C7
Roscadghill Rd TR18 143 C6
Roscarrack TR15 139 B8
Roscarrack Cl TR11 144 E2
Roscarrack Rd TR11 144 D1
Roscarrick Villas TR11 93 D3
Roscarrock Hill PL29 22 D7
Roseacre Dr 8 TR15 140 C5
Roseannon TR11 93 D3
Rosebery Ave PL4 149 C4
Rosebery La PL4 149 C4
Rosebery Rd PL4 149 C4
Roseclave Cl PL7 131 C6
Rosecott Pk EX23 5 A6
Rose Cotts
Camborne TR14 138 E3
Plymouth PL6 129 B8
Stithians TR3 80 F3
Rosecraddoc Holiday Village PL14 38 B2
Rosecraddoc Lodge Holiday Bglws PL14 38 B2
Rosecraddoc View PL14 38 A2
Rosedale Ave PL2 128 D7
Rosedale Gdns PL31 35 B2
Rosedale Rd TR1 137 C5
Rosedene Farm TR3 69 C4
Rosedown Ave PL2 128 A7
Rose Eglos TR11 144 C2
Rose Eglos Cl TR11 144 C2
Rose Gdns PL6 125 E6
Rosehill
Ladock TR2 57 C1
Lanivet PL30 47 C6
Marazion TR17 89 B5
Mylor Bridge TR11 82 A2
Rose Hill
Altarnun PL15 26 C8
Fowey PL23 116 C4
Porthtowan TR4 68 A6
Port Isaac PL29 22 D7
Redruth TR15 140 B5
Sticker PL26 58 F1
Rose Hill Cl PL22 112 C2
Rosehill Gdns TR18 143 B6
Rosehill Mdw TR18 143 B6
Rose Hill Rd PL24 60 B5
Rose Hill Terr PL17 41 A3
Rose Hill Touring Pk TR4 68 A6
Rosehip Cl PL6 125 E7
Rose In The Bush Pk TR12 99 B8
Rose La 23 TR26 141 B6
Roseland Com Sch The TR2 72 A4
Roseland Cres
6 Chacewater TR4 69 A3
Tregony TR2 71 F3
Roseland Flats TR2 82 E1
Roseland Gdns
Bodmin PL31 109 E6
Redruth TR15 140 D6
Veryan TR2 83 F6
Roseland Pk TR14 138 D4
Roselands Rd PL31 109 F6
Roseland Terr TR4 55 F2
Roselidden Parc TR13 146 B7
Roseline Est TR13 80 D1
Roselyon Pl PL24 60 C5
Roselyon Prep Sch PL24 60 C4
Rose Mdw TR3 80 F3
Rose Mdws TR4 55 D4
Rosemellen Terr PL14 113 B4
Rosemellin TR14 138 E4
Rosemellin Com Prim Sch TR14 138 E4
Rosemorran 28 TR26 141 B5
Rosemullion 4 TR6 55 A5
Rosemullion Gdns 3 TR14 138 F7
Rose Mullion Gdns PL17 39 F5
Rosemullion Ho TR1 69 E4
Rosemundy TR5 54 D1
Rosenannon La TR15 139 B8
Rosenannon Rd TR15 139 B8
Rose Row TR15 140 B5
Rose Terr
Gunnislake PL18 40 E5
Mitchell TR8 56 F5
23 Penzance TR18 143 E6
Rosevale TR18 143 D4
Rosevale Cres TR14 138 C4
Rosevale Gdns PL30 59 F8
Rosevalley TR3 69 D3
Rose Valley TR19 75 B2
Rosevallon La PL31 109 C5
Rosevean Ave TR14 138 E3
Rosevean Cl TR14 138 E3
Rosevean Ct 8 PL3 128 F6
Rosevean Gdns PL3 128 F6
Rosevean Ho 7 PL3 128 F6
Rosevean Rd TR18 143 E6
Rosevean Terr TR18 143 E6
Roseveare Cl PL9 136 A8
Roseveare Dr PL26 46 D1
Roseveare Mobile Home Pk PL26 46 D1
Rosevear Rd PL26 47 C1
Rosewall Cotts 16 TR26 141 A5
Rosewall Terr 17 TR26 141 A5
Rosewarne TR13 91 A1
Rosewarne Cl TR14 138 D4
Rosewarne Farm Cvn Pk TR14 138 D4
Rosewarne Gdns TR14 138 D3
Rosewarne Manor Holiday Village TR27 78 F5
Rosewarne Mdws TR14 138 D5
Rosewarne Mews TR14 138 D4
Rosewarne Pk TR14 138 E4
Rosewarne Rd
1 Camborne TR14 138 D3
Carnhell Green TR27 78 F4
Rosewarne Terr TR14 138 D5
Rosewarne (Trng Ctr) TR14 138 D5
Rosewater Cvn Pk PL30 23 D7
Rosewin Mews 3 TR9 45 E6
Rosewin Row
2 St Columb Major TR9 45 E6
Truro TR1 137 D5
Rosewithian Cl TR27 78 E6
Rosewood Cl PL9 135 F5
Roseworthy Hill TR14 78 F6
Rosina Way PL26 59 D7
Roskear TR14 138 E4
Roskear Croft TR14 138 E6
Roskear Fields TR14 138 E4
Roskear Parc TR14 138 F5
Roskear Rd TR14 138 E3
Roskear Sch TR14 138 F3
Roskilling TR13 146 D7
Roskilling Wartha TR13 146 D7
Roskilly Cotts TR19 88 C2
Roskilly's Open Farm* TR12 101 D3
Roskrow Cl TR16 80 A5
Roskruge Cl TR13 146 D8
Ros Lyn TR26 141 C1
Roslyn Cl
St Austell PL25 114 F5
2 St Austell PL25 115 A5
Rosparc TR2 71 D6
Rosparvah Gdns TR18 143 C7
Rospeath Cres PL2 128 D8
Rospeath La TR20 89 C7
Rossett Gdns PL31 35 B1
Rossiter Ho TR19 96 B6
Rosslyn Park Rd PL3 128 D5
Ross St PL2 127 E4
Rossventon TR4 69 A1
Rostalek PL30 24 B2
Rothbury Cl PL6 125 E4
Rothbury Gdns PL6 125 D4
Rothesay Gdns PL5 124 D3
Rougemont Cl PL3 129 B7
Rough La TR3 81 B4
Rough St TR16 80 D6
Roughtor Dr PL32 105 C3
Roughtor Rd PL32 15 D1
Roughtor View PL33 14 D2
Roundhayes Farm Cotts EX23 10 C5
Round Ring TR10 144 D8
Round's La PL34 14 D7
Rous Rd PL12 40 C2
Rowan Cl
Bodmin PL31 109 B4
Plymouth PL7 131 B5
Tavistock PL19 147 C3
Rowan Ct PL12 122 C2
Rowans The
Bude EX23 104 E4
Lifton PL16 19 F4
St Mellion PL12 53 C8
Rowan Way PL6 125 E7
Rowden St PL3 128 E5
Rowdown Cl PL7 131 D4
Rowe's La TR13 146 E8
Rowe St PL11 127 B3
Rowes Terr PL26 58 D5
Row La PL5 123 E2
Rowland Cl PL9 135 E5
Rowse Gdns PL18 41 A3
Row The
Pillaton PL12 53 B7
Portloe TR2 84 A4
Royal Cornwall Hospl TR1 69 E4
Royal Cornwall Mus* TR1 137 C4
Royale Ct TR18 143 F6
Royal Eye Infmy PL4 128 E4
Royalist Ct 14 TR11 145 C3
Royal Navy Ave PL2 127 F6
Royal Par PL1 148 C2
Royal Talbot PL22 112 C2
Royal William Rd PL1 134 A8
Roydon Cl PL15 106 B8
Roydon La PL15 106 B8
Roydon Rd PL15 106 B8
Royffe Way PL31 109 F3
Ruby Terr TR13 92 B8
Rudyerd Wlk PL3 129 D6
Rufford Cl PL2 128 A7
Rule Cross EX23 2 E2
Ruminella View TR12 103 A4
Rumours Apartments TR7 111 B7
Rundle Ct PL14 113 B4
Rundles Ct TR1 137 E3
Runnymede Ct PL6 125 E2
Rush Park Terr PL18 40 F7
Ruskin Cres PL5 124 D2
Ruskin Ct TR9 45 D5
Russell Ave PL3 128 F7
Russell Cl
Gunnislake PL18 41 A7
Plymouth PL9 136 B7
Russell Cl *continued*
Saltash PL12 122 C3
Russell Court Gdns PL19 147 B6
Russell Ct
Plymouth PL1 148 C2
Saltash PL12 122 C3
Tavistock PL19 147 B6
Russell Mews PL31 109 C5
Russell Pl PL1 148 B4
Russell St
7 Liskeard PL14 113 C5
Tavistock PL19 147 C5
Russell Way 4 TR10 144 C7
Russet Wood PL5 123 F4
Rutger Pl PL1 148 A4
Ruthern Valley PL30 34 A1
Ruthven Cl PL6 128 F8
Ruthy's La PL28 107 D5
Rutland Rd PL4 128 F4
Rydal Cl PL6 125 D2
Ryder Rd PL2 127 F4
Rydon La EX22 8 F7
Rye Hill
Ponsanooth TR3 81 B4
Saltash PL12 122 C2
Rylands Terr PL30 24 B3

S

Saffron Cl PL23 116 C4
Sail Loft Flats 2 TR26 141 B6
St Agnes Mus* TR5 54 C1
St Agnes Sch TR5 54 C1
St Albans Pk PL20 42 D2
St Ambrusca Rd TR8 110 A3
St Andrew's CE Prim Sch
Buckland Monachorum PL20 41 F3
Plymouth PL1 148 B2
St Andrews Cl
12 Bere Alston PL20 41 B1
Ponsanooth TR3 81 B4
Saltash PL12 122 C2
St Andrew's Cl PL18 41 A3
St Andrew's Cross 1 PL1 149 A2
St Andrew's Pl PL10 133 A1
St Andrews Rd PL19 147 D2
St Andrew's Rd
Par PL24 60 C5
12 Stratton EX23 4 D1
St Andrew's St
Cawsand PL10 133 A1
1 St Ives TR26 141 B5
St Andrew St
Millbrook PL10 132 E5
Plymouth PL1 148 C2
St Andrews Terr TR3 81 B4
St Andrew's Terr PL24 60 C5
St Annes TR11 93 D3
St Annes Cl
Lelant TR26 77 E4
Whitstone EX22 7 F1
St Annes Rd 17 PL24 60 B4
St Anne's Rd
Newquay TR7 111 A7
Plymouth PL6 125 D6
Saltash PL12 122 E3
3 Trewoon PL25 59 A3
St Ann's Hill EX23 104 F3
St Anta Rd TR26 141 E1
St Anthony Way TR11 145 A2
St Aubyn Ave PL2 127 F5
St Aubyn Cres TR7 111 A6
St Aubyn Est TR14 79 B2
St Aubyn Rd PL1 127 E3
St Aubyns TR20 89 E5
St Aubyn's Rd TR1 137 D3
St Aubyn St PL1 127 E2
St Aubyn's Vean TR1 137 D3
St Austell Bay Bsns Pk PL25 115 E4
St Austell Com Hospl PL26 114 F1
St Austell Hospl PL25 114 A3
St Austell Rd PL24 115 F5
St Austell Row 2 TR2 95 A6
St Austell St
Summercourt TR8 57 C6
Truro TR1 137 D4
St Austell Sta PL25 114 D4
St Barnabas Ct PL1 148 A4
St Barnabas Hospl PL12 122 F2
St Barnabas Terr PL1 148 A4
St Benedicts Cl 13 PL24 60 D5
St Benets Cl PL30 47 E6
St Blazey Rd PL24 60 C4
St Boniface Cl PL2 128 C7
St Boniface Dr PL2 128 C7
St Boniface's RC Coll PL5 124 E1
St Breaca Cl TR13 91 A3
St Breock Prim Sch PL27 108 B5
St Breward Prim Sch PL30 24 B3
St Bridget Ave PL6 124 F1
St Budeaux Ferry Rd Sta PL5 127 D8
St Budeaux Foundation CE Jun Sch PL5 123 F2
St Budeaux Victoria Rd Sta PL5 123 D1
St Buryan Hill TR19 96 F4
St Buryan Prim Sch TR19 97 B6
St Cadocs PL28 31 F7
St Carantoc Way TR8 43 D3

St Catherine's Castle★ PL23 116 B2
St Catherine's CE Prim Sch PL15 106 A4
St Catherines Ct PL23 116 C3
St Clare Flats TR18 143 D6
St Clare St TR18 143 D6
St Cleer Dr PL27 108 D6
St Cleer Prim Sch PL14 38 A3
St Cleer Rd PL14 113 C7
St Clement's Cl TR1 137 E4
St Clement's Hill TR1 137 E4
St Clements Parc TR1 137 E4
St Clement St TR1 137 D5
St Clements Terr 26 TR19 88 C1
St Clement's Terr 3 TR1 137 D5
St Clement Vean TR1 137 F6
St Columb Bsns Ctr TR9 45 E6
St Columb Major Bsns Pk TR9 45 E5
St Columb Major Com Prim Sch TR9 45 D6
St Columb Major Ind Est TR9 45 D5
St Columb Minor Sch TR7 111 D7
St Columb Road Ind Workshops TR9 45 D2
St Columb Road Sta TR9 45 D2
St Crewenna Terr TR27 78 E1
St Cuthbert Cl PL15 106 B7
St Cuthbert's Rd TR7 110 D6
St Cyriac PL30 47 F1
St Davids Cl EX23 4 C8
St David's Rd PL19 147 E5
St Day & Carharrack Com Sch TR16 68 E1
St Day Rd
Redruth TR15 140 C5
Redruth TR16 140 E5
St Dennis Com Prim Sch PL26 58 C8
St Dominic Cl PL31 109 E5
St Dominick CE Sch PL12 40 D2
St Dominic Pk PL17 40 C4
St Dominic Sq 4 TR1 137 C4
St Dominic St
9 Penzance TR18 143 E6
5 Truro TR1 137 C4
St Dunstan's Abbey Plymouth Coll Jun Sch PL1 148 A3
St Dunstan's Terr PL4 149 C3
St Edmunds La PL28 107 D5
St Edward Gdns PL6 125 B1
St Edward's CE Prim Sch PL6 125 C1
St Eia St TR26 141 C6
St Elizabeth Cl PL7 130 F3
St Elvan Cres TR13 91 A1
St Elwyns Rise TR27 142 B6
St Enodoc Cl PL27 108 D6
St Erme with Trispen Com Prim Sch TR4 70 D8
St Erth Com Prim Sch TR27 142 A1
St Erth Hill TR27 77 F1
St Erth Ind Est TR27 77 E2
St Erth Rd PL2 128 D7
St Erth Sta TR27 77 E2
St Eval Pl PL5 123 E4
St Fimbarrus Rd PL23 116 C3
St Francis CE Prim Sch TR11 144 E3
St Francis Ct PL5 124 B3
St Francis Rd TR9 45 E2
St Francis St 6 TR18 143 E6
St Gabriel's Ave PL3 128 D5
St George's Arc TR11 145 B4
St George's Ave PL2 128 C7
St George's CE Prim Sch PL1 148 A1
St George's Cres PL31 109 C4
St Georges Ct
Looe PL13 117 D2
1 Plymouth PL2 127 F4
St George's Hill TR6 55 A4
St Georges Hill Cl 13 TR6 55 A4
St George's Pk PL22 112 C3
St Georges Rd
Nanpean PL26 58 D6
Saltash PL12 122 D3
St George's Rd
Hayle TR27 142 C5
Looe PL13 117 D4
Newquay TR7 110 D5
Saltash PL12 122 E3
Truro TR1 137 B5
St George's Terr
Perranporth TR6 54 F4
Plymouth PL2 127 F4
St Germans Prim Sch PL12 65 A8
St Germans Rd PL17 39 F3
St Germans Sta PL12 65 B8
St Giles Dr PL27 108 C6
St Giles Mews PL27 108 C6
St Giles on the Heath Com Sch PL15 13 F1
St Gluvias Parc TR10 144 D8
St Gluvias St TR10 144 D7
St Golder Rd TR18 143 B3
St Grace's Ct TR2 71 C6
St Helens Wlk PL5 124 C5
St Henry St 4 TR18 143 E6
St Hilary Sch TR20 89 F6
St Hilary Terr PL4 149 C3
St Ive Rd PL14 38 E4
St Ives Bay Chalet & Cvn Pk TR27 78 B6
St Ives Bay Holiday Pk TR27 78 B6
St Ives Holiday Village TR20 77 C3
St Ives Jun & Inf Schs TR26 141 A5
St Ives La TR27 66 B1
St Ives Museum★ TR26 141 C6
St Ives Mushroom Farm TR26 77 A5
St Ives Rd
Carbis Bay TR26 141 D1
Pendeen TR19 75 A1
St Ives Sch TR26 141 B3
St Ives Sta TR26 141 B5
St James Ct
Delabole PL33 14 E2
Plymouth PL1 148 B2
Torpoint PL11 127 B3
St James Mews PL1 148 B2
St James Pl TR13 146 B6
St James' Pl E PL1 148 B2
St James' Pl W PL1 148 B2
St James Rd PL11 127 B2
St James' St TR18 143 E5
St James's Terr TR10 144 B7
St James View TR9 57 D8
St Johns PL19 147 C5
St Johns Ave PL19 147 C5
St John's Bridge Rd PL4 149 B2
St Johns Cl PL6 125 D4
St John's Cl
Helston TR13 146 A6
Millbrook PL10 132 E5
St Johns Ct 7 TR18 143 E5
St John's Ct
7 Falmouth TR11 145 A4
Hayle TR27 142 D6
St John's Dr PL9 135 B6
St Johns Gdns TR11 145 B6
St Johns La PL11 132 B8
St John's RC Prim Sch TR14 138 E2
St Johns Rd
Launceston PL15 106 B4
Plymouth PL4 149 C2
St John's Rd
Helston TR13 146 B6
Horrabridge PL20 42 C4
Millbrook PL10 132 F5
Newquay TR7 110 D5
Plymouth PL4 149 B2
Plymouth, Turnchapel PL9 135 A6
St John's St
Hayle TR27 142 D6
Plymouth PL4 149 B2
St John's Terr
Devoran TR3 81 F6
Pendeen TR19 75 A1
5 Penzance TR18 143 E6
St Johns Wlk TR26 77 A7
St Joseph's Cl PL6 124 F1
St Joseph's RC Prim Sch PL1 127 E2
St Joseph's Rd PL15 106 B8
St Joseph's Sch PL15 106 B7
St Jude's Rd PL4 149 B2
St Julian's Cotts PL10 133 E7
St Julitta PL30 48 A1
St Just Prim Sch TR19 86 E6
St Keri Ct PL15 18 A5
St Keverne Com Prim Sch TR12 101 D4
St Keverne Pl PL2 128 D8
St Keverne Rural Workshops TR12 101 C3
St Kew Com Prim Sch PL30 22 F3
St Keyne Cl TR1 137 C6
St Keyne Sta PL14 51 C3
St Lawrence Mews PL4 149 A4
St Lawrence Rd
Bodmin PL30, PL31 109 A4
Plymouth PL4 149 A4
St Leonards PL31 109 C5
St Leonard's Rd
Launceston PL15 106 B8
Plymouth PL4 149 C2
St Leonards Terr PL31 109 C5
St Leo Pl PL2 127 E4
St Levan Cl 8 TR17 89 C5
St Levan Com Prim Sch TR19 96 E5
St Levan Rd
7 Marazion TR17 89 C5
Plymouth PL2 127 F5
St Mabyn CE Sch PL30 34 D8
St Mabyn Holiday Pk PL30 34 E8
St Maddерns CE Sch TR20 143 A8
St Margarets Holiday Pk PL26 59 A1
St Margarets La PL26 59 A1
St Margarets Rd PL7 130 B7
St Mark's Prim Sch EX23 2 E2
St Marks Rd PL6 125 D5
St Marnarch's PL13 62 B8
St Marnarch's Rd PL13 62 B8
St Martin-in-Meneage Com Prim Sch TR12 100 D6
St Martin's Ave PL3 128 D7
St Martin's CE Prim Sch PL14 113 D5
St Martins Cl
Lewannick PL15 27 B7
St Martins Cl *continued*
Looe PL13 117 D5
St Martin's Cl 2 TR14 138 C2
St Martin's Cres TR14 138 C3
St Martins Rd EX23 7 B8
St Martin's Rd PL13 117 D6
St Martin's Terr TR14 138 C4
St Marwenne Cl EX23 7 B6
St Maryhaye PL19 147 A5
St Mary's PL13 117 D3
St Mary's CE Prim Sch TR18 143 E4
St Mary's CE Sch TR1 137 C6
St Marys Cl PL7 130 D5
St Mary's Cl PL31 109 C4
St Mary's Cres PL31 109 C4
St Marys Ct PL7 130 D5
St Mary's Ct TR7 110 D5
St Mary's Gdns PL31 109 C4
St Mary's RC Prim Sch
Bodmin PL31 109 C4
Falmouth TR11 144 E3
St Mary's RC Sch TR18 143 E7
St Marys Rd PL24 60 B4
St Mary's Rd
Bodmin PL31 109 B3
Launceston PL15 106 C8
Newquay TR7 110 D5
Plymouth PL7 130 C6
St Mary's St
Penzance TR18 143 E6
12 Truro TR1 137 D4
St Mary's Street Mews 10 TR1 137 D4
St Mary St PL1 148 A2
St Mary's Terr TR18 143 E5
St Mary's Terr 4 TR1 137 C5
St Matthews Hill PL27 108 D5
St Maurice Ct PL7 130 F4
St Maurice Mews PL7 130 E4
St Maurice Rd PL7 130 F3
St Maurice View PL7 131 B4
St Mawes Castle★ TR2 95 A5
St Mawes Com Prim Sch TR2 95 A6
St Mawes Terr 8 PL2 127 F5
St Mawgan Cl PL31 109 F5
St Mellans Terr 5 TR12 99 A1
St Mellion CE School PL12 53 D8
St Meriadoc CE Inf Sch TR14 138 C2
St Meriadoc CE Jun Sch TR14 138 B2
St Meriadoc Rd TR14 138 C3
St Merryn Airfield PL28 31 F6
St Merryn Holiday Village PL28 31 F7
St Merryn Sch PL28 31 E8
St Mewan Com Prim Sch PL26 59 A2
St Mewan La PL25, PL26 59 A3
St Michael Ave PL2 127 F5
St Michael CE Prim Sch TR13 146 C5
St Michaels Cl PL15 19 C1
St Michael's Cl
Hayle TR27 142 B4
Plymouth PL1 127 E1
St Michael's Cotts 11 TR18 143 E5
St Michaels Ct
Mawnan Smith TR11 93 D3
18 Penzance TR18 143 E5
St Michael's Ct 7 PL1 127 F3
St Michael's Hospl TR27 142 B4
St Michael's Mount★ TR17 89 B4
St Michael's RC Small Sch TR1 137 C4
St Michael's Rd
Newquay TR7 110 D5
Perranporth TR6 55 A4
Ponsanooth TR3 81 C4
9 Stratton EX23 4 D1
St Michael's St TR18 143 E6
St Michael's Terr
Penzance TR18 143 D6
8 Plymouth, Devonport PL1 127 F3
Plymouth PL4 148 C4
St Minver House Holiday Est PL27 22 A3
St Minver Sch PL27 21 F3
St Modwen Rd PL6 129 F7
St Moritz Ct PL27 21 D5
St Moritz Villas PL27 21 D5
St Nazaire App PL1 127 F2
St Nazaire Cl PL1 127 E2
St Neot Com Prim Sch PL14 36 F2
St Newlyn East Prim Sch TR8 56 B7
St Nicholas' CE Sch PL11 64 C4
St Nicholas Cl TR27 78 C6
St Nicholas Ct 1 TR26 141 B6
St Nicholas Pk PL22 112 B3
St Nicholas St
Bodmin PL31 109 E4
14 Truro TR1 137 D4
St Nonna's Cl PL15 26 C8
St Olaf's Rd 13 EX23 4 D1
St Pancras Ave PL2 128 D8
St Paternus Cl PL15 27 E8
St Pauls Cl PL3 129 C5
St Paul's RC Prim Sch PL5 123 D1
St Paul St PL1 134 A8
St Peter Cl PL7 130 F4
St Peter's CE Jun Sch PL19 147 D5
St Peters CE Prim Sch PL1 148 B3
St Peters Ct PL1 148 A3
St Peter's Hill TR18 143 C1
St Peter's RC Prim Sch PL5 124 B5
St Peters Rd
Plymouth PL5 124 C2
11 Stratton EX23 4 D1
St Peter's Rd TR11 145 B7
St Peters St 16 TR26 141 B6
St Peters Way TR13 98 C8
St Petroc's CE Prim Sch PL31 109 E4
St Petroc's Cl PL31 109 E4
St Petrocs Mdw PL28 107 C5
St Petroc's Sch EX23 104 D7
St Petry TR20 89 E5
St Philip St 8 TR18 143 E6
St Piran Cl PL31 109 B4
St Pirans Cl 2 TR1 137 D4
St Piran's Cl PL25 114 F6
St Pirans Ct
Camborne TR14 138 D3
13 Penzance TR18 143 E5
Tintagel PL34 14 E8
St Piran's Hill TR3 81 D6
St Pirans Ho 15 TR6 55 A5
St Pirans Par 10 TR6 55 A5
St Pirans Parc 14 TR13 98 C8
St Piran's Prep Sch TR27 142 B4
St Pirans Rd TR6 55 A5
St Piran's Rd TR7 110 D6
St Pirans Way TR20 89 D4
St Pol-de-Leon View TR19 88 C2
St Rumon's CE Inf Sch PL19 147 C6
St Sampsons Cl 6 PL24 60 D5
St Sampson's Terr PL23 61 B5
St Saviour's Hill PL23 116 D2
St Saviour's La PL28 107 D6
St Simon's La PL4 129 B3
St Smithwick Way TR11 145 C3
St Stephen Churchtown Com Prim Sch PL26 58 B4
St Stephen Rd PL7 130 F3
St Stephens Com Prim Sch
Launceston PL15 106 B8
Saltash PL12 122 E2
St Stephens Ct PL15 106 B7
St Stephen's Hill
Launceston PL15 106 B7
Saltash PL12 122 C1
St Stephen's Pl PL7 130 E5
St Stephens Rd PL26 58 E1
St Stephen's Rd PL12 122 E2
St Stephen St PL1 127 F1
St Sulien
Luxulyan PL30 48 A1
Luxulyan PL30 60 A8
St Teresa Ho PL4 149 A3
St Therese Cl 20 PL17 39 F4
St Therese's Ct PL1 127 F2
St Thomas Cl
Plymouth PL7 130 F3
Truro TR1 69 F3
St Thomas Hill PL15 106 B6
St Thomas Rd PL15 106 B6
St Thomas' Rd TR7 110 F5
St Thomas St TR10 144 D7
St Tinney Farm PL32 10 D1
St Treath Com Prim Sch PL30 23 E7
St Tudy CE Prim Sch PL30 23 E3
St Uny CE Sch TR26 141 D1
St Uny Cl TR26 77 E3
St Uny Cres TR15 139 F5
St Vincent St PL2 127 E4
St Warren St 7 TR18 143 E6
St Wenn Sch PL30 46 D7
St Winnolls Pk PL13 117 D4
St Winnow Barton Farm Mus★ PL22 61 A8
St Winnow CE Sch PL22 112 F2
Salamanca St PL11 127 B3
Salcombe Rd PL4 149 C4
Salisbury Ope PL3 128 B5
Salisbury Rd
Plymouth PL4 149 C4
Truro TR1 137 B4
Salisbury Road Jun Sch PL4 149 C3
Salmon Row 3 TR1 137 D4
Saltash Bsns Pk PL12 122 C4
Saltash Com Sch PL12 122 E1
Saltash Ind Est PL12 122 D4
Saltash Parkway Ind Est PL12 122 B4
Saltash Rd
Callington PL17 39 F4
Plymouth, Keyham PL2 127 E6
Plymouth PL3 148 C4
Saltash Sta PL12 123 A2
Saltbox Cl TR11 82 A2
Saltbox Rd TR11 82 A2
Saltburn Rd PL5 123 C1
Salt Cellar Hill 10 TR13 98 B8
Saltings Cl TR26 77 E3
Saltings Reach TR26 77 E3
Saltings The TR26 77 E4
Salt Mill PL12 122 F4
Saltponds 27 TR19 88 C1
Saltram House★ PL7 130 A4
Saltram Terr PL7 130 E5
Salts Mdw PL14 50 B6
Sampford Gdns PL20 42 D5
Sampford Terr 6 PL20 42 C5
Sampson Cl PL18 40 D6
Sampson Gdns TR3 81 B4
Sampson's Ct TR27 78 D6
Sampson Way TR3 69 D3
Sampys Hill TR11 93 D3
Samuel Bone Cl PL14 113 D6
Sanctuary Cl TR14 138 C2
Sanctuary La
Helston TR13 146 C6
12 Stratton EX23 4 E1
Sanctuary Lane Flats TR13 146 C6
Sandbank Holiday Flats TR27 66 B1
Sand Bay TR11 145 C2
Sand-Bay Holiday Flats 6 TR6 55 A5
Sandercock Ct PL17 39 F7
Sandfield Cres 3 TR14 138 C2
Sandford Rd PL9 135 F8
Sand Hill PL18 41 A6
Sand Hill Pk PL18 40 F5
Sandhole Cross EX39 2 D8
Sandhurst Terr 1 TR1 137 C5
Sand La PL18 41 A3
Sandon Wlk PL6 125 A1
Sandows La 15 TR26 141 A5
Sandplace Rd
Looe PL13 117 C6
Looe, Sandplace PL13 63 B7
Sandplace Sta PL13 63 B8
Sandra Way PL31 109 C5
Sandyacres
Hayle TR27 78 B6
Phillack TR27 142 E8
Sandy Cl PL14 51 B3
Sandy Cove TR4 68 A7
Sandy Cove Bglws TR20 90 B3
Sandy Cove Travel Lodge TR4 68 A6
Sandy Ct TR8 31 B2
Sandy Hill PL25 114 F4
Sandy Hill Com Prim Sch PL25 114 F4
Sandyhills PL27 21 E2
Sandy La
Harlyn PL28 20 D2
Redruth TR15, TR16 140 D5
Trevone PL28 20 F2
Sandylake La PL22 112 F3
Sandymoor TR14 139 B3
Sandymouth Bay Holiday Pk EX23 4 C5
Sandy Rd
Plymouth PL7 131 C4
Porthtowan TR4 68 A7
Sango Ct PL10 132 F6
Sango Rd PL11 127 A2
Saracen Cl TR10 144 C7
Saracen Cres TR10 144 C7
Saracen Ho 5 TR10 144 C7
Saracen Pl TR10 144 C7
Saracen Way TR10 144 C7
Sarah Cl PL20 41 B1
Sarahs Cl PL28 107 D4
Sarah's Ct PL28 107 D4
Sarah's Gate PL27 32 C7
Sarah's La PL28 107 D4
Sarah's Mdw PL28 107 D4
Sarah's View PL28 107 D4
Sargents Mdw EX23 2 D1
Sarum Cl PL3 128 F7
Saunders La PL11 65 A5
Saunders Wlk PL6 124 D6
Savage Rd PL5 127 D7
Savery Terr PL4 129 A4
Savoy Bldg 3 PL25 114 C3
Sawles Rd
St Austell PL25 114 B2
St Austell PL25 114 D2
Sawmills La TR16 68 D3
Sawrey St PL1 148 A2
Sawyers Ct TR13 92 A6
Scarletts Well Pk PL31 109 C6
Scarletts Well Rd PL31 109 C5
Scarlett's Well Rd PL31 109 B5
Scarne Ind Est PL15 106 C3
Scholars Cl PL14 38 F2
Scholar's La TR13 91 C3
School Cl
Par PL24 60 B4
Plymouth PL7 130 D7
St Columb Minor TR7 111 E6
Tavistock PL19 147 D5
School Dr PL6 125 D7
School Hill
Golant PL23 61 B5
Herodsfoot PL14 50 E3
Lanjeth PL26 58 E4
Mevagissey PL26 73 C4
Padstow PL28 107 D5
Perranarworthal TR3 81 D6
Shortlanesend TR4 69 F6
South Petherwin PL15 27 E8
St Buryan TR19 96 E5
St Keverne, Porthallow TR12 101 D6
St Keverne TR12 101 D4
St Neot PL14 36 F2

School La
Budock Water TR11 144 C3
Gulval TR18 88 E6
Jacobstow EX23 11 A6
Marazion TR17 89 C5
Plymouth PL7 130 E4
Polruan PL23 116 D2
Redruth TR15 140 D5
St Austell PL25 115 C6
St Erth TR27 142 A1
St Hilary TR20 89 F6
Troon TR14 79 E4
Truro TR1 137 C3
School Rd
Breage TR13 90 F3
Landrake PL12 53 C3
Pensilva PL14 38 E5
Summercourt TR8 57 B7
Tavistock PL19 147 D2
School Wlk PL27 108 D6
Sclerder La PL13 62 E4
Scoble's Terr TR1 70 D1
Sconner Rd PL11 127 A3
Scoria Cl TR16 68 D3
Scorrier House Workshops TR16 68 D2
Scorrier St TR16 68 E1
Scott Ave PL5 127 C8
Scott Bsns Pk PL2 128 A6
Scott Cl 2 PL14 38 E4
Scott Hospl PL2 128 A6
Scott Rd
Plymouth PL2 128 A6
Plymouth PL2 128 B6
Scowbuds TR14 138 F5
Scrations La PL22 112 C2
Screech Owl Sanctuary* TR9 46 A3
Seabank TR11 145 B2
Seacroft Rd PL5 123 C2
Sea Front Ct PL13 117 D3
Seagull Tourist Pk PL28 31 F6
Seaholme Ct TR11 145 A5
Sea La TR27 142 D6
Seapoint Ho TR7 110 E6
Sea Rd PL25 115 D2
Seaspray Leisure Flats TR4 68 A7
Seaton Ave PL4 128 E4
Seaton Beach Flats PL11 64 B5
Seaton Bsns Pk PL6 125 B3
Seaton La PL4 128 E4
Seaton Pk PL11 64 B5
Seaton Pl PL2 127 F5
Seaton Valley Countryside Pk* PL13, PL11 64 B6
Seaton Way PL20 42 A2
Sea Urchin TR26 141 E2
Sea View
Crackington Haven EX23 10 C6
Gunnislake PL18 40 E5
Sea View Ave PL4 149 C4
Seaview Cotts 10 TR11 145 B5
Sea View Cotts PL26 73 C3
Sea View Cres 11 TR2 95 A6
Sea View Ct TR11 145 B3
Sea View Pl TR26 141 C6
Sea View Rd
Falmouth TR11 145 B2
12 St Mawes TR2 95 A6
Seaview Terr TR8 57 E6
Sea View Terr
Camborne TR14 138 E2
Carn Towan TR19 96 C7
Helston TR13 146 B6
6 Newlyn TR18 143 C1
Par PL24 60 B6
Penwithick PL26 59 D7
Plymouth PL4 149 B4
Redruth TR15 140 C5
20 St Ives TR26 141 B5
Seawell Rd EX23 104 F7
Second Ave
Plymouth, Billacombe PL9 130 A1
Plymouth, Devonport PL1 128 A2
Plymouth, Weston Mill PL2 127 E7
Sedley Way PL5 124 D3
Sefton Ave PL4 129 B3
Sefton Cl PL4 149 C4
Segrave Rd PL2 128 B6
Seiners Ct 10 TR6 55 A4
Selkirk Ho 5 PL9 135 F7
Selkirk Pl PL5 124 E2
Selsden Cl PL9 136 C6
Sendall's Way PL6 124 F4
Seneschall Pk TR13 146 D8
Sennen Cl PL11 126 F4
Sennen Hts TR19 96 B7
Sennen Pl PL2 127 E5
Sennen Sch TR19 96 C7
Sentry Cl PL27 32 D6
Sergeants Hill TR4 68 F3
Serpell Cl PL6 124 E6
Serpells Mdw PL15 17 F1
Sethnoe Way TR13 91 A3
Seton Gdns TR14 138 B4
Setons The 6 TR14 138 F7
Seven Stars La PL5 124 C6
Seven Trees Ct PL4 149 B4
Severn Pl PL3 129 C5
Sewell Ct PL3 128 E5
Seymour Ave
Newquay TR7 110 E6
Plymouth PL4 149 B4
Seymour Cl TR3 69 C3
Seymour Dr PL3 128 F5
Seymour Mews PL4 149 C4
Seymour Pk PL3 129 A5
Seymour Pl PL1 148 A4
Seymour Rd
Plymouth, Mannamead PL3 128 F5
Plymouth, Plympton PL7 130 C6
Seymour St PL4 149 A3
Shackleton Cres 9 PL27 31 F3
Shackleton Ct PL5 124 E1
Shackleton Dr TR7 111 B5
Shaft Downs La TR27 78 F3
Shaftesbury Cotts PL4 149 A4
Shaftesbury Ct 3 PL4 149 A4
Shakespeare Rd PL5 124 C2
Shaldon Cres PL5 124 B3
Shallowford Cl PL6 129 C8
Shallowford Rd PL6 129 C8
Shapleys Gdns PL9 136 A5
Shapters Rd PL4 149 C2
Shapters Way PL4 135 B8
Sharaman Cl PL25 115 A5
Sharlands Rd EX23 7 B6
Sharon Way PL6 125 A5
Sharpitor Row PL20 42 E4
Sharrose Rd PL9 135 B5
Shaw Way PL9 135 A7
Shearwood Cl PL7 130 C6
Sheep Fair Mdw 14 PL17 39 F4
Sheepstor Rd PL6 125 D1
Sheila's Ct TR26 141 D1
Shelburne Ct TR11 144 F3
Shelburne Rd TR11 144 F3
Shell Cl PL6 125 E1
Shelley Ave PL19 147 D5
Shelley Rd PL25 115 A4
Shelley Way PL5 123 D1
Shepherd's La PL4 149 B2
Sherborne Cl PL9 136 C6
Sherford Cres
Plymouth, Elburton PL9 136 C7
Plymouth, West Park PL5 124 A3
Sherford Rd PL9 136 D7
Sherford Wlk PL9 136 E7
Sheridan Rd PL5 124 C1
Sherrell Pk PL20 41 B1
Sherril Cl PL9 135 F4
Sherwell La PL4 149 A4
Sherwood Dr PL31 109 C5
Sheviock La PL11 65 B5
Shilla Pk PL32 24 A8
Shilson Terr PL15 106 C5
Shipley Wlk PL6 125 A1
Shirburn Rd PL6 129 B8
Shire Horse Farm & Carriage Mus The* TR16 79 F5
Shires Way PL26 46 F3
Shirley Gdns PL5 124 C1
Shoemaker's La PL12 122 E2
Shoemakers Row PL13 63 B7
Shoot Row TR15 140 C5
Shop Hill 3 TR17 89 C5
Shop Pk PL14 38 A2
Shoreline TR7 111 B8
Shores La PL27 21 E3
Shortacross PL14 38 A2
Short Cotts PL11 127 A3
Short Cross Mews TR4 68 C6
Short Cross Rd TR4 68 C6
Shortlands EX22 8 E5
Shortlanesend Com Prim Sch TR4 69 F6
Short Park Rd PL3 128 D5
Shortwood Cres PL9 136 A7
Shrewsbury Rd PL5 124 C4
Shrubberies Hill TR13 98 C8
Shute Hill
Breage TR13 90 F3
Carharrack TR16 80 E8
Helston TR13 146 C6
Lostwithiel PL22 112 C2
Mawnan Smith TR11 93 D3
Pelynt PL13 62 D5
Shute La
Penryn TR10 144 C8
Pensilva PL14 38 E4
6 Porthleven TR13 98 B8
Shute Mdw TR10 144 C7
Shute Park Rd PL9 135 F6
Shutta Rd PL13 117 C4
Sidings The
Bugle PL26 47 C2
Delabole PL33 14 E2
Sidney Terr 7 TR15 140 C5
Silvanus Jenkin Ave PL14 113 E5
Silver Birch Cl PL6 125 C7
Silver Ct 1 TR15 140 B4
Silverdale Ct TR7 110 E6
Silverdale Rd TR11 145 A2
Silver Hill TR3 81 D6
Silvershell Rd PL29 22 D7
Silvershell View PL29 22 D7
Silver St
Bere Ferrers PL20 120 A3
Saltash PL12 123 A2
Silver Terr PL10 133 A6
Silverton Cl EX23 104 E5
Silverton Rd EX23 104 E5
Silver Way TR3 69 C3
Simms Terr PL18 41 A6
Simon Cl PL9 135 E6
Simpsons Ct 30 TR18 143 E5
Singlerose Rd PL26 59 C7
Sir James Smith's Com Sch PL32 105 C4
Sir John Hunt Com Coll (Southway Campus) PL6 124 F6
Sir John Hunt Com Sports Coll PL5 124 D4
Sir Robert Geffery's CE Prim Sch PL12 53 C3
Sir Williams Morles Almshouses PL12 65 A8
Sithney Common Hill TR13 91 C2
Sithney Com Prim Sch TR13 91 B5
Sithney Old Hill TR13 146 A6
Sithney St PL5 123 C1
Six Turnings TR11 82 A2
Skardale Gdns PL6 129 D8
Skardon Pl PL4 149 A4
Skerries Rd PL6 124 F7
Skidden Hill 18 TR26 141 B5
Skinnard La PL18 40 F5
Skitches Cnr EX23 4 D1
Skyburriowe La TR12 99 C6
Skylark Rise PL6 125 E8
Slade Cl PL9 136 A5
Slade Park Rd PL14 38 E5
Slades La 2 TR10 144 C7
Slades Rd PL25 114 E5
Slatelands Cl PL7 131 B3
Slipway PL27 21 D2
Slipway Quay PL12 119 B2
Smallack Cl PL6 124 F2
Smallack Dr PL6 124 F2
Smallridge Cl PL9 135 F5
Smallridge La EX23 4 F1
Smeaton Sq PL3 129 D6
Smithfield Ct TR8 111 B3
Smithfield Dr PL12 122 B3
Smithick Hill TR11 145 B4
Smith's Cotts PL14 113 C6
Smiths Way PL12 122 B3
Smithy Cl PL12 122 C4
Smithy Ct PL32 105 D3
Smithy La TR3 81 F7
Smugglers Row 8 TR11 145 B5
Snell Dr PL12 122 B3
Snowdrop Cres PL15 106 E4
Snow's Pas TR11 145 B4
Socotra Dr 7 PL25 59 A3
Solar Row 6 TR1 137 D5
Somer Ct TR11 145 B4
Somerset Cotts 10 PL3 128 A4
Somerset Pl PL3 128 A4
Somerset Place La 11 PL3 128 A4
Somerville Rd TR6 55 A4
Sona Merg Cl TR18 143 C7
Soper's Hill PL5 120 E1
South Albany Rd TR15 140 C3
Southbourne Cl PL26 58 E6
Southbourne Rd PL25 114 E2
Southcliff TR11 145 C2
South Cliff 18 TR19 88 C1
South Coombe La PL17 39 F8
Southcott Mdws EX23 11 A6
Southdown Cl PL26 58 E1
Southdown Cotts PL10 133 B6
Southdown Rd
Millbrook PL10 133 A6
Sticker PL26 58 E1
South Down Rd PL2 128 B6
South Downs TR15 140 D2
Southdown Terr PL10 133 A6
South Dr
Redruth TR15 140 D2
South Tehidy TR14 138 E8
South East Cornwall Discovery Ctr* PL13 117 C4
Southella Rd PL20 42 D2
Southern Cl PL2 127 F7
Southernhaye PL15 106 C5
Southern Rd PL17 39 F4
Southern Terr PL4 128 F4
Southernway PL9 136 A8
Southern Way PL27 108 C5
Southfield PL12 122 C3
Southfield Rd EX23 104 E5
Southfields EX22 8 A5
Southfields Pl 3 TR26 141 A5
Southgate Ave PL9 135 E4
Southgate Cl PL9 135 E4
Southgate Pl PL15 106 C5
Southgate St
Launceston PL15 106 C5
Redruth TR15 140 C3
South Harbour TR10 144 D7
South Hill
Plymouth, Hooe PL9 135 C5
Plymouth, Stoke PL1 128 A3
South Hill Rd PL17 39 E5
Southlea Terr TR3 80 F3
Southleigh Ho 15 TR1 137 C4
Southleigh Mews 14 TR1 137 C4
South Milton St PL4 149 C2
South Par 33 TR18 143 E5
South Park Cl TR15 140 A4
Southpark Rd PL24 60 C5
South Petherwin Com Prim Sch PL15 27 E8
South Pk
Jacobstow EX23 11 A6
Redruth TR15 139 F6
16 St Columb Major TR9 45 E6
South Pl TR19 86 E6
South Place Folly 5 TR18 143 E4
South Place Gdns TR19 86 E6
South Quay PL28 107 D5
South Quay Hill TR7 110 D6
South Rd
Goldsithney TR20 89 E5
Stithians TR3 80 F3
South Roskear Terr TR14 138 F4
Southside Ope 14 PL1 149 A2
Southside St PL1 149 A2
South St
Fowey PL23 116 D4
Grampound Road TR2 57 E1
Lostwithiel PL22 112 C2
St Austell PL25 114 C3
South Terr
Camborne TR14 138 D2
12 Penzance TR18 143 E4
South Towan TR4 68 A6
South Trelawny Prim Sch PL2 128 A8
Southview PL10 133 A6
South View
9 Horrabridge PL20 42 C4
Liskeard PL14 113 D7
Penryn TR10 144 C8
Plymouth, Crownhill PL5 124 E2
Plymouth, Elburton PL9 136 B6
Porthleven TR13 91 A1
South View Cl PL7 130 D7
Southview Dr PL31 109 E5
South View Parc TR4 68 A6
South View Pk PL7 130 D7
Southview Rd 15 PL24 60 B4
Southview Terr 8 TR19 88 C1
South View Terr
Blackwater TR4 68 E5
Nancegollan TR13 91 B7
Plymouth PL4 149 C3
Southway PL28 20 F2
South Way TR8 111 F3
Southway Dr PL6 124 E6
Southway La
Plymouth, Southway PL6 125 B6
Plymouth, Tamerton Foliot PL6 124 C6
Southway Prim Sch PL6 124 E6
Southwell Rd PL6 124 E1
Sovereign Ct PL7 130 C5
Spargo Ct TR10 93 C8
Sparkatown La PL20 42 E3
Sparke Cl PL7 131 B4
Sparkwell All Saints Prim Sch PL7 131 F8
Spar La TR15 67 D4
Sparnon Cl
Redruth TR15 140 C4
St Austell PL25 114 B4
Sparnon Cross TR13 90 F5
Sparnon Ct TR15 140 C4
Sparnon Hill 1 TR15 140 C4
Sparnon Terr 2 TR15 140 C4
Sparry La TR16 80 F8
Spaven Mor TR14 138 F5
Speares The PL12 122 B2
Spear's Terr TR11 144 F1
Speech La TR3 81 C4
Speedwell Cl
Bude EX23 104 F5
Millbrook PL10 132 F5
Speedwell Cres PL6 129 B7
Speedwell Wlk PL6 129 B7
Spencer Gdns PL12 122 F1
Spencer Rd PL9 135 E8
Spernen Cl TR26 141 C2
Spernen Wyn Rd TR11 145 B2
Spicers La 11 EX23 4 E1
Spindrift TR8 44 C6
Spinnaker Quay PL9 134 F7
Spinnakers TR7 110 A5
Spinney The PL7 131 A4
Spire Ct PL3 129 B5
Spire Hill Pk PL12 122 C2
Spires The TR1 137 C6
Spirit of The West (American Theme Pk)* TR9 46 A8
Spitfire Row PL27 31 F3
Sportsmans PL32 105 C3
Sportsmans Rd PL32 105 C3
Springfield
Horrabridge PL20 42 C4
Portscatho TR2 83 B2
Springfield Ave PL9 136 B6
Springfield Bsns Pk PL15 18 E2
Springfield Cl
Dobwalls PL14 50 E7
Lostwithiel PL22 112 D2
Phillack TR27 142 D7
Plymouth PL9 136 B7
Polgooth PL26 59 A1
St Austell PL25 114 F5
Springfield Dr PL3 128 A4
Springfield Gate PL13 117 D5
Springfield La PL9 136 B7
Springfield Pk
Barripper TR14 79 B5
Mylor Bridge TR11 82 A3
Widegates PL13 63 E7
Springfield Pl 15 TR9 45 E6
Springfield Rd
Falmouth TR11 144 E5
Goldsithney TR20 89 E5
Liskeard PL14 113 E6
Looe PL13 117 D5
Newquay TR7 110 F6
Plymouth PL9 136 B6
Springfield Rise PL9 136 B7
Springfields PL26 47 C2
Springfields Fun Pk & Pony Ctr* TR9 45 E4
Springfield Way
Roche PL26 46 F3
St Day TR16 68 D1
Threemilestone TR3 69 C3
Springhill PL2 128 C8
Spring Hill PL19 147 B5
Springhill Gn PL2 128 C8
Spring Pk PL6 125 E7
Springwell View PL31 109 F5
Springwood Cl PL7 131 A3
Spruce Gdns PL7 131 B5
Spurway Rd PL14 113 D5
Square The
16 Bere Alston PL20 41 B1
Cawsand PL10 133 A1
2 Chacewater TR4 69 A3
Grampound Road TR2 57 E1
Gunnislake PL18 41 A6
Gunnislake, St Ann's Chapel PL18 40 E5
Kilkhampton EX23 5 A6
Landrake PL12 53 C3
Leedstown TR27 78 E1
Lizard TR12 102 F2
Ludgvan TR20 89 A8
Manaccan TR12 101 A7
Marazion TR17 89 B5
Pendeen TR19 75 A1
Penryn TR10 144 D7
Pentewan PL26 73 C6
Plymouth, Stonehouse PL1 128 A2
Portreath TR16 67 C6
Portscatho TR2 83 B2
Praze-an-Beeble TR14 79 B2
Probus TR2 71 C6
Redruth TR16 80 B5
Saltash PL12 122 C3
St Keverne TR12 101 D4
3 St Mawes TR2 95 A6
St Stephen PL26 58 B4
St Teath PL30 23 E7
Tregony TR2 71 F3
Veryan TR2 83 F6
Week St Mary EX22 11 E8
Squire La TR16 80 F8
Squires La TR13 91 C2
Stable Ct PL27 108 C6
Stable Hobba Ind Est TR18 143 B3
Stables The TR14 67 B4
Staddiscombe Rd PL9 135 F4
Staddon Cres PL9 135 E6
Staddon Gn PL9 135 D6
Staddon La PL9 135 B4
Staddon Park Rd PL9 135 E6
Staddon Terrace La PL1 148 B4
Stafford Cl TR7 111 D6
Staggy La TR3 81 F7
Stag La
Plymouth, Elburton PL9 136 B8
Plymouth, Plympton PL9 130 B1
Stamford Cl PL9 135 A6
Stamford Fort Cotts PL9 135 A6
Stamford Hill EX23 4 D1
Stamford La PL9 135 A6
Stamps Hill
Fraddon PL26 57 F8
Indian Queens TR9 45 F1
Stamps La TR15 139 D6
Stamps The PL17 40 D5
Stanborough Cross PL9 136 C7
Stanborough Rd PL9 136 B7
Stanbury Ave PL6 124 F1
Stanbury Cl PL15 13 F1
Stanbury Cross EX23 2 C1
Standarhay Cl PL9 136 C7
Standarhay Villas PL9 136 C7
Stanford Cl 5 TR18 143 D5
Stanford Mews TR9 45 E6
Stanford Terr TR18 143 D5
Stangray Ave PL4 128 D4
Stanharver Cl TR7 111 E6
Stanhope Rd PL5 123 C1
Stanley Ct 4 PL31 109 D5
Stanley Pl PL4 129 B2
Stanley Terr 1 TR15 140 B5
Stanley Way TR15 140 C6
Stannary Bridge Rd PL19 147 D6
Stannary Rd PL26 59 C8
Stantons Row PL14 38 A3
Stanways Rd TR7 111 D7
Staple Cl PL6 121 C1
Stapleford Gdns PL5 123 F5
Stapleton Rd EX23 104 F4
Star Pk PL18 41 A6
Statham Rd PL31 109 D4
Station App
3 Newquay TR7 110 F6
3 St Columb Road TR9 45 E2
St Erth TR27 77 E2
Station Hill
Hayle TR27 142 B5
Lelant TR26 77 E4
Praze-an-Beeble TR14 79 B2
Redruth TR15 140 B4
Station La PL18 41 A3
Station Par TR7 110 F6
Station Rd
Bere Alston PL20 41 B1
Bere Ferrers PL20 119 E3
Bugle PL26 47 C2
Camborne TR15 139 C5
Carnhell Green TR14 78 F4
Chacewater TR4 68 F4
Fowey PL23 116 D5

Station Rd *continued*
Grampound Road TR2 57 E1
Gunnislake PL18 40 F6
Helston TR13 146 C7
Horrabridge PL20 42 C4
Kelly Bray PL17 39 F6
Launceston PL15 106 C6
Liskeard PL14 113 B4
Looe PL13 117 C4
Mary Tavy PL19 30 F5
North Brentor PL19 30 E8
Padstow PL28 107 D5
Par PL24 60 C5
Penryn TR10 144 B8
Penzance TR18 143 F6
Perranarworthal TR3 81 E6
Perranporth TR6 55 B5
Plymouth, Elburton PL9 136 C7
Plymouth, Keyham PL2 127 E5
Plymouth, Plympton PL7 130 E5
Plymouth, Tamerton Foliot PL5 124 A6
Redruth TR15 140 C5
Saltash PL12 123 A2
St Columb Major TR9 45 E5
1 St Columb Road TR9 45 E2
St Mabyn PL30 34 C8
St Newlyn East TR8 56 B7
Truro TR1 137 B4
Yelverton PL20 42 D2
Station View PL19 30 E8
Station Yd 6 PL31 109 D5
Steamers Hill TR27 78 C5
Steamers Mdw TR27 78 C5
Steeple Cl
Plymouth PL9 135 F4
St Ives TR26 141 B3
Steeple La TR26 141 B3
Steeple View Ct TR26 141 C1
Steer Park Rd PL7 131 C5
Steer Point Cotts PL8 136 F2
Stefan Cl PL9 135 B5
Stenalees Hill PL26 59 C7
Stenlake Pl PL4 129 B2
Stenlake Terr PL4 129 B2
Stennack Gdns 14 TR26 141 A5
Stennack Parc TR19 86 F8
Stennack Rd PL25 115 B4
Stennack The TR26 141 B5
Stentaway Cl PL9 135 F8
Stentaway Dr PL9 136 A8
Stentaway Rd PL9 135 F8
Stephens Rd PL14 113 E7
Stephney Cl TR11 144 C2
Steppy Downs Rd TR27 78 A1
Stewarts Rd EX22 11 E8
Stiles The TR8 56 B7
Stillman Ct 7 PL4 149 A2
Stillman St PL4 149 A2
Stippy Stappy 11 TR5 54 D1
Stirling Ct PL5 123 C1
Stirling Rd PL5 123 C1
Stithians Com Prim Sch TR3 80 F4
Stithians Row TR16 80 B5
Stockadon Farm Barns PL12 118 B4
Stoggy La PL7 131 A6
Stoke Climsland Sch PL17 28 D1
Stoke Damerel Bsns Ctr 9 PL3 128 A4
Stoke Damerel Com Coll PL3 128 B4
Stoke Damerel Prim Sch PL1 128 A3
Stoke Hill La PL20 42 B2
Stoke Rd
Bray Shop PL17 28 A1
Kelly Bray PL17 39 E6
Linkinhorne PL17 39 A8
Plymouth PL1 148 A3
Stokesay Ave PL6 125 A5
Stokes La PL1 149 A2
Stokes Rd TR1 137 C5
Stoke Terr PL17 39 E6
Stokingway Cl PL9 135 E5
Stonebarton Cl PL7 130 C6
Stonebarton Rd PL7 130 C6
Stone Chair La TR19 96 B7
Stone Cross PL16 19 F5
Stonehall Flats PL1 128 A1
Stone Hill EX23 4 E2
Stonehouse Bridge PL1 128 A1
Stonehouse St PL1 148 A2
Stonerock Flats PL13 117 C1
Stones Ct 30 TR26 141 B5
Stonewood Ct 4 TR9 45 E6
Stoney Hill PL25 59 A4
Stoney La
Polgooth PL26 59 A1
St Austell PL25 114 C4
Stoney Lands PL12 53 C3
Stony La
Bodmin PL31 34 D1
Gunnislake PL18 40 F5
Stopford Pl PL1 127 F3
Stott Cl PL3 129 D5
Stour Cl PL3 129 D6
Stourscombe PL15 106 F3
Stourscombe Wood PL15 106 F4
Stowe Gdns PL5 124 B2
Stowford Cl PL20 42 E3
Stowford Cross EX22 5 F8
Stracey Rd TR11 145 B2
Strafford Cl EX23 104 C3
Strand TR18 143 C2
Strand St
Padstow PL28 107 D5
Plymouth PL1 134 A8
Strand The
Bude EX23 104 D5
Falmouth TR11 145 C2
Padstow PL28 107 D5
Strangways Terr TR1 137 D3
Strangways Villas TR1 137 D3
Stratton Hospl EX23 4 D1
Stratton Pl TR11 145 A6
Stratton Prim Sch EX23 4 D1
Stratton Rd
Bude EX23 104 F4
Stratton EX23 4 D1
Stratton Terr
Falmouth TR11 145 A6
Truro TR1 137 B4
Stratton Wlk PL2 128 D8
Strawberry Cl TR15 140 B6
Strawberry Cres TR15 140 B6
Strawberry Fields TR16 140 E1
Strawberry Gdns TR16 140 E1
Strawberry La
Hayle TR27 142 D4
Lelant TR26 77 E4
Redruth TR15 140 B6
Stray Park Ct TR14 138 F2
Stray Park Rd TR14 138 E2
Stray Park Way TR14 138 F2
Street-An-Garrow 17 TR26 141 B5
Street-An-Pol 3 TR26 141 B5
Stretyn 5 TR3 81 F7
Strickland Cotts 6 TR18 143 C2
Stringers Hill TR20 88 A5
Strode Rd PL7 130 F6
Stroma Cl PL6 124 F7
Stroud Park Rd PL2 128 C7
Stuart Rd PL3 148 A4
Stuart Road Prim Sch PL1 148 A4
Stuarts Way PL12 53 E5
Stucley Rd EX23 4 D1
Sturdee Rd PL2 128 A5
Stursdon Cross EX23 5 A8
Sugar Mill Bsns Pk PL9 129 C1
Summercourt TR10 144 D7
Summercourt Com Prim Sch TR8 57 C7
Summerfield Cl PL26 73 B3
Summerfields PL12 122 D1
Summerheath TR10 81 C1
Summerhill Rd PL15 106 A5
Summer La PL13 62 D6
Summerlands Cl PL7 131 C5
Summerlands Gdns PL7 131 C5
Summerlane Pk PL13 62 D6
Summerleaze Ave EX23 104 D7
Summerleaze Cres EX23 104 D6
Summer Lodge Holiday Village TR8 45 B2
Summers Cl PL6 129 B7
Summers St PL22 112 C2
Summerville Cross EX39 3 C6
Suncrest PL14 38 A4
Suncrest Est TR9 45 E1
Sunderland Cl PL9 135 A6
Sunderland Rd PL27 31 F3
Sun Girt La PL14 113 C5
Sunland Holiday Est TR16 67 C5
Sunley Orford Ho 6 TR1 137 D4
Sunningdale TR1 137 A4
Sunningdale Rd PL12 122 C2
Sunnybank 23 TR13 98 C8
Sunny Bank
Bodmin PL30 48 E8
Liskeard PL14 113 A4
Sunnybanks PL12 53 E4
Sunny Cnr
Goldsithney TR20 89 F5
Truro TR4 81 B7
Sunny Corner La TR19 96 C7
Sunnycroft PL13 117 C3
Sunny Dene PL5 123 D1
Sunnyside
Carnkie TR13 80 D1
Crantock TR8 110 A3
Menheniot PL14 51 F5
Menheniot PL14 52 B5
2 Perranporth TR6 55 A4
Portscatho TR2 83 B2
7 Redruth TR15 140 B4
Sunnyside Mdw PL32 105 D4
Sunnyside Parc TR15 139 C8
Sunnyside Rd PL4 129 B2
Sunny Terr TR18 143 B2
Sunnyvale Cl TR16 67 C6
Sunnyvale Rd TR16 67 D6
Sunrising Est PL13 117 D5
Sunset Dr 8 TR13 98 C8
Sunset Gdns 9 TR13 98 C8
Sunshine Terr PL19 147 D6
Sun Valley Pk TR9 45 E6
Sunway Cl PL19 147 A6
Sunwell La
Antony PL11 65 E4
St John PL11 132 A8
Surf View TR7 110 A6
Sussex Pl PL1 148 C2
Sussex Rd PL2 127 F5
Sussex St PL1 148 C2
Sussex Terr 5 PL2 127 F5
Sutherland Rd PL4 149 A4
Sutton Ct PL1 127 F1
Sutton Mews 22 PL4 149 A2
Sutton Pl PL4 149 B2
Sutton Rd PL4 149 B2
Sutton Wharf PL4 149 A2
Swaindale Rd 3 PL3 128 E6
Swale Cl PL3 129 B6
Swallow Cl EX23 104 D5
Swallowfield Cl PL24 60 D5
Swallow Ho 13 TR11 145 C3
Swallows End PL9 135 E8
Swan Cl PL10 133 A6
Swan Gdns PL7 130 F5
Swanpool Ct TR11 145 A1
Swanpool Hill TR11 145 A2
Swanpool Rd TR11 144 F1
Swanpool St TR11 145 C3
Swanvale Rd TR11 144 F3
Sweet Briar Cres TR7 111 A4
Swift Gdns PL5 124 C2
Swinburne Gdns PL5 124 C1
Swingate Cross EX22 13 E8
Sycamore Ave
Plymouth PL4 149 C2
St Austell PL25 114 E5
Tavistock PL19 147 C2
Sycamore Cl
Bodmin PL31 109 B4
Polgooth PL26 59 A1
Praze-an-Beeble TR14 79 B2
Rock PL27 21 E3
Sycamore Dr
Illogan TR15 139 D7
Plymouth PL6 125 C7
Redruth TR15 140 D5
Torpoint PL11 127 A3
Sycamore Gdns TR8 57 B7
Sycamore Rd PL12 122 B3
Sycamores The PL25 114 C4
Sycamore Way PL6 125 E6
Sydenham Cross PL19 29 C2
Sydney Cl
Plymouth PL7 130 E4
St Austell PL25 114 C3
Sydney Rd
Newquay TR7 110 D6
Torpoint PL11 127 B3
Sydney St PL1 148 B4
Sylvan Cl PL25 114 E6
Sylvan Ct PL1 128 A3
Sylverton Pl 12 TR18 143 C7
Symons Cl
Blackwater TR4 68 E5
St Austell PL25 115 A5
Symons Hill TR11 145 A5
Symons Rd PL12 122 F2
Symons Row PL14 37 F3
Symons Terr TR15 140 B5
Syra Cl PL30 23 B2

T

Tabernacle St TR1 137 D4
Tackbear Rd EX22, EX23 7 E4
Tailyour Rd PL6 124 F2
Talbot Gdns PL5 127 D7
Talexandra Terr PL15 106 D5
Talgos Cl TR16 140 E8
Talland Ct 29 TR26 141 B5
Talland Hill PL13 62 E2
Talland Rd TR26 141 B5
Talmena Ave PL27 108 A5
Talveneth
Camborne TR14 138 F3
Pendeen TR19 75 A1
Redruth TR15 140 C6
Talvenydh Ct PL31 109 D5
Tamar Ave
Plymouth PL2 127 E5
Tavistock PL19 147 D5
Tamar Bridge PL5 123 A2
Tamar Cl
18 Bere Alston PL20 41 B1
29 Callington PL17 39 F4
Tamar Ho PL1 127 E1
Tamarisk La TR7 111 A4
Tamar Otter Sanctuary* PL15 18 B8
Tamar Pk Cvn Site PL18 40 D6
Tamar Science Pk PL6 125 C4
Tamarside Com Coll PL5 123 E1
Tamar St
Plymouth PL1 127 E3
Saltash PL12 123 A2
Torpoint PL11 127 C3
Tamar Terr
Calstock PL17 41 A3
Horsebridge PL19 29 C1
Launceston PL15 106 D5
Saltash PL12 123 A2
Tamar Units PL15 18 E2
Tamar Valley Donkey Pk* PL18 40 D5
Tamar View
Launceston PL15 106 D5
Milton Abbot PL19 29 C6
St Dominick PL12 40 D2
Tamar View Ind Est PL12 122 D5
Tamar Villas PL9 135 D7
Tamar Way PL18 41 A6
Tamar Wharf PL1 127 D3
Tamblin Ave PL14 50 E7
Tamerton Ave PL5 123 D1
Tamerton Cl PL5 124 A6
Tamerton Foliot Rd PL6 124 D5
Tamerton Rd PL6 121 B2
Tamerton Vale Prim Sch PL6 124 C6
Tangmere Ave PL5 123 E5
Tangye Cl TR16 67 E5
Tangye Rd TR15 139 C6
Tanhouse Rd PL22 112 C2
Tanwood View PL31 109 C5
Tapson Dr PL9 135 A6
Taranto Rd TR13 146 D4
Taroveor Rd TR18 143 E6
Taroveor Terr 3 TR18 143 E5
Tarr PL22 49 E3
Tarrandean La TR3 81 E6
Tarten Cross PL12 53 B4
Tate Gallery* TR26 141 B6
Taunton Ave PL5 124 B5
Taunton Pl PL5 124 B5
Tavern Barn PL23 116 C5
Tavistock Coll PL19 147 A3
Tavistock Com Prim Sch PL19 147 B4
Tavistock Cross PL20 41 C2
Tavistock Hospl PL19 147 B5
Tavistock Mus* PL19 147 C6
Tavistock Pl PL4 149 A3
Tavistock Rd
Callington PL17 39 F4
Launceston PL15 106 D5
Launceston, Stourscombe PL15 106 E3
Plymouth, Manadon PL5 124 E1
Plymouth PL6 125 B5
Yelverton PL20 42 C3
Tavy Pl PL4 128 F4
Tavy Rd
Saltash PL12 123 A3
Tavistock PL19 147 D5
Taw Cl PL3 129 D6
Tayberry Dr TR16 140 F1
Tay Gdns PL3 129 D7
Taylor Cl PL12 122 C3
Taylor Rd PL12 122 C4
Taylor's Cross EX23 5 B7
Taylor Sq PL19 147 B6
Teachers Cl PL9 135 F6
Teats Hill Flats PL4 149 B1
Teats Hill Rd PL4 149 B1
Tedder Rd 4 PL26 59 D7
Tees Cl PL3 129 C7
Teetotal St TR26 141 C6
Tehidy Cl TR14 138 F7
Tehidy Copse TR14 67 B4
Tehidy Country Park* TR14 67 B4
Tehidy Gdns TR14 138 F7
Tehidy Rd
Camborne TR14 138 D4
Tywardreath PL24 60 D5
Tehidy Terr TR11 145 A6
Teign Rd PL3 129 B6
Telcarne Cl TR27 78 D6
Telegraph Hill TR16 68 E1
Telegraph St TR16 68 D1
Telegraph Wharf PL1 134 A8
Telephone La PL26 59 C8
Telford Cres PL5 123 F2
Temeraire Rd PL5 124 D2
Tenacres La PL14 38 E4
Tenby Rd PL5 123 C1
Tencreek Ave TR18 143 E5
Tencreek Cvn And Camping Pk PL13 63 A3
Tenderah Ct TR13 146 C7
Tenderah Rd TR13 146 C6
Tennyson Gdns PL5 124 B1
Tern Gdns PL7 130 F5
Terrace The
Chacewater TR4 68 F3
Crafthole PL11 65 B5
Dobwalls PL14 50 D7
Downderry PL11 64 C5
East Portholland PL26 84 E5
Harrowbarrow PL17 40 D5
Penryn TR10 144 C7
Pentewan PL26 73 D6
Port Isaac PL29 22 E7
Portwrinkle PL11 65 A4
Rock PL27 21 D2
St Ives TR26 141 B5
Yeolmbridge PL15 18 E6
Terra Nova Gn PL2 128 B5
Terras Hill PL22 112 C3
Terras Rd PL26 58 A4
Tethadene PL30 23 E7
Tewington Pl PL25 114 B4
Tewkesbury Cl PL2 128 A8
Thackeray Gdns PL5 124 B1
Thames Gdns PL3 129 D5
Thanckes Cl PL11 127 A3
Thanckes Dr PL11 127 A4
Theatre Ope PL1 127 F1
Theatre Royal Plymouth PL1 148 C2
Therlow Rd PL3 129 B6
Thetford Gdns PL6 129 D8
Theydon Rd TR11 144 F3
Third Ave
Plymouth, Billacombe PL9 130 A1
Plymouth, Camels Head PL2 127 E7
Plymouth, Stoke PL1 128 A2
Thirlmere Gdns PL6 124 F4
Thistle Cl PL6 125 E7
Thomas Bullock Cl PL30 48 C2
Thomas Johnson Ct 6 TR1 137 C4
Thomas St 4 TR13 98 C8
Thomas Terr 5 TR13 98 C8
Thornberry Terr TR18 143 F6
Thornbury Park Ave PL3 128 D6
Thornbury Prim Sch PL6 125 D4
Thornbury Rd PL6 125 E4
Thorn Cl PL15 26 C7
Thorndon Cross EX22 8 F5
Thorne Cross EX23 4 F2
Thornhill Rd PL3 128 E6
Thornhill Way PL3 128 E6
Thorn La PL12 122 C3
Thorn Moor Cross PL15 19 F7
Thornpark Rd PL25 114 E5
Thorn Pk PL3 128 F5
Thorn Terr PL14 113 B5
Thornton Ave PL4 149 B4
Thornton Cl PL26 46 F3
Thornville Terr PL9 135 C7
Thornwell La PL12 53 E2
Thornyville Cl PL9 135 C8
Thornyville Dr PL9 135 D8
Thornyville Villas PL9 135 C8
Three Corners Cl PL32 105 B2
Three Cross TR13 91 F5
Three Holes Cross PL27 34 A8
Threemilestone Ind Est TR4 69 C3
Threemilestone Ret Pk TR3 69 C4
Threemilestone Sch TR3 69 D3
Thurlestone Wlk PL6 129 D8
Tiddy Brook Rd
Tavistock PL19 147 E2
Whitchurch PL19 147 E2
Tiddy Cl
St Germans PL12 65 B8
Tavistock PL19 147 B3
Tideford Cross La PL12 52 F3
Tideford Dr
Landrake PL12 53 A2
St Germans PL12 65 B8
Tideford Rd PL12 53 C3
Tidemill Ho TR11 145 C3
Tides Reach TR7 111 B7
Tillard Cl PL7 131 C5
Tillie St 5 PL17 39 E4
Tilly Cl PL9 135 F4
Timber Cl PL25 114 B4
Tincombe PL12 122 C2
Tincroft Rd TR15 139 B4
Tin La PL4 149 A2
Tinners Dr PL27 21 D6
Tinners Way
Callington PL17 39 F5
New Polzeath PL27 21 D6
16 St Ives TR26 77 A6
Tinners Wlk TR11 145 D3
Tinney Dr TR1 137 F5
Tintagel Castle* PL34 14 B8
Tintagel Cres PL2 128 C8
Tintagel Hotel 8 PL34 14 C7
Tintagel Hts PL34 14 D6
Tintagel Prim Sch PL34 14 C6
Tintagel Rd PL35 9 C1
Tintagel Terr PL29 22 D7
Tintagel Toy Mus* PL34 14 C7
Tintagel Visitor Ctr* PL34 14 C7
Tintern Ave PL4 149 C2
Tiny Mdws
Launceston PL15 18 E1
South Petherwin PL15 27 F8
Tipple Cross PL15 19 C6
Tithe Rd PL7 130 B7
Tiverton Cl PL6 125 B8
Tobruk Rd PL12 122 E3
Toby Way TR7 110 D7
Toddington Lea PL26 58 E5
Tolcarne Cl PL25 114 E3
Tolcarne Mews 7 TR7 110 F6
Tolcarne Rd
Camborne TR14 79 D5
Newquay TR7 110 F6
St Day TR16 68 D1
Tolcarne St TR14 138 D2
Tolcarne Terr TR18 143 C3
Tolgarrick Rd TR14 138 F5
Tolgus Hill TR15 140 A5
Tolgus Pl TR15 140 A6
Tolgus Tin* TR16 67 F5
Tolgus Vean TR15 140 A5
Tolgus Wartha TR15 140 A6
Tollgate Cl PL14 113 B4
Tollox Pl PL3 129 B4
Tollyfrank Hill TR2 83 F6
Tolpedn Flats TR26 141 E2
Tolponds Rd TR13 91 A1
Tolroy Holiday Village TR27 142 C2
Tolroy Rd TR27 142 D1
Tolskithy La TR15 139 E6
Tolticken Hill TR16 67 E6
Toltuff Cres TR18 143 C4
Toltuff Rd TR18 143 C4
Tolvaddon Energy Pk TR14 138 F7
Tolvaddon Rd TR15 139 A5
Tolvan Cross TR12 92 C2
Tolver Pl TR18 143 E6
Tolver Rd TR18 143 E6
Tolverth Terr TR20 88 F6
Tolview Terr TR27 142 B4
Tom Lyon Rd PL14 113 E5
Tom Nicolls Cl 7 PL14 38 A3
Top Hill TR2 57 E1
Top Of The Town Ctyd PL12 122 F2

Top Rd PL11 64 C5
Torbridge Cl PL12 122 D2
Torbridge Rd
6 Horrabridge PL20 42 C4
Plymouth PL7 130 E6
Torbryan Cl PL6 129 E8
Tor Cl
Plymouth, Hartley PL3 128 E7
Porthleven TR13 91 B1
Tor Cres PL3 128 E7
Tor La PL12 122 B1
Torland Rd PL3 128 E7
Torleven Rd TR13 91 B2
Torpoint Com Sch PL11 127 A4
Torpoint Inf Sch PL11 127 B3
Tor Rd
Newquay TR7 110 E6
Plymouth PL3 128 E7
Torridge Cl PL7 131 A6
Torridge Rd PL7 130 F6
Torridge Way PL3 129 C5
Torr La PL3 128 E7
Torr Rd PL3 128 E7
Torr View Ave PL3 128 D7
Tors View Cl PL17 39 F4
Torver Cl PL6 125 D2
Tor View
Bugle PL26 47 C2
Camelford PL32 105 C2
7 Horrabridge PL20 42 C4
Tregadillett PL15 18 C2
Torwood Cl PL31 109 D4
Tory Brook Ave PL7 130 E6
Tory Brook Ct PL7 130 E6
Tory Way PL7 130 D6
Tosberry Cross EX39 3 B8
Tothill Ave PL4 149 B3
Tothill Rd PL4 149 B3
Totnes Cl PL7 131 B4
Towan Blystra Rd TR7 111 A5
Towan Ct PL28 31 E8
Towan Rd
Pentewan PL26 73 D8
Porthtowan TR4 68 A7
Towednack Rd TR26 77 A6
Tower Cl
Pelynt PL13 62 D6
Sennen TR19 96 B6
Tower Ct PL12 122 C2
Towerfield Dr PL6 125 C8
Tower Hill
Looe PL13 117 D3
Wadebridge PL27 108 E5
Tower Hill Rd PL15 13 F1
Tower Mdws TR19 97 A6
Tower Park Est PL13 62 D6
Tower Park Rd PL13 62 C6
Tower Pk
Fowey PL23 116 B3
Lanivet PL30 47 E7
Pelynt PL13 62 D6
Tower Pk Cvn & Camping Pk TR19 97 A7
Tower Rd
Newquay TR7 110 D6
St Erme TR4 70 D8
Towers Cl PL6 125 F2
Tower St PL15 106 C6
Tower View PL12 122 D1
Town Arms Pas PL31 109 E5
Town End PL31 109 C5
Town Farm TR15 140 C3
Town Farm Cl 5 PL20 42 C4
Townfield TR15 139 C6
Town Hill TR5 54 D1
Town Mill Gdns PL19 147 C6
Town Mills PL15 106 B7
Town Mills Flats PL15 106 B7
Town Quay TR1 137 D4
Townsend
Polruan PL23 116 D2
14 Stratton EX23 4 E1
Townshend Ave PL2 127 E5
Townswell Cl PL12 53 E2
Townswell La PL12 53 E2
Traboe Cross TR12 100 D3
Tracey Ct PL1 148 B3
Trafalgar Cl PL5 127 D8
Trafalgar Ct TR18 143 F6
Trafalgar Pl 3 PL1 127 F3
Trafalgar Place La PL1 127 F3
Trafalgar Sq TR1 137 D4
Trafalgar St PL4 149 A3
Traine Brake PL9 136 C1
Traine Rd PL9 136 B1
Traly Cl EX23 104 F4
Tram La TR16 140 E1
Tramway Rd PL6 125 E7
Trannack Com Prim Sch TR13 91 E5
Trannack Mill Ind Est TR13 91 E5
Trannack Terr TR18 143 E7
Tranquil La PL31 109 C5
Transit Way PL5 124 C3
Trasdeves Orch 16 PL17 39 F4
Travellers Rest Pk TR12 99 B8
Travers Cl PL14 113 A6
Treago Gdns PL6 125 C8
Trease TR19 75 A1
Treassowe Rd TR18 143 E6
Treassowe Riding TR20 88 F8
Treator Cotts PL28 107 A5
Trebah Gdns* TR11 93 C2
Treban Rd TR18 143 C4
Trebartha Cl PL17 39 E3
Trebartha Rd TR1 137 F5
Trebarthen Terr TR4 55 D5
Trebarva Cl TR15 140 A6
Trebarvah La TR20 89 E4
Trebarvah Rd TR11 92 E4
Trebarwith Cres TR7 110 E6
Trebarwith Rd PL33 14 D4
Treberran Gdns TR14 138 F6
Treboul Cross PL12 64 F8
Treboul Way PL12 65 B8
Treburdon Dr PL26 46 F3
Treburgie Water PL14 50 D7
Treburley Cl PL15 28 C4
Treburley Ind Est PL15 28 C4
Trebyhan Parc TR3 80 F3
Treby Rd PL7 130 F4
Trecarn Cl PL15 106 B5
Trecarne
Falmouth TR11 144 E5
Tremar PL14 38 A3
Trecarne Cl
Polgooth PL26 59 A1
St Austell PL25 115 B5
Truro TR1 137 E5
Trecarne Gdns PL33 14 E3
Trecarne View PL14 37 F3
Trecarrack Rd TR14 138 F3
Trecarrell PL15 106 C4
Trecarrell Cl PL15 106 D4
Trecerus Ind Est PL28 107 B4
Tredanek Cl PL31 109 B5
Tredarrup Cross PL15 11 A1
Tredarvah Dr TR18 143 C5
Tredarvah Rd TR18 143 C5
Tredaula Manor Cvn Pk PL15 26 D7
Tredavoe La TR18 143 B1
Tredenham Cl 4 PL24 60 C4
Tredenham Rd TR2 95 B6
Tredethy Rd PL30 34 F6
Tredinnick Cotts TR 20 76 A1
Tredinnick La PL12 53 B2
Tredinnick Lane-End PL13 64 A8
Tredinnick Way 12 TR6 55 A4
Tredinnick Wood Cl TR13 146 D8
Tredour Rd TR7 110 E4
Tredova Cres TR11 145 B2
Tredragon Cl TR8 31 C2
Tredragon Rd TR8 31 C2
Tredrea Gdns TR3 81 D5
Tredrea La TR27 77 E2
Tredrea Manor TR3 81 D5
Tredrizzick Cl PL27 21 F3
Tredruston Rd PL27 33 B6
Tredydan Rd PL15 106 B6
Tredynas Rd TR11 145 D3
Tredyson Pl TR11 145 A3
Tre-El- Verne Cl TR1 137 A4
Treen Cotts TR26 75 F4
Treen Flats TR14 138 F3
Treen Hill TR19 96 F4
Treetop Cl PL12 122 D4
Treetops Hill PL13 117 A3
Treeve Farm Ind Units TR27 78 C6
Treeve La TR27 78 C6
Treffry Ct TR7 110 D6
Treffry La PL30 48 C6
Treffry Rd TR1 137 E7
Treffry Way 12 PL24 60 B4
Trefinnick Rd PL17 39 B8
Trefleur Cl 3 PL35 9 C1
Trefloyd Cl PL17 39 E6
Treforda Rd TR7 110 F4
Treforest Rd PL27 108 A6
Treforthlan 7 TR16 67 E4
Treforthlan Cl 6 TR16 67 E4
Trefrew Rd PL32 105 D5
Trefusis Cl TR1 137 F5
Trefusis Ct TR11 145 A6
Trefusis Gdns PL3 129 A4
Trefusis Rd
Falmouth TR11 144 E2
Flushing TR11 145 C6
Redruth TR15 140 C4
Trefusis Terr
Millbrook PL10 132 E6
Redruth TR15 140 C5
Tregadillett Com Prim Sch PL15 18 C2
Tregaer TR11 145 C3
Tregainlands Pk PL30 34 D3
Tregalister Gdns PL12 65 B8
Tregaller La PL15 18 E1
Treganoon Rd TR15 140 D7
Tregargus View PL26 58 B4
Tregarland Cl
Camborne TR14 138 E2
Coad's Green PL15 27 D4
Tregarne Terr PL25 114 C4
Tregarrian Rd TR14 138 F7
Tregarrick PL13 117 B3
Tregarrick Cl TR13 146 B7
Tregarrick Ct PL13 117 B3
Tregarrick La PL13 62 D6
Tregarrick Rd PL26 46 F3
Tregarrick Way PL13 62 D6
Tregarth 12 PL26 59 D7
Tregartha Way PL14 113 D6
Tregarthen 2 TR26 141 A5
Tregarth Pl TR18 143 C4
Tregassack Rd TR20 88 F7
Tregassick Rd TR2 83 B1
Tregatillian Cvn Pk TR9 45 F6
Tregavarras Row PL26 85 A5
Tregavethan View TR3 69 C4
Tregay La PL14 113 C7
Tregea Hill TR16 67 C6
Tregear Cl TR12 99 D6
Tregear Gdns TR1 137 C4
Tregease Rd TR5 54 C1
Tregea Terr TR16 67 C6
Tregellas Rd TR12 99 B1
Tregellast Cl TR12 101 D4
Tregellast Parc TR12 101 D4
Tregellast Rd TR12 101 D3
Tregembo Hill TR20 90 A7
Tregender La TR20 89 B8
Tregender Rd TR20 89 B8
Tregenna Cl
Plymouth PL7 131 C4
Wainhouse Corner EX23 10 F6
Tregenna Ct
Camborne TR14 138 C2
Falmouth TR11 145 C3
Tregenna Fields TR14 138 C2
Tregenna Hill 16 TR26 141 B5
Tregenna La TR14 138 C2
Tregenna Parc TR26 141 C3
Tregenna Pl 4 TR26 141 B5
Tregenna Rd PL30 35 C8
Tregenna Terr TR26 141 B5
Tregenver Rd TR11 144 F4
Tregenver Terr TR11 144 F4
Tregenver Villas TR11 144 F4
Tregeseal Hill TR19 86 F7
Tregeseal Row TR19 86 F6
Tregeseal Terr TR19 86 F6
Tregew Cl TR11 145 B7
Tregew Rd
Flushing TR11 145 B8
Penryn TR10, TR11 81 F2
Treggodick Cotts TR20 143 A8
Tregian Cl TR1 137 F5
Tregidden Hill TR12 100 F5
Tregie TR18 143 B3
Tregiskey Cotts PL26 73 C5
Tregisky La TR12 101 C1
Treglenwith Rd TR14 138 C4
Treglisson Rural Workshops TR27 78 C3
Treglyn Cl TR18 143 B1
Treglyn Farm Cotts PL27 22 B3
Tregoddick Cl TR20 88 B7
Tregolds La PL28 31 F7
Tregolls Cl TR1 137 E5
Tregolls Rd TR1 137 E5
Tregolls Sch TR1 137 F5
Tregoney Hill PL26 73 C3
Tregongeeves La PL26 59 A2
Tregonhay PL14 38 C7
Tregonhayne Ct TR2 72 A4
Tregoniggie Ind Est TR11 144 D4
Tregoning Rd PL11 126 F2
Tregonissey Cl PL25 114 D5
Tregonissey Rd PL25 114 E5
Tregonissy La End PL25 114 E6
Tregonning Cl TR13 90 E3
Tregonning Ct 8 TR6 55 A5
Tregonning Parc 9 TR12 101 C4
Tregonning Rd TR3 80 F3
Tregonning Terr TR13 90 F5
Tregonning View 17 TR13 98 C8
Tregony Com Prim Sch TR2 71 F4
Tregony Hill TR2 71 F3
Tregony Rd TR2 71 D6
Tregony Rural Workshops TR2 71 E3
Tregorrick Rd PL26 114 E1
Tregos Rd TR26 141 C2
Tregoss Rd TR7 110 F6
Tregothnan Rd
Falmouth TR11 145 A5
Truro TR1 137 E3
Tregowris Court Cotts TR12 101 B5
Tregrea TR14 138 E1
Tregrehan Gdns* PL24 115 E6
Treguddock Dr PL27 108 D5
Tregullan TR15 139 C8
Tregullan View PL31 109 D3
Tregullow Rd TR11 144 F5
Tregundy Cl 21 TR6 55 A5
Tregundy Ct 20 TR6 55 A5
Tregundy La TR6 55 A5
Tregundy Rd TR6 55 A5
Tregunna Cl TR13 91 B1
Tregunnel Cvn Pk TR7 110 D5
Tregunnel Hill TR7 110 D4
Tregunnick La PL11 64 B6
Tregunnus La PL11 64 D5
Treguntер Mews TR11 145 D3
Tregurra La TR1 137 E6
Tregurrian Hill TR8 44 D8
Tregurtha Farm Cotts TR17 89 D6
Tregurtha View TR20 89 E5
Tregurthen Cl TR14 138 C2
Tregurthen Rd TR14 138 C2
Tregustick Holiday Pk TR8 44 D6
Treguth Cl TR8 43 B1
Tregwary Rd TR26 141 A5
Tregye Campus (Truro Coll) TR3 82 A7
Tregye Rd TR3 82 A7
Trehaddle TR4 81 B7
Trehane Rd TR14 138 B3
Trehannick Cl PL30 23 E7
Trehaverne Cl TR1 137 C5
Trehaverne La TR1 137 C5
Trehaverne Terr 3 TR1 137 C5
Trehaverne Vean TR1 137 C5
Trehawke La PL14 38 C1
Trehayes Mdw TR27 77 E2
Trehayes Parc TR27 142 E7
Trehaze-Na Cl PL32 10 C3
Treheath Rd PL14 50 E7
Trehill Cross PL12 40 C2
Trehill La PL10 64 B2
Trehunsey Cl TR11 93 E2
Trehurst TR18 143 D4
Trekeen Rd TR10 144 B8
Trekenner Com Prim Sch PL15 28 C5
Trekenning Rd TR9 45 D5
Trekestle Cvn Pk PL15 18 C2
Trekestle Pk PL15 18 C2
Trekye Cl TR16 80 B5
Trelake Rd PL25 114 B4
Trelan TR14 138 F3
Trelander Barton TR1 137 E5
Trelander E TR1 137 F4
Trelander Highway TR1 137 E4
Trelander N TR1 137 F4
Trelander S TR1 137 F4
Trelander Vean TR1 137 F4
Trelantis Est PL28 31 F8
Trelaske La PL13 62 F4
Trelavour Prazey PL26 58 B8
Trelavour Rd PL26 58 C8
Trelavour Sq PL26 58 C8
Trelawne Cl 10 TR3 81 F7
Trelawne Cottage Gdns PL13 62 E4
Trelawne Gdns PL13 62 E5
Trelawne Rd TR3 81 F7
Trelawney Apartments TR7 110 F6
Trelawney Ave
Falmouth TR11 145 B3
Plymouth PL5 123 D1
Poughill EX23 4 C3
Redruth TR15 140 E7
St Ives TR26 141 A5
Trelawney Cl
Bodmin PL31 109 C4
Maenporth TR11 93 E3
Torpoint PL11 126 E3
Warbstow Cross PL15 11 B1
Trelawney Cotts PL15 106 D5
Trelawney Ct PL27 21 E3
Trelawney Est
Madron TR20 143 A8
Ponsanooth TR4 81 B7
Trelawney Gdns PL14 38 D4
Trelawney Hts 19 PL17 39 F4
Trelawney Parc
St Columb Major TR9 45 D5
Warbstow Cross PL15 11 B1
Trelawney Pl
Hayle TR27 142 C6
Penryn TR10 144 C8
Plymouth PL5 123 D1
Trelawney Rd
Bodmin PL31 109 C3
Callington PL17 39 F4
Camborne TR14 138 D3
Chacewater TR4 69 A3
Helston TR13 146 C5
Newquay TR7 110 E5
Padstow PL28 107 D4
Plymouth PL3 128 D5
Ponsanooth TR3 81 B4
Saltash PL12 122 E2
St Austell PL25 114 E5
St Ives TR26 141 A5
St Mawes TR2 95 A6
Truro TR1 137 B5
Trelawney Rise
18 Callington PL17 39 F4
Torpoint PL11 126 E3
Trelawney Terr
Cury TR12 99 B4
Looe PL13 117 C4
Trelawney Way
Hayle TR27 142 C6
Torpoint PL11 126 E3
Trelawny Ct TR14 138 C3
Trelawny Rd
Falmouth TR11 145 B4
Menheniot PL14 52 A6
Plymouth PL7 130 C6
St Agnes TR5 54 C1
Tavistock PL19 147 C6
Treleaver Way TR1 69 F3
Trelee Cl TR27 142 E7
Treleigh Ave TR15 140 B6
Treleigh Com Prim Sch TR16 140 C8
Treleigh Ind Est TR16 140 C7
Treleigh Terr TR15 140 A5
Trelevan Cl PL25 114 C3
Treleven Rd EX23 104 F4
Treliddon La PL11 64 C5
Treliever Cross TR10 81 C1
Treliever Rd
Mabe Burnthouse TR10 81 C1
Penryn TR10 144 B8
Treligga Downs Rd PL33 14 D2
Trelil Cvn Site TR13 146 E7
Trelil La TR11 144 C2
Trelindon PL15 27 E8
Trelinnoe Cl PL15 27 E8
Trelinnoe Gdns PL15 27 E8
Treliske Ind Est TR1 69 E4
Treliske La TR1, TR4 69 F4
Treliske Prep Sch TR1 69 F4
Treliske Rd TR15 140 D6
Trelispen Park Dr PL26 85 C5
Trelispen Pk PL26 85 C5
Trelissick Fields TR27 142 B3
Trelissick Gdns
Callington PL17 39 E3
Feock TR3 82 D6
Trelissick Rd
Falmouth TR11 144 F5
Hayle TR27 142 B3
Trelissick Woodland Wlk* TR3 82 D6
Treloan La TR2 83 B1
Treloar Terr PL15 106 B6
Treloggan Ind Est TR7 111 B4
Treloggan La TR7 111 A5
Treloggan Rd TR7 111 A4
Trelorrin Gdns PL3 128 E5
Trelowarren* TR12 99 F6
Trelowarren Ct 13 PL17 39 E4
Trelowarren St TR14 138 D3
Treloweck TR14 79 A4
Treloweth Cl
Plymouth PL2 128 D8
St Erth TR27 77 E2
Treloweth Com Prim Sch TR15 139 D6
Treloweth Gdns TR15 139 C6
Treloweth La TR27 77 E2
Treloweth Rd TR15 139 C6
Treloweth Terr TR15 139 B7
Treloweth Way TR15 139 C7
Trelowth Rd PL26 59 A1
Treloyhan Cl TR26 141 C3
Treloyhan Park Rd TR26 141 C3
Trelyn PL27 21 E3
Trelyn Rd TR12 101 D4
Trelyon Ave TR26 141 C4
Trelyon Cl TR19 97 B6
Tremabe La PL14 50 E7
Tremabe Pk PL14 50 E7
Tremadart Cl PL14 51 A1
Tremadart Farm Barns PL14 51 A1
Tremaddock Cotts PL14 36 F3
Tremaddock Council Hos PL14 36 F3
Tremaine Cl TR18 143 C7
Tremalic PL13 117 B3
Tremall Parc TR3 80 F3
Tremanor Way TR11 144 D5
Tremar Cl PL14 38 A2
Tremar La
St Cleer PL14 37 F3
Tremar PL14 38 A3
Tremarle Home Pk TR14 138 F5
Tremarne Cl TR3 82 C5
Tremar Rd TR26 77 A7
Tremarren Rd PL27 108 B5
Trematon Cl PL11 126 E4
Trematon Terr PL4 128 E4
Tremayne Cl TR3 81 F6
Tremayne Ho PL31 109 B4
Tremayne Pk TR14 138 F2
Tremayne Rd
Carharrack TR16 80 F8
St Austell PL25 114 E4
Truro TR1 137 C5
Tremayne Rise PL19 147 B5
Tremayne Terr PL13 63 F8
Trembath Cres TR7 110 E5
Trembear Rd PL25 114 A4
Trembel Rd TR12 99 B2
Trembrase TR19 96 C7
Tremeadow Terr
Hayle TR27 142 B4
Liskeard PL14 113 D7
Tremear Gn 6 TR9 45 E2
Tremearne Rd 16 TR13 98 C8
Tremeddan Ct 2 PL14 113 C6
Tremeddan La PL14 113 C6
Tremeddan Terr PL14 113 B4
Tremeer La PL30 23 E3
Tremellin La TR27 77 F1
Tremena Gdns PL25 114 C4
Tremena Rd PL25 114 C4
Tremenheere Ave TR13 146 D8
Tremenheere Rd TR18 143 E6
Tremenva Ct 1 TR13 146 C5
Tremewan 1 PL25 59 A3
Tremodrett Rd PL26 46 F3
Tremoh Ct TR2 71 C6
Tremollett Cotts PL17 28 B1
Tremore Rd TR15 140 D6
Tremorva TR27 142 C6
Tremorvah Barton TR1 137 E5
Tremorvah Cres TR1 137 E5
Tremorvah Ct
Falmouth TR11 144 F1
Truro TR1 137 E5
Tremorvah Pk TR11 144 F1
Tremorvah Wood La TR1 137 E5
Tremough Barton Cotts TR10 81 C1
Tremoughdale TR10 144 B8
Trenale La PL34 14 D7
Trenalt Terr TR1 137 B5
Trenance Ave TR7 110 F5
Trenance Cl TR13 146 B7
Trenance Ct TR7 110 E4
Trenance Cvn Pk TR7 110 F5
Trenance Hill PL25 114 A5
Trenance Inf Sch TR7 110 E5
Trenance La
3 Mullion TR12 99 A1
Newquay TR7 110 E4

Trenance Leisure Pk* TR7 111 A5
Trenance Pl PL25 114 B4
Trenance Rd
Camborne TR14 138 E4
Newquay TR7 110 E5
St Austell PL25 114 B4
Trenant TR16 68 D1
Trenant Cl PL27 21 E5
Trenant Cross PL14 63 A6
Trenant Ind Est PL27 108 D6
Trenant Rd
Looe PL13 117 D5
2 Tywardreath PL24 60 D5
Trenant Vale PL27 108 D6
Trenarren View PL25 115 A6
Trenarth TR10 144 C8
Trenarth Rd TR7 110 E5
Trenawin La TR27 78 E5
Trencher La PL10 132 D2
Trencreek Cl TR4 56 D1
Trencreek La TR8 111 B4
Trencreek Rd TR7, TR8 111 B4
Trencrom La TR26 141 D1
Trencrom Row TR20 77 B3
Trendeal Gdns 1 TR18 143 E5
Trendlewood Rd PL6 125 D7
Trendreath Cl TR26 77 E3
Treneague Pk PL27 108 B4
Trenear Cl TR15 140 D6
Treneere La TR18 143 D7
Treneere Rd TR18 143 D6
Treneglos TR4 81 C7
Treneglos Terr
Gulval TR18 88 E6
Newlyn TR18 143 C3
Trenerry Cl TR1 137 D6
Trenerth Rd TR27 78 E2
Trenethick Ave TR13 146 D8
Trenethick Bsns Pk TR13 146 C8
Trenethick Cl TR13 146 D7
Trenethick Farm TR13 146 B8
Trenethick Parc TR13 146 D8
Trengove PL26 47 C1
Trengove Cross TR11 92 D5
Trengrouse Ave PL11 126 F3
Trengrouse Way TR13 146 C5
Trengwainton Gdns* TR20 88 A6
Trenhaile Terr TR1 70 D1
Trenhayle La TR27 142 B2
Treningle View PL31 109 C3
Treninnick Hill TR7 110 F5
Treninnow & Wiggle Chalets PL10 132 C2
Trenithick Mdw TR4 68 C6
Trenithon La TR8 57 C6
Trennance Ct 6 TR12 99 A1
Trennick La TR1 137 E3
Trennick Row TR1 137 E3
Trennick Villas Ct TR1 137 E3
Trenode CE Sch PL13 51 F1
Trenouth Cl 5 PL14 38 A3
Trenovissick Rd PL24 60 B4
Trenowah Rd PL25 115 C5
Trenoweth Ave TR14 138 B3
Trenoweth Cres TR18 143 B4
Trenoweth Ct TR12 102 F2
Trenoweth Est TR15 140 A8
Trenoweth La TR10 93 B8
Trenoweth Mdw TR12 102 F2
Trenoweth Rd
Falmouth TR11 144 F2
Penzance TR18 143 B5
Trenoweth Terr TR10 93 B8
Trenoweth Vean TR10 81 B1
Trenowth Terr TR2 57 E1
Trent Cl PL3 129 B6
Trentham Cl PL6 125 B6
Trentworthy Cross EX22 3 E2
Trenwith La TR26 141 A4
Trenwith Pl 14 TR26 141 B5
Trenwith Rd TR14 138 B3
Trenwith Sq TR26 141 A5
Trenwith Terr 11 TR26 141 B5
Trenython Rd 10 PL24 60 B4
Treore Cl PL30 23 A6
Treovis Cross PL14 38 C8
Tre-Pol PL26 58 F1
Treraven La PL27 108 C3
Trerew Rd TR18 143 C4
Trerice* TR8 44 D1
Trerice Ct 15 PL17 39 E4
Trerice Dr TR7 111 B5
Trerice Fields TR14 79 B2
Trerice Holdings TR8 44 C1
Trerice Pl TR26 141 A5
Trerice Rd 6 TR26 141 A5
Trerice Terr PL26 58 A8
Trerieve PL11 64 C5
Trerise Rd TR14 138 C3
Treroosel Rd PL30 23 D8
Treruffe Hill TR15 140 B4
Treruffe Terr 9 TR15 140 B4
Treryn Cl PL24 60 B5
Tresaderns Rd TR15 140 A6
Tresahar Rd TR11 145 A3
Tresamble Hill TR4, TR3 81 B6
Tresavean Est TR16 80 E6
Tresavean Hill TR16 80 E6
Tresavean Terr TR16 80 E6
Tresawla Ct TR14 138 F6
Tresawle Rd TR11 145 A6
Tresawls Ave TR1 69 F3
Tresawls Rd TR1, TR4 69 E4
Tresawna Terr TR11 145 B4
Trescobeas Rd TR11 144 E5
Trescoe Rd TR20 88 F6
Trescol Vean Sch TR3 69 C2
Tresco Pl TR11 144 F4
Trescore PL28 31 F7
Trescowe Rd TR20 89 F5
Tresdale Parc TR27 78 D6
Treseder's Gdns TR1 137 D5
Tresevern Hill TR3 80 D4
Tresidder Cl TR11 144 E4
Tresillian Ho TR1 69 E4
Tresillian Rd TR11 144 F6
Tresillian St PL4 149 C2
Tresithney Rd TR16 80 F8
Treskerby TR16 140 F7
Treskewes Est 1 TR12 101 C4
Treskilling PL30 59 F8
Treslothan Rd TR14 79 D4
Tresluggan Rd PL5 123 D1
Tresooth Ct TR10 144 D7
Tresooth La TR10 144 C8
Tresooth Terr TR10 144 D7
Tresowgar La TR2 71 B6
Tresprison Ct TR13 146 E5
Tressa Dowr La TR1 137 F5
Treswithian Barns TR14 138 A3
Treswithian Park Rd TR14 138 B3
Treswithian Rd TR14 138 B3
Tretawn Cl PL30 23 B2
Trethannas Gdns TR14 79 B2
Trethellan Hill TR7 110 C5
Trethern Cl TR14 79 E4
Tretherras Cl TR7 111 A6
Tretherras Rd TR7 111 A6
Trethevy Cl PL14 37 F3
Trethevy Quoit* PL14 38 A3
Trethewey Cl 10 TR9 45 E6
Trethewey Way TR7 110 D5
Trethew Gdns TR14 138 E4
Trethiggey Cres TR8 111 F3
Trethiggey Touring Pk TR8 111 F2
Trethill La PL11 65 C5
Trethorne Leisure Farm* PL15 18 B2
Trethorns Ct TR20 89 A8
Trethosa Rd PL26 58 B4
Trethowan Hts TR1 69 F3
Trethurffe Terr TR9 45 E5
Trethurffe Villas TR2 57 C1
Trethurgy Gdns 17 PL17 39 E4
Tretoil View PL31 109 E2
Tretorvic TR18 143 C8
Tretower Cl PL6 124 F5
Trevadlock Hall Pk PL15 27 A6
Trevail Cotts TR8 43 D1
Trevail Way PL25 114 E4
Trevale TR18 143 C5
Trevalga Cl 5 TR6 55 A4
Trevallack Parc 3 TR12 101 C4
Trevallack View 2 TR12 101 C4
Trevallion Pk TR3 82 B5
Trevallyn Rd PL15 106 B4
Trevance TR10 144 A8
Trevance Pk PL24 60 D5
Trevanion Cl PL27 108 B4
Trevanion Ct
Mawnan Smith TR11 93 D3
1 Newquay TR7 110 F6
Truro TR1 69 F3
Trevanion La PL25 59 A3
Trevanion Pk PL27 108 C4
Trevanion Rd
Liskeard PL14 113 D5
St Austell PL25 114 D2
2 Trewoon PL25 59 A3
Wadebridge PL27 108 B4
Trevanion Terr PL27 108 C4
Trevannion Cl PL6 129 A8
Trevanson Rd PL27 108 A6
Trevanson St PL27 108 B6
Trevarner Way PL27 108 D6
Trevarno Cl PL25 59 A3
Trevarnon Cl TR27 78 D6
Trevarnon La TR27 78 D6
Trevarrack Cl TR18 143 F8
Trevarrack La TR18 143 F8
Trevarrack Pl TR18 143 F8
Trevarrack Rd TR18 143 F8
Trevarrack Row TR18 88 E6
Trevarren Ave TR16 80 A5
Trevarrian Hill TR8 44 D8
Trevarrian Holiday Pk TR8 44 E8
Trevarrick Ct TR26 141 C1
Trevarrick Dr PL25 114 B4
Trevarrick Rd PL25 114 B3
Trevarth Est PL26 73 C4
Trevarthian Ho TR17 89 B5
Trevarthian Rd
St Austell PL25 114 C4
St Austell PL25 114 D4
Trevarth Rd TR11 144 F5
Trevarth Terr TR16 80 E7
Trevarweneth Rd 8 PL24 60 B4
Trevassack Ct TR27 142 D6
Trevassack Hill TR27 142 E6
Trevassack Parc TR27 142 E6
Trevaunance Cl TR5 54 C2
Trevaunance Cove Heritage Trail* TR5 54 D2
Trevaunance Rd TR5 54 C2
Trevaylor Camping & Cvn Site TR19 86 F7
Trevaylor Cl TR1 137 E6
Trevaylor Rd TR11 144 F5
Trevean Cl TR14 138 B3
Trevean Gdns 3 TR18 143 D5
Trevean La TR20 89 F4
Trevean Rd
Penzance TR18 143 D5
Truro TR1 69 F3
Trevean Way
Newquay TR7 110 C5
Rosudgeon TR20 89 F4
Trevear Cl PL25 114 D3
Trevear Rd PL26 58 B4
Trevecca Cotts PL14 113 C8
Treveglos TR27 142 B6
Treveglos Rd TR11 144 E1
Trevelga Ct TR7 111 A7
Trevelgue Ct TR8 44 C6
Trevelgue Cvn & Camping Pk TR8 44 D6
Trevelgue Rd TR7, TR8 44 C6
Trevellan Rd TR11 82 A3
Trevella Rd EX23 104 E7
Trevella Vean TR4 70 D8
Trevelthan Rd 18 TR16 67 E4
Trevelva Rd TR1 137 E2
Trevelveth Rd TR8 110 B3
Trevelyan Cl 10 TR20 89 E5
Trevelyan Rd TR15, TR16 67 E4
Trevelyan Way 5 TR20 89 E5
Trevemper Rd TR7, TR8 110 F3
Trevena Cl TR18 143 C4
Trevena Cross TR13 90 F3
Trevena Dr 10 PL34 14 C7
Trevena Gdns TR11 93 D3
Trevena Lodge 6 PL34 14 C7
Trevena Rd TR18 143 C4
Trevena Terr TR7 110 D6
Trevendon PL17 28 D1
Treveneague Gdns PL2 128 D8
Trevenen Rd TR13 146 C5
Treveneth Cres TR18 143 C1
Treveneth Pl 1 TR18 143 C1
Treven La TR27 78 B1
Trevenna Cross TR8 45 A8
Trevenner Ho 8 TR15 140 B5
Trevenner La TR17 89 C5
Trevenner Mews 6 TR15 140 B5
Trevenner Sq TR17 89 C5
Treven Noweth TR16 68 C3
Trevenson Ct TR15 139 B6
Trevenson La
Camborne, Pool TR15 139 A6
Camborne TR14 138 D2
Trevenson Rd
Camborne TR15 139 B5
Newquay TR7 111 B6
Trevenson St TR14 138 D2
Treventon Cl
Falmouth TR11 144 E4
Portscatho TR2 83 B2
Treventon Rd TR2 83 B2
Treventon Rise 11 TR9 45 E6
Treverbyn Cl
Liskeard PL14 113 E6
Plymouth PL7 130 D6
Treverbyn Com Prim Sch PL26 59 C8
Treverbyn Gdns PL25 114 F4
Treverbyn Rd
Falmouth TR11 144 E1
Padstow PL28 107 E4
Plymouth PL7 130 D6
St Austell PL25 114 E7
Stenalees PL26 59 C8
St Ives TR26 141 A5
Truro TR1 137 E6
Treverbyn Rise TR10 144 A8
Trevere Cl TR27 78 C6
Treverno Rd TR14 138 E6
Treveryn Parc TR11 144 C2
Trevessa Cl PL2 128 D8
Trevethan Cl TR11 145 A4
Trevethan Ct 2 TR11 145 A5
Trevethan Gdns 2 TR11 145 A4
Trevethan Hill 1 TR11 145 B5
Trevethan Pk PL20 119 F4
Trevethan Rd TR11 145 A4
Trevethan Rise TR11 145 A4
Trevethenick Rd TR1 137 E3
Treveth La TR13 146 D8
Treveth Tean TR9 57 E8
Treveth Ylyn TR14 138 F5
Trevia La PL32 105 B4
Trevian Cl 6 TR6 55 A4
Trevia Pk Terr PL32 105 C3
Treviglas Cl TR7 111 D7
Treviglas Com Coll TR7 111 D7
Treviglas La TR2 71 C6
Treviglas Rise TR2 71 C6
Trevilledor Cvn Pk PL27 32 A2
Trevilley La PL30, PL33 23 E8
Trevillick La PL30 23 F6
Trevilling Rd PL27 108 B6
Trevillis Pk PL14 113 B4
Trevilson Cl TR8 56 C7
Trevince Parc TR16 80 F8
Trevingey Cl TR15 140 A3
Trevingey Cres TR15 140 A3
Trevingey Parc TR15 140 A4
Trevingey Rd TR15 140 A3
Trevisker Com Prim Sch PL27 31 F3
Treviskey Hill TR2 84 B3
Trevissome Ct TR11 144 F6
Trevithick PL28 31 F8
Trevithick Ave PL11 126 F4
Trevithick Cl
Newquay TR7 110 F4
St Merryn PL28 31 F8
Truro TR1 137 E6
Trevithick Cres TR27 142 D5
Trevithick Ct
3 Camborne, Illogan Highway TR15 139 C6
Camborne TR14 138 C3
Truro TR1 137 E6
Trevithick Prim Sch TR14 138 D1
Trevithick Rd
Camborne, Illogan Highway TR15 139 C6
Camborne TR14 138 D3
Chacewater TR4 69 A3
Falmouth TR11 144 E5
Plymouth PL5 123 E2
St Austell PL25 114 E3
Truro TR1 137 E5
Trevoarn TR27 142 B5
Trevol Bsns Pk PL11 126 D3
Trevollard PL13 61 F7
Trevollard La PL12 53 D1
Trevol Pl PL11 126 E3
Trevol Rd PL11 126 E3
Trevone Cres PL25 114 A4
Trevone Gdns PL2 128 D8
Trevone Rd PL28 20 F2
Trevoney TR11 144 C2
Trevor Cl PL28 20 C1
Trevorder Cl PL11 126 F2
Trevorder Dr PL25 114 E7
Trevorder Rd PL11 126 F2
Trevorgans Cross TR19 96 F8
Trevose Ave TR7 110 C6
Trevose Cl TR5 54 C1
Trevose Ho TR1 69 E4
Trevose Rd TR1 69 F4
Trevose Way PL3 129 C6
Trevowah Mdws TR8 110 A3
Trevowah Rd TR8 43 D3
Trevozah Cross PL15 28 B8
Trevu Ho TR14 138 E1
Trevu Rd TR14 138 E2
Trevurvas La TR13 90 C3
Trewall Hill PL11 64 D5
Trewan Hall TR9 45 E7
Trewans Terr TR15 140 A6
Trewardreva Cross TR11 92 E4
Trewarlett Cross PL15 28 A7
Trewarne La TR8 111 F3
Trewartha Cl TR26 141 D1
Trewartha Ct 4 PL14 113 C6
Trewartha Est TR26 141 D1
Trewartha Flats TR26 141 D1
Trewartha Rd TR20 90 C3
Trewartha Terr 13 TR18 143 E6
Trewarton Rd TR10 81 D2
Trewarveneth Farm Cotts TR18 88 C2
Trewarveneth St TR18 143 C2
Trewassa Flats PL32 15 F5
Trewavas Cres TR13 146 C5
Trewavas Rd TR18 143 C1
Treweath Rd TR18 143 D7
Treweege Row TR3 80 E4
Treweeks Rd TR19 75 A1
Treweese Cross PL14 52 B7
Treweese Rd
Menheniot PL14 52 B7
Quethiock PL14 52 B8
Trewellard Hill TR19 87 A8
Trewellard Ind Est TR19 86 F8
Trewellard Rd TR19 86 F8
Trewelloe Rd TR20 90 C3
Trewelm La TR16 68 E1
Trewen Rd TR11 144 C2
Trewen Terr TR11 144 C2
Trewern La TR20 87 E6
Trewetha Farm Lodges PL29 22 E7
Trewetha La PL29 22 D7
Trewey Hill TR 26 76 B4
Trewhella La TR20 89 F7
Trewhella Terr TR20 90 A6
Trewhiddle Rd PL25 114 C2
Trewidden Cl TR1 137 E5
Trewidden Ct TR1 137 E5
Trewidden Gdns* TR20 88 A4
Trewidden Rd TR26 141 B5
Trewidland Com Prim Sch PL14 51 C3
Trewince TR11 93 B3
Trewince La
Grampound Road TR2 57 E1
Lostwithiel PL22 112 C3
Porth Navas TR11 93 B3
Trewince Manor TR2 95 C6
Trewince Terr 2 TR18 143 C1
Trewince Villas PL27 32 E6
Trewinnard Ct TR1 137 B6
Trewinnard Gr TR1 137 B6
Trewinnard La TR27 77 E1
Trewinnard Rd TR3 81 D5
Trewinnick Council Hos PL27 32 A5
Trewinnick Rd PL27 32 A5
Trewinnow Cross PL15 27 D6
Trewint Cres PL13 117 D4
Trewint Est PL14 52 A5
Trewint La
Landrake PL12 53 B2
Rock PL27 21 D3
Trewint Rd PL14 52 A6
Trewirgie Gdns TR15 140 B4
Trewirgie Hill TR15 140 B3
Trewirgie Inf Sch TR15 140 B4
Trewirgie Jun Sch TR15 140 B4
Trewirgie Rd TR15 140 B4
Trewirgie Vean TR15 140 B4
Trewiston La PL27 21 E3
Trewithan Parc PL22 112 D2
Trewithen Gdns* TR2 71 E6
Trewithen Parc TR8 56 B7
Trewithen Rd TR18 143 D5
Trewithen Terr TR13 90 D5
Trewithy Ct PL6 124 F1
Trewithy Dr PL6 124 F1
Trewollock Cl PL26 85 C5
Trewollock La PL26 85 C5
Trewoolsta Terr 6 PL14 38 E4
Trewoon Rd TR12 99 B2
Treworden Cl EX23 4 E1
Treworder La PL27 108 F5
Treworder Rd TR1 137 B3
Treworgan Ct TR4 56 D1
Treworgan View TR4 56 D1
Treworlis Cl TR13 146 D8
Treworthal Rd TR3 81 D5
Treworvenneth Dr 9 TR17 89 C5
Trewrickle La PL11 65 A5
Trewyn Flats 41 TR26 141 B6
Treyarnon Bay YH* PL28 20 B1
Treyew Pl TR16 80 F8
Treyew Prim Sch TR1 137 A4
Treyew Rd TR1 137 B3
Trezaise Ave PL26 47 A2
Trezaise Cl PL26 47 A2
Trezaise Rd PL26 46 F2
Trezaise Sq PL26 47 A2
Treza Rd TR13 91 A1
Trezela Rd TR18 143 D6
Trinity Cl
Bere Alston PL20 41 B1
Carnkie TR16 80 C2
Trinity House National Lighthouse Ctr* TR18 143 F5
Trinity Praze TR16 80 C2
Trinity St PL25 114 C3
Trinity Way PL19 147 A4
Tripp Hill PL14 36 F2
Trispen Hill TR4 56 D1
Tristan Rd TR1 137 F5
Trolver Hill TR3 82 B6
Trolvus Vean TR10 81 A1
Troon Com Prim Sch TR14 79 E4
Troon Moor TR14 79 E4
Troon Row TR13 90 F3
Troubridge Rd TR13 146 C4
Trowbridge Cl PL5 124 C4
Troy Ct PL23 116 C4
Truck Hill TR2 71 B6
Trunglemoor Cotts TR19 88 C2
Trungle Parc TR19 88 C2
Trungle Terr TR19 88 C2
Truro Coll TR1 69 E3
Truro Dr PL5 124 A5
Truro High Sch for Girls TR1 137 C3
Truro Hill TR10 144 C8
Truro La TR10 144 C8
Truro Rd
Lanivet PL30 47 F7
St Austell PL25 114 A2
St Austell PL25 114 B3
Truro Sch TR1 137 E3
Truro Sta TR1 137 B4
Truro Vean Terr TR1 137 D5
Truthwall La TR19 86 F7
Tryelyn PL31 109 F2
Tryhornek TR26 77 D4
Trythall Com Prim Sch TR20 76 B1
Trythogga Hill TR18 143 F8
Trythogga Rd TR18 143 F8
Tubbon Hill TR3 81 A4
Tucker Cl PL5 127 F8
Tuckers Cl TR8 111 B4
Tuckingmill Terr TR13 91 E4
Tudor Cl PL9 135 E5
Tudor Ct PL12 123 A2
Tudor Lodge Holiday Pk TR20 89 C7
Tuke Cl TR11 144 E5
Turbill Gdns 4 PL7 131 B5
Turfdown Rd PL30 48 E8
Turf St PL31 109 E5
Turnavean Rd PL25 114 A5
Turnaware Rd TR11 144 E2
Turnpike TR13 146 C7
Turnpike Hill 2 TR17 89 C5
Turnpike Pl PL14 113 B4
Turnpike Rd
Connor Downs TR27 78 D6
Marazion TR17 89 C5
Turnpike The TR19 86 F6
Turnquay PL9 135 C7
Turret Gr PL4 128 F4
Tuxton Cl PL7 131 C3
Twelvewoods Cl PL14 50 E8
Twelvewoods Pl PL14 50 E8
Twinbrook Pk TR11 93 B3
Two Chimneys Cvn Pk TR20 90 B3
Two Hills Pk PL12 122 C2
Two Trees PL27 108 B4
Two Trees Rd PL22 112 F1
Tyacke Rd TR13 146 B5
Tybesta TR2 72 A7
Tye Hill Cl PL25 59 A3
Tyland Rd PL32 105 F4
Tylney Cl PL6 125 B6
Tynance Ct PL26 58 C8

Tyndale Cl PL5 124 B1
Tyringham Pl TR26 77 E4
Tyringham Rd TR26 77 E4
Tyringham Row TR26 77 E4
Tyshute La PL26 59 A1
Tything Wlk 4 PL3 128 E6
Tywardreath Highway PL24 60 C6
Tywardreath Hill PL24 60 D4
Tywardreath Sch PL24 60 D5
Tywarnhale Way TR4 68 A6
Tywarnhayle Rd TR6 55 A5
Tywarnhayle Sq 23 TR6 55 A5

U

Uglow Cl TR14 138 C3
Ulalia Rd TR7 110 F6
Ullswater Cres PL6 124 E4
Umfulla Pl 13 TR26 141 B5
Under Chapel Yd TR18 143 F4
Undercliff TR27 142 D7
Undercliff Rd PL9 135 B7
Underhayes La PL15 106 A8
Underhill Rd PL3 128 A4
Underhill Villas 1 PL3 128 A3
Under La PL15 18 C3
Underlane
 Boyton PL15 13 A3
 Marhamchurch EX23 7 B6
 Plymouth, Plympton PL7 130 C5
 Plymouth, Plymstock PL9 135 E6
Under Rd
 Boscastle PL35 9 C1
 Bridgerule EX22 8 A5
 Gunnislake PL18 41 A6
Underways PL20 41 B1
Underwood Rd PL7 130 D4
Unicorn Cl PL7 130 B6
Union Cnr TR11 144 D5
Union Hill
 St Columb Major TR9 45 E6
 6 Stratton EX23 4 D1
 Truro TR1 70 D5
Union Pl
 Fowey PL23 116 D4
 Plymouth PL1 148 A2
 Truro TR1 137 D5
Union Rd TR11 144 D6
Union Sq TR9 45 E6
Union St
 Camborne TR14 138 D2
 27 Penzance TR18 143 E5
 Plymouth PL1 148 A2
 Truro TR1 137 C5
United Downs Ind Pk TR16 81 A8
United Rd TR16 80 F8
Unit Hos PL27 33 B5
Unity Cl PL6 125 D5
Unity Rd TR13 98 C8
University College Falmouth (Tremough Campus) TR10 144 A8
University College Falmouth (Woodlane Campus) TR11 145 B3
University Coll Falmouth (Annexe) TR11 145 B4
Univ of Plymouth PL1, PL4 148 C3
Univ of Plymouth Bsns Sch PL4 148 C4
Univ of Plymouth (Cookworthy Bldg) PL4 149 A3
Univ of Plymouth The Hoe Ctr PL1 148 C2
Upcott Cross EX39 2 F5
Upland Cl TR1 137 F6
Upland Cres TR1 137 E6
Upland Dr PL6 125 A5
Uplands
 Lostwithiel PL22 112 B2
 Saltash PL12 122 E1
 Tavistock PL19 147 A4
Uplands Vean TR1 137 F5
Upper Castle Rd TR2 95 A6
Upper Chapel PL15 106 A4
Upper Dobbin Cl PL28 20 F2
Upper Dobbin La PL28 20 F2
Upper Eastcliffe Rd PL24 60 D4
Upper Hillcrest 8 TR6 55 A4
Upper Knollys Terrace La PL3 128 C4
Upper Lemon Villas TR1 137 C3
Upper Ridings PL7 131 B7
Upper School La TR1 137 C3
Upperton La PL6 121 F3
Upper Tredrea TR3 81 D5
Upton Cl PL3 129 B7
Upton Cross EX23 104 C2
Upton Cross Prim Sch PL14 38 C7
Upton Mdws EX23 104 C3
Upton Terr EX23 104 C2
Urban Terr PL17 39 F5
Uxbridge Dr PL5 123 E4
Uzella Pk PL22 112 C2

V

Vaagso Cl PL1 127 E2
Valency Row PL35 9 C2
Valentine Row 4 PL17 39 E4
Valiant Ave PL5 124 A4
Vallard's La PL12 53 E4
Valletort Flats PL1 128 A2
Valletort Ho PL1 148 C3
Valletort La PL1 128 A3
Valletort Pl PL1 128 A2
Valletort Rd PL1, PL3 128 A3
Valletort Terr PL1 148 A4
Valley Bglws PL13 117 F5
Valley Cl
 Goonhavern TR4 55 C3
 Truro TR1 69 F3
Valley Gdns 20 TR16 67 E4
Valley La TR3 81 F7
Valley Park La PL26 73 C3
Valley Rd
 Bude EX23 104 E5
 Carbis Bay TR26 141 C2
 Mevagissey PL26 73 C4
 Plymouth PL7 130 B5
 Saltash PL12 122 E2
Valley The TR19 96 E3
Valley View
 Bodmin PL31 109 E3
 19 Illogan TR16 67 E4
 Plymouth PL6 125 D7
 Redruth TR16 140 E1
 St Keyne PL14 51 A4
 St Teath PL30 23 E7
 Wadebridge PL27 108 C4
Valley View Cl PL3 129 B6
Valley View Dr TR1 69 F3
Valley View Pk PL31 34 D2
Valley View Rd PL3 129 B7
Valley View Terr TR3 81 B5
Valley Wlk PL6 125 E6
Vanguard Cl PL5 124 D1
Vapron Rd PL3 128 F6
Varfell La TR20 89 A7
Varley La PL14 113 B5
Varley Terr 1 PL14 113 B5
Vauban Pl PL2 127 F4
Vaughan Cl PL2 128 C7
Vauxhall Ct 10 PL4 149 A2
Vauxhall St PL4 149 A2
Vauxhall Street Flats 19 PL4 149 A2
Vean Rd TR14 138 E2
Vean Terr TR14 138 E2
Vear Ho TR14 138 D2
Vellan Cl TR14 79 B5
Vellandrucia TR3 80 F3
Vellanhoggan Mews TR18 88 E6
Vellan Parc Ave TR27 78 C5
Vellan Vrane TR27 78 C5
Venetian Views TR9 57 D8
Venland Cl 9 PL14 38 A3
Venn Cl 6 PL3 128 E6
Venn Cres PL3 128 E6
Venn Ct PL3 128 E6
Venn Gdns PL3 128 E7
Venn Gr PL3 128 E6
Venn Hill PL19 29 C6
Venn La PL2, PL3 128 C6
Venn Way PL3 128 E7
Venslooe Hill PL14 113 B7
Ventnor Terr TR26 141 A6
Venton Cl PL15 18 B8
Venton East Sq TR19 86 F6
Venton Lace Rd TR2 57 E1
Ventonleague Hill TR27 142 E7
Ventonleague Row TR27 142 E7
Ventonraze TR16 67 E4
Ventonraze Terr 2 TR16 67 E4
Venton Rd
 Falmouth TR11 144 E4
 St Ives TR26 141 C3
Ventonvaise 5 TR6 55 A5
Veor Rd TR7 111 C7
Verdun Terr PL14 113 B5
Vermont Gdns PL2 127 F7
Verna Pl PL5 123 D2
Verna Rd PL5 123 E2
Vernigo Cross PL12 40 B1
Vernon Pl TR11 145 B4
Vernon Villas PL24 60 B4
Veryan CE Sch TR2 83 F6
Viaduct Hill TR27 142 E6
Viaduct La TR14 138 A1
Vicarage Cl
 Budock Water TR11 144 C3
 Menheniot PL14 51 F5
Vicarage Gdns
 Milton Abbot PL19 29 C6
 Plymouth PL5 123 B1
Vicarage Hill
 Budock Water TR11 144 C3
 Mevagissey PL26 73 C4
 10 St Austell PL25 114 C3
 St Day TR16 68 E1
 9 Tintagel PL34 14 C7
Vicarage La
 Lelant TR26 77 E4
 Manaccan TR12 101 A8
 Poundstock EX23 6 F2
Vicarage Mdw PL23 116 C4
Vicarage Rd
 Bude EX23 104 D5
 Plymouth PL7 130 C6
 Porthleven TR13 91 A1
 St Agnes TR5 54 D1
 Torpoint PL11 127 B2
 Tywardreath PL24 60 D5
Vicarage Row TR13 90 F3
Vicarage Terr TR11 92 F4
Victoria Ave PL1 148 A4
Victoria Bsns Pk PL26 47 A4
Victoria Cl PL14 113 C6
Victoria Cotts
 Budock Water TR11 144 C3
 Falmouth TR11 145 B3
 Plymouth PL6 129 B8
Victoria Ct 16 TR18 143 E6
Victoria Gdns
 2 St Columb Road TR9 45 E2
 Threemilestone TR3 69 D3
Victoria La PL12 122 F2
Victoria Mews 18 TR18 143 E6
Victoria Pk PL27 108 D6
Victoria Pl
 31 Penzance TR18 143 E5
 Plymouth, Devonport PL2 127 F4
 Plymouth PL1 148 A2
 Ponsanooth TR3 81 B4
 9 St Austell PL25 114 C3
 12 St Ives TR26 141 B6
Victoria Quay
 5 Falmouth TR11 145 B5
 Truro TR1 70 D1
Victoria Rd
 Bude EX23 104 D7
 Camelford PL32 105 E4
 Plymouth PL5 123 D2
 Roche PL26 46 F3
 Saltash PL12 122 F2
 St Austell PL25 114 F3
 11 St Ives TR26 141 B6
 Threemilestone TR3 69 D3
Victoria Road Prim Sch PL5 123 D1
Victoria Row TR19 86 E6
Victoria Sq
 Bodmin PL31 109 F3
 17 Penzance TR18 143 E6
 Truro TR1 137 C4
Victoria St
 Camborne TR14 138 D2
 St Columb Major TR9 45 E6
 Torpoint PL11 127 B3
Victoria Terr
 4 Liskeard PL14 113 B5
 Nanpean PL26 58 D6
 Plymouth PL4 148 C4
 Portscatho TR2 83 B2
 St Breward PL30 24 B3
Victory Rd EX22 13 A8
Victory St PL2 127 E6
Vigo Bridge Rd PL19 147 C6
Vigo Mews PL19 147 C6
Village Dr PL6 121 C1
Village Farm Cl EX23 7 B6
Village The
 Buckland Monachorum PL20 41 F3
 Duloe PL14 51 A1
Villa Marina TR17 89 B5
Villiers Cl PL9 135 D7
Vincent Way PL12 122 F2
Vine Cres PL2 128 B6
Vinefield Ct TR11 145 B7
Vine Gdns PL2 128 B6
Vine Pl 10 PL24 60 D5
Vinery La PL7, PL9 130 E1
Vineyard The TR3 80 F3
Vingoe's La TR20 88 B7
Vinstone Way PL5 123 D1
Violet Dr PL6 125 E8
Violet La PL19 147 E6
Virgin Hill TR17 89 C6
Virginia Gdns PL2 127 F7
Virgin Pl 16 TR19 88 C1
Virgin St 26 TR26 141 B6
Visicks Works TR3 81 E6
Vivian Cl TR7 110 E5
Vivian Ct TR1 137 D3
Vivian Pk TR14 138 F2
Vivian Rd PL31 109 B4
Vixen Tor Cl PL20 42 C3
Vogue Hill TR16 68 D1
Vogue Terr TR16 68 D1
Vorfield Cl TR15 140 B6
Vosporth Hill TR8 110 A3
Voss Rd PL12 53 E1
Vounder Glaze TR19 86 E6
Voundervour La 20 TR18 143 E5
Vyvyan Dr TR8 44 E3
Vyvyan Pl TR13 146 C5
Vyvyan St TR14 138 D3
Vyvyan's Terr TR14 79 B2

W

Waddon Cl PL7 130 E7
Wadebridge Com Prim Sch PL27 108 C6
Wadebridge Rd
 St Mabyn PL30 34 C8
 St Tudy PL30 23 E3
Wadebridge Sch PL27 108 D6
Wadeland Terr 3 PL14 51 A7
Wadham Cl 4 PL14 113 C5
Wadham Dr PL14 113 D5
Wadham Ho 5 PL14 113 C5
Wadham Rd PL14 113 D5
Wadham Terr 6 PL2 128 A5
Wagg La TR2 71 C6
Waggon Hill PL7 131 A4
Wain Pk PL7 130 F4
Wainsway TR6 55 A4
Wainways EX23 10 F6
Wakefield Ave PL5 123 E1
Wake St PL4 148 B4
Walcot Cl PL6 125 E3
Waldon Cl PL7 131 B6
Walker Lines Ind Est 4 PL31 48 D8
Walker Terr PL1 148 B1
Walkham Bsns Pk PL5 124 B1
Walkham Cl PL19 147 D5
Walkham Mdws PL20 42 C4
Walkhampton Rd PL20 42 C4
Walkhampton Wlk PL6 125 E1
Walkham Terr 4 PL20 42 C5
Walk Terr PL23 116 C2
Walk The PL15 106 C6
Wallace Mews 1 PL31 109 D5
Wallace Rd
 Bodmin PL31 109 D5
 Plymouth PL7 131 A4
Walled Gdn The TR10 144 A6
Wall Gdns TR27 78 E3
Wallpark Cl PL7 130 F7
Wall Rd TR27 78 E3
Wallsend Ind Est PL4 149 C1
Wall Vean TR27 78 E3
Walnut Cl PL7 131 B5
Walnut Dr PL7 131 C5
Walnut Gdns PL7 131 C5
Walreddon Cl PL19 147 B4
Walsingham Ct PL7 131 B6
Walsingham Pl 15 TR1 137 D4
Walters La PL15 18 D5
Walters Rd PL5 123 C2
Waltham Pl PL2 128 A8
Walton Cres PL5 124 C1
Wandle Pl PL3 129 D5
Wansford Mdws PL26 85 C5
Wanstead Gr PL5 124 A2
Wantage Gdns PL1 148 A3
Warbstow Com Prim Sch PL15 11 B1
Warburton Gdns PL5 123 C1
Ward Cl 4 EX23 4 D1
Wardlow Cl PL6 128 F8
Wardlow Gdns PL6 128 F8
Wardour Wlk PL6 125 B7
Ward Pl PL3 129 B5
Warfelton Cres PL12 122 E2
Warfelton Gdns PL12 122 E2
Warfelton Terr PL12 122 E2
Waring Rd PL6 124 D7
Warleigh Ave PL2 127 E5
Warleigh Cres PL6 124 F5
Warleigh La PL2 127 E5
Warleigh Rd 2 PL4 128 E4
Warmwell Rd PL5 123 E4
Warne Cl TR2 71 F3
Warran La PL19 147 C3
Warraton Cl PL12 122 D3
Warraton Gn PL12 122 D3
Warraton La PL12 122 D3
Warraton Rd PL12 122 D3
Warren TR26 141 B5
Warren Cl 18 TR13 98 C8
Warren La PL5 124 A8
Warren Pk PL6 125 D7
Warren Rd TR9 45 F2
Warrens Field PL32 105 D5
Warren St PL2 127 E4
Warren The PL13 62 E1
Warspite Gdns PL5 124 D2
Warton Cl PL5 124 D3
Warwick Ave
 Illogan TR16 67 D4
 Plymouth PL5 124 D3
Warwick Cl PL28 31 F8
Warwick Cres 5 PL27 31 F3
Warwick Dr PL25 115 B5
Warwick Orchard Cl PL5 124 B3
Warwick Rd EX23 104 E4
Wasdale Cl PL6 125 D2
Wasdale Gdns PL6 125 D2
Washbourne Cl PL1 127 E3
Watergate Bay Holiday Pk TR8 44 E8
Watergate La PL30 34 C8
Watergate Rd TR8 44 C6
Watering Hill Cl PL25 114 E3
Waterings Rd TR11 82 A2
Water La
 Crantock TR8 110 A3
 Delabole PL33 14 E3
 Golant PL23 61 B5
 Hayle TR27 142 B3
 St Agnes TR5 54 D1
Waterloo TR1 137 E4
Waterloo Cl
 Plymouth PL1 128 A2
 St Mawes TR2 95 A6
Waterloo Ct PL1 128 A2
Waterloo Pl* TR11 145 B4
Waterloo Rd TR11 145 B4
Waterloo St
 Plymouth PL4 149 A4
 Plymouth, Stoke PL1 128 A3
Waterloo Yard Flats PL1 128 A2
Water-Ma-Trout TR13 146 C8
Waters Ct TR15 140 E7
Waters Edge TR7 110 A6
Water's Edge PL19 107 E6
Watersedge Cl PL25 114 B4
Watersmead Parc TR11 144 C3
Watery La
 Bodmin PL31 109 D5
 Milton Combe PL6 120 D6
Watson Gdns PL4 149 B3
Watson Pl PL4 149 B2
Watts Park Rd PL2 128 C7
Watts Rd PL19 147 B5
Watts' Rd PL4 149 C3
Waveney Gdns PL5 124 C3
Waverley Rd PL5 123 D2
Wavish Pk PL11 126 E3
Waycott Wlk PL6 124 D6
Way Cross PL15 27 B3
Wayfield Rd TR11 82 B2
Wayside Ct TR7 111 A4
Wayside Folk Mus* TR26 76 B5
Wearde Rd PL12 122 E1
Webber Hill TR11 145 B4
Webber St TR11 145 B4
Webbs Ct 9 PL14 113 C6
Webb St PL23 116 D4
Wedgewood Rd PL25 115 A4
Weeks Rise PL32 105 B2
Weeks Row PL18 41 A6
Weekstone Cross EX22 8 C8
Weeth Cl TR14 138 C3
Weeth Com Prim Sch TR14 138 C4
Weethes Cotts 6 TR18 143 D5
Weeth La TR14 138 C3
Weeth Rd TR14 138 C4
Weir Cl PL6 125 F2
Weir Gdns PL6 125 F2
Weir Rd PL6 125 F2
Welbeck Ave PL4 148 C4
Welcombe Cross EX39 3 B4
Welcome Cl TR4 56 D1
Welland Gdns PL3 129 C5
Weller Ct TR11 145 B3
Wellfield Cl
 Coad's Green PL15 27 D3
 Plymouth PL7 131 C5
Well Gdns PL1 148 B3
Wellhay Cl PL9 136 C6
Wellhouse The 8 PL14 113 C6
Wellington Cl TR14 138 C3
Wellington Gdns TR11 145 B4
Wellington Pl
 Falmouth TR11 145 B4
 Penzance TR18 143 D5
 Wadebridge PL27 108 C4
Wellington Plantation TR3 82 B7
Wellington Rd
 Camborne TR14 138 D3
 Porthleven TR13 91 B1
 St Dennis PL26 58 C8
 2 St Eval PL27 31 F3
Wellington St
 Plymouth PL4 149 A4
 Plymouth, Stoke PL1 128 A3
 Torpoint PL11 127 B3
Wellington Terr
 Falmouth TR11 145 B4
 Porthleven TR13 91 B1
 Portscatho TR2 83 B2
 2 Truro TR1 137 C4
Well La
 Constantine TR11 92 F4
 Falmouth TR11 145 B4
 Goldsithney TR20 89 F5
 Lamorna TR19 97 E5
 Liskeard PL14 113 C6
 Looe PL13 117 C3
 St Cleer PL14 37 F3
 St Keverne TR12 101 D4
 Tregony TR2 71 F3
 Tremar PL14 38 A3
 Welcombe EX39 2 E5
Well Mdw PL15 18 A5
Wellpark Rd PL18 40 F5
Well Park Rd PL11 127 B3
Wellsbourne Pk PL3 129 A6
Wells Ct PL10 132 E4
Well St
 Callington PL17 39 E4
 Delabole PL33 14 E3
 Tregony TR2 71 F3
 Tywardreath PL24 60 D5
Well Way TR7 111 C7
Welman Rd PL10 132 F6
Welsby Terr PL14 37 F3
Welsford Ave PL2 127 F5
Welway TR6 55 A4
Wembury Park Rd PL3 128 D6
Wembury Rd PL9 136 A4
Wendron CE Prim Sch TR13 91 F5
Wendron St TR13 146 C6
Wenlock Gdns PL2 128 B8
Wensum Cl PL7 131 A4
Wentwood Gdns PL6 125 E3
Wentwood Pl PL6 125 E3
Wentworth Cl
 Lynstone EX23 104 C3
 Polzeath PL27 21 D5
 Redruth TR15 140 C3
Wentworth Pl PL4 129 B2
Wentworth Way PL12 122 C2
Werrington Dr PL17 39 E4
Werrington Sch PL15 18 F7
Wesley Ave PL3 128 E5
Wesley Cl
 Kelly Bray PL17 39 F6
 Stenalees PL26 59 C8
Wesley Cottage* PL15 26 B7
Wesley Ct
 Penryn TR10 144 C8
 Pensilva PL14 38 D4
 25 Porthleven TR13 98 C8
 Torpoint PL11 127 C3
Wesley La PL12 122 F2
Wesley Pl
 5 Newlyn TR18 143 C2
 Plymouth, Mutley PL3 128 E5
 1 Plymouth, Stoke PL2 128 A4

Wesley Pl *continued*
St Austell PL25 ... 114 F3
7 St Ives TR26 ... 141 B5
Wesley Rd
Cubert TR8 ... 55 D8
Pensilva PL14 ... 38 D4
Saltash PL12 ... 122 F2
Wesley St
Camborne TR14 ... 138 E3
11 Heamoor TR18 ... 143 C7
Redruth TR15 ... 140 C5
Wesley Terr
Bugle PL26 ... 47 C2
Looe PL13 ... 117 D4
Wesley Way PL15 ... 26 B7
Wesley Yd TR7 ... 110 D6
West Ave 4 PL19 ... 147 B5
West Beach Rd TR4 ... 68 A6
West Beckon Cl EX23 ... 2 D1
Westborne Hts TR15 ... 140 B3
Westbourne Rd TR14 ... 138 B4
Westbourne Dr PL25 ... 114 B3
Westbourne La PL14 ... 113 B6
Westbourne Rd PL3 ... 128 D5
Westbourne Terr
Fraddon TR9 ... 57 D8
Saltash PL12 ... 122 F3
Westbridge Cotts PL19 ... 147 B4
Westbridge Ind Est 3
PL19 ... 147 B4
Westbridge Rd PL25 ... 59 A3
West Bridge Rd PL15 ... 106 B7
Westbury Cl PL5 ... 124 B4
Westby Rd EX23 ... 104 E5
West Camps Bay PL11 ... 64 C4
West Charles St TR14 ... 138 D2
West Cl TR13 ... 146 D7
West Cliff TR4 ... 68 A6
Westcliff Flats EX23 ... 104 D6
West Cnr 1 TR3 ... 81 F7
Westcombe Cres PL9 ... 135 D5
West Cornwall Hospl
TR18 ... 143 D6
Westcott PL27 ... 108 A6
Westcott Cl PL6 ... 129 A8
Westcountry Cl PL2 ... 127 F7
Westcove Ho 2 TR7 ... 110 F6
Westcroft Rd PL5 ... 123 D1
West Ct TR7 ... 110 C6
West Devon Bsns Pk
PL19 ... 147 B3
West Down Ct PL13 ... 117 C4
Westdown Rd PL33 ... 14 D2
West Down Rd PL2 ... 128 B6
Westella Rd PL20 ... 42 D2
West End
Goldsithney TR20 ... 89 E5
Marazion TR17 ... 89 B5
Pentewan PL26 ... 73 C6
15 Porthleven TR13 ... 98 B8
Redruth TR15 ... 140 B4
St Day TR16 ... 68 D1
West End Cl TR10 ... 144 C8
West End Cotts PL11 ... 64 B8
West End Ct 2 TR15 ... 140 B4
West End Ind Est TR10 ... 144 B8
West End Sq 7 PL17 ... 39 E4
Westend Terr TR10 ... 144 C8
Westeria Terr PL2 ... 128 C7
Westerlands Rd PL27 ... 108 B6
Western App PL1 ... 148 B2
Western Ave 5 PL14 ... 51 A7
Western College Rd PL4 ... 128 F5
Western Dr PL3 ... 129 B4
Western Pl TR10 ... 144 B8
Western Promenade Rd
TR18 ... 143 E4
Western Rd PL15 ... 106 B5
Western Terr
Bodmin PL31 ... 109 C4
Falmouth TR11 ... 145 A3
Launceston PL15 ... 106 B5
Western Wood Way PL7 ... 131 D5
West Fairholme Rd EX23 ... 104 E7
Westfield PL7 ... 131 A6
Westfield Ave PL9 ... 135 C6
Westgate Mews PL15 ... 106 C5
Westgate St PL15 ... 106 C5
Westground Way PL34 ... 14 D7
Westhampnett Pl PL5 ... 123 F4
Westhaul Pk PL25 ... 115 E4
Westhays Cl PL9 ... 135 F4
Westhead Rd PL10 ... 64 B2
Westheath Ave PL30,
PL31 ... 109 B3
Westheath Rd PL31 ... 109 B3
West Hill
St Austell PL25 ... 114 C3
Wadebridge PL27 ... 108 A6
West Hill Ct 16 PL25 ... 114 C3
West Hill Rd PL4 ... 128 F4
West Hoe Rd PL1 ... 148 B1
West Kitty TR5 ... 54 C1
West La
Crafthole PL11 ... 65 B5
Delabole PL33 ... 14 E2
Landrake PL12 ... 53 B3
Westlake Cl PL11 ... 126 F3
West Looe Hill PL13 ... 117 B3
West Looe Sq PL13 ... 117 C3
West Malling Ave PL5 ... 123 E5
Westmoor Cl PL7 ... 131 C6
Westmoor Cres TR3 ... 81 D6
Westmoor Pk PL19 ... 147 C4
Weston Mill Com Prim Sch
PL2 ... 127 E7
Weston Mill Dr PL5 ... 127 F8
Weston Mill Hill PL5 ... 123 F1
Weston Mill La PL5 ... 124 A1
Weston Mill Rd PL5 ... 123 E1
Weston Park Rd PL3 ... 128 D6
Westover Rd PL17 ... 39 E4
West Park Dr PL7 ... 131 C5
West Park Est PL27 ... 108 D5
West Park Hill PL7 ... 131 B7
West Park Prim Sch PL5 ... 124 A2
Westpark Rd PL27 ... 108 E4
West Park Rd EX23 ... 104 D7
West Pentire Rd TR8 ... 43 D3
West Pk
Perranarworthal TR3 ... 81 D6
Redruth TR15 ... 139 F6
13 St Columb Major TR9 ... 45 E6
Tideford PL12 ... 52 F2
Trewidland PL14 ... 51 C3
West Pl
Falmouth TR11 ... 145 A3
45 St Ives TR26 ... 141 B6
St Just TR19 ... 86 E6
West Point TR8 ... 111 C4
West Porthmear Cotts
PL25 ... 115 B2
West Porthmear Ct PL25 ... 115 B2
West Rd
Looe PL13 ... 117 C4
Quintrell Downs TR8 ... 111 E3
West Rise TR11 ... 144 F3
West St
Grimscott EX23 ... 5 B1
Liskeard PL14 ... 113 B6
Millbrook PL10 ... 132 E5
Penryn TR10 ... 144 C8
Polruan PL23 ... 116 C2
St Columb Major TR9 ... 45 E6
Tavistock PL19 ... 147 B5
West Tehidy TR14 ... 138 F7
West Terr
Hayle TR27 ... 142 B6
Newlyn TR18 ... 143 C3
West Tolgus TR15 ... 139 D8
West Trevingey TR15 ... 140 A3
West Trewirgie Rd TR15 ... 140 B4
Westview TR6 ... 55 B5
West View
Porthleven TR13 ... 91 A1
Tavistock PL19 ... 147 E2
Trevone PL28 ... 20 E2
West View Rd 5 PL20 ... 41 B1
West Villas TR8 ... 57 B7
Westward PL27 ... 21 D5
Westward Rd TR26 ... 141 A6
Westway PL9 ... 135 B5
West Week Cl EX22 ... 11 E8
West Wharf PL26 ... 73 C3
Westwinds PL32 ... 16 A8
Westwood PL14 ... 113 B6
Westwood Ave PL6 ... 125 C6
Wetherham La PL30 ... 23 E3
Wetherham Manor Gardens*
PL30 ... 23 D2
Wharf Rd
Penzance TR18 ... 143 F5
St Ives TR26 ... 141 B6
Wharfside 8 TR18 ... 143 E5
Wharfside Village 9
TR18 ... 143 E5
Wharf The
22 Mousehole TR19 ... 88 C1
St Ives TR26 ... 141 B6
Wheal Agar
Camborne, Illogan Highway
TR15 ... 139 C6
5 Camborne TR14 ... 138 F7
Wheal Alfred Rd TR27 ... 142 F5
Wheal-An-Wens TR17 ... 89 C5
Whealbrake Lodge PL26 ... 58 D6
Wheal Bull PL26 ... 58 D5
Wheal Busy La TR4 ... 68 F3
Wheal Catherine Cl TR6 ... 55 B5
Wheal Damsel Rd TR16 ... 80 E8
Wheal Dance TR16 ... 140 D3
Wheal Dream TR26 ... 141 C6
Wheal Eliza Cl PL25 ... 115 B5
Wheal Fortune La TR15 ... 139 D6
Wheal Friendly La TR5 ... 54 C2
Wheal Gerry TR14 ... 138 E4
Wheal Golden Dr TR8 ... 43 C1
Wheal Gorland Rd TR16 ... 68 D1
Wheal Harmony Terr
TR15 ... 140 B7
Wheal Jane Mdws TR3 ... 69 C3
Wheal Jewel (Gipsy Site)
TR16 ... 68 E1
Wheal Kitty TR5 ... 54 D1
Wheal Kitty La TR5 ... 54 D2
Wheal Kitty Workshops
TR5 ... 54 D2
Wheal Leisure TR6 ... 55 A5
Wheal Leisure Cl 25 TR6 ... 55 A5
Wheal Margery TR26 ... 141 C3
Wheal Maria Cotts PL19 ... 29 C6
Wheal Martyn Mus* PL26 ... 59 B6
Wheal Northey PL25 ... 115 B5
Wheal Oak TR13 ... 146 D8
Wheal Quoit Ave TR5 ... 54 C1
Wheal Ramoth 3 TR6 ... 55 A5
Wheal Regent Pk PL25 ... 115 D3
Wheal Rodney Cvn Pk
TR17 ... 89 C6
Wheal Rodney Holiday Bglws
TR17 ... 89 C6
Wheal Rose 19 TR13 ... 98 C8
Wheal Silver TR15 ... 140 B5
Wheal Speed Rd TR26 ... 141 C2
Wheal Tehidy La TR15 ... 139 E6
Wheal Trefusis TR15 ... 140 D2
Wheal Trelawney TR16 ... 140 D3
Wheal Venture Rd TR26 ... 141 C3
Wheal View PL26 ... 58 B4
Wheal Virgin Ho TR26 ... 77 A6
Wheal Vor TR15 ... 140 D3
Wheal Vyvyan TR11 ... 92 F4
Wheal Whidden TR26 ... 141 C2
Wheatfield Cres TR7 ... 111 A4
Wheatridge PL7 ... 130 B7
Wheel Ayr Terr TR26 ... 141 A6
Wheeler Higman Cl PL26 ... 59 C7
Wheelgate House Sch
TR8 ... 43 D2
Wheelwright Ct PL20 ... 42 E4
Wherry Pl PL23 ... 116 D2
Wherry Way PL14 ... 50 E7
Whieldon Rd PL25 ... 115 A4
Whimple St PL1 ... 148 C2
Whin Bank Rd PL5 ... 124 E2
Whipsiderry Cl TR7 ... 44 C6
Whistley Down PL20 ... 42 B2
Whitby Cres PL6 ... 125 A1
Whitby Rd PL6 ... 125 A1
Whitchurch Com Prim Sch
PL19 ... 147 D2
Whitchurch Rd
Horrabridge PL20 ... 42 C5
Tavistock PL19 ... 147 C3
Whitcross Hill TR15 ... 139 C3
White Acres Holiday Pk
TR8 ... 45 B3
Whitebarrow Cotts PL14 ... 37 A4
Whitecroft Way EX23 ... 5 A6
Whitecross
Blisland PL30 ... 35 D7
Bodinnick PL23 ... 116 F6
White Cross
Cury TR12 ... 99 B4
Redruth TR16 ... 68 D3
White Cross Ct PL4 ... 149 A3
Whitecross Ind Est TR8 ... 45 B2
Whitefield Terr PL4 ... 149 B4
Whiteford Cl 16 PL17 ... 39 E4
Whiteford Rd PL3 ... 128 E6
Whitefriars La PL4 ... 149 B3
Whitegate PL26 ... 58 B8
Whitegate Mdws PL26 ... 58 B8
Whitegate Rd TR7 ... 111 A6
Whitegate Sh Complex
TR7 ... 111 A7
Whitehall Bglws PL30 ... 23 B2
Whitehall Dr
9 Bere Alston PL20 ... 41 B1
Plymouth PL9 ... 136 B7
Whitehall Est PL30 ... 23 B2
White Hart Arc The
PL15 ... 106 C5
Whitehill Cross PL15 ... 19 C6
Whitehill Terr TR13 ... 146 C4
White Horse
Crowntown TR13 ... 91 A6
Nancegollan TR13 ... 91 A6
White House Cl TR26 ... 141 C2
White La PL1 ... 149 A2
White Lady Rd PL9 ... 135 D5
White Lodge EX23 ... 10 C7
Whitemoor Com Prim Sch
PL26 ... 58 E8
Whiterock Cl PL27 ... 108 B5
Whiterock Rd PL27 ... 108 B5
Whiterocks Pk PL18 ... 40 D6
Whiterock Terr PL27 ... 108 B5
White's Cl 3 TR5 ... 54 C1
White Smock Mdw 7 PL35 ... 9 C1
Whitestone Cres PL31 ... 109 C3
Whitestone Rd PL31 ... 109 C3
White Walls Ct 16 TR6 ... 55 A4
Whitewater Ct PL7 ... 130 E6
Whitham Pk PL19 ... 147 C4
Whitleigh Ave PL5 ... 124 E2
Whitleigh Com Prim Sch
PL5 ... 124 D4
Whitleigh Cotts PL5 ... 124 E2
Whitleigh Ct PL5 ... 124 D4
Whitleigh Gn PL5 ... 124 C4
Whitleigh Villas PL5 ... 124 E2
Whitleigh Way PL5 ... 124 C4
Whitley Cl TR1 ... 137 D4
Whitley Grange PL14 ... 113 A6
Whitlieburn Terr PL13 ... 117 C3
Whitpot Hill PL12 ... 64 F8
Whitsam Cross PL20 ... 41 A1
Whitsand Bay Holiday Pk
PL10 ... 132 B3
Whitsand Bay View PL11 ... 65 A4
Whitson Cross PL5 ... 124 C7
Whitsoncross La PL5 ... 124 C7
Whitstone Com Prim Sch
EX22 ... 7 F1
Whitstone Head Sch EX22 ... 7 F1
Whittington St PL3 ... 148 B4
Whitworth Cl TR5 ... 54 C1
Whity Cross PL12 ... 122 A4
Widegate Nursery PL9 ... 136 D8
Widemouth Bay Cvn Pk
EX23 ... 6 E3
Widemouth Bay Holiday
Village EX23 ... 6 F4
Widewell La PL6 ... 125 C7
Widewell Prim Sch PL6 ... 125 B7
Widewell Rd PL6 ... 125 B7
Widey Court Prim Sch
PL6 ... 124 F1
Widey Cross PL6 ... 124 F1
Widey Ct PL6 ... 124 F1
Widey La PL6 ... 124 F1
Widey View PL3 ... 128 F6
Wilcove La PL11 ... 126 E5
Wildebeest Rd 7 PL27 ... 31 F3
Wilderness Rd PL3 ... 128 E5
Wilderness Trail* PL30 ... 48 C5
Wildflower La TR7 ... 111 A6
Wilkes Wlk TR1 ... 137 D4
Wilkinson Rd PL5 ... 127 D8
Willapark View PL35 ... 9 C1
Willas Rd PL16 ... 19 F4
William Edwards Cl
EX23 ... 104 E6
William Evans Cl PL6 ... 124 D5
William Laundry Cl PL14 ... 52 A5
William Prance Rd PL6 ... 125 A3
Williams Ave PL4 ... 129 B1
Williams Ho PL31 ... 109 B4
William St
Camborne TR14 ... 138 D2
Truro TR1 ... 137 D4
William Young Mews
PL14 ... 113 E5
Willis Vean TR12 ... 99 A1
Willkinson Cl PL17 ... 39 E6
Willoughby Pl PL17 ... 39 E4
Willowby Pk PL20 ... 42 D2
Willow Cl
22 Callington PL17 ... 39 F4
Mylor Bridge TR11 ... 82 A3
Plymouth PL3 ... 129 E5
Quintrell Downs TR8 ... 44 E3
Willow Cotts PL7 ... 130 D4
Willow Ct PL6 ... 129 E7
Willow Dr TR14 ... 138 B4
Willowfield TR18 ... 143 C5
Willow Gn PL12 ... 122 D2
Willow Rd PL19 ... 147 C3
Willows The
Bugle PL26 ... 47 C1
Whipsiderry TR7 ... 44 C6
Willow Way PL14 ... 113 B5
Willow Wlk PL6 ... 125 D5
Wills Cl PL6 ... 124 E7
Wills La 53 TR26 ... 141 B6
Wills Moor PL26 ... 85 C5
Will's Row TR15 ... 139 C8
Wilminstone Ind Est
PL19 ... 147 E7
Wilmot Gdns PL5 ... 124 D3
Wilsey View PL15 ... 17 B7
Wilson Cres PL2 ... 128 B5
Wilson Way
Camborne TR15 ... 139 D5
14 Par PL24 ... 60 B4
Wilsworthy Cross EX22 ... 12 C7
Wilton Rd PL1 ... 128 A3
Wilton St PL1 ... 148 A4
Wilton Terr PL13 ... 62 D6
Wiltshire Cl PL4 ... 128 F4
Winchester Gdns PL5 ... 124 A5
Windermere Cres PL6 ... 124 F4
Winding Terr TR10 ... 81 A1
Windmill PL23 ... 116 C4
Windmill Hill
Launceston PL15 ... 106 C5
Saltash PL12 ... 122 E2
St Just In R TR2 ... 82 F2
Windmill Hill Terr PL15 ... 106 C5
Windmill Ho PL23 ... 116 C4
Windmill Ind Est PL23 ... 116 C4
Windmill La PL15 ... 106 C5
Windsor Ct
Falmouth TR11 ... 145 B4
Newquay TR7 ... 110 D5
Windsor Dr PL25 ... 115 C3
Windsor Gr PL31 ... 109 F5
Windsor Hill 8 TR26 ... 141 B5
Windsor Ho 9 PL31 ... 109 E5
Windsor La
Kelly Bray PL17 ... 39 F6
Saltash PL12 ... 122 E2
Windsor Mews PL31 ... 109 E5
Windsor Pl
Liskeard PL14 ... 113 C5
29 Penzance TR18 ... 143 E6
Plymouth PL1 ... 148 C2
Windsor Rd PL3 ... 129 B7
Windsor Terr
Falmouth TR11 ... 145 B4
Penzance TR18 ... 143 D6
4 St Ives TR26 ... 141 A5
Windsor Villas PL1 ... 148 C2
Windsworth PL24 ... 115 F7
Windy Ridge PL26 ... 46 D1
Wingfield PL31 ... 35 B2
Wingfield Mans PL3 ... 128 A3
Wingfield Rd PL3 ... 148 A4
Wingfield Way PL3 ... 148 A4
Winifred Baker Ct 5
PL4 ... 149 A4
Winnard's Perch TR9 ... 32 D1
Winnicott Cl PL6 ... 124 E7
Winnow Cl PL9 ... 135 F4
Winns Row TR13 ... 146 C6
Winsbury Ct PL6 ... 125 A1
Winsor Cotts PL15 ... 106 B7
Winsor Est PL13 ... 62 D5
Winstanley Wlk PL3 ... 129 D6
Winston Ave PL4 ... 148 C4
Winstowe Terr TR8 ... 110 A3
Winwell Field PL27 ... 108 D6
Witham Gdns PL3 ... 129 C5
Withnoe La PL10 ... 132 B6
Withnoe Terr PL10 ... 65 E3
Wixenford Ct PL9 ... 135 F8
Woburn Rd PL15 ... 106 B4
Woburn Terr PL9 ... 135 C7
Wodehouse Terr TR11 ... 145 B4
Wolcocke Cl TR17 ... 89 D5
Wollaton Gr PL5 ... 123 F3
Wolrige Ave PL7 ... 131 B5
Wolrige Way PL7 ... 131 A5
Wolsdon Pl PL1 ... 148 A3
Wolsdon St PL1 ... 148 B3
Wolseley Bsns Pk 2
PL2 ... 128 A5
Wolseley Cl PL2 ... 128 A5
Wolseley Rd
Plymouth, Camels Head
PL5 ... 127 F6
Plymouth, St Budeaux PL5 ... 123 C1
Wolseley Road Flats PL2 ... 127 F6
Wolverwood Cl PL7 ... 131 C3
Wolverwood La PL7 ... 131 B3
Wombwell Cres PL2 ... 127 E7
Wood Acre PL12 ... 122 B4
Wooda La PL15 ... 106 B6
Wooda Rd PL15 ... 106 C6
Woodbine Cotts PL7 ... 130 E4
Woodbine La TR16 ... 67 D4
Woodbury Gdns PL5 ... 124 A3
Woodchurch PL20 ... 42 B3
Wood Cl PL12 ... 122 B3
Woodcock Cl PL10 ... 133 A6
Wood Dr PL12 ... 53 C8
Woodend Rd PL6 ... 125 D7
Woodfield Prim Sch PL5 ... 124 C5
Woodfield Rd EX23 ... 104 E7
Woodford Ave PL7 ... 130 A7
Woodford Cl PL7 ... 130 A7
Woodford Cres PL7 ... 130 A6
Woodford Cross EX23 ... 2 C1
Woodford Gn PL7 ... 130 B6
Woodford Inf Sch PL7 ... 130 B6
Woodford Jun Sch PL7 ... 130 B7
Woodford Rd PL6 ... 125 D6
Woodgate Rd PL14 ... 113 A5
Woodgrove Pk PL26 ... 59 A1
Woodhey Rd PL2 ... 128 A7
Wood La
Landrake PL12 ... 53 D2
Truro TR1 ... 137 D3
Tywardreath PL24 ... 60 D5
Woodland Ave
Penryn TR10 ... 144 B6
Plymouth PL9 ... 136 A8
12 Tywardreath PL24 ... 60 D5
Woodland Cl
Gunnislake PL18 ... 40 F6
Lanivet PL30 ... 47 E7
St Austell PL25 ... 114 E3
Woodland Ct TR1 ... 137 E5
Woodland Dr PL7 ... 130 B4
Woodland Glade PL30 ... 47 F7
Woodland Hts TR1 ... 137 E5
Woodland Rd
Plymouth PL7 ... 130 C6
St Austell PL25 ... 114 E3
Woodland Rise
Penryn TR10 ... 144 B7
Rilla Mill PL17 ... 38 E8
Woodlands
Dousland PL20 ... 42 E3
4 Mullion TR12 ... 99 A2
10 Par PL24 ... 60 C4
Plymouth PL9 ... 135 F6
Woodlands Ct PL5 ... 124 A3
Woodlands End PL6 ... 125 D5
Woodlands La PL6 ... 125 F1
Woodlands Sch PL5 ... 124 B4
Woodlands Terr 3 TR16 ... 140 F1
Woodlands The TR14 ... 67 B4
Woodlands View PL13 ... 117 B4
Woodland Terr
Plymouth PL4 ... 149 B4
4 St Columb Road TR9 ... 45 E2
Woodland Terr La PL4 ... 149 B4
Woodland View
Coombe PL26 ... 58 C2
Lanivet PL30 ... 47 E6
Woodland Way
Gunnislake PL18 ... 41 A7
Torpoint PL11 ... 126 F3
Woodlane TR11 ... 145 B3
Woodlane Cl TR11 ... 145 B3
Woodlane Cres TR11 ... 145 B3
Woodlane Dr TR11 ... 145 B3
Woodley Cl 8 EX23 ... 4 D1
Woodman's Cnr PL20 ... 42 D3
Woodovis Cvn Pk PL19 ... 29 F1
Woodridge Cl TR27 ... 78 E1
Woods-Browning Ind Est
PL31 ... 109 F2
Woodside
Crapstone PL20 ... 42 B2
Penryn TR10 ... 144 B7
Plymouth PL4 ... 149 B4
Woodside Ave PL9 ... 135 C6
Woodside Ct PL7 ... 130 E4
Woodside La PL4 ... 149 B4
Woodstock Gdns PL5 ... 123 D1
Woodvale Terr PL15 ... 106 C5
Wood View TR10 ... 144 B7
Woodview Pk PL9 ... 136 A6
Woodville Cl PL2 ... 127 F7
Woodville Rd
Morwenstow EX23 ... 2 C1
Plymouth PL2 ... 127 F6
Woodford EX23 ... 4 D8
Woodway
Penryn TR10 ... 144 B7
Plymouth PL9 ... 136 A7
Woolacombe Cross PL20 ... 41 C1
Woolacombe Rd PL20 ... 41 C1
Woollcombe Ave PL7 ... 130 F4

Woolster Ct 8 PL4 ..... 149 A2
Woolwell Cres PL6...... 125 C8
Woolwell Dr PL6........ 125 C7
Woolwell Rd PL6 .... 125 D7
Woon La 3 TR3 ....81 F7
Worcester Rd PL25 ..... 115 A4
Wordsworth Cres PL2....127 F7
Wordsworth Rd PL2......127 F7
World in Miniature* TR4..55 E4
Wotton Cross PL12........53 B4
Wreford Cl 11 TR9 ....45 D6
Wren Gdns PL7......... 130 C6
Wren Ind Est TR1 ....69 E4
Wrens Gate PL9 ....135 E8
Wrey Ave PL14.......... 113 C7
Wright Cl PL1 ....127 E3
Wyatts La PL19 ....147 B6
Wych Hazel Way TR7.....110 F4
Wycliffe Rd PL3 ....129 B4
Wye Gdns PL3 .... 129 D7
Wykeham Dr PL2 .... 128 A7
Wyndham La PL1 ....148 A3
Wyndham Mews PL1......148 A3
Wyndham Pl PL1 .... 148 A3
Wyndham St E PL1 ......148 B3
Wyndham St W PL1......148 B3
Wyndham Sq PL1....... 148 A3
Wyndhurst Orch PL27....108 B6
Wyoming Cl PL3........ 129 C6
Wythburn Gdns PL6..... 125 D3

Y

Yardley Gdns PL6 ....125 E3
Yarg Cheese Farm* PL14 .38 D8
Yarrow Mead PL9....... 136 D7
Yealmpstone Cl PL7......131 B4
Yealmpstone Dr PL7 .....131 B3
Yealmpstone Farm Prim Sch
PL7....................131 B3
Yeats Cl PL5............ 124 C2
Yellow Tor Ct PL12...... 122 C2
Yellow Tor La PL12...... 122 C2
Yellow Tor Rd PL12 ......122 B2
Yellow-wort TR16.........80 C3
Yelverton Bsns
Pk PL20.................42 B2
Yelverton Cl PL5.........123 E4
Yelverton Paperweight
Mus* PL20 ....42 C2
Yelverton Terr
Tavistock PL19.......... 147 D6
Yelverton PL20............42 D2
Yeo Cl PL3 ....129 B5
Yeoland La PL20..........42 C1
Yeoland Lane Cvn Pk
PL20....................42 C1
Yeomadon Cross EX22 .....8 E4
Yeomans Cl PL14 .... 113 D5
Yeomans Way PL7 ...... 131 A4
Yewdale Gdns PL6...... 125 D2
Yew Tree Ct TR1 ....137 F6
Yonder St PL9 ....135 B6
York Pl PL2..............127 F4
York Rd
Plymouth PL5............127 E8
Torpoint PL11 ....127 B3
York St
Penzance TR18 .... 143 D6
Plymouth PL1............127 E2
York Terr 7 PL2.........127 F5
Youldon Way PL20 ....42 C4

Z

Zaggy La PL17.............39 E4
Zion St PL1............. 148 C2
Zodiac Ho TR19...........96 E3